MEDIEVAL WARFARE

TRIUMPH AND DOMINATION IN THE WARS OF THE MIDDLE AGES

MEDIEVAL WARFARE

TRIUMPH AND DOMINATION IN THE WARS OF THE MIDDLE AGES

PETER REID

CARROLL & GRAF PUBLISHERS
NEW YORK

Carroll & Graf Publishers
An imprint of Avalon Publishing Group, Inc.
245 W. 17th Street, 11th Floor
New York, NY 10011–5300
www.carrollandgraf.com

AVALON
publishing group incorporated

First published in the UK by Constable,
an imprint of Constable & Robinson Ltd, 2007

First Carroll & Graf edition, 2007

ISBN-13: 978-0-78671-859-7
ISBN-10: 0-7867-1859-5

Printed in the USA

For my wife, Catherine

New Orleans, LA.
May 2007

Contents

Acknowledgements

I would like to thank my editor Leo Hollis for his helpful suggestions and his good humour at all times. I would also like to thank John Welch, my agent, for introducing me to the world of publishing and in particular to my publishers.

I would have found it virtually impossible to write this book without the courteous help given to me always be the staff of the London Library in my search for obscure references, or indeed for many of the books that I needed to read; why is it that they always seemed to be on the bottom shelf of the darkest corner of the deepest dungeon in the building? I would also like to thank the staff at the British Library and the National Archive who were always most helpful.

Certain people helped and encouraged me during the project. I would particularly like to thank Peter Henson, who introduced me to my agent and gave me many useful tips. I would also like to thank Peter Gwyn for his advice about the format of the book, and John Strawson for his advice and encouragement.

Above all I would like to thank Catherine for her indulgence over the past several years as the book took shape, and books and papers took over the dining room. She was always my first editor; she would read through a chapter after I finished it and make helpful suggestions. She would often question why I had written what I had and so would remind me that I was writing for the general reader; she might even point out that what I had written made no sense at all! In effect, not only was she my first editor but she was also my first critic and one I could not have done without.

Illustrations

A surgeon withdraws a barbed broadhead ref: O120 © The Master and Fellows of Trinity College, Cambridge

Passage de la Tyne par les Anglais © Bibliotheque Nationale, Paris, France

Battle of Ecluse, 24th June 1340 © Bibliotheque Nationale, Paris, France/The Bridgeman Art Library

Battle of Crécy in 1346, copy of Froissart's Chronicles (engraving) © Bibliotheque Nationale, Paris, France/Archives Charmet/The Bridgeman Art Library

Battle of Crécy, 26 August 1346 © Bibliotheque Nationale, Paris, France/The Bridgeman Art Library

The Burghers of Calais submitting to Edward III, 1347, English, with Flemish illuminations © Lambeth Palace Library, London, UK/The Bridgeman Art Library

Battle of Maupertuis (near Poitiers) 19th September 1356 (the Black Prince, son of Edward III of England, gains victory over King John the Good of France). King John is taken prisoner. To the Chronicles of Jean Froissart. Besançon, Bibliotheque Municipale © akg-images/Erich Lessing

Rioters pillage a house in Paris, © British Library, London, UK/ © British Library Board. All Rights Reserved/The Bridgeman Art Library

Battle of Agincourt, 1415, English with Flemish illuminations © Lambeth Palace Library, London, UK/The Bridgeman Art Library

The Siege of Mortagne, Vol III 'From the Coronation of Richard II to 1387', by Jean de Batard Wavrin © British Library, London UK/© British Library Board. All Rights Reserved/The Bridgeman Art Library

The Battle of Towton in 1461, illustration from Hutchinsons 'Story of the British Nation' (litho) by Woodville, Richard Caton (1825–56) © Private Collection/The Bridgeman Art Library

The Battle of Towton by permission of the artist Graham Turner, www.studio88.co.uk

The Battle of Bosworth by permission of the artist Graham Turner, www.studio88.co.uk

Preface

This book covers a period of history usually only remembered in England by the battles of Bannockburn, Crécy, Poitiers and Agincourt, and the two general titles of the Hundred Years' War and the Wars of the Roses, and then history passes quickly to the glories of the Tudors and the Elizabethan age. Only scholars have studied the period in any depth and there were few books written for the general reader, indeed I was lamenting this fact when my eldest daughter said, 'Well Dad, there is only one way to solve the problem, you will have to write it'. Without thinking I said I would and that was thirteen years ago. Having started I became more and more interested in the project and this book is the result of my research and reading over the years, and my visits to various battlefields, all of which I have enjoyed doing.

I was determined to put the various wars in their proper perspective. The book was not to be simply about battles but also about how they came about and why. So it includes the whole process from the initial decision to go to war, through the problems of financing it, providing the hardware and the men to fight it, the administration of the war machine, and finally the effects of any one battle on the political situation at the time. This is a wide canvas and one that could not possibly have been done without recourse to the scholarship of others, which I have acknowledged wherever possible in the notes. When there has been disagreement about facts or analysis of facts between writers I have gone back to the original source, and if the resulting research is none too clear I have used my military judgement to produce a probable result.

Life in the period covered was very different from that of today, or even from life during the Napoleonic wars or those in the eighteenth century. Consequently I have included introductory chapters to cover social and financial aspects of the time. I have also included chapters on the very business of waging war and its consequences.

I have both Scottish and English blood, live in England and have a house in France, and therefore I have written this account without prejudice or favour; when in my estimate the armies of one or another do well or badly, I say so. I have also tried to be even-handed over the politics of the day. However, having said that there is no doubt in my mind that England's armies set the standard for the period and whenever possible their organization and tactics were followed by those of her enemies, at least until the emergence of regular armies in France and the modernization of their artillery arm.

The Wars of the Roses would appear to us today to have been a completely unnecessary period of warfare, but set in the political conditions of its day it is hard to see how they could have been avoided. The whole period covered by the book is linked to the emergence, practice and demise of the English way of war in the Middle Ages.

As a soldier I have done my best to put the reader on the battlefield and I have analyzed the results of many of the important battles fought, not just those won by England. However, I would like to express one caution. It is very easy in this day of extremely sophisticated weaponry on the battlefield to dismiss the efforts of the soldiers and their commanders in this period in their battles and sieges as overly simplistic. It is therefore essential that one considers their actions in light of the technology and communications of the times. They were no less intelligent or capable than we are today.

Part 1

BACKGROUND

Chapter 1

The Nation

The King

Why did England go to war against France for more than a hundred years? Why did England and Scotland fight such a bitter war, again, for more than a hundred years? What caused the Wars of the Roses? What course did these wars take and how did politics in France, Scotland and England influence these endless years of war? How did the wars affect the lives of the citizens of the three countries concerned? How was England organized for war? Who paid for the wars? How were soldiers recruited and what were they paid? What actually happened in the battles? What equipment did they use? How were the armies administered? All these questions and many more need to be answered before warfare in the Middle Ages can be fully understood in all its complexity. War in the Middle Ages was much more than an affair between armoured knights fighting as though at a tournament while representing their countries. War then, as now, was a complicated and expensive political act.

All these conflicts were either dynastic struggles or conflicts of over-lordship and all were concerned with the aggrandisement of the English crown and its consolidation or its succession, dealing with a complex network of allegiances. The two best examples of this principle are those which caused the two prolonged foreign wars. One was the relationship between the Kings of England and France over the sovereignty of Aquitaine, and the other the relationship between the Kings of England and Scotland over the sovereignty of Scotland itself. Uniquely, England, due to her island status, was already a nation state by the beginning of the fourteenth century, with systems of government and administration and recognized frontiers. This was probably her major initial advantage over her adversaries in her two foreign wars.

In all three kingdoms of the thirteenth century, wars entered into by the king were considered to be the king's private affair. These had to be paid for from his demesne land and supported, both financially and militarily, by those who owed him allegiance, and by those who volunteered in the hope of winning favour and advancement. In England and Scotland parliament would only assist with a subsidy when the war was in defence of the realm and when it became clear that the king could not meet the expense of the war from his own resources, and they judged the war to be just. Taxing for war in England began early in the reign of Edward I when it became obvious that the existing system could not meet the expense of war overseas or across the borders. Consequently the king would call a parliament to ask for a subsidy or tax to enable him to go to war. In effect the king had to obtain parliament's approval before going to war outside the realm. As wars became more and more sophisticated and more expensive, the power of parliament in England increased at the expense of the crown. Indeed in matters of war it was not long before the kings of England had to answer to parliament for their actions and their failures. Parliament, whose agreement was already necessary for the imposition of civil taxes, became the arbiter of taxation for war.

Where executive action was concerned, government in England was an intricate blend of royal decree, usually issued through the king's council and qualified by parliamentary assent, and legislation initiated by parliament and sealed by the crown. In effect, for all executive purposes the crown stated what it required to be done and the king's ministers put it before parliament where the people's representatives approved it, rejected it, or amended it. In England in the fourteenth and fifteenth centuries, for the most part, power was evenly balanced between the crown and parliament.

In France, however, government was royal government and good government was dependent on strong kingship, indeed it has been said that the French king 'has no other control over him than the fear of God and his own conscience'. There was no parliament in the English or Scottish sense, nevertheless a *parlement* did exist. This was the supreme court of law in the land and as such its principle aim, which it pursued tirelessly, was to uphold the king's law throughout the realm of France, including all the great semi-independent duchies. The exercise of justice was one of the obligations of kingship in the Middle Ages. This role of the French *parlement* was one of the many factors that brought England and France into conflict.

The tool of government in France was a bureaucracy which was apparent in every walk of life and which operated through the *conseil, parlement* and the *Chambres des comptes*. Taxes, which were imposed by the crown and sometimes granted by representative assemblies, the estates,[i] were controlled through the *Chambres des Comptes* in Paris and its tax gatherers were assiduous in their duties. As the imposition of taxes did not require the assent of a parliament as in England, tax gathering became one of the main causes for complaint against the king. The king could call an assembly at which representatives of the people might air their views, but he was not obliged to do so and these assemblies had no official political or financial power.

Throughout the period in England power slipped from the crown to parliament due to the requirements and expense of war and the consequent need for taxation. The English parliament was both the most effective brake and the most effective spur on the actions of the crown in the three countries at the beginning of the fourteenth century where warfare was concerned. By the end of Edward III's reign, although the king was undoubtedly head of the state and the executive, it was parliament which controlled taxation and the income from customs, voted finance, made laws and gave the king's decrees the force of law. Furthermore, in England the king's ministers and officers were not untouchable, they could be called to account in front of parliament.

The main functions of parliament were to raise taxation and approve new laws or changes to the law. The members of parliament, nobleman, churchman or commoner were summoned to serve at parliament by personal writ from the king for a specific parliament. It was the custom to call a spring parliament and an autumn parliament each year and one could be called whenever necessary to deal with emergencies. The actual members tended to be the same people or the holders of the same office from one parliament to another, an exception sometimes being those held to address specific regional problems. Indeed parliaments called outside London were usually called to address specific local

---

i Each major feudatory had an assembly or 'estates'. These bodies could not raise taxes, but could approve a royal demand for taxes; indeed it was considered necessary to receive this approval. However the estates could not frustrate a royal demand but they could delay it or show that it would be difficult to raise or that it would be most unpopular and hence have it postponed or cancelled. The duchies of Aquitaine, Brittany and Burgundy had their own tax-raising powers.

problems; for instance parliaments called at York or Newcastle would be called to address the problems of the north and particularly those concerned with Scotland and the border.

In England the Commons were chosen from members of the knightly classes and educated citizens who between them provided most of the officials of the king's household, the Privy Council and the three offices of state as well as most of the king's ministers. This same group of people provided the judges and lawyers, the sheriffs in the counties, the mayors and the officials of cities. They also provided most of the captains of the king's castles, the majority of the crown's officials in the capital and the shires and the heralds; they often provided the commanders of small independently operating armies detached from the main theatre of events. The principle merchants also came from this part of society and, after 1340, they became the main source of lending to the crown. By the middle of the fourteenth century the Commons were a very important body of men who were politically, militarily and economically powerful and who had a majority say in the governance and well-being of the cities and towns of England. Individually they might not have been able to gather the military power of a magnate, though they might have been just as wealthy, but collectively their power was not to be discounted.

The Knight

In the widest sense the knightly class included the king and the nobility. Nobles were not automatically knights, they had to earn their knighthood on the field of battle or in service to their sovereign; unlike nobility, knighthood could not be inherited. The king was the fount of knighthood founded as a military elite with a code of conduct, the code of chivalry, applicable only to them.

Early in the fourteenth century knighthood was based on the obligation of military service with the accompanying responsibility to be properly equipped for war at all times. As a war instrument a knight was obliged to mount himself, to clad himself in armour and to equip himself with sword and lance and to do the same for his esquire. This was an expensive business;[ii] most knights could only afford this

---

ii As an example knights were expected to have two destriers, or warhorses, These were expensive, a destrier might cost as much as £80, or at today's values at least £50,000 each.

expense if they owned land. Some knights gave their services in exchange for their living as household knights in the personal service of the king, or a tenant-in-chief, living at their lord's expense at court or in a castle, or as tenants on their land; these contract knights were equipped and provided by their masters. Such people could be called out by their patrons for war, for the tournaments or to accompany them on important business, such as attendance at parliament or the assizes. Here it is important to realize that in England the crown could not afford a standing army or police force. Consequently the crown had to rely on the loyalty of its magnates to maintain law and order at home as well as fight abroad.

To be knighted was a great honour and the place of a knight in society was similar in all the countries of the Western Christian world. Knights could and did travel extensively and could depend on the hospitality of their peers in their own and other countries. At the beginning of the period most knights in England, Scotland and the Low Countries spoke French, as did those of Aquitaine, Burgundy and Brittany, and this produced a brotherhood which transcended frontiers and ensured courtesy and honourable treatment. However as the century advanced and war increasingly became the province of professional paid soldiers, so the chivalric ethic of Knighthood waned and at about the same time knights began to speak their national language, thus changing knighthood from an international brotherhood to a national, professional class.

Knighthood was encapsulated in the Arthurian legends which were a civilizing influence on this brotherhood and which became the inspiration for the establishment of the Order of the Garter by Edward III in 1348 and similar orders of knighthood in other countries which followed. Within the Order of the Garter Edward III gathered about him those knights who would be his commanders in war or on whom he could rely for good governance at home during those times when he was himself abroad. Indeed the order was set up 'to the honouring of the soldiery'. These knightly obligations influenced state policy in that it was important for kings to be able to show that they went to war in a just cause, which would remove any doubt a knight might have had about waging war on the common people loyal to the enemy of their lord. The logic centred on the fact that since his lord's cause was just, his lord's enemy's cause could not be, and since the enemy's subjects were supporting an unjust cause they could not claim protection under the code of chivalry. The king, therefore, was under pressure to prove that his cause was just before he went to war. In England, at the beginning of the fourteenth century, this was particularly important because he had to convince parliament of the rightness of his cause in order to solicit a grant of aid, or taxation, without which he probably could not proceed. However by the fifteenth century pursuit of *realpolitik* undoubtedly took preference over the need to show just cause for war.

In the thirteenth century most knights were illiterate but their increasing involvement in government and administration, and their interest in this avenue of advancement, demanded that they could read and write in Latin. These new demands for education saw the founding of universities and borough grammar schools. In addition, in England the development of governmental bureaucracy, of the common law, and of the mercantile class produced a need for an education which not only taught students to read and write in Latin, but also in English and French. Merchants and some members of the bureaucracy had to be able to assess and account, and this too was taught at universities. The educational revolution benefited people from every strata of society, whether peer or peasant, but perhaps most particularly the knightly classes and those aspiring to knighthood.

England had one great advantage in the spread of education over both France and Scotland, where the thirst for education was no less, in that every Englishman spoke English. However, in both France and Scotland three native languages were spoken. In France half the population spoke French, while the other half, from south of the Loire, spoke Occitaine and its local variations, and those in Brittany spoke Breton. In Scotland roughly half the population, those living south of Stirling and east of a line drawn from there to Annan on the Solway Firth, spoke a dialect of English. But for those living north and west of that line, Gaelic was the mother tongue, while in the Hebrides and the Northern Isles, Norwegian was still the main language. Nevertheless, in both France and Scotland the nobility and the knightly classes spoke French regardless of their native tongue.

This development in education amongst the knightly class was one of the factors that gradually changed them from a military elite ready at all times to answer the call of their lord to war, to a group more interested in national and local government as a means to honour and power. For the knight the sword, whilst still available, was gradually replaced by the pen.

The People

The population and wealth of the three main countries were significant factors in their respective war efforts. At the beginning of the fourteenth century the population of France was variously estimated as between 11 million, including the main *appenages*,[iii] and 15 million in 1328,[1] while that of England was between 5 and 7 million and that of Scotland was probably about a million. All three countries, and indeed the whole of Western Europe, had been enjoying the benefits of expanding economies over the past 200 years. It was at this juncture that the Black Death struck.[2]

The plague first arrived in France, probably by ship at Marseilles in December 1347 and by December 1349 had reached the highlands of Scotland and southern Norway; it spread throughout Western Europe, but by 1355 it had largely died out. The populations of France and England were reduced by between a third and a half by this first wave of the plague and then reduced further by successive but considerably smaller epidemics to the middle of the fifteenth century.

At the beginning of the fourteenth century and for the next two centuries life was extremely hard. Child mortality was high and disease rife among the whole population, indeed adults were lucky to live beyond the age of forty years. The majority of the population in all three countries lived and worked on the land on which each country's prosperity depended. Nevertheless many relatively large cities existed. Paris, the largest city in Western Europe at that time had a population of about 100,000; other big cities such as Bruges, Ghent, Rheims, Rouen probably had no more than 20,000 each. Caen, by no means the largest city in France was, according to Froissart, larger and wealthier than London, while Edinburgh had only 400 houses! Records show that at the time the plague hit London it was a city of between fourteen and eighteen thousand households with a total population of between 60 and 70,000.[3] Furthermore due to its banking and financial activities and the wool export trade London was a great deal wealthier than its size indicated. As in France several English cities had sizeable populations; Norwich at 13,000 was probably one of the largest outside London, but York and many others had populations of about 10,000 each.

---

iii A dependent territory given to the son of a king or prince.

Cities not only provided markets but nurtured developing industries and technology, and a thriving trade developed on the continent of Europe, between French cities and cities in the Low Countries, the Holy Roman Empire and Italy. England exported between 30,000 and 40,000 sacks of wool annually while Scotland exported nearly 6,000 sacks. Additionally England exported large quantities of grain to Aquitaine while Scotland exported some 50,000 hides a year to the Low Countries and the Baltic. Scotland, and later England, welcomed Flemish cloth makers to their countries and before long both were exporting cloth. Scotland's overall annual export trade in the mid-fourteenth century amounted to between £30,000 and £35,000 while England's yearly exports must have totalled about £200,000.[iv]

In England nearly a third of the crown's wealth came from the custom on the wool export trade which increased the total income of the crown to much the same as that available to the King of France. Consequently, although the taxable population in England was little more than half that of France, the sums available for financing war were comparable. In Scotland the wool trade with Flanders brought in about a fifth of that of England's and the customs on this represented perhaps a third of the crown's income at the beginning of the period, to nearly half at the end. In general, since in Scotland the crown's war expenses were much less than those of England, and since it received subsidies from France from time to time, the finance available to the crown in Scotland to pay for war would have been proportionally much the same as in England. However the size and type of the war machine needed by Scotland was very different from that required by England and of course she was not conducting a war overseas.

There can be little doubt that war severely damaged this trade for both countries, since all overseas trade had to be transported by ships, which were easily intercepted and seized by the enemy. Internal trade in France was frequently interrupted and damaged by the many English incursions and by the depredations of the free companies.

---

iv It is difficult to equate these figures with modern-day values. But if the figures are multiplied by 640 it gives a fairly realistic figure in modern terms, i.e., Scotland's export trade would have been the equivalent of about 20 million pounds, which for a population of under a million was quite significant. By the same measure England's exports would have been well over 130 million pounds. See also footnote 1 in chapter 5 for comparative monetary values between the fourteenth and fifteenth centuries and today.

Damage to trade was a cogent factor in the negotiation of the innumerable truces agreed by all three countries throughout the period from time to time.

Trade depended on communications and those on land were abysmal. The majority of the land was forested and the infrequent earth tracks through the forests scarcely reduced their significance as obstacles to armies or for trade. Very few bridges crossed the rivers, and since drainage of the land had not yet begun, all land either side of rivers and even quite small streams was boggy and often impassable except during the height of summer. Fields as they are known today did not exist, arable land was ploughed and planted in small strips close to the villages, and all land in England and Scotland over 500 feet was quite wild and seldom cultivated or used as pasture. In France, due to the larger population and internal trade, the roads were better and the area under cultivation proportionally larger than in England. Travel by land was difficult, slow and full of hazards. Roads were simply earth tracks which in winter would become ever wider as each traveller tried to avoid the worst of the mud and puddles and which in summer became rutted dusty lanes baked hard. In France most cities and towns of any size were walled and the walls incorporated a citadel or chateau (castle), even the small market towns and villages in Gascony and the Dordogne, the bastides, were walled and fortified or had a fortified church as a place of refuge. In England the major cities in the north were walled and boasted a castle, but in Scotland most towns were without walls except for those close to the border and castles only existed at strategic points, although large land owners probably had a keep or peel as a refuge.

Notwithstanding the difficulties a great deal of travel took place; people moved about for trade, on government business, on church business, to supervise widely scattered estates and for war or the tournaments. Most travel on land was by horse or mule and most baggage was carried on sumpter horses. Baggage wagons came in all sizes from small single horse carts through two- and four-horse vehicles to the very large eight-horse wagons found on the continent. The nobility travelled in some style in large parties with some of their knights, with heralds and pages, chaplains, chamberlains and treasurers, and many of their other household officers together with an escort of mounted men-at-arms or archers.[4] Many horses and wagons were required as they travelled accompanied by a household in miniature reflecting all the departments of their normal domestic scene. They carried with them cooking utensils, gold and silver plate, beds, linen, clothes, armour and weapons, jewellery and money; naturally many retainers went with them to serve them and to guard and maintain the baggage. All these articles had their own particular type of packaging, an iron-bound chest or a bundle wrapped in a barehide; armour was carried in a barrel with sand and oil so that the motion of the wagon or horse kept it clean. Often food and wine were carried, as was fodder for their horses.

Lesser people generally travelled together in a party for protection and companionship and travelled in as much style as they could afford.[5] Knights and noblemen when travelling generally stayed overnight in the houses or castles of their peers as guests; other people stayed at inns where replacement horses could usually be hired if required. The knightly classes travelled to war in much the same manner as they would in peace, which accounts for the attraction of the baggage train to the victors after battle and to its huge collective value. Knights travelled extensively all over Europe in search of glory, honour and fortune, and as a consequence there was a constant flow of ideas and materials between them particularly in warlike matters, clothing, the arts and to a lesser extent the very business of good living. Clerics and merchants also travelled widely in Europe returning with new ideas and new markets. Travel, even in wartime, nurtured a flowering of knowledge and of the arts.

Chapter 2

Preparing for War

The Call to Arms

The administration of war in England and its organization over this period was a constantly evolving system, so much so that the details of that which applied in 1314 were very different from those of 1485. Nevertheless, in each case, the call to arms was initiated by or through the king, aided by his close advisers and council comprising the king's ministers: the chancellor and the treasurer, as well as the justices of both benches, generally the escheator-general,[1] the sergeants,[2] some of the principle clerks of the chancery and some of the bishops, earls and barons chosen by the king.

During Edward II's time a baronial council was formed and this had to be consulted by the king when consultation with parliament was not required. Early in Edward III's reign the council included some thirty-five professional men including both the keeper of the Wardrobe and the treasurer of the Wardrobe. However by 1376 the official element of the council, represented by the ministers of the crown, had been reduced to three, the chancellor, the treasurer and the keeper of the privy seal;[3] this was later increased to five by Richard II. Richard II's privy and great councils were gradually integrated and, largely due to Richard's capricious style of government, parliament took a much greater interest in the council's membership. Nevertheless the council continued to exercise its direction of war effort and the supervision of foreign affairs.

The council was a flexible instrument, members, apart from the paid ministers of the crown were called individually, according to the business in hand. However, notwithstanding this flexibility, the king needed to be able to discuss certain matters of state, foreign affairs or war, in secret with only a few close advisers and ministers present and so the secret or privy council was born. After discussion in the privy council any course of action decided upon would be put before the council as a whole. The council could accept or reject the views of the privy council and it alone could proclaim an act or issue an ordinance in the king's name, however it had no power to make a grant (of taxation) or to repeal a statute.

During Henry IV's reign the council continued as the main instrument of government concerned with the direction of war and foreign policy; it also raised loans for the prosecution of the war against France. Events in 1411–12 are a good example of the council's responsibilities. In 1411 the full council, under the influence of the prince of Wales (later Henry V) decided to support the Burgundians against the Armagnacs in France. The king and his close advisers agreed with them that an expedition should be sent in support of Burgundy but asked the council to consider how best they might finance it. In 1412, however it was the king and his close advisers who decided that they should withdraw their support for the duke and instead support the Armagnacs and required the council to organize[4] another expedition. In 1415, the council also accepted responsibility for the reinforcement of castles and the provision of military supplies, and agreed to double the number of ships, presumably warships, in the king's service.[5] Finally before Henry left for France he advised Bedford 'to do all things with the consent of the council'.

After Henry died in 1422, and by the terms of the Treaty of Troyes, the governance of the two kingdoms, inherited by Henry VI, became two separate administrations and therefore the council in England was no longer responsible for the direction of the war in France. This became the responsibility of a council set up by Bedford, the regent, in France. However, notwithstanding the separation of responsibilities for the war, the council in England still remained responsible for the war effort at sea in addition to the payment of all reinforcements before they crossed the Channel. It also remained responsible for affairs in Aquitaine and for the security of the northern border and the south coast. All this was expensive and indeed the treasurer to the council reported in 1429 that the government's deficit was running at an annual loss of £20,000.

During the Wars of the Roses the council continued much as it had in Henry VI's earlier years, though perhaps with a wider remit, parliament often being content for it to take responsibility in new areas, albeit on a temporary basis. However the council still remained the agency through which foreign policy and war outside the national borders were conducted, raising finance for expeditions overseas or across the northern border which it did by raising loans and, or, by asking parliament for a grant in aid or taxation.

It was then up to parliament to decide if the request was in the national interest and therefore if it deserved parliament's endorsement, and if so how the necessary finance was to be raised and how much was to be levied. Parliament was given this responsibility in 1311 when Edward II was forced to agree that, among other things, the king should consult parliament before declaring war and that he should obtain their permission to leave the country. It had always been the king's right to act in defence of the realm but the raising of taxes to meet the costs of war outside the national boundaries was parliament's responsibility. The king had to obtain parliament's consent to the raising of taxes before they could become law. In 1327 in order to get parliament's approval for taxes to support his campaigns Edward III had to agree that in future parliament's assent would also be necessary before armed forces could be used outside the realm.[6] Parliament's support therefore was essential for successful hostilities and this support was dependent on the leadership shown by the king. Parliament's approval during the successful wars of Edward III and Henry V is in marked contrast to the lack of support given during the reigns of Edward II, Richard II and Henry VI who failed as war leaders. In effect war had to be popular to secure support in parliament and it was only popular when it was successful.

Throughout the period the crown, in need of taxation, released more and more power to parliament in exchange for underwriting the cost of war. This enlargement of parliament's role was manifest in the increasing consultation that took place between successive monarchs and parliament. In 1331 the king's income from all sources amounted to a mere £72,514 2s 10d, barely enough to meet the expense of a campaign into Scotland; even a short foray across the border would cost about £30,000. Consequently when Edward III decided to go to war against France while he was still at war with Scotland, his revenue could not possibly meet his war outlay. He therefore had to devise ways of raising cash from within his own prerogative and when this could not meet his expenses he had to entreat parliament for a subsidy or aid. Parliament of course would not give something for nothing and so every time this happened a little more power slipped from the crown to parliament. Parliament's assent was necessary for the use of force beyond the national borders but not if an invading force threatened England's borders. This particularly applied in the north of England concerning defensive measures against incursion by the Scots.

When parliament agreed that war was necessary it then had to ensure that sufficient finance was forthcoming to pay for it. This it did by imposing taxes or 'lay subsidies'; it could also grant a subsidy or levy on wool exports over and above the custom duty, which the king would collect on trade both exported and imported. In 1338, for example, the king instituted a customs levy of 40 shillings per sack of wool exported for English merchants and 60 shillings for aliens, all sacks being required to be shipped from and to designated ports.

In 1337 Edward III laid claim to the throne of France, while he was still heavily involved in his attempt to conquer Scotland. The cost of the war against Scotland was barely met by the usual crown receipts and consequently Edward III decided to extend the practice of purveyance to the wool trade by compulsorily purchasing 30,000 sacks of wool at a fixed price. Purveyance was a system instituted in time of war by which the king could obtain supplies or commodities at a fixed price for a fixed quota; the king of course fixed the price and ensured that he got the supplies he needed at below market value.

The commons influence on government and its interest in the appropriation of funds raised by taxation for defence and warlike purposes increased throughout the fourteenth and fifteenth centuries. Indeed as early as 1377 the Lords and Commons required that treasurers be appointed to see that money granted for particular projects was actually spent on the project stipulated in the grant. In 1388 dissatisfaction with the government came to a head and 'The merciless parliament' purged the royal court and council. In 1406 they nominated a committee to work with the King's council to negotiate a defence plan for shipping and the ports with the 'Merchants of England'. In 1442 the Commons put forward a scheme for the king's approval for a standing naval force to provide defence for the southern counties. In the fifteenth century parliament directed that the proceeds of the tax obtained from tonnage and poundage be spent only on coastal defence and that the tax on wool be spent on the defence of Calais.[7]

War was a costly condition and as has been seen parliament kept a wary eye on the king's war expenditure and his need for cash. A full-scale operation in France in Edward III's reign, such as the Crécy campaign, cost about £150,000 and the siege of Calais probably cost more. To balance this, the king's receipts in 1345–6 came to £153,900 and those in 1348 were £142,548 7s 1d,[8] this was clearly not enough to pay for war against both France and Scotland at the same time. This shortage of cash to pay for war continued throughout Edward III's reign. Matters did not really improve during the reigns of his grandson Richard II or that of Henry IV, although it was never such a large problem probably because war was not such a prominent or constant occupation.

However, when Henry V came to the throne war once again became a central issue for both the crown and parliament and Henry was every bit as short of cash as was his great-grandfather. So much so that in 1414 he felt obliged to convince parliament of the justness of his case for the throne of France. A diplomatic embassy sent to France claiming all the old Plantagenet lands in addition to the crown itself had been rejected by France, and Henry claimed there was no other way to settle the issues than by war. However this was insufficient to pay for Henry's ambitious plans and he was forced to send commissioners to raise loans to meet the shortfall. Among other loans he received £32,000 from the city of London, £44,243 from the bishops and nearly £9,000 from various religious orders, all guaranteed against future taxation and customs dues.[9] In addition to his ordinary revenue Henry was voted extra grants by parliament in 1415, 1416 and 1417. All told until 1422 Henry's revenue for the seven years, including grants by parliament, loans and ransoms of French nobles taken at Agincourt, amounted to the staggering sum for those days of £945,166. However his expenditure over the same period amounted to £976,099.[10]

After 1418 public opinion was increasingly of the view that the conquered province of Normandy and other parts of northern France should shoulder the major part of the financial burden of the war. To meet the costs of war in France Henry and his successors relied on taxes obtained in Normandy and in due course on other parts of conquered France. Taxation in Normandy was already well organized before the arrival of the English and Henry benefited from a revenue bureaucracy already in place. Although he appointed Englishmen to the major posts, in general, he simply left the system to continue its work.

Revenue came from two main sources: the taxation formerly imposed by the French, and rents from lands belonging to French overlords and bishops who failed to swear fealty to King Henry and whose lands were confiscated as a result. Taxation, included the *aides,* a tax on sales, the *gabelle,* a tax on salt, and the *fuage* or hearth tax. These sources of revenue were used for the normal administration of Normandy, and increasingly for the costs of the war in northern France. The total revenue from all sources in Normandy in 1419 amounted to approximately 182,275 *livres tournois* (lt) or about £27,620; of which about 40 per cent came from domaine income and 40 per cent from the taxes.[11]

The parliamentary grants of direct taxation made in 1415 and 1416 met the costs of the army and the shipping for the invasion of France in 1415, the subsequent capture of Harfleur and the march to Calais via the battlefield of Agincourt. This was Henry's most expensive time, however his renewed efforts to conquer Normandy in 1417 and its subjugation, and that of other parts of France, until his death in 1422 still required sums well in excess of his normal revenue. To meet this specific grants had to be voted by Parliament to keep his ambitions alive. Luckily for Henry his victory at Agincourt made the war popular in England and the continuing revenue from captured lands in Normandy and ransoms contrived to keep it so.

It is legitimate to ask if the Normans had cause for discontent over the rate of taxation imposed. When Henry V had concluded his conquest of Normandy in 1418 and established his administration he eased the tax load by reducing the *gabelle* from the rate imposed by the French crown and it was only raised to its former rate in November 1424. Nevertheless the continuing campaigns to extend the English dominion into other parts of France, to clear out resistance within the borders of 'English' France and to secure that which had already been conquered demanded an ever-increasing call on the pockets of the mainly Norman populace. Indeed it has been estimated by Newhall[12] that by the end of 1424 the average Norman taxpayer was paying tax at a rate of just over 10 *sous tournois* (2s 2d sterling) per year, two and a half times what he had paid in 1418. This should be compared with what the average English taxpayer was paying in England, about 1s 9d sterling. However, judged by the wages of carpenters in Normandy at that time of 9d a day with the wage of a carpenter in the English Army of 6d a day, the Norman taxpayer was paying less tax per head, relative to earnings, than his English counterpart. Perhaps therefore any discontent was not so much with the rate of taxation as it was with the fact of its imposition by an alien nation to pay for a war against the other inhabitants of France, their fellow citizens.

By the end of 1424 the treasuries of Normandy and conquered France were running at a deficit. Perhaps this encouraged the view that an extension of the frontiers of 'English' France would help to meet the cost of the occupation and the security of the whole. Probably the normal revenues of Normandy and 'English' France would have been sufficient to meet the costs of the defence and security of the conquered territories alone. However, England persisted with aggressive campaigns of aggrandisement to secure their conquests, culminating in the disastrous siege of Orleans in 1428–9 which heralded the gradual decline of English fortunes and their eventual enforced withdrawal from France. Suffice it to say that by 1430 the cost of the defence of Normandy had to be underwritten by the exchequer in England once again.

Indeed after 1430, when England was very much on the defensive in northern France and was constrained largely to within the borders of an impoverished Normandy, the Normans found it more and more difficult to find the £33,000 Sterling from taxation needed to pay for its defence. Consequently parliament at home was increasingly asked to subsidize the defence of Normandy from taxation in England, not a popular matter. This aid came as an annual subsidy to the governor and also as reinforcements initially indentured for six months, but which by 1435 had become an annual reinforcement in order to maintain sufficient English forces in Normandy for its defence. The duke of York, as governor, managed to negotiate a subsidy of £20,000 to cover the cost of wages to his army with parliament in 1440. This, when added to the annual cost of the provision of troops to top up the garrison and to provide a field force, became a considerable charge on the exchequer. Furthermore this subsidy was in addition to the revenues obtained from taxation within Normandy. The cost of subsidizing Normandy amounted to about half of the total lay and clerical subsidy in any one year in England and was certainly more than the country could afford or wished to disburse.

This effort in both men and money was expended in order to maintain an army establishment of a little over 6,000 men whose total cost was estimated by the council in England in 1441 at about £60,000 annually. These men were distributed among thirty-eight different garrisons and included the personal retinues of the field commanders and the master of the Ordinance. Soldiers from garrisons regularly took part in sieges of French-held castles and towns but most of the operations in the field were carried out by the personal retinues of the commanders, aided by troops sent out specifically from England and indentured for the campaigning season. The number of these soldiers each year varied from 800 to 2,700 depending on the operational situation and the size of the subsidy voted by parliament.[13]

Although the cost of war in France between 1418 and 1430 was largely borne by the French people of Normandy, it must not be forgotten that the exchequer at home was still responsible for meeting much of the cost of the war effort as a whole. This meant that parliament had to pay for all reinforcements until they left English shores and was responsible for the payment of all warlike stores not manufactured in Normandy. Parliament also had to pay for the war at sea and to be prepared to underwrite the costs of war in Aquitaine, which was primarily the responsibility of the government in Bordeaux. Additionally the ongoing costs of the war against Scotland had to be met. After 1430 the exchequer at home bore the brunt of all war expenses particularly during the last twenty years of English rule in France as England's grip on Normandy gradually diminished. Overall between the start of the Hundred Years' War and its end in 1453, the cost of the war to England must have exceeded crown and parliamentary receipts by a substantial amount. Certainly it was not until well into Edward 1V's reign that the crown's income from all sources, including parliamentary grants, exceeded its outgoings.

Henry VI having virtually no war expenditure after the English were expelled from France in 1453 nevertheless had to maintain the garrison of Calais. This was met from the wool subsidies and customs, which parliament had granted him for life. However this income only came in after the wool was sold and therefore he had to obtain loans of about £1,000 per quarter from the mayor and merchants of Calais. He secured the loans by the simple expedient of selling licences for a monopoly of the export of wool through the staple free of customs dues.

In the Wars of the Roses the financing of war by each side depended very much on whether they were in power or not. This war was of course a civil war and therefore financing by parliament through general taxation was not attempted, nevertheless parliament would still have had to back any external war requirement. In this war one side was always seen to be in rebellion against the other and so the side being rebelled against was able to call out the shire levies for forty days without pay. Each side, when in power, was able to call on the income from the Duchy of Lancaster and could also expect the income from customs dues. But a large slice of their income for war came from loans raised in the city of London, at the staple, from alien bankers and from individuals. In this the Yorkists seem to have been more successful than the Lancastrians. Income also came from the forfeited estates of those in rebellion. However a large part of the military effort in the war by both sides came from the services offered by individuals and their retinues.

The Call-up

The administration of war remained remarkably similar throughout the period from the early fourteenth century to the late fifteenth. Once the decision to go to war had been endorsed by the council and put before parliament, and parliament had agreed and offered finance, it was then up to the council to put the administrative wheels into motion. In the early fourteenth century prior to the muster of an army the council was responsible for issuing the writs of array while the chancery was responsible for issuing the summons for service for those knights with an obligation for knight's service. It also issued protections against the obligation to serve by those knights owing a knight's service but who had paid fines in lieu of military service. Meanwhile the exchequer paid the arrayers and the troops in transit. Once mustered, however, the Wardrobe, another government office, became the principle administrative agency for the army in the field. The Wardrobe was also responsible for the valuation of warhorses and for keeping a register of them, as well as for the purchase of supplies and the provision of expendable war stores such as arrows and cannon balls. In the middle of the fourteenth century the Wardrobe handed over responsibility for the recording of war contracts and service to the exchequer.

During Henry V's invasion and subsequent subjugation of Normandy the financial administration of war was split between the exchequer, which remained responsible for financing that part of the war effort incurred in England, and the treasurer of war who was responsible for all expenditure in the field. The latter became in essence a paymaster-general for the forces and was the exchequer's representative in the field where he was also treasurer of the royal household and head of the Wardrobe. The treasurer of war was not only responsible for the pay of the field army but also for all incidental war costs, such as the buying of powder and shot, bows and arrows and other war materiel. He was also responsible for the cost of supplies and provisions for the army in Normandy and northern France, in short he was responsible for all administrative and supply services with the army in the field. The treasurer of war also received the balance of any monies raised by parliament for the pay of reinforcements until they had embarked, and his office also received money voted by the council in Normandy for war purposes other than that for the garrisons.

Henry V's system for the pay, administration and supply of his armies in Normandy probably grew out of a system initiated by Edward III for his armies in Scotland. In 1336, Edward was obliged to keep a large military presence in his garrisons in occupied Scotland yet, unable to supervise them personally, he appointed Henry of Lancaster as his 'captain and leader' with the full subordinated powers of the king himself. This appointment was approved by parliament in 1337. However by April 1338, the English had been driven out of all Scotland, so the appointment itself gradually became defunct. Nevertheless it became the blueprint for similar appointments in Aquitaine and later in Normandy under Henry V and Bedford.

How was the army mobilized? Once finance had been approved and parliament had given its assent to war outside the national boundaries the council first sent the king's requirements and orders to the sheriffs of counties, the mayors and aldermen of cities and towns, the wardens of the march with Scotland, the admirals, the keepers of the maritime lands, the captains of royal castles and the constable of the Tower of London. The council could initiate two types of 'call-up', which were executed by the sheriffs: the first was that for defence of the realm and the second for war overseas or across the northern border. Both of these systems of mobilization relied on the shrieval summons in which the county arrayers, under shrieval orders, would call on men between the ages of sixteen and sixty to answer the county levy for service within national boundaries. Commissions to array men were also sent to the mayors of towns to raise the town's levies. The men raised in this fashion were paid by their county or town until they reached the county boundary after which they were at the king's wages. The call-up lasted for forty days. However men could exempt themselves from service by paying a fine, which was scaled by the arrayers according to the man's resources.[14] This was a useful arrangement since it collected money to pay for other men or for war munitions and supplies; it also had the great merit of ensuring that unenthusiastic men were not conscripted to join the army.

There were two forms of array: the general array and the selective array. The former was used to raise the local levies at a time of danger when large numbers of semi-trained troops were required. This call-out was used to meet an invasion scare or at a time of raids either along the south coast or the Scottish border; men thus raised were usually equipped to the minimum standard.[15] The selective array was used to raise troops for service abroad either in France or Scotland; for these operations fit, well-trained and well-equipped men were required, and so men with war experience would find themselves selected. However by the end of the fourteenth century it was more usual to fill the ranks of armies for service abroad from paid volunteers, and the raising of men by the general array became strictly for home defence alone.[16]

The king could also call out the feudal levy, that is a levy of all those who held land direct from the crown who had been obliged to render military service to the crown as a consequence of their title to the land be they the higher nobility to quite humble knights. It also included some spiritual leaders such as the bishop of Durham – even the nunnery at Wilton owed a knight's service! These tenants-in-chief were not obliged to meet their obligations in person and could pay someone else to serve in their place, or pay a fee in lieu of service. Once Edward III went to war against France he found the feudal system of obligatory service unsuitable for a long period as it was also subject to the forty days call-up and it failed to provide the necessary numbers for protracted operations in Scotland and France. Although he relied on this system initially to provide him with the nucleus of his mounted men-at-arms, he was obliged by 1337 to increase the voluntary paid element of this arm of his army.[17] As a consequence the indenture system incorporating contracts of service came into being.

The principle behind feudal service to the king applied in the relationship between major landholders and their dependents, who were also obliged to answer a summons from their lord to go to war when called. This relationship was a factor that contributed to what became known as bastard feudalism. A tenant-in-chief's retinue would be made up of knights holding land from him together with knights of his household, his servants and yeomen who worked the land.

The same system applied for the recruitment of artisans for the army, the carpenters, masons, miners, saddlers, armourers, bowyers, fletchers, blacksmiths and carters. The council would say how many and of what trade they wanted, which counties and towns they were to be recruited from, and the sheriffs and mayors would meet the requirement. War stores such as bows and arrows and arrowheads, horseshoes, field anvils and bellows, horseshoe nails and nails used in the construction of bridges and siege engines would be ordered similarly. These stores would be delivered to the muster point or the port of embarkation, or in some cases to the Tower of London by wagon or riverboat, or by coastal shipping. All war stores were paid for initially by sheriffs and mayors who then had to be reimbursed by the exchequer. Armour and weapons were made at the Tower of London, or at armouries supervised by them. When artillery, both siege and field, became part of the necessary weaponry of war the Tower became responsible for their manufacture and for the manufacture of iron cannon balls. The Tower was also responsible for the supply of gunpowder and for the provision of appropriate wagons on which to transport the guns, powder and shot. All of this would take at least three months for a small expedition into Scotland or a short raid across the Channel, and took much longer for a full-scale expedition, particularly across the Channel.

Edible stores had to be bought and gathered through purveyance. The council would again state what it needed, where it was to be delivered and by when. The sheriffs would then appoint the purveyors who bought the provisions that were then delivered to a designated warehouse at the port or muster point. Once delivered the supplies had to be packed and if necessary salted for shipment. Again this took time, but since these were all perishable stores the process had to be completed quickly. There was also the risk that bad weather might delay sailing resulting in shiploads of perished provisions. In this case the supplies would be offloaded then sold for the best price that could be obtained, and new supplies purveyed. Fodder and oats had also to be provided for the horses for the time on board ship and the first few days after landing.

The supply of horses was of great concern in the Middle Ages. In England's case almost all soldiers rode to war during the Hundred Years' War and against Scotland. In the Wars of the Roses both sides made extensive use of the shrieval summons and the town levies, and these soldiers generally marched on their feet, but even so the numbers who rode to battle were still very large. An indication of the numbers of horses taken and used by the various ranks of the army in the campaigns in France comes from a detail of Sir John Chandos's retinue on his return to England in 1363. Knights were allowed four horses each, esquires three and men-at-arms two.[18] Using these numbers and adding one horse for each archer we can get a very good idea of the minimum number of horses required for a campaign. As an example, approximately 14,000 horses had to be available, paid for and transported across the channel.

These are formidable numbers but must have been easily available since all knights were obliged to keep two warhorses, and also because all forms of transport on land depended on the horse. The king would almost certainly have provided his household knights and men-at-arms with horses from his own resources. Likewise the magnates would have done the same for their household knights, but most others who answered the call to arms with their retinues would have expected individuals to come mounted appropriately. Warhorses, or destriers, were valuable and the king was required to make good any losses. Consequently destriers were valued and catalogued by the Wardrobe. It is not clear however if he was obliged to do so for all horses, though it is probable that he did so for coursers, which were often used in place of destriers.

Fourteen thousand horses need a great deal of fodder. At a typical cavalry ration of 20lb of hay and 8lb of oats per day it comes to a total of 175 tons of food per day. Bearing in mind that provision might have to be made for about the first five days in a hostile country, plus possibly two days aboard ship, assuming the ships were able to sail shortly after the horses came aboard, a total of 1,225 tons would have had to be collected and shipped. In addition, straw would have been put down on the decks of ships with horses aboard. In case the expedition was delayed from sailing by contrary winds more fodder would have had to be available at the port. However, if the expedition was to land in friendly territory then the amount needed initially on disembarkation would have been arranged previously by the Wardrobe, so reducing the total amount to be shipped on board.

Land Forces

We have seen how the war machine was mobilized by the government down to the level of the sheriffs and mayors, but how did these officials actually select those who were obliged to go to war under the shrieval summons? Arrayers would select men who met the necessary physical standard, and in the case of archers that they were competent bowmen. These men would, if it were necessary, be clothed, equipped and mounted. They would then appoint a leader who was required to take them to a holding place until transit instructions were received, or send them directly to a port. The only men excluded from this process were those who lived at seaports where they were needed to man warships or merchant ships used as transports, either as seamen or archers.

The leaders of the arrayed men were responsible for handing the group over to the king's officers at the port in the south or the muster point in the north. The leaders were mounted, carried the wages of the group and were responsible for their pay. Their active service was deemed to begin when they reached the muster point or port and it was from this moment that their contracts began and the king became responsible for their pay.[19] The sheriffs and captains were eventually reimbursed the expense of getting them from the county boundary to the muster point. This became the normal arrangement from about 1340 until the end of the Hundred Years' War by when all war service had become voluntary paid service.

The arrayed men who made up English armies were divided according to their means. The knights and men-at-arms came from those who owned more than 450 acres of land or 60 marks worth of moveable property. The archers and hobilars came from those who owned more than 60 acres, while the bill-men were freemen who owned more than 3 marks worth of moveable property.[20] This guide for the arrayers ensured that those chosen within in any one group had the necessary resources to meet the obligations of that group.

Knights had both a military and a judicial obligation whereas a man-at-arms had neither, although he was obligated to answer a call to arms when the militia was called out.[21] Both classes were armed and equipped in a similar manner and would have carried out the same role in war. War was a knight's profession, however, and he would certainly have had better arms and armour than his militia equivalent. He would also have been more skilled in the use of arms through tournaments and constant practice, and his horses would have been more familiar with the noise and shock of battle. He was required to be properly equipped, having at least two warhorses and he had to equip his esquire similarly; this was a very expensive business. Knights generally came from a particular social class but their accolade had to be earned at war or in the tournaments. In contrast a man-at-arms achieved his position purely as a result of his wealth, which ensured that he could afford the weapons and armour of this position and could mount himself appropriately; he could of course be promoted to knighthood in war.

Hobilars and archers had similar obligations. Each type of soldier had to arm himself according to a laid down requirement and hobilars and mounted archers were also expected to mount themselves. Even bill-men were expected to possess appropriate arms for their military position. As indentured service became normal, however, it became the responsibility of the magnates and captains to ensure that those in their retinues and companies were properly armed, armoured and mounted for their role in battle. The magnates and captains would expect their men, of whatever rank, to report properly equipped and mounted as they had had to have been under the old shrieval summons.

Contracts or indentures were made between the king or great lord and a captain for a company of a specific number of men-at-arms, hobilars, mounted archers, foot archers, armed bill-men etc., for a specific time. The leader of any company or retinue would have contracted appropriate men to himself to fulfil his side of the contract. Originally these contracts were for forty days extendable by mutual agreement, but the initial contract would later be specified for a quarter year or a half, or for the duration of a campaign, or sometimes at the king's pleasure. Many examples of these contracts exist today. In 1341 Thomas Beauchamp, earl of Warwick, was contracted for forty days to provide a company of 100 men-at-arms, 40 armed men and 100 archers, while the earl of Northampton was indentured to provide 280 men-at-arms, 200 armed men and 250 archers.

The captain of a company had certain responsibilities to his men. He was obliged to equip them, pay them and to see that they were adequately provisioned; indeed apart from the personal loyalty factor the only factors that insured against desertion were pay and the prospect of plunder. Captains of companies were themselves, of course, paid for their services and received wages for their men, together with allowances for provisions and fodder from the government of Normandy out of taxation raised in Normandy.[22]

It is generally assumed that the men in armed retinues and companies for service in France during the conquest of Normandy and other parts of northern France were soldiers recruited in England. This may have been true early in the conquest, but by the time it had turned into an occupation and men were needed for periods of six months or more it was no longer a purely English army. Commanders like the duke of York, Talbot, Scales and Fastolff certainly retained the services of men they knew from home as their captains and lieutenants, and the same applied to many of the men-at-arms and archers in their companies. Nevertheless the majority of their men were recruited from professional Anglo-Norman soldiers living in Normandy, where of course many of the great captains were extensive landholders. These men came from a growing pool of experienced, but unemployed, soldiers already in France.

Captains were discouraged from recruiting too many foreigners but by 1440 nearly half the men in retinues and companies came from this source. Most of them would have been English or Anglo-Normans, but there would also have been a few Germans, Flemings and many Frenchmen from Normandy, Brittany, Gascony, and Burgundy. This reservoir of unemployed veteran soldiers was available to the highest bidder which put a premium on good and regular pay and the prospects of success, plunder and profit. Successful commanders such as Talbot would have found it easier to recruit the men they needed than those who were not so successful.

The type of contract in use at the end of the Hundred Years' war was used throughout the Wars of the Roses between magnates and captains, and between captains and individual soldiers. These contracts were used all the way up the social scale from the esquire with a few archers to the magnate with a huge retinue, and between the magnate and his sovereign. An interesting detail of these contracts is that pay seems to have been given to meet the soldiers' expenses only.[23] In other words it was given to cover the cost of his food and clothing, and presumably also the cost of forage for his horse. There does not seem to have been any element in his pay to pay for his actual service. Perhaps plunder was expected to cover the cost of the soldier's service. In a civil war where popular support was essential, however, plunder could not be allowed free rein.

Wars and campaigns did not only involve soldiers; there were specialist tradesmen, without whom the armies could not operate. These men included carpenters, miners, smiths, armourers, fletchers, bowyers, masons, saddlers, farriers, ditchers, pavillioners, bakers, butchers and wagoners. Initially artillerymen were considered artisans but it wasn't long before they too were listed as soldiers in medieval armies. All these tradesmen could be arrayed by the arrayers just like a soldier and would serve under similar terms. They could also be indentured to serve a particular captain or to be part of a magnate's retinue, as can be seen in Henry V's preparation for the Agincourt campaign: Nicolas Frost, a bowyer, received a writ to make and repair Henry V's bows; Stephen Ferrour was required to provide iron and horseshoes, smiths and all the things that farriers might require together with whatever was necessary for their conveyance.

Another group of camp followers were the household staffs of the king, the prince of Wales and other great captains who would take some of their personal staff with them when they went on campaign. Presumably they continued to be paid what they had received at home, with the possible addition of a war bonus and an allowance for the rigours and dangers likely to be met. These great men were always expected to keep a good and bountiful house, no matter what the circumstances. Consequently they took with them a chamberlain, clerks, physicians, priests, minstrels, tailors, bakers, butlers, pavillioners, farriers, and sometimes even falconers and huntsmen. The household staffs would be a part of a privy baggage train guarded by members of the magnate's retinue but subject to the overall directions of the captain of the army's baggage train. It is no wonder that the baggage train was such a magnet to the other side and that great booty was taken from a defeated medieval army.

Voluntary service in English armies for service abroad or into Scotland was normal; certainly this was so from Edward III's reign until the Wars of the Roses. For those who volunteered from the lower echelons of society the rigours of campaigning were not that different from those of their daily lives, and they might enrich themselves through plunder. Convicted felons, and many volunteered for service, did so in the hope of earning a pardon through good war service. The knightly classes, of course, were brought up to consider that war was their business and as a result they volunteered for service; they would hope to win their spurs and gain fame and fortune in war. The motive to gain renown and possibly a fortune through war remained for the nobility and knightly classes throughout the period until the end of the Wars of the Roses, by which time other avenues of advancement became less risky and more profitable. Voluntary service, therefore, was normal for almost the entire period under review.

Taking into account the many arrayed, voluntary or indentured soldiers, all of whom were in the service of the king who was obliged to pay their wages. How much did he pay? By 1350 a scale of wages was applied to everyone from an earl to the armed foot soldier; the pay was good for a mounted archer, the same as that paid to a skilled craftsman at the time. The daily pay for an earl, who would normally command a division of the army, was 6s 8d or £126 10 shillings per year – about the equivalent of a major general's pay today, who also commands a division. A banneret was paid 4 shillings per day, a knight 2 shillings, a man-at-arms 1 shilling, a mounted archer 6 pence, a foot archer 3 pence and an armed foot soldier 2 pence.[24] Additionally a 'war bonus' or 'regard' was paid every quarter to the leader of a group.

A comparison of these wages with those paid eighty years later is of interest. Before his invasion of France in April 1415, Henry V published a daily scale of pay for the army. This stated that a duke would receive 13s 4d, an earl 6s 8d, barons or bannerets 4s, knights 2s, men-at-arms 1s, and archers, both mounted and foot, 6d.[25] This pay scale did not change. Henry V also instituted a form of pension when in 1416 he declared that those who died at the siege of Harfleur would have their pay for the whole period of the siege paid to their relatives. He also ordered that the relatives of those killed at Agincourt, or who died during the march from Harfleur to Calais, should be paid the same as those who survived the campaign.[26]

During Henry VI's reign, John Talbot, as an earl and acting in the capacity of a lieutenant general in Normandy, received precisely the same figure of 6s 8d per day in 1442 as did an earl in 1350. However he also received a 'regard' of 100 marks per quarter for every thirty men-at-arms in his retinue. Additionally he was paid a 'pension pour son estat' as one of the two lieutenant generals in Normandy of about £500 per year, which was later reduced to £220 per year when his pay as a marshal was doubled. He also received an allowance to cover his expenses.[27] These were good earnings by any standard but probably the 'regard' was passed on to his men. As befitted their extra responsibility captains of companies and garrison commanders received additional wages over and above their wages as knights or men-at-arms.

However Talbot and other captains had considerable expenses to meet in the war. Their main expenses involved the prompt payment of wages to their retinues and to any garrisons they captained. Also, in the case of senior commanders, they had the expenses of their personal military and household staffs. Of course they received wages from the crown for the soldiers in their retinues and for those serving in the garrisons of which they might be captain – these were not only paid in arrears but they were not necessarily paid when they were due. Furthermore, there was often a shortfall in the reimbursement, and it is doubtful if the crown met all their expenses. Since one of the attractions of service under the crown with a great captain such as Talbot was the good and regular pay, it was incumbent on the captain to ensure that pay was paid when it was due. Any shortfall therefore would have had to be met from his personal income.

The same problem confronted lesser captains, though on a smaller scale. Captains received pay for their companies on the basis of the numbers and rank of the soldiers in the company, and because pay was paid in arrears it invited petty dishonesty. However, unless ample plunder was available, it is unlikely that a dishonest captain would keep his soldiers for long – there were always other captains on the lookout for good soldiers. Nevertheless, it is known that profits of war were used as wages during periods of financial crisis. Edward III may have done this in the 1350s, and it is known that Henry V did so on his campaigns in France.

The wages bills for campaigns, which had to be met by parliament, were considerable and it explains parliament's pecuniary interest in the campaigns. In the case of the French campaign of 1369, initial payments to Edmund, earl of Cambridge (Edward III's third son) and the earl of Pembroke for a campaign out of Gascony into Périgord was £19,500 for wages and regards, and a further £2,000 for shipping. This was approved by parliament at the end of January. In February prests, or loans, were issued by the exchequer totalling £1,060 4s 1d. These loans were simply an advance on wages, which would normally have been expected at the muster when the captains would have had to account for the number and type of soldier on the payroll. The prests were necessary to enable captains to recruit the number and type of soldier required and to give the soldiers something to live on until they reached the theatre of operations.

Pay in Normandy was the responsibility of the treasurer-general of the Normandy government and the process of mustering was the responsibility of the two marshals of France in Normandy. The latter would provide the lists of retinues, companies and garrisons, and the number of men in them by rank, while the former would ensure that the wages, in cash, were delivered as required. Obviously the bureaucratic process involved took time and therefore all wages were paid in arrears and generally monthly or at the end of short contracts. Sometimes the crown defaulted in the payment of wages leaving the captain to pay his troops out of his own pocket. A good example of this concerns Talbot's claim for accumulated arrears of pay from 1435 to 1436 amounting to a total of £3,800. The crown agreed this sum but consented only to pay the amount outstanding in instalments. Other examples include the £38,666 owed to Richard, duke of York and the £19,000 owed to Humphrey, duke of Buckingham as captain of the garrison at Calais.[28] This Calais garrison constituted the only 'regular' forces of the crown and they were paid by the exchequer in England. The numbers in the garrison varied a little from year to year, depending on the threat, but in 1451 they numbered a little over 1,000 men. Their wages over the three years from June 1451 to June 1454 averaged over £17,000 per annum.[29] This was a large sum of money and when non-payment sometimes occurred it was the cause of frequent mutinies. Generally the expense was met from the income from the wool staple. It was relatively easy to coerce money from the company to pay for the garrison, since otherwise the garrison would simply steal the wool kept in the warehouses and sell it for themselves.

Training

Although there is no mention by the chroniclers of any training being done it is inconceivable that some sort of group training was not carried out while in camp before embarkation or before a campaign began. Some form of training would be done to familiarize the soldier with his leaders, to the orders that could be given in battle and to explain what was expected of him on receipt of those orders. Also, he would need to be familiar with his leader's banners and those of other leaders in the army, including the heraldic devices used by them on their surcoats and later with their badges. This sort of training would have engendered a feeling of comradeship, and would have built up morale and encouraged confidence; it would also have been important to prevent boredom and keep the soldiery out of mischief while waiting to embark or before setting out on campaign.

Of course all those who volunteered were already expected to be able to use their weapons effectively. Indeed youths of noble or knightly birth were expected to be good horsemen and proficient in the use of their arms; 'using jousts, learning to run with a spear and handle an axe, sword and dagger, wrestling ... leaping, running, to make them hardy, free and well bred; so that when the realm in time of need had their service in deeds and enterprises of arms, they might be more apt to do honourable service'.[30] These same young men took part in tournaments, which were held regularly across the country. It was a place at which young men could first impress themselves on princes and the great magnates and played an important part of their training for war.

There were two sorts of tournament, the joust and the *mêlée*. The former was derived from the twelfth-century Pas d'Armes when a knight would post himself at a bridge, ford or narrow pass and challenge anyone of knightly rank who wished to pass to fight him for the privilege of doing so. The latter would be given time to don his armour and then battle would begin. This form of the sport gradually developed into the joust where two knights would gallop at each other fully armed and armoured with couched lances but separated by the tilt, a long wooden fence or barrier covered with cloth. The joust was a trial between individuals and tested their skill at arms and horsemanship. The *mêlée*, in contrast, was initially a friendly battle fought between invited teams, rather like football teams. However they gradually evolved into a very serious affair indeed, often involving more than a hundred knights a side and fought over a wide area of countryside.[31]

Before any particular joust or *mêlée* began the decision had to be taken as whether it was to be fought *à l'outrance*, to the death, or until surrender, with sharp weapons of war, or *à plaisance*, with rebated weapons and cronelled lances where the aim was to score points. The weapons of the *mêlée* were essentially those of mounted warfare: the lance, the sword and the mace or hammer. Generally, the lance was carried in the hand and was the first weapon to be used, once broken, the sword, which was carried on the sword belt, was used for close fighting. A mace or hammer was carried on the saddlebow and would be usd either instead of the sword or if it broke or fell from the hand.

Teams entered for either type of *mêlée* usually came from a particular magnate's establishment or from a garrison, and they formed in effect, a squadron of heavy cavalry which fought as such if they were well trained. They followed their leader in a compact group for the initial charge with the couched lance and having pressed this home against the opposing team would then reign in, turn about, close ranks and carry out a second charge. The combat would then deteriorate into a series of individual fights with sword and mace or axe, in which a successful knight would come to the aid of a hard-pressed colleague. All this was excellent training for war since the controlled and disciplined heavy cavalry charge could be decisive in battle, and the ability to reform and come back into the fight was often a crucial factor. Of equal importance was the ability to fight as an individual on horseback in the general press of battle, and to be able to both recognize and come to the aid of a comrade in distress. This often saved the day, or at least saved a friend's life or his ransom.

However, after the English copied the Scots and fought mainly on foot in battle, it became essential for knights and men-at-arms to be as formidable on their feet as they had been when mounted. The weapons favoured by knights in this form of combat were the poleaxe or the two-handed sword; these fights could also be fought *à l'outrance* or *à plaisance*. A famous *mêlée à l'outrance* was the Battle of the Thirty fought in 1351 between the English garrison of Ploermel and the French garrison of Josselin in Brittany.[32] It was agreed that the *mêlée* should be fought by thirty knights, or men-at-arms, a side on foot; the weapons were not specified. Most of the participants were mercenaries. The French won this arranged battle killing nine of the English for the loss of six of their own men. All the participants were wounded and the surviving English were taken prisoner. One version of this renowned fight says that the French won because a French knight left the fight, mounted his destrier and charged the close-packed and dismounted English so scattering them.[33] A famous fight on foot with poleaxes *à l'outrance* was fought by Sir Richard Beauchamp, earl of Warwick, against his challenger Sir Pandolf

Malateste in Verona in about 1410; he wounded his opponent and the fight was stopped.[34]

The archers trained constantly while the bill-men, coming mainly from the town militias, most probably received some training in arms. Archers came from both the country and the towns, and both the nobility and the gentry were competent archers since they used bows and arrows when hunting deer, wild boar and wolves. Indeed archery was a competitive sport and competitions were popular throughout the Middle Ages in England. However, constant practice was needed to become a competent archer. Royal edicts made sure that archery skills were maintained: Edward III was particularly concerned that the practice was being neglected and thought that 'whereas the people of our realm, nobles as well as commons, usually practised in their games the art of archery ... now the art is almost totally neglected.' He was worried that the 'kingdom becomes truly short of archers', consequently he encouraged men on feast days 'to exercise themselves in the art of archery'.[35] However he need not have worried, not only was archery a popular sport in which good archers achieved renown, but the possibility of finding plunder in France was high and the pay of an archer in the army was good.

Provisioning

Once an army had been assembled at the muster point in the north for a campaign into Scotland, or had disembarked from ships in France, they not only had to be prepared to meet their enemy in battle but they had to feed themselves and this was their biggest problem. Indeed the campaigns into Scotland were nearly always cut short because of a shortage of supplies or fodder. This is not surprising bearing in mind that Edinburgh, the largest city in Scotland at the time probably had no more than perhaps 4,000 citizens, and the size of a city, of course, reflected the size and productivity of the countryside around it. In the case of Edinburgh the area must have been relatively poor to sustain what was, even in those days, a fairly small city. Therefore the problem of maintaining an army of between ten and twenty thousand strong in that area must have been Herculean. The problem was not as acute in France but it certainly existed.

Instances of how campaigns in France were affected by the need to provision abound. In August 1346 Philip VI of France was able to catch up with Edward III's army after he had crossed the Seine because it needed to gather provisions and forage on the way, a slow business. How then was this problem overcome? All armies in the Middle Ages expected to live off the countryside to a certain extent and therefore had a well-organized system of harbingers under the marshals to glean food and forage from the country through which they passed. In friendly areas the provisions would be paid for or at least tallies, which could be redeemed for cash later, would be given in exchange. However in hostile territory the necessary supplies were simply taken at the point of the sword. Harbingers therefore went on their foraging way with an escort of mounted soldiers. They would pack the provisions that they either bought or took onto seized carts, and found the necessary horses to draw them. Harbingers were often the first to know that an enemy army was nearby when they met those of the other side, and they would be used deliberately to deceive the other side as to the whereabouts of their own army or its intended direction of march.

Soldiers would also forage for themselves, as soldiers have always done; a chicken here or a piglet there for the pot were considered legitimate additions to the rations. Also, all soldiers carried an iron ration on their saddles and probably also a hay-net of forage for their horses. Merchants were often encouraged to follow an army and they provided many of the goods that the army wanted – at a price. If purveyance rules were enforced the prices offered might not offer sufficient profit for merchants to take the risk of operating so close to an army, particularly if the enemy was anywhere near. Merchants were always reluctant to go into Scotland and in France would not go far from the army's bases in Calais, Brittany, Aquitaine or Normandy.

Campaigns into Scotland were whenever possible supported by sea. Provisions came by sea to Berwick, Leith or Stirling, but from there on all supplies had to be carried by the individual soldier or on wagons, indeed storms at sea often curtailed an invasion of Scotland. Wagon trains in Scotland had to be well protected as the Scots always had well-organized guerrillas operating behind an invading English army, and the wagon train was a juicy target. English armies in France were always supported by sea when practical, and also along the rivers by boat. But generally, with the exception of *chevauchées*, most expeditions of any size were accompanied by a wagon train. Wagon trains also accompanied armies in the Wars of the Roses where harbingers too were used. Wagons generally carried rations for about a week for the army and were packed with barrels of salted fish and meat, and wheat for bread; wine was also carried as it was used to purify water. The wagon trains included the army's baggage wagons as well as the private wagons of the senior commanders. The baggage wagons carried tents, pots and pans for cooking, spare clothing and footware, and all the myriad tools and materials that the artisans needed for their work. There were also wagons loaded with spare weapons and armour, and replacement bows and arrows.

Wagon trains could be very large and were a constant source of worry for an army commander who had to allocate men to protect it. However, they could also be a source of strength when an army was in a defensive position, as was the case at both Crécy and Agincourt. Taking the size of wagon trains in the seventeenth century as a guide an average English army in the Middle Ages of 10,000 men would have needed between 1,500 and 2,000 carts to carry provisions for them for a month – an unrealistic length of time. Nevertheless about 400 carts would be needed for a week for 10,000 men, or between 120 and 150 for each division of the army.[36] Three such wagon trains for the divisions would each take up about 4 miles of road space and would move relatively slowly; marching men on foot would leave them well behind. These numbers only covered the number needed for provisions, but when the number required for all the war stores and baggage are added, the numbers of wagons must have grown by a further 50 for each division.

Artillery

Siege trains were also an encumbrance on the roads and tracks and they were often very large. In the fourteenth century a battery of four guns was really about the smallest effective artillery force for a fairly small siege, but by the end of the Hundred Years' War siege trains consisting of twenty or thirty guns were quite normal. Initially the barrel of each gun was lifted off its cradle and loaded onto a special cart, the cradle was then loaded onto another. The loading and unloading had to be done with a crane, which also had to be carried on a cart, probably only one for each battery of four guns. Cannon balls also had to be carried; originally they were of stone, but later they were made of iron and several wagon loads were needed for each battery. Lastly there were the powder wagons to carry the gunpowder or the ingredients to make it on site. A fully equipped forge formed part of every siege train. This adds up to about 22 wagons per battery of four guns, or over a hundred for a major siege. These wagons carried a heavy load and needed four horses each to draw them. Once again they would have had an escort of soldiers in addition to the gunners themselves.

At the time of the siege of Harfleur in 1415, guns were cast and were about 12ft in length with a bore of over 2ft, and could cast a stone of 400lb. However, due to their great weight they had not yet superseded the old-fashioned siege engines which relied on torsion, tension and counterpoise to hurl a stone of nearly the same weight to about the same distance. The advantage of the gun lay in its ability to throw a stone with much greater force and therefore its effect on the walls of a fortress was greater, and it could make a breach in less time than that taken by the conventional siege engine. Loading the guns was a simple matter of rolling or ramming a stone ball down the barrel and tamping it with wadding, then fitting the chamber which held the charge. Each gun was furnished with two or three removable chambers, known as thunder boxes; these were filled with gunpowder by a spoon, and fired by a firing iron, a heated iron wand, which was inserted down a tube into the chamber. The chamber mouth was closed with a tampion or bung made of softwood to act as a wad between the charge and the stone cannon ball. When the bung had been rammed in with a pusher, the box was lifted into the breach by the handle and clamped in its place. The gun was now loaded and ready to fire. After firing the barrel was washed out with a mixture of vinegar and water and the chamber was changed for a new one already charged. The rate of fire was very slow, perhaps ten rounds an hour. Each large gun had its cradle of elm or oak, in which it was set with a packing of hay or tow at each side. It had a pair of wooden gemels on which it could be raised or lowered by means of chains, pins, pulleys and levers.[37]

The first manuscript mention of cannon was in the 'Registro delle Provisione' of Florence in 1326, while the earliest known picture of a cannon is in the 'Milemete Ms' at Oxford dated about 1325. Cannon were used at the siege of Calais in 1346 when all the guns, shot and powder held at the Tower were sent to aid the siege. Since those early days and by the end of the Hundred Years' War guns had developed into fairly sophisticated weapons; they had become essential in both siege and field warfare. Indeed nearly all the characteristics and details of artillery that can be seen today were already present in embryo then.

Cannons, even in Henry V's time, were most unpredictable and there were three main reasons for this. First, they used gunpowder made with coarse saltpetre, which burnt slowly; secondly, the barrels were made of long strips of iron welded together by hammering when hot and then bound by steel bands; and thirdly because the early shot, being made of stone, did not fit the barrels sufficiently tightly. However by the middle of the fifteenth century cannons had become quite sophisticated weapons. Finer saltpetre was used in the gunpowder producing a quicker burn, often to the detriment of the gun crew standing behind because the breech ends of cannons were not yet made strongly enough to resist the pressures with the new gunpowder. The most significant advance made in the propellant was when the French master gunner, Jean Bureau, set up a powder mill in 1429 in which the ingredients of the gunpowder were properly mixed into grains which stopped the gunpowder from breaking up into its separate constituents.

Stone shot was replaced by cast-iron shot in the last quarter of the fourteenth century; it was made the same size as the stone ball it replaced. However it wasn't long before the significance of muzzle velocity was realized and both the cannons and their shot became smaller and more effective. Initially the cast-iron shot was cast to fit particular cannon, but soon the size of cannon became roughly standardized in various sizes and cannon balls were produced in quantity to fit the standard cannons, small irregularities being neutralized by wadding. Likewise, once cannons and shot became reasonably standardized and gunpowder reliable, charges began to be measured with knowledge of the probable effect so they were able to be varied according to the range required for any particular standard size of cannon. Good gunpowder increased the range of cannons up to a maximum of about 2,500 yards. The barrels of cannon were soon cast in bronze but due to variations in the alloy were still not very reliable or safe; however, by the mid fifteenth century this problem was largely overcome and artillery entered the modern age.

The English might have used cannon in war before the French – 'gonnes' are mentioned in accounts of the siege of Berwick in 1333 and some accounts say the English used them at Crécy. Cannon were certainly used at the siege of Calais in 1346. It is also likely that the English put cannon on board ship before the French; Richard Beauchamp, earl of Warwick, for instance, had guns on board his carracks in 1404. However there can be little doubt that it was the French who developed most of the innovations which made cannon such an important weapon, largely thanks to the interest shown by Charles VII and the innovations of his master gunner Jean Bureau.

In England the keeper of the Wardrobe was responsible for ordering and making cannon until Henry V's reign when a new office became responsible, that of the master of the ordnance. Gun founders, who made the cannon, were established at the Tower of London, the crown's main arsenal, where iron cannon balls and gunpowder were both made and stored. Henry VI neglected his artillery until forced to take an interest as a result of the Wars of the Roses. However it was Edward IV who elevated the position of master of the ordnance to his household as he took a great personal interest in the artillery. Nevertheless artillery was never used to its full potential in these wars, being used in one siege only, that of Bamburgh. Field artillery was only used at the battles of Empingham in 1470, Tewkesbury in 1471 and Bosworth Field in 1473. Guns were moved about the country many times as a threat, particularly against Lancastrian-held castles in the north, although they were not used, and no doubt, since they were impressive weapons, they gained prestige wherever they went. Handguns made their appearance towards the end of the fourteenth century but were used in the Wars of the Roses mainly by mercenary troops.

Guns were very expensive to make and to use, and consequently it was usually only kings who could afford them, although it is clear that some noblemen and some cities owned cannons. The cities of London and York certainly had cannons and both the Lancastrians and the Yorkists had them in their armies. Whether they kept the cannons from the royal arsenal after their leader lost the throne or whether they were made at other arsenals is not clear. Warwick certainly had them on his ships, so presumably they could be bought from or made at other arsenals besides the Tower, or perhaps they were bought in France or Flanders. It is interesting to note that in 1456 the Scottish parliament thought it 'speedful that the king make request to certain of the great barons of the land that are of any might to make carts of war, and in each cart two guns, and each of them to have two chambers, with the rest of the gear that pertains thereto, and a cunning man to shoot them'.[38] Later acts refer only to carts of war and do not include references to guns, presumably because guns were much too expensive for even the greatest lords to afford. Artillery therefore became a weapon of war owned exclusively by kings; this was certainly so in France and it is reasonable to assume that the same applied in England.

Armour constantly changed throughout the period, getting gradually lighter and more efficient. The changes that took place are referred to in the following chapters as and when they occurred. The catalyst for change was undoubtedly the use of the longbow used in mass. First the longbow forced the armoured knight and man-at-arms to fight on his feet because too many horses were killed or wounded in the arrow storm. As a consequence armour had to be made lighter and more flexible and be able to resist double-handed weapons such as the poleaxe; it also had to be able to deflect an arrow loosed from close range. All this dictated the gradual change from mail armour to plate. However plate armour was expensive and good plate armour was very expensive, so only relatively rich men could afford it. Archers and bill-men certainly could not afford this type of armour, but they wore the best they could afford provided it still allowed them to do their job. All three types of soldier were expected to come to the muster with appropriate protection as the crown did not provide it. The same applied to their weapons. Nevertheless armourers, smiths, bowyers and fletchers were all members of the support services provided by the crown. New bows were often required on campaign, arrows also. The smiths had to sharpen and repair weapons and the armourers repaired armour. This mainly took the form of attaching new straps to plate armour or welding on new rivets. However the crown did provide replacement weapons, which were carried in the baggage train. Of course after a successful battle many good weapons and armours were found on the battlefield. The latter served to uprate the armour of men-at-arms, archers and bill-men, and good armour became part of the profits of war, since it could be sold to a knight for a good price.

Chapter 3

The Army at War

The Chevauchée

Warfare in the Middle Ages was cruel, barbarous and bloody. Battles, even skirmishes, always involved hand-to-hand fighting in which men hacked and thrust at the men opposite, whether on foot or on horseback. Indeed even when archers in large numbers formed a major part of armies, and later when artillery and handguns appeared on the battlefield, battles could only be won by hand-to-hand fighting after closing with the enemy, and this, the ultimate aim, was the only way to defeat him. The firepower of archers merely reduced the numbers of opponents before the moment of contact, giving the side with the most archers an advantage in the hand-to-hand fighting that followed. Everyone from the king to the lowliest bill-man was prepared to meet his opponent face to face.

This had tremendous consequences for the leadership of kings and princes and for charismatic captains like Henry of Lancaster, Richard earl of Warwick and Talbot. Robert I, Edward III, the Black Prince and Henry V were admired and respected universally for their bravery and courage in battle. To their men, the knights, men-at-arms, archers and bill-men who made up their armies, they were above mere heroes. The fortunes of them all rested on the conduct of their leaders, and to see and hear of their king fighting bravely in the midst of the carnage around them gave the whole army great confidence. The death of a prince in combat, or his flight from the field of battle, or the taking of a king as a prisoner spelt the defeat of his army.

Wars in the Middle Ages are usually depicted by the chroniclers as a series of battles and sieges in which knight fought valiantly with knight under the rules of chivalry and the loser was treated with courtesy. Much was made of the panoply of war and the nobleness of the magnates involved, but the reality was very different. Knightly virtues were extolled by knightly society and practised in battle, but only represent a small part of the warlike activity undertaken by knights in war. Most operations of war were either sieges or *chevauchées*, an offensive march by an army through enemy territory, and smaller raids, and were concerned with the destruction of the resources of the enemy. The real struggle in the war against Scotland and France was economic. The instrument used was unrelenting military pressure applied where it would be most effective and the destruction of the everyday means of life of the populace at large.

The invasion and devastation of foreign lands did not only have an economic effect but also impressed upon the inhabitants that their king did not care for them and could not protect them. If France allowed foreign armies to march throughout the length and breadth of the land without let or hindrance then clearly she was not interested in the welfare of her citizens; and consequently loyalties might change. In those areas where local ties were stronger than national ones, a strategy of destruction was designed to impress upon those in authority that their best course would be to show loyalty to the king of England rather than to the king of France. The intent therefore was political as well as economic; it showed waverers the might of the English king and the weakness of the French. The policy had similar objectives in Scotland where there had always been an English faction.

In both countries, where occupation was impractical if not impossible, war became a matter of attrition in which the French and Scottish economies were to be weakened by the destruction of their resources and by the curtailment of their trade by any means. The facts of war were well known and understood by the kings of England, France and Scotland, as well as by the dukes of Brittany and Burgundy and by the counts of Flanders, who all condoned the wars of destruction carried out in their names whilst bewailing the effect of this policy on their own citizens, towns and countryside.

Once Edward III and his successors realized they were never in a position to occupy the whole of Scotland or France permanently they had either to defeat them in a decisive battle or exhaust them to win the crown of France and the overlordship of Scotland. English campaigns in France do not appear to have been devised to draw the French into a decisive battle; nevertheless the strategy of the raid in force achieved this on three occasions and was close to exhausting French resistance twice. English armies invading Scotland always hoped to bring the Scots to a decisive battle, which they achieved twice; on the first occasion they were defeated, on the second they were victorious but failed to achieve their political aim.

This style of warfare with its looting and burning persisted even to the time of Henry V's occupation of Normandy in 1417. Henry intended to occupy all of northern France before taking the crown; consequently he did his best, on pain of death, to stop the inveterate looting and burning. When Henry died in 1422 his brother the duke of Bedford continued this policy in Normandy, but in those parts of France beyond the limits of the English occupation, the old practice of loot and burn prevailed.

The brunt of this type of warfare fell, as always, on the ordinary citizens of the towns and countryside. When a friendly army passed their way nearly every store of grain, hay and wine was taken for the army's needs and many head of cattle, sheep and pigs were slaughtered for their sustenance. If the local inhabitants were lucky all this would be paid for in due course but it meant a lean year ahead. If the army was hostile all this was inevitable and carried out more thoroughly over a wider area, without of course any form of payment for supplies taken. Furthermore all villages, farms and isolated buildings were put to the torch. Towns on the army's route were razed to the ground. Any town that offered resistance was stormed and sacked, and its citizens put to the sword. Townsmen, villagers, farmers, peasants and their families were lucky to be left alive. Indeed once an army had passed through an area the survivors counted themselves poor from that day regardless of their former station. 'Devastation' was the apt word used at the time to describe this systematic looting, sacking and burning of a whole province or area.

However the morality of this behaviour was beginning to be questioned. Christine de Pisan[1] pointed out that the 'goode simple folk were bound to suffer' but that 'the gentlyman of arms ought to kepe hem self as moche as they can that they destroye not the goode symple folke.' Honoré Bonet, another writer of the Middle Ages,[2] said:

> in these days all wars are directed against the poor labouring people and against their goods and chattels. I do not call that war, but it seems to me to be pillage and robbery. Further, that way of warfare does not follow the ordinances of worthy chivalry.

In 1339, when Edward III invaded France from the Low Countries to take pressure off Aquitaine, he moved slowly into Picardy with a small army of English, Flemings and Germans, hoping to goad Philippe of France to battle by the destruction wrought. In total 174 parishes were destroyed, mainly by fire, and all portable and valuable goods were carried off. The total number of people who became destitute in this area of some 2,300 square miles ran into thousands including noblemen, churchmen, burghers, farmers and peasants. Several hundred men, women and children were slaughtered. Pope Benedict XII was so distressed that he gave a grant of 6,000 gold florins (about £1,075 or well over half a million pounds at today's values) to the diocese to relieve the immediate suffering. This was Edward III's first *chevauchée* in France and one in which he perfected what he had already perpetrated in Scotland in his invasion of 1333. He proudly described his operations in Picardy to his fifteen year old son, the prince of Wales, thus: 'the country is quite laid waste of corn, of cattle and of any other goods.'[3]

In 1345 the Scots crossed the border near Carlisle and did in England what the English had so often done in Scotland: they laid waste the countryside for some 750 square miles from the Border to the Lake District and from the sea to the Westmoreland hills. Every parish in the area was burnt and looted and thousands were made homeless. The following year they did the same the other side of the Pennines and devastated Northumberland. So effective were these Scottish raids that Edward III complained, 'While we are away, the Scots invade our country and commit murders, depredations, burnings and other crimes.' This was written shortly after the completion of his own successful march through Normandy, described succinctly in official letters as, 'He passed through France to Calais wasting and destroying.'

French sources describe the extent of the damage by these raids as appalling, which is evident from the promptness of measures taken to make good the damage. The *ville* at Carcassone,[i] which was utterly destroyed by fire by the army of the Black Prince on 6 November during his *chevauchée* of 1355, is a good example. Carcassone was a politically important city to King Jean because he needed its support

---

i Most large cities in France were walled, the *cité* and generally a chateau were within the walls; the former was usually garrisoned by the *cité* and the latter by the local magnate. However, suburbs grew up outside the walls and these were called the *ville*.

in the south of France to stiffen the loyalty of the local magnates. Therefore on 22 November he ordered the count of Armagnac to take immediate steps to repair the damage and to put the city into a state of defence against the possibility of future attack. He also made timber available from the royal forests for the rebuilding of churches and hospitals and impressed masons and carpenters for the work. The complete task, including the repair of the city walls was finished by April 1359.

Brutal though the strategy of devastation was it is important to realize that it was not unexpected, indeed it was common to all nations and not confined solely to the English. This was the reality of war for the civilian population, for the soldiery it represented food and profit. The instrument of devastation, the *chevauchée*, was a ruthlessly efficient operation. Unprotected towns and villages were pillaged and then burnt to the ground while the surrounding countryside was systematically laid waste. The usual means of destruction was fire and had been since the earliest of times; buildings were mainly built of wood and easily destroyed. The exceptions, made of stone, were the monasteries, abbeys and churches which were usually forbidden territory to the soldiery; and castles, keeps, city walls and towers all of which were defended and difficult to destroy by an army without siege equipment. All carts and wagons found in the countryside were invariably set alight unless needed to carry loot or supplies; on the Crécy campaign all ships found in the harbours of Normandy were first looted and then, unless required, burnt.

Most English armies operating in France had first to cross the Channel. Sometimes the armies landed at friendly ports, such as Calais, Bordeaux or Brest, but some had to land in hostile territory, and in these cases the disembarkation would take a logical course. Ships would be beached or anchored offshore and unloading would be across the beach or by the ships' boats. If enemy attacks were considered a possibility a barbican of a ditch and palisade would be built to protect the landing area. Archers and dismounted men-at-arms would have formed a defended beachhead behind which horses and men would have disembarked, to be followed by carts with war stores and provisions. As soon as sufficient horses had been landed mounted patrols would press inland to provide a piquet line to give ample warning of any enemy hostile move. In Henry V's invasion of 1415, guns were also unloaded, as they were needed for the siege of Harfleur.

On the Crécy campaign men and horses were rested for two days on disembarkation. The pause would be longer for the longer crossings and it was usual to rest for some five days after the voyage from Plymouth to Bordeaux. The usual routine for an army once it had set out on its offensive campaign involved marching, gathering supplies of food and forage, pillaging and destroying by fire all that was not eatable, transportable or valuable. Occasionally the siege of a fortress or the storming of a town would interrupt this progress, and sometimes a skirmish would occur between rival foraging parties or advance guards, but very, very rarely a full-scale battle. Indeed the pitched battles of Crécy, Poitiers and Agincourt were not characteristic of the Hundred Years' War as a whole. Pitched battles only took place when there seemed to be no alternative.

Most of the army on these operations was mounted so the force moved rapidly on two or three axes with scouts out ahead and flank guards posted. The columns could be up to ten miles apart and with the flank guards included might cover a frontage of nearly 20 miles. Everything in between would be ransacked and burnt, and civilians, if they were foolish enough to stay behind to protect their property, would be lucky to escape with their lives. Edward III himself said that his forces burnt and destroyed on a front of 12 to 15 leagues, between 36 and 45 miles, on his Cambrésis campaign.[4] Once launched the *chevauchée* spread terror far and wide and the army usually came across abandoned farms and villages. The people either hid in the forests until danger had passed or fled to the nearest walled town. There they stiffened the resistance of the townspeople who, if they didn't surrender when called upon to do so, offered furious opposition to the army trying to enter and ultimately led to the inevitable sacking of yet another town. Unfortunately, such was the lack of control where plunder was concerned, that towns were just as likely to be sacked whether they surrendered or not.

In setting out on *chevauchée* the overall aim might be to devastate the lands of a certain duchy or county as part of the economic process of war, and where possible to take particular towns and fortresses. Nevertheless the actual day-to-day route of the army was influenced largely by the availability of supplies and fodder as well as the state of the local tracks, and the whereabouts of suitable bridges and fords. On *chevauchée* it was impracticable to have a long line of communication back to a secure base and though armies carried emergency supplies they expected to live off the countryside, so victualling and foraging parties went about their business daily. Consequently the army tended to go where sufficient supplies were thought to exist and as a result, due to the pressing need to feed itself, the army ensured that the devastation was carried out where the economic effect would be greatest. Wherever the army halted it was invariably forced to continue on its way after it had consumed the locally available supplies, even in the richest areas, often after only two or three days.

Although devastation might have been the order of the day, specific prohibition against destruction, particularly of church property, was often ordered and many examples exist. In 1333 when Edward III destroyed Dunfermline he spared the Abbey and again when he devastated the lands around Elgin he spared the town because he liked the church there. In France he ordered Mont St Martin to be spared in 1339, and in 1346, having practised what he was pleased to call 'maximum damnum' within sight of Paris, he ordered that there should be no burning on the Feast of the Assumption. In 1359 he ordered that the Abbey of Pontigny, the burial place of a former archbishop of Canterbury, should not be touched. At Caen Edward III instructed his marshal, Sir Godfrey D'Harcourt, in the words of Froissart 'to have it proclaimed in his name that none should dare, on pain of the gallows, to start a fire, kill a man or rape a woman'. But notwithstanding these very explicit orders many crimes were committed for as Froissart also points out: 'in an army such as the King of England was leading it was impossible that there should not be plenty of bad characters and criminals without a conscience.'

During the early years of the Hundred Years' War the chances of this type of operation being visited upon the south of England seemed high. France was the most powerful country in Western Europe and she carried out many successful raids on the south coast; yet, year after year, it was Edward III and his commanders who launched successful *chevauchées* deep into the heart of France from their bases in Brittany, Calais and Gascony. This had a salutary effect on both antagonists. In England confidence and scorn gradually replaced a formerly deep-rooted respect and awe of the chivalry of France, the finest in Europe – while in France a haughty and arrogant optimism steadily degenerated into a feeling of despair and apprehension whenever the prospect of battle with the English loomed. Indeed after

Poitiers the English began to despise the fighting qualities of the French; Higden, a contemporary of the times, said of the French: 'just as the courage of the French is greater than other men's in the first assault, so afterwards is it weaker than women.'

The *chevauchées* were an undoubted success, but they left such hatred in their path that it stiffened the resistance of the defeated. Perhaps, in the long run, the policy of devastation was an unsuccessful political strategy for it failed to achieve the English aims and failed to make friends and cement loyalties. The majority of the soldiers who took part in these *chevauchées* were perfectly normal English and Gascon citizens at home: knights in their manors, yeomen and peasants on their farms or artisans from the towns. Chivalrous thoughts may have prompted the actions of individual knights in battle but in the daily work of devastation such thoughts must have been far from their minds.

Sympathy for the people in the lands through which they rode must have entered everyone's thoughts from time to time and no doubt individual acts of clemency occurred. As an example, the actions of Sir Thomas Holland at the sacking of Tankarville in Normandy during the Crécy campaign were noted by Froissart: 'He was able that day to prevent many cruel and horrible acts which would otherwise have been committed.' In this case Sir Thomas Holland was initially protecting people of the knightly classes and while doing so was so distressed by what he saw being done against the common people that he rode through the streets with sixteen other knights to try and put a stop to it. But incidents like this, which showed the chivalrous and humane side of the knights, must have been comparatively rare for them to be mentioned by the chroniclers.

Until about 1380, the leaders of the companies brought from England were mainly men drawn from the knightly classes, while their commanders, the men who agreed the policy and gave the orders, were all of the nobility or of the blood royal. Presumably therefore they could have stopped the destruction if they had so wished. This was probably not the case later in the Hundred Years' War when professional armies began to replace those raised largely on a class and feudal basis, and when a share of plunder augmented wages. It was certainly not so in those companies where the captain was a successful man-at-arms who had gathered about him other itinerant soldiers of fortune. These companies included English, Flemish,

French, Gascon, Scottish and German soldiers, whose wages, unless the company was under contract to some magnate, came from the booty they managed to win or extort, and whose loyalty was solely to the person who could ensure their continued prosperity and success. These so-called free companies proliferated in France in the second half of the fourteenth century.

Every enemy citizen was fair game and no distinction was made between combatant and non-combatant. However, in the absence of internationally recognized laws of war certain conventions became established among the knightly classes in their dealings with each other in war and their behaviour was at all times guided by the chivalric code to which they all aspired. These conventions related in the main to the relationship between victor and vanquished or besieger and besieged, and concerned only nobles and knights and all well-born women who might have been present in a besieged castle or town. The conventions were concerned largely with the treatment of the vanquished and allowed for the ransom of prisoners. These conventions were relatively easy to apply since nearly all of the knightly classes throughout Western Europe and the British Isles could speak some French until the end of the Hundred Years' War.

But for the common soldiers, the archer, the hobilar and many of the men-at-arms, however, knightly ethics were not of their concern and were certainly no restriction on their conduct. These soldiers were serving in a foreign country, subject neither to its laws nor to those of their own country, unfamiliar with the language and, almost certainly in France after Crécy, contemptuous of its people. Under these circumstances when devastation was the agreed strategy ordered by the leaders of English armies, and no internationally recognized law existed to curtail the actions of the soldiery, it is hardly surprising that atrocities took place.

Many examples exist of the cruelty of English leaders to those they had defeated. One of the more notorious was after the Battle of Halidon Hill in 1333 and the subsequent surrender of Berwick. Edward III ordered a hundred captives to be put to death, presumably for treason. Again, he ordered the entire population of Caen to be put to the sword after having pillaged and burnt the city in 1346; fortunately this order was never carried out due to the intervention of Sir Godfrey d'Harcourt; nevertheless over 3,000 of the citizens were killed during the sack. At Calais in July 1347 the civilians were forced to leave because of lack of food, only to be left to starve to death between Edward's siege lines and the walls of the city.

Brutality was not restricted to Edward III alone. An infamous example occurred towards the end of the Hundred Years' War in 1440 when Talbot caused 300 men, women and children to be burnt alive in a church at Libons.[5] Even as late as March 1449, when England's hold on Normandy was looking decidedly precarious, their lust for plunder was allowed free rein. The duke of Somerset, Henry VI's lieutenant general in Normandy, authorized François de Surienne, an Arogonese knight, and his English mercenaries to sack and burn the town of Fougères, on the Norman-Breton border.

However, the question must be asked, would English armies have been any less rapacious if the strategy of devastation had not been an agreed policy? Was the discipline in the army and in the various semi-independent companies good enough to overcome the temptations that came their way? The answer to both questions is 'no'. It must be remembered that no formal disciplinary training took place and no military law existed until 1385. Also, many volunteers, English, Flemish or Gascon, were lured in large part by hopes of plunder and profit. Discipline was clearly good under battle conditions, and certainly better than that of the French until towards the end of the Hundred Years' War. But discipline in battle was a very different matter from discipline in a small foraging party well away from authority. So when sack was the order of the day it is hardly surprising that excesses took place and the treatment of non-combatants in enemy territory was appalling.

The Arthurian ethic and the code of chivalry would ensure that knights took no part in the inevitable pillage and rape. This may well have been generally the case but the fact that they benefited from the ransoms and a share of the spoil makes it difficult to absolve them from the more grisly events involved with sack and pillage. It is therefore inconceivable that many a knight did not take an active part. It would have been unlikely that rich knights and knights of renown would have dismounted from their horses to take an active part in the sack of towns or the burning of villages and farms. It would have been difficult for a man in full plate armour and wearing a surcoat to take a personal hand in this activity, if not for practical reasons then at least because he would not wish to be recognized in the act and have his honour impugned. Nevertheless many knights would have directed operations from horseback and might even have cut down civilians trying to escape.

The army's leaders undoubtedly found it difficult to prevent the looting and burning of property, including church property, but clearly they did try on occasion. However the fact remained that the policy of devastation covered an innate lust for plunder. The fact that these acts were covered in war by an economic strategy designed to destroy the means of life in enemy territory opened up an avenue of opportunity for all those who went to war.

Plunder was often used as a substitute for wages when the latter were in arrears and it is clear that prospects for plunder encouraged recruitment. Indeed the booty gained from a successful campaign and the ransoms of prisoners of war enabled Edward III and other commanders to pay their troops well and reduced the demands on the taxpayer at home. Thus, campaigning in France became a popular national enterprise in stark contrast to the War in the North where booty was much more difficult to come by, ransoms not so frequent or so assured and the conditions on campaign very much harder. Troops were encouraged before battle by promises of booty. Edward III before the naval battle of Sluys is quoted by Froissart as saying, 'each man may keep whatever he can seize', and before the Battle of Poitiers the prince of Wales is reported to have said to his archers, 'the desire of the rich spoyle of the Frenchmen doth stirre you up to follow your fathers' steps.'[6]

Before the expedition of 1359 set out, knights, squires and men-at-arms flocked to Calais to await Edward's arrival; some came to 'advance their honour' but many more came to 'loot and pillage the fair land and plenteous realm of France.'[7] The prospect of loot was also a factor that determined the direction of the army. When Sir Godfrey d'Harcourt advised Edward III to invade Normandy before the Crécy campaign, he said, 'In Normandy you will find populous towns which are completely undefended where your men will have such great plunder that they will be better off for twenty years to come.' He stressed this again when he said, 'we will enter the richest country in the world and the most plenteous and we will have our way, for they are simple people who do not know what war is.'[8]

Writing of the sack of Caen, Froissart tells us that the English loaded their ships with 'cloth, jewels, vessels of gold and silver and many other treasures which they had in great plenty', and after the

Battle of Crécy the English were 'rejoicing, so great were the spoils'. The capture of the French camp after the Battle of Poitiers revealed so much booty that all who fought there

> became rich in honour and possessions, as much from the ransoms of captives as from the gain of gold and silver which was found there in the form of vessels, and gold and silver belts, and precious jewels, and chests crammed with costly and weighty girdles and fine cloaks.[9]

There was so much rich booty at Poitiers that fine French armour and harness was left lying on the battlefield, while at Castelnaudary in 1355 English soldiers found so much silver and coinage that they disdained fine clothes and furs. These riches accompanied a nobleman or rich knight everywhere he travelled, both in peace and war, and were considered essential symbols of his place in society to be displayed whenever possible. Consequently soldiers of all ranks made their fortunes from these expeditions.

Since the earliest times booty had been shared out in an army on an ascending scale depending on rank and deeds done, a general principle that applied throughout the Middle Ages. Plunder was considered a legitimate spoil of war and after a successful action or operation most plunder would be shared out among those who took part. In due course most valuable items ended up in the hands of the knightly classes; the common soldier, having no baggage wagon or sumpter, always wanted cash and he sold the larger items which he could not carry to members of the knightly class. In Edward III's armies each company was required to have an official, the *butiner*, whose sole function was to distribute the plunder according to the convention of the day. In Normandy, in Henry V's and Bedford's time, each garrison was required to have a controller, one of whose functions was to ensure that the king and his lieutenants received their due share of any plunder or ransoms taken locally by the garrison. The actual share that an individual received was strictly regulated and enforced.

Many examples of the distribution of booty exist in the chronicles. Booty was divided on the basis of a third for the captain and the remainder for the taker; often the remaining two-thirds was pooled among all the troops of a retinue or company and divided equally among them. The taking of booty was encouraged by commanders, even by kings. Edward III was not averse to the practice; indeed in 1340, on returning from Flanders, he 'distributed the spoils among his earls'. It was said of Henry of Lancaster after his campaign of 1345 in upper Gascony that his 'liberality and munificence attracted recruits ... for when he took a town he kept very little or nothing for himself but let the army have it all.'[10]

An official division of plunder seems first to have been codified by Richard II in 1385 in his Ordinances of War. In these ordinances it was laid down that one third of a soldier's profit of war went to his captain who was obliged to give one third of his profits to his master and so on up the ladder of authority to the king himself. Consequently the king received the 'thirds of the thirds of the thirds' of all the profits of war.[11] Nevertheless it appears that the division of profits had not always been on the basis of thirds, both Edward III and the Black Prince demanded a moiety of ransoms and spoils of war in particular cases.[12] The official division of a third of all profits to the leader at all levels of the army was written into contracts of service from about 1370 when virtually all military service was by indenture. Every step in the hierarchy therefore had a pecuniary interest in the profitable execution of war and in all things that could possibly make war prosperous, including the encouragement of looting.

Discipline

Warfare, as ever, demanded good discipline and clear authority on operations, and although a rank structure like those in modern armies did not exist, punishment for military ill discipline was harsh and swiftly executed. Authority at the beginning of the period was linked to social position. The king, prince or royal duke was commonly the commander-in-chief, a divisional commander was an earl while a banneret, a baron or knight was a senior commander under an earl. Knights would often captain a company of men-at-arms and mounted archers, and a vintenar, an experienced soldier, would be put in charge of twenty foot soldiers. However, running through this generalized pyramid of authority ran the thread of loyalties founded on the existence of retinues. Retinues varied from the very large belonging to a king or an earl to those of a handful of men-at-arms and archers owing loyalty to a specific knight. These retinues, along with their commanders, would be placed under the command of a particular banneret or earl who was appointed by the army commander.

Each earl either singly or jointly commanded divisions of up to two or three thousand men. Each division would be made up of the retinues of the earls plus the commands of several bannerets who would also have their own retinues, plus those of the knights allocated to them under their command. The king would normally command one of the divisions whose mainstay would be his own retinue. Archers and bill-men mustered under shrieval summons would be allocated in vintaines, platoons of twenty men, to where they were needed to augment the retinues. Gradually as the armies became more professional and the feudal obligation became redundant, captains would answer the call to arms complete with their companies on indenture or contract. These professional bands together with the indentured retinues of the knightly classes made up the armies of the later fourteenth century until the end of the Hundred Years' War and into the Wars of the Roses.

Authority and a chain of command therefore certainly existed, and this denoted a disciplinary code and a scale of punishment for military offences when on operations that was very different from the common or civil laws at home. The latter were certainly applicable while the army awaited embarkation in England or was encamped at the muster point near the northern border. However the laws of France or Scotland were deemed irrelevant once the army was on operations in either country and England's common law was not strictly applied. Nevertheless law of a sort was clearly enforced from time to time on the soldiery in their relations with the foreign civilian population by the commander-in-chief when it served his purpose to do so, but it was not consistent and not deemed essential. In Aquitaine the English soldiers were subject to the laws of the duchy, where their king was duke. Later, Henry V applied the civil laws to his garrisons when English armies occupied Normandy.

Punishment for military offences could be very severe, but no record of a scale of punishment or disciplinary code seems to exist for the times of Edward III, although the code produced on the authority of Richard II in July 1385[13] would appear to codify what was already normal practice. However, it is not too difficult to produce a possible scale of punishment that would have been accepted by society at the time and which would have met the needs of the armies for the fourteenth and fifteenth centuries. For an army on the march in enemy territory, punishment short of hanging must have been difficult to impose. Reprimand and threat would have been used and on occasion a soldier would have had an ear cut off for disciplinary reasons. Flogging does not seem to figure as a punishment since a soldier with a sore back would not have been able to carry equipment and weapons nor wear armour. However, once soldiers received regular pay on operations it opened up another avenue of punishment, for it is well known that a soldier is hurt most in his pocket. The duke of Bedford during his regency in Normandy in the 1420s issued orders to the effect that any soldier who took goods from non-combatants without payment would have the value docked from his wages.

However, in the Middle Ages many soldiers followed their calling solely because of the prospect of plunder. It is conceivable therefore that when a share of plunder was distributed throughout the ranks of the army, the withholding of a soldier's share of the booty for disciplinary reasons would have been an effective punishment. A suitable scale of punishment for the age might therefore begin with a reprimand and move up through default of plunder, confiscation of plunder, fines and stoppages of pay to arrest and imprisonment, loss of an ear and ultimately to hanging. With such a scale available commanders should have been able to impose discipline and thereby have prevented the destruction, slaughter, rape and pillage if they had so wished. The fact is that except in certain cases destruction and pillage were part of the orders of the day, and slaughter and rape unfortunate side issues of such a policy. There can be no doubt that the problem of discipline with regard to the treatment of the non-combatant was made more difficult when sack was ordered one day and restraint the next, as for instance during the prince of Wales's *chevauchée* through Languedoc and Roussillon in 1355.

Henry V issued ordinances setting out his disciplinary code before his invasion of France in 1415. It listed a series of crimes and punishments that in general had been accepted as crimes by soldiery against the civilian population for some time, and was part of the growing recognition that certain things should not be done in war against the non-combatant. The great difference between Henry and his predecessors, and indeed his enemies and their predecessors, was that Henry did his best to enforce it. Henry's disciplinary code was probably based on that of Richard II and importantly it included what might be called purely military crimes, in addition to crimes against the non-combatant.

The purely military sections of these ordinances deal with matters that are at the very heart of the problem of the maintenance of discipline, particularly in an army culled from so many disparate elements. It begins, under pain of death, by forbidding any man from going ahead of the army, except those authorized by the 'herbergers' or victualling officers to buy or take provisions for the army. It also expressly forbids any man from going in front of the banner of his lord or master when the army, or his part of it, was in battle array. This was essential to maintain ordered ranks, particularly when advancing into battle. The names of offenders would be taken and given to the constable and the marshal who would set up courts martial under specific royal officers to try offenders.[14]

Violent resistance to arrest was punishable by death, as was the wounding of a royal officer in the course of arrest. Anyone found guilty of leaving the ranks, for plunder or to take prisoners while in action, would be put 'from his horse' and fined. He was also required to give adequate surety for his future behaviour before he was allowed once again to take a full part in the life of the army. Any man who stole from rations or forage already gathered and assigned by the king's herbergers was liable to have his horse and harness confiscated. The confiscation of horse and harness was not only a significant financial loss but, perhaps more importantly, in an army where the majority rode to war, it reduced the offender to the ranks of the foot soldiers and to half his former pay.

Every soldier was obliged, under pain of death, to obey the orders of his superior officer in all 'lefulle things'. He was obliged to keep 'wacche and ward' when required, or in modern parlance to be detailed for sentry or picquet duty. Any failure to do so was punishable by the arrest of 'his body, horse and harness' by the marshal for a period agreed between the marshal and the man's captain. Furthermore any man detailed for these duties who left his post without permission was liable for 'smytyng of his heede that departed otherwyse'! Punishment for mutiny and desertion was severe. 'Any man escrye his own name or the name of his lord or master, to make a rysing in the people, by which any affray might fall in the ooste [host] shall be drawn and hanged'. While any man that 'raiseth a banner and called people togidre without licence' would also be drawn and hanged and all those who followed him would have 'theire heedes smyten of'.

In an effort to maintain the discipline of the host when in battle array any man who cried havoc and all who followed him would be arrested, lose their horses and harness, be fined, and be required to give surety against their future good behaviour. However the man who first cried havoc would also be imprisoned at the 'kynges wylle'. Furthermore a man 'that crieth mounte' in battle would not only lose his horse and harness and be fined but have 'his body to the kynges wille of his liffe'; an important clause when knights and men-at-arms fought on foot but had their horses held close at hand by grooms. A man who 'broke no array ne goo of the ooste without licence', or in other words broke ranks in the face of the enemy, faced severe punishment, while any man who made an 'assault without his capiten his will it be' did so under threat of imprisonment.[15] Finally, the military crime, which exists today, of stealing from a comrade, was severely punished.[16]

Other aspects of these ordinances related mainly to the taking of prisoners, the levying of ransoms, and the division of ransoms between the man who took the captive, his captain and the king, and the giving of safe conduct. As to the division of ransom and plunder, the ordinances once again legalize the division and state the traditional view 'that everyman pay his thirdes to his capitayne, lorde, or master, of all maner wynyng by wares'. An interesting aspect was that racism was strictly forbidden, not on moral grounds but for the maintenance of discipline. It was necessary to prevent brawls, an important factor in an army drawn from many different nationalities including the Welsh, Irish, Gascon, Flemish, German, Norman and of course the English; offenders could be put to death for 'noys making'.[17] Captains of garrisons had specific disciplinary powers over their garrisons, the members of which were obliged by law to be obedient to their captain. Captains of garrisons of fortified towns had the right to detail soldiers to duties of watch and ward, a duty normally carried out by watchmen appointed and paid by the local city council. They were also obliged to judge all disputes and to suppress all disturbances within the garrison and they were specifically required to keep a prison.

Other aspects of the disciplinary code dealt with the legitimacy of orders given before specific tactical situations. As an example of this type of order, all archers were ordered to provide themselves with an 11-foot stake, sharpened at one end, before the Battle of Agincourt. And before the Battle of Cravant, men-at-arms and mounted archers were ordered to dismount and leave their horses half a league in rear on pain of death in order to ensure that everyone, less those specifically ordered to remain mounted, fought on foot. Later, at sieges, every soldier was required to bring a 13-foot fagot so that fascines could be made to fill ditches at the foot of castle or fortress walls. Every group of seven men-at-arms were obliged to provide a scaling ladder while archers had to provide a pavisse for each pair.[18]

Henry V's disciplinary ordinances were mainly applicable to an army in the field, but once the occupation of Normandy was complete the ordinances had to be modified so that they were appropriate for an army of occupation. In particular the taking of plunder had to stop, payment had to be made for provisions, and the local population treated with courtesy and consideration. Much was achieved by the simple expedient of regular pay and provisions. But Bedford, during his regency, made quite sure that his captains knew where to draw the line by including reference to the various disciplinary ordinances in their contracts of service, and by proclaiming the ordinances, publicly, in both English and French. Everyone therefore knew what the law was concerning the behaviour of the army and its relations with the civilian population.

Bedford's ordinances generally tightened discipline and at the same time made the military in garrisons subservient to the civilian authorities wherever possible. For example, an ordinance issued in October 1442 made it illegal for captains and lieutenants of garrisons and companies, and others, to issue private safe conducts. This practice enabled soldiers to arrest people on suspicion of crime or active opposition and then to release them for ransom after selling a safe conduct. Another ordinance, issued a few days later, ordered all itinerant men-at-arms who were not part of a recognized company or retinue, to report to a garrison commander and place themselves under his authority on pain of severe penalties. Yet a third, issued the same month, gave power to local officials to punish any breech of the ordinances by imprisonment, and forbade soldiers from arresting civilians and from keeping them in their own prisons. Any seizure of goods or arrest of persons under suspicion of breaking the law was to be carried out by officers of justice only, who were locally appointed.

Seizing provisions without payment was a common practice until the ordinances of 1423, which were republished in September 1428. These laid down that any civilian could make a complaint against an individual soldier or against a captain concerning the seizure of provisions, or even against his behaviour. Any such complaint had to be made before the local officer of justice and if proven, the culprit had the value of the seized goods stopped from his pay at source. Indeed the ordinances went so far as to state that before any captain could claim his pay, or that for his company, the ordinances had to be cried aloud so that any would-be complainant could receive redress on the spot if the complaint was found in his favour. Furthermore no captain could claim his pay, or that of his company, until he could show a certificate, drawn up by the local *baillis* or *vicomtes*, to state that he had discharged all valid complaints made against him. The *baillis* were the highest judicial officials in the district and were always Englishmen in Normandy, and the *vicomtes,* their junior officials in the villages and small towns, were all Normans.

It would be wrong to infer from this that the soldiery were always lawless; this was far from the case and indeed there are many recorded cases of soldiers reporting the illegal behaviour of others or of preventing it – presumably because the soldiers wanted their pay and captains needed to draw the pay for their companies but could not do so if incidents involving their soldiers remained outstanding. So the need for pay ensured that by and large the garrisons were well behaved and the inhabitants, while not necessarily pro-English, were at least no worse than indifferent to them and were at times quite friendly; indeed many soldiers married Norman girls and settled in Normandy.

Unfortunately although the soldiery in garrisons and those in retinues became reasonably well behaved as a result of the ordinances, it did not entirely put an end to the pillaging and extortion, even in Normandy, by bands of unemployed soldiers who were virtually outlaws and who claimed no master. However, perhaps the report of the *vicomte* at Gaillard should be allowed to speak for the garrisons. He found the captain, his lieutenant and retinue conducted themselves so well that none had reason to complain and that while 'zealously guarding the castle, they lived like simple persons of the country, paying their way without seizing or exacting anything from the people.'[19]

Profits and Hazards
Plunder was undoubtedly a source of profit, but the other great source of enrichment came from the taking of prisoners and their subsequent

ransom. Ransoms provided an equal if not greater source of income to the spoils of war and often represented a fortune for those lucky enough to capture some great commander or rich nobleman. The possibility of ransom provided an incentive to take prisoners when the potential captive was clearly a noble or rich knight; the alternative on the battlefield for the soldier was to kill or severely wound the man he was fighting and put him out of the battle. This was done reluctantly if it was clear he was a rich or important man. All commanders understood the impulse to capture prisoners and did their best to stop it during battle, since it broke up the ranks and reduced the number of fighting men in the line, while increasing those guarding prisoners at the rear.

Before the Battle of Poitiers the Black Prince made a proclamation that no man should linger over his prisoner during the battle on pain of forfeiting him, although once the battle was clearly won a free-for-all ensued. The scramble for captives, according to the Chandos herald, affected knights, squires and archers who were to be seen 'running in every direction to take prisoners'. Froissart said that so many prisoners were taken at Poitiers that they outnumbered their English captors by two to one. The most notable prisoner of all, King Jean, was in some danger from the press of men-at-arms around him all claiming to have captured him after the battle. Froissart reports that he said, 'do not quarrel among yourselves over my capture, for I am a great enough lord to make each one of you rich.' So great was Jean's ransom that according to one chronicler when but half was paid, England was already so flooded with gold coin that the exchange rate for silver dropped by 4d.[20]

The process of ransom payment was complex and frequently involved lengthy and expensive litigation before the captor was paid. Additionally a prisoner who was ransomed was expected to pay for his maintenance whilst a prisoner. As Christine de Pisan wrote,[21] the captor 'ought to take heed that the ransom be not so cruell that the man be not undoo thereby, and his wiffe and children distroied and brought to poverty'. Unhappily, for those who were taken prisoner, this convention was already being forgotten by greedy captors, French and English, by the end of Edward III's reign.

Ransoms were not a one-way business for many Englishmen were taken by the French and ransomed. William Montacute, first earl of Salisbury, captured at Lille in 1340, had his ransom paid by the king.

Ralph, later first earl of Stafford, was captured in 1342 and exchanged for a French prisoner. In 1351, after the 'Combat of the Thirty', both Sir Robert Knollys and Sir Hugh Calveley were taken prisoner and later ransomed. Sir Thomas Felton was taken prisoner in 1367 and his release was secured by the king on payment of a ransom of 30,000 Lt (£6,600), met by the ransoms of French prisoners. John Holland, earl of Huntingdon and future duke of Exeter, was taken prisoner at Baugé in 1421, together with the earl of Somerset and Lord Fitzwalter; John Holland was imprisoned for four years and eventually exchanged for a French prisoner, together with a ransom. Robert Hungerford, Lord Boleyn, was captured in 1422 and remained imprisoned for seven years before his mother was able to raise the ransom of £14,000 for his release.

Not surprisingly the greatest fear, after death, of an esquire who was not the cadet of a rich or noble family was to be taken prisoner. Since they aspired to knighthood they would be dressed and armoured as richly as possible, often in armour taken from the dead off the battlefield, and it would be difficult for them to convince their captor that they were in fact penniless. Indeed they would have been foolish to try since their lives would have been spared solely because their captors thought, from their armour, that they were rich and important men and could stand a ransom. Consequently they could be saddled with a ransom which might make them paupers or prisoners for life.

There was, however, one way round this dilemma which seems only to have been used by the poorer, fringe elements of knighthood – those who hoped to make their fortune and their way in society by means of the sword. Ever since the days of William the Marshal in 1177 poor knights and esquires had on occasion entered into contract with another similarly placed soldier to be 'brothers-in-arms'. These contracts would be lawfully drawn up, signed and sealed before witnesses, as a precaution against fraud. In effect the sealed contract became an insurance policy against the possibility of ransom after capture in battle and could also make provision against other calamities. Many examples exist from the Hundred Years' War although it was not a common practice. The brothers-in-arms would contract to share all war profit. This would be lodged and invested safely and, if necessary, it would be used to meet a ransom within certain agreed limits.

If the ransom exceeded the agreed limit the free 'brother' would offer to act as hostage for his brother-in-arms so that the latter could return home and raise the ransom. When one or both of the brothers-in-arms were married, provision would be made for widows and children of either partner should one be killed in battle or on campaign. The contract would provide an annuity for life for the widow coming from her husband's share of the accumulated invest-ments from war until his death in battle. Children were also covered by the contract in the event of their father's death, with the surviving brother-in-arms being obliged to maintain them and to educate them. These contracts between brothers-in-arms were business partnerships and were an early form of insurance trust. They were enforceable at the court of chivalry.[22]

In principle all prisoners belonged to the king, but providing the king received his share the crown had traditionally waived its right to ownership. Exceptions were made in the case of royal prisoners and those of the highest rank; in effect those that had a political value remained the property of the crown. Disputes often arose between those who claimed to have captured a certain prisoner. The case of King Jean of France is a good example. He was first made a prisoner by Denis de Morbeque, a knight from Artois who had been banished from France for murder; he received the king's right gauntlet as a token. Moments later a brawl broke out and the king was snatched from Morbeque. He was saved from this mob by the earl of Warwick and Sir John Cobham who said the king was lawfully the prince's prisoner. Later a Gascon, Bernard de Troyes, claimed to be the rightful captor. The case was eventually referred to King Edward for settlement.

Henry V, in order to stop this sort of quarrelling and to prevent the enmity it could provoke, set out certain rules in his Ordinances of War concerning the taking of prisoners and their subsequent ransom. The basic rule said that he 'that taketh the feithe of a prisoner first shal have him'. Once a prisoner had been taken the captor had to show his prisoner to his captain and notify the constable and the marshal, giving details of his prisoner. Having done this the constable and the marshal could give the prisoner safe conduct in the king's name. This enabled a prisoner, on release, to return to his demesne to gather his ransom money before returning with it to the place stipulated for payment.

Ransoms of prisoners of war together with plunder made up the coin of war and the king's share of the total was sizeable. In addition to his income from all ransoms and plunder the king also received the indemnities of subdued towns on their surrender after resistance. This could be a very large sum; that of Rouen, for instance, was 300,000 *écus*, or about £99,000; an enormous sum, larger than the total of all annual receipts to the English exchequer at that time.[23] Another source of income for the crown was that the king had a quarter share of the value of all prizes taken at sea, as well as a share of the value of their cargoes.

After the crown as the war supremo had taken its share of all booty, prizes, ransoms and indemnities, the profits of war were distributed among two groups, the common soldier and the magnates, knights and captains. The soldiers, including the archers, some men-at-arms and the bill-men, received their share by custom as the majority and an essential part of any army, and of course they were largely the people who did the actual looting. The magnates, knights and captains received their third share because they provided the commanders and constituted the dominant arm, the backbone of the army. For the ordinary soldier, the archer or the common man-at-arms, the prospect of booty must have been the major attraction of military life. Most of a soldier's profit of war in a field army was taken in the form of loot or booty during raids and was quickly translated into cash. However for garrison troops in unsettled times in the border areas the imposition of the illegal *rachâts*, or protection money, on the surrounding countryside provided some extra income and relief from the boredom of fortress life

Most of the soldiers' 'profits of war' would end up in the pockets of the tavern and brothel keepers in Gascony, or later in Normandy, and therefore remained, so to speak, in the country of origin. Some soldiers, more careful than the rest, might come home with a small fortune, sufficient perhaps for them to buy some land and their share of plunder would thereby add very slightly to the enrichment of England. The magnates and knightly classes were more prudent with their profits of war and most invested it in land in England if they survived their term of service. It is only possible to hazard a guess at the combined total of all the profits of all the knightly classes for the whole of the war, but it must at least have equalled those of the crown. However, as has been shown, these profits were not all one way, as many knights were themselves taken prisoner and had to pay a ransom, which, if they were lucky would be paid out of their own war profits, but if they had none could impoverish them for life. Nevertheless the profits of the knightly classes from the war must have added considerably to England's wealth. It is only possible to estimate the total from these sources but it would be surprising if the total of the crown's income from the Hundred Years' War did not greatly exceed £1,000,000.[24]

Lands given by the crown as a reward for faithful service in the wars, particularly in Normandy after Henry V's conquest, hardly added to the profits of war since few were profitable enough in unsettled times to enable the new owners to enrich themselves back in England. Most of these grants of land required the owners to garrison castles within their French domain and to live on their new estates, a stratagem designed to bolster the defence of the duchy. Sir John Fastolff, who was one of those given lands in France, nevertheless managed to turn a pretty profit from these and transfer them to England. He is also a good example of how a prominent soldier with a shrewd business mind invested his profits of war in the fifteenth century.

Fastolff's military career began in 1415 when as an esquire he first went to France; he was knighted in 1416 but his first important appointment came in 1421 when he was made the captain of the Bastille de St Antoine in Paris. He was made grand master of the duke of Bedford's household and a member of the French council of Normandy and English occupied France, until 1439. In 1424 after the Battle of Verneuil he was promoted to banneret and in 1426 he was made a garter knight and a baron of France. He undoubtedly achieved fame and prominence on the battlefield, but did he make his fortune? His first notable profit of war came for his services at the Battle of Verneuil when he received a purse of 20,000 marks[25] (probably marks of silver, about £13,300) as a share of the booty plus a reward for outstanding service. The total of his profits from the war over a period of eleven years, from when he first went to France as a penniless esquire until 1436, amounted to the staggering figure of £20,743 of which he deposited about £7,443 in England. Most of these profits were invested in land and buildings and other items such as furniture and plate. By 1445 the total annual income from lands, both bought and inherited, had increased to £1,061. Sir John invested

in real estate in London, giving him an additional annual income of
£102 and a house on the Thames near the court. He also rebuilt his
manor at Caister, a residential castle, which still stands today. He had
properties in France, which in 1445 gave him an annual income of
over £401. Yet seeing the writing on the wall, he prudently sold off
these properties before the end of the war.

The combined value of his estates and properties, which he had
bought from war profits, had a combined total of some £16,183. To
which should be added possessions worth well over £4,000. At
today's values the total would amount to about 13 million pounds.
However that was not all as Sir John was also involved in the coastal
shipping trade on the east coast: grain, malt, wool, cloth and bricks
mainly between Yarmouth and London, but sometimes as far north as
Newcastle. He owned a small merchant fleet, which by 1446 included
eight ships. Sir John Fastolff had done exceedingly well out of his war
in France, and many others did likewise during the course of the
Hundred Years' War. Consequently it is not surprising that the war
never lacked for volunteers when the war was going well; neither is it
surprising that support for it, in parliament, was always forthcoming
when profits were high.

The Hazards of War
For those who could not command a ransom to be in a defeated army
or defeated garrison was a grim prospect indeed, and for obvious
reasons this meant the majority in any army or garrison. War brought
profit and death. To be on the winning side led to great profit, but to
be the losers generally meant loss of life for all but the rich, and they,
in a civil war, might well lose their heads for treason.

In hand-to-hand fighting there would have been many wounded
and the wounds would have been horrific; axes, swords, glaives,
halberds and pole-axes could all sever limbs, cleave the skull or
behead a man. Good armour could prevent or deflect these cuts, but if
the weapon penetrated the armour there was likely to be a jagged cut
to the bone. All pointed weapons including the sword, various staff
weapons, the horseman's lance, the spear and arrow could inflict deep
punctures through gaps in armour or between the plates, and deal a
fatal wound to the body, one that might well not be instantaneous.
Pole-axes, war hammers and maces could dent or crush helmets
inflicting severe head wounds, or they could break limbs and

shoulders. Arrows from the longbow and bolts from the crossbow could penetrate all but the very best plate armour, indeed arrows were known to penetrate the mail on a knight's thigh, go through the saddle and kill the horse underneath, and knights could be pinned to their horses by arrows. Primitive handguns, when they appeared, were quite capable of penetrating the best of armours. Many severely wounded men or those who missed their footing would simply fail to get up again because of the press of bodies from others on top of them.

At the end of a fight a battlefield would be littered with the dead and the dying. The screams and groans of the wounded added to the frenzied shouts of those still fighting, but the cries of the wounded continued long after battle was done. What happened to them? If discipline in the victorious army was good the first to search the dead and the wounded would be the heralds of both sides to identify fallen knights by their surcoats or badges. If the wounded man was a particularly prominent person he might receive the last sacrament from a priest. All members of the knightly classes would then be buried in hallowed ground whenever possible.

The wounded men-at-arms, archers, crossbow-men and bill-men were simply despatched with neither ceremony nor mercy. Indeed as no facilities existed to cope with the wounded on the scale that might be needed after a pitched battle, and as resuscitation was so primitive and uncertain, probably the most merciful course was to despatch badly wounded men as soon as possible. All of these would be buried in communal burial pits but not before they had been stripped.

The fate of the wounded was uncertain and, even for a rich nobleman, none too hopeful, but men survived the most dreadful wounds. Some medical facilities did exist on the battlefield, but generally only for the richest men, purely because they were the only people who could afford to employ the physicians and surgeons. These doctors were a rare breed, and those who were prepared to go on campaign were rarer still; very few knights could afford or provide the facilities and the living that these men needed. Edward III had a private physician and a private surgeon who accompanied him everywhere with their own staffs, even on campaign.[26] Henry V had a 'phisitian' with his own bodyguard of three archers and also three master surgeons each with nine more under surgeons, medical orderlies, with him in his retinue on the Agincourt campaign.[27] French and

Burgundian armies also had rudimentary medical facilities. No doubt many soldiers and women camp followers had an expertize in the use of healing balms and ointments made from herbs, as undoubtedly did the nuns and monks in the priories and abbeys of the day.

Surgeons and physicians could certainly attend to quite severe wounds and many of the wounded survived both their wounds and the medical attention they received. There were medical schools at Oxford and at the priory of St Bartholmew in London, with others at Paris and Montpellier, Florence and Bologna. Medical practice in the Western Christian world had received a boost during the Crusades from the Islamic world, where it was more advanced. Evidence from illuminated manuscripts and the accompanying text shows that surgery for battle wounds was well advanced. Physicians had knowledge of the internal and external application of medicines and ointments and how to prepare them. A miniature from a thirteenth-century manuscript shows a physician examining a man with sword wounds to the stomach. The accompanying text says: 'If one has been struck down with a sword, apply to the wound the herb *senecion* [groundsel] beaten with salt-free grease until it is like liquefied wax; this will heal the wound very quickly.'[28]

Doctors practised cautery to staunch blood from a wound or to prevent the spread of infection, and they were quite adept in the suturing of flesh wounds after cleansing. They were also capable of amputating limbs where they deemed it necessary. Another illumination, from a fourteenth-century manuscript, depicts a man receiving a sword cut to the head during a brawl. The caption reads:

> If the skin and cranium are cut open with a sword or similar weapon, or by a blow with a rock or some such object (a mace?), so that the skin hangs down or is cut, excise the hanging skin through the middle down to the fractured cranium. Then separate it from the projecting cranium with a rasp and suture from both sides.[29]

Surgeons were well aware of the need to get rid of pus and infected blood from the area of a head wound and would make appropriate incisions to drain the wound.

Barbed arrows were a common cause of wounds and surgeons had to know how to extract them. If the head of the arrow together with the barbs had penetrated right through the body or limb it was a simple matter to pull the arrow out through the body and then treat the wound as any other. However, if the arrowhead was still imbedded in flesh the following procedure was adopted:

> If it is possible to use large forceps we carefully grasp the barbs with the forceps and, bending them back to the stem of the arrow, retract it. But if this is difficult, we work a small iron or bronze tube onto one of the barbs, retracting that barb into the tube. Then doing the same to the other barb we, with much care and diligence, skilfully extract the arrow. We can do this also with two goose quills.[30]

All surgery, however, had to be done without anaesthetic and the shock from an operation coming on top of the wound itself must have killed many a battle casualty. Nevertheless herbal recipes, henbane and opium, soused in boiling water or burnt, were given to inhale and this reduced pain.

Chapter 4

The War at Sea, the Ships and their Crews

England's need for secure lines of communication between the homeland and various theatres of war, and her need to protect her own coasts and trade across the Channel and the North Sea, dictated her naval policy. As reported in the Commons, 'The Navy is the chief support of the well-being, earnings and prosperity of your kingdom.'[1] During this period England also faced a very real threat of invasion from France and had to contend with raids along her southern coast. Edward I claimed the 'Sovereignty of the Seas' and had done so since 1293 when a combined English-Gascon fleet defeated a Norman fleet off the coast of Aquitaine. Nevertheless England had no real concept of seapower as it was understood in later ages. Indeed she simply indulged in a policy of taking the cheapest option that would allow her to meet her needs on an ad hoc basis.

The sea then, as now, was a great avenue for trade and all three of the main belligerents had substantial trade around their own coasts, with each other and with other countries in northern Europe, the Baltic and in the Iberian peninsular. The chroniclers often exaggerated the numbers of ships used to transport an army across the Channel to bring lustre to the name of the king, as did Froissart – 'At last with a thousand ships and smaller vessels they began to sail' – in his description of Edward III setting out for France. The exchequer rolls show that Edward III had an invasion fleet of over 700 ships before his Crécy campaign in 1346, using 700 English ships and 38 Continental ones to enforce the blockade of Calais and to provision his troops at the siege. Henry of Lancaster's army for his campaign in Gascony was carried to Bordeaux in 152 ships; 75 ships were used to transport reinforcements to the Black Prince before his 1355 Poitiers campaign; 256 ships were arrested for John of Gaunt's expedition in 1369 for the short crossing from Sandwich to Calais, 72 of which were over 100 tons. Henry V is reputed to have assembled 1,500 ships for his invasion of France in 1415, a figure that might well be an exaggeration. However Henry's army was larger than any previous invading army and everyone was mounted, which meant more horses had to be carried across; also artillery and siege equipment had to be shipped. Because the average size of ships had grown in the intervening sixty-nine years it is probable that only about 1,000 ships were actually used. The supply and maintenance of the garrison at Calais required about 140 average-sized ships a year just to take rations and forage across the Channel,[2] to which must be added ships needed to transport war stores, and of course those used to carry wool across to the staple. There were also regular convoys to and from Bordeaux. These large numbers of ships were needed during periods of active operations and all needed warships to escort them.

Nonetheless there was no standing navy. When a navy was required it was culled from the existing commercial fleets and appropriate ships were arrested in port. Any cargo on board was offloaded and the ship was then fitted out either as a transport or as a warship. The former might not need any alteration except perhaps for accommodation for a larger crew. The average merchant ship probably had no more than 12 or 14 sailors aboard for a 30-ton ship, but one of 500 tons had a crew of between 30 and 50 men.[i] Merchant ships arrested for use as horse transports needed extensive alteration, as did those destined to be men-of-war.

Except for a short crossing, when they would have been carried on deck, most horses were probably stabled between decks and therefore a minimum height of about 8 feet was required to stable a destrier on board. The horses would be stabled head to head across the beam of the boat with a companionway between the two lines of horses and another along each side of the ship behind them. The horses were stabled in slings, but they were not raised off the deck; they still stood on their hooves, the slings simply preventing them from slipping when the ship rolled or pitched. It is probable also that padded screens would have been hung between the horses or that stalls would have been built for each horse to prevent them damaging each other.

When horses were carried on the open deck special hurdles to separate the horses into stalls were ordered before embarkation. But

---

i All ships' tonnage are given in tonnes burthen, a measure of the amount of cargo they could carry. It is possible that sizes might have been in tuns, a measure of volume.

how they were actually fastened to prevent the horses from slipping or damaging each other is pure surmise. Of course, if one horse slipped on a heaving deck it could not only hurt itself but also the horses nearby. Destriers were expensive animals and so something substantial was needed. Perhaps two lines of stalls would have been set up on deck suspending the hurdles between each stall. The horses would then have been secured closely together, tails outwards, with a companionway between them so that grooms could feed and water the horses on passage and the decks kept clean via the scuppers. Quite clearly for any voyage across the Channel, the transportation of horses posed considerable administrative problems and always required some construction on deck or between decks by shipwrights.

An accurate estimate of the number of ships needed to transport horses in an invasion fleet can be gauged from the size of a small shire horse or large hunter, horses that most nearly equate in size to a destrier. These horses were about 7¾ft from nose to tail and about 2¼ft wide. Fifty of these horses, stabled as described, would need a hold not smaller than 21ft wide and about 72ft long. Judging by a reconstruction of a cog[3] of 1350 which was 65½ft on the waterline with a beam of 23½ft and draught of 10ft, any cog over about 65 tons would have been able to carry fifty horses. On this basis a cog of about 30 tons could certainly have carried thirty horses. Consequently some 400 ships of between 30 and 70 tons would have been required to ship all the horses needed by Edward III's expedition in 1346, well over half the fleet.

Examples of the number of horses shipped exist in the records. In 1359 after Edward III's Rheims campaign, 6,313 horses of the knightly classes were shipped home,[4] additionally the horses of some 7,000 hobilars and mounted archers have to be added to this total, unless they were sold off at the end of the campaign. The Issue Roll of Thomas de Brantingham shows that 8,464 horses were shipped out of Rye for Sir Robert Knolly's expedition in 1370.[5] Henry V shipped sufficient horses to Normandy for his Agincourt campaign in 1415 to mount 2,000 men-at-arms and 8,000 mounted archers, in addition to those required to haul his artillery and his baggage wagons; in all between 14,000 and 16,000 horses.

One problem that had to be faced by the planners was the location of the landfall – where was the expedition to land? If the landing was to be at a port with quays then cogs were suitable ships, but if it was to be over open beaches, as were the landings before both the Crécy and Agincourt campaigns, then cogs were not the most suitable ships for the job. Under these circumstances barges or balingers, shallow-draught oared sailing boats, were used. Finding 400 of these of the appropriate size and shape would have severely disrupted coastal and perhaps cross-Channel trade. Adapting ordinary merchant ships to be horse transports was clearly a long business requiring much early planning. The work of conversion could be carried out by competent shipwrights at almost any port, but the ships themselves had to be arrested well before the muster date to give time for this work to be done and also to allow time for them to sail from the port where they had been arrested to the port of assembly. Furthermore this all added to the expense of the expedition as did any compensation paid to the owners for altering their ships. The bill for altering merchant ships into warships was even larger, but luckily not every ship used on these expeditions was a warship or a horse transport; many carried soldiers or cargoes of munitions or provisions. The latter needed no alteration, but those acting as troop transports probably needed some form of rudimentary accommodation arranged below decks for anything other than a short crossing of the Channel.

Ships hired or arrested early in the fourteenth century as troop transports had very few creature comforts. Normally the only cabin aboard, if one existed at all, would be that of the master, and a privy at the stern rail would be an extravagance. Magnates who hired ships for themselves and their retinues, and those arrested for the king and his household, had to be made habitable. Cabins were made by erecting canvas screens or putting up temporary walls of hurdles, even so privacy was a luxury afforded by very few. Beds and other furniture were brought aboard as well as chests holding clothing, while bare-hides and barrels holding arms and armour had to be stowed where they could be got at in a hurry. These attempts to civilize a ship for a channel crossing really only applied to the longer voyages, although kings, princes and the higher nobility doubtless always had private cabins aboard, no matter how short the crossing. Chapels were usually set up with as much style as was possible in the available space and bearing in mind the probable crossing time; kitchens were also set up. By the middle of the fourteenth century ships had become quite large and sophisticated and the facilities available on board ship for VIPs were much as they were two centuries later.

Warships needed most alteration. In the period before about 1400, warships merely became so by virtue of the fact that they had a fighting crew on board. This meant that they had a large compliment of men-at-arms and archers aboard in addition to the normal crew of sailors, because they fought enemy warships by grappling and boarding. But in order to let the fighting crews do their job merchant ships were converted to warships by building substantial high castles both at the bows and the stern of each ship, and a topcastle at the top of the mainmast where archers were stationed. These alterations were time consuming and expensive but only a relatively small number of warships were needed – perhaps thirty or forty to escort an invasion fleet of several hundred ships.

However, escorting an invasion fleet was not the only task for which warships were needed. They were also used in raids on the French coast and to protect the south coast at home from French raids. They carried out sweeps along the French and Flemish coasts from the Zwyn estuary to the Cherbourg peninsula, and they had to deter Scottish warships from raiding down the north-east and north-west coasts. The king's ships generally carried out these tasks, being ordered and paid for by the crown. Some of these ships were built as warships from the start but most were large merchantmen bought by the crown and then fitted out as warships when the need arose. The navy, if it can be so called, consisted of the king's ships, the number in service varying greatly.

At times when no threat existed the king's ships were either sold off or allowed to rot. It was certainly cheaper to arrest appropriate merchant ships and convert them to warships than it was to maintain a permanent fleet of king's ships. The number of king's ships varied considerably according to the threat, the offensive need and the expense of keeping them ready for sea. Except during times of concentrated military activity, maintaining king's ships was a very low priority. The expression of power through the naval arm seems only to have been understood by Henry V and Richard III, since they were the kings who maintained a fleet of king's ships and used them effectively. Edward III and Edward IV, both of whom built king's ships, failed fully to understand the implications of so doing. The duke of Bedford clearly understood the value of the fleet while he was regent, as did the earl of Warwick who owned his own fleet and used it to good effect between 1457 and 1464 in the power game of the Wars of the Roses.

Following the Battle of La Rochelle in 1372 Edward and parliament realized that English naval forces were inadequate, and as a result an urgent naval building and buying programme was begun; by April 1373 the king had forty-four ships, soon to be joined by a further twelve. In 1410–12, according to John Starlying's accounts, Henry IV had seven ships. Henry V's fleet varied considerably. A list made after the Battle of the Seine gives 3 carracks, 3 cogs, 8 barges and 10 balingers; in a second list compiled in August 1417 there were 8 carracks, 3 cogs, 1 barge and 9 balingers. Another list from a later period gave 17 carracks, 7 cogs, 2 barges and 12 balingers, but these had been reduced to 3 by 1436. Most of them were sold shortly after Henry V's death. This may seem an appaling waste of a valuable element in the Hundred Years' War, but the whole of northern France was in English hands as well as Aquitaine. Furthermore Henry VI was the designated king of France as well as England, and once again the crown was in debt; so why not capitalize on this asset? Why would they need this expensive fleet? Nineteen of Henry V's ships were disposed of after his death between 1423 and 1425 for which the exchequer received £1,000. Edward IV had 2 or 3 ships in 1468–70 and gradually increased the size of his fleet to 7 by 1480 when, on going to war against Scotland, he increased the fleet to about 15 ships. Richard III owned 10 ships, 7 of them inherited from Edward IV and 3 that he bought.[6] This accounts for what might be called the 'Royal Navy' throughout the Hundred Years' War and the Wars of the Roses.

Richmond[7] makes the point that the 'keeping of the seas' in the fifteenth century was a matter of having a fleet of king's ships assembled and at sea each year before the enemy. Constant patrolling of the Channel throughout the year was not an option. Ships were unable to stay at sea for long periods and weather conditions in the winter were usually too difficult for ships to put to sea with a war compliment of men-at-arms and archers on board. Consequently naval activity was limited to a season of some seven months between April and October and the initiative at sea passed to the country which first managed to assemble and deploy a fleet during that time. The battle of Sluys in 1340 was fought to disperse a French fleet massing for an invasion of England. The Battle of Winchelsea in 1350 was fought to intercept a Castilian fleet in French service. The Battles off Harfleur in 1416 and that off the Chef de Caux in 1417 were fought to disperse French fleets attempting to prevent or interfere with Henry V's siege of Harfleur. These were all actions based on good intelligence and carried out by fleets, sometimes augmented by pressed ships that were assembled and ready for sea or already at sea. Naval battles were uncommon, so the payment for and assembling of a fleet of king's ships was not primarily to fight the enemy at sea.

The king's navy, when it existed, was there to show the power of the king. The king's fleet showed the enemy that this power existed and was ready for action by raiding the enemy's coastline. Once this was achieved the enemy fleet was forced onto the defensive protecting its own ports and coastline; in effect the fleet's main purpose was to carry out sea-borne *chevauchées* where and when they were needed. Of course naval squadrons were also used for other, secondary, tasks. They were used to escort invasion fleets across the Channel, to escort the wool convoys going to the staple at Calais and on occasion to protect the fishing fleets in the North Sea and off Iceland.[8]

Many of these tasks were undertaken by ships in the king's service as distinct from king's ships; the latter were owned and crewed by the crown, whereas the former were pressed ships taken into temporary service and often converted into warships. In the fourteenth century some of the king's ships were galleys used primarily as scouts along vulnerable shores to give warning of the approach of French or Castilian ships and stationed in ones and twos along the coasts.[9] These galleys were largely replaced for this purpose by balingers in the following century.

Once guns had become reasonably reliable on land they were very soon mounted on ships, indeed the first mention of them was on Castilian galleys sailing between Barcelona and Alexandria in 1370. The first gun to be fired at sea was apparently by an English ship, the *Christofre de la Tour*, in about 1410. The inventory for this ship taken from John Starlying's accounts[10] showed that she carried three iron guns with five chambers and one handgun; also a barrel of gunpowder. This same ship carried thirty-six pavises, painted wooden shields, which were hung along the bulwarks in the waist of the ship to give some protection to the soldiers in the waist. Judging by these the *Christofre* was a fairly small ship, perhaps 75ft on the waterline.

By about 1470 guns were mounted on carracks and large merchantmen were armed with five guns on the quarterdeck. Warships carried guns in the waist of the ship and could theoretically fire a broadside, though it is not known if they did. Light swivel guns were mounted on the top-castles and also on the taffrail overlooking the waist. In 1485 another king's ship, the *Mary of the Tower*, a much larger ship, carried 130, many of them hung on the rails round the fore and after castles. A barge in the inventory, the *Marie de la Toure* had one iron gun with two chambers and one brass gun with a single chamber. Among the king's ships listed by John Starlyng in addition to those above, the *Bernard* had two iron guns, the *Carake* one, while the *Mary of Weymouth* had both an iron gun and a brass gun. It is not known how these guns were placed on board; indeed it is not even known how they were used. Although warships had, by then, entered the Nelson age there is no record of any warship firing a broadside at an enemy ship, indeed gun battles at sea have not been recorded.

How was the process to assemble a fleet or to build king's ships set in motion? Who carried out the executive action? As with the armies the process began at the king's council. Once the decision had been made to go on campaign the king's officers had to decide how many ships were needed for any particular occasion and the king's council then set the executive wheels in motion. The first thing that was needed was of course money and once again parliament was asked to provide the necessary finance. However, there was already a division of responsibility. Parliament provided the finance for the various fleets once they had agreed to go to war and for the warships that were needed to escort them and for ships that were to operate from English ports. However it seems that the king paid for his ships from the exchequer, and so strictly speaking they were his property in the same way as were those of Richard Neville, earl of Warwick during the Wars of the Roses.

Once a ship was requisitioned on the orders of the king's council, it was paid for by the port authorities at the port where it had been arrested for a period of three weeks, as were its master, the crew and any archers assigned to it. Presumably payment for the ship was to compensate against loss of commercial profit and was extra to that needed to ready the ship for war as either a transport or a warship. However, this three weeks' payment failed to cover the many cases when a ship was arrested, told to sail to the port of embarkation for an expedition and was then required to wait for several weeks before the expedition sailed. The payment also failed to cover the case when a ship was held up by adverse winds from reaching its destination on time.

Consequently in 1373, due to pressure from the Commons in parliament, payment for the use of the ship became regularized by a payment of 3s 4d per ton of cargo capacity per quarter-year in the king's service.[11] This payment was intended to cover compensation for the wear and tear of the ship in the king's service and the loss of its use for commercial purposes. Henry V must have paid out at least £15,000 for his invasion fleet covering the six months from their arrest to their release.

The cost of building king's ships has not always been recorded but examples exist that indicate that they were expensive, as indeed was a permanent conversion of merchantman into warship. Wylie[12] estimated that Henry V paid a total of £24,337 for his naval building programme during his reign. Earlier Robert II of Scotland (1371–1390) paid over £300 to convert merchantmen to warships to protect Scottish trade.[13] The cost of individual ships bought by Edward IV is known, for example the *Carvel of Leybourne* cost £133 6s 8d in 1463; another ship was bought for £170 in 1467. The *Falcon* was bought in 1475 for £450, but the most expensive ship was bought from Genoese merchants in 1481 for £1,000.[14] The maintenance of king's ships was also expensive; examples given by Richmond for the period between 1420 and 1422 include the *Thomas*, purchased about 1412, which had £529 7s 4½d spent on her to keep her seaworthy, only to be sold in 1423 for £133 6s 8d.[15] The *Jesus*, a large ship of 1,000 tons and built in 1415–17 had £403 6s 9¼d spent on her to preserve her seaworthiness.

In the period between 1436 and about 1461, during Henry VI's reign, when the king's ships had been reduced to three or less, and the building or buying of ships to increase the fleet was deemed too expensive or was too low a priority, a new way of exercising some power at sea was devised. Licences were issued to merchants and shipowners to keep the seas at their own cost. This seemed an inexpensive innovation – the merchants were keen to have official sanction to protect their ships by force and the crown had no need to maintain expensive king's ships. These licences were to equip and man a certain number of ships for a stated period to keep the seas; any prizes taken were to be theirs. The licences generally stipulated that the owners should not be liable for offences committed by those on board. In due course licences for some thirty ships were issued in 1436 but this practice was soon stopped. It caused too many problems for the government. It was rightly held responsible, internationally, for the actions of the armed merchant fleet and had to pay compensation for the damage done; indeed it had to pay £4,500 compensation to the Burgundians alone. The actions of armed merchantmen, which were little short of sanctioned piracy, caused a great deal of anger in the Hanse and other trading countries, as well as reprisals against English merchants on the Continent. In effect, although it may have temporarily kept the seas, it caused so much damage and ill feeling that it might have been more cost effective to maintain and use a small fleet of king's ships. After this experiment and until Edward IV began to build up a fleet of his own ships, fleets were assembled for a specific operation by indenture. Once the commander was chosen and the task agreed ships and men were selected and paid by indenture, like any other military expedition.

Once parliament had authorized the necessary finance, the king's council, as the executive authority, sent out orders to the king's sergeants-at-arms at the ports to requisition ships in peacetime. However in wartime or during periods of tension admirals were appointed to take charge of all ports and shipping north and east or south and west of the Thames. Admirals had greater authority than the sergeants-at-arms but still relied on them for the actual business of arresting ships. These admirals were empowered to arrest ships, organize convoys, impress sailors, detail arrayed men such as archers and men-at-arms to specific ships and impose discipline over the men serving aboard the ships of an assembled fleet.[16] The admirals also administered the maritime law, such as it existed at that time.

Those ships destined to become king's ships or warships then became the responsibility of the clerk of the king's ships, who was normally resident at the Tower of London, and who supervised the conversion of merchant ships to warships. The sergeants-at-arms would be ordered to arrest ships of a certain size and to impress crews when necessary. Merchantmen would often only have a maintenance crew aboard when in port and awaiting a commission; sailors and archers would then have to be pressed to enable the ship to put to sea. The writ to the admirals and sergeants-at-arms generally stipulated that ships must be 'prepared for war and furnished with men, victuals and other necessaries and brought to the port of … by such and such a date.'[17]

This seems a relatively straightforward procedure; it was simple and efficient and worked well during successful times, but when the fortunes of war were not so good resistance to the arrest of ships was not uncommon.[18] Nevertheless although the procedure was simple, the conditions of the times within which this had to be accomplished made it troublesome. The fastest communication was by horseback along roads, which were little more than cart tracks. The admirals' writ might have to be taken from London to Bristol, or London to Newcastle, a three-day journey at the very least. The sergeants-at-arms at the various ports on receipt of the writ had to assess and requisition any appropriate ships in port and then prepare them for war. This process could include off-loading a cargo or preparing a ship as a horse transport. If a ship was to be converted into a warship the responsibility was then handed over to an officer of the clerk of the king's ships. When the ship was ready to put to sea the crew would have to wait for suitable winds and leave on an ebb tide.

The journey then might take anything up to five days for a relatively short trip from say, Harwich to Portsmouth, depending on the winds; and of course a wind that was fair for that voyage could be contrary for a ship sailing up channel from Plymouth. When individual ships arrived at the port of assembly they might still have had to be loaded with supplies before men or horses embarked. If, due to a storm or the late arrival of several ships, the embarkation were delayed stores would begin to rot and would need to be off-loaded and replaced by fresh stores. The king or the officer in command of the expedition would travel with his retinue and household staff in one of the king's ships and a magnate might requisition a ship for his own use, but otherwise the retinues and companies would be allocated to a ship by the marshals at the port of embarkation. The assembly of a large fleet quite clearly took a long time so it is hardly surprising that expeditions seldom left on the appointed day.

Sailors were not as well paid as soldiers, the normal daily wage for a sailor being 3d and the master of a ship between 9d and a shilling per day, depending on the size of his ship. However Henry V only paid his masters 6d a day, sailors 3d and ship's boys half that.[19] Consequently a smallish cog might cost its owners 4s 9d a day while at sea and a large ship of over 500 tons with a peacetime crew of forty sailors, not uncommon by the time of Henry V, could cost about 10 shillings a day. Crewmen's pay actually remained at 3d a day throughout the period, regardless of the size of ship; however the pay of ships' masters varied considerably. Again taking the average size of the ships in his invasion fleet for the Agincourt campaign as 45 tons, and the average crew size as 35 sailors per ship, the ships' crews in Henry's invasion fleet must have cost about £1,300 per day, excluding the pay of ships' masters, a further £25. To this had to be added the cost of the archers to protect each ship, about £150 per day. The daily wages bill for the sailors and the ships' masters for Henry V's fleet would have been about £1475, a not insignificant amount; when added to the amount paid to the owners for the use of the ships, about £7,500, the cost of transporting his army across the Channel and supporting it thereafter for six months would have been about £255,000. This outlay would have been reduced as soon as and whenever it could be and consequently although king's ships may have been retained in service for six months it is unlikely that all the arrested ships would have been; most would have been released as soon as the army had been transported across the Channel. Therefore it is unlikely that the actual cost would have exceeded £85,000.

Not only were sailors not particularly well paid but they also had a hard life. Normally the master hired a crew who had to provide for themselves or be provisioned by the master at their expense. If this was to be the case the master was obliged to give them meat three days a week and on other days bread, cheese and pickled fish. Wine was served morning and evening, and figs and prunes whenever they were available.[20] Double rations were to be served on major feast days. As to discipline, the master was empowered to keep order and could strike a sailor once, however if he did so a second time the sailor could defend himself. Certain disobediences could be punished by ducking a man on the end of a rope from the yardarm, while if he killed another sailor he would be tied to the dead body of his victim and both would be thrown overboard. To sleep while on watch was a severe offence, because it endangered the whole crew; in this case he had a pail of water thrown over his head, he was then stripped naked and beaten by the whole crew; he also had his wine stopped.[21] Any sailor who deserted his ship would be hung from the yardarm if he were caught.

All sailors had to be prepared to do any job concerned with the sailing of the ship and to go ashore for provisions and water. Sailors had to bring their own weapons for defence and were obliged to defend their ship. Every ship detailed a sailor to keep a diary, or log, of the day's events, which could be used as evidence at any subsequent enquiry. Each ship also carried a cook and a cat among its crew, and a lodesman or pilot was responsible for navigation. In any ship converted to a warship, or in king's ships, the master became a sailing master and the captain of the ship was generally the captain of the soldiers on board; this of course had reference to the way in which ships were fought in those days.

Navigation was almost one of the black arts. Rudimentary compasses existed on ships but the only means of timekeeping and therefore longitudinal position was by the use of hourglasses; sextants and chronometers had not yet been invented, so there was no way of getting a precise position, and charts were non-existent. Consequently ships' masters would never know exactly where they were when offshore. Even when hugging a shoreline they had to rely on good visibility and their own experience to estimate where they were. To add to their difficulties there was no way of communicating from ship to shore, or for that matter from ship to ship apart from a trumpet call or a hail when alongside. However the arms of the home port were often painted on the bows of a ship and recognition flags were flown; king's ships had the royal arms painted on the hull and generally on the mainsail.[22] When the difficulties of navigation are added to the problems of sailing to windward in a cog, which could, at best, sail at between 75 and 80 degrees to the wind, it can be seen that sailing offshore or along the coastline was a hazardous business.

The problems of gathering a fleet for an expeditionary force, or even for a small resupply convoy, loading them and then sailing for a specific destination to arrive by a certain date were clearly extremely difficult. Nevertheless the English did this, not just once, but many times across the Channel to Normandy, to Brittany and to Calais. They also sailed down the Channel for the much longer voyage to Bordeaux and even to Portugal. However it must be stressed that this capability was not confined to the English alone – all the belligerent countries were able to do this and did so frequently. To add to the difficulties there was only one lighthouse in the fourteenth century, at St Catherine's Point on the Isle of Wight, no charts or bouyage; however, pilotage of a sort would have been available at the better ports, although ships' masters would have been wary of accepting boats of any sort alongside if piracy was common in the area. Some ports had quays, wharves and docks equipped with windlasses and derricks, but certainly not all. Consequently many cargoes had to be loaded and unloaded by small boats to a ship at anchor.

Notwithstanding the difficulties of navigation there was a great deal of commercial and warlike shipping activity in the waters around the coasts of the British Isles and France throughout the fourteenth and fifteenth centuries. One of the problems faced by all sailors was that the cogs used then, while being quite seaworthy, were not able to cope with the weather conditions and seas that might be met in the middle of the North Sea or the Bay of Biscay. Also, since reliable navigational instruments had not yet been designed to enable ships to sail across the open seas, there was no guarantee that they would arrive at their point of destination. Consequently trade routes generally hugged the coasts, although ships did sail directly across the Channel from the Devon ports to Brittany, a distance of about 120 miles, or across the southern North Sea from about Great Yarmouth to the Flemish coast. Scottish traders taking wool to Flanders or hides to the Baltic were therefore vulnerable to English warships and privateers off the East Coast of England before striking out across the North Sea. Likewise French ships taking armour and weapons, or gold or even men-at-arms to the aid of their ally Scotland had to run the gauntlet of the English coast. Things were no different for the English, their merchant ships carrying grain to Aquitaine or shipping wine on the return journey had to sail along the south Breton coast having crossed the Channel. English warships or convoyed expeditions to Aquitaine similarly had to run the gauntlet of French warships and privateers out of the south Breton ports and La Rochelle. A friendly or at least neutral Brittany was therefore essential to English interests in Aquitaine and dominance of the Channel north of Dover was vital to England's wool trade with Flanders, on which so much of the financing of the war with both France and Scotland depended. So important was the export of wool to England that when the staple was moved to Calais the wool convoys were usually escorted.

In the context of England's wars in the Middle Ages it is important to realize the intensity of the war at sea and the importance of sea power to England. In her wars with Scotland she had to be able to victual her garrisons in castles as far north as Aberdeen, while also protecting her own coastline against Scottish raiding. England also endeavoured to impose a blockade on Scottish trade with the Continent. None of this was easy, as the Scots were quite capable of embarrassing the English at sea. She was, for instance, able to threaten and raid the English west coast down the Irish Sea as far south as Holyhead with a fleet of galleys. She also raised a fleet to transport an army of 6,000 men to Ireland in 1315. In the North Sea the Scots raided down the English east coast, and together with Flemish and German privateers preyed on English shipping to such an extent that English merchants called upon the king for protection and compensation.[23] Later in the fifteenth century, while Henry V was trying to conquer northern France, the Scots, with French and Castilian[24] help, were able to land an army of about 6,000 men in France to the aid of her ally.

All this offensive activity had to be countered by the English at sea while maintaining her normal trade with the Continent and along her own coasts. Edward II was obliged to maintain a fleet in the Irish Sea; he required the Cinque Ports to provide ships to patrol the narrow seas and prevent interference by the French. Ships from Great Yarmouth and the Norfolk ports were tasked to frustrate the activities of Flemish privateers. In the north-east Edward maintained a fleet drawn from local ports to deter Scottish raiding and in 1315 was forced to convoy and escort his supply ships and merchantmen sailing into Scottish waters. This was not sufficient to deter the activities of Flemish privateers or to dominate the northern seas where the war at sea reflected much the same pattern as the war on land. However this period was only a phase in the war at sea; generally when one side was dominant on land it was also dominant at sea. Consequently Scottish seaborne offensive activities gradually declined as Edward III increased his grip on southern Scotland, and when this began to ease so the Scottish seaborne threat increased. Scottish sea power remained a potent threat throughout the fourteenth and fifteenth centuries and one that England had to confront and dominate, particularly in the Irish Sea.

Sea power was even more crucial in England's wars with France, enabling England to land expeditionary forces in France fourteen times during the Hundred Years' War, five of which were major expeditions across the Channel. Once Henry V had established the English presence in northern France, and until the English were finally driven from all of France less Calais in 1453, there was constant communication between the two countries that France was unable to disrupt. In addition to this five battles were fought at sea, only one of which was initiated by the French; indeed, except for attempts to disrupt the siege of Calais and to threaten Henry V's landings off Normandy,

France was content to let England play the lead in the war at sea. This does not mean that France took no initiative at sea – she did so frequently with her Castilian allies, but only to raid the south coast of England or to interfere with England's trade. In short, freedom of passage on the seas was essential for England's welfare and security, and while she was unable to dominate the seas she was certainly able to control the seas sufficiently for her purposes when it was important to her.

Another aspect of the conflict at sea was that a great deal of piracy, or licensed privateering, took place against merchant shipping at the beginning of the fifteenth century. All three belligerents indulged in this profitable activity, notwithstanding the many truces throughout the wars between the English, the French[25] and the Scots. France entered this activity with royal ships 'armed and arrayed for war' and seized English ships on their way to or from Aquitaine, largely by ships under the control of royal officials out of La Rochelle, St Malo and Harfleur. The French tally of seized English ships in 1401 alone amounted to fifty-two and a further twenty were captured in 1402; piracy at this rate continued into the next year.

The Scots also enjoyed this unofficial war at sea and seized English ships whenever they could off the north-east coast of England and in the Irish Sea. In 1402 the admiral of Scotland, the earl of Crawford, sailed to France to appeal for military aid against the English. As part of that aid the French provided several ships to accompany Crawford back to Scotland together with a contingent of French men-at-arms. These ships, with Crawford's small squadron, were assembled at Harfleur and preyed on English shipping on their way back to Scotland. They were credited with the seizure of twenty-five English ships on their three months' voyage; the French ships sailed under the Scottish flag and were serving under Crawford's command but in fact they sailed under the strict instructions of the French government.

The seizure of ships did not necessarily entail the capture or sinking of the ships concerned, but it certainly involved the boarding and inspection of cargoes. If the cargo belonged to or was assigned to a belligerent, it was seized as contraband of war and the ship was escorted into the arresting ship's home harbour from which it might, or might not, be released. Neutral vessels were often arrested at sea and their cargoes seized if they were taking supplies to an enemy, as happened in the case of three Hanseatic ships arrested by the English in 1402 which were taking goods to Scotland. Again the Franco-Scottish fleet seized a Dutch ship in the Channel and took the cargo because it belonged to an English merchant. Castilian and Flemish ships also suffered the indignity of arrest at sea, this time by the English – in the summer of 1402 twelve Castilian ships were stopped by the English of which seven had their cargoes seized since they belonged to French merchants. Eight English ships were seized by the Castilians, at least half of which were taken off the coast of Portugal, an English ally, at a time of conflict between Castile and Portugal. In the same period fourteen Flemish ships were stopped by the English, of which three had their cargoes seized because French merchants owned them.

The English were well organized in this undeclared war at sea. Henry IV divided his resources for this sanctioned piracy into two fleets: one, the southern, with the primary aim of defending the Channel coast out of Dartmouth, Fowey and Southampton; and the other, the northern operating out of the east coast ports. Each fleet was under the control of an admiral and was made up of armed merchantmen, that is to say ships, like those of the French, 'armed and arrayed for war', although they were not king's ships and do not appear to have been ships arrested for the king's service. Nevertheless they were very willing servants of the crown and arrested foreign ships at sea on orders. They were probably not paid by the crown but received their profit, and therefore their wages, from the value of the cargoes they seized.

At a time when warfare at sea mirrored that on land, warships, and probably privateers, were crewed by large numbers of men-at-arms and archers, consequently men of note would be appointed to captain a ship and they would have many knights in their retinues on board. These gentlemen were valuable since they could command a ransom. When ships met in battle and an enemy ship surrendered all prisoners became the property of the crown. If the victorious ship was a king's ship the king traditionally took only half the value of the prisoners, the prize itself and any cargo it was carrying, the other half being shared out among the owners and the crew. If the victorious ship was not a king's ship the crown only took a quarter of the total value of the prize, the crew and any cargo, the other quarter going to the owner of the victorious ship[26] and the remaining half being shared out among the master and crew. This encouraged privateering at a time when the crown could not afford to build and commission royal ships. English fleets seized at least sixty French ships in the two years to 1402. This semi-official unpaid service on behalf of the crown may have been solely retaliatory for damage done to English shipping by the French and Scots in the same period, but the English seem to have been very successful and it was certainly profitable.

Piracy was endemic along the coastlines of the three belligerents throughout the period and was not specifically directed at ships of other nationalities. It was a lucrative trade. Of the English ships involved those out of Devon and Cornish ports were perhaps the main offenders, with ships out of the Isle of Wight, the Cinque ports and the East Anglian ports providing healthy competition. French ships from the Norman and Breton ports were every bit as voracious as were their English rivals. Flemish ships, like those of Castile, Scotland and the Hanse, were as good as those of France and England at preying on merchant ships. In times of war piracy became legalized by the issue of royal licences to ships' captains who then became privateers in the crown's service. Most of these privateers were well-known pirates, some even well born like Edward Courtenay, son of the earl of Devon. Another was the respected official John Hauley, several times mayor of Dartmouth and collector of customs who was made admiral of the West in 1400, a time when legalized piracy was at its height. The earl of Warwick indulged in piracy with his fleet of ships out of Calais during the Wars of the Roses.

The war at sea was every bit as intense as the war on land, furthermore it did not necessarily stop when a truce was declared or a treaty signed. An ancient custom of the sea gave forty days grace after a truce had been agreed during which prizes could lawfully be taken.[27] This was about the maximum time a ship could be expected to be at sea early in the fourteenth century. It would therefore be reasonable to assume that all ships that had been at sea at the time a truce was negotiated would have returned to port within that time and would then learn of the truce. However by the middle of the following century ships were able to remain at sea for much longer periods, and so the war at sea often continued right through a truce. In effect, either due to war between belligerents, sanctioned privateering or piracy, the war at sea never really ceased.

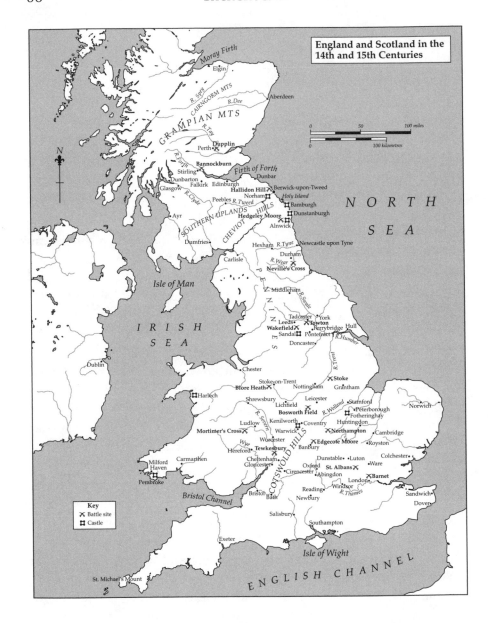

England and Scotland in the
14th and 15th Centuries

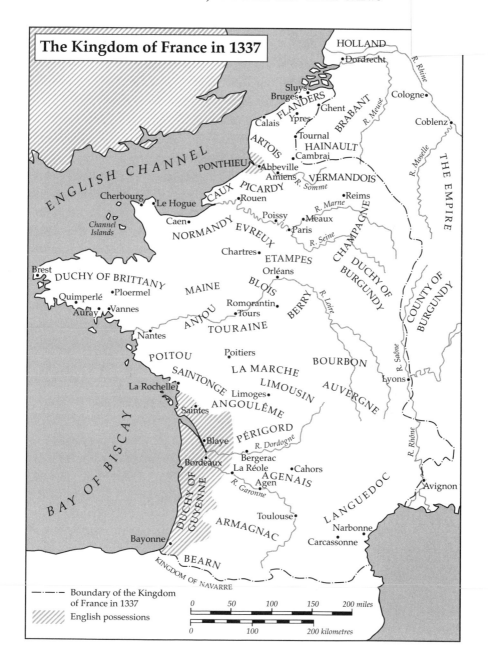

The Kingdom of France in 1337

HOLLAND
•Dordrecht

R. Rhine

Sluys
Bruges• FLANDERS
Calais •Ghent BRABANT Cologne•
Ypres• R. Meuse
•Tournai Coblenz•
ARTOIS HAINAULT
•Cambrai R. Moselle
•Abbeville VERMANDOIS
PONTHIEU Amiens R. Somme THE EMPIRE
CAUX PICARDY •Reims
Cherbourg •Rouen R. Marne
Le Hogue Poissy •Meaux COUNTY
Caen• •Paris CHAMPAGNE OF
Channel NORMANDY EVREUX R. Seine DUCHY BURGUNDY
Islands Chartres• ÉTAMPES OF
Brest Orléans BURGUNDY
DUCHY OF BRITTANY MAINE BLOIS R. Loire
Quimperlé •Ploermel Romorantin• BERRY R. Saône
Auray •Vannes •Tours
Nantes ANJOU TOURAINE BOURBON
POITOU Poitiers Lyons•
La Rochelle SAINTONGE LA MARCHE AUVERGNE
Saintes LIMOUSIN
Limoges• AUVERGNE
ANGOULÊME R. Rhône
•Blaye PÉRIGORD
Bergerac R. Dordogne
Bordeaux• La Réole •Cahors
AGENAIS
Agen• Avignon
R. Garonne LANGUEDOC
DUCHY OF ARMAGNAC
Bayonne GUYENNE Toulouse• Narbonne•
BÉARN Carcassonne•
KINGDOM OF NAVARRE

ENGLISH CHANNEL

BAY OF BISCAY

- · - · - Boundary of the Kingdom
of France in 1337

////// English possessions

0   50   100   150   200 miles

0   100   200 kilometres

Part 2

THE WAR IN THE NORTH

Chapter 5

The Bannockburn and Weardale Campaigns

Robert Bruce discomfited the king and all the barons of England at a place in Scotland called Stirling, in the year of our Lord 1314.[1]

The 'War in the North' had been ongoing for eighteen years before the Battle of Bannockburn. It began when Edward I invaded Scotland in 1296 to enforce his claimed overlordship on John Balliol who had been declared the rightful king of Scotland by Edward I at the parliament of Norham in May 1291. This declaration was made by Edward after learned assessment of the claims of various candidates on the death of the actual heir, the 'Maid of Norway', at the request of the Scots. Edward in accepting this task avowed that he was the overlord of the Scottish king and to emphasize this he renounced the quitclaim of Canterbury in 1296. But the Scots took little notice of Edward's claim believing, perhaps naively, that he referred to lands held by Balliol in England, which were extensive. Balliol did homage, as it was thought, for his English lands. This apparently simple misunderstanding gave Edward the excuse he needed to realize his ambitions, but it also committed England to what must have seemed an endless war and one without much honour and no profit.

Not long after Balliol had been crowned, Edward decided to test his claims to overlordship in the field of jurisdiction by offering justice to a Berwick man dissatisfied with a verdict at Balliol's court. In 1294 he summoned Balliol, the king of Scots, and several of his foremost magnates, to render military service for him in Gascony, a summons which neither Balliol nor his magnates answered. Consequently a council of twelve assumed power in Scotland in July 1295 and set up a government in Balliol's name. One of their first acts was to conclude an alliance with Philip IV of France against whom Edward was on the verge of war.

This act by the Scottish government, together with a refusal to deliver three Scottish castles to Edward as surety in a Scottish case being heard by an English court at Westminster, gave Edward the justification he needed to go to war against Scotland. He immediately gathered a large army and on 26 March 1296 crossed the Tweed where he took and garrisoned three castles, then stormed and sacked the town and castle of Berwick.[2] He then moved on up the coast and defeated a small Scottish army at Dunbar and marched north through Scotland as far as Elgin, which he reached on 26 July.

Believing he had impressed the nobility and people of Scotland sufficiently to cower them he returned to Berwick. Here he received the homage of many of the earls, bishops and barons of Scotland, but certainly not all. It was said that:

All those who were with the English were merely feigning, either because it was the stronger party, or in order to save the lands they possessed in England; for their hearts were always with their own people, although their persons might not be so.[3]

Satisfied with his achievements, Edward returned to England, leaving John de Warenne, earl of Surrey, and Hugh Cressingham in charge.

Scottish resistance to the English grew and under William Wallace and Andrew de Moray they found the leadership they needed. As English-occupied castles began to fall de Warenne and Cressingham moved north with an army to confront and destroy the Scots. The armies met at Stirling Bridge on 11 September 1297, where not only were the English heavily defeated but the hated Cressingham was killed and de Warenne only just escaped to Berwick.

The following year Edward crossed the Tweed once more and defeated a Scottish army under Sir William Wallace at Falkirk on 22 July. Wallace became a fugitive and Edward once more established his overlordship. But the English victory at Falkirk was not decisive. The Scottish council appointed Robert Bruce and John Comyn as the 'Guardians of the Realm of Scotland' and the Scots gradually recovered their country, leaving the English in control of only the border counties and the Lothians. Edward invaded the country again in 1300 and 1301, wintering at Linlithgow and returning south in 1302. He invaded again in 1303 and held a parliament at St Andrews in March 1304. His only gains from this concentrated effort being the castles of Bothwell in 1301 and that of Stirling in 1304; meanwhile resistance continued.

In August 1305 Sir William Wallace was found guilty of treason and was hanged, drawn and quartered. Many other Scots, nobles, knights and common men were to suffer the same agonizing death and many of their womenfolk were to be dreadfully humiliated: the countess of Buchan and Lady Mary Bruce, for example, were said to have been imprisoned for four years in cages hung outside the castle walls at Berwick and Roxburgh.[4] But these atrocities simply stiffened resolve and defiance spread. Robert Bruce was crowned king of Scots on 25 March 1306 and intensified his campaign to oust the English. After many vicissitudes and many reverses, Edward was at last stirred to deal with Robert himself and, although very ill, he led a campaign to Scotland in the summer of 1307: he had barely crossed the border near Carlisle when he died.

Edward II was a man of very different calibre to his father and the Scots knew it. Robert Bruce now began an active campaign against the English in Scotland, taking castle after castle and razing them to the ground to prevent the English from making use of them and to remove the need to garrison them. He avoided formal battle whenever he could and then only when relatively small forces were involved and the ground was in his favour. He began a sustained guerrilla war which was, in the main, successful. He also began to raid into England on a large scale. For the first time since 1296 the English were beginning to realize what war really meant.

It was said of Robert Bruce that 'there had never been in former times any other king in Scotland who so grievously harassed the English as this one in his day.'[5] Indeed the damage done to England's wealth and pride by Scottish raids into England were such that Englishmen south of the border as far as Lancashire and Yorkshire lived in constant fear of the Scots. In response Edward II carried out two abortive campaigns into Scotland in 1307 and 1310 but achieved nothing.

In the summer of 1313 Sir Philip Mowbray, captain of the besieged English garrison at Stirling castle, offered to surrender the castle to king Robert I, the Bruce, if it had not been relieved by an English army by mid-summer the following year. Sir Philip galloped south under safe conduct to tell Edward II of his deal with Edward Bruce, the Scottish king's brother.

Edward, in consultation with his council and with the approval of parliament immediately set in motion the administrative arrangements necessary to gather together the largest army that had yet been seen on English soil. Everyone wanted to be in on this expedition. The Scots were finally going to get their comeuppance and the rewards in land would be great.

A quick decisive battle with the odds very much in his favour and with little risk would do wonders for his popularity, and the defeat of Scotland would give him land with which to reward faithful service. France was neutral, if not friendly, while the Pope, helped by English gold, was convinced of the righteousness of England's cause.

Edward began preparations in earnest in November 1313. He warned his supporters in Scotland that he would bring an army into Scotland in the summer of 1314 and he sent out writs to eight earls and eighty-seven barons demanding their presence with their retinues at Berwick on 10 June. The levies from England and Wales were called on to provide 16,000 and 9,000 footmen respectively; the Welsh contingent included 3,000 archers; a further 4,000 men were to be summoned from Ireland. Knights from Western Christendom were invited to come and share the glory and the spoils. Ships were arrested to provide support along the east coast and up the Firth of Forth to the gates of Stirling itself. A baggage train of 106 horse-drawn carts and 110 ox-drawn wagons[6] was assembled; the army was to lack for nothing on the march. Edward was so confident that he created the earl of Pembroke viceroy of Scotland before even setting foot across the border.

In the event the huge army which gathered near Berwick numbered about 2,500 cavalry, including over 1,000 knights and 1,500 mounted men-at-arms, 3,000 archers and some 16,500 footmen. It crossed the border on 17 June 1314. This army, which was organized into ten 'battles' or divisions, pushed on in some haste for Stirling Castle had to be relieved by 24 June to prevent its surrender to the Scots and they had about 120 miles to go. They reached Edinburgh, some 35 miles from their goal, on 21 June but after two forced marches and little rest got to within striking distance of Stirling on the 23rd.

The Scots meanwhile had not been idle. They had good intelligence of the progress of the English army, and while it was making its ponderous advance Robert gathered his small army south-east of

Stirling. He organized it into four divisions; Randolph, earl of Moray's of 500 men, his own of 2,000, his brother Edward's of 1,000 and Douglas with a further 1,000. He kept a force of 500 knights and men-at-arms ready for mounted action under the marshal, Sir Robert Keith, and had about 1,000 of what the Scots called the 'small folk' – those with less than £10 in goods and therefore volunteers not liable for the levy. The Scottish army also had a small company of archers armed with the longbow, perhaps as many as 300. He despatched James Douglas and Sir Robert Keith with a number of 'well-horsed' men to watch the English advance from Falkirk east of the burn at Bannock and south of the River Forth. Robert had decided to meet the English army between the burn and Stirling Castle about 1½ miles away. He recognized the danger of having the garrison of Stirling at his back and so he detailed a small part of his army to maintain the siege and to prevent a sally from the castle.

The approach to Stirling Castle from Falkirk crossed the burn at Bannock, which ran in a north-easterly direction to the River Forth. The burn, which had steep banks, could be forded where the old Roman road crossed it; this road then led up rising ground to the castle on its rock through the New Park with its scattered trees. To the west of the old road and a little way from it the park joined thick forest, the Torwood, which stretched nearly to Falkirk. There was another track, which crossed the burn, some 500 yards to the north that joined the old road halfway towards the castle beyond St Ninian's kirk; the burn itself was tidal from about 400 yards north of this crossing to the Forth.

These two routes made up the main approach, all on firm ground. There was an alternative and shorter route, which crossed the burn much closer to the Forth across several hundred yards of boggy ground and thence uphill to the castle. The boggy area was bound to the north by the Forth and to the south by a small tidal creek called the Pelstream, which flowed into the Bannock burn. Between the creek and the burn there was an area of reasonably firm ground, the carse, with good going up the hill to the park across a steep grassy bank.

Robert deployed his army on the high ground overlooking the main approach across the burn and about 500 yards from it. His own division backed by his brother's stood astride the old road facing the crossing of the burn; Douglas's division was behind this on higher ground but facing the north-east and flanking the other approach, and Randolph's division was on his left flank. The 'small folk' were stationed higher up the slope near the woods and behind the divisions of Edward Bruce and Douglas. Robert, concerned about the burn crossing, turned it into a formidable obstacle for heavy cavalry by digging and camouflaging pits about two foot wide and knee deep in a belt several yards deep either side of the old road where it issued from the burn on the north-west side. The scene was set.

Although both armies were typical of armies of that period certain differences need to be emphasized. The knights and men-at-arms of both sides wore armour consisting of a mail hauberk sometimes topped with an armoured coat generally made of leather, with many small plates riveted to it. They also wore mail leggings down to and covering the foot; on top of this they wore plate armour over their lower legs and forearms and steel gauntlets. They protected their heads with a bascinet or skullcap of steel to which was attached a tippet of mail, the aventail, which hung over the neck and shoulders and over which they would wear a great helm. They carried a shield, a sword and a lance and very often an axe or mace on the saddlebow.

In Scotland however, where there was very little armour-making capability, there was a great shortage of modern armour most of which had to be imported from France or Flanders; it was very expensive and could only be afforded by the wealthy. Consequently, in general, the Scottish knights were not quite as well protected as their English opponents.

The English were well horsed while the majority of Scottish knights and men-at-arms rode a lighter type of horse, a courser. This put them at a decisive disadvantage when pitted against properly mounted heavy cavalry.

Foot soldiers on both sides were similarly dressed with a brigandine, a reinforced jacket made from boiled leather, or an aketon, a sort of quilted and padded tunic with long sleeves and skirts. All wore either a steel pot helmet or a kettle hat with a wide brim. Very few could afford mail armour but in due course veterans would acquire suitable protection taken from casualties after battle. All foot soldiers carried a sword or an axe as well as a staff weapon or, if an archer, a longbow and quiver. However the staff weapon of the English foot soldiers was generally a bill, a cleaving weapon, whereas that of the Scots was a 12-foot spear, a thrusting weapon.

At this stage in warfare English foot soldiers were organized in loose groups of twenty under a vintenar, giving themselves sufficient room to wield their bills. Scottish foot soldiers, in contrast, were assembled in compact masses of several hundred spearmen leavened and led by knights and men-at-arms on foot known as a schiltrom. The English foot soldiers could be ridden down by a cavalry charge, unless well covered by their own archers or obstacles, or forced back into a confused mass by the determined advance of a schiltrom and then cut down by mounted knights. The schiltrom was itself relatively immune to a cavalry charge but could be broken up by concentrated fire from archers and would then be vulnerable to cavalry. Archers, unless firing from behind cover and protected at close quarters by bill-men or spearmen, were themselves vulnerable to cavalry. In all phases of battle in those days the mounted knight *en masse* was ultimately decisive, but to get to the moment of decision required the co-operation of all the elements of an army. In order to achieve this they had to be grouped correctly for the battle ahead, stationed on the ground best matched to their capabilities and be committed at the opportune moment. This required good generalship and good leaders. At Bannockburn the Scots had the best general and the best leaders.

Scottish soldiers normally fought on foot, even the knights, and although most soldiers would be mounted for a march, only a small proportion of the knights would remain mounted for battle.

In England at that time there was a great social distinction between the knight and the common soldier raised by the summons. The latter would have had little training and was largely ignored by the knightly class who nevertheless recognized that they provided the base from which they and the archers could operate.

The Scots had had nearly two months to gather and train their army at Torwood and many of them had recently been on operations. Edward Bruce had been raiding in Cumberland while Douglas and Randolph had lately captured both Roxburgh and Edinburgh. Very few soldiers on either side had experienced a pitched battle before.

On 22 June the Scots had withdrawn to their positions behind the Bannock burn where they slept the night; the 23rd dawned a fine warm day and the Scots had all morning to improve their position.

The English meanwhile reached Torwood at about midday on the 23rd, after yet another forced march. Sir Philip Mowbray, governor of Stirling Castle, met them there; he had ridden from the castle unseen by the Scots, with a small escort. He warned the English commanders that the Scots had improved the natural defences of the approaches and that they were ready in position to receive the English, pointing out that by the terms of the surrender agreement the English army had no need to go any further as, having arrived within three leagues of the castle it was officially relieved. However Edward II and his barons had not come all this way simply to achieve a technical relief of the castle, they intended to teach the Scots a lesson they would never forget, and besides there was land and honour to be won! They resolved to give battle.

The English decided on a two-pronged advance by their cavalry. The vanguard, under the earls of Gloucester and Hereford, were to advance out of the Torwood, astride the old road, cross the burn at the ford and continue on their way towards the castle. A smaller force of 600 knights, under Sir Robert Clifford and Sir Henry Beaumont, were to cross the burn at the track about 500 yards to the right of the main advance and get between the Scots and the castle to cut off their retreat.

The Scots watched the vanguard in all its glory, shining armour, glinting weapons, bright pennons and colourful trappings, as it issued from the forest edge and made its way down to the ford. But they could not see the smaller force to the right, due to the high banks of the burn.

The English vanguard lost its cohesion as riders pushed forward to the burn or waited their turn at the ford. As they fanned out again on the other side many of them fell foul of the pits which disorganized them still further; knights were thrown from their horses and horses lamed. Meanwhile one knight, Sir Henry de Bohun, several yards ahead of the rest on the old road, saw King Robert on a grey palfrey inspecting the ranks of his division about a hundred yards ahead. He immediately couched his lance and charged up the old road hoping to kill or capture the king of Scots. With only an axe in his hand but mounted on his lighter and more handy horse, Robert cantered to meet him. As de Bohun was nearly on him he swerved his horse away, stood up in his stirrups and split de Bohun's helmet and skull with one blow of his axe as he thundered by.

The Scots let out a cheer and charged down the slope at the English knights who were still trying to extricate themselves from the pits. Under these circumstances the 12-foot spears of the Scots were deadly weapons and the English very soon withdrew beyond the burn after suffering many casualties. The Scots were called back by Robert and returned to their positions.

Meanwhile the force under Clifford and Beaumont, having crossed the burn unseen and remaining undetected by riding under the lee of the grassy bank, were suddenly seen near St Ninian's Kirk right below Randolph's small division of 500 spearmen. Randolph quickly marched his division forward to bar the advance of the 600 English knights. The latter could not ignore such a challenge and without more ado they spurred their horses and charged the Scots, who were drawn up in their schiltrom, spears out, like the spines on a hedgehog. The horses of the leading knights were soon spitted on the spears and the thrown knights quickly killed; the rest started to mill around the schiltrom trying to force their way through the frieze of spears. Horses, wounded and maddened by the spears, threw their riders who were soon killed on the ground. Without accompanying archers, there was no way the mounted knights could break the schiltrom. This fight went on until the late afternoon when Randolph, sensing that the English knights were no longer so keen, began to press them himself with his division. Before long the English called off the struggle and galloped off, some to seek refuge in the castle and the others back whence they came. The English had suffered many casualties that afternoon, and pride had taken a catastrophic fall. 'The English had been put out of countenance and were exceedingly dispirited by what had occurred.'[7] In contrast Scottish morale was high. The Scots had lost only one spear-man from the fighting that day and their foot soldiers had mauled two powerful bodies of fully armoured knights putting them to flight; 'From that hour great fear was set up among the English and greater boldness among the Scots.'[8]

After the two skirmishes it became clear that the English army was not going to attack again that day and so Robert relaxed his guard and the army moved back to the edge of the woods for food and rest. He offered to withdraw that night to the wilder country north-west of Stirling, as he wished to preserve Scotland's army for future operations, and the odds for the morrow were still heavily against them. But his knights and spearmen voted to stand firm and to fight it out the next day. Indeed they demanded that the battle should begin at dawn. That night Sir Alexander Seton came to Robert secretly from the English camp and advised him that if he wished to defeat the

English, now was the time as they 'have lost heart and are discouraged.'

The immediate problem facing the English army was where to camp for the night. They had to find water for their horses and grazing, while maintaining their threat to the Scots; the only possible place seemed to be the carse, between the creek and the burn down towards the Forth. By the time 2,000 horsemen had trampled the grass in this restricted space it was, in the words of Sir Thomas Gray,[9] 'a bad, deep, streamy morass.' The large body of foot soldiers, not yet committed, settled down the other side of the burn, footsore, weary and apprehensive about the coming events in the morning. The whole English army spent the short night in fear of a Scottish attack, infantrymen under arms and the knights and men-at-arms still in armour, their horses still bitted and saddled with loosened girths.

Apart from forming up the horsemen in the morning in front of their night positions and facing the Scots up the slope, the English seemed to have no definite plan of battle for the next day. They seemed to believe that the Scots would remain up the slope in their positions ready to receive an English cavalry attack, which they would carry out in due course after the horses had been watered and fed. There was no plan to use the infantry.

The Scots on the other hand knew just what they had to do. Robert knew the English dispositions from his patrols during the night. He knew that the burn separated their knights and men-at-arms from their infantry and that the tide would be coming in, making the burn a formidable obstacle. He realized that their horsemen would find it difficult to manoeuvre or to go much faster than a trot over the ground they had chosen. He knew that with the creek on their right, the Forth behind them and the burn on their left the English knights were hemmed in, and the tide would be on the flood. Their only way out was uphill through the Scottish schiltroms, over the creek or the burn. Robert decided to attack the English knights and men-at-arms before they could come out of their restricted positions and form up in battle array. His army slipped out of the woods in good order and was well down the slope before dawn.

Dawn was at 3.45 a.m. on 24 June 1314, and as it became light the Scots halted in their schiltroms about 300 yards from the English cavalry lines, knelt and prayed, then stood up ready for battle under their banners. With Edward Bruce's division on the right, Randolph's in the centre and Douglas's on the left, they were in echelon from the right so that Edward Bruce's division was ahead of the division to its left and so on. Robert Bruce's division was in reserve and Keith's cavalry covered the open ground on the left flank. The archers were on the left of Douglas's division. The order to advance was given and the Scots pressed forward determined to drive the English into the Forth.

The English meanwhile could not believe their eyes; surely the Scots were not so foolish as to challenge them in open ground with footmen? By God, they were! Knights hurriedly tightened girths and mounted, but they were all so pressed together that only the van under Gloucester and Hereford, which had spent the night in front of the others, was able to form up in any semblance of order. They charged uphill as soon as they were ready onto the spears of Edward Bruce's division. Many of the English and Welsh archers, seeing the problems ahead, quickly crossed the burn and took station on the English right flank and at right angles to it, to bring flank fire to bear on the advancing Scottish schiltroms. They drove off the few Scottish archers by weight of fire and the advantage of range. English longbows were made of home-grown or imported Spanish yew; this wood was scarce in Scotland and they were unable to import yew from Spain so most of their longbows were made of elm, which could not match the English bows for range.

Battle was now truly joined. The English van met the spears of Edward Bruce's division in a terrific clash of arms as it marched implacably downhill and reeled back after some fierce close-quarter fighting. In the words of Sir Thomas Gray:

> the Scots came in line of schiltroms and attacked the English columns, which were jammed together and could not operate against them, so direfully were their horses impaled on the spears. The troops in the English rear fell back upon the ditch of Bannockburn tumbling one over the other.[10]

The other two Scots divisions from the first line closed with the remaining English cavalry who were now mounted but had insufficient room to wield their weapons effectively, their horses, slipping in the mud and wounded by spears, threw many a rider who was quickly overcome by the Scottish spear-men. The Lanercost chronicler described the scene:

(the Scots) advanced boldly upon the English ... of a truth when both armies engaged each other, and the great horses of the English charged the spears of the Scots, as it were into a dense forest, there arose a great and terrible crash of spears broken, and of destriers wounded to the death. And so they remained without movement for a while. Now the English in the rear could not reach the Scots because the leading divisions were in the way, nor could they do anything to help themselves, wherefore there was nothing for it but to take flight.[11]

Chaos and panic began to spread as the Scots pressed on down the slope. On the Scottish left flank the English archers were beginning to cause casualties when Keith's 500 horsemen swept down and cut them to pieces, allowing the Scottish archers to come back into range and pour a murderous fire into the English mass. Seeing how things were going, Robert then marched his own division to the left of that of Douglas into the area vacated by the English archers and soon began to press the English back.

The English army was now trapped; it had no escape and insufficient room to make use of its potential; order and purpose were gone and panic ensued as they saw yet another Scottish division, the small folk, coming down the hill in good order under their banners. It was now a case of every man for himself. The Scots, who had proved to be unbreakable, kept pressing the English towards the Forth; many tried to escape this way but drowned.

Edward II was nearly captured, his horse was speared and many Scots hands tried to pull him down but he fought bravely and was saved by his own efforts and by the gallantry of Aymer de Valence, Earl of Pembroke, and Sir Giles d'Argentan. He was escorted off the field towards Stirling Castle followed by nearly 500 of his household knights. Sir Giles, seeing that the king was safely on his way turned back saying, 'I will bid you farewell for never yet have I fled from a battle, nor will I now', and he spurred his horse back into the press never to be seen alive again. The only real example of leadership by the English knights was shown by Pembroke who, after escorting the king to Stirling Castle, went back and found about 3,000 of the Welsh contingent in the Torwood, many of whom were from his estates in Wales. He organized them and led the majority all the way back to safety at Carlisle over the Lowland hills and moors.

Edward II reached Dunbar and from there sailed for Berwick and home, but his party was harried by Douglas the whole way and suffered many casualties. The English lost thirty-four barons and several hundred knights killed in the battle, to which can be added perhaps another hundred killed as they escaped to England. Nearly a hundred other barons and knights were taken prisoner immediately after the battle to which should be added those taken at Bothwell and Stirling castles and some others taken on their way to England. The Scots lost comparatively few men and their only notable casualty was Sir John Airth who was in charge of the baggage train and was killed by the earl of Athol in an act of treachery as he was on his way to join Bruce's army.

In terms of the profits of war the Scots captured the complete English baggage train which must have been worth well over £100,000 and they probably received an equal amount from ransomed prisoners. Scottish hostages held by the English, including Robert's wife, daughter and sister were released.[12]

English leaders learnt a great deal from this battle, which they were not slow to put into practice in the future. In the past, English armies fighting in Scotland, Wales or Ireland had always been vastly superior in both numbers and quality to those of their enemies, who had to rely on a form of guerrilla warfare. But on the continent the battles in which they had been engaged were nearly always battles between mounted knights and the English army was designed to meet this contingency. Bannockburn was the first time that a superior English army had been defeated in battle by a much smaller force. Also it was the first time that English mounted knights in a large formed body had been defeated by the common soldier on his feet supported by armoured knights marching in their midst. It was a revolutionary concept and the English leaders took due note of it. They also noted the effectiveness of their archery fire; initially their archers had managed to drive the Scottish archers out of range and they were beginning to affect the main battle when the Scottish cavalry, in their turn, drove them off the field.

The Scots on the other hand learnt little from their experiences at Bannockburn. They failed to appreciate that one of the main factors that contributed to their victory was the excellent discipline and order in their army compared with that of the English. They also appear to have thought that the soldier on his feet in large tight groups was the only answer to the problems they had in raising sufficient men-at-arms and archers to meet the English armies on a more equal basis. Consequently, in the future, they continued to rely on their dismounted ability regardless of the factors that might influence an impending battle.

English military leaders now realized that the knights mounted and *en masse* were not infallible and could not always be relied upon to overcome properly organized and well-disciplined infantry unless they had the support of archers. Furthermore they saw that archers by themselves were vulnerable and needed the protection of infantry and some form of obstacle. They also realized from the skirmish between the opposing archers, early on the second day at Bannockburn, that archers won their firefight by virtue of the weight of fire they could bring to bear. In other words, the multiple of the rate of fire times the number of archers was a decisive factor, and clearly the greater the number of archers deployed the more effective they would be.

Following Bannockburn English leaders appreciated that knights must on occasion fight on foot and that ordinary bill-men needed the presence of dismounted armoured knights to stiffen the ranks. Perhaps they also realized at last that the common soldier had his place in the order of battle, and that if well led and trained he could also win battles. They further noted, indeed they had probably always known, that no matter how the various elements of the army were to be grouped for battle a proportion of the knights should always be held in reserve, mounted and ready for any opportunity that might present itself; or at least have their horses ready at hand.

They had had an object lesson in the fact that the choice of ground on which to offer battle could be a battle-winning factor in itself. Clearly, from their subsequent battles against both the Scots and the French, they now realized that, whenever possible, battle should only be offered on favourable ground. Furthermore they had seen and felt at first hand that ground could be improved as an obstacle artificially and realized that defended ground should include obstacles to obstruct or canalize an enemy advance. These were salutary lessons, which the English understood and applied in the future, however they had two more lessons to learn from their northern neighbours: the advantages that came from strategic mobility and self-reliance.

When the Scots took Berwick in 1319, Edward II moved north to take Berwick in July with a formidable army but was thwarted because Bruce sent Sir James Douglas with a strong raiding force into Yorkshire to capture the queen who was then at York. This, however, he failed to do although he did achieve some success. This Scottish raid forced the English to abandon their efforts to retake Berwick and the English army withdrew. A two-year truce was then agreed. As soon as the truce expired in the summer of 1322 the Scots again crossed the border in force and swarmed as far south as Preston, Lancashire. In retaliation Edward wasted the Lothians but was soon forced to withdraw, pursued by Bruce who followed the English army into Yorkshire where he nearly captured Edward near Rievaulx.

In 1326 Scotland and France signed the treaty of Corbeil, the most cogent aspect of which was that Scotland and France undertook not to make peace or truce with England should the other be still at war with her. This ensured that from that day on England had to be prepared to fight a war in two very different theatres, several hundred miles apart at the same time, if she decided to go to war against either.

Edward II was deposed in 1327 and Queen Isabella became regent during Edward III's minority, although she was to prove no more successful against the Scots than had her husband. In that year, Robert the Bruce, though an old man and suffering from leprosy, was very much in control of events. The truce negotiated in 1323 between Edward II and Robert ended with the accession of the young Edward III in 1327. Robert decided in April of that year to demonstrate his defiance and to take advantage of political weakness in England, where Queen Isabella, the queen mother, and her lover Roger Mortimer, Earl of March, manipulated the council set up to rule during Edward's minority for their own ends. Meanwhile Isabella's government received intelligence of Scottish intentions and issued a general summons in Edward's name, applicable to every shire, to provide men for a large army which was to operate in the north; the feudal summons went out to five earls and twenty barons who were ordered to join the army with their retinues. The army was to be supported by sea and fifty-five ships of over 60 tons burthen were arrested of which some thirty were assembled at Great Yarmouth. There then followed a pause to see what the Scots would do; with luck this show of strength would overawe them sufficiently to keep them on the defensive and on their own side of the border.

Robert's response was immediate and unexpected: he sent his brother Edward to land in Ulster with a small force to obtain the support of the Irish for a combined landing in Wales where they were assured of an enthusiastic reception. Nothing actually came of this grand idea but it certainly wrong-footed the English. The Scots moved quickly and crossed the border in three large bands under the earls of Mar and Moray and Sir James Douglas, and made their way south across the wild country of Westmoreland between Carlisle and Durham, travelling fast and undetected.

All the Scots were mounted – knights on destriers or coursers and the spearmen and archers on hacks or ponies. As Froissart said:

> These Scottish men are right hardy and sore travailing in harness and in wars; for when they will enter England, within a day and a night they will drive their whole host twenty-four mile, for they are all a-horseback; the knights and squires are well horsed, and the common people and others on little hackneys and geldings; and they carry with them no carts nor chariots.[13]

The animals could survive on bad grazing and were accustomed to harsh conditions. The men, knights included, expected to live off the land. Meat would be found on the hoof and everyone carried oatmeal; water was always available in the burns. Wine, considered an essential commodity in the Middle Ages to purify water, would be found by and by in the sacked villages and manors. The Scots always marched in this fashion. Indeed they needed to be highly mobile, as their strategy was generally to avoid pitched battle against the English who could always raise larger and better-equipped armies, and to concentrate on quick plundering raids and the harassment of English armies on the march.

The main English army gathered meanwhile at Durham while a smaller force assembled at Carlisle, between them hoping to deny the Scots passage south of the rivers Tyne and Eden. The English army would have been between three and four times the size of the Scottish army and the proportion of men-at-arms to foot soldiers would have been about the same in each army. To this army of about 3,500 men-at-arms and about 11,000 foot soldiers should be added about 8,000 archers. Apart from the men-at-arms, about a third of the English foot soldiers were mounted like their opponents, but the archers still marched on foot. This army had to be supported by a large and comprehensive baggage train of many carts that drew its supplies from Newcastle to which they had been brought by ship.

The English commanders knew that the Scots had crossed the border and their scouts were finally alerted to their presence by the smoke of burning farms and villages in the area south of Hexham, between the rivers Tyne and Wear, far south of where they were expected. The English army immediately set out in pursuit, but very soon the 3,500 men-at-arms and a similar number of hobilars left the marching foot soldiers and archers far behind, as they did the baggage carts. As night drew near the mounted part of the English army halted after a frustrating day to wait for the baggage carts and foot soldiers to catch up. They had been following the signs of smoke all day but were unable to catch the Scots; that night they could see the fires of burning houses and perhaps the cooking fires of the Scots, but come daylight their enemy was nowhere to be seen. The next day the pattern repeated itself. The English van never caught up with the Scots; whenever they were spotted they would invariably melt away before the English could bring them to battle.

That night the English commanders met to decide how they could force the Scots to fight and prevent them from burning and pillaging the country. They decided that they could do nothing about the devastation, but that if they were to picket the River Tyne at the crossings they would bar passage to the Scots. They would then be forced to fight as they withdrew back to their own country with their plunder and the cattle they would be driving. Having resolved on this plan they left their camp site at midnight, each man with a loaf of bread tied to his saddle or carried on his back, and they marched north to the crossings between Haydon Bridge and Hexham leaving their baggage carts behind. They rode all that night and the next day in pouring rain and arrived on the Tyne early that evening at the point where the Scots had crossed on their way south.

Surely they surmised they had the Scots now. The English army straggled in during the night; they had nothing with which to make fires or to cook, and indeed they had nothing to eat apart from a loaf of soggy bread each and nowhere to shelter. Their horses had no forage or oats for the second day running and since they had no picket ropes or hobbles their riders had to hold them by the harness all night. The next day it rained hard all day and the river swelled to a raging torrent. They sent a foraging party with sumpters to purvey provisions and the majority of the army had something to eat that day. This routine continued for eight days during which it rained for most of the time. Everyone was getting hungrier. Saddles got soaked, weapons rusted and the padded aketons worn by most of the men became heavy and sodden with rain. Horses developed saddle sores and many that needed shoeing had to do without.

Neither army knew where the other was. However the Scots were used to the conditions and to living rough; besides they had plenty of meat and oatmeal and, by this time, wine also; they could always find shelter in a farmhouse or village before they burnt it down. Froissart described the Scots succinctly: 'The Scots are a bold, hardy race, and much inured to war.'[14]

On the ninth day the king promised that whoever first brought word of the Scots would receive a hundred pounds of heritable rents from land and a knighthood.[15] The army marched hither and yon for the next three days without sight or knowledge of the Scots when on the fourth day after crossing the Tyne an esquire brought news that they were camped on a hill about 12 miles away.

The hill on which the Scots were positioned overlooked a fast-flowing river and dominated the only feasible crossing point. Many English knights crossed over to the Scottish side to make a challenge but there was insufficient room to deploy. The English army then dismounted their men-at-arms and formed up on the flat ground on the north side of the river and marched to the crossing point opposite the Scots, hoping to overawe them. The Scots simply fired arrows, threw rocks and yelled insults at the English who saw that the Scots were in an impregnable position. The English then withdrew a little way and sent heralds to the Scots to say that they would allow them unhindered passage of the river and room to form up in battle array if they would only accept the challenge of battle. The Scottish army, being about one-third the size of the English, was not to be tempted.

A stalemate continued for a further three days, until on the fourth day, shortly after dawn, the English suddenly realized that the Scots had broken camp and left silently in the night. They found them on another hill a few miles away beside the same river and in an even stronger position.

Once again the English sent out heralds to ask the Scots to come and do battle with them on ground that was more favourable to the English, and once again the Scots declined. That night Sir James Douglas with about 200 men-at-arms crossed the river out of sight of the English position and rode through the English camp. They caused many casualties and much chaos. Le Bel says they killed more than 300 men and even cut the guy ropes on King Edward's tent, before returning to their own positions well content with their night's work. Morale among the English continued to fall.

That night the Scots quietly withdrew and rode north fast.

Afterwards some of the English army went to view the Scottish campsite. They found over 500 cattle newly slaughtered, the Scots being unable to drive them away. They also found over 400 cauldrons made of cowhide filled with meat and water, ready for boiling, and more than a thousand spits with meat ready for roasting and several thousand old shoes made of rawhide with the hair still on. Living off the countryside was, for the Scots, second nature; providing they could find cattle or sheep they could live in very harsh conditions for a considerable time. The English army got back to Durham thirty-two days after leaving it on their way to Newcastle and after twenty-six days on campaign. They had totally failed to bring the Scots to battle or prevent them from devastating the country between the Tyne and Wear. Edward III, just sixteen years old, was humiliated.[16]

How did the balance sheet look after this campaign to overawe the Scots? It is unlikely that the total bill including equipment, transport and compensation, was much less than £180,000. This was a huge sum, more than double crown income for any one year, but the greatest cost was to English pride and prestige. Edward III never forgot his first campaign.

Politically it was a real setback to England and led to the treaty of Northampton in 1328 in which England at last, but reluctantly, recognized the sovereignty of Scotland. Perhaps it is worth quoting the relevant part of the preamble to the treaty signed in Edward's name.

We, and certain of our predecessors as Kings of England, have tried to assert rights of rule, dominion, or superiority over the realm of Scotland and in consequence a grievous burden of wars has long afflicted the realms of England and Scotland ... on behalf of ourselves, our heirs, and all our successors ... assent that the realm of Scotland, defined by its true marches as they existed ... In the time of Alexander ... shall remain forever to Lord Robert, King of Scots and to his heirs and successors, divided in all things from the realm of England, entire, free, and quit and without any subjection, servitude, claim or demand.[17]

Both the campaign and the subsequent treaty were clear messages to the French that their ally could play a most useful part in their dealings with England.

For the Scots this campaign was a triumph; they had humiliated England at very little cost to themselves. But, and perhaps more importantly, they had brought home to the people of northern England and to the crown the realization that continuing war between the two countries was going to be expensive and that Scotland too could field a devastating offensive.

English leaders, and particularly Edward III, realized that their armies, and particularly their archers, had to be mounted for the march in the future, recognizing that the mobility thus gained would give them a battle-winning factor. However they also realized that their armies had to learn to live off the country, although clearly baggage carts had their place when conditions allowed. The great *chevauchées* of the English in the Hundred Years' War were born of the Weardale campaign where the English learned many valuable lessons from the Scots. However the Scots success in the campaign ensured that Edward III would not rest until he had forced them to renounce the treaty of Northampton. So far as he was concerned the Scots were still his subjects and he was going to force them to acknowledge his sovereignty. This could only be done by war and he watched for the first political opportunity to declare it.

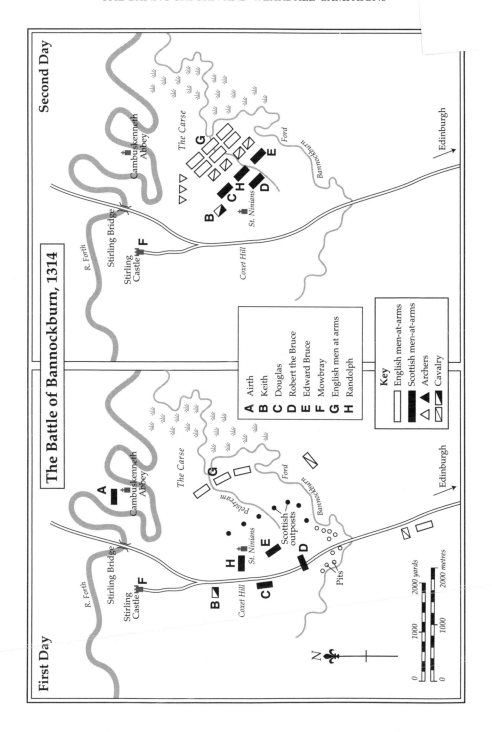

The Battle of Bannockburn, 1314

First Day

Second Day

R. Forth
Stirling Bridge
Stirling Castle
Cambuskenneth Abbey
The Carse
St. Ninians
Coxet Hill
Pdstream
Ford
Bannockburn
Scottish outposts
Pits
Edinburgh

Key
A Airth
B Keith
C Douglas
D Robert the Bruce
E Edward Bruce
F Mowbray
G English men at arms
H Randolph

English men-at-arms
Scottish men-at-arms
Archers
Cavalry

N

0   1000   2000 yards
0   1000   2000 metres

Chapter 6

The Battle of Halidon Hill

'Verily the Scots are the Antidote to the English'[1]

Edward III was so mortified by his first campaign against the Scots in the Weardale that he resolved to settle the Scottish question once and for all, and in this he was strongly supported by his barons who thought the treaty of Northampton was demeaning and dishonourable. Fortunately for him the means was at hand. When Robert died in 1329, Edward Balliol, John Balliol's son, decided to make a bid for the throne of Scotland. In fact the crown had passed legitimately to Bruce's infant son, David II, who was in France, and the country was governed in his absence by the regent Donald, earl of Mar. Nevertheless, with the active support of a group of magnates known as the 'disinherited', Balliol took steps to seize the crown. These barons, who were mainly English, had achieved their titles and land through marriage and had lost their lands by refusing to acknowledge Bruce as king of Scotland. Edward III calculated that his support for Edward Balliol's bid for the Scottish throne in return for Balliol's acceptance of him as the overlord of Scotland would make him the *de facto* ruler. He therefore actively supported Balliol's efforts, which culminated in the Battle of Dupplin Moor in August 1332.

At Dupplin Moor a big Scottish army marched on foot over open ground to get to grips with the smaller Anglo-Scottish army of Edward Balliol already drawn up in position, on foot, and with a large number of English archers in support. The Scottish army was eventually put to flight by a combination of murderous archery fire while pressing Balliol's army in front, and a lack of order and discipline in their own ranks. The Scots advanced in schiltroms, each a solid body with frontages of much the same length as their flanks, giving them great penetrative powers against a line of dismounted men-at-arms and bill-men but making them very vulnerable to archery fire. They advanced on foot over unsuitable ground against an enemy already on dominant ground supported by massed archers firing from the security of protected positions on the flanks. They were unable to disperse the enemy archers because they had dismounted all their men-at-arms and they could not defeat them by weight of fire because they had failed to raise sufficient archers of their own. Indeed the Scots tended to use the few archers they had as skirmishers and never managed to assemble sufficient archers to produce the weight of fire needed to win battles. Although at Dupplin the Scots managed to close with the Anglo-Scots to their front, it was the English archers who won this battle 'at a distance' and from the flank. The tactics used at Dupplin Moor by the Anglo-Scottish army were to become the basis for all the subsequent battles fought by the English, both in Scotland and later in France.

Politically the battle at Dupplin put Edward Balliol on the throne of Scotland. He was driven out three months later but not before he had rewarded Edward with virtually half of southern Scotland, including the town, county and castle of Berwick. As a result Edward became lord of southern Scotland. He quickly put his own officials into positions of authority as sheriffs and coroners and as constables of the castles, which he filled with his own garrisons. His collectors of customs and his tax gatherers began the business of milking revenue from Scotland to set against his growing need for cash. However the town and castle of Berwick, which had been recaptured by the Scots in 1318, remained in Scottish hands with a Scottish garrison.

After their defeat at Dupplin Moor the Scots reverted to Robert I's successful strategy against the occupying English forces of a combination of guerrilla warfare and the destruction of captured castles within Scotland. Their riposte to the English presence was always the offensive raiding into England and they were aware that they should avoid offering battle to English armies, which were invariably larger and better equipped. While this strategy may not have produced stunning victories it had the merit of putting English forces onto the defensive in Scotland and of forcing English armies out of Scotland after short campaigns; it also took the war into England at every opportunity. It was effective and it made the English despair of ever finishing the 'War in the North'.

However, new personalities were now in command on both sides; Robert I was long since gone as was the mediocrity Edward II. Early in 1333 Edward gave leave to Balliol to invade Scotland once again. He crossed the border with his army in March 1333 and after taking the stronghold of Oxnam and wasting the land on his way, he invested Berwick, establishing a blockade by sea and surrounding the town. But Berwick was no longer an easy victim; its stone walls, first built by Edward I, had recently been repaired by the Scots and they had a competent garrison under their commander Patrick, earl of Dunbar and March. Berwick was quite capable of withstanding a lengthy siege. In retaliation and in an attempt to draw off the Anglo-Scottish army the Scots raided into Northumberland and Cumberland in two separate expeditions, and harried the counties before returning north with their booty.

These raids gave Edward III the excuse he needed to justify his preparations for war. Two months later he arrived at Tweedsmouth with a large army to reinforce Balliol's besieging army before Berwick. He crossed the Tweed and immediately took charge of the operation. At that time if a walled town or fortress could not be taken quickly by surprise or treachery the besiegers were in for a long sojourn outside the walls. There was no way of telling how long a siege might take, but success by starvation took time, and often quite a long time, while assault, though quick, could be very expensive in man-power and might not be successful. It was not unknown for a besieging army to run out of supplies quicker than the besieged and then the siege would be raised, or a relieving army might approach to drive away the besiegers. Either way, to be successful, the besieging army had to have an adequate and secure supply system to meet its needs over the anticipated length of the siege.

Edward had organized just such a system. He appointed a 'receiver of the king's victuals' in March at Newcastle where appropriate warehousing was requisitioned and where he intended to set up his base of operations. The Florentine banker Mancent Francisi was commissioned to purvey 15,600 quarters of wheat and 22,100 quarters of other victuals in February.[2] Merchants were encouraged to ship supplies up the east coast to Newcastle. Indeed nine east coast ships discharged cargoes at Newcastle amounting to 1,500 quarters of wheat, 200 quarters of beans and peas and 100 quarters of oats, but this was only a small part of what was required, and what was collected and shipped. The sheriffs of sixteen midland and southern counties were ordered to secure 12,000 quarters of wheat and another 12,000 quarters of oats by purveyance to be delivered in two halves, the first by 14 May and the second by 24 June. Altogether twenty-two ships were used to transport the supplies north, six from Hull and the remainder from ports between Southampton and Newcastle.[3] Later these same ships were used to support and supply the army as it marched north up the east coast of Scotland. A large English army found it impossible to live off the land in Scotland as good grazing was scarce and the army soon ran out of grazing wherever they halted, even for a short time. Indeed the authors of the *Chronicle of Lanercost* observed: 'The English do not willingly enter Scotland to wage war before summer, chiefly because earlier in the year they find no food for their horses.'[4] Consequently without proper supply arrangements English armies could not stay in Scotland for long.

However not all resupply could be ship-borne – some supplies had to move with the army and of course supplies had to be moved from the warehouses at Newcastle to the army camps near the border. Edward, foreseeing this need, required the larger abbeys to furnish the necessary wagons, large carts drawn by five horses; it is doubtful if this was a voluntary contribution, more a donation in lieu of taxation. These large carts would have been in addition to the carts belonging to the barons and their retinues, and the sumpter horses belonging to the knights and men-at-arms. This was a formidable supply organization and it catered for the needs of an army that was expected to carry out a siege; however because sumpters were included it also allowed part of the army to be as mobile as their enemy, if the need arose. Such a large and slow-moving supply train would need an escort, particularly in Scotland where, as Edward was well aware, easy targets like this were soon taken unless well protected.

Edward knew that he would have to take Berwick before he could advance further into Scotland as it would lie across his lines of communication; he also wanted to use it as his main ship supply point and advance base for his campaign. He appreciated that in order to take Berwick he would need a siege train and so he took the necessary steps to provide one well in advance. On 24 March two 'war engines' were ordered and a special troop of carpenters, smiths and ropers was collected to fell appropriate oak trees and make the engines. The engines were probably trebuchets because stone masons and quar-rymen, included in the construction troop, were ordered to make 700 stone shot. The crews of these engines embarked on board three ships at Hull on 16 and 17 May for the passage direct to Berwick, together with the engines and the shot.[5] Edward also transported guns by ship to the siege. It was said in the *Brut*[6] that Edward

> made many assautes with gonnes and with other engynes to the toune, wherwith thai destroiede mony a fair hous; and cherches also were beten adoune vnto the erthe, with gret stones, and spitouse comyng out of gonnes and of othere gynnes.

So effective was the bombardment that a parliamentary petition of 1334 tells of the town as being mainly destroyed.[7]

The administrative arrangements made by Edward for his army show how well he prepared for his campaigns; the detail of the planning and its firm execution were unusual for the fourteenth century. Edward showed imagination in his forward planning and he made provision for every contingency. His strategic appreciation was outstanding, in particular he correctly guessed that, providing the Scots retaliated to Balliol's invasion as he expected, with a raid across the border, he would be able to persuade a reluctant parliament of the justness of his cause. Because of the time it took to make the necessary administrative arrangements he must have planned his campaign long before Balliol actually crossed the border.

The English reaction to the two Scottish raids was not the usual call-up of the local levy and the barons of the north to carry out a defensive operation that would drive the Scots back behind the border. It was a well-planned invasion of Scotland with a view to ending the 'War in the North' once and for all. Furthermore Edward needed his puppet king, Balliol, to exercise kingship in Scotland once again in order to give legitimacy to his own claim as the overlord of Scotland and to the lands in southern Scotland already ceded to him by Balliol the previous year. He intended to have what he considered was justly his.

How large was his army? It is known that Edward sent out writs for service to one hundred military tenants and that writs were also sent to the arrayers of ten northern counties and to the marcher lords. These measures were expected to provide 15,000 footmen and 1,500 mounted infantrymen; most of this force was to be archers. In addition there was the array of fencible men between the ages of sixteen and sixty from the four northernmost counties. There were also many volunteers in search of fame and fortune to add to the ranks of the men-at-arms. Normally not more than about 85 per cent of the arrayed men actually made the muster and a proportion would desert between the muster and the campaign. It would be reasonable, therefore, to expect at least 14,000 infantrymen in Edward's army from the writs of array, of whom about 3,000 would have been mounted at this stage in his reign and probably a little over half of the remainder would have been archers, say 6,000. It is not known how many knights and men-at-arms he had with him, but judging by the number of writs sent out there would have been about 2,500. To this army should be added the smaller volunteer army of Edward Balliol, complete with its own complement of men-at-arms and archers, which was to became a division in the combined English army. It was probably about a third of the total arrayed force with the same balance between men-at-arms, archers and bill-men. This then was a combined army of some 20,000 arrayed men and volunteers, of which at least 8,000 were archers, and with about 3,000 men-at-arms; a large and well-balanced army for this period of the fourteenth century. The fencible men were probably called up to provide a form of home guard to watch the crossings into England while Edward and his army moved north into Scotland; it is unlikely that any of them took part in the campaign.

As to the Scots, the chroniclers mention 60,000 footmen and 3,650 men-at-arms, 140 new-dubbed knights and 55 great lords. These, as was so often the case, are impossibly exaggerated numbers given by the chroniclers as a form of propaganda to glorify the later English victory. The Scots had never been able to put large armies into the field. Even at Bannockburn, where the Scots fielded their largest army, they had no more than perhaps 7,000 men including their knights, men-at-arms, spearmen and the 'small folk', so it is unlikely that they fielded many more to oppose Edward's army. Furthermore, their army was a raiding army that had just been operating south of the Tweed in England. An army of between 4,000 and 5,000 mounted infantrymen and perhaps 1,000 men-at-arms seems reasonable with maybe a further 1,500 mounted archers. Practical considerations therefore limit the size of the Scottish army to not more than 7,500, although 6,000 is a more likely figure, all of whom would have been mounted for the march. Consequently the English army must have been about three times the size of the Scottish army in total and had more than three times as many men-at-arms and between five and seven times as many archers.

Edward arrived at Tweedsmouth on 9 May, crossed the Tweed and joined Balliol before Berwick, which he had been besieging for two months. On 27 June, after a prolonged bombardment, Edward attempted to take the town by assault with a simultaneous attack by land and sea. The attack failed and a short truce was agreed while the Scots put out the fires in the town.

The garrison of Berwick, had sustained their defiance for three months and had been subject to continual bombardment and many assaults. They were weary of the siege and decided to negotiate an honourable truce. Accordingly, on 28 June, they agreed to surrender both the town and castle unless a relieving army raised the siege before 11 July, and to show their good faith they surrendered twelve hostages.

On 11 July a Scottish army under Sir Archibald Douglas, the Guardian, which had been north of the Border, crossed the Tweed into England unobserved in an effort to compel Edward to lift his siege of Berwick. They burnt Tweedsmouth in full view of the English army standing impotently on the north bank of the Tweed, and passed reinforcements and supplies into Berwick across a broken bridge before moving on south. The besieged garrison considered that the Scottish army had relieved them and they sent messages to Edward to this effect claiming the return of the hostages, and refused to open the gates of Berwick. Edward however asserted that since the relief had taken place across the Tweed from England and not from Scotland it did not come within the terms of the surrender agreement, and therefore in his view Berwick had not been relieved. Edward might well have been right but clearly the agreement, which was by word of mouth only, was not explicit enough, and failure to meet his understanding of the conditions hardly merited the ruthless act that was to follow. To show his displeasure and frustration he had the most prominent of the hostages, Thomas Seton, son of the warden of the town, hanged outside the city walls in full view of his mother and father.

The Scots in Berwick, fearing for the lives of the remaining hostages after the death of Thomas Seton, negotiated an extension to the truce. The conditions were complicated and explicit and to avoid the misunderstanding of the previous truce were written down and sealed by both sides. The truce gave three conditions for the lifting of the siege, one or other of which had to be met. By the first condition the Scots had to defeat Edward's army on Scottish soil. By the second a force of 200 Scottish men-at-arms had to fight their way through a similar number of English men-at-arms to the gates with the loss of no more than 30 men. And in the third, the same number of men had to force their way over the ford in the Tweed at Berwick Stream and into the town. If one or other of these conditions were not met by vespers on 19 July, they would surrender the town and castle at sunrise the following day. The indentures setting out the conditions of surrender also allowed for the return of the hostages, and the safety of the garrison and their goods. Any who decided to continue to live in Berwick would receive the king's peace, while those who wished to leave could do so with their belongings under safe conduct. The terms were generous.

Edward also allowed three Scottish knights to ride south under safe conduct to find the Scottish army and to appraise them of the situation at Berwick. The Scottish army meanwhile, considering they had relieved Berwick, had marched south and threatened to take Bamburgh Castle, where Edward's queen, Philippa, was staying, hoping to force Edward to raise the siege of Berwick and return to England. But Edward ignored the threat, well knowing that Bamburgh could stand a long siege and rightly surmising that Douglas had no siege engines with him. Douglas presumably hoped to surprise the castle garrison for he didn't stay there long before moving on to ravage other parts of Northumberland. He and the army were found near Morpeth having failed to lure Edward south from Berwick. He now knew the terms negotiated by the earl of March concerning the surrender of Berwick and, well knowing its importance to Scotland, felt he had no choice but to march north and do battle.

The Scots who had received the surrender terms for Berwick at Morpeth, about 15 miles north of Newcastle, had only a few days to march to a meeting with Edward's army if they wished to relieve the siege of Berwick. They had to march 45 miles to cross the Tweed between the castles of Wark and Norham, both in English hands, and then march some 15 miles by the shortest possible route to Berwick to fight a battle; in fact they went via Duns. Almost certainly they had less than a week for this.

The Scottish army crossed the Tweed and spent the night of 18 July in the park at Duns, about 13 miles due west of Halidon Hill and 11 miles north of the Tweed. Sir Archibald Douglas would have known from his scouts that the English army was positioned on Halidon Hill and he would have known from both the scouts and Sir William Keith that this was a formidable and numerous enemy. Sir William actually thought that the English army was not as large as the Scots', but he would not have been able to see the whole army from the walls of Berwick. However, Douglas certainly did not know that the English army was about three times as large as his own. He knew he would not be able to march directly to Berwick without inviting an attack on his left flank from the English on the hill. Consequently he decided to march to the north of Halidon and approach the English positions from the north-west under cover of the Witches Knowl atop Bothul Hill which was a little higher than Halidon.

Halidon Hill is 537 feet above sea level and lies about 2 miles north-west of Berwick. It dominates the landward approach to Berwick and the road north to Edinburgh, and lies equidistant from the sea to the east and the Whiteadder Water about a mile away to the west. Its crest runs in a north-easterly direction. The Whiteadder Water flows into the Tweed about 1½ miles to the west of Berwick. The crossing over the Tweed at Berwick Stream was only fordable at low tide. The ground was marshy for a considerable distance either side of the Tweed and the Whiteadder Water, indeed the boggy ground stretched all the way to the foot of the hill.

The English army was commanded by Edward III, a young man of twenty, who, like the Scots, had not been tried in battle but who was to make his mark as both a strategist and a tactician. He was also to show ruthlessness not seen since the days of his grandfather. His army was divided into three divisions commanded by Balliol, the earl marshal with Sir Edward Bohun, and himself. All his commanders had seen active service before. Edward posted 200 picked men-at-arms between the hill and the Whiteadder, due west of Berwick and on the edge of the marshy ground to meet the conditions of the surrender terms, in case the Scots tried to force their way through with their body of 200 men-at-arms. But he appreciated that the whole Scottish army would probably attack, and so he deployed the majority of his army on Halidon Hill with his division in the centre flanked by that of the earl marshal on his right and by Balliol's on his left. He posted his archers on the flanks of each of his three divisions, which were in a line following the curve of the crest of the hill. His dismounted men-at-arms were in the centre of the ranks of the infantry in each division. He might well have prepared his positions by planting stakes into the ground in front of his archers and along the front of his divisions; most of his army was probably stationed out of sight on the reverse slope of the hill. He left 500 men outside the walls of Berwick to deter a sally in support of the Scottish army, and he probably also picketed the ford at Berwick Stream. Edward himself took post in the centre of his division in the front rank. A proportion of his knights' and men-at-arms' horses were held just behind the position ready to mount and charge, or pursue a defeated enemy. He was ready, rested and confident.

On 19 July the Scottish army rode to the north side of Bothul Hill where they dismounted and formed up in their schiltroms. The *coup de main* party of 200 picked men-at-arms also dismounted but stayed as a body and joined the schiltrom of Sir Archibald Douglas, presumably hoping to force their way through the English ranks towards Berwick. The horses were either attended by grooms or picketed. The English positions were less than a mile away from the Witches Knowl. The Scots would have to march down the face of the hill in full view of the English, cross a bog between the two hills and then up the other side to the English positions about 500 yards from the bog. Difficult though it was, this approach was the only feasible line to take, unless the Scots marched nearly to the coast across the front of the English positions, inviting flank attack once they had cleared Bothul Hill. The English position was well chosen.

The Scots marched down from the Witches Knowl in good order, knights and men-at-arms in armour, spearmen in their aketons or brigandines and helmets, under the banners of their leaders, their relatively few archers out in front. The armour of the knights of both sides was similar and showed many improvements over that worn at Bannockburn; protection came from wearing several layers of different materials over a wool shirt. First came the aketon, a thick, stuffed and padded garment, which hung to the knees; then the hauberk of banded mail, which had loose sleeves and hung from the neck to the knees. On top of the hauberk the richer knights would have worn a breastplate and a back plate, but all would have worn a gambeson on top of the hauberk. The gambeson was another thick padded garment stuffed with wool and generally quilted in vertical lines. Finally, on top of this came the cyclas, a loose-fitting linen or silk robe that stopped short of the knee at the front but hung below it at the back and was often embroidered with the wearer's coat of arms. In addition to these general body defences knights would wear steel gauntlets, kneecaps of either steel or cuir-bouilli, steel plates over their forearms and a camail of mail fastened to the round basinet and falling over the shoulders; over the basinet a knight would wear a great helm. If mounted a knight would carry a shield in addition to the usual weapons of lance, sword and mace or axe. Foot soldiers would have been dressed much the same as they had been at Bannockburn, though they would have updated their personal defences by items scavenged from battlefields. It seems unlikely that an arrow would penetrate the defences of the mounted knight, but bows were becoming more powerful and arrowheads were being devised that could certainly do so. It is equally unlikely that a knight would be able to march on foot about a thousand yards, much of it uphill, cross a bog and then fight in all of this armour without dying of heat exhaustion. The Scottish knights must surely have discarded much of this, or, since they were a raiding army, had never set out wearing it in the first place; certainly the English arrows would not have had such a devastating effect if they had been wearing the full armour. The English knights on the other hand were almost certainly dressed in the full armour available to them; they of course would not need to march anywhere on foot as their horses were close by behind them.

The regent of Scotland, Sir Archibald Douglas, was the commander of the Scottish army; he was a competent commander of a large raiding force but was so far untried in pitched battle. He had as his division commanders the Earl of Moray and Robert the Steward, both young men, inexperienced in battle. The Scottish deployment had Moray's division on the right, Robert the Steward's in the centre and Douglas's on the left. After crossing the bog the Scots paused and reformed. Each division had about 2,000 men, spearmen and men-at-arms, close packed in a schiltrom, men-at-arms in the front ranks, with a frontage of perhaps eighty men spread over 100 yards and twenty-five ranks deep. This was a formation that was very difficult to stop once it had gained momentum, providing it could keep its cohesion. Their discipline was good and they were eager to close the gap and get to grips with their enemies, about six minutes' march above them. The English waited for their assault in silence, drawn up in their three divisions of about 4,000 men each, with the men-at-arms in the front rank like the Scots. Each division had a frontage of about 300 yards and some ten ranks deep, with its complement of 2,500 archers stretching out from both flanks towards the enemy advance,[8] like the horns of three bulls side by side.

The arrows began to fly as soon as the massed Scottish ranks came within range about 250 yards from the English line. The Scots would have had about three or four minutes of the arrow storm to endure before they could come to grips with their enemies. During this time each archer could have let loose at least thirty arrows so that the schiltroms would have been the targets of over 200,000 arrows before the close clash of arms. Their own archers were soon driven off by the weight of English fire, which had the advantage of numbers, range and of firing downhill. Each Scottish division made for the centre of the opposing division, Moray's against Balliol's, the Steward's against Edward's and Douglas's against the marshal's. Showers of arrows fell among the Scots, so that it was described 'as thik as motes on the sonne beam.'[9] Indeed, by the time the leading Scottish division, Moray's, had come up to Balliol's, 500 of their fighting men had already been slain before ever sword crossed sword. The other two divisions suffered a similar fate. But now, as the leading ranks began to fight hand to hand, the ranks behind them were subject to murderous arrow fire from the flank at close range. Notwithstanding the carnage caused by the constant rain of arrows into their flanks all three Scottish divisions got to grips with their opponents and fierce fighting took place. But the ceaseless rain of arrows soon began to tell and the schiltroms had lost their momentum. The English now had more men at the three points of contact than the Scots and gradually the Scots were forced back, slow retreat got quicker and soon retreat became flight and flight rout. As soon as they realized that the day was theirs English men-at-arms ran back to their horses, mounted and hunted down fugitive Scots who were slaughtered without mercy wherever they were found. 'There might men see the douztynesse of the noble King Edward and of his men, how manliche thai pursued the Scottis, that flowen for drede.'[10] Scottish knights and soldiers failed to get away, not only because they had a long way to go to safety, hotly pursued by mounted English men-at-arms, but also because their horses had been ridden away by the grooms as soon as they saw the schiltroms repulsed. Quarter was not given by the English men-at-arms, nevertheless some prisoners must have been taken, for the next day Edward ordered the execution of prisoners and one hundred were beheaded.[11] A few knights were kept for their ransom value but most perished. The Scots once more had been beaten 'at a distance' by English archers of whom there were more than the whole Scottish army put together.

Media exaggeration was present even in those days. The chroniclers put the Scottish losses at between 35,000 and 60,000, and the English at only one knight, one esquire and twelve footmen! However that may be, what is certain is that the Scots lost five earls and the guardian, Sir Archibald Douglas, as well as many knights, men-at-arms and spearmen. Indeed it was said that the Scottish wars had come to an end 'for no man remained of that nation who had either the influence to assemble or the skill to lead an army.'[12] But the pundits were wrong; most importantly for Scotland, Robert the Steward, heir to the throne after David II, managed to get away from the battlefield and escaped to Dumbarton Castle across the Clyde, in territory loyal to the cause of King David, from where he began the fight back.

To what extent this victory can really be attributed to Edward III, a young man of twenty years is arguable. He had never before been in battle although he had been on active service; however he had with him several commanders who had been at Dupplin Moor of whom the most influential was probably Sir Henry Beaumont, one of the disinherited who claimed the earldom of Buchan through marriage. He was an experienced soldier who as a young man had fought with Edward I in Flanders in 1297, and also in Wales; he had fought at Bannockburn and was largely responsible for the victory at Dupplin Moor. He knew from experience of the value of fighting in a defensive position on ground of one's own choosing, and he fully understood the power of the longbow used *en masse*. Almost certainly he was Edward's main adviser, but whether he acted as a chief-of-staff is not known. Someone, and probably not Edward, was responsible for the grouping and positioning of the English army. Perhaps it was settled at a council of war, a common occurrence in the Middle Ages before an impending battle, at which the senior commanders gave their views and the king or whoever was acting in his stead made the final decisions. Either way Edward, who had the responsibility, made the right decisions on that fateful day and he never forgot the result or how it was obtained.

It is possible that the Scottish commanders were unable to see the size of the English army because of their positioning on the top of the hill, and if this was so then there is some excuse for their attack up the hill and against the odds. A sea mist, common at this time of year, might have disguised the English or Edward might have placed part of his force out of sight on the reverse slope. It is likely that the Scots were unaware of the full size of the English force, otherwise they would have been more likely to have chosen the option in the terms of surrender of attempting to force their way with 200 men-at-arms.

If the 200 picked Scottish men-at-arms had failed, Berwick would have surrendered, but that would not have been disastrous and anyway the surrender terms were generous; after all the Scots had recaptured Berwick before and could do so again, as indeed they did several years later. The 200-man option would have left them with an army in the field capable of doing grievous harm to the cause of Balliol and Edward, and would, of course, have left them with their more experienced commanders. Either the Scots had an overweening confidence, or the weather prevented them from seeing the size of the English army, or they lost sight of their war aim, the independence of their country. The 'Scalacronica'[13] gives another reason; it says that Sir William Keith, as warden of Berwick, threatened to surrender the town if the guardian failed to take up the challenge implied by the surrender agreement. After he had obtained the guardian's promise to attempt the relief of Berwick by battle, he then rode back to Berwick to take up his duties as warden and took no part in the battle itself. Berwick was a red herring, but it showed how shrewdly Edward had judged the Scots.

Concerning tactics on the ground, there is no doubt that the schiltrom was a most effective formation because it produced an overwhelming number of men at the point of contact, while being immune to a cavalry charge during its assault. However, it had been shown at Dupplin Moor to be very vulnerable to archery fire during the attack, both on the march to contact once in range and into its flanks during the hand-to-hand fighting that followed. Since the Scots must have realized that they would suffer grievous loss from the archers one has to ask why they did not direct their advance at the archers rather than at the lines of men-at-arms at their front. They could have driven the archers into the men-at-arms, once up with them, and would then have been able to attack the English line from a flank. The men-at-arms would have been disorganized by the rush of archers seeking safety and would have been facing the wrong direction, meanwhile the Scottish schiltroms would not have suffered so much from the effects of flanking archery fire. Presumably the conventions of war at that time, with its emphasis on honour, deemed it necessary for the knights of one side to make for the knights of the other. The English, who fought by the same unwritten laws, would have realized this and placed their archers accordingly, well knowing that the Scottish schiltroms would direct their advance straight at the centre of each of their three divisions.

The Battle at Halidon Hill had confirmed a style for the English that was born at Duplin Moor. It depended first on an advantageous choice of ground for the battlefield, one that gave good fields of fire for the archers, that was not easy to outflank and which gave the dismounted men-at-arms some advantage against an advancing schiltrom. Secondly, it depended on the use of archers *en masse* firing from the flanks of the main position, and thirdly, on dismounting the men-at-arms to form the mainstay of the position. Lastly it was realized that where possible a mounted reserve should always be kept close by so that mounted action was possible.

When two other lessons learnt from their Scottish campaigns are included, that of being strategically mobile, by having the whole army mounted, and the ability to live off the countryside without baggage trains, the English clearly felt ready to challenge the French at war. One question however remained: would their tactics stand up to the mass mounted charge usual on the Continent and loved by the French? Would a mounted charge behave much like a schiltrom and would it recoil under an arrow storm? Would dismounted men-at-arms be able to withstand the shock of a mounted charge even after it had been disrupted and reduced by archery? The battles to come in France would give them their answer.

Chapter 7

The Battle of Neville's Cross and the Capture of a King

'All that country was in a state of war'[1]

Following the Battle at Halidon Hill Edward rapidly overran the south of Scotland and soon held all the major fortresses as far north as Perth. But he was unable to extend his grip on the country north of the River Dee, or indeed to the area west of Dumfries or into the Highlands, even though English armies went into Scotland every year for the next five years. Despite the grievous losses at Halidon Hill, armed resistance began again, first in Cowal, then Bute followed by Renfrew, Cunningham, Kyle, Carrick and Galloway, and even in the lands ceded to Edward by Balliol. The lands north of Stirling, which had not been overrun by the English, joined in what had become a general uprising.

Edward was now obliged to take action to restore his authority so he crossed the border once again in 1335 and again in 1336, in a campaign noted for its savagery, and speed of movement. As an example, he rode out of Perth with no more than 400 men-at-arms and 400 archers on 12 July and set off to the north straight through the middle of the Highlands via Blair Atholl. On the 17th he marched north to Forres, burnt the town and devastated the countryside nearby before riding on to Elgin and Aberdeen, both of which he burnt. Moving south he was at Forfar on 26 July and back in Perth on the 27th fifteen days after he had set out, having ridden about 230 miles, relieved a castle, burnt three towns and devastated the countryside on his route.[2]

In 1337 in response to vigorous Scottish campaigning in which they took the English-held castle of Perth and destroyed all the English-held forts in Kincardineshire and Fife Edward crossed the border intent on raising the siege of Stirling Castle. Even in the part of

Scotland ceded to him and his successors by Balliol, it was very difficult for Edward to exert his authority without great expenditure in men and resources. The ceded lands included the better part of seven southern counties and encompassed the area from Berwick west to Wigtown, and from the border near Carlisle in the south to Linlithgow on the Firth of Forth, and it included the Scottish capital of Edinburgh. These lands remained hostile. Edward provided inadequate protection for his administrators who were easily overcome by the Scots whenever they ventured from the safety of their castles, and indeed they were afraid to do so. He provided only forty-eight men-at-arms and seventy-two hobilars to escort the sheriffs of Peebles, Edinburgh, Dumfries and the constable of Jedburgh Castle[3] on their rounds, collecting taxes and imposing Edward's law. He had run out of money and could not pay for any more on a permanent basis. Already by mid-October 1334, only fifteen months after Edward's crushing victory at Halidon Hill, his chamberlain in Berwick was complaining that he had been unable to collect taxes from the county for the previous four months. Edward was unable to impose his will after five major expeditions into Scotland, and the occupation of the southern counties and some of the northern castles.

He had failed in his primary aim of the subjugation of Scotland. The devastation wrought by his armies merely stiffened resistance and encouraged yet more recruits to the cause of David II in a bitter guerrilla war under the able leadership of Sir Andrew Moray, the new regent, made more effective by the rugged Scottish countryside. Conventional fourteenth-century armies were not designed to fight a guerrilla war. He was unable to victual his castles at Edinburgh, Stirling and Perth by land, and as they were all essential to his occupation he had to supply them by sea. Indeed the era of war renewed by Edward's ambitions in Scotland and which was to last for a further hundred years simply stoked the fires of revenge which by 1337 had initiated a new period of Scottish raiding as Edward became thoroughly involved in his war with France.

Gradually Scotland struck back; in the period between 1337 and 1341 English forces were driven out of Annandale to the north and west of the River Solway, and the castles of Perth and Edinburgh were recaptured. In 1342 the castle at Stirling was starved into surrender and Balliol, Edward's puppet king who was paid a pension of 50s[4] a day by Edward in 1339, fled back to England. The same year David II and Queen Joan, Edward III's sister, returned from France where they had been given asylum. It was now England's turn to experience the ravages of war once again. The north of England again lived in constant fear of raiding and the payment of Danegeld to buy off Scottish raiding parties and armies became common practice once more. Indeed even the Bishop of Durham considered raising a local tax in 1344 to buy off the Scots for a few months. In reply England raised armies that were too large for the Scots to face. They would invade Scotland for a few weeks and then either because it was too expensive to keep such a large army in the field, or because of a lack of forage and provisions, they would have to return whence they came. All the time the army was in Scotland stragglers and provision carts would be picked off by guerrillas and parties of reinforcements would be ambushed and destroyed or captured. When, in due course, the army returned south of the border and was disbanded, the raiding would begin again.

This pattern continued until 1346, when the Scots overreached themselves. They invaded England in October in response to calls of help from Philip VI who had been defeated at Crécy in August and was being hard pressed by English armies. The Scots crossed the border near Liddell, north of Carlisle, and marched by way of Hexham into the counties of Durham and Yorkshire to waste and burn there. The Scots camped on the 16th near Durham at Beaurepaire where the monks offered them £1,000 to leave the place without harm, payable two days later. Meanwhile the archbishop of York had assembled the northern army at Barnard Castle and marched north to meet the Scots. A raiding troop under William Douglas accidentally discovered the English army on the 17th and informed David II who immediately marched his army to Neville's Cross and deployed them on high, broken ground to await events. Having learned the lesson of Halidon Hill, the Scots decided to await an English assault. When the English army arrived and took up positions on a hill opposite both sides stood to arms watching each other for seven hours. Finally the English advanced their archers and began to pour a withering fire into the Scottish ranks; unable to respond or take cover from the hail of arrows they finally put their heads down and charged the English line. Many of the Scots were felled by the arrows but those who made the English positions were soon being forced back by the more numerous English men-at-arms. Seeing what was happening to David's division, Robert Stewart and the Earl of March, who commanded the largest Scottish division which was in echelon behind, withdrew and made their escape together with most of their division. David and his own division continued to fight courageously against the whole English army until he was wounded in the face by an arrow and they began to retreat. David himself was surrounded but, despite his wounds, refused to surrender; he was soon overpowered and taken prisoner.[5]

Neville's Cross was not a lucky affair won by a few locally mustered yokels. The north of England had been put into a state of defence after 1338. The border fortresses had been repaired and garrisoned and the indenture and mustering process for all the available trained manpower north of the Trent had been allocated for service in defence of the realm in the north. Indeed, some 8,000 archers and hobilars were available for muster and the magnates of the north could be counted upon, by indenture, for some 500 men-at-arms and an equal number of archers over and above those already indentured for garrison service.[6] This pool of soldiers was amply large enough to meet any invading Scottish army – Froissart states that the English army at Neville's Cross included 1,000 men-at-arms, over 1,000 hobilars, 10,000 archers and 20,000 from the levy. These are almost certainly exaggerated figures, but the numbers of all but the levy were certainly possible and would have outnumbered the Scottish raiding army. However, in order to raise these numbers, two problems had to be overcome: first, the finance to pay for such a large force had to be available, and secondly the army had to be assembled at the right time and in the right place.

The first problem was overcome by retaining in York most of the revenue from taxes gathered from north of the Trent. The second problem had been overcome by an organizational change in the composition of English forces. Following their experiences in the Weardale campaign of 1327, most English soldiers were now mounted to give them a mobility equal to that of the Scots, and therefore the actual mustering of an army took far less time than it had formerly. Since the whole of the north of England was in a state of defence, regular meetings of northern magnates took place to review their defence needs and to take any action deemed necessary to counter possible Scottish incursions. Finally, intelligence about Scottish intentions was good. In this particular case the northern lords realized that a Scottish invasion was imminent some weeks before it began, and indeed they were given even more time than usual to prepare as the Scots foolishly wasted time in a petty siege of the peel of Liddesdale.

The Battle of Neville's Cross taught the English yet another valuable tactical lesson: they realized that massed archers could be used to attack. This was the first time that they had used their archers in this way; they had forced a dismounted enemy to abandon a well-chosen defensive position purely by archery fire. This would not have been possible if the Scots had retained a mounted reserve who could have charged the archers and forced them back behind their own dismounted men-at-arms. This was a valuable lesson and one that the English were to use to good effect in France.

Following Neville's Cross, English forces quickly overran the south of Scotland once more and reoccupied the border counties of Berwick, Dumfries, Peebles, Roxburgh and Selkirk. In 1347 Edward's puppet, Balliol, once again led an army into Scotland as far as Glasgow. But the old pattern reasserted itself and by 1356 the Scots had taken back all the latest English gains with the exception of the castles of Berwick, Roxburgh, Lochmaben and Caerlaverock from where Balliol tried to assert his authority as King of Scotland. Meanwhile the raiding over the border began again and soon reached unacceptable proportions. Edward was forced to adopt a purely defensive strategy on the border while he sought a profitable peace. The latter seemed within his grasp since he held David as his prisoner, and David's ransom alone might reimburse him some of the expense of his Scottish endeavours.

Edward would have been wise to negotiate a peace with Scotland a decade before turning against France. He could have done so after the Battle of Halidon Hill in 1333 and he could probably have concluded a favourable peace in 1337 when he was undoubtedly in the stronger position. But any peace would have involved recognizing Scotland as a sovereign nation, something he was most reluctant to do, and for its part Scotland would only sign a peace treaty providing England recognized her independence. And so Edward went to war with France while he was still at war with Scotland. When Edward was militarily involved over the Channel the Scots would invade the north of England, and when Edward invaded Scotland the French would raid or threaten invasion of the south coast, or take offensive action against the English in France. England had overreached herself and she was saddled with a war on two fronts.

Edward III was adept at taking the calculated risk and clearly knew of the many and ancient links between France and Scotland when he first broke the treaty of Northampton in 1333. He certainly knew of the treaty of Corbeil (1326) guaranteeing mutual aid and co-operation between France and Scotland against English aggression. It must have been a factor in his calculations when he turned against France in 1337. A major consideration must have been that if he could subdue Scotland quickly French political and military pressure on their behalf would end.

The quick defeat of the Scots would enable him to concentrate his forces against France, while the containment of France would enable him to deal with the Scots more quickly; the two wars were inextricably linked. He suspected that France had made preparations for the invasion of England through Scotland. Indeed, it is known that Philip VI of France made plans for the provision of an army of 1,200 men-at-arms and several thousand soldiers in 1335 or 1336 to land in Scotland, and join the Scots in an invasion of England across the border; in the event nothing came of these plans. Some French men-at-arms did come to Scotland but they soon left having failed to understand the pattern of warfare in the north. There can be little doubt that the Franco-Scottish connection, while in no way being a prime cause for war, was certainly a subsidiary factor in Edward's appreciation before going to war with France.

Edward's sustained effort to subdue Scotland between 1332 and 1337, whilst being a military failure, notwithstanding the victory of Halidon Hill in 1333, was an economic disaster. His income from Scotland never exceeded £2,000 per annum and was not always obtainable, yet his expenses were enormous; his occupation of southern Scotland virtually froze the Scottish export trade and he therefore never benefited from the customs on wool and hides. His expenditure to cover the costs of occupation alone from 1333 to 1337, including the maintenance of the garrisons and the repair of the castles at Roxburgh, Edinburgh, Stirling and Perth, amounted to some £10,000 per year.[7] In addition to this, lesser garrisons had to be maintained at fortresses throughout the south of Scotland together with a fleet in the North Sea. The fleet was essential to bring supplies to the castles accessible by sea, to protect his supply routes up the east coast, to frustrate Franco-Scottish threats of combined operations across the border and to prevent landings down the east coast of England. Furthermore, because of the increasing confidence and audacity of Scottish arms, he was obliged to maintain garrisons and castles across the north of England and keep the country north of the Trent on a war footing. All this was expensive.

A short expedition into Scotland of two weeks by an army of some 8,000 men would have cost about £30,000, while full-scale expeditions such as those of 1335 and 1336 must have cost more than £70,000 each. Adding all this together, Edward's expenses in pursuit of his Scottish ambitions between 1332 and 1337 would have cost him well over £300,000, while his income from Scotland for the period could barely have reached £10,000. Edward's Scottish campaigns were a huge drain on his resources at a time when he needed all his revenue for his venture in France. Indeed his total revenue in 1331 was only £72,514 2s 10p,[8] or about the cost of a full-scale invasion of Scotland. This drain on his resources obliged him to demand a custom on wool exports from parliament in 1337, which netted him about £30,000.[9] Nevertheless this was still insufficient to balance the books and in order to meet the expense of his war with France while he was still inextricably involved with Scotland he was forced to go cap in hand to the Lombardy bankers to make up the deficit. In 1337 he borrowed a little over £130,164.[10] This pattern was to continue for much of his reign while he continued the simultaneous war with both France and Scotland; indeed this financial pressure was only relieved during times of truce.

Edward was now saddled in the north with a war he couldn't win and one he was reluctant to stop except on his terms. However, with King David II his prisoner he began to make overtures for peace from 1347 onwards. Negotiations were opened with the regent, Robert Stewart, David's half-brother and his heir. Edward's initial offer to relinquish English conquests in the south of Scotland and to return David to his kingdom in exchange for £40,000 seemed reasonable. But the Scots would also have been obliged to recognize one of Edward's sons as David's heir to the Scottish throne. This was rejected by the Scots who had no wish to see an Englishman on their throne or to see their independence lost after David's death. Two similar offers were made in 1352 and 1353 but were also rejected. At about this time Edward dropped his support for Balliol and began to promote

David's cause in the hope of promoting his own, by force if necessary. Initially David was attracted by Edward's proposals and the prospect of his own freedom, however the Scots said they would elect another king unless David defied Edward's schemes and backed his Scottish supporters in the war with England.

In March 1355 the Scots received 40,000 *deniers d'or* from the French,[11] presumably to encourage them to cross the border, and on 6 November, while Edward was away in Calais, the Scots took the town of Berwick, but failed to take the castle. Edward received the news on or about 19 November on his return to England and immediately set out for the north, gathering a large army on his way. He crossed the border, retook the town of Berwick and went on his way to Edinburgh. His route took him via Roxburgh where his puppet Balliol on 20 January 1356 ceded the Kingdom of Scotland to him. Edward then proceeded to burn his way north in his new realm of Scotland in what was remembered for a long time in Scotland as the 'Burnt candlemas'. However, and not surprisingly, the Scots failed to appreciate their new 'king' and opposed him in every way, by guerrilla warfare and a 'scorched-earth' policy, so perhaps there was some excuse for the ferocity shown by his army. But events then followed the familiar pattern. The English had invaded Scotland with an army so large that the Scots could not possibly face it; consequently the Scots withdrew but remained in contact, cutting off stragglers and preventing resupply along the land route. The English burnt and harried wherever they could and relied on resupply by sea, but ultimately, the ships failed to arrive due to adverse weather conditions. Although Edward probably hoped to be crowned at Scone, the failure of his resupply by ship forced him to withdraw; after two weeks his army was back across the border and the Scots once more resumed their raiding into England. The military effect of the Scottish raid to take Berwick ultimately benefited their paymasters, France, because as a result Edward was unable to take part in a three-pronged offensive, planned for the summer of 1356, in France.

However, following the Battle of Poitiers in September 1356, at which King Jean II of France was captured, England was in a strong negotiating position. Edward now had the kings of both France and Scotland as his prisoners. Now, with France in no position to help, the Scots, who were as tired of the war as were the English, quickly concluded a truce in October 1357. By its terms the Scots were obliged to pay a ransom of 100,000 marks[12] for King David's release, the crucial point being that David was referred to as the king of Scotland and the English made no mention of their territorial claims north of the border. Also, by virtue of the ransom, Edward received some recompense for the expense of his Scottish venture. Although Edward's campaign into Scotland in 1356 can hardly be called a military triumph it was certainly a political success and was, ultimately, financially profitable. The fact that France was not able to demand a place at the negotiating table undoubtedly made matters easier for England and more difficult for Scotland.

However the signing of this truce was made possible largely because Scotland was as weary of the war and wanted peace as much as England. The fact that the truce was kept by the Scots was thanks mainly to David who kept his unruly barons in check and presided over an era of increasing prosperity in Scotland.[13] It is significant to note that even at the height of the war trade continued between Scotland and England. Scotland imported large amounts of grain from England throughout the war and exported hides and fish, but perhaps the most extraordinary trade was in English wool. England sent over 6,600 sacks of wool into Scotland for re-export between 1362 and 1377 and Scottish merchants then sent them on to Flanders. This thriving trade flourished because the custom on wool exported from Scotland was significantly lower than that imposed in England.[14] Other aspects of the intercourse between Scotland and England during times of war were that many Scots lived in England and had land in England or business interests there. Also, many licences were given by the English government for Scots to travel south to study at their universities.[15] Sea-borne trade down the English east coast became difficult during actual hostilities, but once campaigning stopped trade began again.

This war certainly drained the English treasury but it also impoverished the people and realm of Scotland; both countries wanted and needed peace. The truce negotiated in 1357 lasted for twenty years and during that time neither England nor Scotland launched major expeditions against the other. This does not mean to say that all hostilities ceased as raiding on a minor scale continued across the border by both sides.

This endemic border raiding can in no way be compared with that of the invasions carried out in times of war, which might have involved anything up to several thousand mounted men, including men-at-arms and archers under the full panoply of war, which burnt and devastated whole counties. Because of her geography England was more vulnerable to this style of warfare than Scotland. The Pennine hills divide England east from west, with the one gap at Hexham. Therefore any large-scale Scottish raid on the west could, and did, go south as far as Penrith and west to the coast, while a similar raid in the east could penetrate as far as York and often further. Indeed, after Bannockburn the Scots raided as far south as the Humber and the Trent. Also, any Scottish raid crossing the border in the west could easily cross the Pennines to the east, and vica versa, via Hexham, giving them considerable strategic flexibility. In contrast, the geography of southern Scotland breaks the country into two relatively small areas: one in the east lying south of the Lammamuir hills and east of Ettrick forest, and the other in the west bounded by the Solway Firth and the Cheviot hills to Dumfries. To England the profits of war were nothing like as accessible as they were to Scotland. Indeed they were only reachable when a full-scale invasion was undertaken with a large army, supported by sea, able to penetrate beyond the first natural barriers – even then the profits never matched the outlay. For Scotland the profits were always tantalizingly near and not too difficult to take.

Although the war in the North ebbed and flowed neither side managed to stage and carry out a decisive campaign or battle. Both Bannockburn and Halidon Hill were considered so by the antagonists at the time but they fell short of this promise, and the war simply festered on and on. By the early 1370s the Scots were in the ascendant once again and many petitions were sent to parliament in England expressing dissatisfaction with the government's defence of the border. They demanded that the defences of the cities of Carlisle, Newcastle and Berwick were put into a proper state of repair, and that the marcher lords should live in their castles and ensure they were fortified, garrisoned and victualled.

The war must have seemed very remote to the majority of Englishmen, although they would have heard about it from returning soldiers and from the pulpit on victorious occasions, however those higher up the social scale were well aware of it through taxation, purveyance and curtailment of trade. Those who lived in the northern counties had to live under constant threat of the violence of war and experienced at first hand what English soldiers were to mete out to the French year after year. English and Welsh soldiers had earned an unenviable reputation for their rapacity during expeditions into Scotland during the middle 1330s; it was said that only the lives of women and children were safe while not a man was spared. Farms and villages were burnt and pillaged and all stores of food and forage not destroyed by the retreating Scots would be seized by the army or burnt. It is not surprising that the Scots took every opportunity to repay the English in kind. Notwithstanding the reputation of English soldiers there can be little doubt that when the Scots had the upper hand the people of the north rightly feared for their lives. Although the common soldiers of Scotland were no worse than their English or French equivalents, they were certainly brutal and greatly feared in the north of England.

The cost of the 'War in the North', or series of wars, to England was enormous and far exceeded crown revenues during the reigns of Edward II and Edward III. Edward II inherited debts of some £200,000[16] in 1307 from his father's Scottish campaigns. His campaign for the relief of Stirling Castle that terminated at Bannockburn must have cost well over £200,000. The total cost of the 'War in the North' from 1314 to Edward III's accession in 1327 is difficult to calculate but it certainly far exceeded crown receipts in England and English income from Scotland. The cost of the war to Edward III was no less debilitating. The Weardale campaign cost about £180,000 and the armies for the campaigns of 1332, 1333 and 1337 would have cost about £90,000 between them, while the military costs of the campaigns of 1335 and 1336 would have exceeded £140,000. Indeed it was not until Edward III was thoroughly embroiled in war with France in the 1350s that the outlay for his Scottish venture at last came within his means,[17] but by then he had been forced onto the defensive in the north for economic and military reasons. England was simply not wealthy enough nor had sufficient resources to fight two separate wars at the same time.

There can be little doubt that the 'War in the North' cost England dearly and ravaged the northern counties. So far as the Scots were concerned the war devastated its marcher areas but in the main it had its greatest effect on Scottish trade, since their trade routes to France and the Low Countries had perforce to be along the English east coast. Also, Scotland received handsome subsidies from France from time to time. A sum of 40,000 *deniers d'or* was handed over in September 1356 and 50,000 marks were probably given in 1359. There can be little doubt that the raising of an army for service in Scotland cost the Scots a great deal less than the English since they relied almost exclusively on the general array to raise an army in defence of the realm. Also King Robert's statute 'Of Armyn in Tym of War' obliged all men to own arms on a scale relative to their property, a measure that took the cost of the provision of arms off the crown. Furthermore the arms and practice in their use was regularly checked at 'Wappinshaws' (weapon shows) by the sheriffs. From these means it can be seen that Scotland generally had sufficient trained military manpower to meet its needs on very nearly a no-cost basis. The general array was similar to the English equivalent, under which an individual was obliged to give forty days service to the crown in defence of the realm without pay; the only drawback to the general array was that it took a long time to assemble. The array was supplemented by the feudal host, which together with a shrieval summons gathered the men-at-arms, essential for the armies of the time. However, for an invasion of England, as distinct from raids, the feudal retinues, sometimes partially paid for by the French, were augmented by large numbers of volunteers attracted by the lure of plunder, as indeed were English volunteers for the war in France. Indeed the English who gloried in the triumphs of their *chevauchées* in France were obliged to experience the terror and devastation of this mode of warfare at home in the north, courtesy of the Scots.

It seems amazing that England, a far richer country, with a population about six times as large, was unable to defeat Scotland decisively and to occupy it permanently. But England became heavily involved in its war with France, whereas Scotland had only the one enemy to face and she was helped in various ways by her French ally. Scotland too had an immeasurable advantage in her geography. Also she was not plagued by chronic lack of funds as were both Edward II and Edward III. Scottish kings did not have to pay for their armies under their system of muster, and Scottish parliaments were always willing to vote funds in defence of the realm. The fact is that England was never willing to expend either the necessary wealth or the manpower to subdue Scotland; perhaps she underestimated the size of the task. Although both Edward I and Edward III certainly had the will to do so they hadn't the resources, while Edward II had neither the will nor the political backing to deal with the Scots. Furthermore the English nobility, who were essential to any policy of aggrandisement, were really only enthusiastic when their interests were at stake or land was promised. Except for the nobility of the north, the first did not apply and the second was unattractive, bearing in mind the hostility of the population. Meanwhile parliament, always concerned with the financial cost, gradually became more and more defensively minded. Consequently Scotland remained a dire threat, a prickly problem and a constant matter for concern throughout the period.

The fact remains that England's best course of action concerning the Scots, once they had embarked on hostilities against France, was to negotiate a proper peace and for both sides to put in place the necessary border controls to execute it. Unfortunately England never entered into negotiations with any honesty because they considered the Scots to be in rebellion against their lawful masters, while the Scots, who may have wanted peace providing their independence was recognized, never had sufficient governmental authority over their border nobles to enforce it. The 'War in the North', fought by the English in the belief that the Scots were obstinate and rebellious vassals, was fought by them with the bitterness of a civil war; while the Scots fought with patriotic fervour and determination in what was to them a war of independence. Indeed the Declaration of Arbroath sent by eight earls, thirty-one barons and the rest of the nobility and the community of the Realm of Scotland to the Pope in May 1320 sums up the Scottish view admirably. The Scots fought 'not for glory, nor riches, nor honours, but for freedom alone, which no good man gives up except with his life.'

In a similar situation to that which existed in France over the sovereignty of Aquitaine, England wanted a negotiated peace providing Scotland recognized the king of England as her overlord, while the Scots were ready to negotiate a peace providing the English recognized the sovereignty of Scotland. As these positions were mutually irreconcilable the issue had to be settled by force of arms. Success in this war was governed by the relative cost of the war to each side and their wish to meet it. National will was of course greatly influenced by national commitment to the cause and in Scotland the latter was very much stronger than it was in England.

Part 3

THE HUNDRED YEARS' WAR

Chapter 8

The Crécy Campaign

'The might of this kingdom most standeth upon archers which are not rich men'.[1]

Edward had been at war with Scotland for the previous ten years when he turned against France. His last campaign across the border with Scotland had been in 1337 and this war had impoverished him financially. Yet he felt that the issues at stake in France were so important that he went to war against her whilst still being at war with Scotland, France's ally, and when he was in debt.

On land the Hundred Years' War, as this war was eventually called, was fought almost entirely in France, despite the fact that the French and their Castilian allies raided the south coast of England and the French threatened invasion on more than one occasion. Nevertheless it was the English who took the war to France in an effort to settle the issues at stake. The major issue concerned the sovereignty of the duchy of Aquitaine. Aquitaine had come to Henry II in 1152 on his marriage to Eleanor, Duchess of Aquitaine, and the divorced wife[i] of Louis VII of France, as part of her dowry and in accordance with normal feudal practice. Following his marriage Henry II became the de facto Duke of Aquitaine, and his heir and successors inherited the title and duchy as dukes de jure. At the time of his marriage to Eleanor, Henry II was lord of more of France than the French kings themselves, and probably because of this the problem of the sovereignty of Aquitaine and the relationship between the English king-duke and the French king was not raised at the time. French kings turned a blind eye to this tricky problem leaving the English king-duke sovereign in Aquitaine because they lacked the power to contest the issue. The link between England

---

i Eleanor and Louis were divorced on grounds of consanguinity after fifteen years of marriage and after she had borne him two daughters.

and Aquitaine brought wealth to the duchy through the wine trade, while the English administration ensured a degree of peace and security to this quarrelsome corner of France.

However, increasingly during the twelfth and thirteenth centuries the Capetian Kings of France began to insist that the homage due to them by the great feudatories, Normandy, Burgundy, Brittany, Flanders and Aquitaine, should be liege homage. When King John came to the English throne in 1200 he inherited title to Normandy, Maine, Anjou, Touraine, Poitou, the Santonge and Aquitaine, but his titles would only be confirmed if he did homage for them. King John failed to do this and so in 1203 and 1204 Philippe-Augustus invaded and conquered Normandy and Anjou, territories which John never recovered, and neither did his eldest son Henry III.[ii] Throughout both reigns discontent over the 'English' territories in France was always close to open warfare. Unfortunately for his successors Henry III validated his Treaty with Louis IX in 1259 by accepting that he was Louis' vassal as a peer of France. So the English king-duke of Aquitaine was without doubt the vassal of the king of France and was required to do him liege homage for the duchy.

The duchy was forfeited in Edward II's reign following the burning of a new French bastide, St Sardos, by the English and Gascons in 1323. A truce was quickly arranged and in 1325 Prince Edward, later to become Edward III, aged thirteen and acting as his father's proxy, did homage for the duchy and paid a fine for the destruction wrought in 1323.

In 1329 Edward III did simple homage for his duchy and elevated this to liege homage in 1331. It was hoped at the time that this would lead to lasting peace in the area, however, out of exasperation at the many perceived acts of rebellion by the Anglo-Gascons in defiance of the liege homage done to him by their duke, Philippe VI once again confiscated the duchy on 24 May 1337. This act triggered the Hundred Years' War. Although each individual act of aggression and defiance by the Anglo-Gascons might have been relatively small, the cumulative effect finally broke Philippe's patience. He thought that by confiscating the duchy he had finally settled the matter. But he had totally underestimated his young cousin who had no intention of

---

ii Edward I's father.

giving up a territory which yielded revenue greater than that of the whole of England.[2]

When Edward III came to the throne in 1327, his uncle, Charles IV, was king of France, and he died in 1328 leaving no direct heir. The French nobility had then to adjudicate between rival candidates for the throne of France. The two leading aspirants were Philippe, Count of Valois, regent of France and nephew of Philippe IV, and Edward III, Philippe IV's only grandson. The French nobility claimed that the Salic law applied in this case; this meant that as Isabella, Edward's mother, was ineligible to inherit the crown, she would not be able to pass it on to her son; consequently they elected Philippe of Valois to be their king. This seems to have been a device used to deliberately bar Edward from the succession since this law had not been applied in France previously and was not applied in cases of inheritance to lands and titles. Edward was a minor under the regency of his mother Isabella and she was under the influence of Roger Mortimer, the Earl of March and her lover. The French nobility did not want her meddling in French affairs. Many believed Edward's candidature the stronger of the two as Philippe IV's direct descendant; but apart from making his claim Edward took no further action at the time. However, when Philippe of Valois, now Philippe VI, confiscated the duchy of Aquitaine in 1337, Edward formally laid claim to the throne of France, and in January 1340 he assumed the title 'King of France', so by-passing the problem of the sovereignty of Aquitaine. At the same time he quartered the arms of France with those of England so that all could see that he was the lawful king of both countries.[3]

In the fourteenth century the responsibilities and obligations of the feudal system did not allow for the waging of a just war by anyone against his sovereign, and therefore Edward, as Duke of Aquitaine, could not legitimately wage war against Philippe of France, his rightful sovereign. If he did so he could not lawfully remain the Duke of Aquitaine. This had implications in the wider context of Western Christian Europe; the Pope would undoubtedly condemn such a war and would threaten excommunication. Papal condemnation would prevent other princes, dukes and counts from declaring for Edward and he would then find it difficult to recruit allies. Edward had a legitimate claim to the throne of France. Although Edward's claim to the throne of France and his declaration might have been on unsure ground, particularly as Philippe had been on the throne of France for twelve years when Edward finally made his claim, it had enormous propaganda value, making it possible for him to wage a just war. It also made it possible for Frenchmen to join his cause with a clear conscience!

There was another cause for the war and it had to do with England's northern neighbour. The 'auld alliance' between Scotland and France sealed by the treaty of Corbeil, which was often renewed, remained in force throughout the Hundred Years' War. Only by pressure of successful war on France could Edward force France to renounce the treaty. The Hundred Years' War had its roots in these three distinct problems. Although they were three separate matters they were inextricably linked and could only be settled by agreement with France.

This war which began on 24 May 1337 was not a war of continuous battle but of continuous cause. The causes remained, unchanged and unsettled throughout the 116 years of the war. To those who lived at the time of the war there were many periods of active warfare separated by lengthy periods of peace and truce. Indeed over the Hundred Years' War as a whole more than half of the period was taken up with a truce of some kind.

England's political purpose in the war is quite clear; it was to retain Aquitaine in full sovereignty in perpetuity. From the earliest days of the war it seemed that the most satisfactory path to the achievement of this aim was to claim, and gain, the crown of France itself. This was a legitimate claim, and to wage war to secure this glittering prize would ensure that the initial aim was achieved, whereas simply securing the frontier of Aquitaine would not. However other problems could also be settled if Edward gained the throne of France: the treaty of Corbeil would be revoked and he could subdue Scotland without the threat of French interference; England's wool market in Flanders would be assured and her trade to Aquitaine and the Continent uninterrupted. These political objectives formed the basis of English strategy throughout the Hundred Years' War.

When the French confiscated the duchy of Aquitaine they immediately took steps to occupy it and the small Anglo-Gascon garrison put up a robust defence. To divert French attentions from Aquitaine Edward III, with German and Flemish allies, launched an invasion of northern France from Flanders; this achieved very little but had the merit of taking pressure off Aquitaine and giving Edward time to reinforce his garrisons there. Notwithstanding these operations in northern France, England went in constant fear of a French invasion of the south coast and early in May 1340 Edward received intelligence of a French fleet massing in the Zwyn estuary in Flanders. This was a golden opportunity and Edward decided to take advantage of the French preparations, while at the same time eliminating a threat to England and any threat of intervention to his own expeditions across the Channel.

When he heard of the French fleet's assembly he was himself preparing an expedition to Flanders. He had with him some forty ships but this would not be enough to ensure a safe crossing with such a large French fleet in the Zwyn estuary. He therefore called for reinforcements of both men and ships and set out on 22 June with about 120 armed ships manned by 2,000 men-at-arms and as many archers,[4] with the declared aim of destroying the French fleet. He arrived off the coast of Flanders the next day and found the French fleet at anchor in the river.[5] On the morning of the 24th he sailed in among the French ships and battle commenced.

A contemporary account says they sailed towards the French at sunrise.[6] They noted that the French ships were chained together with large chains making it difficult, if not impossible, to get between them. The French ships were all equipped with castles, wooden breastworks and other barriers. The English ships, which must have been close by and had dropped anchor, then weighed anchor and hoisted sail, as if to sail away. The French weighed anchor, let loose the chains and made to chase the English, whereupon the latter turned about and sailed into them. According to this account there were 300 English ships and 500 French, certainly an exaggeration. The English archers and crossbowmen fired so rapidly, 'like hail falling in winter', that the French had to keep their heads down behind their barriers. Meanwhile the English men-at-arms boarded the French ships and, after much fighting, killed or took prisoner all the French soldiers and sailors, and captured or sank all but twenty-four ships and galleys, which escaped. This account also states 'our artillerymen shot so fiercely'; this could be interpreted that some English ships had guns on board, which was just possible, or that some ships had small trebuchets mounted on the forecastle, which was also possible.[7]

Sea battles at that time were fought in the manner of a battle on land. It would therefore not be unrealistic to assume that Edward's victory was almost certainly due to the accuracy and rate of fire of his archers firing down onto the mass of French men-at-arms on board the packed ships. This would make it possible for his own men-at-arms to board enemy ships with a numerical advantage and then to fight an already dismayed and demoralized enemy. It must not be forgotten that the armour worn by men-at-arms at this period was mainly chain-mail and that this was easily penetrated by arrows fired from a longbow.

The successful battle at Sluys forced the French to the negotiating table to sign the Truce of Esplechin on 25 September 1340. This truce settled none of the main issues of the war, and Edward only agreed to it because he was virtually bankrupt and could no longer pay his troops, but it gave him breathing space to repair his finances and put Aquitaine on a proper war footing. The English pressure in the north had served to relieve French pressure on Aquitaine and was a strategy used throughout the Hundred Years' War whenever it was appropriate. It was not a strategy confined solely to the English; the French put pressure on England through their ally Scotland. However, within the year another war theatre opened up in Brittany and it was from these three theatres of war – Aquitaine, Flanders and Brittany – that Edward pursued his ambitions in France.

Brittany became a theatre of war as a result of the factional warfare between Jean de Montfort and Charles de Blois over the succession to the dukedom. Edward's support for the Montfort cause was substantial and quickly established an English presence in Brittany. Edward III gave military help to Jean de Montfort and, in exchange for Montfort's recognition of him as king of France, confirmed him in the earldom of Richmond, which had been held by the Montforts since the twelfth century. But most importantly Edward was allowed to install English garrisons in the south Breton ports.

Jean de Montfort was taken prisoner at Nantes in the summer of 1341 but his wife, Jeanne, kept his campaign alive throughout the winter of 1341–42. Edward, always with an eye for the main chance, sent a small force to her aid under Sir Walter Manny in the spring of 1342. In August of the same year Edward sent another small army to Brittany under William de Bohun, Earl of Northampton. This army landed at Brest and after destroying eleven Genoese galleys[8] stationed there marched south and took Vannes. Northampton then marched across Brittany and defeated a French army under Charles de Blois at Morlaix on 30 September 1342. Operations in Brittany at this time were on a relatively small scale and, with the exception of the Battle of Morlaix, warfare between the two Breton factions was largely by skirmish and ambush. However, the scale of warfare changed when Edward landed at Brest in October the same year with an army of about 5,000 men.[9] He pillaged the countryside and recaptured Vannes, which had recently changed hands; he then marched east with the intention of besieging Rennes. A large French army barred his path but before the two armies could meet in battle papal legates from Avignon arranged a temporary truce, which was extended to three years in January 1343 at Malestroit in an effort to stop the war from spreading. Despite the truce, Charles de Blois continued his operations against Jean de Montfort in whose support the English armies continued their operations. The truce was meant to apply to all the theatres of war, but minor operations continued along the frontiers of Aquitaine, as they did in Brittany.

Edward had intended to invade France on three fronts in the summer of 1345. His grand strategy was to include an invasion of northern France from Flanders, another expedition to Brittany and a land campaign in Aquitaine to clear the French from the area between the Dordogne and Garonne rivers, so consolidating his position in the duchy. The Flanders campaign petered out after the death in a riot of Van Artevelde, the burghers' leader, and Edward's own expedition could not be mounted in time for the summer campaigning season. However, Henry of Grosmont, Earl of Derby, landed at Bayonne on 6 June 1344. After resting his horses and men for a week he then marched to Bordeaux, recruited Gascon knights and men-at-arms to join his small English army of some 900 men-at-arms and 2,000 archers, and was soon in action. He cleared the French garrisons from between the two rivers and defeated a French force at Auberoche in October; he then recaptured the fortresses of La Reole and Aiguillon on the Garonne in December. His operations put the French in the area on the defensive and it was not until 1346 that they were able to take the offensive in Aquitaine when Jean, Duke of Normandy,[iii] invested Aiguillon with a large army in April.

In Brittany that summer French arms under Charles de Blois were still very much in evidence, as they invested the three principle English

---

iii Eldest son of Philippe VI of France and later to become King Jean II.

garrisons in Brittany, those of Brest, Lesneven and La Roche-Derrien, in the late spring of 1346. These garrisons were below strength and vulnerable, and might well have been lost had it not been for an incident involving Sir Thomas Dagworth, the deputy lieutenant in Brittany. He was visiting other English garrisons in the duchy with an escort of about eighty men-at-arms and a hundred archers, and was surprised shortly after dawn near Finisterre on 9 June 1346 by Charles de Blois with about 2,000 men. Dagworth took up a strong position on a hill and faced the French. His company fought throughout the day until the French withdrew at nightfall leaving many dead and wounded.[10] This spirited action relieved the pressure on the besieged English garrisons and stabilized the situation in Brittany to England's advantage.

Edward had been unable to organize and carry out his planned invasion of France in the summer of 1345, largely due to a lack of finance. But his intention remained. He sailed for France the following summer with his army in 1,200 ships[iv] for the invasion of France and landed on 12 July. He had originally intended to sail for Bordeaux[11] but contrary winds forced him to land at La Hogue in the Cotentin with an army of nearly 11,500 fighting men,[12] a paltry force when compared to the size of the forces available to the French king. When they first landed it is doubtful if anyone at the time thought that this invasion would be anything but a raid in force, a *chevauchée*; certainly the French did not take it particularly seriously until Edward reached the Seine. This he did on 7 August having plundered Normandy and sacked Caen for the loss of perhaps 600 men. His sailors also found and burnt seventy-one ships with castles fore and aft in the harbours along the Norman shore.

Once news reached him of Edward's landing and subsequent operations, Philippe VI began the process of assembling his feudal army. Philippe decided to restrict Edward's army to the south of the Seine if he could and prevent him from linking up with his allies, the Flemings. He therefore destroyed the bridges downstream of Paris and ordered the feudal contingents to assemble at Rouen, a strategically sensible decision. Meanwhile he waited for news of the Anglo-Flemish army coming south from Flanders and that of his son, Jean,

---

iv Generally those over 30 tons burthen.

Duke of Normandy, coming north from his unsuccessful siege of Aiguillon in Aquitaine. Philippe's intention was to force Edward to give battle south of the river, however his destruction of the bridges had the effect of driving Edward eastwards, posing a threat to Paris. This was an unforeseen advantage which was certainly not planned by Edward who, with the possibility of being caught between the armies of Duke Jean to the south and Philippe's to the north was anxious to find a way across the river and meet up with his Flemish allies.

Philippe shadowed Edward's army from the north bank of the Seine as it marched east along the south bank of the river, but Edward bluffed him into coming south to protect Paris. The city seemed under direct threat when Edward's patrols burnt the suburbs of St Cloud and St Germaine en Laye, the latter only a few hundred yards south of the walls of Paris itself. Philippe was in a quandary, Paris stretched across both banks of the Seine and the citizens were in panic. Something had to be done. He hurried east to protect his capital after evacuating the garrison and civilians from Poissy and destroying the bridge. The English army immediately repaired the bridge and established a bridgehead on the north bank. Thinking that he intended to assault Paris, Philippe sent Edward a formal challenge to battle between 17 and 22 August outside the southern walls of the city; it was delivered on the 14th. French sources say that Edward accepted the challenge. However there seems no reason why he should have done so except, perhaps, to lure the French army south of the Seine. Nevertheless Philippe duly marched his army through Paris and across the Seine on the 16th, and deployed his army on his chosen field of battle. As soon as he had confirmation of this Edward crossed the Seine with his army at Poissy and began his march to the north for a rendezvous with the Anglo-Flemish army under Count Henry of Flanders, which was making its way south towards Amiens.

Philippe had been outwitted. Nevertheless, although Edward had stolen a march on him, Philippe moved his army with some speed, indeed he covered the 70 or so miles from St Denys to Amiens in three days. By the time Edward's army reached Beauvais on the 18th, Philippe was at Clermont-sur-Oise, 15 miles to the east; Edward had been delayed by the need to gather food and forage. On the 20th, Philippe's advance guard reached the Somme, with Edward still some 25 miles to the south-west. As he now held all the crossings of the

Somme to the north and the Seine to the south, and his army blocked the way out to the east, Philippe had good reason to think that he had Edward trapped. Philippe stayed in Abbeville on 23 and 24 of August, while Edward and his army stayed near Acheux, some 8 miles to the south-west and 6 from the Somme at Blanchetaque. A prisoner informed the English that there was a causeway here across the river, some 2,000 yards long, wadeable at low tide and where the river was bordered by marshes for about a mile on each bank. Edward marched his whole army to the crossing during the night of the 24th so as to be ready to march across as soon as the tide would allow.

Early in the morning the vanguard could see that the French had stationed about 300 men-at-arms and perhaps 3,000 infantry, including a large contingent of Genoese crossbowmen, overlooking the causeway. The English would have to fight their way across. The element of surprise was lost, as the vanguard had to wait until well after dawn before the river was fordable. At about 8.00 a.m., a hundred men-at-arms and an equal number of archers led by the Earl of Warwick, Sir Hugh Despenser and Sir John Cobham, waded across the waist-high water under fire from the crossbowmen. The English archers could not immediately return the fire with any accuracy since the toe of a drawn bow would have been below the water level, but as soon as they were able they returned the fire with interest and drove the French from their positions. The men-at-arms then quickly established a bridgehead, which was soon reinforced. The French fled and by 10 o'clock the whole English army had crossed, though not without casualties.

Philippe meanwhile, thinking that Edward had his back to the sea and was still south of the Somme, was advancing from Abbeville south of the river to give battle; by the time he arrived at Blanchetaque the whole English army had crossed and the tide was in flood. There was no way across now for a further four or five hours. Edward and his army had escaped the trap. They may have been out of immediate danger but they were tired and had run out of provisions. A raiding party was sent to Le Crotoy, 2 or 3 miles away on the coast, and it ensured that the army fed well enough that night; furthermore, Philippe's diffident approach allowed them sufficient rest to raise their morale. They spent that night in the forest of Crécy, but not before Edward had sent four of his most experienced officers on reconnaissance to find a suitable defensive position to the east of the forest overlooking the French army's probable route from Abbeville to Boulogne. Edward's army was fed, rested and ready for battle.

After their disappointment at Blanchetaque the French marched back to Abbeville where they spent the night of the 25th. Next morning they set off for the Boulogne road via Saint-Riquier, hoping to prevent Edward marching north to join his Flemish allies. Edward seemed to have no such intention. He must have realized that his tired army, which had marched some 150 miles since crossing the Seine at Poissy nine days before, could not keep ahead of the French whilst also gathering provisions on the way; besides, he had made up his mind to fight.

Early on the morning of 26 August Edward marched his army out of the forest and they took up the positions assigned to them between the villages of Crécy and Wadicourt. The English army was divided into three divisions or battles: vanguard, centre or mainguard and rearguard. The van, which took post on the right of the English positions, was nominally under the Prince of Wales, then fifteen years old, with the earls of Oxford and Warwick, both experienced soldiers, as his principle officers. With him also were Count Godfrey d'Harcourt and four Knights of the Garter, Sir Thomas Holland, Sir John Chandos, Lord Burghersh and Sir Ralph Stafford, as escorts and advisers. The prince was well guarded and advised by some of the best and most experienced soldiers in the army. The rearguard, commanded by the Earl of Northampton with the Earl of Arundel as his deputy, both experienced and able soldiers, was to the left of the van. Edward kept the centre under his own command and his division took up positions between and to the rear of the other two divisions. He had all the horses of the army penned in a circular laager, made up of baggage wagons and supply carts, behind his own division, where the grooms and servants were expected to provide the defence. With the forest behind them and all the horses held in the laager it was quite clear to the army that Edward intended to stay and fight.

The numbers in the English divisions vary according to the source and the exact number is not known, but the van, or Prince of Wales's division, was undoubtedly the largest and the king's the smallest. It seems that there were at least 2,400 men-at-arms in the army with a further 1,700 light horse who would have fought on foot with the men-at-arms, a total of about 4,000. There were probably about 6,000 archers some of whom would have been from the Welsh contingent, and about 2,000 Welsh spearmen. At this stage in the evolution of English armies the proportion of archers to men-at-arms was about three to two, and therefore the estimated numbers at Crécy would seem about right. If a figure of 700 men-at-arms were given for those in the King's division, he would then have had about 1,000 archers with him. Similarly, if the Prince of Wales's division had 2,000 men-at-arms, it would have had some 3,000 archers, while the Earl of Northampton's division would have had the remainder of the men-at-arms, about 1,300 and perhaps 2,000 archers. These figures agree with those of Jean Le Bel[13] for the men-at-arms, but he says there were 10,000 archers present at the battle; a possibility but no one really knows for sure. The Welsh spearmen would probably have been distributed across the front between the two leading divisions where suitable ground existed.

There is some controversy over the positioning of the English archers; Geoffrey le Baker,[14] says that they were placed on the flanks of the whole army 'like wings'. But Jean Froissart,[15] says that they were placed 'en herce', or like a harrow, though it is not clear what he meant by this. One explanation is that he meant small groups of archers were placed forward of the line of men-at-arms along the whole line, others that he was describing a formation in which the archers were on the flanks of and slightly forward of each division.[16] Edward was also well aware of the need to produce concentrated archery fire following its successful use at Halidon Hill. This factor would ensure that Edward and his commanders kept the archers in fairly large groups so that the officers in charge of them could direct their fire, both as to target and timing. It is therefore doubtful that the archers were distributed in small groups all along the front as some have claimed, or solely on the flanks of the whole position. The fundamental point rests on the range of the longbow, about 250 yards, and the need to be able to cover the frontage of each division with flank fire. This allows for a maximum frontage for each division of about 500 yards, with a maximum gap between the two front divisions of a further 500 yards, and if necessary an ability to cover another 250 yards outwards at either flank of the whole position. These frontages would allow the men-at-arms of each division to be between four and six ranks deep, depending on the division and the room each man-at-arms needed to wield his weapon effectively. This meant that ideally the army had to find a defensive position with secure flanks not more than 2,000 yards apart, with good visibility to the front and flanks and to which any enemy attack would if possible be uphill. An added bonus would be if the position were to the flank of the probable line of approach of the French army. The position chosen at Crécy met all these criteria.

The English position was on high ground looking south-eastwards across a small valley to ground of an equal height opposite. The valley was deepest in front of the Prince of Wales's division and tapered off to a gentle rise in front of Northampton's; the former was further down the slope than the latter, about 300 yards from the valley floor. Separating the two was a line of cultivated terraces some 350 yards long, almost certainly an obstacle to the heavily armoured cavalry and probably where the Welsh spearmen were stationed; another smaller group of terraces was to the right of the Prince of Wales' division and guarded his flank. The king's division was further up the slope and positioned in front of a thick hedge running along the track between the villages of Crécy and Wadicourt; immediately behind the king's position was a windmill which was where Edward placed himself. He could watch the battle unfold from his position and could, if necessary, march his division forward to reinforce either of the other two should they need it, or to either flank should the French begin to outflank the English position. The Amiens-Boulogne road ran obliquely across the front of the English position on the face of the hill opposite to Wadicourt, and it was along this road that the French army was advancing. Beyond Crécy, on the English army's right flank, ran the little River Maye.

The two armies at Crécy were dressed and equipped in much the same fashion. Knights wore armour that was more efficient and lighter than that worn at Halidon Hill, which for the English was important, now that they had adopted the Scottish habit of fighting on foot whenever a suitable defensive position could be found. The gambeson was no longer worn, making the wearing of armour not quite so hot to fight in. The hauberk was generally made of chain mail, with back and breast plates worn over it, while the lower body was protected by overlapping horizontal hoops of steel loosely riveted together and fastened to the back and breast plates allowing full body movement. The upper legs were protected by mail leggings and cuissarts, a new form of armour made of padded leather with strips of steel riveted to it and strapped round the thigh; the cuissarts were brightly coloured. The lower leg was armoured with plate armour over the shins and strapped on over the mail leggings. The arms were protected in a similar fashion to the legs. Steel gauntlets were worn and caps of steel or *cuir-bouilli* defended the knees and elbows; bands of loosely riveted steel guarded the shoulders. On top of their armour all knights wore the jupon, a tightly fitting sleeveless garment sometimes padded but always finished in an expensive cloth such as silk or velvet, and beautifully embroidered with the knight's heraldic arms. The conical bascinet, with or without a visor, was replacing the helm, and the camail, a curtain of mail to the shoulders, was attached to the bascinet by lacing.

The knight was well protected and could move easily without getting too hot. He could, for instance, run to his horse and mount should it be necessary, and he could certainly fight and march on foot; nevertheless, as the forthcoming battle was to show, it did not provide a complete defence against arrows from the longbow. Destriers were protected on the head and neck by armour of *cuir-bouilli*, or steel plate, and many were furnished with trappings, loose linen hangings, to give some protection against arrows, and embroidered or painted with the owner's arms. Mounted knights carried a small shield on which their arms were painted. The ordinary man-at-arms would be armoured as well as he could afford and many would wear good armour, which they might have taken off a dead knight or from a prisoner. They were easily identified having no heraldic devices on their jupons, if indeed they wore one at all; perhaps they wore the Red Cross of St George on a white jupon as Edward III had included in his articles of war.[17]

All knights and men-at-arms carried the same weapons when mounted – the lance, sword and axe, mace or hammer – however when fighting on foot they used a shortened lance, or an infantry bill or spear, and carried their swords at the belt in case of need.

The English foot soldiers, the archers and bill-men, were dressed much as they had been in the Scottish wars. They wore aketons or brigandines for bodily protection and 'kettle hats' on their heads (similar to the British army helmet during the Second World War), generally worn over a mail camail reaching over the shoulders. Some, who had been on campaign before, might also have a mail hauberk, while others might have used the gambeson of the previous era, now discarded by knights. Most would have worn gauntlets and some protection for the shins and arms picked up on a previous battlefield. The main weapon of these foot soldiers was the longbow for the archers, and either the bill or the pike for the bill-man; both the archer and the bill-man carried a sword and often a buckler; archers might also carry a mallet or an axe.

French infantrymen were made up of professional mercenaries like the Genoese crossbowmen and the peasant levy, the latter conscripted from the local area, wearing a wide variety of clothing often with no protection at all and often equipped with weapons adapted from agricultural implements. The armed peasant was no match for his English opponent who was an experienced, well-trained and disciplined soldier, by now much respected by the knights of England. The peasant levy was assembled in huge numbers and was significant only in its mass; it was treated with contempt by the chivalry of France, had no recognized leaders and was seldom committed to battle. Indeed the men-at-arms were generally so numerous that they were able to win battles entirely on their own by one magnificent charge, a fact that fuelled their arrogance and their scorn for those who fought on foot. Nevertheless the peasant levy had a role to play – they made the host look even more impressive than it would have done otherwise and they scavenged the battlefield after the knights had won the day.

In contrast, the Genoese crossbowmen were a respected body of mercenaries who fought under their own officers in formed bodies; they were a skilled group of soldiers. They took the place of the English archer in the French army, which at this time had no archers, and they were well paid by the crown. The crossbow, or arbalest, was a powerful weapon fired from the shoulder like a rifle, but it had a very slow rate of fire. Whereas a good crossbowman might loose off three bolts in a minute, a good archer would fire twelve arrows, and an archer who could not achieve ten aimed arrows a minute had no place in the English army. The crossbow was accurate and had greater penetration than the longbow; perhaps its great advantage was that crossbowmen could do their job without a great deal of training. But this hardly made up for its slow rate of fire, its shorter range at that time, and its clumsiness at close quarters.

While the French made their ponderous way out of Abbeville, Edward rode among his soldiers, talking to them and encouraging them. He ensured that every man knew his place and that his officers knew what was expected of them. He ordered his men to dig knee-

deep, foot-square holes across the front of their positions to break up
a cavalry charge, a trick learnt from the Scots at Bannockburn, and
when he was satisfied that all was ready he told everyone to eat, rest
and prepare himself for battle. Knights, archers and bill-men sat down
on the grass and awaited events. The English were rested, fed, at peace
with their maker and ready to do Edward's bidding from an excellent
position. The time was about 10 o'clock in the morning and they had
a long wait ahead of them.

Philippe, meanwhile, who had hastened out of Abbeville with his
eager army shortly after dawn, had no real idea where the English
army was. But they knew they had crossed the Somme at
Blanchetaque, they could see the smoke from the burnt villages of
Noyalles and Crotoy, and had no doubt been told by local peasants
that the English had passed to the east of the forest of Crécy. When
Philippe was a little way north of Saint-Riquier he was advised that it
would be prudent to send a reconnaissance party forward to find the
exact position of the English army. At that time his army was strung
out on the road to Abbeville and he had only his personal retinue with
him. A party of knights was sent forward under Miles de Noyers, his
standard bearer, to take a close look at the English positions. By the
time they returned with their report Philippe and the van were about
3 miles from Edward's army. He called a halt and gathered a council
of war to decide what to do.

Some of the council were for pressing on with the encircling
movement to get between Edward and his allies, then halt and allow
the whole army to catch up, let it rest, regroup and attack the English
at leisure the following day. Others were all for attacking the English
straight off the line of march without waiting for the whole army to
catch up. There were, they said, sufficient of them at hand to do the
job and if the English wanted to fight on foot so much the better; it
would make their task all the easier. Philippe did not agree and
ordered a withdrawal into camp for the night. But the haughty nobles
in the van said it would be shameful to retire and meanwhile those
further back on the road would not accept that they should halt; they
knew by now that the enemy had been sighted and they kept pressing
forward. Philippe and his marshals were unable to stop this undisci-
plined forward movement, each arrogant knight competing with his
neighbour as to who should be first to earn glory against the English.
At this stage it should not be forgotten that there was great political

pressure on Philippe to achieve a positive result as soon as possible. Despite Philippe's preference for the former course of action he gave in to his more hot-headed advisers. At about 5.00 p.m. on 26 August, the French attack at Crécy went on its proudly ill-disciplined way.

By all accounts the French army was very large, probably more than 12,000 men-at-arms, about 6,000 Genoese crossbowmen and enormous numbers of the peasant levy and some say as many as 60,000. It was not a disciplined force and it had no acknowledged hierarchy of command under the king other than the Constable of France and the marshals. Command of the men-at-arms was given on the basis of social prominence and not on military experience, thus the king's younger brother Charles Duke of Alençon commanded the leading cavalry division, while the king himself with the Duke of Lorraine commanded the remainder. There appears to have been no organization within the cavalry divisions, simply a mass of impetuous knights and their feudal retinues vying one with another to be the first to draw blood. The Genoese crossbowmen were commanded by their own officers, Carlo Grimaldi and Otto Doria, but some 300 men-at-arms in the retinue of the blind King John of Bohemia were up with them. Philippe's army was therefore roughly grouped into these three divisions as they wheeled off the road and tried to align themselves opposite the English position, ready to attack.

The English first became aware that the French had arrived and were intent on battle when they saw the Genoese wheel off the Wadicourt road from behind the south-east point of Crécy forest. English trumpets called the men to arms and all stood up. Archers strung their bows and stuck ready arrows in the ground by their feet; knights put on their helmets and drew their swords; the banners of the earls and bannerets were unfurled and held aloft on lances. A murmur of talk went along the lines of armoured men as the Genoese took up their battle formation, to be followed by an awed silence as more and more brilliantly coloured horsemen in glinting armour on caparisoned horses swung off the road and milled about behind the Genoese. Twelve thousand of them loosely marshalled under their banners and spread across the slopes opposite, more than the whole English army put together. English soldiers crossed themselves and waited for the stern test ahead.

The French meanwhile were vying and bragging as to who would capture the most valuable prisoners as they looked across at the silent and contemptible little army opposite, one moreover that had foolishly decided to fight on foot. They saw that even the knights and great men were on foot as they picked out the banners of the Prince of Wales, of Warwick and Oxford, Northampton and Arundel, even of King Edward himself. This was going to be easy: the sooner the Genoese loosed their bolts and got out of the way the better; they could then sweep the English away in one glorious charge. There was much pushing and shoving as each knight did his best to be in the leading division under Charles of Alençon. They unslung their lances and shields, and secured their helmets; the horses felt the excitement and were eager to be away as before a race. The finest and most numerous chivalry of Western Europe was impatient to be off.

The Genoese meanwhile had been drawn up in two or three lines and had spanned[v] their crossbows ready to fit the bolt.

Their trumpets sounded the advance and their banners, born aloft, were carried forward in front of them as they advanced slowly down the slope towards the nearest English division, that of the Prince of Wales. They had already marched the 15 miles from Abbeville that day on foot and were tired and perhaps reluctant to enter the fray; they stopped three times on the way from their start line to their first firing position some 250 yards from the English line. However, since they had marched straight off the road into battle it is probable that the halts were necessary to dress their ranks. As was usual for them, they fired off the odd bolt as they approached the English, probably to gauge the range, and when they had judged that the range was about right they halted, gave a great shout and loosed a volley at the English. This apparently had little effect and as they bent to span their crossbows and reload, they heard the whistling and soughing of the approaching arrow storm as perhaps 25,000 English arrows sped on their way 'so thickly and evenly that they fell like snow'[18] into their ranks.

The English archers produced such a concentrated weight of fire that the Genoese broke and fled, having never before been opposed by massed archery fire. The crossbows of the time had laminated horn

---

v A crossbow at that time had a stirrup at the front end and in order to span the bow the crossbowman put his foot into the stirrup on the ground, fastened a hook, which was hung from his neck, around the bow string and pulled upwards until the trigger latch caught the string. The crossbow was then cocked ready to place the bolt before firing.

bows and had a similar range to the longbow, but they were firing uphill and this shortened their effective range to well within that of the longbow. There had also been a short, sharp rainstorm as they marched down the slope towards the English line and this may have weakened the crossbow strings. The longbow strings would also have been affected, but it took much less time to unstring and brace the longbow with a new dry string than it did the crossbow, so perhaps the archers changed wet for dry while the crossbowmen did not. Indeed the Genoese had had to march to within effective longbow range before being able to loose their bolts at the English; furthermore, they fired into the setting sun and at extreme range, giving Edward's army a huge initial advantage. There was one other factor which prevented the Genoese from being as effective as they might have been. They usually took aim from behind a pavise, a large wooden shield, to give them some cover while they spanned the crossbow for another shot; the pavises were carried by a paviseur, one for each crossbowman, but on this occasion their pavises were still packed on baggage wagons, which were somewhere on the Abbeville road. Crossbowmen also went into action with pikemen to give them some protection at close quarters; whether the pikemen were in fact the paviseurs without their pavises is not known, but Jean Le Bel states that the two types of soldier marched forward together under their commanders without pavises.

Unfortunately for the Genoese their troubles were not yet over. As they ran out of longbow range, Alençon's division rode them down. He was a hot-headed and impetuous young man, and he was impatient to get at the English. According to Froissart, King Philippe, on seeing the fleeing Genoese, called out 'Quick now, kill all that rabble, they are only in our way.' Alençon, hearing these words, clapped spurs to his horse and charged into the ranks of the Genoese, cutting and hacking as he went, closely followed by the other knights of his division. Few of the Genoese who ran from the arrow storm survived the attentions of their allies, the French men-at-arms, and several of the latter must have met their end at the hands of the Genoese. The English simply watched and poured arrows into the heaving mass whenever it came within range. It must have been some time later than 7.00 p.m. that the French men-at-arms finally completed the discomfiture of the Genoese and turned their attentions to the English, who were still waiting patiently for them.

The men-at-arms in the leading French division under Alençon got themselves into some sort of order and advanced on the Prince of Wales's division. Some say the French advanced at the trot because the destrier, due to the weight of the rider and his armour, could not canter or gallop. But this is unlikely since the weight of the rider together with his armour and saddle would have been about 250lb, well within the limits for a powerful horse. It is reasonable to assume that the French knights would have started at a trot and then spurred into a gallop just before hitting the lines opposite them. The French knights, however, very soon experienced the arrow storm themselves, something a few had met before near Finisterre at the hands of Sir Thomas Dagworth's small force, and some at Blanchetaque, but nothing on the scale they experienced now. It would have taken the French about thirty seconds to cover the 250 yards through the arrow storm to the front of the Prince of Wales's division and during that time the archers of the division could have loosed some 18,000 arrows at the approaching horsemen. It is also possible that archers from Northampton's division were in range, so increasing the number of arrows loosed. As the arrows struck home horses were felled, pinning their riders to the ground, knights were wounded and killed, and an eager, relatively well-ordered attack degenerated into a strug-gling mass of wounded horses and riders. Loose horses driven mad by the arrows and the noise they made, having thrown their riders, added to the chaos. The longer the confusion continued the greater the number of arrows struck home; it is probable that before the survivors had extricated themselves from the mess and galloped out of range, a further 45,000 arrows had been fired at the heaving mass of French men-at-arms. In total possibly as many as 88,000 arrows were loosed by the archers, mainly of the Prince of Wales's division, at the Genoese and the first cavalry charge. This number amounts to about thirty arrows per archer of this division alone, and so far as is known they were each issued with two full quivers at the start of the battle, or forty-eight arrows.

The effect of the repulse of Alençon's division on the watching knights with Philippe must have been shattering, but the French knights were brave, and there were still some 8,000 of them who had not yet been committed. The English army watched as successive lines of French horsemen thundered towards them, only to wither away under the arrows into bloody heaps of struggling men and horses. The few who got close enough to cross swords were soon struck down, either by English men-at-arms and bill-men or by the archers firing at them in flank. Nevertheless the French men-at-arms mounted some say as many as sixteen attacks until evening. A knight would rally perhaps several hundred others and they would trot forward under their banners then charge up the slope only to be cut down by the arrows once they came within range. According to Froissart, one such attack, led by Jacques d'Estracelles, came up by the flank of the archers, probably using the dead ground on the English right, and closed with the Prince of Wales's division. They attacked this with such ferocity that Northampton felt it necessary to send reinforcements from his division and the king was asked to move his division forward to the prince's aid. But Edward could see from his position that the situation was not as serious as was made out. He asked the messenger, Sir Thomas of Norwich, if his son was dead, stunned or wounded.

'No thank God,' came the reply, 'but he is very hard pressed and needs your help.' The King replied:

Sir Thomas, go back to him and to those who sent you and tell them not to send for me again to-day, as long as my son is alive. Give them my command to let the boy win his spurs, for if God has so ordained it, I wish the day to be his and the honour to go to him and to those in whose charge I have placed him.[19]

By 10.00 p.m., as it was getting dark, the furious and despairing attacks of the French knights finally ceased. It was then the turn of the peasant levy. Stiffened by some knights marching on foot, they made one last desperate attempt to close with and defeat the English army. They marched down the hill in a solid mass and started up the slope towards the waiting English, only to be greeted once again by showers of arrows as they came in range; unprotected as they were, they simply broke and ran for safety out of range.

Sometime between 10.00 p.m. and midnight, the surviving French finally drew off, leaving their dead and wounded on the battlefield. Convinced that the day was lost Philippe left late that night with an escort of five knights and forty-two men-at-arms, and rode to the castle of Labroye, then to Amiens. By mid-day the following day he had crossed the Somme.

Once Edward was certain that the French had had enough and had withdrawn, he walked with some of his knights down to his son, embraced him and congratulated him on winning the day. Many of the English army had not been engaged by the enemy who had mainly attacked the Prince of Wales's division. However there were so many French men-at-arms that it is likely that some would have made for Northampton's division on the left of the English line where the slope was more gentle. Edward ordered the army to light fires, to keep watch, and to eat and sleep in their battle positions in case the French should mount an attack during the night or at dawn the next day. He gave dinner to his principle officers and retired to his tent for the night.

Dawn on the 27th found the English army still in its ranks, but very soon after in the early morning mists the inevitable murder of the wounded and pillage of the dead and dying Frenchmen began. In case the French were regrouping for further attacks, Edward sent out a strong force of 500 men-at-arms and 2,000 mounted archers on a sweep of the immediate neighbourhood. This force came across several thousand of the peasant levy who were still making their way to join the main French army, having not heard of their defeat. The peasants were scattered with heavy casualties. Later the English force came across a large party of French knights and men-at-arms who were also on their way to rendezvous with the main French army, equally ignorant of the catastrophe which had befallen them. They even thought that the approaching knights in the mist were French but soon realized their mistake as the English knights charged into them; some got away, but most were killed. This English fighting patrol returned before noon and reported the area clear. Only now did Edward relax his guard. He ordered heralds to identify the dead and to arrange the burial of knights and nobles in hallowed ground.

Crécy was the first major battle on the continent of Europe in which an English army practised what had been learnt on the Scottish campaigns; the shock of the French defeat and the manner of it sent tremors throughout the chivalry of Western Europe. Edward's army was largely mounted for the march but was clearly designed to fight on foot due to the high proportion of archers in the army who could only use their weapons while standing on the ground. French armies, if the peasant levy is discounted, had their main strength in the mounted men-at-arms who fought on horseback. French armies always included crossbowmen, but their rate of fire was so slow that they could be ridden down and dispersed by determined men-at-arms, something that could only be done to archers if heavy casualties were accepted or other factors intervened. Viollet-le-Duc sums up the French military scene:

> France possessed excellent troops [the knights and men-at-arms], men brought up to the use of arms from childhood, brave to rashness, but she had no armies; her infantry was made up merely of hiring Genoese, Brabançons, Germans and of irregular troops from the good cities, badly armed, without any notion of executing manoeuvres, undisciplined, and in an action, more a source of embarrassment than any real assistance.

In contrast, 'The English began at this period to bring into the field an infantry which was numerous, disciplined, skilled in the use of the bow, and even already supplied with fire-arms'.[20] Thus it can be seen that, for the French, a new era had dawned; for the first time the nobleman on his horse could be struck down by the common man on his feet, or as Froissart put it, 'by archers who are not rich men'. Furthermore, this could be done without even the need to cross swords – the nobleman would not know who had struck him down. The whole ethic of knighthood and of honour in war was challenged and society was in danger of being changed for ever.

There can be little doubt that the English tactics relied on the combination of the firepower of the archers and the staunchness of the dismounted men-at-arms fighting on foot in full armour. This tactic depended on fighting from a prepared defensive position and relied on the premise that the enemy, French or Scottish, would always attack them. This premise was only valid if sufficient provocation had been given to goad the enemy to attack, or that he was sufficiently arrogant to attack anyway regardless of the circumstances. Both these conditions existed at Crécy. Assuming the tactic used at Crécy was designed – and the large number of archers would indicate this – rather than forced on them by a much larger army, then English tactics on the battlefield were undoubtedly defensive within a strategy that was clearly offensive. However, it is doubtful if Edward really expected things to work out the way they did. After all, he only had the experience of Halidon Hill on which to base such a tactic, hardly sufficient basis on which to design the tactics to defeat the greatest military power in the west. Nevertheless many of his senior commanders had been present at Dupplin Moor as well as at Halidon Hill, and Edward himself had drawn up the allied army at La Capelle in October 1339 on his Cambrai campaign specifically to profit from similar tactics. The deployment and integration of the two elements of his army, men-at-arms and archers, had almost certainly been discussed and agreed as the battle tactic that they would employ when circumstances allowed, and it is probable that all commanders down to bannerets knew of it and understood it. It is therefore unlikely that he was forced into this solution by pressure from the French, although he probably did not expect the stunning victory that was his. The archers certainly won the day but victory was achieved by Edward's superior generalship, by the support of very good commanders, by good leadership and discipline, and by the fighting qualities of all his soldiers. It is interesting to note that Perroy[21] believed that Edward won the battle as a direct result of his inferiority in men-at-arms. This forced him to fight on foot on favourable ground, which included a point from which Edward could watch the enemy's movements. It also forced him to position the 'despised infantry' behind hedges and fences and to instruct his archers to fire at the horses of the French knights. All apparently despicable, or at least unfair and dishonourable in the French view! But they are all marks of good generalship – something that the French sadly lacked at Crécy.[22]

Edward had also shown great understanding of the need for sound administration in gathering his army and transporting it to France. This appreciation of the part that good administration plays extended all the way from the factory, so to speak, to the battlefield itself. As an example, each archer had been issued with two quivers of arrows before the battle, or some 288,000 arrows for the whole archer contingent. It is known that archers were supplied with fresh arrows during the battle by grooms and others running between the battle-lines and the wagon laager, where carts loaded with fresh arrows were parked. It is also known that archers had to run out in front of the battle-line in quiet moments to gather arrows off the ground so that they had some ready for the next assault. It is not unreasonable therefore to say that some 300,000 arrows and possibly more had been loosed against the French during their attacks. This was foreseen and planned for by Edward in his preparations for the campaign during the previous year. Good generalship, good leadership, good administration and good discipline, plus a plentiful supply of arrows, won the Battle of Crécy; another battle won at a distance.

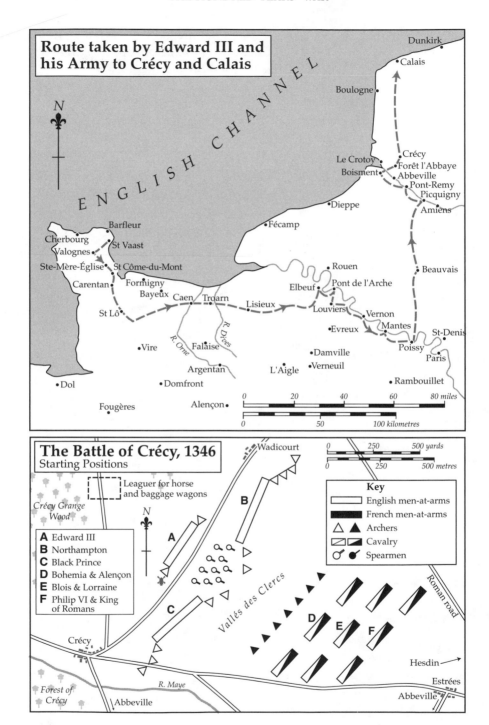

Route taken by Edward III and his Army to Crécy and Calais

The Battle of Crécy, 1346
Starting Positions

Leaguer for horse and baggage wagons

Crécy Grange Wood

A Edward III
B Northampton
C Black Prince
D Bohemia & Alençon
E Blois & Lorraine
F Philip VI & King of Romans

Key

English men-at-arms
French men-at-arms
△ ▲ Archers
Cavalry
Spearmen

Chapter 9

The Siege of Calais

'I am not disposed to do very much to suit his plans and convenience'.[1]

At Crécy a battle had been won but, unless Edward now opted for peace, the war still had to be fought because his claim to the throne of France and for sovereignty over Aquitaine remained to be settled. Furthermore he had received aids and subsidies from parliament expressly to achieve his claims and if he wished to retain the confidence of parliament he had to continue to pursue them. Now that he had achieved a notable victory, he pondered what he should do next. Edward was well aware of the huge military resources available to the French and the speed with which they could again muster a large cavalry army; he was also aware that his own army was badly in need of replenishment. The army needed many mundane things essential to its well-being: horseshoes, nails and harness for the horses, boots and clothing for the soldiers, new tentage, replacement armour and weapons, and above all fresh bows and a new supply of arrows. After the battle his only link with England was through the small port of Le Crotoy on the Somme, which probably dried out at low tide and was not easily defended; it was an unsuitable base from which to maintain a threat in northern France. He decided therefore to continue his march north and to seize Calais. He expected it to fall relatively quickly, as the news of his victory at Crécy would have preceded him. With Calais in his hands he would have a new strategic perspective; it would give him a base in northern France from which he could assist his Flemish allies and maintain a constant threat towards Paris. He sent messengers home from Le Crotoy to report his victory and to demand reinforcements of men, war material and supplies to be sent direct to Calais, together with siege engines and all the cannon kept at the Tower of London. He gathered his army and set out for Calais, which he reached on 4 September having despoiled the countryside on his way. He burnt the buildings outside the town walls of Hesdin, Montreuil and Boulogne, stormed and sacked the town of Etaples and burnt the town of Wissant to the ground.

Jean du Fosseaux, the lieutenant governor in Artois, having news of the English army's plundering march through Normandy, its crossing of the Seine and onward march to the north, considered it prudent to prepare Calais to face a possible siege. He took over command of the citadel in mid-August and the town garrison was put under the able leadership of Jean de Vienne; together they prepared the defences of Calais and ensured that stocks of supplies for the garrison and civil population were gathered in. They were prepared to make any siege a long one and they certainly expected to hold out until Philippe and his army came to their rescue, which they expected would be before the winter set in.

Calais was well protected by natural and man-made features. It was a town laid out in a grid within a rectangle of defensive curtain walls about 1,000 yards long on the two longest sides and about 300 yards on the other two. There were square towers about every 50 yards along the walls and a round tower at each corner; the whole was protected by a moat, single on the coast side and double on the other sides. Between the moat and the shore on the side by the sea was a fortified dyke and beyond it lay the entrance to the harbour, which was on the north-west side of the town. There were dunes beyond the moat on all the other sides and marshes beyond the dunes on the east and south sides. At the north-west corner separating the town from the harbour was the citadel, a formidable defensive complex of a circular keep and a square bailey surrounded by its own system of walls and moats.

Calais would be an extremely difficult town to take; its defences, manned by an efficient and motivated garrison, would make successful assault a doubtful and bloody option. Furthermore, its natural defences of water, sand dune and marsh made it virtually impossible to sap the walls to make a breach, and the same factors made it very difficult to set up siege engines or cannon. With such good defences the citizens and garrison of Calais faced the immediate future with confidence, notwithstanding the firm ground on the southern approaches to the town from which the town could be bombarded. However the defenders had this area well covered out to the limit of cannon range by their own cannons and engines mounted on the town's walls. This area of hard ground stretched all the way to the Boulogne–Gravelines road. This road ran from west to east from about a mile south of the town wall near the church of St Pierre. There was also another road leading south from Calais to St Omer along a hard causeway through the marshes for about 6 miles. To the south-west of Calais the Boulogne road crossed the little river Ham at the Nieulay bridge and shortly after climbed onto firm ground at the heights of Sangatte.

Edward and his officers confirmed all these factors as soon as they arrived before Calais on or shortly after 4 September. Of course they would have already known a great deal about the town and its defences from information supplied by merchants, as seems clear from the request for cannons and siege engines sent from Le Crotoy shortly after Crécy. Edward decided from the beginning that an assault was out of the question and that his only course was to starve the garrison and citizens into surrender; to do this he had to establish a blockade of the town by sea and prevent relief and supply by land. The neighbourhood of Calais was already gleaned of supplies by the Calais garrison so, initially, he was forced to rely on supply by ship for his army direct from England; later he was able to open a supply route from Flanders along the Gravelines road. However, as all war stores and many of the supplies needed by the army had to come from home by ship, he had to maintain sea communications across the Channel for the whole period of the siege. Edward also had to maintain the morale and fitness of his army in unhealthy conditions over a prolonged period. Calais would be a stern test of his administrative ability.

When it arrived before Calais Edward's army was probably about 10,000 strong, but he had called for reinforcements to make good his losses and to replace many of his Crécy veterans whom he sent home on completion of their contracts. Walter Wettwang, the keeper of the wardrobe, the household office responsible for the army's pay overseas, paid the 'wages of war' for 31,294 men for 496 days indicating that most of those at Crécy had been replaced twice over. The size of the army at Calais was probably never more than about 12,500 but a figure of 32,000 has been suggested; perhaps some exchequer accounts have not survived. Sumption[2] supports his figure of 32,000 men by saying that 736 English and allied ships had poured reinforcements across the beach by July. Possibly the reinforcements landed by

July 1347 were actually the changeover of the besieging garrison; after all, June was the start of the normal campaigning season. For comparison it should be remembered that even if the besieging force was as large as 12,000, it would have been as large as the population of most provincial towns in England, France and Flanders and at 32,000 perhaps as large as half of that of London before the plague.[3] It would seem therefore that the higher figure is unlikely.

As soon as they arrived outside Calais the English army set about their siege preparations with urgency and method. They surrounded the three landward sides of the town with a trench system to prevent a sortie by the garrison and to protect their main camp near the church of St Pierre. They built temporary barbicans around the bridge at Nieulay and the bridge across the Ham on the St Omer road, which they garrisoned. They picketed and patrolled the road leading to Gravelines and their Flemish allies, and they prepared an area between Calais and Sangatte for resupply across the beach by ship. Edward's army made themselves as safe and as comfortable as their circumstances allowed, while maintaining a tight grip on Calais. Froissart paints the picture:

> He [Edward] commanded to be built between the town and the river and the bridge of Nieulay, *hôtels* and houses, which were constructed of timber frame-work and orderly set in rows and streets, and the said houses were covered with thatch and broom … and there were, in this new town built for the king, everything required for an army, and more besides; and a place was set apart for holding a market every Wednesday and Saturday, and there were mercer's wares, butcher's meat, cloth, stores and all other necessary things … and the whole of these matters came to them every day, by sea, from England and likewise from Flanders.

This siege town was called Villeneuve-la-Hardie and people said that its market was just like those of Arras or Amiens.

Despite the attractions of Villeneuve-la-Hardie, and it undoubtedly had its taverns and brothels in addition to its houses, the army was there to prosecute the siege. Soldiers would do a spell in the siege lines followed by some 'Rest and Recuperation' in Villeneuve before another spell in the trenches, a monotonous existence that continued for the whole of their contract of service. Desertion grew and soldiers bribed sailors on board ship to smuggle them home where with any luck they might avoid the sheriff's men. Sickness also increased with only brackish water to drink, rudimentary drainage and the vapours of the marsh all about them. Nevertheless their case was better than that of the garrison and citizens of Calais who after two months badly needed resupply. Edward also adopted a policy of aggressive patrolling beyond the immediate neighbourhood of Calais. Strong patrols were sent out as far as St Omer, where several hundred English archers and men-at-arms under Sir Thomas Beauchamp, Earl of Warwick, joined forces with the Flemings for a while. Indeed Edward, and his Flemish allies, dominated the whole of Artois outside the French garrison towns.

However things did not all go Edward's way. Individual merchant ships were frequently lost to French pirates and warships, so much so that Edward began a convoy system across the Channel. The first convoy of twenty-five ships carrying much needed victuals was intercepted on 17 September by a fleet of Genoese galleys, recommissioned by Philippe earlier in the month and operating out of the Somme; every English ship was sunk and all the crews killed. This forced Edward to escort the convoys with warships and to put archers on board all merchantmen crossing to Calais; yet another expense to be borne by his exchequer. Edward's blockade of Calais by sea up to the middle of November was not entirely successful either, understandably so since his blockading ships could not remain on station as warships did four centuries later. Blockade was enforced by a series of sweeps from the English Channel ports, which may or may not have come across a French blockade-runner. French ships, on the other hand, simply had to run down the coast from Dunkerque or up from Boulogne whenever the coast was clear and the wind in their favour, and ships frequently slipped into Calais harbour with provisions and reinforcements for the garrison. The harbour had its own defences and was protected by the citadel; also, it was out of reach of English cannon. Indeed the French managed to break the blockade in the second week of November with a convoy of ships, which reprovisioned Calais with sufficient supplies to last until the spring.[4]

About the same time, in Jean le Bel's words:

When the men of Calais saw that king Edward would not leave that winter and that their provisions were insufficient, they sent out five hundred people and passed them through the English forces. When the noble king saw these poor people sent out of their town he had them all brought before him and gave food and drink generously to them; when they had eaten and drunk well, he allowed them to pass through his army and gave to each, out of love for God, three old pennies sterling, and had them conducted safely beyond his camp.[5]

During the winter, resupply for either side by ship was a rare occurrence and the English besiegers had to rely on escorted supplies arriving down the Gravelines road from Flanders. Shortly after the French convoy reached Calais in November Edward made a determined effort to take Calais by assault and again in February, but both failed. Meanwhile Philippe managed to get two convoys into the harbour at Calais without loss, the first in mid-March and the second early in April.

At this time Philippe's preparations for the relief of Calais were frequently interrupted by the actions of Edward's allies the Flemings, who maintained an active and aggressive policy along the borders of Flanders and Artois. In consequence the French were obliged to keep large garrisons in the towns of St Omer, Aire, Béthune, Lille and Tournai. Also, as they never knew where the Flemings would strike next, they found it necessary to keep a mobile reserve in the area of several hundred men-at-arms. Edward endeavoured to co-ordinate his deep patrols into Artois with those of his allies and in April they mounted an unsuccessful joint operation to surprise the garrison at St Omer.

Such minor operations on the borders of Artois and Flanders, sustained by English gold, certainly tied down large numbers of expensive French troops at a time when Philippe was having difficulty in raising both men and cash for the relief of Calais. He also wanted to restore French fortunes in Aquitaine, where the Earl of Derby had had considerable success before the winter set in. But both kings knew that the siege of Calais was the important operation; prestige and strategic position rested on the outcome. For his part Edward probably realized that unless he cut Calais off from the sea the stalemate could go on for a very long time indeed. It was quite clear that in order to do this he had to prevent the French from using the harbour which was protected by both the citadel and the Rysbank, the spit of sand between the harbour and the sea, which the French occupied. Edward first cleared the French from the sand spit in a limited operation. Next, according to Froissart:

> he ordered the building of a lofty fort, made of heavy timbers, on the edge of the sea, and equipped it with bombards, espringals and other heavy pieces of artillery; there were forty men-at-arms and two hundred archers, and thus they could keep so close a watch on the harbour of Calais that nothing could come in or out without being destroyed by them.[6]

This fort was built after the second French convoy had got through at the beginning of April and before the end of the month, henceforth it would be very difficult if not impossible for the French to send in another relief convoy.

The French made another attempt to resupply Calais by sea in June, with eleven merchantmen escorted by ten galleys and twenty-one armed ships, but as they cleared the mouth of the Somme on their way north they were attacked and scattered by a much larger English war fleet. They made their last attempt to get into Calais in July with eight unescorted barges full of supplies and armed men, but they were spotted and all were captured. Calais was now truly cut off from the rest of France and their only hope lay in a relieving army. As an indication of hardening attitudes on both sides, in July, Jean de Vienne took the drastic measure of expelling some 500 men, women and children, mainly the aged, the sick and the wounded, all useless mouths for the defence. These citizens of Calais had to take their luck with the English but Edward and his army ignored them and would not allow them to pass through their lines; they remained in no-man's-land until they died. In mitigation of Jean de Vienne's action, he had heard that Philippe was on his way with a relieving army and so with luck the expelled citizens would not have to wait long for succour.

Meanwhile in Brittany French arms suffered another setback. A small English and Breton force under Sir Thomas Dagworth at La Roche-Derrien captured Charles de Blois, the French claimant for the duchy, in June. This was bad news for Philippe who was on his way to Calais with a relieving army and who was now forced to send troops to Brittany to restore French authority there. Flemish activity along the border with Artois still tied down large numbers of French troops in the northern garrison towns and in their mobile forces. Philippe was beset with difficulties, nevertheless he gathered an army of perhaps 20,000 men, of whom some 11,000 were mounted men-at-arms, and was on his way to Calais. There were two possible approaches and Philippe decided on the less risky and more direct route from the south.

When the French army arrived at the heights of Sangatte on 27 July, they were met with a depressing sight, and must have wondered how they could defeat this professional army, not significantly smaller than themselves. Skirmishers on both sides were soon in action and the tower west of the bridge was quickly taken, but nothing of significance occurred that day. Philippe had probably made up his mind that the task was beyond him and his army when he first saw the English lines, but his commanders now confirmed it. After four days of fruitless negotiations in which the French acknowledged the loss of Calais but failed to offer any compromise over the big issues of Aquitaine and the crown of France, Philippe finally sent a challenge which Edward declined.

According to Froissart, the challenge was presented by Sir Eustache de Ribemont and three other knights. They arrived before Edward, bowed and said:

Sire, the King of France has sent us to inform you that he has come to this place and halted on the hill of Sangatte with the intention of fighting you, but he cannot see any way by which to reach you. Yet he would dearly like to in order to raise the siege of his loyal town of Calais. He sent out his marshals to try to discover some way of approaching you, but the thing is impossible. He would therefore take it as a favour if ... you would agree on a place where we could fight each other.

Edward replied:

My lords, I fully understand the request which you bring from my adversary ... Kindly tell him that I have every right to be where I am and where I have been for nearly a year ... and he could have come to me sooner if he had wished. But he has let me stay for so long that I have spent heavily and I believe I have now done enough to be shortly master of the town and castle of

Calais. So I am not disposed to do very much to suit his plans and convenience, or to let slip the thing I have so strongly desired and bought so dearly. Tell him that if he and his men cannot get through that way, they must go on looking until they find another.

After four days of abortive negotiation the garrison assumed that they were not to be relieved. On the night of 1 August they signalled to the French army from the tower of the castle that they could hold out no longer and that they were going to ask for terms of surrender. The same night Philippe and his army marched away and left Calais to its fate.

The next day Jean de Vienne, with the consent of the people of Calais, stood on the battlements and asked to speak to Sir Walter Manny about surrender terms. Manny, accompanied by three of the king's counsellors, carried a sombre message: it was not Edward's intention 'that you should go in peace, you must submit yourselves entirely to his will to be killed or ransomed as he chooses.' Sir Jean replied:

We can not consent to what you request. We in this town are a handful of knights and esquires who have served our lord as loyally as we know how – as you would have done in a like situation – and have suffered much distress. Humbly beg the king therefore to receive us with mercy.

Sir Walter and the others returned to the king and repeated what they had heard. They begged him to show mercy because 'if you put these people to death as you propose, they will do the same thing to us in a similar situation, even though we were simply doing our duty.' Edward relented, but said that six of the most prominent citizens should present themselves in their shirts, with halters round their necks and bearing the keys of the town and citadel. Edward intended that they should die. In due course the six citizens came out of the town as directed to be met by a large crowd of English and Flemish knights, and soldiers drawn up either side of a dais on which sat Edward, his queen and his council. The six citizens fell on their knees and begged for mercy; most of the knights present said they should be spared. Sir Walter said that the king should beware of doing something in cold blood that he would regret and for which he would be remembered evermore, but Edward said, 'I will not change my mind. Send for the executioner. These men of Calais have caused the death of so many of my men that these six must die.' At this Queen Philippa pleaded with her lord on her knees to show mercy; after a little while Edward reluctantly relented and handed custody of the six to his queen, who had them dressed and fed before releasing them. So the siege of Calais ended on 3 August 1347.[7]

Edward evicted the citizens of Calais without their possessions and in the clothes in which they stood, but gave them bread and wine before they were expelled. The principle officers of the garrison were sent back to England for ransom as prisoners and the soldiers were disarmed and expelled; the spoil of the town was considerable and many of the victorious army became rich following the surrender. Edward then took steps to repopulate the town with Englishmen, offering free grants of land and houses, and within three months over 200 had taken up the offer.

Edward had taken Calais as a result of his patience, resolution, organization and administration, and his appreciation, after two failed attempts, that further assaults would be costly and not necessarily successful. In stark contrast Duke Jean of Normandy had failed to take Aiguillon in Gascony the previous year. He had a much larger army and he made many costly assaults, but he failed to appreciate the difficulties of his task and failed to organize the proper supply of his army or to cut off the garrison's supply route down the River Garonne. The siege of Calais is a good example of the old military maxim of 'maintenance of the aim', something that was not very common in the Middle Ages. Edward knew what he had to do and how he wished to do it; as the sole and undisputed commander he put it into practical effect with relentless efficiency. As Hewitt so aptly wrote, the siege of Calais was 'an exercise by blockade rather than a military exploit.'[8]

However, after the successful siege, although morale in the English camp was high, staleness had set in; soldiers were going home to their families and those who had to stay had nothing in particular to do. At home Edward was heavily in debt and parliament was reluctant to give another subsidy to allow him to go on the offensive. The English war machine was as tired as that of the French. In these circumstances the papal legates found it relatively easy to persuade both sides to sign a truce for a year in September 1347, to be renewed on an annual basis.

The truce was only partially effective, operations continued on a small scale in one theatre or another over the next few years but general war was avoided and Edward was confirmed in his gains in Calais, Flanders, Artois, Brittany, Poitou, Aquitaine and even in Scotland. The two contentious issues of the sovereignty of Aquitaine and the crown of France again were not addressed. In 1348 disaster, in the guise of the Black Death, struck both France and England and left them severely underpopulated. With insufficient workers on the land food production fell, and many fields and pastures reverted to scrub or bog. This had a knock-on effect: peasants were required to work longer hours and consequently asked for higher wages, causing inflation and reducing money values; at the same time fewer people were available to provide the revenue needed to maintain the military effort and taxes were increased. This burgeoning economic problem seems to have affected France more than England. The latter had the income from the wool trade to set against the reduction in revenue, but France had the additional problem caused by the devastation of the English *chevauchées* to contend with. Of course the plunder taken by the English on their many raids made a not insignificant contribution to the English economy at France's expense.

In August 1350 a significant action took place at sea. By an agreement made between France and Castile in January 1347, Castile agreed to provide naval support for France providing France financed it. The first payment was made and a fleet fitted out in 1349; it sailed the same year for Sluys to discharge cargo in the normal process of trade. When the second payment was made early in 1350 this fleet loaded up with the cloth and linens of Flanders for the return journey. The Castilians were well aware that an English fleet lay in wait for their return through the narrow waters of the Channel and equipped themselves accordingly with 'powerful artillery', and iron bars and heavy stones to throw into the English ships in the hope of holing them. Each ship had a complement of men-at-arms and cross-bowmen, and was well prepared for battle. According to Froissart 'there were forty big ships all sailing together' and were at least ten to one in men following their hire of mercenaries in Flanders; both numbers are probably exaggerated.

The English fleet, which Edward had gathered, was well manned with many men-at-arms and archers. As soon as he heard that the Spanish fleet was ready to sail he put to sea and waited at anchor for three days off Dover. In due course the lookouts saw the Spanish ships on the horizon bearing down fast with a following wind. The Castilians could have sailed right through the English fleet if they had so wished but they were confident that they could defeat them and so were quite prepared to offer battle. The fleets clashed at about four o'clock in the afternoon, ships grappling with each other while the fighting men tried to board and overwhelm their enemy. However, after a stiff fight, the Spaniards drew off and sailed away down Channel. They lost fourteen ships either sunk or captured, while Edward lost at least two ships – his own and that of the Prince of Wales. The English fleet sailed home to drop anchor near Winchelsea after nightfall. This sea battle cleared the northern Channel of Castilian ships and galleys based on Sluys, which had been preying on English merchant shipping throughout the summer, but perhaps more importantly they were never again stationed so far north.

Interestingly naval battles at sea remained a matter of hand-to-hand fighting after grappling, even though in this battle Froissart mentions the use of powerful artillery. He probably refers to small trebuchets, which were often carried on board ships in the bows; they fired heavy stones or bundles of burning cloth dipped in tar. However the reference could refer to small early cannon which were beginning to make their appearance at sea.

Another point of interest concerns the ships themselves. Froissart paints the picture 'The Spanish ships being bigger and higher than theirs they were able to shoot down at them and hurl the great iron bars which did considerable damage.' And again when Sir Robert of Namur's ship was grappled by a Spaniard the Spanish ship hoisted its mainsail and dragged the English ship away to be overcome at leisure because 'The Spaniard being the heavier and taller ship, its advantage was too great to be resisted.' Nevertheless, although the Castilian ships had the advantage of size they were clearly not as manoeuvrable as those of the English.

The tempo of the war dropped over the next five years, almost certainly due to the ravages of the plague and perhaps partly due to the fact that Philippe VI died on 22 August 1350. His son Jean succeeded him. Jean seemed more concerned with the intrigues of his cousin, the young king Charles of Navarre, who was also a contender for the throne of France, being the grandson of the Count of Evreux, the younger brother of Charles of Valois, Jean II's grandfather. Edward III, seeing in these intrigues a possibility to destabilize the governance of France, cultivated Charles of Navarre as an ally and contented himself with threats of new invasions of France while he sought a favourable settlement to his territorial claims, which were extensive.

However, operations continued in Brittany, Gascony, Poitou and the Calais pale throughout the period from 1349 to the Black Prince's great raid into Languedoc in 1355. In Brittany, after Sir Thomas Dagworth's murder, the new king's lieutenant, Sir William Bentley was every bit as active as his predecessor. In 1352 Bentley went onto the offensive against an increasingly active Franco-Breton army under Guy de Nesle, marshal of France; the armies met at Mauron, not far from Ploermel on 14 August. This battle is interesting because it shows that the French had obviously given much thought to the tactical problems presented to an attacker by the new English tactics and especially by the longbow used *en masse*. Mauron was the last of four small battles that took place in this relatively quiet time of the war which illustrate the development of French tactics between Crécy in 1345 and Poitiers eleven years later.[9]

At Lunalonge in Poitou, in 1349, the French met a mainly Gascon force under the seneschal of Bordeaux and the Captal de Buch. The Gascons, like the English, had dismounted for battle, while the French, under Jean de Lille and Marshal Boucicault, divided their force into two, but remained mounted. One part of the French army outflanked the Gascons and made for the horse lines where they drove off their horses. This cut off the Gascons' means of retreat but the French then failed to return and attack the Gascons from behind; the other force rode at the dismounted Gascon men-at-arms but were repulsed with some loss, the combination of dismounted men-at-arms and flanking archers again proving decisive.

In April 1351 a small French army was defeated by an Anglo-Gascon force at Taillebourg, not far from Saintes in Poitou. This time the French dismounted most of their men-at-arms but retained a mounted squadron on each flank; unfortunately their attack was so badly co-ordinated that the Anglo-Gascons were able to defeat each element separately. Another battle in June 1351 in the Calais pale shows a further tactical development on the part of the French. The captain of Calais, John de Beauchamp, was raiding near St Omer when he was caught by the French under Beaujeu, who attacked the English on foot. Beauchamp's men dismounted for battle but the French overwhelmed them and killed or took prisoner over 700 of the English. It is not clear how they did this; perhaps they were much stronger or the English archers were not deployed on the flanks. This was their first success against the English and Gascons and, importantly, it gave them a growing confidence.

At Mauron the following year the French tried yet another development, this time Guy de Nesle, according to the *Chronique Normande*, dismounted all but 700 of his men-at-arms and led them in person on foot at Bentley's army. The 700 remained mounted under the Sire de Hangest and were placed on the French left wing with the specific task of riding down the archers on the English right wing while the dismounted men-at-arms closed with the English line. Bentley adopted the usual English formation and deployed archers on each wing of his dismounted men-at-arms; however, he also made best use of the ground by stationing his army at the top of a slope and in front of a thick hedge. De Nesle's dismounted right wing made for the archers on the English left and although easily repulsed, forced the archers to fire to protect themselves rather than bring fire to bear on the flank of the main body of the French. Hangest's mounted squadron on the English right cut the archers to pieces and so once again there was no archery fire into the main body of the French, which was able to close with the English unmolested. The main body was finally repulsed after a fierce struggle, possibly because by that time the archers on the English left were free to add their fire into the flank of the French men-at-arms.

It is interesting to note that the last time cavalry were used specifically to cut down archers was at Bannockburn by the Scots in 1314. Throughout Edward III's campaigns in France the French suffered because they had no archers, their own crossbowmen were largely ineffective in any battle in the open and if they wished to fight the English on more equal terms they had to find a way of neutralizing this huge English advantage. The French had certainly proved that they were every bit a match for the English either mounted or dismounted, but were severely handicapped without this essential new arm.

Edward planned that 1355 would be a decisive year of action in France. He was going to lead an army into Picardy from Calais,

Lancaster was going to invade Normandy in support of Charles of Navarre and the Black Prince was to go on *chevauchée* into the lands of Jean d'Armagnac, the French king's lieutenant in Languedoc. In the event Edward crossed over to Calais with a sizeable army and set out on 2 November 1355, leaving, as he thought, a settled situation at home on his northern border, where a truce had been negotiated. However Edward needed to gather as much of his available force as he could and so he allowed Henry Percy, Earl of Northumberland, to come south with his retinue from his watch on the border, where he was a warden of the march with Scotland, and join the army for the expedition into France. Consequently the border, though quiet, became vulnerable. In France Jean was well aware of Edward's preparations and probably of his intentions, and took appropriate measures. Jean gathered an army under his command and concentrated it to the north of Amiens to await the English. This was a strategically sensible position as he could not have been sure where the English would land, whether at Calais, in Normandy or Brittany – at one time or another rumour would have indicated all three.

Jean also took the precaution of alerting his Scottish allies, who, by the terms of the treaty of Corbeil were obliged to wage war against England if the English invaded France. He also sent the Scots a handsome sweetener of 40,000 *deniers d'or*, but the Scots needed little urging once they knew the border was unguarded. There can be little doubt that Edward must have received the disquieting news that the Scots were once more on the warpath while he was himself marching through northern France and he realized that the north of England was threatened. In fact, when he got to Calais he learnt that the Scots had not crossed the border but had taken the town of Berwick, where the castle still held out.

He embarked at Calais with most of his army and landed in England on 19 November. He then travelled north to Durham, where a large army had mustered, and marched on Berwick, having sent Sir Walter Manny on ahead with sufficient force to relieve the castle, which he did. When Edward reached Roxburgh he was met by Edward Balliol, who was recognized in England as the lawful king of Scotland and who, fearing that he would be blamed for this latest Scottish offensive, promptly surrendered his kingdom to him. Edward now called himself the king of three kingdoms, though he was only recognized as such in England. The Scots had achieved all that their French ally wanted. They had probably forced Edward to abandon his French campaign without crossing the border, at least as it had been before Edward I captured Berwick, thus ensuring that the border here was constantly in dispute. Edward granted a truce for ten days but then, sensing some trickery on the part of Sir William Douglas, marched up to Edinburgh burning and devastating the land on his way. Edward was back in England after a fortnight.

The second planned expedition, that of Henry of Lancaster, never crossed the Channel, due mainly to the news of Charles of Navarre's reconciliation with King Jean. Although these two planned expeditions into northern France never got under way, they nevertheless kept Jean guessing about English intentions, and more importantly, forced him to make the necessary preparations to be able to marshal armies and be ready to meet the English. This was an expensive business; the French armies at that time were embodied for forty days in defence of the realm without pay, but the crown had to pay for every day over the limit. Daily pay scales[10] included 20 sous de Tours for a knight banneret, 10 sous for a knight, 6 or 7 for an esquire, 15 deniers for a crossbowman and 1 sou for a foot sergeant.[i] The crossbowmen were largely mercenaries and so had to be paid for the whole of their service. The peasant militia does not seem to have been paid at all, presumably because their service always came within the forty-day limit and they only served within France; it was of course easy enough to call up a fresh lot before the initial forty days expired. The cost of keeping armies available and fortifications in a good state of repair on top of the damage done to the economy by the plague was a heavy burden on the people of France and only tolerated in the expectation of success.

The third expedition of 1355 set out as planned. Edward, the Black Prince, rode out of Bordeaux on 5 October at the head of an Anglo-Gascon army of perhaps 5,000 men. He had arrived from Plymouth

---

i The French monetary system was similar to the English in the Middle Ages. The livre, Tournois, Parisis or Bordelais (the different names simply referred to the different places in which the coinage was minted) was divided into 20 sous and each sou into 12 deniers, thus 240 deniers (or pennies) made up one livre or pound. However the livre was only valued at between five or six shillings sterling. Therefore the knights daily pay in France was the equivalent, at best, to two shillings sterling, exactly the same rate that Edward III paid his knights.

on 29 September with an English army of about 1,000 men-at-arms, 1,000 mounted archers and some 600 foot soldiers, over half of whom were archers.[11] The English contingent included the retinues of the earls of Suffolk, Warwick, Oxford and Salisbury, as well as Prince Edward's own, and they were joined at Bordeaux by eight Gascon magnates and their retinues. Practically the whole force was mounted for the march, enabling the expedition to rely on its mobility and speed of movement for safety and success as it burned and plundered its way across Armagnac and Languedoc. The raid almost reached the Mediterranean beyond Narbonne on its outward march before returning to La Réole on the Garonne in English Gascony on 2 December after a march of about 600 miles.

During the course of its march the army burnt some thirty market towns and bastides, took many fortresses, made innumerable people homeless and carried off an enormous amount of valuable booty; in the process an untold number of perfectly innocent people were killed. Chandos Herald wrote: 'He [the Prince] rode towards Toulouse, there were no towns which he did not lay waste. He took Carcasonne, Béziers and Narbonne and laid waste and harried all the countryside as well as many towns and castles.'[12] The prince's army having no siege train had not attempted to take the fortresses and *cités* of Carcasonne and Narbonne, which were both very well fortified and garrisoned, but they destroyed the *villes*, or suburbs, outside the walls. Likewise he did not attempt to take Toulouse into which Jean d'Armagnac and his army had withdrawn, indeed he by-passed it to the south, fording the rivers Garonne and Ariège in flood, the French having destroyed the bridges. Jean d'Armagnac never offered battle on Edward's outward march and although he moved out of Toulouse, apparently to cut off the prince's army on its return, he took good care not to meet him in battle.

Although the Black Prince's *chevauchée* did not change the political scene in France as a whole, it limited French influence in the south-west and cost the French crown a great deal in lost taxes,[13] the payment of reparations, the restoration of fortresses and towns, and above all in prestige. This *chevauchée*, while achieving little of military value, must nevertheless be accepted as a political and economic success for English Aquitaine and a further blow to French authority and morale. On his return to Aquitaine the Black Prince dispersed his army and sent them to winter quarters in the border fortresses; he himself spent the winter at Libourne, a port upriver from Bordeaux. During the winter the prince's commanders carried out many offensive raids, up the Dordogne valley towards Rocamadour; along the Garonne into the Agenais; up the valley of the Lot to Clairac; and into Poitou from the Saintonge. All this activity and the inevitable destruction which accompanied it served to weaken the French crown's authority and French morale in the area. The cost to France was astronomic, so much so that Jean II felt obliged to demand of the *Estates* in Paris approval for the necessary finance to keep 30,000 men in the field for a year. This could only come from yet more taxation on the suffering French people, many of whom refused to pay.

Edward III meanwhile was determined to pursue his just demands and planned three expeditions for the summer of 1356 in the hope of forcing King Jean to the negotiating table and the achievement of his ambitions.

It is pertinent to ask why the French had no archers as it is quite clear that English armies achieved their superiority through this arm. Archery had become a tradition and a sport in England but there was no equivalence in France. French noblemen used a crossbow or a short bow when hunting, and the use of the longbow was a rarity; furthermore, the French had basically two classes of people, the noblemen and knights, and the peasants; there were no yeomen, which was the class from which the archers came in England. Citizens of towns in France who might expect to be called up for service in defence of their town used the crossbow, a much more suitable weapon with which to defend the walls of cities and castles.

Furthermore the French had no need to encourage archery since, until meeting the English in battle, the chivalry of France had been powerful and numerous enough to win battles on their own. Finally they despised the peasant levy, which was untrained and poorly armed, and led, and they did not want to encourage people from this class to use and become efficient with a weapon that would enable them to challenge the baronial classes. After Crécy the French clearly realized that either they had to overcome their disadvantage by tactical means, as is seen from the smaller battles between 1349 and 1352, or they had to create such an army in sufficient numbers to influence the outcome of battles, which would take years, if not decades. However, until such time as they did they would always face the English under a disadvantage. As a consequence French armies were only prepared to meet the English if they had an enormous preponderance of men-at-arms. They became afraid of the prospect of pitched battle against English armies.

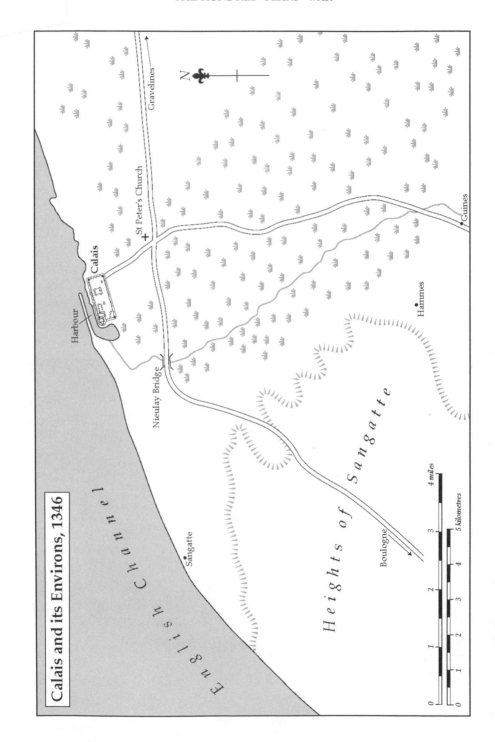

Calais and its Environs, 1346

Chapter 10

The Battle of Poitiers and a King Ransomed

'My dear Lord you have with you here the whole cream of your kingdom's nobility, pitted against what in comparison is a mere handful of the English.'[1]

There was to be no let-up on Edward III's part in his war with France, and he remained as determined as ever to gain the crown of France and sovereignty over Aquitaine. Parliament still considered his war a just war and continued to underwrite it, while his nobles and captains, rich from the profits of war with France, backed him unreservedly. Furthermore, the victorious English campaigns and the opportunity for plunder ensured plenty of volunteers for his armies in France. The year 1356 was to be one of decision. He planned to take the offensive himself in Picardy while the Black Prince, in a separate offensive, was to drive north to the Loire from Bordeaux. Henry, duke of Lancaster, meanwhile was to land in Normandy with a smaller force to distract the French from the other two offensives and ultimately join up with the Black Prince.

Edward's hopes of an offensive in Picardy were dashed by events in Scotland early in the year, ensuring that he never crossed the Channel, another example of the treaty of Corbeil in operation. The Scots certainly helped their French allies with their border activity, though it is doubtful if those who had their homes burnt and their menfolk slaughtered by Edward's response saw much advantage in the treaty for them. At about this time the Scots also gave aid to France in a more direct manner: a small force of about a hundred men-at-arms and a similar number of mounted archers under the command of Sir William Douglas arrived in France to join their French allies. They were immediately put on King Jean's payroll. This was the first Scottish contingent to see service in France.

Lancaster, who was to land in Normandy with an army and raise the Navarrese supporters before turning into Anjou to link up with the Black Prince's army somewhere about the Loire, was greatly helped by an incident in France in April. Jean II, who had been suspicious of Charles of Navarre's motives and actions, became concerned by the Dauphin's friendship with Charles and suspected that they were plotting treason. He heard that they were to be together in Rouen where his officers surprised them one evening at dinner and arrested them. Charles was imprisoned in Paris and four of his Norman barons were summarily executed for treason without trial. As the Dauphin was duke of Normandy and Charles the count of Evreux, the duchy with its Navarrese faction was incensed and likely to greet Lancaster with open arms; his expedition was politically opportune and astutely directed.

Lancaster landed at La Hogue in Normandy on 18 June 1356 and was met by Charles of Navarre's younger brother Philippe. Lancaster,[2] who had brought 500 men-at-arms and 800 mounted archers with him, was joined by Philippe's 100 Norman men-at-arms and by Sir Robert Knolles, who rode up from Brittany to join the expedition with a further 300 men-at-arms and 500 mounted archers. This was a small but highly mobile army, adequate for its task of relieving the three Navarrese fortresses of Evreux, Pont d'Audemer and Breteuil, all in Normandy and under siege by the French, and a sizeable reinforcement for the Black Prince should the two forces manage to link up. But it was woefully inadequate should Lancaster meet up with the main French army, then at Dreux in Eastern Normandy. By all accounts the French army was large with possibly as many as 8,000 men-at-arms and some 30,000 infantry including some 2,000 mercenary crossbowmen. Even at the lower estimates available the French army was at least ten times the size of Lancaster's force, with about eight times as many men-at-arms.

Lancaster was an experienced soldier who knew the value of speed and surprise in an operation of this sort; he had a highly mobile and well-disciplined force and realized that the possibility of being brought to battle by King Jean's large army was high. He probably knew that a French army was already in the field, that it had left Paris on 1 June and had reached Chartres on the 9th. We do not know exactly how Lancaster organized his little army for the march but his first objective, Pont d'Audemer, was some 125 miles distant from La Hogue and his prime consideration would be to raise the siege as quickly as he could. He left La Hogue on 22 June after resting the horses and his men for four days, a prudent precaution as they had been on board ship for fourteen days having embarked on 4 June. He needed his men and horses fit and well for he was going to press them hard.

He set off for Pont d'Audemer on the most direct route possible, by-passing St Lo and Caen, both well garrisoned, and arrived seven days later on 29 June, having averaged some 18 miles a day. The French besiegers, forewarned, fled, leaving all their siege equipment behind. He then made for Breteuil, some 30 miles to the south and 24 miles north-west of Dreux; as yet he had had no definite news of the French army. On his way to Breteuil, on 3 July, he took the town and castle of Conches, having entered them without loss; that same day he moved on south to the great fortress of Verneuil about 8 miles away and demanded its surrender, only to have the gates shut before him. He assaulted the town successfully that afternoon but one tower of the castle took two more days to subdue, and cost him several casualties.

Although it has been suggested that Lancaster used the siege equipment found at Breteuil, it is more probable that the quick surrender was due to his reputation and the threat posed by his army, combined with low garrison morale and no news of the whereabouts of the French army that persuaded the garrison commanders to obtain honourable terms of surrender.

Where was Jean's army? It had certainly reached Chartres on 9 June and the only possible reason for it to have marched that far south-west of Paris must have been that Jean had received news of the Black Prince's intentions for a summer campaign. Particularly since Lancaster's army had not yet arrived at La Hogue and the only English army in France at that time was that of the prince's in Aquitaine. Nevertheless Jean clearly considered Lancaster's army the greater threat at the time. The prince's army had not yet gathered for its summer campaign, and he can have had no idea how small Lancaster's army was when he set out for Dreux. This was a good place from which to cover Paris or the crossings of the Loire until he had more definite intelligence of Lancaster's movements and intentions.

Elements of Jean's army set out for Pont d'Audemer, no doubt to secure it against Lancaster, but they ran into their own besieging force hastily fleeing from the English and realized they were too late. Jean's army must have left Dreux on the road for Evreux and Rouen, anxious to prevent a replay of Edward's Crécy campaign by denying the crossings of the Seine, and would have been somewhere north of Evreux by the time Lancaster had taken Conches. The two armies would have passed about 12 miles apart, Jean going north and Lancaster south. Jean then turned south and eventually caught up with Lancaster's army at Tuboeuf on 8 July where he had stopped for rest on his way back from Verneuil. Both armies were in sight of each other and night was not far off. Jean, cautious as ever, instead of launching his advance guard at Lancaster's smaller army immediately, sent heralds to Lancaster proposing battle the next day. Lancaster returned a suitably equivocal reply as night fell, then during the night his army silently withdrew and Jean's huge army woke next morning to find themselves in sole possession of the suggested battlefield.

Lancaster's army rode hard all that day and had reached Argentan, 35 miles away, by evening. He clearly believed he was being followed by the French army and was off again early the following morning, reaching Torigny in the evening, an astonishing march of over 50 miles. He was now in safe territory and the tempo relaxed. He arrived once more at Montebourg on 12 July, where Sir Robert Knolles had been left in charge, twenty-four days after setting out. What had Lancaster achieved? In purely military terms he had done what he had set out to do: he had relieved, re-victualled and reinforced the Norman Navarrese garrisons at Pont d'Audemer and Breteuil. He had also taken many prisoners and much booty, captured several fortresses and taken 2,000 horses – all this from under King Jean's nose and the very real threat of his large army, which, once Lancaster got to Pont d'Audemer, was never more than a day's march away. It was an impudent raid and an insult to King Jean, but it had its reward in the political domain. Philippe of Navarre crossed to England and did homage to Edward III for his Norman lands, so giving credence to Edward's claim that he was the lawful king of France.

Once Jean realized that he was not going to catch Lancaster he turned back and invested Breteuil in the hope of gaining some kudos from his abortive campaign. But events were pressing in on him; finance was still a problem and the great magnates of France remained reluctant to follow him to war against the English. Rumours of the Black Prince and his intentions persisted and the only thing he could be sure of was that Edward III was tied up with Scotland and was most unlikely to cross the Channel. However Breteuil was proving no sinecure. In order to reduce the fortress he used all the devices that technology could provide including artillery and a great siege tower, or cat, but the defenders ably countered his efforts, neutralizing Jean's artillery with their own and destroying his great cat with their artillery fire.[i] At this low point rumours were confirmed that Lancaster was moving into Brittany and that the Black Prince was again on the march; he had left Bordeaux on 6 July, marched to Bergerac via the fortress of La Réole and then set out for the north on 4 August.

King Jean immediately assumed that the prince was making for Paris, some 250 miles away. He concluded the siege of Breteuil and returned to Paris in mid-August. Strategically Paris was the right place to be at the time. Politically, victory in battle with the English was now essential; he had to march to confront the prince and the sooner he did this the better.

The Black Prince arrived at Périgueux on 7 August with the intention of marching on Bourges, some 200 miles to the north, where the Comte de Poitiers, one of the king's sons, was gathering an army. However he was unsure of Jean d'Armagnac's moves to the east of Aquitaine and so had to leave part of his army, mainly Gascons, to watch his eastern borders. Nevertheless his army was quite substantial, and some 6,000 all told set out on *chevauchée*. On 23 August the army reached the River Indre at Châteauroux having taken three castles, two fortified churches and several towns. On 28 August he crossed the River Cher near Lury; this was an important political milestone as the Cher used to be the old north-eastern boundary of the Angevin lands in France; he was now in the undisputed domain of the king of France.

Contact was now made for the first time with the French army by a patrol under Sir John Chandos and Sir James Audley: apparently Jean was at Orleans on the Loire and intended to fight the English between there and Tours. Jean had moved quickly once he had received confirmation of the Black Prince's move north. He had sent out orders for his army to muster at Chartres, but by the time the prince had reached the Cher elements of Jean's army were still on their way to the muster. They were diverted to cross the Loire at their nearest point and presumably join up south of the river. They crossed at Orleans,

---

i At about this time the word 'artillery' covered both siege engines and the new guns, of whatever sort.

Meung, Tours and Saumur; Jean crossed with his own retinue at Blois leaving sufficient force north of the Loire to deter a possible move on Paris by Lancaster.

The prince must have had some knowledge of Jean's movements and the scattered spread of his army for he marched west along the north bank of the Cher towards Tours. Perhaps he wanted to join up with Lancaster or defeat each main French contingent separately. Lancaster meanwhile had turned away from the Loire having reached Angers, which was held by a strong French garrison, and was unable to cross the river. The prince reached the Loire about 18 miles upriver from Tours on 7 September and his advance guard arrived outside the city walls the following day. A reconnaissance soon showed that without a siege train there was no way that he would be able to force a crossing of the river and take Tours, where the king's eldest son, the Dauphin, duke of Normandy, was in command. Furthermore, without news of Lancaster and with Jean's army closing in on him from the north-east, his position was beginning to look precarious. He decided to turn for home in Bordeaux with his prisoners and loot intact.

King Jean crossed the Loire on 10 September, the same day that the Black Prince decided to head for home. The two commanders were less than 40 miles apart. Jean marched about 20 miles the next day reaching Amboise, while the English concentrated at Montbazin; the armies were then about 12 miles apart. Both armies rested on 12 September but the next day the prince's army marched 30 miles to La Haye on the river Creusen, about 12 miles north-east of Chatellerault, while the French covered 24 to Loches; they were now about 16 miles apart. The following day the French marched to La Haye and the English to Chatellerault. The English remained at Chatellerault on 15 September, while the French marched the 33 miles to Chauvigny, 15 miles due east of Poitiers. Both armies rested on Friday the 16th; the English had now been at Chatellerault for two days and the French, had they but known it, had outflanked the army of the prince. On the 17th, Saturday, the English marched 30 miles to cut the Poitiers-Chauvigny road about 4 miles east of Poitiers, while on the same day the French marched along that road to Poitiers. Neither army knew exactly where the other was as they set out that morning. Jean correctly assumed that the prince was marching for Bordeaux, and was presumably hoping to cut him off and bring him to battle, while the prince was hoping to ambush the French army on the Poitiers-Chauvigny road or to get clean away to Bordeaux. Both were surprised when the English vanguard ran into the French rear-guard near the farm of Charbotrie on the Poitiers road where a sharp skirmish took place; many prisoners were taken by the English and the rest were killed or put to flight.

These marches and rest days deserve some analysis, since if King Jean's intent really was to get behind the English and cut their withdrawal route to Bordeaux, why did he rest all day on 16 September? As for the Black Prince, why did he wait two whole days at Chattelerault if his aim was to get away from the threat of battle with the French army only a day's march away? There would seem to be no rational reason for Jean's pause unless he never intended to do battle with the prince, or that he was waiting for elements of his army to join him after crossing the Loire. The latter is the more likely. But the most probable reason is that the army either had to wait for its baggage train to catch up, or that its herbigers needed a pause to gather food and forage, which the army badly needed by that time. As much of his army had still not reached him, he decided to gain the city and fortress of Poitiers from which he could bar the Prince's southward march and on which his army could converge before marching out to battle.

The prince's conduct is equally strange for if he was really in a hurry to get home, or if he was afraid to join in battle with Jean's army, why rest for two days? The reason again is almost certainly because of the need to collect food and forage for the army. It is also clear that the prince was anxious to have news of Lancaster since, as he said in his letter of 22 October to the mayor of London,[3] he had heard from Lancaster that the latter was trying to march towards the prince. He therefore waited two days for Lancaster at Chatellerault.

The English, tired after their forced march of thirty miles and short of food and water particularly for the horses, needed to look for a place to spend the night where the horses could be properly watered and where the baggage wagons could catch up. Some believe the army spent the night in woods near the farm of Charbotrie and marched to its battle positions next morning across the front of the French army outside Poitiers. But it is unlikely that the farm would have been able to water at least 8,000 horses. It is probable therefore that the army would surely have pressed on to the river Moisson, between three and four miles away, less than an hour's ride. The farmer at Charbotrie would probably have told them anyway, being anxious to see the last of them; but importantly it had the tactical advantage of being to the south of the French army.

Hewitt[4] says that the prince moved on south after the skirmish and by early morning on Sunday 18 September was encamped on the northern side of Nouaillé Wood. However Geoffrey Le Baker's chronicle,[5] a prime source for the battle and the days preceding it, after telling of the skirmish continues:

> As night approached, our men rested in a forest; and the next day continued towards Poitou. Our scouts discovered that the usurper had drawn up his men in battle order; and soon after other scouts came in with reports that he was moving in our direction and advised the Prince to choose a place for battle and draw up his troops in case the enemy caught us unawares.

Geoffrey Le Baker seems to be referring to the night of Saturday 17 September in the first part of the sentence when the army spent the night in a wood, possibly Nouaillé Wood, and the Sunday morning in the second when they continued their march south. Was this march 'towards Poitou' simply the baggage wagons moving to cross the River Moisson and the ordered watering of horses in the morning? The remainder clearly refers to the initial moves on Sunday morning when the Prince thought he would have to fight a battle. Hewitt's interpretation seems the most realistic, bearing in mind the army's pressing need to water their horses on the Saturday night.[6]

Froissart[7], writing about events after the skirmish on the Chauvigny-Poitiers road, says that the English spent the night in a strong position, among hedges, vines and bushes, a description that fits the ground immediately north of Nouaillé Wood. He also says that next morning (Sunday 18 September), Sir Eustace de Ribemont confirmed this in his reconnaissance report to King Jean. Froissart goes on to say that the French army closed up to the English positions and prepared for battle on the Sunday morning.

No one knows exactly what happened but it makes more military sense for the prince's army to have spent the night of Saturday 17 September, in the wood of Nouaillé and not in woods near Charbotrie. Furthermore that the march 'towards Poitou' simply refers to the rearward movement of the wagon train and the morning watering of horses. If this were so then, that Saturday evening, the marshals would have found a reasonable defensive position outside the wood on the north-west side facing the direction from which the French could be expected. Under these circumstances Sunday 18 September would have turned out to be a busy but not a frenetic day. The prince's army moving down by divisions to water their horses at the river before returning to their allotted battle positions could easily be misconstrued as the initial withdrawal to Poitou and home.

It therefore seems probable that the Anglo-Gascon army arrived at Nouaillé sometime late on Saturday 17 September and would have been led to their bivouac areas in the wood by the marshal's officers. The army was tired and short of food and the baggage train had not yet arrived, but there was work to be done. The marshals had to show the prince and his commanders and staff the positions they had chosen for battle before it got dark. A war council would then have been called to settle the battle plan and this would have been passed on to subordinate commanders. Apart from the feeding of men and horses, much administrative work had to be done before the dawn: weapons to be sharpened, armour to be repaired and arrows issued. Finally, when it arrived, the baggage train had to be led aft across the river to relative safety.

When Sunday dawned all the usual chores of a cavalry army were attended to and soon after scouts would have come to the prince's tent with the first news of French movements. Indeed the scouts of both sides had found their enemy, the French army now knew exactly where the English were and closed up to their positions during the morning, taking up their own about 1,500 yards away to the north-west. This was a time when commanders would look to their positions; they would scan the ground looking for the defensive weak points and consider how to improve the natural defences of the position with artificial obstacles. They would consider the most likely avenues of enemy attack, where to place their archers to provide flank fire into the approaches and where to station the men-at-arms to oppose any approach. They also had to decide where the horses should be held and where wagons with spare arms and arrows should be put. While this was going on they could see elements of the French army arriving on the hill opposite. This was a very large army, estimated[8] to consist of about 8,000 men-at-arms and 2,000 crossbowmen, as well as the lightly armed, poorly trained and inexperienced peasant levy who could have been anything from 16,000 to 30,000 strong. Other estimates give the number of men-at-arms alone at 13,000 and the total number at anything up to 60,000. Lord Bartholomew Burghersh who was present throughout the campaign wrote in a letter that the French army was 11,000 strong, but this almost certainly referred to the men-at-arms alone.

What would the waiting English and Gascons have seen across the valley? Most of the French would have been hidden from view behind the hill opposite but from time to time groups of men-at-arms on horseback would have been seen as knights and their retinues joined up with the army and others took a look at the English. The armour of the knights in both armies showed some improvements over the armour worn at Crécy. More plate armour was now being used, mainly as individual pieces, particularly the breast and back plates and the articulated plate defences of the shoulders and lower abdomen, all worn over the mail hauberk. The arms and legs were still protected by plates or a mix of plates and cuissarts. The richer knights were already beginning to wear complete suits of plate armour, giving them good protection against arrows. The usual head protection was still the conical basinet, with a mail camail laced to it to protect the neck; some knights wore a helm over the basinet and a few wore a crest on top of the helm. Many basinets had a visor, which covered the face, the so-called 'pig-faced' basinet.

All knights wore the jupon over their body armour, emblazoned with their heraldic arms. Knights still carried a shield, about 2 feet long and 18 inches across the top, painted with their arms; any knight with a retinue or who was a banneret or higher carried a pennon of his heraldic colours on his lance. Horses were armoured more efficiently against arrows on the head, neck and breast with either steel or 'cuir bouilli' armour and carried trappings, again of the principle colours of the owner's coat of arms, hanging loosely from the withers and across the back to protect the legs and flanks. The knights made a bold and colourful scene with their armour glinting in the sun with the many colours of their jupons, shields and trappings. This was the picture so often recalled by the chroniclers: the brave outward panoply of chivalry, soon to be bloodied by battle. But the glitter and the colour had its purpose in battle: one protected and the other identified; the bravery of the knights was never in doubt.

According to Burne, the Anglo-Gascon positions were about 500 yards to the north-west of Nouaillé Wood on high ground which sloped in a south-westerly ridge from a high point in the east to a marshy depression in the west.[9] This depression ran down to the Moisson river to the south, the river flowed from east to west behind Nouaillé Wood and met the depression about a thousand yards west of the wood; the wood itself was about 1,500 yards north to south and some 500 yards wide. At the south-eastern end of the wood was the village of Nouaillé with a bridge across the river. Some 600 yards north of the wood and running across its front from near the high point in the east to the marshy depression in the west was a thick hedge with a ditch on its northern side which ran along the forward slope of the ridge. There were two gaps in this hedge where two tracks ran through it, the eastern one disappearing into the woods and leading to the village and bridge of Nouaillé, and the western going south-west of the wood, to the Gué de l'Homme, a ford. The two tracks converged about 400 yards north of the hedge and went on to Poitiers about 4 miles distant. A further 500 yards north of the track junction, and parallel to the hedge was another ridge and it was behind this that the French army gathered. The ground between the hedge and the north ridge was covered with vines on the south slope of the ridge and with thickets of thorn bushes on the opposite side in front of the hedge, not easy country to march or ride across. There was a farm just east of the track junction, thought to be that of Maupertuis, and the village of Beauvoir some 800 yards to the east of the high point.

The prince decided to take up positions behind the hedge, which meant that for the most part the actual Anglo-Gascon positions could not be seen from the French positions. However a very detailed and accurate reconnaissance report was given by Sir Eustace de Ribemont to King Jean and his principle officers at about mid-morning on the English position and their activities. According to Froissart, Ribemont reported:

We have seen and observed the English. We would estimate their numbers at two thousand men-at-arms, four thousand archers and fifteen hundred light armed men ... they are in a very strong position, and though we are convinced they only have one division, it is extremely skilfully placed. They have chosen a length of road strongly protected by hedges and bushes, and they have lined the hedge on both sides with their archers ... one must

go that way before one can fight them. There is only one way in
and out of that hedge, through which perhaps four men-at-arms
could ride abreast. At the end of the hedge, among vines and
thorn bushes, between which it would be impossible to march or
ride, are their men-at-arms, all on foot, and they have placed
their archers in harrow formation in front of them.

Ribemont concludes that it is a very skilful piece of work and would
not easily be overcome.

On being asked by King Jean how he would advise the French army
to proceed Ribemont replies:

with everyone on foot, except for three hundred of the most
vigorous and experienced knights, mounted on first rate horses,
to break through those archers and scatter them. And then your
formations of men-at-arms would follow quickly on foot and
engage their men-at-arms hand-to-hand.

King Jean had received similar advice from Sir William Douglas,
who had joined the French army with a small Scottish contingent of
men-at-arms and archers and accepted this plan of battle. Sir
William's advice was that the best way of coping with the arrow storm
was for the men-at-arms to march on foot. Their armour and shields
would give them good but not complete protection against the
arrows, and they would avoid the chaos and confusion caused by
wounded and terrified horses, and the casualties caused by falling
horses killed by arrows. The French now knew how large the Anglo-
Gascon army was and they had a good understanding of the English
position, though not many had seen it, and, providing they followed
it, they had a sensible battle plan.

Early on Sunday morning the French army was still in the fields
outside Poitiers and would have to march along a single track from
Poitiers to reach the Anglo-Gascon position. Assuming they left
shortly after dawn, the head of the column of men-at-arms would
have arrived behind the north ridge at about 8.30 a.m., though no
doubt the marshals' officers would have arrived earlier to show
people where to go. However the column of between 8,000 and
13,000 men-at-arms would have been about 5½ miles long and so the
tail of the column would not have arrived behind the north ridge

much before 10.00 a.m. and probably later – perhaps giving rise to the English observation that the French were being reinforced throughout the day. The crossbowmen marching to the French assembly area could have arrived before the last of the men-at-arms if the French order of march included groups of them with each division – an unlikely event since it is doubtful that the French army was sufficiently well organized or disciplined to have allowed for such a contingency. Consequently the crossbowmen probably set out after the last of the column of men-at-arms had left the overnight camp area, say at about 9.15 a.m., and would have arrived at their assembly area at about 10.30 a.m. Some of the peasant levy probably set out at much the same time as the men-at-arms and would have marched across country alongside the track, but many would have set out later. It is difficult, therefore, to believe that the whole French army would have gathered behind the north ridge much before about midday on 17 September. At this point Cardinal Talleyrand de Périgord, an emissary of the Pope, had come to offer his good services to arrange a truce and prevent battle. The cardinal asked King Jean to delay his attack and to allow him to negotiate a truce with the prince, suggesting that if he could get the prince to surrender and thereby prevent casualties more honour would redound to the king's name. King Jean was happy to allow him to go ahead on his peace mission. The cardinal rode over to the Anglo-Gascon positions and asked to speak to the prince, who received him courteously and suggested that a truce be declared to allow delegates from each side to meet in no-man's-land to hammer out a solution agreeable to both sides.

So Sunday 18 September was declared a day of truce by both sides. Initially, the French demanded that four-fifths of the English army should become their prisoners and that the prince and his men should surrender unconditionally, a proposal which the cardinal clearly found unbelievable and the English rejected out of hand. The prince then offered to give up all the towns and castles he had captured as well as all his booty and prisoners, and to swear not to take up arms again against the king for seven years, in return for free passage back to Aquitaine. The king rejected this and demanded that in addition to all that the Prince had offered, he, the prince, together with one hundred of his knights, should surrender unconditionally. The prince rejected this saying that he was not empowered to negotiate and that the king must do so with his father Edward. Finally, the French suggested a combat between a hundred knights from each side to settle the issue, presumably as to whether the prince and his army should have free passage to Aquitaine or whether he should surrender unconditionally. This was also promptly rejected.

So the scene was set and the two armies prepared for battle on Monday morning, 19 September. The negotiations, which had taken place most of the day from mid-morning, had allowed late-comers to reach the French and had given the Anglo-Gascons time to improve their defences. Trenches were dug on the open right flank of their positions and wagons were dragged into place on the same flank in an effort to produce an obstacle to cavalry; the archers dug holes in front of exposed positions. Seen from the front, the Anglo-Gascon position now had a continuous obstacle right across their front. Beginning at the western end with the marshy ground in the depression, moving on to the hedge then the trenches and wagons, and ending close to Nouaillé Wood in the east, in all some 1,200 yards long. There were only two ways through this position: one, the gap in the hedge on the track to Nouaillé itself, identified by Ribemont; and the other the gap in the hedge where the track to the Gué de l'Homme went through and was almost certainly known about by the French.

That Sunday night, while the French were feasting and preparing for battle, the English were debating what course of action they should take on the morrow. There were three courses open to them: they could stand and fight; they could withdraw with their booty and prisoners during the night; or they could abandon their booty and make a hasty retreat home. They soon gave up the third course as the booty was of course one of the principle reasons for setting out on the expedition in the first place. It represented their profit and would certainly pay for the expedition and more; abandoning it would make the whole expedition a loss-making venture both in honour and value. They were prepared for the first course and obviously felt confident about the outcome, but realized it would be a close run thing. However the second course had its attractions, providing they prepared for it during the night, although it had the risk of being involved in a running fight all the way back to Aquitaine during which they could easily lose their profit.

It seems that the war council resolved on the second course and decided to make an orderly withdrawal from their positions at dawn, if not before. As a first precaution those wagons not involved in the defensive position, and not carrying spare arms and arrows, were withdrawn across the river during the night. This was to be followed at dawn by the withdrawal of the earl of Warwick's division, the vanguard, by the track to the Gué de l'Homme. Next the prince's division would withdraw through the wood and finally the earl of Salisbury's division, the rearguard, would withdraw down the track to Nouaillé and its bridge. This was a sensible plan because if it could be executed without interference from the French it would put the river between the two armies. In furtherance of this plan all the horses were to be kept in the hands of grooms out of sight on the reverse slope of the hill, but close behind the positions, so that squadrons of each division and the archers could fade quietly and quickly away when so ordered. Presumably if the intention had been to adopt the first course and fight it out, the horses would have been picketed in the wood well behind the position as was normal to prevent individuals from mounting before ordered.

Come the Monday morning both sides were up and ready early and the earl of Warwick's division had already begun its quiet withdrawal; the baggage wagons and escort were south of the river. The French scouts however had spotted this movement and reported it. King Jean did not want his prey to escape; he and his knights were eager to begin the business of the day. At this point the cardinal intervened once more and was given leave by the king to ride over to the prince to try, for the last time, to achieve an honourable settlement. But the prince sent him away empty-handed. While this last effort for peace was going on many French knights must have appeared on the north ridge making their intentions quite clear; much of Warwick's division was back at the ford. Someone, either from the prince's entourage or from Warwick's own divisional rearguard, must have galloped back to Warwick to recall him and so by the time the first French attack reached the Anglo-Gascon line Warwick was back in position with his division.

How were the two armies deployed? The Anglo-Gascons were divided into four groups. On the left was Warwick's division, close up to the hedge, denying the gap at the track and with its left down into the depression near the marshy ground; it included about 1,000 men-at-arms and perhaps the same number of archers. On the right and set back from the hedge and perhaps a hundred yards from Warwick's right was the division of the earl of Salisbury, made up roughly of the same number of men-at-arms and archers. Behind and overlapping the other two was the prince's division, which probably had slightly fewer men-at-arms but a similar number of archers to the other two; behind the prince's division was a small mounted reserve of men-at-arms and mounted archers under the Capital de Buch. The prince himself, together with his immediate advisers Chandos and Audley, took up a position on the highest ground from where he could see the battle develop. No doubt also there would have been several esquires with him ready to take orders to his divisional commanders at a gallop should the need arise. The archers were mainly stationed on either flank of the leading divisions as at Crécy, but undoubtedly some would have been posted among the men-at-arms all along the line.

The French, following the battle plan suggested by Ribemont, were arrayed in three large dismounted divisions, stacked one behind the other. The first under the command of the duke of Normandy, the Dauphin, of about 2,000 men-at-arms; the second, about the same size, under the duke of Orleans; and the third and by far the largest of between 5,000 and 6,000 men-at-arms under the command of King Jean himself. The king was also nominally in command of the whole French army but, apart from approving the initial grouping and dispositions of his army, he was unable to exercise command properly during the battle because he was never in a position to see what was going on. He had stationed himself with his division behind the north ridge. In front of the dismounted divisions of the French army were two mounted squadrons of about 150 men-at-arms each under the two marshals, Clermont and Audrehem.

The French opened proceedings with an attack some time after 8.00 a.m. by the two mounted squadrons, with the intention of scattering the archers and making an initial penetration of the Anglo-Gascon positions for the dismounted divisions to exploit soon after. This was a realistic tactical ploy since armoured knights in partial or complete plate armour, with the additional protection of shields mounted on horses armoured from the front, would have been very difficult to bring down by archery fire. Indeed this could only be done with any certitude if the horses presented their flanks to the archers or the archers managed to run to a flank. However the gaps and the tracks that led to and through them split this attack into two diverging halves, each making for a different gap. Audrehem's squadron opposing Warwick's division found the gap on the track to the ford barricaded and veered off to its right where it was broken up with many casualties by the archers hidden behind the hedge firing into the horses' flanks. Clermont's squadron on the English right opposite Salisbury's division had more success; he forced his way through the gap and then led his leading files to his right behind the hedge to clear the archers and to help the other squadron, by this manoeuvre threatening Warwick's right flank. Salisbury was quick to see the danger and promptly moved his division forward to close the gap before the majority of the squadron had got through the hedge. Both French squadrons were decimated and took no further part in the battle; of the two marshals Clermont was killed and Audrehem taken prisoner.

The Anglo-Gascons had won the first round. Clermont had shown good tactical sense but Salisbury's feel for the battle, his quick thinking, and the rapid response of his division had overcome an initial crisis. However the French had already made one cardinal error: the Dauphin's follow-up division had set out too late. The battle plan required them to come up to the Anglo-Gascon line very shortly after the cavalry attack on the premise that it would have scattered the archers and made an initial penetration. But aside from the fact that the cavalry aim had not been achieved, they delayed their start until it must have been clear to them that the cavalry attack had failed. Indeed, allowing for an approach speed of about 2 m.p.h. for armoured men marching uphill they could not have arrived at the Anglo-Gascon line until some twenty minutes after the cavalry charge. This gave plenty of time for the archers to retrieve spent arrows, for wounded men to be taken out of the line, for prisoners to be taken and moved to the rear, and for commanders to encourage their men and close ranks. But perhaps more importantly the Anglo-Gascon line now seems to have moved forward so that it was stationed in front of the hedge ready for the hand-to-hand fighting that was obviously about to begin. None of this would have been possible had the Dauphin set out as planned.

By the time the Dauphin's division came up to the Anglo-Gascon line they would have been hot, out of breath and facing relatively fresh men. It would have been normal to have halted just outside arrow range to dress their ranks and catch their breath before pressing on into the arrow storm which they would have to endure for perhaps three minutes, a storm made up of as many as 90,000 arrows. This obviously caused many casualties, but the French pressed on to the almost arrow-free zone just in front of the Anglo-Gascons and soon fierce hand-to-hand fighting took place, mainly with Warwick's division. The prince became concerned as to the outcome and sent men-at-arms from his division forward to reinforce Warwick's, keeping only a small number with him as a reserve in addition to those of the Capital de Buch. It is not known how long this hand-to-hand struggle lasted but the result was a close-run thing and eventually the Dauphin drew off, defeated but in reasonably good order, leaving an exhausted Anglo-Gascon army still in possession of the ridge.

At this stage the Anglo-Gascon army might be forgiven for thinking that they had won the day. They might have seen Orleans' division marching off away from the field of battle and they had put that of the Dauphin's to flight, but they could not have seen King Jean's division, stationed even further to the rear and behind the north ridge. When King Jean's huge division hove in sight over the hill in front, the prince showed his generalship. He realized that if the king's division was allowed to reach his positions his army would be overwhelmed by sheer force of numbers. He could still withdraw but would probably not get his booty away with him; he therefore resolved to take the offensive and counter-attack the king's division halfway up the slope before it could reach him.

Consider the two adversaries, the French under their king, hot from their march but in good heart. Their morale possibly not as good as it might have been having seen the remnants of the Dauphin's division withdrawing and the whole of Orleans' division marching away from the battle. But the honour of France was at stake and their king was at their head – for the chivalry of France that was enough to inspire them to great deeds. The men-at-arms of the king's division were at least as numerous as the whole Anglo-Gascon army put together, including the archers and 'light armed men'; the majority of them were knights and those who aspired to knighthood.

Meanwhile, across the way, the Anglo-Gascon army was exhausted and thirsty, its numbers reduced by the fight with and repulse of the Dauphin's division. Many wounded men, both theirs and their enemy's, lay on the ground about them, groaning and calling for water. Men-at-arms had broken lances and swords, archers had run out of arrows and they were even reduced to pulling them out of wounded and dead men lying on the ground; all were suffering from the lassitude experienced by men throughout the ages after the excitement and effort of battle. And at this moment the largest of the French divisions appeared over the hill. The Anglo-Gascons could see this huge mass of armoured men coming inexorably towards them, a mass twenty to thirty ranks deep extending across their whole front of now not much more than the distance between the two tracks. Geoffrey Le Baker writing some four years later said: 'The great number of the enemy frightened our men.' And again how a member of the prince's staff on seeing the king's division cried out: 'Alas, we are beaten', and the prince's retort: 'Thou liest, thou knave, if thou sayest that we can be conquered as long as I live!'

Taking account of casualties, the mounted reserve and those who had left their positions to go in pursuit of the Dauphin's defeated division, the English defensive line would have been about 700 yards long and some seven ranks deep. A defensive line of men-at-arms would have been relatively loose, each man in the front rank a few feet from his neighbour, not shoulder to shoulder, and those in the second rank covering the spaces in between, and so on, for the next rank and those behind. This was necessary in order to allow sufficient space for each man to use his weapon effectively – weapons like bills, halberds, pole-axes and glaives were all mainly slashing weapons and needed space, although they all also had points and could be used as pikes. A formation like this allowed for quick support from those behind for any hard-pressed individual in front and allowed space for archers to engage the enemy head on, although the majority of archers would have been on the flanks of the English army. One of the effects of their massed archery fire was that it compressed an advancing column into its centre, so making it far more difficult for the men-at-arms in the approaching column to use their own weapons effectively.

This was a time for cool leadership and discipline; both were displayed in abundance. The prince having decided to counter-attack now had to carry out the necessary regrouping to put his plan into action. He assembled all the unwounded men-at-arms of the army into one division, less his own small reserve and that of the Capital de Buch. He ordered the Capital to take his small squadron of mounted men-at-arms and archers round his right flank to take up positions out of sight and behind the hill to his right front, with orders to attack the king's division in the rear. He also ordered the men-at-arms in his small reserve, perhaps 150 men, to mount their horses and warned the dismounted division to follow up the counter-attack of his mounted reserve as quickly as they could. The archers were to move forward and to the flanks in order to be able to fire into the column of the advancing men-at-arms from a flanking position. This activity and the knowledge that they were going to attack the oncoming mass opposite would have put heart into his army and morale would have lifted.

When all was ready and the advancing Frenchmen were halfway up the slope the prince led the mounted men-at-arms charging down the slope, lances couched. The mass of the French dismounted men-at-arms absorbed the shock of the charge only to be hit by the dismounted men-at-arms following on. The whole front was now engaged in a bloody close-quarter fight and the flanks of the French column were being driven in towards the centre by the fire from the archers who, once they had run out of arrows, joined in the close-quarter battle with their swords. At this point the Capital's squadron struck the French from the rear. Suddenly the spirit of the king's division gave way and every man sought safety for himself.

The king, however, armed with his battleaxe and with his fourteen-year-old son by his side fought bravely on with his guard about him until it was clear that he had lost the day; no one wished to strike him down. There was a ring of dismounted men-at-arms about him all quarrelling as to who would take him prisoner when Sir Dennis de Morbeque, a banished knight from Artois, stepped forward and accepted his surrender. Quarrelling again broke out and the king was in some danger from the press when the earl of Warwick and Sir John Cobham rode up to claim the king in the prince's name. The battle was over and the pursuit was on; the prince's army pursued the fleeing French to the gates of Poitiers 4 miles away. Over 2,000 French knights and men-at-arms lay dead on the battlefield and many more were killed in the pursuit; a further 2,000 were taken prisoner, including King Jean and his youngest son Philippe. The English and Gascon casualties were relatively light. The Anglo-Gascon army stayed that night on the battlefield and the next day they resumed their march to Bordeaux.

The Frenchman Edouard Perroy[10] wrote that the English were forced by their inferiority of numbers 'to resort to stratagems unworthy of knights.' But in fact the French army was beaten by better generalship, leadership, discipline and morale, and by far superior firepower. The choice of ground, the regrouping during the battle, the move to the offensive and the launch of a mounted attack at the critical moment in the battle, and the outflanking move are all indications of good generalship and good control. Once battle had come to close quarters, the effectiveness of the archers and the men-at-arms and the manner in which they co-ordinated their activities, showed the value of training and experience of an army that had been together on active service for over a year. In this respect it is inter-esting to note Viollet Le Duc's[11] comments on the French and English armies: 'the organisation and discipline of the English troops gave them an incontestable superiority over the troops of France.'

There is some controversy over whether the counter-attack was mounted or not; Froissart writes that it was so, Chandos Herald does not specifically mention it, though he does say that Sir James Audley was mounted as was the prince and that the knights couched their lances. But the argument really turns on whether there was time for the Anglo-Gascon men-at-arms to mount and carry out such an attack or not. The horses of the prince's small reserve were only some 200 yards behind them in the care of grooms. It is therefore a reasonable assumption that they could easily have been mounted in the twenty minutes available to them between the time that the king's division hove in sight and before they could have come up to the Anglo-Gascon line. A mounted counter-attack seems therefore to be a most likely course of action. But judging by the fact that mounted knights rescued King Jean from a quarrelling ring of dismounted knights and men-at-arms, it would seem likely that only the prince's small reserve and the Capital's squadron were in fact mounted, perhaps 300 horsemen all told.

The French had much to learn from the Battle of Poitiers. They clearly had not yet understood that the style of warfare had changed. While they fought with all their old bravery and panache, they were handicapped by their inveterate ill-discipline, their recklessness and by desertion. Furthermore, although following the battles of Crécy and Morlaix they had attempted to find a tactical answer to massed archery fire, they do not seem to have understood that close co-ordination between the mounted and dismounted elements of their army was essential. And this, combined with their usual superiority of numbers, would have provided the answer in the short term, particularly in the timing of attacks and the setting of objectives. In the longer term of course they had to develop their own force of archers. For instance, if the Dauphin's attack at Poitiers had been launched at the right time to support the mounted attacks of Audrehem and Clermont, their chances of success, notwithstanding the archers, would have been high. The plan was sound and the mounted squadrons were given the right objective but, for one reason or another, the cavalry attack was unsupported. Likewise the timing of dismounted attacks to maintain pressure on the Anglo-Gascon position was crucial. The plan called for a quick follow-up and if the king's division had not been more than ten minutes behind the Dauphin's the Anglo-Gascons would not have had time to regroup. Indeed they would not have had the time to collect fresh arrows or to mount their horses, or even to have rested and quenched their thirst. Under these circumstances the Anglo-Gascons would almost certainly have been totally overwhelmed. All these points are matters of generalship and training, and all were within the capability and understanding of the French. Yet they were not done due to bad discipline, diffident commanding and the fact that the overall field commander, the king, was never in a position to see what was happening.

Although qualification for high command in the two armies was very similar throughout the war, at the time of the Battle of Poitiers French armies seemingly laboured under the tradition that only highborn members of the nobility were fit for command. The higher that a man was in the social hierarchy the more qualified he became for high command. Indeed, command as exercised by the English at that time appeared to be unobtainable in a French army of the day, because feudal superiority was deemed the best command attribute, and rivalry and lack of discipline among the chivalry of France made the exercise of high command difficult. Contrast this with English armies where the aristocracy also received high command, but only after they had gained considerable experience in war and regardless of their relative social position. Knights were often given independent commands, particularly in minor operations, and some were made king's lieutenants of provinces; indeed knights were ennobled as a consequence of their ability in war. In this respect it is interesting to see the large proportion of mere knights among the founder members of the Order of the Garter,[12] a military order composed largely of

Edward III's 'fellow soldiers' and formed 'to the honouring of the soldiery'. These knights of the Garter were Edward's army commanders and in effect were promoted above the nobility for military purposes; no member of the aristocracy would complain about being put under the command of a knight of the Garter.

However it must not be forgotten that in feudal times a king's duty was to lead his armies in battle, and of course if he were present on the battlefield he would naturally take command. Nevertheless, any inexperience on the part of the king could be overcome with the help of advisers. So, providing the aristocracy was willing to take orders from their sovereign, then perhaps the solution to the problem of command of feudal armies was at hand. Edward III at Hallidon Hill was inexperienced and yet he took command of the English army, and the Black Prince was even more inexperienced at Crécy, but both had experienced soldiers, knights, at their side to advise and guard them. King Jean II had the sound advice of Ribemont and Douglas before the Battle of Poitiers and yet he failed to put their advice into practice; his divisional commanders and two marshals, and indeed he himself, seem not to have understood the essentials of their battle plan. Perhaps discipline in the French army was just not good enough to put the plan into effect. Furthermore Jean had the experienced knights Sir Geoffroy de Charny and Sir Eustace de Ribemont close by him for advice and support during the battle so he cannot be faulted on that score. However, he himself, so far, had had an inglorious military career, which only included the unsuccessful sieges of Aiguillon and Breteuil, and of course he missed the Battle of Crécy. His divisional commanders were his sons, the Dauphin and the duke of Orleans; the former was twenty-one years old and the latter nineteen, neither had had any previous military experience though presumably they had experienced soldiers to advise them. In both countries the nobility was a military nobility, but contrast the experience and the execution of high command between the French divisional commanders, the Dauphin and Orleans, on the one hand, with their English counterparts, Warwick and Salisbury on the other. Also consider the differences in experience and execution of command between the two commanders-in-chief, King Jean and the Black Prince; these are so marked that this fact in itself could be a major reason for the extraordinary victory at Poitiers of the Anglo-Gascons.

This battle was an appalling blow to France, its prestige and to the honour of its knightly classes. The whole country was stunned by the grim news from Poitiers. Twice, in little over a decade, French armies had been ignominiously defeated by smaller English armies and now she had lost her king, as well as many of the chief men in the kingdom. But not all was lost: Charles, the Dauphin and duke of Normandy, heir to the throne, had escaped the carnage; he was to prove to be France's most valuable asset in the forthcoming struggle. The prince's army, astonished at its victory but weary and hungry, attended to the wounded, buried the dead and then settled down for the night on the battlefield. Next morning they began their march to Bordeaux and arrived in triumph several days later.

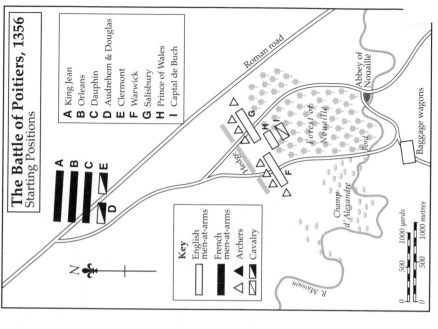

The Battle of Poitiers, 1356
Starting Positions

A King Jean
B Orleans
C Dauphin
D Audrehem & Douglas
E Clermont
F Warwick
G Salisbury
H Prince of Wales
I Captal de Buch

Roman road

Abbey of Nouaillé

Forest of Nouaillé

Ford

Baggage wagons

Hedge

Champ d'Alexandre

R. Miosson

Key
English men-at-arms
French men-at-arms
Archers
Cavalry

500   1000 yards
500   1000 metres

N

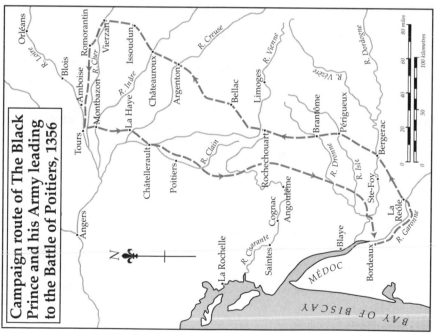

Campaign route of The Black Prince and his Army leading to the Battle of Poitiers, 1356

Orléans

R. Loire

Blois

Amboise
Romorantin
Vierzan
Tours
Montbazon R. Cher
La Haye Issoudun
R. Indre
Châteauroux
Argenton
R. Creuse
R. Vienne
Bellac
Limoges
Brantôme
Périgueux
R. Vézère
R. Dordogne

Châtellerault
R. Clain
Poitiers

Rochechouart
Cognac
Angoulême
R. Dronne
R. Isle
Bergerac

Ste-Foy
La Réole
R. Garonne

R. Charente
Saintes
Blaye
Bordeaux

MÉDOC

La Rochelle

Angers

BAY OF BISCAY

N

0   20   40   60   80 miles
0   50   100 kilometres

Chapter 11

The Rheims Campaign and the Prince in Spain

'We may lose more in one day than we have gained in twenty years'[1]

Henry, duke of Lancaster, who had marched south from Normandy after his successful march in the duchy, failed to get across the Loire to support the prince and returned to Brittany, where he was the king's lieutenant. Following the Battle of Poitiers a two-year truce was signed between England and France at Bordeaux on 23 March 1357. This truce was important because warfare had become generalized throughout France after Poitiers, with numerous minor operations. They included the factional fighting in Brittany, the Navarrese operations in Normandy, the depredation of the Free Companies in central France and the peasant rising of the *Jacquerie* at a time when the traditional hierarchy of authority in France had been temporarily swept away at Poitiers. This truce was not only designed to bring peace between France and England, but also to give a measure of lawful authority to the French and English authorities over the various warring factions and the Free Companies operating in France as a whole. But the truce failed to prevent the unrest, the brigandry and the petty military operations which blossomed in France at that time under Charles's weak initial authority. Many incidents were carried out by redundant English soldiers operating as small bands of brigands who terrorized the countryside, sometimes under the blind eye of English authority. However, and more seriously, Lancaster himself ignored the truce.

On 3 October Lancaster, in direct contravention of the truce, laid siege to Rennes. His army was far too small to take the city by storm and as he had no siege equipment he was obliged to settle down and starve the city into surrender. This was no easy task as Charles, now regent of France in the absence of his father in captivity, sent forces under Bertrand du Guesclin to raise the siege. This he failed to do but he did manage to get supplies into the city, which prolonged the siege and forced Lancaster onto the defensive while continuing his siege. The citizens eventually bought him off with a payment of 100,000 crowns. Other English captains operated on the borders of Aquitaine or in Normandy under the guise of assistance to Charles of Navarre. During this period the depredations of the Free Companies caused real hardship to the inhabitants of central France. They terrorized the populace while living off the countryside, and pillaged from peasant and noble alike; they imposed *pâtis* on all whom they could force to pay. These companies would seize a castle as an operating base and only move on when the surrounding countryside was sucked dry. Some of the companies were very large; that of Sir Robert Knollys was said to be 3,000 strong. Such companies were much too formidable to be stamped out by the retinue of the local count; only royal authority could raise the necessary forces to do the job and this authority did not exist following Poitiers.

In Paris Etienne Marcel, a rich bourgeois cloth merchant, backed by the *estates,* assumed power with the help of Charles of Navarre's supporters in Paris. Things got out of hand in February 1358 when some of the mob broke into the Dauphin's apartments when he was in council and murdered two of his officers in his presence. Charles of Navarre had wisely left Paris by this time and the Dauphin escaped in March. Meanwhile, outside Paris in the countryside to the north the peasants rose up in revolt against their masters. These *Jaques* numbering several thousand then went on the rampage, burning and looting any castles and manors they could overcome and killing, torturing and raping those caught inside. Marcel sent troops from Paris to assist the *Jaques*, an unwise move. The *jaquerie* were finally cut to pieces by forces of Charles of Navarre near Meaux, north-east of Paris, while Marcel and some of his close supporters were killed by his former followers in Paris in July. The Dauphin then returned and began the difficult business of bringing some order to the affairs of France where Charles of Navarre remained in defiance of the regent and an unknown quantity in the confrontation between France and England.

Edward III meanwhile seemed to be genuinely interested in peace, providing it gave him what he wanted, and as he held Jean II in captivity he entered into negotiations with French envoys for his release. A draft treaty, the First Treaty of London, was agreed between the two kings in May 1358 in which an enlarged Aquitaine, including the Limousin, Poitou and the Saintonge, were to be ceded in full sovereignty. Ponthieu and Calais were also to be ceded and France was to renounce its alliance with Scotland; in return Edward was to give up his claim to the throne of France. The problem of where the actual borders of this enlarged Aquitaine lay could be settled in due course. Jean, in accordance with normal medieval practice, would nevertheless still have to buy his freedom with the payment of a massive ransom of 4 million crowns, about £666,000 sterling. This tentative agreement between the two kings was rejected by the English parliament who felt that more should be extracted from a defeated France, and particularly a divided France with its severe internal difficulties. Parliament also felt that King Jean should be required to use his good offices with his kinsman, the Pope, to settle certain outstanding differences between the curia and the country.

A new attempt, the Second Treaty of London, was made and signed by the two kings in March 1359. In this the old Angevin provinces of Anjou, Maine, Normandy and Touraine were to be added to the territories to be ceded to England in full sovereignty in addition to the overlordship of Brittany. These demands amounted to virtually half of France in exchange for Edward's promise to drop his claim to the whole. This was preposterous and not unexpectedly these outrageous terms were rejected by the Dauphin in council and by the *conseil* in Paris in May. Edward was furious that a defeated France should have had the temerity to reject his peace proposals and resolved to settle the issue once and for all by force of arms. He clearly felt that in France's confused state he stood the best chance he had yet had to achieve his goals, and if he could invade with a large army and carry out a quick and decisive campaign he might yet be crowned king of France. He set his eyes on Rheims, the city where French kings were traditionally crowned, and planned his greatest campaign.

Edward hoped to cross the Channel in good time for a summer campaign, but as these expeditions took several months to organize it is probable that he began his preparations while the peace treaty was still being negotiated. He probably never expected his terms for the Second Treaty of London to be agreed by the French. In the event the vanguard of his army did not cross until early October. Edward, a good organizer, appreciated that following the devastation caused by the many English *chevauchées*, the Free Companies and the *jaquerie*, his army was unlikely to be able to live off the land as English armies had done in the past. His intention was to strike deep into the heartland of France, at Rheims about 175 miles south-east of Calais, his intended starting point. He realized that the army would have to be self-contained for a large part of the campaign.

A comprehensive wagon train would therefore be essential and to this end he had at least 1,000 large four-horse wagons made[2] and transported across the Channel to Calais. Everything that the army might need was provided for.

Edward had made it known that he was going on campaign in the summer and as a result many volunteers in search of plunder flocked to his standard, at Calais, so many in fact that they constituted a threat to the security of Calais itself. However, when Lancaster landed in Calais with 2,400 troops on 1 October, he immediately took his own force and most of the foreign volunteers on *chevauchée* in the direction of Paris. In England preparations went ahead apace: shipping was arrested and assembled at Sandwich; knights, magnates and their retinues converged on the assembly areas; archers and footmen were conscripted by array, as were numbers of non-combatant artisans.

As always the total number in the army is a matter of conjecture and ranges from 100,000 to fewer than 6,000 combatants; 20,000, including non-combatants, is a well reasoned figure.[3] But figures[4] in the household accounts of William Farley give a more accurate picture. They show that the Black Prince and Lancaster were with the army. Also that the army included 10 earls, 70 bannerets, 870 knights, 3,800 men-at-arms, 5,500 mounted archers, 300 men of the household for administrative duties, 30 grooms and porters, 200 artisans and 1,100 Welsh foot, making a total of 11,880 including the administrative personnel. To this has to be added a possible 1,500 foreign volunteers who served under Sir Walter Manny's banner without pay, and the 3,000 in Sir Robert Knollys' company who marched up from central France to join the army, probably at Rheims, making the expeditionary force about 16,400 all told. The hierarchy of the expedition also included John of Gaunt, Edward's third son, later to become duke of Lancaster when Henry of Grosmont died, and Lionel, earl of Ulster. Included in the figures were the retinues of the earls, barons and the more prominent knights including the Welsh knight Oweyn Charleton who led the well-organized contingent from north Wales. The non-combatants included all those artisans who were so essential to ensure the army could overcome all the many administrative problems they were likely to meet; the smiths and armourers, the bowyers and fletchers, the saddlers and farriers, the millers and cooks, and the carpenters and miners. The wagon drivers, who do not seem to have been included in Farley's figures, would have added at least another 1,000 to the total. If Sir Walter Manny's and Sir Robert Knollys' companies and the wagon drivers are excluded the total still represents one of the largest expeditionary forces put across the Channel.

In addition to the troops and non-combatants, thousands of horses would have been shipped across. The chief men would have had at least four warhorses each and the knights two, accounting for some 2,500 horses, to which should be added a further 3,800 for the men-at-arms and 5,500 for the mounted archers. Additionally the hacks of the chief men and knights would have added a further 1,500 horses to the total. Also there were the sumpter horses, the horses of private baggage wagons, the horses of the households of the royals and the magnates, and the draught horses for the wagon train to be shipped across the Channel. All told, the army probably shipped well over 16,000 horses to Calais for the campaign and of course those who came with Sir Robert Knollys' and others who joined at Calais would have come with their own horses. The total of men, horses and wagons would have required a very large number of ships to transport them across the Channel in one lift. However, as the crossing was made at the shortest point to a secure base, many of the troops and horses would have been ferried across over several days with a rela-tively small number of ships. Lancaster, for example, arrived at Calais with his retinue twenty-seven days before the king so it is probable that other contingents crossed during that time, and perhaps even after the king himself had landed.

Edward arrived at Calais on 28 October and promptly recalled Lancaster from his raid, who then joined the army a few days later on the march. The army set out on 4 November on its way to Rheims in three columns,[5] the king's division going via Arras and St Quentin to the rendezvous near Craonne, about 20 miles north-west of Rheims. The Black Prince's division went on a more southerly route via Montreuil, Hesdin and Albert, crossing the Somme near Bray, then on to Ham and Laon and finally to the rendezvous. Lancaster's division marched in the centre between the two others. When the Black Prince got to Hesdin he was about 24 miles from his father's division and from then on the two flanking divisions were on converging courses. This ensured that, taking into account Lancaster's division in the centre and the flank guards and scouts from each division, no division was out of touch with the one on its flank. More importantly, the army could easily be concentrated for battle should it be necessary, the flanks being less than a day's march away from each other. Presumably Edward divided his army on the march in this way to give it the best possible chance of living off the countryside. He also hoped that they might confront the French for a decisive battle, but the regent, Charles, realized that his best strategy was to stay in the castles and fortified towns and not give Edward the opportunity to meet him in battle. The English army had no siege train and was therefore in no position to conduct quick sieges, the army would either have to take castles and fortified cities by assault and suffer casualties, or by starvation. Charles and his army were safe.

After a miserable march in pouring rain, the different divisions met at Craonne on 29 November and from there marched to their siege positions on or about 4 December. The prince's division went to the north of the city, the king's to the south and Lancaster to the east. The siege of Rheims now began. It was a leisurely affair and largely involved a simple blockade: no trenches were dug round the city and the walls were not sapped, no assaults were mounted and no bombardment by either siege engines or artillery took place. Edward expected the citizens to surrender the city to him once they realized that there would be no relief by the regent. He wanted an acquiescent population for his forthcoming coronation as king of France and consequently the siege was to be non-violent, an almost unheard of thing in medieval times. Unfortunately the regent Charles had had plenty of warning about Edward's campaign and his objectives, and therefore the citizens of Rheims were well stocked with food and supplies of all sorts, the city walls were put in a good state of repair and the garrison reinforced and ready. Christmas came and went and still the citizens refused to open their gates to Edward. The weather was wet and cold and the horses picketed outside suffered badly, as did the men on duty outside the walls and away from their billets in the surrounding villages and farms. Edward refused to order an assault, largely because he knew he could not control his troops after the city had been taken. To maintain discipline and occupy his troops he sent his captains on deep raids into the surrounding countryside. One went to St Menehould 45 miles to the east, another to the walls of Paris 90 miles away to the south-west and others went to the north and south of Rheims.

However, by 10 January, when all the raiding parties had returned to their bases, Edward had to decide what to do next. He could either assault the city, which he was most reluctant to do, or maintain his passive siege. He decided to raise his siege and march to the dukedom of Burgundy which lay about 100 miles to the south; his army should be able to replenish their provisions and take much plunder. Furthermore, a march to Burgundy had the political advantage of neutralizing the duke, the most powerful vassal of France and therefore one who could be bound by his homage to King Jean to come to the regent's aid. Edward's army set out on 12 January, pillaging and burning as it went and capturing some towns and fortresses on its way before establishing itself in northern Burgundy by the end of January. There now followed a month of greedy pillage and destruction in the lands of the duke, Philippe of Burgundy, which had so far avoided the ravages of war, while negotiations took place between Edward and Philippe. These were concluded on 10 March with a three-year truce and a declaration by the latter of non-intervention in Edward's war with the regent. The duke also agreed to pay a huge danegeld of 200,000 *moutons d'or*, about £33,300, to ensure that the English army left his lands, which they did five days later when the agreed sum had been paid.

Edward still hoped that his primary aim to be crowned king of France could be secured, perhaps in Paris, and so he marched his army to the city's gates devastating much of the countryside on its way. Whilst on the march Edward was told that a French fleet had descended on Rye and Winchelsea. However, a small but adequate force was quickly on its way and after a sharp fight the French were driven back to their boats with heavy loss. In France, after a leisurely march covering about 70 miles in twenty-six days, the English army arrived outside the walls of Paris on 7 April. On 10 April, a deputation came from the city to treat for peace. They met Edward's negotiators at the abbey of Cluny but the two sides failed to agree terms.

Two days later the English rearguard made a demonstration in front of the walls while the rest of Edward's army withdrew to the south-west towards Chartres. Edward and his army now wandered like a lost tribe. Rheims had not fallen because he did not want to damage the sacred city and he had not attempted to take Paris because an assault without supporting artillery and siege engines would have been a risky and costly affair. Most exasperatingly, Charles would not allow a French army to meet Edward in battle. Charles's policy of passive resistance from the safety of defended castles and walled cities was beginning to show results. The French did not follow up the English withdrawal from Paris but instead sent another delegation to negotiate peace terms. The embassy caught up with the English army at the end of April and on 1 May negotiations for a truce began at Brétigny, near Chartres, and were concluded a week later. Froissart says that Edward was obdurate about his claim to the throne of France and if it had not been for Lancaster's advice the truce would probably not have been agreed at all.[6] However, in July 1362, Edward appointed the prince of Wales, prince of Aquitaine. The prince was to be his vassal and lieutenant, much as Edward had been previously when he held the duchy of the king of France. This was a significant political step because Edward did not yet hold Aquitaine in complete sovereignty, and would not until the details of the treaty had been complied with, which was not scheduled until November of the same year. From the French point of view he was therefore still acting as the king of France, which of course he still claimed to be although he had agreed to surrender his title in the treaty. Edward had unnecessarily jumped the gun and had made himself look insincere.

The truce was to last until 29 September 1361; while treaty negotiations took place the Black Prince and the Dauphin agreed a draft treaty for their sovereigns to sign. Under the terms of the draft an enlarged Aquitaine, basically the inherited duchy of Eleanor of Aquitaine, was ceded in full sovereignty, together with Calais and the county of Ponthieu.[7] In addition Edward agreed to renounce his claim to the throne of France and king Jean agreed to renounce his suzerainty over Aquitaine, these renunciations being conditional on the transfer of territories. King Jean's ransom was agreed at 3,000,000 gold crowns, about £500,000, a huge sum for those days and one which would impose a heavy strain on French resources. Jean was to be released from his comfortable custody at the Palace of the Savoy as soon as the first 600,000 gold crowns had been paid at Calais; the remainder of the ransom was to be paid over the next six years in annual payments of 400,000 gold crowns each. This treaty was signed in Calais by the two kings in October 1361, but with what was to turn out to be a very significant but probably necessary amendment concerning the transfer of the various ceded lands, castles and towns.

The amendment dealt with what were known as the 'renunciations', a technical problem dealing with the changeover of sovereignty because one sovereign had to renounce sovereignty over a particular area of land, castle or town before the other could accept sovereignty over it. Most of these were French to be ceded to England although some were due to go the other way, mainly in Normandy. It was recognized that the transfer of sovereignty to different administrations would take some time to implement and Edward would only agree to renounce his claims to the throne of France once the transfer had been completed. The amendment was therefore separated from the main body of the treaty into a separate document with the proviso that the transfers were to be completed by 1 November 1362. The actual transfer of sovereignty was probably impossible to accomplish within the time limit set and therefore the most important part of the treaty, apart from the actual agreement of peace, the renunciations, were unlikely ever to be completed. This left a loophole for either sovereign to resume the war whenever he wished on the premise that the treaty had not been complied with.

As a result, the treaty of Brétigny became a flawed document once it had been agreed to separate out the renunciations from the main body of the treaty, and in reality it settled nothing. It was unrealistic to expect all the renunciations to be completed on time and therefore the renunciations as a whole would become null and void. This was unlikely to happen while Jean remained king of France as he and Edward had become good friends during his captivity but it left the way open for the Dauphin, Charles, to dispute the treaty should it not be completed in its entirety before Jean's death.

Once the draft treaty was agreed at Brétigny and signed by the Dauphin and the prince of Wales, Edward left for home with his sons, leaving Honfleur on 28 May and arriving at Westminster the next day. The army under Lancaster's command marched to Calais at the end of a militarily disappointing campaign but one which reaped a potentially huge political bonus for Edward who could now claim that the enormous expense of his war with France had been worthwhile. In 1363, in an attempt to cement good relations with the Flemings,

Edward established the wool staple at Calais and opened negotiations with the count of Flanders for the marriage of the count's only daughter to his youngest son, Edmund Langley, earl of Cambridge. Margaret of Flanders was heiress to all the count's lands, which included the counties of Burgundy and Artois, in addition to Flanders. This suggests that Edward's territorial interests in France had not been satisfied by the Treaty of Calais, which had not yet been concluded because all the renunciations and therefore the transfer of territories had not been completed. Certainly Charles the Dauphin saw it in this light. When his father died in London in April 1364, having not renounced sovereignty over Aquitaine, and Charles became king of France, he persuaded the Pope, Urban V, not to give his blessing on this marriage. At the same time he began his own negotiations with the count for the marriage of Margaret to his brother, Philip the Bold, duke of Burgundy. This marriage eventually took place in 1369 and gave birth to the quasi-state of Burgundy.

When Edward made his eldest son prince of Aquitaine, he intended Aquitaine to be a self-governing vassal state with the prince at its head, to be financially independent of the exchequer at home; the principal posts were to be distributed among both Englishmen and Gascons. Unfortunately the Black Prince appointed his cronies to the most lucrative posts, furthermore, without the financial reserve of the exchequer in London, he was obliged to increase taxes to meet the costs of his own household, his administration and the defence of the principality. Perhaps this would not have mattered too much under normal circumstances but, as a result of the Treaty of Calais, new loyalties had to be cemented. Those who had always been loyal subjects of the king of France were now expected to give their loyalty to the king of England, which needed tactful handling. But instead they had to pay heavier taxes in order to pay for an English administration and, so far as they could see, the lavish lifestyle of the prince. However this was simply an excuse, in fact many of the Gascon lords within the new boundaries of Aquitaine claimed special privileges for their counties, and towns did the same, exempting them from taxes imposed by Bordeaux on traditional grounds, but with very little substantial evidence. Exasperation followed by anger and discontent spread throughout the newly acquired territories, and even within the old boundaries the Gascons were more than a little concerned.

Sir John Chandos, as the king's lieutenant in France, was required to supervise the handover of territories after the treaty, and to accept the homage of the principle Gascon nobles and of the towns newly incorporated into Aquitaine. He had virtually completed this task by the time the prince arrived in June of 1362. This was no easy task and he needed a sizeable force to accomplish it. Sir John Chandos had been taking the homage of the magnates, towns and fortresses in the name of king Edward, but when the prince arrived in Bordeaux as prince of Aquitaine this homage had to be taken again in the prince's name. In the south, Gaston Phoebus, count of Foix and Béarn, would only give homage for two of his viscounties, saying that he had never given homage for Béarn to anyone but would do so if the prince could show that he should.[8] Gaston was to remain an ambiguous vassal in the future. Another powerful man was Jean d'Armagnac, the prince's principle opponent on his *chevauchée* of 1355, who was count of Armagnac and Rouergue. He gave his homage freely enough, but when the prince levied the *fouage* or hearth tax at a harshly high rate he refused to allow it to be levied in the Rouergue, a poor county. So the seeds of future discontent were sown.

When Jean II died in April 1364, Charles the Dauphin became king of France and immediately began to undermine the prince's position in Aquitaine by offering pensions and land without a great deal of success.

Meanwhile a French army under Bertrand du Guesclin defeated the Navarrese army at Cocherel in May 1364. A peace treaty between Charles of France and Charles of Navarre was then signed the following year thus putting out of play one of Edward's useful, though untrustworthy, allies in France. This set-back was balanced by the Battle of Auray on 29 September 1364 at which the Anglo-Breton army of Jean de Montfort, not only defeated their Franco-Breton enemies but killed Charles de Blois and took du Guesclin prisoner. Superficially this could be taken as bolstering the English position in Brittany and settling the political future of the duchy. But it failed to do so because although the problem of the Breton succession was now solved with English help, Jean de Montfort, who remained pro-English, nevertheless gave homage for his duchy to Charles V who recognized him as the lawful duke.

Meanwhile another scenario opened. In London in June 1362 an alliance had been signed between Edward and Pedro, king of Castile.

It was signed by Pedro to balance the support given by the French to his enemy Pere III of Aragon, and to Enrique of Trastamare, his half-brother and rival for the throne of Castile. Edward signed for practical reasons. The English had been opposed at sea by the galleys of Castile as allies of France and in French pay since the beginning of the Hundred Years' War. They had disrupted trade and carried out many effective raids against the south coast and indeed comprised the enemy fleet at the naval battle off Winchelsea in 1350. The alliance removed the threat from the Castilian fleet and came into force in the summer of 1364, however it also pledged English support to Pedro should French troops invade Castile itself in support of France's allies in the area. It was not thought in London that this was very likely. However, as part of a scheme to employ the Free Companies, which were ravaging central France, Charles V commissioned Bertrand du Guesclin, who had been freed on ransom, to recruit some of the Free Companies to go on crusade against the Moors in southern Spain. Du Guesclin's army, which included three companies commanded by English captains, Sir Hugh Calveley, Dagworth and Elmham, set out from Montpellier at the end of 1365.

It soon became clear that the purpose of this expedition was to put Enrique on the throne of Castile, which du Guesclin's army achieved after a short but efficient campaign in June 1366. Pedro retreated to the south losing support as he went so he decided to invoke the Anglo-Castilian alliance and pleaded with the prince in Aquitaine for support; he achieved this in July and preparations went ahead. However, some inkling of the real purpose of du Guesclin's expedition must have reached London early in 1366 because by June of the same year reinforcements of men-at-arms and archers were being arrayed for service with the prince and ships were being arrested for their transportation. The campaign was planned at Bayonne in September and presented no problems, but the conditions of support for Pedro from the prince and from Charles of Navarre involved much horse-trading. Charles was a party to the proceedings and the campaign because his tiny kingdom controlled the passes across the western Pyrenees into Spain. A pro-French king on the throne of Castile was seen as a threat to England, through their fleet. Consequently, Edward III partly underwrote the campaign by shipping 10,000 lb of gold,[9] perhaps then worth about £150,000, to Bordeaux. This was about the cost of a major expedition into France but would not in fact cover the costs of the campaign. However the prince and the Gascon lords expected it to be profitable. There were also to be territorial concessions along the Biscay coast to both Charles of Navarre and the prince; the latter was to receive the county of Vizcaya. This would effectively close the bases from which a Castilian fleet could operate against England, provided the prince took control of the county once Pedro was put on the throne of Castile.

The army of the prince included his own and John of Gaunt's, now the duke of Lancaster's, retinues and those of the principle Gascon lords; also several of the Free Companies joined him, notably that of Sir Hugh Calveley. The army totalled between 6,000 and 8,000 men of whom some 2,000 were English archers. Sir Hugh had been serving under du Guesclin in Spain, but declined to operate against the prince. Forces promised by Charles of Navarre were an unlikely asset as information had reached the prince that Charles had entered into negotiations with Enrique of Trastarmare with the aim of opposing the prince's army at the crossings of the Pyrenees, despite the undertakings he had given at Libourne. On hearing this the prince sent messengers to Calveley, who was still in Castile, to invade Navarre. This had the desired effect and Charles quickly came to heel.

Leading elements of the prince's army set out from Dax on 14 February for the pass across the Pyrenees at St Jean-Pied-de-Port and the whole army was assembled at Pamplona, the capital of Navarre, by the end of the month. Enrique's army joined forces with du Guesclin and the combined army then moved north to cover Vitoria only to find that the prince was already there. Enrique decided to base himself on the castle of Zaldiaran, about 10 miles to the west and began guerrilla operations against the prince's army.

The guerrilla operations forced the prince to move away and he marched south-east to Logrono which he reached on 1 April. Enrique shadowed the prince's move and marched south to Najera, about 15 miles to the west of Logrono, which he also reached on 1 April. The next day Enrique's army moved out to the open to take up battle positions facing east and during the night prepared for battle. The prince's army marched to the north-west during the night and took up battle positions overlooking the Castilian left flank, catching Enrique and du Guesclin by surprise. They had sent out scouting patrols during the night but had failed to discover the flanking movement or to find the final Anglo-Gascon position. Early in the morning of 2 April 1367 the Franco-Castilian army hastily turned their front to face the Anglo-Gascons. It is probable that they were in the middle of doing so when the vanguard of the prince's army, under Sir John Chandos and John of Gaunt, attacked the mostly French vanguard of the Franco-Castilian army under du Guesclin.

The prince had dismounted most of his army, leaving only his rear-guard under Sir Hugh Calverley and Jean d'Armagnac still mounted. The English advanced under a hail of supporting archery fire and a fierce fight followed. But the Castilian wings fled the battle before they could be engaged by the flanks of the prince's army which now turned inward to embrace the French in the centre where his main body had joined the vanguard. The battle was soon over and many prisoners taken, including the French marshal, Audrehem, and du Guesclin, but Enrique escaped. The prince wrote to his wife Joan in Bordeaux on 5 April, sending a copy to Edward III in London, telling her that between five and six thousand of the Franco-Castilian army had been killed. Also, besides certain named individuals, up to 2,000 noble prisoners were taken;[10] these are almost certainly exaggerated figures but they indicate a handsome victory for the prince and his army. This victory depended on three factors: the prince's leadership; the desertion of the Castilians; and, once again, the effect of massed archery fire which the Castilians had never before experienced. This was the second time that massed archery fire had been used effectively by the English to support an attack in a major battle, the first being at Neville's Cross in 1346.

A few days after the battle the prince and his army moved to Burgos, the Castilian capital where Pedro had already established himself, and negotiations began concerning the amount owed by Pedro for the aid given him by the prince and his army. The final agreed figure was the colossal sum of 2,720,000 gold florins (over £450,000) which increased every day that the army remained in Castille. The prince, naturally, was not inclined to leave until he had received a sizeable portion of his costs, however there was really no way that Pedro could raise such a large sum. There were also diffi-culties about the transfer of the county of Vizcaya; agreement about these two matters were finally settled at a signing ceremony on 2 May but still failed to provide either the gold or the county. In fact only a small part of the sum due was ever paid and Vizcaya never declared its allegiance to the prince. During the summer the prince was forced to move first to Valladolid and then to Soria in search of food and forage for his army, until finally in July, with many sick, he decided to cut his losses and return to Aquitaine; he himself was seriously ill, probably with dysentery. In August the army retraced its steps through Navarre and the prince took his leave of Charles on 29 August at the same pass he had entered six months before, and arrived at Bordeaux early in September.

The prince's intervention in Castilian affairs was certainly a military success, but it left an unsettled political situation in Castile itself where Enrique, with French and Aragonese help, continued his fight for the throne. Indeed in March 1369 his army met and defeated Pedro at Montiel, where Enrique later murdered him. Once crowned, Enrique again put the Castilian galleys at the service of France. Politically the Spanish campaign may have been less than satisfactory, but financially it was a disaster. Pedro paid very little of the huge sum he owed before he was defeated. Furthermore the Gascon lords and the Free Companies, who had been led to believe that plunder would be plentiful, came back virtually empty handed and demanded to be paid for their services.

The prince was now faced with the problem of paying off his army from an empty exchequer in Bordeaux. He was short of about three-quarters of his total costs and was therefore forced to demand money owed him by some of the Gascon lords, which was unpopular. The two disgruntled lords, Jean d'Armagnac and Arnaud d'Albret, then disputed payment of the *fouage* on their domains and appealed against its imposition. When they failed to obtain satisfaction at the court in Bordeaux they appealed to London, and failing to obtain satisfaction there took their case to Paris and appealed to Charles V.

Charles took legal advice and considered most carefully whether or not he had jurisdiction over the lords in Aquitaine. He decided that because the renunciations by his father, Jean II, and Edward had not been made he still had lawful authority over the courts in Bordeaux. Charles received the appeals on 3 December 1368 so publicly made the statement that Aquitaine remained subject to his sovereignty. Edward III quickly responded and on 3 June 1369 he resumed the title of king of France; Charles riposted with the confiscation of Aquitaine in its entirety on 30 November and the Hundred Years' War began again. Politically nothing had changed after thirty-two years of inter-mittent warfare. In those years France had been ravaged and defeated, her king taken prisoner, the chief men in the land killed or ransomed, the wealth of the country drained away and, notwithstanding the confiscation, about half of France remained in English hands.

In due course the prince received the balance of his loan to d'Armagnac who had been given a pension by Charles of £17,000; similarly d'Albret was promised the balance of his English pension over the next four years from Charles in addition to a pension of £10,000.[11] Neither of these pensions was ever paid in full, but clearly the fact that both lords had turned to the French crown for the satisfaction of their grievances meant that they accepted Charles's sovereignty, which Charles shrewdly cemented with his promise of pensions. They felt they would be better off financially if they declared for Charles than they would be if they remained loyal to the near bankrupt prince of Aquitaine. Clearly the barons of south-west France, who were fiercely independent were available for hire to the highest bidder.

The year 1369 was one of tentative warfare as each side probed for weak points as they drifted into general war. John of Gaunt, duke of Lancaster, landed at Calais in September with an army of about 5,000 where he was joined by a further 1,000 foreign volunteers before going on *chevauchée* into Normandy. In the same year the prince lost two of his finest commanders in quick succession, Sir James Audley and Sir John Chandos.

Both the French and the English planned major military ventures for 1370. The prince and his army were based in the area of Angoulême, while the French marshal, du Guesclin, who had been recalled from Spain, was about 60 miles to the east about Limoges. On 21 August the duke of Berry and his army joined du Guesclin and they immediately surrounded the city. Limoges was a municipality divided in two: the walled city, dominated by the cathedral and under the lordship of the bishop; and the town, walled and dominated by the castle with a strong English garrison. Berry made no attempt to assault or indeed to besiege the walled town but concentrated on the city and its small garrison, soon entering into negotiations with the bishop, Pierre du Cros, a friend of the prince. The city surrendered on 24 August almost certainly because of its inadequate garrison in the face of a sizeable army, and to protect the inhabitants and the cathedral. The garrison of the town took no part in this affair and the French departed the same day leaving a garrison of about 500 in the city. The prince reacted angrily to what he saw as the treachery of his friend the bishop and although bedridden, he accompanied his small army, carried on a litter. The army of about 1,000 men-at-arms, 1,000 mounted archers and some foot soldiers arrived outside the walls of Limoges on 14 September. He could not afford the time for a conventional siege so he mined the walls which were successfully fired on 19 September when a large breach opened in front of his troops, who swarmed into the city to plunder and to kill. It was estimated that some 3,000 people were in the city including the French garrison who fought bravely in the streets until finally overcome. The action ended, according to Froissart, with 'men, women and children begging for mercy from the prince on their knees but he was so inflamed with anger that he would not listen. Neither man nor woman was heeded, but all who could be found were put to the sword', and 'More than three thousand persons, men, women and children, were dragged out to have their throats cut.' The city itself was 'sacked without mercy, then burnt and utterly destroyed.[12]

This dramatic description might have been based on Chandos Herald's laconic sentence: 'But everyone there was killed or taken.' This probably refers to the French garrison only since no other source, not even the chronicles of the abbey of Saint-Martial in Limoges, mentions a massacre, though they do refer to 300 dead.[13] The massacre of the inhabitants of a stormed city was countenanced by the laws of war, such as they were in the Middle Ages.[14] Certainly this happened from time to time but the 'massacre' at Limoges, which is often quoted as an instance of the brutality and callousness of English soldiers of the day, is rightly questioned.[15] Nevertheless the siege at Limoges tarnished the Black Prince's reputation and he returned to England in 1371, a sick man, accompanied by his brother, the duke of Lancaster.

The fortunes of war did not favour England in the early 1370s. The decade began with Sir Robert Knollys' expedition which landed at Calais and looted and burnt its way to the gates of Paris where once again Charles V refused to let his army fight the English who, after burning the villages on the outskirts, marched away in disgust. Edward III had clearly failed to realize that the character of the war was changing. He could certainly send his commanders rampaging through France on *chevauchée,* and indeed planned to do so again, but France was no longer on the defensive. Charles V, while avoiding the challenge of yet another Crécy or Poitiers, was determined to carry out an offensive policy and in Aquitaine did so by a number of small operations aimed at vulnerable English positions where loyalty to England was questionable. These quick raids were very difficult to counter along the new long frontiers of Aquitaine, and almost impossible to prevent as du Guesclin showed when he took Poitiers in 1372 and most of Poitou soon after. England suffered yet another set-back when the mayor of La Rochelle overpowered the English garrison and opened its gates to du Guesclin in June; as the French gradually tightened their grip on Aquitaine the Saintonge declared for France. England's problem was that she did not have enough loyal troops to garrison all the important places adequately.

In an effort to retrieve the situation Edward sent the earl of Pembroke, his newly appointed lieutenant, to Aquitaine with reinforcements and sufficient money to pay the garrisons, but they were attacked at sea on their way to Bordeaux. Castilian galleys caught the convoy in June 1373 off La Rochelle and inflicted a disastrous defeat; Pembroke together with the reinforcements for the army in Aquitaine ended as prisoners in Spain and the army's pay was sent to the bottom together with most of his fleet. An account in the *Chronique des Quatre Preimers Valois*[16] says that the English fleet was at anchor by La Rochelle when the Castilian galleys first hove in sight. The English immediately sallied out to engage the Castilians, but the tide was on the turn, it was getting dark and so they returned to their anchorage by La Rochelle. Pembroke gave orders that they would again sally out at high tide when he expected the Castilians to close with them. However the Castilian commander ordered his galleys to attack the English at first light at low tide. This is exactly what happened; the larger ships presumably were on the mud until the tide rose, while the Castilian galleys, being shallow-draft vessels could manoeuvre at will. The galleys attacked with fire and oil setting fire to most of the English ships and after a fierce fight Pembroke surrendered. This was a severe blow for English Aquitaine where Pembroke was expected to take the offensive. However it shows the importance of the prince's earlier Castilian campaign in the wider context of the war at sea.

After an abortive expedition in 1372, an army of about 6,000 men,[17] half of whom were archers, was mustered and transported across to Calais in July 1373 where foreign volunteers joined them. The army, under the command of John of Gaunt, duke of Lancaster,

set out on 4 August 1373; he was accompanied by the earls of
Stafford, Suffolk and Warwick, and among the eight bannerets, all
experienced soldiers, was Sir Hugh Calveley. Jean de Montfort, duke
of Brittany, joined the expedition with his retinue of 299 men-at-arms
and 300 archers, the largest foreign contingent.

The aim of Lancaster's *chevauchée* was twofold: first to reinforce
Aquitaine; and secondly to bring the French to a decisive battle.
Consequently the final destination was to be Bordeaux but its route was
to be bound by two factors: the army was to go where it could feed and
forage itself; and to go via sensitive areas, which the French might be
tempted to defend with a field army. Herein lay the two factors which
ultimately ensured that the expedition failed to achieve its objects in full.
The army was fully mounted and could have marched 20 to 30 miles a
day, but because it started out from Calais and marched towards Paris it
had to cover ground that had often been devastated by English armies
before, most recently by Sir Robert Knollys. Consequently it was
unlikely that food and forage for the army in the area would be
available. Therefore, like Edward III's expedition to Rheims in 1359–60,
it had to take its initial supplies with it in a wagon train, which, at most,
could only manage 10 miles a day. However the planners had forgotten
or ignored this factor when they planned the expedition and failed to
include a siege train because it would slow the army down, though no
more so than the wagon train that they had included. This was a real
error of judgement since the French were content to shut themselves up
in their walled cities until the danger had passed.

Lancaster's army therefore made its slow, ponderous way through
Artois, Picardie and Champagne, then through Burgundy, past
Auxerre and Nevers to the Auvergne, down the valley of the River
Allier. The army was shadowed the whole way by Philippe who never
offered battle but who was quick to cut off stragglers and foraging
parties. The English army meanwhile thoroughly devastated the
countryside, burning and looting where they could. By November
Lancaster's army was east of the Puy de Dôme near Clermont and
Philippe had marched away to Paris. The English still had to cross the
mountains of the Auvergne, a cold and barren land in winter, before
they could reach Aquitaine. They turned west, and came out of the
mountains, down the valley of the Dordogne and finally marched into
Bordeaux on Christmas eve, a bedraggled and starving army
marching on its feet but still well disciplined.

What had this *Grande Chevauchée* achieved and at what cost? The army that reached Bordeaux twenty weeks after leaving Calais and after a march of some 550 miles was about 4,000 strong, having lost a third of its strength from casualties, sickness and desertion, and virtually all its horses. The expedition cost the government about £82,250 for wages and transportation across the Channel, plus a further £13,623 3s 4d in gifts and loans to John de Monfort.[18] It had failed to bring the French to battle and it failed to redress the declining situation in Aquitaine or relieve the pressure in Brittany; it also failed to take any town or city of importance. Nonetheless it did bring some much-needed reinforcements into Bordeaux, although many of the survivors took passage to England as soon as they could afford it. In chivalrous terms Lancaster's exploit was much admired by friend and foe alike and he ended his campaign with enhanced prestige. But his army, which had gained a great deal of booty during the march, had had to abandon most of it before they got to Bordeaux where they arrived penniless and in poor shape.

The English had failed to understand that the day of the *chevauchée* was over and that war in the south had become a defensive war; the devastation of land, farms, villages and towns and the collection of plunder, the English way of total war, no longer achieved political results. This was not attractive to the adventurous knights and professional soldiers who expected to make their fortunes out of the *chevauchées*. They were not interested in service for purely defensive operations without booty, within what was called friendly territory, and so volunteers were not so forthcoming as once they had been, and since they expected good pay they were expensive. Even so, despite this restriction profits could still be made by astute and unscrupulous men in authority such as William Latimer, who was accused by the 'Good Parliament' of 1376 of extorting £83,000[19] in Brittany between 1369 and 1371. However, notwithstanding the occasional profit made by individuals, the government at home was disenchanted with the war and none too keen on war expenditure – people at home were beginning to complain of the heavy burden of tax levied for a war without profit.

John of Gaunt's *chevauchée* was the last important English campaign of the decade. By 1373 the French had reduced English Aquitaine to a mere strip along the Biscay coast from Bordeaux to Bayonne; even the Albret lands had gone over to France and the great fortress of La Réole had been taken. In the north, England held on to Calais and Cherbourg, while in Brittany she retained only Brest and Auray. With the exception of these ports along the French seaboard, all Edward III's gains in his long war with France were reduced to less than he had held when the conflict began, and none of his political ambitions had been achieved. Edward in his dotage took less and less interest in government and was by now incapable of taking an active part in the war himself. Furthermore, with the exception of John of Gaunt, duke of Lancaster, all his famous captains who might have restored the situation were either dead or, like their sovereign, too old to lead a campaign. Nevertheless, his ambitions remained and he pursued his claim for sovereignty in Aquitaine through the courts, arguing the feudal ramifications of his case within the details of the treaty of Brétigny. By 1375 both England and France were thoroughly tired of the endless war and after protracted negotiations Lancaster agreed a two-year truce at Bruges. Jean de Montfort greeted this truce with some dismay – he was leading an Anglo-Breton army in Brittany in an attempt to re-establish himself there and his expedition was cut short by the truce. The truce was also unpopular in England, a country used to military success in France, because it failed to honour any of Edward's achievements agreed in the Treaty of Brétigny. Nevertheless the truce recognized the status quo in France at the time and was no doubt accepted in England as inevitable following the general failure of English arms over the past five years. Indeed the truce was a sad epilogue to a period of great English military endeavour and must have been a huge disappointment for Edward III who died on 21 June 1377 the year after his son, the Black Prince.

Chapter 12

The Tyrant and the Usurper

'The French want to pay us out of what is already ours'[1]

Before Edward died he planned one more expedition to France to set out as soon as the truce was over at the end of June. This was to be Richard's, now the prince of Wales, introduction to the glories of war; the expedition was to be commanded by Lancaster and to include Jean de Montfort and Thomas of Woodstock, the earl of Buckingham. The expedition included some 2,000 men-at-arms and the same number of mounted archers; seventy ships were pressed for its transportation and protection;[2] but the expedition was cancelled on Edward's death. Richard II, son of the Black Prince, succeeded his grandfather at the age of ten but obviously was not yet ready to rule. In the absence of a ruling monarch a regency council appointed by parliament and headed by Lancaster directed the government. Lancaster's two younger brothers agreed to serve on this council and a regent was not appointed. Meanwhile across the Channel the French had also planned offensive operations to be carried out as soon as the two-year truce was over. These plans included a resumption of raids on the south coast of England, which began within a few days of Edward's death.

A Franco-Castilian fleet burnt and plundered Rye and Hastings and later landed on and devastated the Isle of Wight; they also attacked the fishing fleet at Yarmouth. These attacks brought fears of a French invasion and the government was under pressure in parliament to protect the coast. Unfortunately, there were no seaworthy king's ships available to counter this activity. Suitable ships had to be arrested and then converted to warships. This took time and money, but by September over 150 ships lying in the Thames[3] had been taken into royal service. In due course Buckingham sailed with a fleet to clear the seas in November and returned in January having put a relief garrison into Brest and having failed to meet the Franco-Castilian fleet.

In England the prosecution of the war no longer remained the first priority of the regency council or of parliament and thoughts turned towards peace, when an event took place which affected relations between England and France, and indeed between England and Scotland. Two popes were elected in 1378, one in Rome, Urban VI, and another in Avignon, Clement VII, thus producing a schism in the Church. The schism ensured that relatively neutral and impartial mediation between the two most powerful military nations in the Western world was no longer possible, each Pope now canvassed both diplomatic and military support among the princes of Western Christendom. France and Scotland gave their support to the Pope in Avignon while England supported the Pope in Rome. Peace could no longer be pursued through the good offices of the Pope at a time when both major contestants were feeling their way to a rapprochement. Indeed a French proposal, which might have secured peace, the betrothal of Richard II to a Valois princess, was rejected by Richard's councillors under the influence of the papal authority in Rome.

Notwithstanding the increasing desire for peace after Edward III's death, the French raids on the south coast stirred parliament into action. There was a need for ships and for improved security at English bases across the Channel. While objecting to pay for war overseas, Parliament agreed to provide the necessary funds by the imposition in 1378 of a graded poll tax. The lowest band of this tax set at 4d per annum was a heavy imposition on serfs who earned no money, and by their very station in life were forbidden to seek employment beyond the manor where they worked. The poll tax precipitated the peasants' revolt of 1381 which began in the summer in Kent under the leadership of Wat Tyler and ended in London. The peasants, who were well armed and included many soldiers from the French wars, burned several manors and Lancaster's palace of Savoy before storming the Tower of London where they killed the archbishop of Canterbury. They then demanded to see the king. Richard, accompanied by several men-at-arms, met them at Smithfield and there the Lord Mayor killed Tyler and the mob was dispersed.

The war meanwhile dragged on. England sent reinforcements to Gascony in 1378 and 1379 but no offensive operations were undertaken. In December parliament agreed to underwrite an army of 4,000 men under de Montfort's command in Brittany, but this army, reduced to 1,300 men because finance was not forthcoming, never reached its destination. Having embarked at Southampton in December it was scattered by gales, which wrecked most of the ships.[4] In the winter of 1380–81 the council sent Buckingham on *chevauchée* from Calais but this failed to achieve anything of note, either politically or militarily. This parliament while being prepared to grant funds for home defence and the war at sea, was not prepared to raise taxes for the war in France. Consequently English garrisons in France were no longer paid adequately and had to rely on *pâtis* and ransoms for their sustenance, an unpopular practice.

Charles V died in 1380 and his son Charles VI, who succeeded, was a minor. Thus councils dominated by royal dukes ruled both monarchies. In 1382 France had to deal with a troublesome peasantry, caused as in England by the imposition of heavy taxes. In Flanders the burghers of Ghent under Philip van Artevelde defeated count Louis de Male and overran the province. Count Louis appealed for help to his son-in-law, Philippe of Burgundy and van Artevelde did likewise to Richard. The latter was prepared to lead an army into Flanders but was thwarted by parliament, which was not prepared to provide the necessary funds. Philippe, in contrast, used French troops to defeat the burghers at Roosebeke in November. Count Louis died the following year and Philippe of Burgundy became the count of Flanders. England had lost an opportunity but tried to retrieve the situation the following year. In April, urged on by Pope Urban VI, Henry Despenser, bishop of Norwich, landed at Calais on 'crusade' against the anti-pope of Avignon with about 2,000 men and invaded Flanders. This was actually a hard-headed decision by the English government to do something about the situation in Flanders after the battle of Roosebeke. Also, they were concerned with the possible disruption of the wool trade. But the government was in no position to mount a royal expedition to Flanders though that is what the country, and particularly the merchants, wanted. The bishop had some minor success and then laid siege to Ypres before hastily withdrawing to Gravelines for evacuation before a large French army. This, the last excursion from England across the Channel in the 1380s, achieved absolutely nothing and Bishop Henry Despenser was impeached on his return to England.

In 1385 the Scots poured over the border at the east march, aided and abetted by the French. This may have been the Scottish contribution to French plans for a joint Franco-Scottish invasion of

England, since it was clear that the French were gathering their forces at Sluys for an invasion across the Channel. In response Lancaster persuaded Richard to divert his attention from France to Scotland and to defeat the Scots before the French were ready. Richard, who had just reached his majority, had been granted generous funds by the autumn parliament of 1384 for an expedition to the Continent in 1385, with the proviso that if he decided to use the grant for an expedition elsewhere, the grant itself would be halved. However, as he intended to deal with Scotland before France was ready to invade he announced the call-up of the feudal levy, something that had not been done since 1327. This would reduce the cost of the army to him, but also, realizing that large numbers would not answer the call, he would collect scutage from the absconders, a sum of about £12,000. However the parliament of 1383[5] forced Richard to withdraw this levy. In the event an army of about 4,500 men-at-arms and about 9,000 archers was raised, mainly by contract.

In due course the army crossed the border on a 6-mile front, destroying everything in its path, and marched to Edinburgh, where they burnt Holyrood and the abbeys of Melrose and Newbattle; they then returned to England two weeks after they had first crossed the border. The expedition achieved nothing and seems to have had no political aim except perhaps to boost Richard's standing with a mainly warlike nobility and to overawe the Scots. It certainly did not reduce the Scots' capacity to wage war across the border.

The French meanwhile were pressing ahead with their invasion plans and the population in the south of England and in London went in real fear of a French invasion, well knowing what it portended for them. However, the government was confident enough of its ability to defeat any invasion on land for it to make plans to destroy the invasion fleet after it had disembarked the army, leaving it with no means of escape. Perhaps it was fortunate that their confidence was never put to the test. The French had gathered an army of 30,000 at Sluys for the invasion and some 1,200 boats of various sorts to take them across the Channel. In the end they delayed their invasion because Philippe of Burgundy fell ill and the invasion was finally cancelled in November because fine weather for the crossing could not be guaranteed at that time of year.

Following Richard's Scottish campaign, events in Portugal influenced the political scene in England. The duke of Lancaster, after his first wife died, married Constanza, daughter of the deposed king Pedro of Castile and consequently, on Pedro's death, had a legitimate claim to the Castilian throne. However, he had never pressed his claim largely because during Edward III's dotage and the Black Prince's illness he was needed at home, and when Richard ascended the throne he was wanted to lead the regency council. But when Richard reached his majority in 1385 and established his own council, Lancaster was free to pursue his ambitions in Spain, which Richard encouraged. Richard himself was proving to be a capricious and intolerant ruler, gathering about him a group of favourites who were both grasping and dishonest. In the same year an event in the peninsula offered Lancaster the opportunity to intervene in Iberian politics. King James of Portugal defeated the Castilians at the Battle of Aljubarotta in Portugal and Lancaster decided that the time had come for him to make his bid for the crown of Castile. In 1386 Lancaster sailed for Galicia in north-west Spain with an army having arranged with Richard for a loan from the treasury of 20,000 marks and the transportation of his army, all to be repaid when his kingdom had been won. Unfortunately this was the very time when the French were once more making a determined effort to gather the necessary forces to invade England.

Although the invasion force never actually sailed, both Richard and parliament regretted Lancaster's absence at a time when they needed his advice and leadership; indeed, it was a blunder of some magnitude. Feeling against the government for the inept way it had handled affairs in France and for exposing the country to the risk of French invasion grew. This, coupled with corruption by Richard's officials, culminated in demands by the autumn parliament for the dismissal and impeachment of Michael de la Pole, the chancellor, who was held generally responsible. However, Pole's impeachment – he had recently been made earl of Suffolk by Richard – reflected dissatisfaction with the financing and finances of the royal household and Richard's use of the signet to by-pass the normal procedures for obtaining finance from the treasury. Of course, Suffolk's willingness to do the king's bidding in matters normally subject to parliament's approval aggravated the case against him, and Suffolk was charged among other things with malversation of crown revenue and maladministration.

But perhaps the main charge against Suffolk, which he refuted, was that he had failed the people of Ghent when they had asked for help following the Battle of Roosebeke in 1382. Like the other cloth cities in Flanders Ghent had been involved in a long struggle for independence from its French overlord, Louis de Male, who owed allegiance to the French crown. When de Male died he was succeeded by his son-in-law, Philippe of Burgundy, a prince of France, who was determined to enforce his authority on the cities of Flanders. The Battle of Roosebeke, in November 1382, seemed to have settled the issue and the Treaty of Tournay was signed with the duke of Burgundy on 18 December while the ambassadors of Ghent were still in London, and consequently English help was never sent. The main result of the capitulation of Ghent and the occupation of Bruges and Ypres by Burgundian forces was that it had an immediate and adverse effect on England's wool trade, and Suffolk was held to blame.

Nevertheless, Philippe of Burgundy, the victor of Roosebeke, was not slow to realize that Flanders' economy depended in large part on the continuation of the wool trade with England, and consequently he took a less belligerent view of England's support for the citizens of the cloth cities. Suffolk was imprisoned and parliament reorganized the administration of the royal household in October; the transfer of funds from the exchequer to the royal household without parliamentary approval then ceased. Parliament appointed a 'continual council' to govern for a year against the king's wishes. As Keen said: 'the first great crisis of the reign had commenced.'[6]

This crisis divided the governance of the land between a 'war party', headed by Buckingham, recently made duke of Gloucester and the earl of Arundel, the senior members of the continual council, and a 'peace party' headed by Richard himself and supported by Robert de Vere, earl of Oxford. The peace party had its origins and motives in Suffolk's realization that the war was bankrupting the crown and peace was essential. However the war party, currently in the ascendant, reflected the views of the majority in the country.

Richard having protested to parliament that the formation of the council ran contrary to the royal prerogative and the law of the land, and with the example of Edward III before him as precedent, left Westminster and set up an alternative council, with Suffolk, Oxford, Burley and others. In the summer of 1387, Richard and his advisers put certain questions to a group of judges, including the Chief Justice of the Common Pleas, concerning the legal position of the royal prerogative. As a result, the law of treason was extended to include those who obstructed the king in the exercise of his royal authority. Treason, formerly a crime of armed disloyalty to the crown, had now become a political crime and consequently peaceful opposition to the policies of the government, or in other words to the king, became a dangerous game.

These judgements quite clearly challenged parliamentary authority in its dealings with the crown, and carried with it the threat of forfeiture of land and execution for treason of those opposed to the king's policies, but not in arms against him. Accordingly when Richard returned to Westminster in November, Gloucester, Arundel and Warwick gathered their retinues and confronted the king 'appealing' five of his favourites to answer a charge of treason because they had exercised undue authority over the king. This charge fell within the meaning of treason as it had been in the time of Edward II. In due course Henry Bolingbroke, earl of Derby and Lancaster's son, and Mowbray, earl of Nottingham, joined the original appellants. Those appealed would be held under arrest until the next parliament, but de Vere escaped and gathered an army in Cheshire of between four and five thousand men to aid the king. De Vere's army was scattered on its way to London by the forces of the appellants at Radcot Bridge on 20 December.[7]

Before matters could proceed parliament made a solemn declaration that the lords in parliament took precedence over all other courts of law in the kingdom and that therefore the lords in parliament were within their right to judge the charge. The five, the earls of Oxford and Suffolk, Archbishop Neville, Sir Robert Tressilian the Chief Justice of the King's Bench and Sir Nicholas Brembre, a former Lord Mayor of the City of London, were duly found guilty of treason. Tressilion and Brembre were executed, the others fled the country; a further five of Richard's supporters were impeached for treason and found guilty, four of whom were executed. This purge of the king's favourites put the king on a collision course with the appellants and he was determined to exact his revenge in due course.

Although the war party was now in the ascendant it was failing to prosecute the war with any real success. In 1388 Lancaster returned from Spain having failed in his bid for the crown of Castille but having come to an accommodation with Juan of Trastamara, the king, by betrothing his daughter to Juan's heir. Gloucester and Arundel meanwhile tried once more to take the offensive against

France. This time they successfully recruited Jean de Montfort to their enterprise but de Montfort backed down on hearing that Lancaster, who was the king's lieutenant in Aquitaine, refused to go onto the offensive in the south-west of France. Arundel returned home from Brittany to the disappointment and ire of parliament having simply raided Isle d'Oleron off La Rochelle.

Disappointment in war continued for the council, this time in the north of England. The Scots crossed the border in the east under Douglas and in the west under Fife. Douglas penetrated beyond the Tyne and was surprised by Hotspur, the earl of Northumberland's eldest son, at night near Otterburn. Douglas lost his life in the confused fighting which followed but the earl of Dunbar came up with the main Scottish army and defeated Hotspur's army, taking him prisoner before returning across the border. Notwithstanding Gloucester's and Arundel's continuing view that war with France was of the first priority, parliament was tired of subsidizing failure, and negotiations for a truce with France were begun before the end of the year. A truce was agreed and signed at Leulinghen in June 1389 for three years and was later renewed for a further period while ways were explored for a permanent peace.

At home Lancaster provided a calming influence on the political scene where Richard now ruled in his own right; he chose an experienced council to aid and advise him. Nevertheless the bitterness and feuds caused by the political troubles of 1387–8 still simmered beneath the surface; so much so that Richard was forced to promise in council that he would not harm any lord for things done in the past. But he was a wilful and fickle tyrant and no one trusted him to keep his word. Richard's promise provided no security for the appellants and those associated with them, or for any who had opposed him before. The problem was made worse by Richard's Francophile views, which placed many who favoured war with France in opposition to the king.

In France similar problems arose. Charles VI came to the throne in 1380 aged eleven, and the governance of France passed to the regent, his uncle Louis, duke of Anjou, and a Council of State of fifty members, with an inner council of twelve. In 1382 Anjou gave up his position as regent and left France for Naples, where he had been declared king by Pope Clement. His two brothers, Jean, duke of Berry, and Philippe, duke of Burgundy, together with their cousin the duke

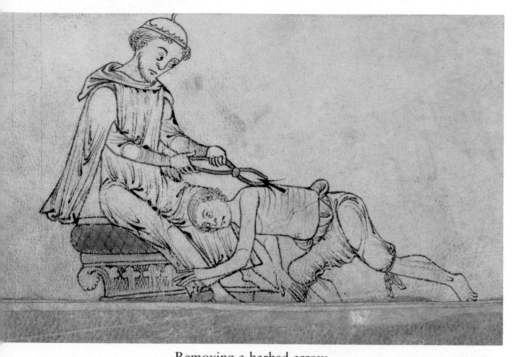

Removing a barbed arrow

A Scottish position in the Weardale Campaign

The Battle of Sluys

The Battle of Crécy. A stylized and inaccurate view of the battle by a fifteenth-century painter showing mainly that the chief men were present

The Battle of Crécy. Another stylized
impression of the battle; note the cannon

The chief citizens of Calais handing over the
key of the city to Edward III after its surrender

The Battle of Poitiers. The Prince of Wales
did not meet King Jean in battle on foot

Looting. The usual practise of an army after
a successful siege and during a *chevauchée*

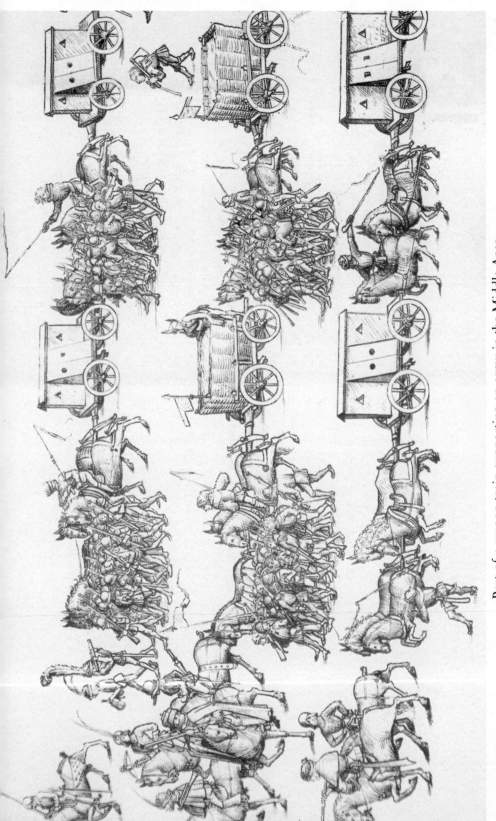

Part of a wagon train supporting an army in the Middle Ages

The Battle of Agincourt, as depicted by an artist shortly after the battle

The siege of the English castle of Montague on the Gironde by the French

The Yorkist army forcing the Lancastrians
across the river Cock at the Battle of Towton

Yorkist Archers in action at the Battle of Towton

The Charge by Richard III and his knights against Henry Tudor at Bosworth Field

of Bourbon, soon gathered the reins of power into their own hands. Young King Charles, in accordance with the wishes of his father, although only thirteen years old, came of age the same year but still remained very dependent on his uncles and to all practical purposes left the governance of France in their hands. In 1385 Charles married Isabella of Bavaria and in 1388 the council finally handed power over to Charles, then nineteen. His first act was to dismiss his royal uncles from his council and to replace them with his father's ministers – as in England the king and his council wanted peace.

The problem remained of how to turn the wish into fact. Both kings recognized that the key to the problem lay in Aquitaine and the vexed dilemma of sovereignty. A solution seemed to lie with Lancaster who had been made duke of Aquitaine for life by Richard in 1390. If Charles were to recognize this appointment and Lancaster established his own line of hereditary dukes in Aquitaine, giving homage directly to the kings of France, then the problem might well have been solved. However, there were also territorial problems. It seems that France was prepared to cede lands in Aquitaine provided Calais and lands elsewhere were returned. But as Gloucester remarked:

The French want to pay us out of what is already ours ... if Calais and the other lands which they are demanding were given back to them they would be masters of all their maritime frontiers and all our conquests would be lost.[8]

Even Richard baulked at the return of Calais, for he had returned Cherbourg to the new king of Navarre in 1393 who then promptly sold it on to the French. The loss of both Calais and Cherbourg would leave the whole of the eastern Channel open to French pirates and expose the south coast of England to the probability of raids whenever Anglo-French relations deteriorated. More importantly it would inevitably disrupt the wool trade on which so much of England's wealth depended, particularly since the wool staple was at Calais; it would also deny England a most important base from which to threaten the very heart of France. Long-term peace eluded the negotiators for the time being, nevertheless both Richard and Charles were determined to achieve it despite opposition in their kingdoms. Peace plans received a set-back in August 1392 when Charles went mad for the first time and power returned to the royal dukes.

According to Palmer,[9] the territorial issues had been solved, as had the problem of liege homage for Aquitaine, providing the plan to alienate the duchy to Lancaster and his heirs was accepted by all parties. However, the plan was vehemently opposed in parliament in January 1394, which Richard, having the means and the power, chose to ignore. But in Aquitaine the Gascons also firmly rejected this solution because by alienation of the duchy to Lancaster and his heirs it separated them from the crown of England. Richard sent Lancaster to Bordeaux with a small army of 1,500 men in November the same year in an unsuccessful attempt to overawe the Gascon *estates* and the principle barons. This failed and Richard was forced to recognize that the Gascons were greatly concerned about who held the 'proprietary right' over the duchy; this, in their view, should remain with the kings of England. Consequently the peace treaty foundered, once again, on the problem of the sovereignty of the duchy of Aquitaine.

Queen Anne died in 1384 leaving Richard free to remarry and when Richard married Charles VI's eldest daughter Isabella, a child of six, by proxy in 1396, it opened the possibility of peace through a dynastic alliance. Finally a long-term truce, to last for twenty-eight years, was signed in 1398. Richard had now achieved peace with France, but the issues that could once again lead the two countries to war remained. France was now, in royal eyes, a friend and no longer an enemy, though the war party in England, led by Gloucester, was still deeply suspicious. These suspicions were alerted when Richard, at his wedding near Calais, promised Charles that he would persuade the Church in England to support the Pope in Avignon in preference to the Pope in Rome. This was a grave error. Henceforth the church also opposed him in addition to the appellant lords, the war party and those opposed to the dynastic alliance with France. However, since the country was now at peace he was free of parliament's control of war finances and therefore of interference in his management of the treasury, and he could now turn his attention to matters at home.

As part of the wedding settlement Charles had agreed to provide a dowry of 800,000 livres for Isabella, but Richard was prepared to reduce this in exchange for a promise that Charles and his uncles Burgundy and Berry would agree to support him 'against all manner of folk ... and to sustain him with all their power against any of his own subjects.'[10] If this was accurately reported then it shows that Richard expected to face problems at home including armed rebellion; it also shows the extent to which Richard was prepared to go with his new-found friends against his own people to maintain himself in power. He had certainly not forgotten his humiliation at the hands of the Lords appellant, and they knew it; certainly his magnates and landowners expected trouble ahead. However his immediate problem lay in Ireland, where Irish chiefs were making life difficult. Richard landed at Wexford with a large army in 1394 and marched to Dublin. As in Scotland, this show of force overawed the Irish who melted away in front of him and Richard returned to London well satisfied with his military venture, having achieved nothing.

At home the political scene, which had been bubbling with unrest since the events of 1387–8 suddenly erupted. Thomas Haxey, a clerk in the king's service, presented a petition to the spring parliament of 1397. This, among other matters, complained that 'the great and excessive charge of the king's household be amended and diminished.'[11] This was virtually the same charge that had been brought by parliament in 1387 and, as at that time, Richard reacted with anger and a determination to put an end to parliament's interference with the royal prerogative and his regality. Haxey was charged with treason and the lords in parliament, at Richard's behest, endorsed the ruling of the judges in 1387 saying that 'if anyone … shall move or excite the commons of parliament or any other person to make remedy of any matter which touches our person or our government or our regality, he shall be held a traitor.'[12] There is a thought that the king himself put Haxey up to present his petition in order to clarify this aspect of the laws of treason before moving against the Appellants.[13] Haxey was condemned as a traitor early in February 1397 but was pardoned by the king himself in May of the same year.

Backed with this edict from the Lords, now the highest court in the land, Richard struck during the autumn parliament in 1397. Gloucester, Arundel and Warwick were arrested for allegedly plotting against the crown and were charged with treason, found guilty and all three were sentenced to death. Warwick's sentence was commuted to banishment to the Isle of Man, Arundel was beheaded and Gloucester, Richard's uncle, was murdered in prison in Calais, almost certainly on Richard's orders. Gloucester's estates were divided between the king's supporters. Richard was now firmly in the saddle and he took the opportunity to cow parliament into agreeing that henceforth it should hand over its power of restraint over the crown to a council appointed by the king himself. Having now usurped parliament's traditional role as a counterweight to an over-powerful monarch, it seemed that none could touch him, and the aristocracy, particularly the lords in parliament, went in fear of trumped-up treason charges and the subsequent forfeiture of their land and the loss of their heads. All in all, England was in a very unhappy state and for the moment war with France was far from people's minds.

The following year Richard was given the opportunity to settle old scores with the last two appellants. In January Bolingbroke appeared before the king in parliament and accused Mowbray of treasonable advances, which he alleged had been made to him the previous month. Richard decided that a special committee should investigate the allegations, and it was decided that it was a matter of honour to be decided by a judicial dual. However, as the contestants appeared before Richard at Coventry in September ready for combat, Richard stopped proceedings and banished both lords from the kingdom, Mowbray for life and Bolingbroke for ten years. Four months later, in February 1399, Lancaster died and Bolingbroke should have inherited his vast estates and fortune. But Richard was determined to prevent this and so by an alteration to the terms of appointment of the committee in 1398, it was recalled to consider the charge against Bolingbroke once again. This time they did Richard's bidding and banished Bolingbroke for life, disinheriting him of his father's lands, which consequently reverted to the crown, causing much unrest among the nobility. Shakespeare encapsulated it thus:

> Think what you will, we seize into our hands
> His plate, his goods, his money, and his lands.[14]

Problems in Ireland now attracted Richard's attention once again; the previous year the king's lieutenant was killed and Richard decided to crush the Celtic chieftains once and for all, and sailed for Ireland with a considerable army only two weeks after he had made the decision to confiscate Bolingbroke's estates. This was a grievous error, the country was in an unsettled mood and in fear of the king; Henry Bolingbroke, who was in Flanders, was determined to regain his lawful inheritance. While Richard was away in Ireland Henry landed on the Yorkshire coast with a band of friends and marched inland to Doncaster, where he was joined by the earl of Northumberland and his armed following. The Percys, as marcher lords, had what was virtually a private army paid for by the crown to secure the East March on the northern border, and this nucleus of an army was now committed to help Henry. From this point on Henry's support grew, while those who had supported Richard began to make themselves scarce or openly changed sides. Richard returned to Wales from Ireland early in August to retrieve the situation, but by the second week his cause looked doomed. Henry was in Chester with a sizeable army while Richard was virtually alone. Northumberland and Bishop Arundel met Richard at Conway to make demands on Henry's behalf. These included that his entire estate should be restored to him and that a parliament be summoned to legalize the matter. Furthermore, Richard should give up five named members of his council to parliament to face proceedings of impeachment. Richard had no choice but to agree. Richard was then escorted to Chester to meet Henry, but was taken in ambush on the way and made a prisoner.

Parliament was summoned in his name and Richard was imprisoned first at the Tower and then at Pontefract Castle, never to be seen in public again. He was deposed by parliament on 29 September 1399 and parliament withdrew its fealty to him the following day, strictly speaking, because the king was not present; these actions were taken by an assembly in parliament and not parliament itself. The same day, in the absence of a direct heir, Henry, as the son of John of Gaunt, duke of Lancaster, Edward III's third son, claimed the throne by blood and by conquest before an assembly of bishops and magnates in Westminster, a claim which was confirmed by parliament later. There was in fact another claimant living from a senior, though female line; he was the child Edmund Mortimer, earl of March, the great-grandson of Edward's second son, Lionel duke of Clarence, through the latter's daughter, Philippa. Sir Richard of Bordeaux, formerly king Richard II, died in Pontefract Castle on 14 February 1400, some say murdered on Henry's orders, others that he died of self-starvation.

The deposition of Richard was a turning point in the Hundred Years' War. Possibilities of peace had lain with Richard particularly through his marriage with Isabella of France, but he had been deposed without an heir. Isabella was only ten at the time. The long-term truce signed the previous year now looked unlikely to last a further year, let alone twenty-eight. Charles VI was more than concerned at the deposition of his son-in-law and although Queen Isabella was returned to

France in 1401, she went without her dowry. Relations with France were soured and England was in no way ready to renew the war.

Problems, including armed insurrection, confronted Henry IV from the very beginning of his reign. His first action, in 1400, was to summon Robert III of Scotland to do him homage; when this was ignored he invaded Scotland to no good purpose and little success. This rather unnecessary venture was presumably done in order to impress his barons who had backed him to the throne, however as he marched south from Scotland in September he went on to north Wales in a show of force. Here Owen Glendower, taking advantage of the unsettled conditions in England, had risen in rebellion. Glendower, supported by the Welsh in large numbers, burned Ruthin and other towns in the area, expelled English garrisons and declared himself prince of Wales. Henry again went into Wales with an army in 1402 but, as in the other Celtic countries, the Welsh gave way before him and Henry found himself entangled with an endless series of skirmishes and petty sieges; the decisive battle eluded him. During this first campaign Edmund Mortimer, earl of March, was captured by Glendower and offered for ransom, but Henry was content for Mortimer, a rival claimant for the throne of England, to remain a prisoner. Mortimer later married Glendower's daughter and joined the rebels. Meanwhile in the north, Harry Hotspur, the earl of Northumberland's son, defeated a Scottish raid led by Douglas and Fife at Homildon Hill in September 1402, thus securing the northern border for the time being.

Politics in England at that time were very much a matter of shifting alliances among the magnates and the king, and 1403 saw a significant change. The Percys and the Mortimers, lords of the marches with Scotland and Wales respectively, became allied when Mortimer's sister married Harry Hotspur. When Henry failed to pay Mortimer's ransom and to support his claim to the throne, Hotspur sought to help his brother-in-law by coming out in rebellion in Cheshire. Northumberland, irked by Henry's refusal to pay for his forays into southern Scotland and for his failure to pay his expenses as warden of the East March, decided to throw in his lot with his son.

Things were rapidly moving to crisis and Henry's crown no longer looked secure. Henry marched to Cheshire where he met and defeated Hotspur at Shrewsbury in July 1403 before either Northumberland's forces or those of Mortimer and Glendower could intervene. Hotspur was killed in the fighting and Northumberland, on hearing that both his son and his brother had been killed in the battle, submitted to the king at York, where he was stripped of his appointments and withdrew to his estates. The French sent a small force to aid the Welsh rebels in 1405 but Glendower was not finally defeated until 1410. Northumberland rebelled again in 1405 and was driven into exile in Scotland by his chief rival in the north, Rupert Neville, earl of Westmoreland and warden of the West March. He invaded the north of England from Scotland in 1408 but was defeated and killed at Bramham Moor by Henry's forces under the sheriff of York. With Northumberland's death Henry was at last secure on his throne and he was able to turn his attention to his greatest problem, lack of cash.

Somehow he had to increase the royal revenues which had dropped from those in Richard's early reign by about £26,000 annually[15] almost certainly due to falling customs duty on the wool trade because of the unsettled conditions in Flanders. He therefore entered into negotiations with Jean of Burgundy to find a mutually satisfactory solution. At home, Henry was wary of asking parliament for grants from taxation after his promises to reduce taxation on his accession, and he was therefore forced to remain on the defensive against France, notwithstanding French operations in Gascony, and raids against the Isle of Wight and the south coast. England retaliated with raids on the Normandy coast but Henry's government was not able to do more than cover the cost of the Calais garrison and of a fleet to prevent further French raids across the Channel. But despite his efforts he was finally forced to appeal to parliament for funds. Parliament agreed to provide sufficient finance to enable the king to embark on a more offensive policy, providing the king agreed to certain checks and impositions on the royal household and the king's government. Parliament's demands included that they should be allowed to appoint treasurers of war to supervise the spending of their specific grants and also, although they refrained from demanding to be able to approve nominations, that they expected to be informed of all appointments to the king's council. These demands, to which Henry agreed, passed yet more power from king to parliament as a result of the costs of war, but they ensured that Henry had the necessary financial resources to enable his government to prosecute the war with France.

Throughout this time Henry maintained the fiction that he was king of France, whereas, in contrast, Charles VI failed even to recognize him as the lawful king of England, let alone of France! Indeed Charles, in the absence of a recognized king in England, had appointed the Dauphin as duke of Aquitaine in 1402. This irritating and provoking appointment was made notwithstanding the fact that Henry believed that Aquitaine was his in full sovereignty by the treaty of Brétigny. He had already, legally, given the dukedom of Aquitaine to his son Henry, the prince of Wales, in liege homage in October 1399. As a result of the appointments of the two royal princes the Gascons now had a choice, but they remained loyal to their English duke and his overlord, the king of England. Sufficient of the magnates and cities in Aquitaine remained loyal to their English overlord to defend the duchy against invasion by the duke of Orleans, who was determined to prosecute the war against England, between 1402 and 1407. Indeed, at this time France was the more dominant of the two countries and it is possible that she could have driven the English out of Aquitaine if it were not for problems within France itself.

These problems concerned the prosecution of the war with England and the government of France. Orleans, together with the dukes of Berry and Bourbon, formed the war party and wished to conduct a more aggressive war policy, while Burgundy with his Flemish interests at heart was keen to promote peace with England to maintain the wool trade. Indeed Burgundy signed a mercantile truce with Henry in 1407, which relieved pressure on Calais and ensured the smooth working of the wool market, and thus the vital wool revenue for Henry. Both French parties did their best to finance themselves and their duchies from royal revenues and to reduce the royal domain during the periods of Charles's madness; both parties needed the power and prestige of France to back their private ventures, respectively, in Italy and the Low Countries. Things came to a head when Orleans was assassinated on Burgundy's orders in 1407 and civil war followed. Bernard, count of Armagnac, whose daughter married Orleans' son Charles, took up the challenge posed by the duke of Burgundy and consequently France became divided between the Armagnac faction and that of the Burgundians. Basically the Armagnacs held all of France south of the Loire, less Aquitaine, while the Burgundians held most of the north including the duchy and the county of Burgundy, Flanders and most of the Low Countries.

Brittany remained largely neutral in the quarrel, as did Normandy with her divided loyalties, but most importantly, at that time, Burgundy had the support of the citizens of Paris.

The Armagnacs put Paris under siege in 1411 and Burgundy appealed to Henry IV for English troops to raise the siege. Some 800 men-at-arms and 2,000 archers under Arundel landed at Calais and marched to Meulan where they joined Burgundy and his army; the combined army then stormed the Parisian stronghold of St Cloud, raising the siege. Arundel and his army returned to Calais and Burgundy drove the Armagnacs across the Loire. The following year England was again asked for help by the Armagnacs who offered to pay for English assistance. In due course an army, 4,000 strong, under Thomas, duke of Clarence, landed in Normandy and marched south to join the Armagnacs in Poitou but arrived too late to take any part in the French quarrel. Clarence then marched on to Bordeaux, burning and looting on the way; the English were finally bought off by the promise of payment of 210,000 gold crowns and handsome payments to individual commanders.

Earlier in 1412 the French royal dukes signed a treaty at Bourges, following the announcement by parliament in England that the duchy of Aquitaine was annexed to England and that the Gascons were subjects of the English crown. This treaty offered to restore Aquitaine 'to the king of England as his by hereditary right',[16] however this gift and others were not within their power to grant and the treaty was hardly worth the paper it was written on, though it inclined parliament and Henry to support the Armagnacs. Peace between the warring parties in France was short lived and was shattered in Paris in May 1413 when Burgundian supporters slaughtered those of Armagnac. Calm was eventually restored and the riots quelled. Prominent citizens appealed to the Armagnacs to bring their troops into the city to maintain order and in August the Dauphin, Louis, answered their call. Jean, duke of Burgundy, was forced to flee the city and took refuge in Flanders. France was now well and truly a divided nation; the Dauphin and the Armagnacs were firmly in control of Paris, Normandy and the south of France. But duke Jean was safe in Flanders plotting to divide France and extend his own domains with, if he could arrange it, the help of the English.

Henry IV died of leprosy on 20 March 1413, leaving a united country which had enjoyed domestic peace for some six years, though there were still undertones of opposition to the king centred about the person of Edmund Mortimer, earl of March. Henry also left the English possessions in France much as they had been when he came to power fourteen years previously. The war, though in a state of truce, was mildly active and England was well placed to face whatever problems the war might bring in the next reign. Financially and militarily she was in a better state to prosecute the war than France, and undoubtedly the payments to the commanders of Clarence's army by the Armagnacs made the greedy English eager to resume the war. Furthermore, the young James, heir to the throne of Scotland, was taken prisoner at sea on his way to France, putting England in a strong position vis-à-vis France's ally Scotland, which to a certain extent closed the door at England's back should she decide to take action across the Channel.

The new king of England, the 25-year-old Henry V, a proven commander in the field and an able administrator, was keen to cross the Channel and emulate the deeds of his great grandfather. France on the other hand was split between two hostile factions with a mad king, divided nobility, finances in disarray and a hesitant heir to the throne. The stage was set for dramatic events – if ever there was a time for England to seize the initiative and establish her hereditary rights within France, it was now, and Henry V soon made it clear that this was exactly what he intended to do.

Chapter 13

The Agincourt Campaign

'and behold a white horse: and he that sat on him had a bow; and a crown was given unto him: and he went forth conquering, and to conquer.'[1]

When Henry V came to the throne on the death of his father in March 1413 the political scene was, for the Middle Ages, relatively settled. The king's council and parliament worked well together and the relative powers and areas of influence of these two bodies were well defined. Trade was booming and the country prospered. Abroad, confrontation with France over Aquitaine had quietened, largely due to the civil war between the Armagnacs and the Burgundians. France was in no position to press the king of England over the vexed question of the sovereignty of the province. Indeed English armies had recently been solicited for their help in France, first to one side then the other. The northern border had been quiet ever since March 1406 when the young king of Scots, James I, was taken prisoner on his way to France. In this favourable setting Henry V soon made it known that he intended to claim his 'rightful inheritance', the crown of France. The majority of his nobles and the Church gave him their backing. All seemed set fair for him to achieve his ambition.

But it was essential that, if he should venture abroad, he should leave a quiet and contented country behind him. This in effect meant that the nobility should support him wholeheartedly. Unfortunately there remained a small number of disaffected but influential barons from his father's reign, who might be encouraged to take advantage of his absence abroad. These peers or their families had had their land taken from them or been dishonoured in other ways by Henry's father when he usurped the throne from Richard II. They had either supported Richard, or if they were supporters of Henry Bolingbroke they had only supported him to regain his inheritance and not to seize the throne. Henry V on his accession made a generous gesture to these people. His first act was to grant the earl of March full title to the family lands. He then restored Hotspur's son, the late earl of Northumberland's grandson, to the family title and lands, and followed this by restoring Thomas Holland to the title and lands of his father John, earl of Huntingdon, who had been summarily beheaded in December 1399. His next act was to remove the stigma against the house of York, recorded in parliament in 1399; the old duke of York had been in charge of the government at the time that Henry Bolingbroke landed in England and had opposed him. This astute move made his son, Edward, duke of York, a staunch supporter. These acts of generosity converted potential troublemakers into friends and allies. Henry clearly intended to rule with the solid backing of a contented nobility and to this end he elevated his brothers, John and Humphrey, to the dukedoms of Bedford and Gloucester respectively, and made Richard Langley, York's younger brother, earl of Cambridge. Finally, to extirpate the past, he had the body of Richard II disinterred from its grave at Langley and re-buried with much pomp, at Westminster.

It was equally important that Henry should leave a settled border with Scotland before turning on France. To this end he kept Murdoch, the young earl of Fife and son of the duke of Albany, regent of Scotland, a prisoner in the Tower together with the young James I. Consequently he was in a position to force a renewal of the truce of 1414 with the Scots to last for a year. Additionally he appointed his brother John, duke of Bedford, as a warden of the Scottish march together with Ralph Neville, earl of Westmoreland. He also began a programme of reinforcing the garrisons of the marcher castles and repairing them where necessary.

With matters at home now settled Henry turned his attention to France. The quarrel between England and France had simmered down over the past six years and if Henry wished to fan the flames he needed a cause. This cause had to be sufficiently grave for him to be able to demand justice from the French, and sufficiently plausible for him to be able to persuade parliament to support him. Providing the French rejected his demands and parliament found them just he could go to war, and if parliament agreed that his quarrel was just they would find the necessary finance. The cause of course was to be the age-old one of the sovereignty of Aquitaine, to which was added the dukedom of Normandy and all the other territories of the old Angevin empire, as well as the crown of France itself. These were preposterous claims, but were largely those set out in the Treaty of Brétigny in 1360, which France had signed but never implemented and now rejected out of hand. Furthermore, they said that Henry, as the son of a usurper, had no valid claim even to the dukedom of Aquitaine. Nevertheless Henry had made his bid and began negotiations to achieve them. He maintained diplomatic relations with both sides in France's internal quarrel, favouring first one side and then the other, promising either aid or neutrality, and all the time forcing the French to improve their offers in answer to his ambitious claims.

Events in France helped Henry considerably. The peace of Auxerre between the Armagnacs and the Burgundians had dashed English hopes of concessions, cemented by Clarence's expedition in aid of the Armagnacs in 1412, and had left Duke Jean of Burgundy in control of Paris. But in 1413 riots in the capital forced Jean to flee and civil war broke out again leaving the Armagnacs in control of Paris and the government. The civil war raged through Picardy and Flanders until August 1414 when peace was agreed at Arras. Both sides now made overtures to Henry hoping to enlist his aid in their quarrel and Henry was content to keep them both on a string. At one point it was suggested that Henry might marry Jean's daughter allowing the Burgundians, with his help, to settle the French quarrel once and for all.

Meanwhile a truce was arranged in January 1414 between Henry and the Armagnac government in Paris so that negotiations over Henry's claims could continue. These negotiations now included the hand of Charles VI's daughter, Katherine, in marriage and a colossal dowry of a million crowns in addition to the old claims of title and land. The Armagnacs were willing to meet many of Henry's demands but they were not prepared to provide such a large dowry. The fact is that the Armagnacs needed a neutral England as a temporary measure as they concluded their civil war with the Burgundians. Henry, on the other hand, wanted war as soon as possible while the French were still distracted by their internal troubles. The truce between Henry and the Armagnacs was extended to August 1415 but it was nothing more than a smoke screen behind which Henry prepared for war.

While the negotiations dragged on, Henry mobilized his resources. In the autumn of 1414 he convinced parliament of the justness of his

cause and parliament duly voted him the necessary funds. His aim
was no less than the conquest and occupation of Normandy on a
permanent basis as a necessary preliminary to his claim to the throne
of France, and if necessary security for the future sovereignty of his
duchy of Aquitaine. To do this he first had to assemble a fleet to both
transport his army across the channel and to supply it once across,
and he then had to gather an army that could both travel fast and
undertake a siege. He would need soldiers to garrison captured towns
and fortresses, and an artillery siege train to batter castle walls and to
bombard towns; he needed artisans able to construct siege engines on
site and a baggage train capable of carrying all the assorted stores
necessary to conduct a siege. This army also had to have a highly
mobile element to carry out the conquest of Normandy and to
threaten Paris if not the whole of northern France. His strategic
purpose deemed that he should have what was to be in effect a regular
army, available for field and garrison duties throughout the year and
able to conduct a campaign in the winter months when the largely
mercenary armies of the French and Burgundians would have been
dispersed. In order to achieve this he would have to provide regular
pay and reinforcements for the army and ensure that sufficient
supplies were always available.[2] This needed adequate financing on a
guaranteed basis, something which parliament had just granted him,
but which his predecessors in England had never experienced and
which his French enemies had always failed to achieve.

Once finance was assured, indentures were sent out to recruit both
mounted and foot archers, men-at-arms, gunners and artisans. In all a
force of between 10,000 and 12,000 men was to be mustered. About
10,000 of them would have been soldiers, including engineers and
miners, and most would have been mounted. The army's tail would
include upwards of 2,000 administrators and craftsmen such as
smiths, armourers, bowyers, fletchers, carpenters, saddlers, surgeons
and waggoners, as well as the wagons needed to carry them all, and
the guns, powder and shot. He issued instructions to the warden of
the Tower of London to prepare guns, siege engines, powder and
stone shot. Orders were sent to sheriffs of counties and the aldermen
of cities and towns to make bows, arrows, bow-strings, swords and
other weapons for his army; these would in fact be reserve stores as all
the retinues would come fully armed. His preparations for war, begun
in April 1415, were complete by the end of July. Notwithstanding his

own duplicity he told a French embassy that he had tried to find common ground with the French about his just demands but had been frustrated by the dishonesty of France.

While negotiations were continuing and as part of his preparations for war he sent orders to his admirals and to the sheriffs to arrest suitable ships to be assembled at Southampton by 1 August 1415.[3] This was a process that might take up to three months; many of the ships had to be modified for war and had to have war crews put aboard. Altogether some 1,500[4] ships gathered in Southampton and the adjacent waters to transport his army to France, the majority of them being hired from Holland and Zeeland;[5] even this large number was not enough and orders were sent out for more. In the event there were insufficient ships and some of the troops had to be transported in a second wave. Embarkation took three weeks under Henry's personal supervision and the armada sailed on Sunday 11 August. Henry embarked at Porchester on the *Trinity Royal*, a large, newly launched ship of 540 tons with a crew of 300 sailors and soldiers.[6] The fleet was escorted across the Channel by three large warships, six barges and six balingers.[7] All seemed set fair.

However the assembly and embarkation of his expeditionary force suddenly took second place in Henry's priorities at that time. All was not as peaceful as it seemed at home; there were still influential people who resented his position as king, people who supported Richard II or the closest survivor to Richard of the blood royal, the young earl of March. These people saw Henry V as an unlawful sovereign, being the son of the usurper Henry Bolingbroke. Unbeknown to Henry, a plot to kill him before he sailed for France was quietly hatched. The earl of March suddenly requested an audience of the king at Porchester, where Henry was quartered while supervising the embarkation of his army. March revealed all. He had been approached by his brother-in-law, the earl of Cambridge, to join him in a plot to overthrow and kill Henry, and presumably put March on the throne.

It was a formidable plot combining the forces of the Percys and Mortimers with those of Scotland and Wales. The plotters, including the earl of Cambridge, Lord Scrope and Sir Thomas Grey, were seized at once. Grey was summarily tried and executed, but Cambridge and Scrope demanded to be tried by their peers. This was allowed, but the court under the duke of Clarence and including twenty peers found them guilty of treason and plotting regicide, and they were beheaded.

Henry kept the destination of his expeditionary force secret and to the surprise of most of his army and all of the French his point of entry on 14 August 1415, after a three-day crossing, turned out to be the Chef de Caux just west of Harfleur. This was a good choice as it controlled access to the River Seine and as a result controlled traffic along the river from the sea to Rouen and Paris. The royal shipyards of France, where they made their galleys and king's ships, were at Rouen. Harfleur had also been one of the main bases from which English shipping had been harassed by French privateers and pirates, and from which raids on the south coast had been mounted. Most importantly it provided a safe anchorage for his ships as well as a good harbour, secure under the guns of the city.

It took some three days to disembark the horses, guns, siege engines, wagons and all the men from Henry's invasion fleet before the army was ready to march the 3 miles from the invasion beaches to the fortified town. Henry, who had made his camp in some splendour and luxury on a hill about a mile from the town, pushed an advance guard out to a position between this and the town and strengthened the position to the north of the town to guard against attack from this direction. During the night of 18 August the duke of Clarence, accompanied by the earl of Salisbury, marched around the north of the town to the eastern side with a large number of men and several guns to close the only route open to the French garrison. Unfortunately this move was too late to prevent a company of 300 men-at-arms under the lord de Gaucourt from entering the town.[8] On arrival Clarence was lucky to surprise and capture a relief convoy bringing gunpowder, guns and crossbows to the town from Rouen.

Harfleur proved to be a harder place to take than Henry and his army had anticipated. Not only was it strongly fortified, but also the captain of the original garrison of 400 men-at-arms was a tough and resourceful soldier, the lord d'Estouteville.[9] The reinforced garrison, now some 700 strong, was energetically and skilfully led. It was well provisioned with guns, powder and shot, and there were ample provisions within the town to eke out their resistance for about a month, during which time they fully expected to be relieved by a French army coming from Rouen. The defences included a thick surrounding wall protected by twenty-six towers and with three strong barbicans guarding the gates. These strong defences had been improved by building earthworks and wide water-filled dykes, which protected the approaches to the barbicans outside the town's three gates; there was also a stone-lined moat along the walls on the north-east side as a protection against mining. Added to this, once news of Henry's landing reached them the garrison breached the dykes and flooded the low-lying areas between the town and the sea.[10]

Henry had a problem: he needed Harfleur as a base for his conquest of Normandy and he had to take it quickly before either a relieving army or sickness forced him to raise the siege and sail away. His army had burnt the suburbs and cleared away all obstructions from in front of the walls; they had then built a system of trenches and palisades right round the walls so that the town was cut off from the outside. Unfortunately many of the English positions were in unhealthy areas and in the heat of summer it was not long before dysentery and fever began to take their toll. The garrison of Harfleur also had guns mounted on the walls and towers, which made the establishment of batteries within range of the walls a hazardous business. Guns could only be placed after trenches had been dug so that they could then be dragged to their firing positions under cover. The tedious process of entrenchment and embankment took about a week before the English guns were able to begin their own bombardment. Henry had twelve large guns, larger than the French had seen before, and he took a personal interest in their placing and laying; not only were they capable of causing great damage to the walls but they could also reach and demolish buildings in the centre of the town.[11]

While this was going on Henry's army attempted to mine the walls, a tactic that was largely neutralized by skilful French counter-mining. The French also tried to mine the English artillery positions but without success. The garrison carried out many sorties with mounted men-at-arms and on one occasion captured three English knights; on another, towards the end of the siege, they reached the gun positions and set two gun emplacements on fire. However the guns and supporting siege engines maintained their bombardment day and night and although, after a month, the walls and much of the town beyond were severely damaged, Harfleur was still not taken. Nevertheless progress was being made; by 16 September Henry's guns had so battered the main barbican protecting the south-west gate that the French were forced to abandon it. The English took possession of the barbican the next day allowing them to drag their guns even closer to the walls. The French made one last sally on the following day but were driven back in confusion, and as the plight of the citizens was now getting desperate and disease was rife the garrison commander offered terms of surrender. These Henry ignored, offering his own terms instead which the French found too demanding to accept.

Following the rejection of terms the bombardment continued more fiercely than before. The French then again offered terms, asking for a truce until 6 October by which date they would surrender if they had not yet been relieved. Henry once again rejected the French offer. He was in a hurry as time was running out if he was to make his bid for the French crown before the winter. The French however were getting desperate with sickness, shortage of food and the bombardment, and so they offered to bring their surrender date forward to 22 September, unless previously relieved, terms which Henry quickly accepted. Relief failed to appear and Henry marched in that day. Harfleur surrendered after thirty-eight days of an intense and rigorous siege in which Henry had had to use every resource available to him. The cost had been high: Henry had lost about a quarter of his army through sickness and enemy action, indeed according to Monstrelet[12] over 2,000 died and a further 2,000 were sent home sick. Of those who remained most were debilitated by dysentery or fever.

Henry now had four possible options. He could return to England leaving a garrison to defend his new-won base; he could march the 450 miles to Bordeaux in English Aquitaine, or march the 160 miles to Calais. He could march to Rouen and thence to Paris in the hope of taking the French capital and seat of government. He could, of course, stay at Harfleur and await reinforcements from home, but this was soon discarded, as the army needed to get away from the unhealthy air of the estuary. Paris was too great a gamble – not only would he have to meet the forces of Armagnac France but probably also those of Burgundy; politically this did not make sense since it would tend to bring the warring factions in France together to oppose him. Bordeaux was too far away and was quickly discarded. To return home by ship would be seen as weakness by the French and, perhaps more importantly, by parliament who, having ensured that Henry had the necessary finance, expected a handsome profit, and anyway, Henry was determined to emulate his great-grandfather and go on *chevauchée*. Before finalizing his decision Henry sent a herald together with the lord de Gaucourt to the Dauphin at Rouen challenging him to mortal combat, a fairly safe bet as the Dauphin was a fat and idle eighteen year old, the winner to wear the crown of France. Henry gave the Dauphin eight days for a reply. Receiving none within the time limit Henry took the decision to march to Calais leaving a strong garrison of 300 men-at-arms and 900 archers at Harfleur[13] in addition to the siege train and most of the baggage. Reinforcements had been received and so, notwithstanding many desertions, Henry was able to set off with an army of between six and seven thousand men on 6 October. They took with them barely sufficient rations for the next eight days,[14] the time Henry reckoned it would take him to march to Calais.

French actions before the invasion and reactions to the actual invasion may be seen as hesitant and dilatory, first, in their response to Henry's invasion preparations, which they knew about and, secondly, to the invasion itself. But it must be remembered that Charles VI was going mad and that the Dauphin, the head of state in the king's absence, was an inexperienced, dissolute and sickly young man who had never been on campaign and was despised by the nobility of France. Furthermore France was riven by the antagonism of two powerful political groups, the Burgundians and the Armagnacs. Nevertheless the council in Paris was stirred to action by the invasion and writs of service were sent to all the military vassals to serve under the Dauphin. This dilatory action was too late to relieve the siege of Harfleur or to oppose Henry's march north from there to the Somme. However, it is unlikely that they could have mustered sufficient of their feudal vassals in time to have had a realistic chance of relieving Harfleur before it fell.

Also, for the honour of France, the French wanted to defeat Henry in the field in one glorious battle and this is what they set out to do. It would, of course, take time to gather the overwhelming force that they considered necessary. Initially they intended to concentrate their army at Rouen, a strategically sensible place from which to bar any advance by Henry either towards Paris or north to Calais. But by the time the many contingents of their largely feudal army had begun to collect Harfleur had fallen and Henry was already on his way to Calais. The senior commanders nevertheless gathered at Rouen where the Dauphin met them to discuss the strategy of their campaign and to decide on their future moves. They now ordered the army to muster at Abbeville from where they could bar Henry's march to Calais. Once

Henry knew their muster point he must have realized that the French had no intention of fighting him south of the Somme, but probably intended to defeat him while crossing the river or keep him south of the river until his army starved.

The army left Harfleur without carts, wagons or guns and marched off in three columns with scouts out ahead and to the flanks, and with their rations carried on sumpters. They marched up the coast towards the Somme, burning and looting as they went; they even burnt the abbey of Fécamp, dragging out and raping women who had taken refuge there. Their route took them via Montevilliers to Arques, a small town on the river Arques about 4 miles south-east of Dieppe. Shots were fired at them, probably for honour's sake, from the castle at Arques without harm before the governor of the town and castle, under threat of an assault with all that that implied, allowed them free passage over the river; he even gave the army fresh bread and wine. The army then went on its way and arrived at Eu, near the mouth of the River Bresle, on 12 October, and here they met organized resistance for the first time. Part of the French army had been quartered there and on the approach of the English vanguard they came out of the town to bar the way, a sharp fight followed and they were soon repulsed, but not without casualties to both sides. The French then withdrew and the citizens of Eu came to an agreement with Henry to spare the town.

Henry arrived opposite Abbeville on the evening of 13 October only to find the bridges destroyed and the French army in force on the opposite bank. His army was now in a difficult position: they were unable to cross the Somme at Abbeville and a withdrawal to Harfleur would look cowardly. But Henry decided to press on. He felt confident but his army was in a sad state, many of his soldiers were still suffering from dysentery contracted at Harfleur and although they started out with provisions for eight days most were extremely hungry. He had to find a crossing point so that he could march north to Calais and safety, but as he marched up the Somme the French shadowed him from the far bank. He could see that the French army was five or six times as large as his own and realized that he faced a daunting prospect. The English army was nearly out of provisions and after only a week on the march was already exhausted. But Henry had good commanders and battle-hardened men, and he himself was a respected and determined leader, full of courage; he seemed not unduly deterred by the prospect ahead.

However to the English soldiery the prospect seemed to be one of either starvation or annihilation, probably both, and they looked for a miracle to get them out of the mess. Indeed a priest who accompanied the expedition and wrote an account[15] of it said: 'I, who write, and many others looked bitterly up to heaven, and implored the divine mercy and the protection of the Holy Virgin.'

On 14 October the main body of Henry's army passed about 3 miles to the south of Amiens, still following the river upstream. On the 15th they came to the castle and village of Boves and were fired on from the castle. However after a parley the garrison agreed to let the army pass without hindrance providing no damage was done to the houses of the village and to the surrounding vineyards. The next day the army slowly went on its way and arrived by Corbie, only 3 miles from Boves on 17 October. Part of the French army was quartered here and on seeing the English close by sallied out to fight them; another sharp fight followed before they were driven off.

It soon became obvious to Henry that he had to steal a march on the French. With luck he might find an unguarded crossing point where he could cross unopposed, but if he had to force a crossing he needed the extra time in hand to do so before the main body of the French could come up. This is exactly what he achieved, either by luck or design. The army marched from Corbie to Nesle in a day, a distance of 20 miles in a south-easterly direction; this took them away from the Somme, which continued in an easterly direction before swinging sharply south at Péronne. Henry marched across the loop in the river and on reaching Nesle was only about 2 miles from it. The French meanwhile, who had been marching along the north bank of the river round the outside of the curve, had only managed to reach Péronne, some 10 miles to the north when Henry had reached Nesle. At this point fortune smiled on the English; Henry was told that fords existed not more than 2 miles away.

He immediately sent a mounted scouting party to the ford with orders to seize it if they could. This they did as it was unguarded; the army's prayers had been answered and once again lady luck had favoured the English. They reported back that the river was only as deep as a horse's belly, that there were two fords there, and that the approaches were very boggy for about a mile. The French had also felled trees across the track to make it difficult for more than a single file to pass along it. Notwithstanding the difficulties, Henry quickly took advantage of the situation. He sent a strong advance guard to cross the river with orders to establish a defensive position on the far side behind which the rest of the army could cross in relative safety. He then organized a party to improve the track, sending others to the nearest villages to bring wood and anything else that would firm up the going leading into and out of the river. The army was organized so that all the baggage animals crossed by one ford while the soldiers crossed by the other. While all this was going on a French party of men-at-arms stumbled on the English advance guard, which had just crossed the river and realizing that the English were already too strong for them to attack drew off without a fight. The French now knew that the English had crossed the Somme. The unopposed crossing, which had begun at about 1.00 p.m. in the afternoon, was complete before nightfall some four hours later on 19 October.

A very different situation now faced both antagonists. The English could set out for Calais and home, while the French, if they wanted to avenge the fall of Harfleur, had to offer battle. Of course morale in Henry's army must have risen as soon as they crossed the river, for although they realized they would have to fight their way back, they were at least going home. If the French offered battle, then so be it, Henry's army would give a good account of themselves. The French, as at Crécy many years before, were haughty and full of confidence – after all, they were at least five times as many, fit and well mounted. Furthermore the princes of France, the Dauphin and the dukes of Orleans and Bourbon, felt they now had the opportunity to shatter Henry's presumptuous claim to the throne of France at a blow. Morale was high and they were all for battle; how could their magnificent army possibly fail? With any luck they might even avenge King Jean's capture at Poitiers by taking Henry himself prisoner.

Three French heralds arrived at Henry's camp the day after he had crossed the Somme to tell Henry that the French commanders intended to offer battle. They wished to know by what route Henry intended to make for Calais so that the French army could bar his way and ensure that battle took place! According to the chroniclers, Henry replied:

Straight to Calais, and if my enemies attempt to prevent me, it will be at their peril. I shall not seek them, but the fear of them will not induce me to deviate from my route, nor will the sight of them cause me to quicken my pace.[16]

After this exchange the English army expected battle the next morning and prepared for it, furthermore from that time on all knights and esquires wore full armour.[i] However when morning came there was no sign of the French, so the army started on its march north to Calais.

At this time the French army was already at Péronne 10 miles to the north of the crossing point. This meant that they were always between Henry's army and his destination and unless Henry could by-pass them and once again steal a march the French would always be in a position to choose the time and place of battle. Henry's route took him past Péronne to Albert, then to the east of Doulens to Freven and thence to Maisoncelle, a distance of about 56 miles which he covered in four days, fast going for an unfit and hungry army. The French meanwhile, on quitting Péronne, made for Bapaume and St Pol, presumably on their way to Fruges. Apart from seeing a body of French men-at-arms near Péronne the English saw no sign of the French army until they reached the River Ternoise on 24 October. After a brief fight with some French men-at-arms, Henry's army then crossed the river and made its way towards Maisoncelle. But before the advance guard under the duke of York got there a scout came galloping up to him to say that the French, in vast numbers, were advancing between woods only about a mile to the north of Maisoncelle. York verified this personally before passing it on to Henry.

The French barred the way and were clearly ready and eager for battle. Henry, expecting to be attacked, drew up his army in as good a defensive position as he could find, and as he was a good commander he almost certainly rode forward with his escort to see the French for himself. It looked to him that the French intended to encircle him, their army was large enough to do this and the ground would be no obstacle, so he adjusted his positions accordingly. But the French had no such intention, they were simply marching to the villages of Agincourt and Ruisseauville for the night. When this became clear the English army stood down and made camp just to the north of

---

i Usually when on the march and until a major engagement became probable knights and men-at-arms wore half-armour or jacks with leg armour, giving them greater mobility and freedom of action.

Maisoncelle. The two armies were now about 1½ miles apart and battle was inevitable in the morning. The French, confident in their numbers, spent much of the night drinking and gambling. The English, having made their peace with God, settled down to get as much rest as they could. Luckily the village of Maisoncelle gave them food, so that many had at least something to eat after eight days without rations and existing solely on what they could scavenge. It rained heavily all night and both sides waited miserably for the dawn. Henry, who had seen the ground over which they would have to fight, as indeed had the duke of York, sent out reconnaissance patrols to verify certain aspects before calling for a council of his commanders at his lodging in Maisoncelle. Plans for the battle were drawn up and everyone knew his place for the morrow and what he had to do.

Dawn came and after hearing Mass Henry's army marched out to take up their battle stations, as indeed did the French. They made a brave show, the men-at-arms in plate armour, the knights with colourful heraldic tabards covering their armour, and banners held aloft on lances. The dismounted men-at-arms carried pole-axes, halberds or shortened lances as well as their sheathed swords. Plate armour had replaced the mail and part plate of the days of Poitiers. This could deflect arrows and prevent penetration, and as a result most hand-held weapons were now designed to crush rather than pierce the armour of an adversary. A secondary result was that men-at-arms on foot now needed both hands to wield their weapons and so shields were no longer carried. The mounted archers, dressed and equipped with agility in mind, wore helmets, mail armour or brig-andines or jacks and thigh boots, and all were armed with swords and perhaps bucklers as well as their bows and quivers with up to forty-eight arrows. Since leaving Corbie all the archers had been ordered to carry 6-foot stakes, sharpened at one end. They were now hammered into the ground at an angle in front of their positions facing the enemy and about breast high on a horse; the protruding end would have been sharpened to a point as protection against cavalry attack. The English army was drawn up in three divisions, York's on the right and lord Camoy's on the left. Henry's division, the main body, was drawn up in the middle and slightly to the rear of the other two. The baggage and the non-combatants were in the rear near Maisoncelle.

Once again there is controversy about the positions of the archers; three views prevail. Harris says they were in a triangular position between York's division on the right and Camoys' on the left, and just in front of the main body, the outer flanks of the two divisions being protected by the woods. This isn't a very sound tactical ploy since a cavalry charge at the centre of the English line would scatter the archers and leave a hole in the English positions, it therefore seems an unlikely formation. However two possibilities remain, either of which could have been meant by the writings of the chroniclers. The archers were either stationed on the outside flanks of the two flanking divisions only, or both there and also between the three divisions. The deciding factors must be the length of the English line and the range of the bows. In this case, assuming that Henry only had about 1,000 men-at-arms with him and that they were formed up in three or four ranks, the line would have been about 500 yards long. Each man would have had about 3 feet of space either side of him to be able to wield his weapons effectively. This would mean that if the archers were stationed on the outside flanks of the flanking divisions only they would have been able to reach the centre from either side with an overlap in the middle. It is therefore probable that most of the archers were posted here on the flanks of the English position, the remainder being spread across the front among the ranks of the men-at-arms. The archers, some 5,000 of them, would have taken up position behind their stakes with their own outside flanks resting on the woods. Deployed like this they represented both a formidable obstacle to cavalry and a very firm fire base from which to shoot, from a flank, at any attack on the English line of men-at-arms. The archers of course would have had to be able to defend themselves as well as fire into the flanks of any advancing French formation attacking the English line. Their positions must therefore have reached well forward of the line of men-at-arms to ensure that the maximum number of bows could bear on an advancing enemy at all times.

The English deployed a few hundred yards north of Maisoncelle, between the road to Calais on their right and a local track from Maisoncelle to Agincourt, about a mile and a quarter away, on their left. Beyond both roads were woods which were thick enough to act as an obstacle to cavalry. The distance between the woods was about 800 yards at the English end and widened to about 1,200 yards at the French. The French also deployed between the two woods, with their right by Agincourt and their main body just in front of a track which ran from Agincourt eastwards to the village of Tramecourt about a thousand yards away in the woods. The ground was flat and planted with young corn near to the English positions but still ploughed nearer the French. It had rained heavily throughout the night making the going soft and difficult for armoured cavalry to move over, and very tiring for the dismounted men-at-arms in full armour.

The French would have had great difficulty deploying their huge army in the narrow confines between the woods; there was simply not enough room for them to be spaced out properly and this may account for the very large number of ranks facing the English. They deployed in four main groups. In the first division facing the English and stretched right across the available space were about 8,000 men-at-arms under the constable D'Albret. Because of the need for space to wield their weapons they could only have had about 400 men in the first and subsequent ranks, making the first division about twenty ranks deep. 800 mounted men-at-arms under Clignet de Brebant were supposed to be on the right flank with a further 800 under the count of Vendome on the left. These were picked men with the task of riding down the English archers, but in the event only about half this number arrived in time to take part in their charge. They and all the other mounted men-at-arms made a brave sight as they sat astride their horses, fully armoured men on horses which were themselves armoured on the head, neck and breast and caparisoned in the heraldic colours of their riders. The French archers and crossbowmen, about 5,500 all told, stood in their ranks behind the first division of dismounted men-at-arms. Behind the archers came yet another division, not as large as the first but formidable nevertheless, with perhaps 5,000 men-at-arms. Finally in rear of all the rest of the army were yet more men-at-arms, a body of men almost as large as the first division. Some say they were mounted others that they were on their feet; if the latter then their horses were close to hand just behind them.[17]

The French had taken up a defensive position across the Calais road, knowing that the English had to go that way, and were therefore content to be attacked. They knew the English had to force their way through or starve. Unfortunately they appear not to have thought too deeply about their own deployment believing that overwhelming superiority would win the day. They had a massive advantage in cavalry numbers, perhaps 21,000 men-at-arms, all of whom could fight mounted or on foot, and yet they chose a battlefield where they could not be used to their full effect. They had about the same number of archers as the English and then placed them behind the twenty or so ranks of the first division. Deployed in such a position they would have been about 60 yards behind the first rank of men-at-arms allowing the English archers, who would have been out of range, to fire at the French men-at-arms of the first division with impunity. Finally, their divisions were so large that they were unwieldy and difficult to command. Their army commander, the constable, d'Albret, was on his feet in the centre of the first rank, undoubtedly in the position of honour, but a position from which he could not hope to influence the battle or control his own forces. Indeed, it was not certain that anyone was in command.

Both armies began their deployment early in the morning on St Crispin's day. The English army, under Henry's command marched out in its three divisions to take up the positions agreed the night before. As the English army was at least five times smaller than the French, and as they were both deploying into similar positions, it must have taken the French about five times as long to take up their battle formation. It is surprising that as all this must have taken place in full view of the English, and only some 1,200 yards away, that Henry did not attack while the French were deploying and before they had time to organize themselves properly. However this was Henry's first set-piece battle and so presumably he wished to fight the battle in his defensive position in the traditional English fashion, waiting for the French to attack him, something the impetuous French traditionally did. Perhaps by the standards of the day it would have been a dishonourable move and therefore unthinkable. Proceedings were delayed perhaps by Henry's effort in his just cause to seek a way of avoiding battle. He sent heralds to the French to demand a parley to this end and shortly after negotiators from both sides met to see if battle could be avoided. This failed as both sides demanded impossible conditions to avoid the forthcoming battle.

In due course both armies were ready and committed to battle, but nothing happened. They stood watching each other, neither side being willing to take the initiative. The usual French tactic was to charge when ready, either mounted or on foot, but in this case they had decided to force the English to attack, well knowing their desperate need to get to Calais. After waiting like this for several hours, some

say as long as five hours, Henry lost patience and at about eleven
o'clock in the morning ordered his army to advance to the attack.

Once again the positioning of the archers is important. In the
original defensive position it made good tactical sense for the majority
of the archers to be massed on the two wings, but in a general advance
this was no longer the case. Sir Thomas Erpingham, marshal of the
archers, was probably ordered to redeploy more of the archers along
the whole front of the English army, so forming the first line of the
attack, while the remainder stayed on the flanks. The men-at-arms
marched immediately behind the archers as one concentrated body,
probably in three ranks. Once the archers in the front came within
easy range of the French men-at-arms, but outside the range of the
opposing archers, they would have halted. Then, while the men-at-
arms continued their advance, they would have concentrated a withering fire over their heads and into the French ranks. Later, just before
the two lines of men-at-arms closed they would have doubled forward
to a position from which they could fire at the French archers. The
movements of the archers, after they had been spread across the front
of the English men-at-arms, are speculative because such detail is not
recorded. But the archers were skilled soldiers while their commander,
Sir Thomas Erpingham, a knight of the Garter and an experienced
officer, would have directed the fire of his archers to the best
advantage. It will be recalled that in the original position the flanking
archers had hammered their stakes into the ground as an obstacle
against cavalry attack. It is unlikely that there was time for all the
archers to uproot their stakes, march forward with them and then
replace them in the ground at the end of the advance. But
undoubtedly some archers managed to do so, probably two or three
archers shifting and replanting one stake between them. It is therefore
probable that the majority of the stakes were left behind when Henry
called for a general advance and as a result the archers would have
been vulnerable to a determined cavalry attack in the new position.

The constable, on seeing the English advance, ordered his first
division to move towards the approaching English, but the remainder
of the French army seems to have stayed in its initial positions, thus
leaving their own archers even further behind the front rank of their
men-at-arms. Carrying out these orders must have taken a little while,
because the English had closed to within 200 yards before the French
began their own advance. The French first division would have been

under archery fire from about the time the order was given to advance until the opposing lines of men-at-arms closed, indeed it might have been the trigger for the French advance. In contrast the French archers, because of their position, were not able to bring their bows and crossbows to bear on the advancing English. When eventually they could do so they were themselves under fire from the opposing archers, and the opposing men-at-arms were already furiously involved in hand-to-hand combat. At the same time as their first division began its advance the French loosed their two cavalry wings which due to indiscipline had no more than 300 horsemen ready.[18] Both wings did their best to charge the archers opposite them but were unable to gather any momentum due to the very heavy going and were driven off with many casualties by the archers. Riderless horses and others, driven mad by the arrows and totally out of control, galloped into the ranks of their own advancing men-at-arms, causing disruption and some casualties.

Henry, seeing this and before the opposing ranks closed, ordered his men to quicken their pace to take advantage of the confusion opposite. The French also speeded up to get out of the arrow storm; the closer they got to the English men-at-arms opposite them the less likely they were to be spitted by an arrow. A great clash of arms took place all along the line. The French naturally closed into three groups, each going for the banner of one of the three principle English commanders they could see opposite. At first the English were forced back by the sheer weight of the French attack but they managed to absorb the shock and then began to push the French back. It may seem extraordinary that a mere 1,000 men-at-arms could repulse some 8,000, particularly since in terms of courage, morale and ability there would have been little to choose between them. But the French would have been disorganized after facing the loose horses and the arrow storm, and, perhaps more importantly, the men-at-arms had insufficient space around them in which to wield their weapons effectively. The English had room to fight but the French had not, they were compressed by their very numbers and by the shape of the battleground, which narrowed as they approached the advancing English. Unfortunately for them the problem was made worse by the fact that those in the ranks behind pressed forward in order to get away from the fire of the English archers which now also came at them from the flanks.

As the French went back so the chaos in their ranks became worse and great piles of dead and wounded lay across the front. The front ranks of the French which had led the initial attack fell back onto the second who were themselves compressed by those behind, so increasing the confusion in their ranks. The carnage continued and increased. English archers who had run out of arrows now joined their comrades in armour and with their swords, mallets or staff weapons picked up off the ground, added to the number of Englishmen engaged in the hand-to-hand fighting. The going under foot was soft and slippery and as knights and men-at-arms in armour fought for their lives too many just slipped and were trampled under foot by friend and foe alike, or were simply killed on the ground where they lay. The piles of French dead and wounded grew and made a virtual parapet across the battlefield which the English men-at-arms and archers had to climb over to get at those behind.

The French archers made no impression on the battle, although many of them followed the advance of the first division only to be driven off by English archery, after hastily firing a few arrows to not much effect. Indeed, apart from this action, they are never again mentioned by any of the chroniclers; presumably, on seeing how the battle was going they simply melted away into the woods either side. Having destroyed the first French division, the English army advanced into the second division of men-at-arms, some of whom put up a stout resistance but most took to horse or withdrew into the ranks of the division behind them. The fourth French division of some 8,000 men-at-arms took no part in the battle itself. They too, left the battlefield in groups although some seemed to be on the point of counter-attacking.

Some from this division were the unwitting cause of a disgraceful, but understandable, incident behind the English lines, though they were not involved in it. These horsemen carried out a raid on the English baggage train in the rear near Maisoncelle where the non-combatants and sick were placed. This area, protected by twenty men-at-arms and twenty archers, was also where all the prisoners were held. Prisoners normally gave their word of honour that they would not try to escape once they had surrendered, however it was not unknown for them to do so, and to take up arms again if the opportunity arose and there was any advantage in doing so. Henry was told of the raid when the fourth French division seemed to be about to mount a counter-attack. He knew that the prisoners, helped by the men-at-arms in the raid, could easily rearm and return to the battle at his back. It was said that the number of prisoners at this time outnumbered the English men-at-arms by two to one,[19] in other words about 2,000. He therefore ordered all the prisoners to be put to death. At first the guards refused to kill the prisoners, but eventually 200 archers were ordered to carry out the butchery or hang. The raid itself was beaten off with many casualties and the expected counter-attack never materialized. Henry's order to massacre prisoners who had already surrendered was a grave and shocking breach of the laws of chivalry by which they all fought. It seems, however that most prisoners were taken before this stage of the battle and that as many as 1,000 of them reached Calais, therefore a significant proportion of them must have survived the 'massacre'. Also, Henry apparently sent counter-orders as soon as he realized that the fourth French division was not going to enter the battle. Perhaps the whole incident has been exaggerated; it certainly does not seem to have been in character since Henry was bound by the laws of chivalry. As Allmand points out, no contemporary French chronicler condemned Henry's order, perhaps because the French unfurled the 'Oriflamme', a war banner held aloft when quarter was not an option.

The French were thoroughly defeated and those who remained standing or were still horsed left the battlefield as quickly as they could. Once again the English were too exhausted to give chase. The battle lasted about three hours[20] and, once Henry was sure that the French would not mount another attack, he gave orders for the heralds to go out and list the dead. When this was done Henry's soldiers scavenged the battlefield, stripping the dead of anything valuable including their armour. The English dead numbered between 300 and 1,000 according to French sources and from 22 to about 100 by English chroniclers. The dead were put into a barn and burnt, while the bodies of the duke of York and the earl of Suffolk, the only two notable English casualties to be killed, were boiled so that their bones could be carried home for church burial. The duke of York is said to have died from a blow to the head, however others said he died from suffocation having slipped and fallen after being wounded and then been buried beneath the press of dead Frenchmen who fell on top of him. Henry himself had been in the thick of the fighting and had received a blow on his helmet, while his brother, Humphrey, duke of

Gloucester, was badly wounded; he recovered at Calais. The bodies of notable French casualties were carried off the battlefield for burial, either at their homes or in the nearby church at Hesdin. However, 5,800[21] dead were buried the next day in three large trenches on the battlefield in ground that was later consecrated by the bishop of Guisnes.

The French dead included three dukes, five counts, over ninety barons and between 1,050 and 2,000 knights: these were in effect the French combatant officers commanding divisions and lesser groups within them. The loss of these commanders and their experience would be sorely felt in any future army raised by France, or indeed in any future conflict between the Armagnacs and Burgundians, since the dead were mainly followers of the Armagnac cause. But two prominent Burgundians, the duke of Brabant, and his son the count of Nevers were both killed; the former was Jean of Burgundy's brother. Perhaps 4,000 to 5,000 other 'well-borne' men, probably esquires and those aspiring to knighthood, were also killed. Estimates of the number of the dead among those not entitled to 'coat armour', vary upwards from 4,500, but about 6,000 would probably be correct, making the total French dead between 12,000 and 13,000.[22] Despite the 'massacre' of the prisoners during the battle, many more were taken after it was all over, among them the duke of Orleans, the count of Richmond (later the duke of Brittany), the count of Vendôme and marshal Boucicault.

It was a very sad day for France – 'ceste malheureuse et douloureuse journee',[23] and one that came entirely of their own making. It came from incompetent leadership, bad deployment and bad choice of ground, failure to take account of the sodden condition of the battle-field and a total failure to understand how archers should be used. Henry himself, apart from attributing his victory to God, credited his army's success to the insubordination and tactics of the French and from want of a strong man in command.[24] Examples of French ill discipline abound. They include the large number of French horsemen detailed for the initial attack who failed to arrive in time and who might well have turned the scales early in the day. Also, the general quality of leadership that allowed the leaders of retinues to leave their own soldiers leaderless somewhere in the back ranks, or even still in camp, in their eagerness to fill the honourable places in the front rank. And, something which was a general failing of French medieval armies of the time, the hauteur that enabled them to believe that only men of rank could vanquish the English; 'base-born' men were not needed. Also it has to be asked why did the French command, who chose the battleground and who held the initiative in this respect, choose the field of Agincourt for their battle? They had a superiority in men-at-arms of about 20 to 1 and about the same number of archer and crossbowmen as the English. Why choose a battlefield which favoured the English? If they had chosen open ground for their battle, ground over which they could have ridden and moved at will without restriction, they could have done what they had always dreamt of, brushed the English army away in one glorious charge! But their commanders were not capable of appreciating their advantages. They had lost heavily at Crécy by trying to defeat the English by cavalry alone on ground that favoured the defence. Poitiers was a close-run thing; they had nearly overwhelmed the English by copying their style of battle, of fighting mainly on foot. This time they would prevail. The French battle tactics followed the successful ones of their enemy without understanding why they had evolved. Their problem was that no one had critically analysed these former battles. It is of interest to note that at long last the French were able to put a significant number of archers into the field some seventy-eight years after they had first come against them, although they clearly failed to understand the way they should be used.

For the English there can be no doubt that Henry's leadership and his ability as a commander were prime factors in their victory, as was the disciplined contribution of the English archers. The men-at-arms also achieved a Herculean victory against all the odds, aided by the archers in the hand-to-hand fighting. Another contributory factor was the discipline shown by the advance of the English army on the battlefield. It would have been extremely difficult to keep the dressing of the line of armoured men-at-arms and archers over heavy going for some 800 yards but, in contrast to the French, they achieved this. Perhaps the essence of victory lay in the very fact that the English army was so small compared with that of the French for the battle-field chosen by the French. Another point of interest is the impact made by the English archers fighting unhindered by armour in the close-quarter fighting where they were able to profit from their greater mobility. This factor was not entirely lost on the military minds of the time, who, for the future, commissioned plate armour that was even lighter than that used at Agincourt but, due to improved technology was probably more effective. Nevertheless it took another hundred years before most armour was discarded, leaving only helmets and breastplates to be worn in battle.

Except for those in the cavalry squadrons detailed to attack the English archers and possibly those in the French fourth division, the French commanders were all dismounted. In contrast it is probable that the English commanders remained mounted until the first clash of arms. This particularly applies to Henry, as he seemed to have a good grasp of the battle. The English commanders must then have dismounted since Henry had part of the circlet on his helmet knocked off during the battle and the duke of York was killed in the hand-to-hand fighting. There were obvious advantages and disadvantages for the commanders to remain mounted for as long as possible. The ability to see what was going on was the main advantage but set against that was the fact that the mounted commander became a target for crossbowmen and archers. Nevertheless, it is probable that the English commanders remained mounted until the last possible moment and then had their horses taken to the rear.

That night most of the English army had their first proper meal for days, having found ample food in the French camps. The next morning, Saturday 26 October, Henry's army left their camp at Maisoncelle and marched up the Calais road past the battlefield. They found many wounded French soldiers still lying there whom they either put out of their misery or, if they looked to be worth a ransom, took prisoner. The army took two days to march the remaining 35 miles to Calais via Fruges and Guines. Henry entered Calais on 29 October, the day on which news of the battle of Agincourt was received in London. Although food and beer had been sent across the Channel to Calais for the returning army it was insufficient and many went hungry, so much so that many a soldier sold his captive or his plunder cheaply in order to buy food. The army was keen to get back home but the vast fleet that had been assembled to carry them across to Harfleur at the beginning of the campaign had already been dispersed. Some ships did come over and took many home, but the majority of the captains of retinues were simply paid 2s a man plus 2s for their horses and then told to organize the passage of their retinues themselves.[25] This was done and most were soon home; Henry however stayed in Calais until 16 November when he sailed to Dover arriving the same evening after a stormy passage.

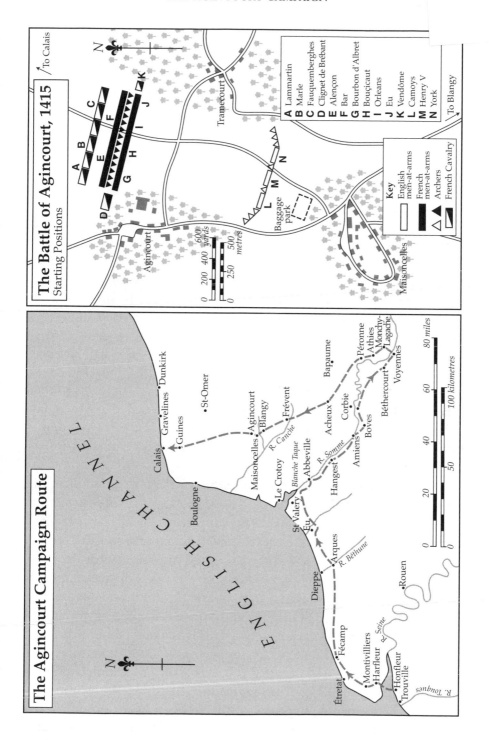

The Battle of Agincourt, 1415
Starting Positions

To Calais

Agincourt

Tramecourt

Baggage Park

Maisoncelles

To Blangy

Key

	English men-at-arms
	French men-at-arms
	Archers
	French Cavalry

A Lammartin
B Marle
C Fauquemberghes
D Clignet de Brébant
E Alençon
F Bar
G Bourbon d'Albret
H Bouçicaut
I Orleans
J Eu
K Vendôme
L Camoys
M Henry V
N York

0 200 400 600 yards
0 250 500 metres

The Agincourt Campaign Route

ENGLISH CHANNEL

Dunkirk
Gravelines
Calais
Guines
St-Omer
Boulogne
Agincourt
Blangy
Frévent
Maisoncelles
R. Canche
Le Crotoy
Blanche Taque
Abbeville
Acheux
Bapaume
Péronne
Athies
Monchy-Lagache
Voyennes
Béthencourt
Corbie
Amiens
Boves
Hangest
R. Somme
St Valery
Eu
Arques
R. Béthune
Dieppe
Fécamp
Montivilliers
Étretat
Harfleur
Honfleur
Trouville
R. Touques
Seine
Rouen

0 20 40 60 80 miles
0 50 100 kilometres

Chapter 14

The Conquest of Normandy

'Every Divided Kingdom shall be Laid Waste'[1]

When he arrived in England after his triumph in France Henry was greeted with great pomp and affection all the way to London, which he entered on 23 November, where special processions and banquets were held in his honour. He had won his stunning victory at Agincourt and had taken the fortified port of Harfleur, thus giving him yet one more option for any future invasion of France, but he was no nearer the crown of France. Meanwhile in France news of their defeat shocked the population,[2] her main army in the north had been routed and dismembered, and many of her leaders had either been taken prisoner or were lying dead on the battlefield. In terms of their civil conflict Agincourt had undoubtedly weakened the Armagnacs more than the Burgundians, who had hardly been involved, and in their on-going quarrel the balance of power now shifted towards Duke Jean of Burgundy.

Parliament met on 6 November to advance the tenths and fifteenths that had been voted to Henry for the expedition before he set out. These taxes, which were due to be collected in February 1416 and again a year later were to be available immediately so that Henry could pay off the creditors who had loaned him money for the expedition. But parliament realized that further expeditions might be necessary and to enable Henry to plan and fit out another expedition the commons granted him a subsidy on wool exports for life of 4 marks on each woolsack exported. This was a huge sum by the standards of those days. As England exported 40,000 sacks in a good trading year and seldom less than 20,000, this represented a maximum of about £35,500 annually and exclusively for war against France. There were also taxes on imported wine and other merchandise in addition to a further tenth and fifteenth to be levied in November 1416. Quite clearly the country, as represented by parliament, was in Henry's thrall: rebellion against a king who brought such success against the traditional enemy was unthinkable. Henry was secure on his throne. The country looked forward to further glorious victories and much profit at the expense of France. Parliament clearly thought that one more swift and decisive expedition would achieve Henry's goals and that it would be worth the cost. How wrong their appreciation proved to be; France may have lost a battle but she was far from losing the war.

Henry realized that a policy based on raids and *chevauchées* would not achieve his aims and that nothing less than the occupation of France would do. This was a colossal task and one that even he recognized to be beyond his means. However he reasoned that he stood a good chance of achieving his desires if he could play one side off against the other. After Agincourt he held as his prisoners the dukes of Orleans and Bourbon, both royal princes, who were nominally the Armagnac leaders. Jean of Burgundy remained excluded from Paris and, he who held Paris held France, therefore the Armagnacs were France. Jean, the Dauphin, died in 1417, leaving his younger brother Charles as the heir to his father the mad king Charles VI. The new Dauphin was with and under the influence of the Count of Armagnac, the new constable of France. Politically France could not have been more divided and Henry realized that the sooner he seized the opportunities open to him the easier his task would be.

Henry already possessed three bases in France – Calais, Harfleur and Aquitaine – but none of them was entirely suitable for his purpose. Calais and Harfleur were too small and Aquitaine was too far away from Paris to put immediate pressure on the seat of government in France. Henry needed to be close enough to Paris to threaten if not to occupy it and also close enough to home to be able to maintain easy sea communication. Moreover, he had to occupy a large enough area to give him the depth of territory he would need to absorb any French counter-offensive. He therefore decided to invade Normandy south and west of the Seine, conquer it and occupy it. This was something entirely new, previously England had been content simply to pillage France and for that she needed temporary control of the narrow seas and fast-moving armies, but occupation required different resources and different stratagems.

During the winter of 1415/16 Sigismund, the Holy Roman Emperor, resolved to settle the Great Schism in the Church, which had led to the election of two popes in 1378, Urban VI in Rome and Clement VII in Avignon. He had been the prime mover in setting up the general council of the Church at Constance to settle this problem, among others. He felt that the problem itself had continued over the years because of 'the discords among the kingdoms' of Europe, and in this he was right. Popes needed the secular backing of princes and princes needed the spiritual backing of popes; so when regal ambitions clashed each antagonist needed the backing of the Church; having two popes made this problem easier but made the maintenance of peace more difficult. Between 1378 and 1417, when the Great Schism was resolved, the chances of peace brokered by the Pope between England and France were slim.

However Sigismund sent an embassy to Paris to try and secure peace between England and France, and also visited England, where he was entertained lavishly by Henry. But Sigismund came up against the same impasse: the French would not increase their offer and the English would not reduce their claims. Nevertheless Sigismund called for a meeting between Charles VI, Henry and himself, probably at or near Calais, to discuss a three-year truce. The Count of Armagnac, now the constable, convinced them that he could defeat England militarily and persuaded the council to reject Sigismund's overtures.

The count, confident that the threat posed by Duke Jean of Burgundy was containable, switched France's considerable military resources away from the defence of Paris to the ejection of the English from Harfleur, which he put under siege by land and sea. Several French ships crossed the Channel and raided the south coast but before English ships could be gathered to attack them they were dispersed by stormy weather. Disappointed by the French, Sigismund turned to Henry for his support on the question of the Great Schism and signed the Treaty of Canterbury in August 1416 which underwrote their mutual support in seeking their just rights in France. Henry was now free to go ahead with his ambitious project; he had overcome the diplomatic hurdles and had isolated France.

In August, on the very day that the treaty was signed, a fleet of some 100 ships under the duke of Bedford, probably balingers but including four carracks, carrying 7,000 soldiers of whom over 4,000 were archers, sailed for the mouth of the Seine. Here it defeated the French blockading fleet of eight carracks and eight galleys based at Honfleur on 15 August 1416. The action began in the early morning and lasted several hours, the Franco-Genoese fleet losing some 1,500 men killed and 400 prisoners taken, while the English lost about 700 men.[3] It was clearly a hard-fought struggle but the French grip about Harfleur was finally broken. The French were forced to lift their siege and they withdrew their army to Rouen and further east towards Paris. The garrison immediately took steps to repair the walls and improve the defences of Harfleur, and did so to such good effect that the French realized that it was now, like Calais, too well defended to be taken without a great effort.

Jean of Burgundy had met Henry and Sigismund in Calais in October to discuss the possibility of a grand alliance between them and probably also to ensure England's wool exports to Flanders in the event of renewed war between England and France. The wool trade was vital to both parties. It seems that, although Jean of Burgundy was unwilling to take up arms against France as an ally of England, he was willing to do homage to Henry as king of France, once he had conquered a sizeable portion of the country.[4] Jean and Henry had many meetings and as a result Henry believed Jean would not interfere with any English initiative in France and, indeed, might even join him in a joint military effort.

While these discussions were taking place, Burgundy went on the warpath and his armies operated against Armagnac forces in raids towards Paris from both Burgundy and Flanders throughout the summer and autumn of 1416. These raids, devastating the countryside and taking several towns and castles, were eventually contained by the Armagnacs, but it distracted them from their preparations to meet the main threat, an English invasion. The containment of both threats required a great deal of money and the French government had none, or at least insufficient for the task, so once again the hard-pressed French people were subjected to yet more taxation. To show the French people that their taxes were being put to good use in the war, the French government foolishly extended their military activity by taking the offensive against the English in Aquitaine, besieging the Gascon fortress of La Réole without success and with some loss.

The French expected Henry to invade in the summer of 1417 aided by Duke Jean of Burgundy, but they also thought any landing would simply presage another *chevauchée*. Nevertheless these two perceived threats were enough to split the deployment of French forces to meet any landing by Henry and any threat from Jean at the same time. Henry had decided to land in Normandy. He needed to establish himself in a prosperous area and one that could supply the needs of his army of some 12,000 men; the environs of Calais, after much military activity in the area, were barren and therefore unsuitable. Nevertheless he knew that nine large Genoese carracks were still based at Honfleur at the mouth of the Seine opposite Harfleur on the left bank and these had to be eliminated before he could cross the Channel safely. The Earl of Huntingdon was despatched with a squadron of ships to attack the carracks off the Chef de Caux on 25 July,[5] capturing several ships and scattering the rest. The way was now clear for Henry's invasion.

Henry's plans had been completed by early spring 1417 and all was ready by the third week in June, though there was a delay due to contrary winds.

Henry embarked his army of about 10,000 men on 23 July but was not able to sail before 30 July. No doubt he waited for news from Huntingdon before sailing and presumably got this before he cleared the English coast. After a two day crossing he landed on the French coast near the mouth of the River Touques between Honfleur and Deauville in Normandy on 2 August. He quickly took the castle at Deauville and six days later the castle at Touques, about 2 miles upriver, surrendered. The English army now had a small, reasonably secure bridgehead, allowing disembarkation and the off-loading of horses and stores to begin in earnest. Henry needed to be sure that the French army was too far away to interfere with his plans before he moved westward to Caen so he sent the duke of Clarence up the river Touques to Pont l'Eveque and Lisieux, the route by which the French would have to come if they intended to interfere, but there was no sign of the enemy. Clarence pushed on to Bernay and then turned about and marched for Caen. The king, on learning that there was no sign of the French, also marched from the bridgehead towards Caen. After a quick march Clarence reached Caen on 14 August and began to invest the city.

Ships that had discharged their cargoes were quickly released and sailed back to Southampton to embark a second contingent under the earl of March to reinforce Henry's army in Normandy. However, 239 ships, probably carrying the army's cannons, their crews and horses, and all the supporting equipment, sailed down the coast and up the River Orne towards Caen to discharge their loads there before returning across the Channel.[6] Balingers patrolled the Normandy coast between Harfleur and Caen, and west towards the Cotentin. Henry was concerned that the French might interfere with his plans from the sea; they were certainly in a position to do so, with the necessary ships in the ports of the Cotentin and in northern Brittany. However, English ships now controlled the coast from Calais to Caen and English troops garrisoned all the ports along this coastline with the exception of Honfleur, Dieppe and Boulogne. But a significant threat remained further up the Seine at Rouen, where French royal ships, particularly galleys, were built and Honfleur posed another threat. Clearly Henry had to close the Seine to French sea and river traffic and in due course he would have to take Honfleur.

As soon as he had subdued the surrounding countryside he turned his attention to the siege of Caen which he bombarded for over two weeks prior to an assault over the walls on 4 September. Once inside the town the army indulged in all the usual atrocities of the times. English soldiers plundered and looted as they wished, indeed it was said that the English herded men, women and children into the market place where over 2,000, a most unlikely figure, were apparently massacred.[7] The citadel surrendered sixteen days later. In due course Henry restored order in both the old and new towns of Caen but not until many citizens had lost their lives and much booty had been taken at the point of the sword. As Henry claimed the throne of France he could not be seen to treat the citizens of Caen as enemies, however he could treat those who opposed him as traitors and this he did to many of the citizens, expelling them from the city and confiscating their property. Several of the surrounding towns and villages on hearing what happened at Caen, decided out of fear to accept Henry's peace and declared their loyalty to him. Although it was always difficult to prevent the sack of a city after an assault Henry was in no hurry to restore order. He allowed his army ample time after the assault to sack Caen thoroughly as part of a deliberate policy aimed at coercing Norman towns and cities to declare for him. The immediate effect of the fate of Caen was that it significantly enlarged his foothold westwards towards Bayeux and south to Thury-Harcourt without the need for active operations. Following the Battle of Agincourt in 1415, and the assault and subsequent treatment of Caen two years later, English arms were held in awe and dread; French garrisons were faced with a difficult choice should an English army come their way. Garrisons might well resist in the name of their sovereign and then march off with honour leaving the citizens to their fate. However it was not unknown for town councils to persuade a garrison to withdraw, as did that of Pontoise when faced with a Burgundian army on 11 September.[8]

There can be little doubt that Henry's cause in Normandy was significantly helped by Jean of Burgundy's operations against the Armagnacs about Paris. Indeed the captain of the citadel at Caen, which surrendered on 21 September, had asked the government in Paris for reinforcements before the English invested the city, but was told that the government was wholly occupied with the Burgundians and could not help. This preoccupation with the Burgundian menace helped Henry in two ways: it inclined Norman towns to declare for him when his forces appeared because they knew their own government was unable to help; and it ensured that Henry had a largely unopposed campaign in Normandy during the first crucial days. It also influenced Henry in his choice of future operations after Caen.

Henry had four courses open to him. First, he could do as most medieval armies did and go into winter quarters in and around Caen. But he clearly felt that he must make the most of the opportunity presented to him by the French civil war to occupy as much of northern France as he could while the opportunity lasted. He therefore discarded this option. Second, he could cross the Seine, take Rouen and advance into northern Normandy. However such a course, apart from entailing a lengthy siege of Rouen, had the danger of bringing his forces into contact with those of Burgundy, which were advancing down the Oise valley towards Paris and in doing so providing him with a guard against Armagnac forces from the east. Third, he could turn west and advance up the Cotentin to Cherbourg, thus removing the threat of interference by sea. Fourthly, he could enlarge and consolidate his holding by marching south towards Maine and thus putting pressure on the duke of Brittany for his active support, or at least for his neutrality. He decided on the latter course and began a winter campaign at the beginning of October. Honfleur, at his back and still in French hands, remained a threat so he attempted to take it unawares before marching south, but this failed and he was obliged to leave forces to contain the threat both by land and sea.

Henry's army quickly overran southern Normandy. By the beginning of November he held an area bounded by Verneuil in the east, on the direct route to Paris, and Alençon in the south including nineteen castles and fortified towns. This gave him a defensive line inland from the sea for some 35 miles to the south guarding his conquests against either of the warring French factions from the direction of Paris or from Tours. Henry's quick occupation of southern Normandy, however, was matched by Burgundy's equally quick advance down the Oise, across the Seine west of Paris to Chartres where he set up his headquarters. From here he intended to supervise operations to link his advance towards the Loire with that of another Burgundian army coming from Burgundy along the same river to join at Tours. Thus Burgundy's operations, while ostensibly bottling up the Armagnacs in Paris and the Isle de France, and cutting them off from the possibility of aid from Provence and Languedoc, had the added advantage of preventing Henry from moving east towards Paris. Jean could now justify his claim as the defender of the capital. Both Henry's and Burgundy's moves southwards caused panic in the councils of Anjou and Maine who called for aid from the government in Paris. The latter replied that they were in no position to send an army to help, but gave them authority to negotiate a truce with Henry.[9] Burgundy, they said, was not to be trusted; he had set up a rival government, which had no authority and the councils were not to negotiate with him.

While Anjou and Maine waited for a reply from Paris, Henry occupied castles about Le Mans, a city he intended to invest and then assault. Meanwhile the Burgundians marched towards Vendôme, only 35 miles north-east of Tours, matching Henry and always keeping between Henry and Paris. Anjou and Maine were rightly fearful of the consequences of resistance to the English but so too was Brittany. Duke Jean V went in person to Henry in October to negotiate his neutrality and in due course a truce was signed on 16 November by Henry with the duke and the councils of Anjou and Maine to last until the following September. This secured Henry's southern and western boundaries as far as the Loire and the frontier with Brittany. He now turned his attention to the Cotentin peninsular, but he couldn't trust either faction in France not to intervene while he moved against Cherbourg; the Burgundian army was at Chartres to the east and the Armagnacs held various fortresses to the north-east. Consequently he reinforced his frontier garrisons and carried out defensive patrolling towards Chartres and the Armagnac fortresses of Evreux and Dreux. Burgundy however moved away from Chartres to Troyes, south-east of Paris, early in December and any possible threat to Henry went with him.

With the surrender of Falaise after a battering from Henry's artillery during a siege that lasted from 1 December to 16 February, Henry had accomplished all that he had set out to do during the winter. In March 1418, 2,000 reinforcements arrived under Sir Thomas Beaumont, duke of Exeter and the duke of Clarence. Western Normandy remained to be subdued; nevertheless he turned his attention to the protection and administration of his conquests. He decided to divide his army into a field army and a garrison army – the former with the immediate task of overrunning the Cotentin and western Normandy in general, and the latter with the problem of protecting the eastern and southern frontiers of the conquest. The latter were divided into four sectors each under a commander who was responsible for several garrisons and castles, including some well behind the frontier from which reinforcements could be summoned in an emergency.[10]

The French meanwhile were more concerned with their own problems than with the English. The Armagnacs, while holding Paris and its neighbourhood, a corridor along the Seine to Rouen and parts of northern Normandy, together with isolated fortresses such as Evreux, Dreux and Honfleur, were locked in a life-and-death struggle with the Burgundians. The latter held the strategically important fortress of Pontoise, at the junction of the Oise and the Seine, and also Meulan, Beauvais and Arras, and north to Flanders. South-east of Paris the Burgundians held Troyes and, of course, their base, the duchy itself. The struggle between the two factions centred about Paris, by far the largest and richest city in France. Whoever held Paris held France and would then be responsible for the governance of France and for co-ordinating opposition to the English. And taxing the Parisians necessarily provided the main source for the means to pay for the men-at-arms and archers needed to expel the English and pacify France.

Early in 1418, in an effort to exert their authority and to remove the Burgundian noose about Paris, the Armagnacs, who held Paris, carried out a limited offensive to the south in which they took Etampes and cleared the southern routes out of Paris. They then attempted to do the same to the north by putting Senlis under siege, but the Burgundians riposted in March and April by sending a force south from Arras to Pontoise threatening Paris, and another north-west from Troyes. These two moves forced the Armagnacs to lift their siege of Senlis and hurry back to Paris. However, it was the Burgundians who made the significant gains. They enlarged their hold in Normandy north of the Seine where Dieppe and Rouen opened their gates to Burgundian forces in January 1418; these were strategi-cally important additions to Burgundian-held territory, Dieppe being a vital Channel port and Rouen, the capital of Normandy, a royal arsenal and dockyard. Both cities were crucial to Henry's plans of conquest and it was unfortunate because their new allegiance to Burgundy would inevitably force the Burgundians and English to confront one another. In the spring the Armagnac towns and fortresses of Evreux and Louviers changed loyalties and invited the Burgundians in. The Burgundians immediately taxed the citizens of these towns and also demanded payment of all taxes that were in arrears before they arrived. It was not long before all four towns regretted their change of loyalty; nevertheless Evreux did not remain in Burgundian hands for long.

While the French were preoccupied with their civil war the English were allowed to subdue western Normandy at their leisure and Henry was given time to pause and regroup for the next stage of his conquest. By mid-March Bayeux, St Lô and Coutances had all fallen. Very soon after, Avranches and Pontorson also fell and, following a peaceable proclamation, most of the smaller towns and villages voluntarily accepted Henry's peace. Evreux gave up on 20 May, to be followed on 23 June by the surrender of Louviers. With Evreux in his hands Henry now controlled all Normandy west and south of the Seine. His frontier ran from Avranches in the west, through Domfront, which was now under siege by Clarence and was expected to fall shortly, and Alençon towards Verneuil in the east, and then north along the River Eure to the Seine at Pont de l'Arche. All the towns and cities mentioned were walled and had fortified gateways, and often a chateau as well. This meant that once they had been taken or had declared their loyalty to Henry, and had been garrisoned by his forces, they became part of his defences for the duchy and any attempt to push the English out of Normandy could only be done by retaking these places.

Henry now had sufficient depth of territory behind garrisoned fortresses to be able to withdraw into this safe haven should it become necessary. But more importantly western Normandy now gave him the base he needed from which to occupy the rest of Normandy and then threaten and perhaps occupy the whole of France north of the Loire and to the east of Paris. His occupation of western Normandy also gave him a new source of revenue and manpower, both essential to his ambitions in France and part of his bargain with parliament; the war was to pay for itself and the conquered province would have to bear the greater part of the cost. Also, the space gained in western Normandy gave him two operational options; he could strike deep into Anjou and Maine or cross the Seine and take northern Normandy and thus threaten Paris. He chose the latter course and set his captains on the road to Rouen, the key to the Seine and northern Normandy, and the seat of government within the duchy.

Pont de l'Arche, garrisoned by the Armagnacs, some 5 miles north of Louviers, was Henry's next target; it lay upriver from Rouen on the south bank and if taken would cut river traffic on the Seine as well as open the road to Rouen from the east. The English advance guard quickly made a pontoon bridge for the whole army to cross on 4 July. With the English army on both banks of the river the captain of the garrison at Pont de l'Arche sued for terms and agreed to surrender the castle on 20 July if he had not been relieved by either faction before then. Henry's next objective was clearly the city and fortress of Rouen, the capital of Normandy. Rouen lay some 8 miles away downriver from Pont de l'Arche and was garrisoned by the Burgundians. The last thing Henry wanted was to have a Burgundian army marching to the relief of Rouen from the direction of Paris. Burgundy, who had entered Paris on 14 July after a pro-Burgundian coup, and who now controlled the city, replied that he would shortly be marching against the English but he did nothing to either strengthen the garrison or to put his army into the field to make good his threat to Henry.

The castle at Pont de l'Arche duly surrendered on 20 July. Meanwhile Burgundy had his hands full with problems in Paris and had insufficient resources to contest northern Normandy at the same time. Notwithstanding the threat of intervention by Burgundy, Henry decided to go ahead and besiege Rouen. Meanwhile the last remaining French stronghold in the south of Normandy, Domfront, surrendered on 22 July 1418, after a four-month siege.

Rouen, which had been expecting a siege ever since Louviers fell in the spring, had been reinforced by 300 men-at-arms and as many archers shortly after. The walls had been repaired and all boats on the Seine had been burnt, as had the suburbs. Citizens were conscripted to carry out duties of watch and ward on the city walls, and food and supplies sufficient to withstand a long siege had been taken in; they were as ready as they could be to face a siege. But Henry's army had an awesome reputation and the garrison and citizens realized that their only real hope of survival lay in Jean of Burgundy and his army in Paris. However he found it difficult to maintain trade and to import food from the surrounding countryside, because although he controlled the routes into Paris from the north and the south-east the Armagnacs controlled all the rest. Now that Burgundy had the king in his power in Paris as well as Paris itself he began to exercise the powers of a regent and discharged those of government.

Duke Jean realized that the key to northern Normandy lay in Rouen and furthermore that he had to confine Henry to the south of the Seine if he was to have any chance of evicting the English from France. To this end he launched a diplomatic campaign to collect allies, to patch up his differences with the Armagnacs, and to gather funds. He convinced Castile that Henry was their enemy to such good effect that the Cortes voted sufficient funds to equip a fleet of galleys for use by the French against the English. He sent the Dauphin's wife, whom he had been holding in Paris, back to her husband, who was with Armagnac forces in the south, in the hope that they might concert their operations against the English. He hoped to operate north of the Seine leaving the Dauphin to operate against the English in Aquitaine and across the Loire into southern Normandy. He made an alliance with Scotland who promised aid, indeed the duke of Albany, the regent, lent him 30,000 Livres (about £6,000). All this took time during which no active operations were initiated against the English in northern Normandy, who after overrunning the countryside about Rouen settled down to besiege the city on 29 July.

Intermittent skirmishing went on along Henry's southern borders with both Armagnac and Burgundian forces, which also did their best to fight and frustrate each other. This enmity between the two factions prevented concerted action against the English who, although losing some small fortresses and towns in the south, nevertheless tightened their grip on Normandy as a whole; both French factions were increasingly worried that the English would next strike south towards the Loire. In fact, Henry never wavered from his aim to conquer northern Normandy, and while reinforcing his garrisons in the south moved Warwick's division to the north of the Seine, thus denying the Burgundians the northern approaches to Rouen with the possibility of raising the siege from that direction. As Rouen was a river port it was important that the river was closed to French shipping coming upriver from the sea while it was kept open for use by Henry's ships. A successful siege would depend on being able to replenish his army by ship direct from England, particularly if the siege proved to be a long one. Indeed this is exactly what Henry had arranged and supply ships kept his army fed during the course of the winter throughout the long siege.

The Burgundians were well placed to interfere with the siege should they wish to do so, providing they could co-ordinate the actions of their forces. Their army was in and about Paris and they held all the fortresses along the river east of Pont de l'Arche as well as the area north and west of Rouen towards Dieppe. Warwick's division detailed for the task of isolating Rouen from the north and from the sea by-passed Rouen and surprised the garrison of Cadence on the Seine, halfway between Rouen and Harfleur. He followed this up with the capture of Quilleboeuf, nearer to Harfleur, so denying the lower Seine to the French while opening it to Henry's ships; this allowed him to patrol the river right up to the walls of the city. Meanwhile the main part of the army closed up round the city. The garrison refused to surrender and a lengthy siege began. Back in western Normandy Cherbourg surrendered to Gloucester on 29 September 1418 after a siege of five months. Henry now had the whole of lower Normandy west of the Seine in his grasp with the exception of Honfleur, which was surrounded; its capability to interfere by sea was neutralized by ships out of Harfleur on the other side of the Seine estuary.

Three factors – the unlawful taxation to pay for men-at-arms, companies living off the countryside without payment, and unrest in Paris – contributed to the difficulties confronting the French authorities in their efforts to wage war against the English. It also alienated the people of the countryside and the citizens of the major towns. Indeed the government's efforts were largely ineffective, not only for the reasons given, but also because the French were, as after Crécy, reluctant to meet the English in a set-piece battle for fear of another

Agincourt. Henry's task was therefore a great deal easier than it might have been if France had been united, and he took every advantage of this state of affairs.

The citizens and garrison of Rouen experienced all the usual privations of a siege, including bombardment, disease and starvation. Burgundian forces, sent piecemeal on the road from Paris for the relief of Rouen, either faded away at the prospect of action against the English or else never arrived because of a lack of food. This and lack of cash always prevented the assembly of a sufficiently large force to pose any real threat to the English army; the small parties sent were simply eliminated. Nevertheless the French did make an effort to assemble an army west of Paris in order to raise the siege, but once again this came to nothing because of a shortage of food, or so it was rumoured in Paris. About the same time, in November, the Burgundians tried to raise an army at Troyes, in the heart of the duchy, for operations against the English or the Armagnacs, but this also came to nothing. The duke, sensing unrest in the city, left Paris with the king shortly after to set up his headquarters at Pontoise where he remained for a month during fruitless negotiations with Henry. Armagnac forces, meanwhile, raided up to the walls of Paris from the south, even while Jean of Burgundy was trying to co-ordinate their respective forces against the English. The citizens of Rouen were now starving, reduced to eating dogs, rats and mice and those of Paris sent delegations to the duke at Pontoise pleading with him to raise the siege. The Burgundian army, however, was keen to withdraw due to lack of provisions.

As soon as news of the Burgundian withdrawal reached them the garrison and officials of the city began negotiations for surrender with the English, and agreed to open their gates on 19 January 1419 after a relentless siege which had lasted nearly six months through a very cold winter. Henry, who intended to rule Normandy from Rouen, was obliged to be diplomatic and show clemency towards the city and its surviving inhabitants. As a result the city was not sacked, indeed by the standards of the day and judged by his treatment of the citizens of Caen, Henry was extremely lenient. He fined the city 300,000 crowns (£50,000) and those citizens who were willing to take the oath of fealty were given the King's peace and allowed to keep their property; furthermore the city was allowed to keep the ancient privileges granted by the French crown.

Once Rouen was safely in his hands Henry sent his captains on raids up to the walls of Paris. He of course realized that if a city the size of Rouen could defy him for six months Paris, which was well garrisoned and with strong walls, would take even longer. Furthermore, with a Burgundian army at Beaumont-sur-Oise and an Armagnac army not far away near Dreux, his army if stretched around Paris in siege lines would be very vulnerable to attack. He was also well aware that provisions for his army would be hard to find after the Burgundian army had been forced to move on by a shortage of supplies in the area, although of course he would have been able to bring supplies upriver from the sea by boat. He therefore dismissed the idea of taking Paris at this juncture and instead concentrated on securing his hold on Normandy. He sent Exeter and his division towards Dieppe to clear northern Normandy while Salisbury cleared the banks of the Seine towards Paris. Gaillon and Vernon yielded on 3 February, Mantes and Meulan on the Seine on 5 February and Dieppe surrendered on 8 February, by which time all the fortresses west of the Rouen-Dieppe road towards the sea had transferred their allegiance to Henry. After a thrust by Warwick to the River Bresle in mid-February, Normandy had indeed been conquered. In July the English occupied Pontoise at the junction of the Oise and the Seine, about 20 miles north-west of Paris. Henry could now put diplomatic pressure on the French from a position of some strength. He still intended to conquer France north of the Loire and to occupy Paris and only then could he have himself declared king of France.

After Rouen had been taken and while neither French faction controlled Paris, it seemed to Henry that the balance of advantage lay with Jean of Burgundy. He therefore welcomed a delegation from the Burgundians and met Duke Jean and the queen, Isabella, at Meulan on 30 May; Princess Katherine accompanied them. At first the negotiations went well from both points of view and took realistic account of Henry's strong position after his conquest of Normandy. Duke Jean and Queen Isabella conceded Henry's right in full sovereignty to Aquitaine, Normandy and Calais, and were prepared to give the hand of Princess Katherine in marriage with a suitable dowry. But Henry would only renounce his claim to the throne of France if he also received the old Angevin lands. This was too much for the Burgundians who were concerned that many of their own followers would desert them if they agreed to this.

It must have been clear to Duke Jean that the negotiations were not going to lead to a settlement because he opened discussions with the Dauphin well before the impasse arrived. In fact his delegation failed to turn up for the talks scheduled for 3 July and on 11 July Duke Jean and Queen Isabella were reconciled with the Dauphin at a meeting in Pouilly. A further meeting was arranged at these talks between the Dauphin and Duke Jean to take place at the bridge at Montereau on 10 September to discuss their differences and to co-ordinate action against the English. Urgency now entered the proceedings between the French factions; Henry began a push towards Paris as soon as the temporary truce, arranged between himself and Jean for their talks, expired on 29 July. On 10 September Jean duly walked onto the bridge over the Yonne for his personal meeting with the Dauphin, when the barriers were closed behind him and he and his party were cut down and killed at a sign from the Dauphin.

The murder of Duke Jean of Burgundy, together with Henry's threat to Paris, triggered the Anglo-Burgundian alliance, sealed on Christmas Day 1419 by Jean's son Philippe. Although Henry did not enter Paris at this stage he was clearly the master of the political situation in France and he made his demands quite clear. He intended to have the crown of France and although he was content to leave the mad old king, Charles VI, on the throne until he died, he expected to be appointed his successor. Philippe was not in a position to oppose this. Queen Isabella tried for reconciliation with the Dauphin without success and, with no avenue out of their quandary, the queen and Philippe signed their alliance with Henry. Henry now had Philippe of Burgundy, Queen Isabella and King Charles in his power and their first step was to declare the Dauphin guilty of treason and banned from Paris for his part in the murder of Duke Jean. But the most important aspect of the negotiations that had first opened between Henry and Philippe after Jean's murder came with the signing of the treaty of Troyes between France and England on 21 May 1420.

By the terms of the treaty Henry was to be the lawful successor to Charles VI on the latter's death and the crown would pass to Henry's heirs forever. The governance of France would remain French with their system and their officials, and the two kingdoms would be kept administratively and politically separate. Normandy and Aquitaine, however, would remain under English control until Charles's death. Henry and Philippe agreed to restore all the lands held by the

Dauphin and his supporters to the crown. Philippe of Burgundy received certain valuable lordships and a promise of aid from Henry to avenge his father's death. Henry was to marry Princess Katherine who would bring a substantial dowry, and finally he was to become regent of France during Charles's lifetime. Henry had apparently achieved all that he had ever dreamt of.

Although the treaty produced a military alliance, larger and more potent than that immediately available to the Dauphin, it did not result in peace. Indeed Henry had committed himself to continuing warfare against the forces of the Dauphin. Parliament recognized this but took note of the fact that the two administrations were to be kept separate and therefore welcomed the fact that once Charles died it would no longer be called upon to act as treasurer for Henry's campaigning in France. It seemed that Henry had made good his promise to parliament and might even soon be in a position to repay some of his debt. However, the Dauphin was not without resources of his own. He held all of France south of the Loire, excluding Aquitaine, together with several fortresses near Paris and along the borders of English Normandy. Furthermore he had a valuable ally in Scotland, which now, in response to appeals for help, sent a welcome reinforcement of an army 6,000 strong under the earls of Buchan and Wigton, with a promise to send another contingent later.[11] This Scottish expeditionary force was transported by a Castilian fleet, paid for by the French, which sailed down the Irish Channel probably to land at La Rochelle. They might have landed in Brittany but as Duke Jean was in treaty with Henry and had apparently forbidden such a course,[12] it is unlikely. The Castilian fleet sailed to France without interference from the English, but lost six ships on the way.[13] The forces available to each side were now balanced as the Burgundian army was never larger than about 6,000 strong and although the forces available to the Dauphin were more numerous than those in Henry's pay, they could not match their quality and experience.

The Dauphinists took advantage of the inevitable disarray in the Burgundian camp after the murder of Duke Jean and before his son Philippe could take over, and in 1420 went on the offensive locally from their fortresses in the north of France and around Paris. They harassed the English in northern Normandy, looted and burned about the capital and pressed the English along their southern frontier, operations which were easily contained by the earl of Salisbury, the king's lieutenant in the south-west, who himself riposted with a raid to Le Mans. The Dauphinists also tried to pressure the Bretons into neutrality or even active support, but the duke appealed for support from Henry and the French failed in their attempt.

Shortly after he had signed the treaty of Troyes, Henry V married Katherine of France at Troyes on 2 June 1420; a very short two-day honeymoon followed before Henry was again on campaign. Dauphinist forces held much of the countryside around Paris including many of the fortified towns and castles, all of which Henry had undertaken to eliminate by the Treaty of Troyes; he therefore set out to meet his obligations and by November he had taken Sens, Montereau and Melun. Notwithstanding these successes Henry found he lacked the necessary resources to clear northern France of Dauphinist forces and so returned to England to obtain more money and men, rather as parliament had feared would happen.

While he was in England he left his brother Thomas, duke of Clarence, as his lieutenant in France. Thomas, an experienced but headstrong soldier, had been raiding out of Normandy into Maine and along the Loire, and having failed to surprise Angers was on his way back to Normandy. He was at Beaufort, 15 miles east of Angers on 22 March 1421 when he was told of a mainly Scottish army encamped near Baugé 10 miles away to the north-east; this army under the earl of Buchan had marched to intercept Clarence. Against advice Clarence set off immediately with only 1,500[14] men-at-arms and no archers. Baugé lay on a slight ridge some 300 yards from the little River Couosnon, which ran through marshy ground, and overlooking a bridge. When Clarence and his men-at-arms were a little way from the bridge a Scottish reconnaissance patrol saw them and managed to warn their main body in the town before Clarence reached the bridge. Some of the Scots rushed down to the bridge and got there the same time as the English and a fierce fight ensued for its possession. However the river was only about 3 yards wide so the remainder of the English waded across the river and through the boggy ground outflanking the Scots on the bridge, who then pulled back to the village of Vielle Baugé, close by the town. The English chased them back and bottled them up in the village church before Clarence, realizing that his little force was becoming scattered, called everyone back and rallied them at the bridge. Meanwhile the earl of Buchan, the commander of the Franco-Scottish army of between three and five thousand men, mustered them in battle order out of sight behind the village and below the ridge before marching them over the top to engage the English. Clarence, on seeing the leading elements of the enemy, immediately mounted and charged up the slope with all those near him, but by the time he got to the ridge the Franco-Scottish force was coming over it. The two sides met in a sharp encounter, Clarence was overwhelmed and his small force cut to ribbons; he himself was killed and most of his force were either killed or taken prisoner. This significant skirmish took place in the late afternoon and probably lasted no more than half an hour; by the time Salisbury came up with the mounted archers and some men-at-arms it was already getting dark. The English found the bodies of Clarence and others in a cart being taken off the field but no formed body of enemy soldiers; they then withdrew whence they came. The Franco-Scottish army spent the night in Baugé itself before marching off early next morning to cut the English army's line of withdrawal to Normandy, which they failed to do; Salisbury evaded them and got safely home.

Baugé had one serious diplomatic result for Henry: it convinced Duke Jean of Brittany that his destiny lay with the Dauphin. After months of negotiation with both the Dauphin and Henry he finally signed an alliance with the French on 8 May 1421, and immediately endorsed his signature by promising to send a large body of men-at-arms and archers to join the Dauphin at Le Mans. The forces available to the latter were now quite sizeable. In addition to his own army he had 6,000 Scots and, in due course, perhaps 5,000 Bretons; furthermore there was another contingent of Scots under the earls of Douglas and Mar on their way. The Bretons and Scots were no peasant levy but tough, well-armed and experienced professional soldiers. With his added strength the Dauphin advanced into Normandy from Le Mans but was checked by Salisbury, the French army being reluctant to close in battle, notwithstanding the recent gain at Baugé.

Henry returned to Calais in June with reinforcements of some 4,000 men and immediately set out to finish the war. He marched south to Paris to muster his forces and challenge the Dauphinist army about Chartres. The latter, still reluctant to meet the English in a set-piece battle, withdrew to Vendôme. Henry then besieged and took the Dauphinist fortress of Dreux in July and August and then took Chartres before marching to the Loire at Orleans without encountering the Dauphinist army. He then marched north again and put Meaux, to the east of Paris, under siege in October with his Burgundian allies. These operations relieved pressure both on the capital and on Normandy. However there was a great deal of minor activity along English Normandy's southern frontier. Dauphinist raids commanded by Jean Aumâle, count of Harcourt, while not being a threat to the conquest, were nevertheless debilitating and needed to be stopped, as also were the operations of Marshal Severac and Breton raids into south-western Normandy. Henry gave the task to Salisbury who, in December, raided south to Dangeau, whereupon Aumâle withdrew; but no sooner had Salisbury stabilized the situation than the Scots took Avranches in January 1422; once again it was Salisbury who was sent to restore the fortress to English hands. This pattern of raid and counter-raid was to become a constant irritation for the English forces in Normandy, who were not going to be allowed to enjoy the fruits of their conquest in peace. There is no doubt that Henry could have put a stop to the pattern if only he could bring the French to battle, but the French avoided this. Two possibilities remained: he could either extend his conquest to the Loire or withdraw into Normandy. However, by the Treaty of Troyes Henry had undertaken to fight the enemies of the king of France for whom he had become regent by the same treaty. The Dauphin controlled much of Maine, Anjou and Blois north of the Loire, and most of France south of the river; Henry, as regent, was obliged to clear this of Dauphinist forces. If he could achieve this it would extend his conquest to the Loire and establish him even more firmly in northern France.

But the siege of Meaux dragged on throughout the winter and the town did not surrender until 10 May 1422, seven months after it was first put under siege. The surrender, however, brought diplomatic success: Jean of Brittany, who had been equivocal in his support of both sides in the war, finally threw in his lot with Henry and swore to recognize the terms of the Treaty of Troyes; he then withdrew his forces from the Dauphinist army. During the siege Henry continued his diplomatic pressure on the Dauphin by negotiating with Sigismund, the emperor and feudal overlord, for the transfer of the Dauphiné and parts of Languedoc from the Dauphin to him. But the siege severely depleted Henry's army by sickness, mainly dysentery, and Henry himself became ill. With Meaux safely in his hands Henry next set out in July to besiege Cosne-sur-Loire but was so ill that he had to be carried on a litter. He died on the way at Bois de Vincennes on 31 August 1422.

Baugé, although only a skirmish, was important. The heir to the thrones of England and France had been killed in battle, which in itself was of enormous propaganda and morale value for both the French and the Scots and a blow to England. It was important also because it showed that English arms were not invincible. Providing their archers could be separated from their men-at-arms, the latter were seen to be much the same as anyone else's. The battle came at a time when the French were badly in need of a morale booster, however it is doubtful if the French realized that their success was due in large part to the separation of archers from men-at-arms. Baugé also shows the extent to which Franco-Scottish co-operation had evolved in their wars with England; for France this was a politically important skirmish in which the Scots formed the major part of a Franco-Scottish army under the command of a Scot and operating in France. The Scottish division at Baugé, later expanded to about 7,000 men, helped to produce armies in the field as large as France might have done had she not been divided. But perhaps more importantly it gave confidence to the French.

Chapter 15

The Rise of Bedford and Talbot

'During the time men live without a common power to keep them all in awe, they are in that condition which is called war.'[1]

Henry's death was an unexpected blow for England, nevertheless he had achieved almost all that he had dreamt of in France. He had conquered Normandy, secured Paris and by the terms of the Treaty of Troyes had obtained the throne of France for his infant son Henry VI, the mad king Charles VI's grandson. However, the fact that half of France, that south of the Loire less Aquitaine, was loyal to the Dauphin, who did not recognize Henry VI as the lawful king of France, made the claims on the infant's behalf rather hollow. Also, neither Philippe of Burgundy nor Jean of Brittany had pledged their loyalty to the new infant king. Burgundy, however, maintained the understanding that he had had with Henry V and while not openly acclaiming the new king nevertheless was prepared to continue military co-operation with the English for so long as it was useful to him. This was important, for by the Treaty of Troyes Henry V had committed England to a continuation of the war. Henry had elected to defeat the Dauphin Charles, who had been disinherited by his father, and to that end John, Henry's younger brother and duke of Bedford, was obliged to clear Dauphinist forces from north of the River Loire and from about Paris in a continuation of Henry's policy. This commitment was also one of the main reasons why Philippe of Burgundy was happy to support the English; it was of course the Dauphin who had arranged the murder of his father, Duke Jean the Fearless.

The mantle of responsibility in France had fallen on Bedford since he became regent after his brother's death and he therefore became responsible for enacting the terms of the treaty. His first task was to obtain recognition of the treaty of Troyes from Burgundy and Brittany.

One aspect of the Treaty of Troyes was to have an unseen influence on the war as a whole: the treaty stipulated that England and France should be treated henceforth as two separate kingdoms although Henry V's successors would wear the crowns of both. This meant that Normandy, Aquitaine and Calais would revert to the French crown once Charles VI died and, since an English king would also then be king of France, the old problem of the sovereignty of Aquitaine seemed now to be settled. However the regency council in England and parliament were also conscious of Henry's commitment in the treaty to treat the governance and administration of the two kingdoms separately. In practical terms it meant that parliament in England was no longer responsible for financing the war in northern France; henceforth it had to be paid for from taxes levied in Normandy and in other parts of conquered northern France including Paris. As a result parliament ceased to underwrite the war in France for the next seven years. However parliament at home remained financially responsible for fitting out and maintaining the fleet, and for raising and paying reinforcements until they arrived in Normandy. The garrisoning of Calais also remained a responsibility of the government at home. Aquitaine continued to be administered mainly by Gascons and the army there was mainly Gascon with a leavening of English troops. War and administration in Aquitaine was financed, in the main, by the Gascons themselves as was now going to be the position in Normandy.

The lack of treasury funds from England meant that Bedford was now short of gold for war in France. This financial shortage had the effect of changing the strategy of the war from one of offence against the Dauphinists on all fronts to one of defence of the English conquests. Henry V's untimely death gave England another problem in its association with France. His infant son, Henry VI, had inherited the two crowns and so Bedford became the regent in France while his younger brother, Gloucester, became protector in England during Bedford's absence in France. Consequently Gloucester chaired the regency council when Bedford was in France but was always subject to it. In effect the two crowns became separated with a regent of France having regency powers in England but only when in England, and a protector in England who became the *de facto* ruler of England in the absence of the regent, but having no powers in France. In due course this was to have serious consequences for the prosecution of the war in France and for England's cause in France as a whole.

Henry V's death spurred the Dauphinists to offensive activity. In January 1423 they took the fortress of Meulan, about 31 miles downstream of Paris, and their Scottish allies took Gallardon, 10 miles north-east of Chartres. However, shortage of funds prevented them from exploiting their limited success. Following this burst of activity, English troops took three major fortresses so clearing the Dauphinists from the area between Paris and Chartres. However the Dauphinists were by no means cowed; they held the whole of France south of the Loire except for Aquitaine and some strongpoints north-east of Paris and in Picardy. They were probably in a better financial position than Bedford and could raise a large French field army of possibly 10,000 men. They could also count on the services of a sizeable Scottish army of about 6,000 men under the earl of Buchan. According to Newhall the original Scottish army of about 6,000 men which took part in the fighting at Baugé was said to have been reinforced with a further 8,000 men in 1422–3.[2] However, since the Scots never managed to raise more than about 7,000 even in defence of the homeland, it is doubtful that the Scottish contingent in France, all told, would have been much larger at any one time.

Bedford was determined to continue Henry's policies in northern France. This entailed keeping duke Philippe of Burgundy true to his commitment made at Troyes and clearing Dauphinist forces from north of the River Loire. Normandy was to remain English and like Aquitaine was sovereign to England until such time as Henry VI came of age, when it would revert to the crown of France, which of course Henry VI would wear by the Treaty of Troyes. Unfortunately this neat political solution foundered before it was born. The mad king Charles VI died in September 1422, and as a result the Dauphin declared that he was the Valois king of France as Charles VII. Bedford was no longer going to issue orders to the French in the name of their own king. Although Bedford proclaimed Henry VI king of France in Paris, an absentee infant did not carry the same ring of authority as a resident.

In the military sphere nothing very much of note took place in the year following the deaths of the two kings. Operations were characterized by raid and counter raid, and by the seizure and loss of various castles and fortified places. Nevertheless, the operations of the Anglo-Burgundians had a purpose. The Valois held various strongholds to the north-east of Paris in Champagne which constituted a threat to

Paris and to Burgundian territory in the area. They also had a small army in the field in Picardy, which took Le Crotoy at the mouth of the Somme in 1423. This was more than a nuisance and French possession could not be allowed, as they would interfere with England's sea communications between Calais and Caen. A three months' siege and blockade was envisaged and an army of about 1,500 men, mainly gathered from garrisons in Normandy, was detailed for this task together with four great ships and three balingers.[3] The siege began on 24 June and was to last for nearly nine months.

As will be seen, the garrisons in Normandy and elsewhere in France were often milked to provide elements for a field army, and garrisons might be taken from a fortress to man a more important place or a newly taken fortress. Garrisons varied in size a great deal. The smallest Norman garrison was at Pont d'Ouve and had only 3 men-at-arms and 9 archers, while a larger fortress such as Gisors had 60 men-at-arms and 180 archers. The total number of soldiers in garrison in 1419 was estimated by Newhall[4] to be 4,213, divided on the basis of three archers to each man-at-arms. Generally garrisons were established along the frontier of English Normandy, along lines of communication, guarding river crossings and at important ports. The most important, including those at the administrative centres of Rouen and Caen, were royal garrisons and were considerably larger than the others, the remainder being feudal garrisons captained and garrisoned by those who had been enfeoffed.

Bedford decided to clear Champagne and Picardy of Valois forces before turning south and moving into Maine and Anjou. He despatched the earl of Warwick to deal with the Valois forces in Picardy and the earl of Salisbury into Champagne after he had recovered the fortress and bridge of Meulan on the Seine. If Bedford was to advance south to the Loire he had to be sure of the neutrality of Jean, duke of Brittany, and of the active support of Burgundian forces. To this end he espoused Philippe of Burgundy's younger sister Anne. He also called a meeting at Amiens in the spring of 1423 where he agreed a mutual defence pact with the dukes of Brittany and Burgundy. The subtle aspect of the agreement was that Bedford signed it as regent for Henry VI, king of France, and thus both Burgundy and Brittany had implicitly recognized Henry VI as their king. In May Bedford journeyed to Troyes to receive the hand of his betrothed,

Anne of Burgundy. He now also had a personal tie with Philippe of Burgundy and had isolated Charles within France.

In the summer of 1423 Salisbury was on his way to begin operations in Champagne and had got as far as Montaiguillon near Previns, which he put under siege. Shortly after, in July, the Dauphinists launched an offensive north-eastwards towards Auxerre and Troyes, the Burgundian headquarters, their first objective being the Anglo-Burgundian fortress of Cravant which controlled the bridge across the River Yonne some 15 miles upstream from Auxerre. Bedford reacted quickly and sent the earl of Salisbury with an army of about 4,000[5] to raise the siege. Salisbury met up with a Burgundian contingent at Auxerre where he held a council of war with his Burgundian allies. Here they agreed to certain articles of war, which survive to this day. These concerned command, the taking of prisoners, discipline, the provision of scouts on an equal basis and the problem presented by the horses once the order to dismount had been given – they were to be led at least half a mile to the rear. Charles had gathered an army variously estimated at between two and three times that of the Anglo-Burgundians who were given as 4,000 English and 1,000 Burgundian.[6] The French army included a large Scottish contingent, perhaps as many as 6,000, under Sir John Stewart of Darnley.

Cravant lies on the right or east bank of the river at the foot of steep hills, which rise to a height of 980 ft some 2½ miles to the north. Immediately to the north of them is an escarpment, which runs down to the river. Both sides had scouts out and it was not long before the French realized that the Anglo-Burgundians were advancing down the right bank from Auxerre, knowing that the Franco-Scots had lined the escarpment. Salisbury, on seeing the enemy position, realized it was far too strong to attack and so withdrew and crossed the river at Vincelles about a mile downstream from the escarpment, before marching down the left bank towards Cravant. The Franco-Scots watched Salisbury's crossing and then kept pace with the English until both arrived at the bridge opposite the town. Here there was a strip of land between the town and the river perhaps 160 yards wide and it was on this strip that the Franco-Scots drew up their army.

A Scottish contingent had secured the bridge but otherwise the Scots were drawn up on the right, or northern half of the Franco-Scottish line, while the French held the left. The Anglo-Burgundian army arrived opposite the bridge and town still in their order of march: Lord Willoughby and the advance guard first, then Salisbury with the main body and finally the Burgundian rearguard. They took up positions with the advance guard opposite the French and the main body opposite the Scots; the Burgundians provided the second line. Willoughby's men attacked the bridge and a fierce but indecisive fight developed. While this struggle was going on and the two sides waited and watched each other Salisbury suddenly plunged into the river crying 'St George, banners advance' and his men-at-arms closely followed him. At this time, providing their morale was about the same, the men-at-arms of one side were every bit as good as those of their opponents. In this case the morale of the Scots was certainly as good as that of the English, and French morale was as good as that of the Burgundians, but crucially, with memories of Agincourt, French morale was not as good as that of the English. The Anglo-Burgundian army crossed the river, some 60 yards wide, in the face of an enemy about twice as large and immediately pressed them hard. How was this done?

Once again the archers are the crucial element. In an English army 4,000 strong, at least 3,000 of them would have been archers and each division would have had its own contingent in the same proportion of one to three. So Willoughby's division would have had about 1,000 archers, probably drawn up on its right or southern flank, and Salisbury's about 2,000 drawn up on its left or northern flank. The whole Anglo-Burgundian line of men-at-arms would not have been longer than about 400 yards, so enabling the archers at either end to cover the centre of the line. Possibly of more importance, the archers could also cover the whole depth of the Franco-Scottish position right up to the walls of Cravant itself from their safe positions on the left bank of the river. The archers would have poured a devastating fire into the ranks of the Franco-Scots who would have come under fire from the walls of Cravant as well. This archery fire would not only have caused heavy casualties but would also have disorganized and disrupted the Franco-Scots.

As Salisbury's army climbed out of the river it was engaged immediately by the French and Scots, while the garrison of Cravant watched the action from the walls of the town. Salisbury's division was making little headway against the Scots when Willoughby's division, having taken the bridge, began to get the better of the French opposite them. At this crucial time the Burgundian garrison in Cravant made a sortie into the back of the French on the left flank who immediately panicked and escaped as best they could to the south, leaving the Scots and many of their comrades to face the whole Anglo-Burgundian army by themselves. They fought bitterly but were eventually overwhelmed. The most reliable source[7] of casualty numbers gives the French as having 1,200 killed. The number of Scots casualties is given variously as between 2,500 and 4,000, but many would have been taken prisoner; all in all the Franco-Scottish army lost over 2,000 as prisoners. Both the French and the Scottish contingents lost their commanders. The count of Ventadour and Sir John Stewart of Darnley, the constable of Scotland, were taken prisoner along with many others, but importantly for the Anglo-Burgundians the Dauphinists' offensive came to a speedy end and they withdrew beyond the Loire. The allied victory at Cravant removed the Dauphinist threat to Burgundy and allowed the allies to raid as far as Macon down the valley of the Nivernais, a tributary of the Yonne, well behind and to the east of the Loire.

For the French Cravant was a disaster, however the Dauphinists gained a small but morale-boosting victory in Anjou, many miles to the west of Cravant. Sir John de la Pole had been ordered to mount a siege of Mont St Michel in July, but disregarding his orders and assuming the French would have all their field forces at or near Cravant, many miles to the east, raided down to Angers. On his way back, laden with booty, he was surprised a few miles west of Laval by a French force of about 1,500 men under Aumale on 26 September. The two sides were about the same size but this time the French severely mauled the raiding force, regaining the booty and taking Sir John prisoner. This little episode was important because, for a while, it curbed English intrusion into France south of Fougères, from which they had been raiding into Anjou. However the French were in no position to go onto the offensive, not so much because of Cravant but because, once again, they were short of cash.

After Cravant the tidying up continued in Champagne and Poitou. Mont St Michel continued to hold out and remained a threat; indeed the besieging forces could more accurately be described as containing forces to prevent the garrison from raiding into Normandy if and when the English army left for operations elsewhere. Many castles changed hands during the winter months of 1423, particularly in the area to the north and north-east of Paris in a surge of activity to clear the area of Dauphinist forces. However the Dauphinists also had their successes. They surprised the Burgundian garrison at Compiègne, which changed hands again in April, and they captured Beaumont-sur-Oise from which Bedford quickly evicted them. They surprised Gaillon, which was later taken by Lord Scales in July, the garrison was massacred and the defences torn down. Le Crotoy, at the mouth of the Somme, finally surrendered in March 1424. Bedford was reinforced in April that year by a further 3,400 men under Talbot who landed at Calais; Guise came under siege in May. These actions cleared Ponthieu and much of Hainault of the Dauphinists and both the English and the Burgundians began to concentrate their efforts against the Dauphinists south of Paris: the latter for their part were keen to extend their operations against the English in southern Normandy. The area between a line drawn through Rennes, Laval and Chartres to Paris in the north and along the Loire from Angers to Orleans became the battleground. Whoever dominated this area and held Paris would be in a winning position to impose or reject the conditions of the Treaty of Troyes. From a Dauphinist point of view the line of the Loire was not really a secure feature since it could be turned, or at any rate easily crossed, in its upper reaches about Nevers by Burgundian forces operating out from the Cravant area towards Bourges. So it became important for the Valois to dominate not only the area north of the Loire but also that to the east of it. The scene was set for a final test of strength.

Early in 1424 both sides concentrated on mustering field armies, both Bedford and Charles having, unusually, sufficient cash to raise and pay them. The French and their allies the Scots had suffered grievously from the battle at Cravant and immediate steps were taken to make good the losses. Charles raised some 8,000 French troops for his army and paid for a further 1,000 mercenaries from Lombardy. This of course required large sums of money and in order to pay for his new army Charles declared a levy applicable throughout France south of the Loire, less of course Aquitaine. But he also enticed a large Scottish reinforcement under the earl of Douglas to serve under his banner.[8] Charles hired Castilian ships to transport them and they arrived in France in April 1424. The number of men in this reinforcement varies from source to source, but bearing in mind the size of the Scottish population it is unlikely to have exceeded 3,000 men. Also it is probable that Scottish casualties at Cravant were not as bad as they were reported and that perhaps as many as 4,000 survived. Together with the reinforcements, these numbers would account for the numbers in the Scottish division later at Verneuil. The reinforcements would have sailed together in an escorted convoy of about twenty ships. However once again, why didn't the English attack such a tempting target? Probably because, as before, they sailed down the Irish Channel to France and also perhaps because many of the ships from Henry V's navy were already rotting on the mud in various English Channel ports.

As a result of these various measures Charles managed to raise a field army by the early summer of 1424. However, field armies were expensive and he could not afford to raise one and then not use it. It had to be used as decisively as possible. The garrison at Gaillon was being besieged by a force under the earl of Suffolk. The garrison had agreed to surrender on 14 August if they had not been relieved by then[9] and this seemed to a hesitant but rather more aggressive council an ideal objective for Charles's newly raised army.

Bedford too had not been idle since the Battle of Cravant; he made plans to push south into Maine and Anjou, but first he had to collect a field army. He recalled Salisbury from a successful raid into Valois territory from the far south of Burgundy and other commanders from raids elsewhere, and he squeezed about 2,000 men from the Normandy garrisons. But the kernel of his new field army was the reinforcement in April, which had come over with Lord Talbot and landed at Calais. All told Bedford managed to gather a field army of about 10,000 men, made up of 1,800 men-at-arms and 8,000 archers,[10] with possibly 500 Bretons. The numbers in the Franco-Scottish army are not known for sure but all agreed that it was larger than the English; there were probably about 10,000 in the French contingent under Aumale and Narbonne, and possibly as many as 6,500 Scots together with 500 Lombard cavalry, say 17,000 altogether.[11] Both armies had reason to make for the same place, Ivry on the River Eure some 22 miles due west of Paris.

Bedford mustered his army at Evreux, about 20 miles north-west of Ivry, where a force of about 3,000 Burgundians under L'Isle Adam joined him. He marched to Ivry and accepted the garrisons surrender on 14 August before returning to Evreux the day after to observe the feast of the Assumption in the cathedral there. He also sent Suffolk with a force of 1,600 men to shadow the movements of the French.

On learning how large the French army was, he sent Salisbury with another force to back up Suffolk. The French meanwhile heard from their scouts that the surrender had already taken place, apparently they thought it was due on 15 August, and so they retraced their steps towards Verneuil. They took the city by a ruse and stayed there for the night. The English spent that night at Evreux, about 25 miles away, with Suffolk and Salisbury camped in between. The French now debated what they should do. They knew that Bedford was at Evreux with his army; they had a choice, indeed the strategic initiative lay with them. But decision making was not a strong point among the French at that time. Some were for disengaging and withdrawing back behind the Loire; the Scots and the younger French commanders wanted to engage the English; but the more circumspect suggested that they should campaign in southern Normandy, taking small fortresses along the southern Norman border. While they debated the die was cast.

Bedford was already on his way. He, perhaps foolishly, released the large Burgundian contingent to continue siege operations in Picardy and so they marched off after the surrender of Ivry. He spent most of 16 August marching south towards Verneuil, collected Suffolk and Salisbury on the way and spent the night at Damville, 12 miles from Verneuil. Early the next morning he was on the march once again. The French meanwhile realized from the reports of their scouts that the English were marching south, apparently intent on battle, and that they were too late to put any plan into action other than to prepare to meet them. They moved out of Verneuil early in the morning of the 17th and took up their battle positions. The Damville road ran north-east out of Verneuil for about 3 miles before entering the forest of Piseux. The ground was flat with a slight dip towards the forest and there was a farm about 1½ miles along the road from Verneuil.

The Franco-Scottish army deployed about halfway along the road towards the forest with the Scottish division under Lord Douglas to the right of the road, and the French under Aumale to the left. Two small mounted groups of perhaps 500 horsemen each were stationed on the flanks, a French squadron to the left of the French division and a Lombard squadron to the right of the Scots. The whole front extended perhaps 1,000 yards in three lines. There were some French crossbowmen interspersed with the men-at arms all along the front.

The English scouts would have told Bedford about the French positions before they debouched from the forest and no doubt Bedford
and Salisbury would have cantered up the rise to look at the French
position before giving out their orders for the English deployment. As
the English marched out of the forest, Bedford took his division to the
right of the road and Salisbury went to the left. They then dismounted
and waited. Nothing happened for four hours though the English tail
was very busy. The baggage wagons were formed into a wagon laager
near the forest and the horses were cobbled in pairs, nose to tail and
tethered just outside the laager; the pages and grooms provided what
baggage guard there was. Bedford's army settled into their battle
formation; archers were stationed on the flanks of each division and
importantly, a reserve of about 2,000 archers was stationed to the
rear of Bedford's division, but rather nearer the baggage than the line
of men-at-arms.

As at Agincourt the English archers carried sharpened stakes to
protect their positions and no doubt the reserve of archers also
hammered stakes into the ground around their position; they had
plenty of time and were ready. But the main body having stood in
formation for so long suddenly, at about four o'clock in the
afternoon, marched forward to just beyond bowshot range from the
Franco-Scots and halted; the accompanying archers tried to hammer
their stakes into the hard ground once more. The French had also
advanced, but while the English archers were planting their stakes the
French suddenly loosed their mounted squadrons at the archers. The
French squadron to the west of the road swept the archers away
before they were ready and galloped on towards the reserve of archers
who drove them off. But the Lombard squadron veered off from the
archers on Salisbury's left flank and failed to make proper contact;
almost certainly they had never before faced massed archery and they
didn't much like the experience. After their failure they galloped on to
the baggage laager, which they penetrated. They cut down many of
the guard and then looted several baggage wagons before they were
driven off by the reserve of archers. Both squadrons took no further
part in the battle. Meanwhile the two enemy lines marched towards
each other to begin the clash of arms. After about forty-five minutes
the English men-at-arms in Bedford's division sensed that their opponents were not as keen as they had been and before long some turned
and ran, soon to be followed by the whole of Aumale's French

division. Bedford's division pursued them to the walls of Verneuil where many met their end in the town ditch outside the walls. However, to the east of the road Salisbury's division was having a hard time, the fight was bitter and furious, and the Scots would not give way. But circumstances were against them; their allies the French had turned tail and run; Bedford, on seeing Salisbury's division hard pressed, reformed his division and attacked the Scots from the rear. Meanwhile the reserve of archers marched to the left of Salisbury's division and began to pour a lethal fire into the ranks of the Scots. Surrounded and outnumbered by about two to one, the Scots, having rejected quarter before the battle began, had no option but to sell their lives dearly and die bravely. The battle finally ended when not a Scot was left standing.

Verneuil was a crushing victory. The only French field army had been totally destroyed and the Scottish division had ceased to exist. Bedford wrote that the heralds had counted 7,262 enemy dead, mainly Scots. The French had lost their best commanders: Aumale, Narbonne and Ventadour were all killed and the duke of Alençon and marshal Lafayette were both prisoners. The Scots lost Douglas, his son James and the earl of Buchan. One of the most important results of the battle was that the Scots never again put a complete army into the field under the banner of the king of France, although they continued to send groups of a few hundred until the end of the war. The strategic importance of the battle was that it forced the French back behind the Loire, leaving the counties of Maine and Anjou open to exploitation by the English, as well as clearing French forces from the south of Normandy. In terms of morale this battle was a shattering blow to the French: twice in two years they had suffered a crippling defeat at the hands of the English; at Verneuil their allied army had suffered almost as many casualties as they had at Agincourt. It must have seemed to the French that they could never beat the English in a set-piece battle.

Ten days after the battle Bedford and Burgundy went on the offensive. Bedford contented himself with overrunning Maine and Anjou, his original plan, rather than making a single powerful raid with his triumphant army to Bourges, Charles's administrative head-quarters. Had he done this he might have finished the war at a stroke and dictated terms to Charles. But he went back to Rouen and sent Sir John Fastolf and lord Scales to campaign in Maine and Anjou, most of which they overran. Salisbury and Suffolk began the advance to the Loire, and Burgundy carried out a successful campaign in the south towards Macon, only 40 miles from Lyon and the Dauphinée, and bordering the duchy of Bourbon. Politically, militarily and financially matters were going well for Bedford in France; in particular the cornerstone of the Treaty of Troyes, the Anglo-Burgundian alliance, was working well.

Then like a bolt from the blue a problem arose from an unexpected quarter. Bedford's young brother Humphrey, duke of Gloucester, fell in love with Jacqueline, countess of Hainault and Holland in her own right; or perhaps it would be more accurate to say that he fell in love with her counties. She had come to England after quarrelling with her boorish husband, Jean of Brabant; they were a childless couple and Humphrey soon obtained papal dispensation to marry her. Humphrey and his bride were much admired, but he had ambitions of his own on the Continent and, once married, he immediately set about recovering her inheritance. Unfortunately, Philippe of Burgundy was Jean's heir and was bound to support Jean in any confrontation over the inheritance of Hainault and Holland, which in due course would become his. Gloucester styled himself count of Hainault, Holland and Zeeland, and raised an army 5,000 strong to wrest his wife's inheritance. He crossed the Channel with his army and landed in Flanders in October 1424. But after restoring her lands to his wife he went on *chevauchée* into the lands of Jean of Brabant. His army burnt and pillaged its way to Brussels but as Philippe of Burgundy assembled his forces to oppose them they withdrew back to the coast and embarked for England.

Gloucester left his bride in Hainault, presumably to administer her counties, while he went back to England. But meanwhile Jean of Brabant died and Philippe advanced into Hainault to take over what he considered to be his counties. He took Jacqueline prisoner, but she escaped and returned to England. This was a thoroughly unnecessary and unsuccessful venture, which seems to have set out without the blessing of the council. Gloucester's subsequent actions show what a shallow and greedy man he was: having failed in Hainault and Holland, he obtained a papal bull to nullify his marriage to Jacqueline, whom he discarded so that he could marry her lady in waiting! Certainly Humphrey's abortive action angered Philippe sufficiently for him to publicly vilify Bedford at a meeting in Paris.

Gloucester had very nearly undone all Bedford's patient diplomatic efforts. Indeed if it hadn't been for Bedford's wife, Anne, it is probable that Philippe would have reneged on the agreement made at Amiens, but luckily Burgundian and English troops never met in battle and so the issue was papered over. Nevertheless, Philippe opened communications with Charles the Dauphin while remaining questionably loyal to the Amiens agreement. He clearly calculated, and he was a scheming man, that he had more to gain for the present by remaining an ally of England than by openly changing sides; besides, the English were far too strong and might turn on Burgundy and ruin her. For the English Philippe was seen as an unreliable ally from that time on.

This meddling by Gloucester had the effect of closing down the operations in Maine and Anjou while Bedford did his best to limit the diplomatic damage. Luckily it was during the winter months and nothing of importance occurred. Salisbury, however, went back to England and returned to France early in the summer of 1425 with reinforcements. He continued the offensive into Maine in 1425, capturing Le Mans on 10 August and Mayenne soon afterwards. By the end of the summer the county of Maine had become part of 'English France'. But at the end of that year Bedford had to return to England, called back by the chancellor, Henry Beaufort, bishop of Winchester. Beaufort was Henry V's half brother and he and his cronies dominated the council. Gloucester opposed him because they frustrated his attempts to wield power in England where he was protector and not regent, and was always subject to the council; indeed Gloucester bore his uncle a personal grudge for he believed that it was Beaufort who had prevented him from being declared regent in Bedford's absence. There was a subtle difference between a regent, who exercised kingly powers, and a protector who did not. The latter simply provided the chair at the council and displayed the hollow trappings of kingship. Gloucester didn't like this, he wanted real power and he blamed Beaufort for his lack of it.

In 1425 Beaufort and Gloucester had a confrontation at London Bridge which nearly came to blows but was only prevented by the intercession of the archbishop of Canterbury and the king's cousin, prince Peter of Portugal,[12] who was in London at that time. Tempers cooled and matters returned to normal, but enmity and fear now resided in the council. It was this incident which prompted Beaufort to write to Bedford begging him to return to England as soon as possible. His letter indicated the way things were going: 'If you tarry, we shall put this land in peril with a battle. Such a brother you have here.'[13] Bedford needed no second bidding – he was back in London by December 1425.

Bedford was absent from France for the whole of 1426, but apart from activity on the borders of Brittany nothing very much happened that year. Duke Jean of Brittany once again changed sides and declared his support for the Dauphin. This provoked a response from the English who sent a small force under Sir Thomas Rempston to invade the duchy. They penetrated some way towards Rennes the capital of Brittany before withdrawing to the small walled town of St James de Beuvron on the Normandy/Brittany border. Duke Jean's brother, Arthur of Richemont, newly made constable of France, decided to punish the English intruders. He had besieged and taken the English fortress of Pontorson about 5 miles due south of Mont St Michel in January and was clearly a threat to the English containing forces. On hearing that Rempston's force had settled into St James, only 10 miles to the south-east, he decided to eliminate them and thus strengthen his hold about Mont St Michel. He arrived outside the walls of St James with an army said to be 16,000 strong, together with an impressive artillery train. He set up his guns and began the systematic destruction of the walls, soon making two breaches. Rempston and his small force of 600 were clearly in some danger but they decided on an unusual ploy. They left some of their force to guard the breaches and the remainder quietly crept out from a sally port, stole behind the French positions without being seen and then suddenly attacked them from behind with much shouting of 'Salisbury, St George'. The French, thinking perhaps that Salisbury had actually arrived on the scene with an army, panicked and ran back to their camp. Here the panic spread and during the night the French burnt their tents and withdrew, leaving their guns behind.[14] Richemont hurried away to Bourges where, apart from trying to retrieve his reputation, he impressed on Charles that something had to be done about the organization and pay of the French army if they were ever to meet the English on equal terms.

However, the incident of St James was not yet quite over. The earl of Suffolk, hearing of Rempston's audacious victory and fearing a return by Richemont, marched to St James from Avranches with about 1,500 men to support the small English garrison. Finding no sign of the French, he and Rempston with their combined force of over 2,000 men marched on Rennes. This put the fear of God into Duke Jean and, although Suffolk's small force halted at Dol de Bretagne, which they occupied, Jean applied for a three month truce. This Suffolk granted and it led to the treaty which Duke Jean signed with Bedford in the summer of 1427 accepting the Treaty of Troyes and recognizing Henry VI as the lawful king of France.

Bedford returned to France, accompanied by Lord Talbot, in March the same year with 1,200 reinforcements and a new artillery train. Talbot had evolved a style of warfare based on his experiences in Wales and Ireland where for the most part he was fighting guerrilla forces in countries in which the majority of the inhabitants opposed the English. Set-piece battles were unheard of; action took the form of short, sharp raids against armed gatherings of fleeting opponents based on information obtained and were carried out with ruthless efficiency. This he was now about to practise in France. He was soon in action as he joined his father-in-law, the earl of Warwick, at the siege of Pontorson, which was taken back in May 1427. Later that year he replaced Sir John Fastolf as governor of Maine and Anjou, based in Alençon, and prepared for a spring offensive against pockets of resistance around Laval and Le Mans. He first moved against Laval, which he took in a lightning raid, burning towns and destroying castles on the way. He returned to Alençon only to hear that a French army under La Hire had taken Le Mans, bottling up the English garrison in the castle. He moved with his customary speed and took the French army by surprise in a dawn attack on 27 May, exacting vengeance on collaborators with the French. Maine was now securely part of English France and in making it so Talbot became feared as a decisive and ruthless commander.

With the western and southern borders of Normandy secure after taking Pontorson and occupying Maine, Bedford could now concentrate his efforts against the Dauphinists north of the River Loire. However, they still held the fortified town of Montargis, between Orleans and Sens on the River Loing, a tributary of the Seine about 60 miles south of Paris, and a threat to communication between the English and the Burgundians. Bedford resolved to take the town before launching his offensive to clear the area north of the Loire. He sent the earl of Warwick to invest the town in July 1427 with about 5,000 men and an artillery siege train. Superficially this should have been a relatively easy siege, but there were problems. Montargis was well protected on its southern and eastern sides by the River Loing and by dykes on its northern and western sides. It was strongly fortified, had a resolute garrison and was very well situated. Warwick occupied the open ground about the road from Paris and his forces surrounded the town along both banks of the river. He opened proceedings with an intense artillery bombardment on 15 July, but after six weeks had made little progress. Meanwhile the Dauphinists decided to send John du Dunois, the bastard of Orleans, with 1,600 troops to relieve the town. They managed to get a messenger into the town to co-ordinate their action with the garrison and then took the English by surprise. They approached from the south and when the English saw them they rushed to engage them. The garrison then opened the sluice gates on the dykes, cutting Warwick's forces in two, and attacked them from behind. Warwick suffered many casualties, lost most of his artillery and was forced to raise his siege.[15] Montargis remained a Dauphinist fortress throughout the remainder of the war and the English then concentrated their efforts on the Dauphinist enclave north of the Loire. Montargis was perhaps an indication of things to come – it was a small but significant rebuff for the usually victorious English and was no doubt noted by Philippe of Burgundy, even though the English commanders might have brushed its significance aside. The French had proved that they too were quite capable of bold offensive action against the odds.

In July 1428 Salisbury occupied Paris mainly to prevent Burgundy from establishing himself there and indulging in political mischief. Later the same month Bedford called a council of war in Paris at which his principle commanders, Salisbury, Suffolk, Talbot and Warwick were present. The council had been called to decide on future action and after some argument it was decided to cross the Loire and march on Orleans, taking it as a prelude to an advance on Bourges, the Dauphin's base. Once the decision had been taken to cross the Loire, Orleans had to be taken. If it was taken it would breach the Dauphinist frontier of the Loire and, most importantly, the English would be able to march to Bourges forcing the Dauphinist army to meet them in open battle. However Bedford was apparently against a siege at this time, because it would tie up his only field army, but was presumably outvoted at the war council in Paris.

Political problems confronting Bedford still centred on the division of responsibility between the crown in England and the crown in

France. The economic burden of the war in France fell on the people of Normandy, and perhaps those of Paris and Maine. As a result Normans were faced with an ever-increasing burden of taxation although at the same time Bedford never had a sufficiency of cash to recruit field armies that were large enough to take the offensive conclusively.

The earl of Salisbury was given command of the army of some 5,000, which included the 2,500 men he had recruited to his banner in England, about 1,500 garrison troops and possibly as many as 1,000 Burgundians. After a rapid campaign in which some forty towns and villages were captured, including Meung and Jargeau, both of which were fortresses guarding bridges over the Loire either side of Orleans, the army arrived opposite Orleans on the south bank. Orleans was now separated but not cut off from Dauphinist France and the army should have been able to prevent supplies from reaching it along the river. The army's first task was to take and clear the suburbs, which they did quickly. But then they had to consider their task most carefully. Orleans was a walled city on the north bank of the river. There were five entrances to it, one by a bridge across the river where it was about 400 yards wide, and four others with gateways protected by towers and barbicans. The bridge was guarded at its south end by two towers, Les Tourelles, which were also protected by a barbican. The massive city walls protected by towers and bastions stretched for about 2,000 yards. It was a formidable fortress and made more so by French preparations. They had destroyed many buildings on the outskirts of the city so that their cannon had a clear field of fire and they had had time to stock up on provisions. The garrison was large, about 2,400 indentured soldiers augmented by a further 3,000 town militia. Orleans had seventy-one guns, cannons and bombards, probably made of bronze. One cannon lent by Montargis, called *Rifflard*,[i] fired stone cannon balls weighing 100 lb and needed twenty-two horses to drag it to its firing position. These cannon were able to cover Les Tourelles and its approaches by fire. They had one innovation, a gun with a very long barrel, which could reach the island of Charlemagne in the Loire about 800 yards from the city walls.[16] At this time small cannon, called culverins, were coming into

---

i Most cannon and bombards of any size were always named in the Middle Ages.

service on both sides; they fired a stone shot of between 9 and 20 lb. Their great advantage was that they could be moved easily from place to place and could therefore quickly cover any threat; they were the forerunners of dedicated field artillery. These were formidable defences manned by a large garrison; indeed if the city militia is included it was as large as the combined Anglo-Burgundian army besieging them. However they had one debilitating factor: their morale was low and they were terrified of the English and what they might do to their city; nevertheless they were not yet in a mood to surrender. As will be seen the morale factor was to become crucial in this siege.

Salisbury considered that the key to the defences was Les Tourelles. It is difficult to see why he came to this conclusion as it opened up the most difficult path for an assault into the city across the bridge. He bombarded the towers and the barbican for two days and then tried an assault, but the defenders resisted so fiercely that he called off this attack before his casualties mounted. He then called up his engineers and miners to sap the walls. No sooner had this begun than the French left Les Tourelles and withdrew across the bridge destroying two of the arches on their way. Salisbury now had one end of the bridge but was no nearer taking the city. The usual way to carry out a siege was for the besiegers to circumvallate the walls with a system of trenches and gun positions to enclose the garrison, before bombarding one or more points in the walls, followed by an assault through any breach made. But in this case the Anglo-Burgundian army was too small to man such a system of trenches. Salisbury therefore planned to establish a blockade about the city, to prevent reinforcement or replenishment, by building a series of forts or *bastilles* around it while he continued his bombardment and prepared to mine the walls. This bombardment was intense – for instance, on Sunday 17 October 1428 the English fired 124 'pierres de bombardes et de canon' into the city of Orleans.[17] Some of the shot weighed as much as 116 lb.[18] The English army gradually increased its pressure and was close to launching an assault when Salisbury was fatally wounded by a cannon shot on 24 October while on reconnaissance at Les Tourelles. He died on 3 November and command of the army devolved onto Suffolk, a reliable but conventional commander and one not noted for his flair or for taking risks. He withdrew the army into winter quarters in the nearby towns, leaving a garrison in Les

Tourelles and the church of the Augustins immediately to its south. The siege, which had started so promisingly, had lost its way.

It may be that going into winter quarters in the surrounding villages was a sensible thing to do, but it must have given the French a respite and also given them the wrong impression. It certainly did not impress Bedford who, having no confidence in Suffolk, appointed Talbot as joint commander of the army and ordered them to reopen the siege of Orleans. Under Talbot, the army began by putting Salisbury's plans for a series of blockading forts into action. They first made a fortified base camp around the church of St Laurent on the north bank of the river; this *bastille* was about 1,000 yards downstream of the city's walls. Next they built a fort on the island of Charlemagne to link up with the garrison at Les Tourelles and then, over the next four months, built four further forts, those of La Croix Boisée, London, Rouen and Paris, with interconnecting trenches north-eastwards from St Laurent. Finally, they fortified the derelict church of St Loup, about a mile east of the city walls on the north bank. All the forts were well out of gun range from the city walls. However, although they controlled the river at Jargeau and Meung they failed to string chains across the river nearer to Orleans and thus were unable to prevent boats from reaching the city. Also they left a gap in their blockade almost 2 miles long between the fort of Paris and the church at St Loup.

Early in February Sir John Fastolff set out from Paris with 300 wagons loaded with herrings and other supplies for the besieging army at Orleans, in preparation for Lent. He had a mounted escort of 1,000 archers, some of the Paris militia and the men-at-arms of his own retinue. The escorted convoy reached the village of Rouvray, 5 miles north of Janville, where it spent the night of 11 February. Early next morning as they set out they saw French scouts on the skyline to their south-east. These were the scouts of Clermont's 4,000-strong army which, having been forewarned of the convoy's route and timings, had positioned itself to bar its way. This army was on its way to relieve the siege at Orleans but Fastolff's convoy was a tempting target, and anyway it would provide a welcome present for the garrison and citizens of Orleans. However Fastolff was no novice. As soon as the French scouts were seen he halted his convoy and formed a circular wagon laager with two entrances, both covered by archers and protected by the archers' stakes. Once Clermont saw what

Fastolff had done he halted his army out of bowshot range and brought up his artillery. He then opened fire on the wagon laager. Fastolff's little force soon suffered from the bombardment and it is unlikely that they could have stood it for long, but they didn't have to. Lack of discipline in the French army and the Scottish contingent with them came to the rescue. Before the artillery had done its work a large number of dismounted French and Scots charged one of the entrances of the laager, only to be forced to retreat with many casualties by the archers. As the survivors ran back out of bowshot range, mounted French men-at-arms then charged the archers. Many of their horses were wounded on the stakes before they were also bloodily repulsed. As they drew back Fastolff ordered his own men-at-arms to mount, they charged out through both entrances and put Clermont's army to flight. So ended the 'Battle of the Herrings'. Fastolff delivered his supplies to the army and then returned to Paris for more.

This little battle should have been a significant reverse for the Dauphinists since Clermont's army was marching to raise the siege at Orleans and it, together with the garrison, would have far outnumbered the Anglo-Burgundian army. However, in the end it had little effect on the outcome of the siege, although at the time, once the garrison heard of Clermont's defeat their morale sank and negotiations were put in hand for their surrender.[19] But this possibility was premature and took no account of the many factors in their favour. The Anglo-Burgundians were unable to close the approaches to the city from the north-east or down the river from below Jargeau, consequently replenishment and reinforcements for the city and its garrison flowed into the city along the river. The garrison was now larger than the besieging forces and had more guns. Also a large Dauphinist army was based at Blois only 34 miles downriver from Orleans. No English garrison would think of surrender with so many factors in their favour. The only negative factors were that the initiative was held by the English and that the morale of the garrison was low, but this was about to change.

Politically also things were about to change and problems beset Bedford in Normandy. Here the activities of the 'brigands' increased and, due in part to increased taxation, many Normans actively supported them.[20] These bands were usually put down or driven away by the garrisons from the fortified towns and castles, but while the garrisons were away at the siege of Orleans the brigands thrived.

English Normandy needed their garrisons; they were misemployed on siege work at Orleans. On the diplomatic front problems were beginning to arise between the English and the Burgundians. Duke Philippe was piqued that Bedford had not allowed him to take up the Dauphin's offer in which he shrewdly offered to cede Orleans to him early in 1429;[21] an offer clearly designed to open a wedge between Burgundy and Bedford. Also, English troops had occupied Paris in July 1428, ostensibly to ensure its defence and to bring a degree of calm to this excitable city, but actually to keep it from Duke Philippe's grasp. These two incidents probably prompted the withdrawal of Burgundian troops from the siege of Orleans in April 1429. Bedford had to mollify Philippe with gold or greater influence, or he would move over to Charles; he was beginning to be an unreliable ally who exacted a high price in cash for his questionable loyalty.

These many problems in the spring of 1429 undoubtedly affected the strategy and field performance of the Anglo-Norman army and their garrisons in France. In part to balance the withdrawal of the Burgundian contingent from the siege of Orleans in April, Bedford asked the council for reinforcements and was sent a derisory 100 men-at-arms,[22] an addition that could hardly match that which Charles received when Jeanne d'Arc came to see him in March.

It is easy to say that the English soldiers were better than their opposite numbers in the French and Scottish armies, but the history of warfare in the Middle Ages does not bear this out. How then did the English at Cravant and Verneuil achieve such overwhelming victories? They certainly did not display outstanding or innovative battle tactics, indeed they were rather conservative in their ideas. The archers in English armies were certainly one factor and we know that the French were not able to produce the large numbers of archers usually found in English armies. But why on a man-to-man basis, dismounted, were the English able to defeat often four times their number of French men-at-arms who individually were no less courageous or capable than they were? Certainly the archers produced large numbers of casualties, although by this time plate armour was so efficient that it could often deflect arrows and prevent penetration. But the hail of arrows had another effect: it tended to force the lines of men-at-arms in towards their centre so causing disruption and more importantly compressing the ranks so that the men-at-arms had insufficient room to wield their staff weapons effectively. No such handicap confronted the English.

Like the French, the Scots could never raise the large number of archers, which was such a characteristic of English armies and so vital an element in their success in battle. By this time the proportion of archers to men-at-arms in English armies had risen to about four to one, however in French armies it was still below one to four, and in Scottish armies rather better at about two to one. These proportions give an indication of the make-up of the three national armies. In an example of say 10,000 men each, an improbably large size for a Scottish army, the make-up of the armies would be very different. An English army of this size would include 2,000 men-at-arms and 8,000 archers. A French army of the same size would have 8,000 men-at-arms and 2,000 archers or crossbowmen, while a comparable Scottish army might include 500 men-at-arms, 2,000 archers and 7,500 infantrymen. These Scottish infantrymen were not men-at-arms in plate armour, though some might have been lucky enough to pick up armour off the battlefield. They were dressed much more like English archers, with a helmet of sorts and a mail camail. They probably wore a brigandine with, if they were lucky, some pieces of plate armour protecting their arms and thighs; they were thus very vulnerable to archery fire and not as well protected as the English men-at-arms in a hand-to-hand fight. However, they were much more mobile and agile; indeed many of the Scottish 'casualties' at Cravant had probably escaped up the hills to the north of the town where they could not be pursued by the English men-at-arms. Considering the proportions between the various elements of their armies and the difference of equipment between them, it is easy to see why the English generally seemed to come out on top. Their archers were nearly always able to inflict so many casualties on the men-at-arms and infantrymen opposite them, and cause so much disruption before the hand-to-hand struggle, that their own disciplined and cohesive group of men-at-arms were able to win the day. Where English archers were not present, were scattered or were surprised, English armies were not any more successful than the armies of their enemies, providing they were of similar size. Cravant and Verneuil therefore were victories due to English military organization and deployment and their commanders ability to profit by them.

Chapter 16

The Two Kings of France

'Archers, noble soldiers and others besieging the good city of Orleans, go away, for God's sake, back to your own country.'[1]

Jeanne d'Arc arrived before Orleans on 29 April 1429 having marched from Blois. She had set out from her home in Domremy on 28 February the same year on her mission, in obedience to and guided by her 'voices'. Her mission was to rid France of the English, but first she had to convince Charles VII and his council that she could do this. She therefore travelled to Chinon for an audience with the king, at which she asked for an army and said she would raise the siege of Orleans. Against much scepticism and antagonism her wishes were granted and an army 4,000 strong under the command of the duke of Alençon was placed at her disposal. In a very short time she had converted this hesitant and apprehensive French army, fearful of meeting the English in battle, into an army of fervent crusaders. They reasoned that with her at their head, God must be on their side and so they could not fail. However Alençon, the commander, did not entirely trust the 'voices' and, though he supported the maid faithfully, he allowed his military experience to guide him. They marched to Orleans from Blois along the south bank, contrary to Jeanne's wishes to march by the north bank where they would have encountered five strong English forts. The French by-passed Beaugency and Meung to the south and marched past the English outposts at Les Tourelles and Les Augustins without being seen.

They made for the south bank of the river opposite Chécy, about 3 miles upstream of Orleans and no doubt marched across the loop of the river well south of the English positions. Before arriving there Alençon had been in touch with Dunois, the garrison commander at Orleans who had entered Orleans with a reinforcement of 500 men-at-arms earlier in the siege, and between them they hatched a successful plan. It seems that the army had actually been escorting supplies for the citizens and garrison, and had not been intending to raise the siege at all. However the problem remained of getting this large resupply into Orleans. Dunois collected boats and barges from along the north shore and sailed them up to Alençon's army with a favourable wind, once loaded they returned on the stream. Dunois knew that Jeanne intended to enter Orleans so came to greet her and to escort her into Orleans. To facilitate this he had arranged a suitable foray at St Loup to distract the garrison and ensure a trouble-free entry, although it is probable that the garrison of St Loup was too small to interfere. Jeanne, the maid, crossed the river at Chécy and entered the city along the north bank by the east gate in the evening of 29 April to a rapturous welcome.

Alençon meanwhile marched his army back to Blois to collect a second convoy for the beleaguered city. On 3 May French soldiers from the garrisons of Gien, Montargis, Château Reynard and Châteaudun began filtering into Orleans. Meanwhile Alençon's army returned along the north bank of the river and entered the city between the easternmost fort and St Loup on 4 May. Early that morning Jeanne had ridden out from Orleans at the Porte de Paris with 500 men to meet the army and second convoy, which entered the city later in the morning. That same day they heard that Fastolff was coming from Paris with another convoy of supplies and reinforcements for the English.[2] The French commanders must have felt that they had to take action against the English soon if they were going to at all before Fastolff's reinforcement could reach them and while they still had a comfortable superiority in numbers. Alençon's army of 4,000 then joined the garrison, which now totalled 7,000 indentured soldiers and 3,000 militia, more than double the size of the besieging English army. It must not be forgotten that the initial Anglo-Burgundian army of about 5,000 men had had to provide garrisons for Chartres, taken on the march to Orleans, and also for Beaugency, Meung, Jargeau and Chateauneuf. These together must have accounted for about 800 men, and then with the loss of the Burgundian contingent of 1,000 men it is unlikely that the besieging army now numbered more than perhaps 3,500 men.

To distract attention from Alençon's army while he passed a convoy of supplies into the city, another diversionary attack was mounted on the fort at St Loup. In the midst of this attack Jeanne suddenly galloped up to the attackers and so inspired them that they took and burnt this English outpost, taking forty prisoners and leaving 114 dead. St Loup was about 3 miles away from the English base at St Laurent and perhaps 2 from the fort of Paris, and was dreadfully isolated. Talbot, realizing what was happening, galloped off with a small force from the base and collecting more soldiers from the other forts endeavoured to put a stop to the attack on St Loup. But his way was barred by a much larger force from Alençon's army and when he saw the fort at St Loup go up in flames he called off his attempted relief. It must now have dawned on Talbot and his commanders that something had changed in the French camp. English soldiers probably only learnt about the maid from their few comrades who struggled back to them from the burnt fort of St Loup.

But Bedford certainly knew of her and her mission and it is possible that his senior commanders knew of her too for *la pucelle*, the maid, wrote him a letter on 22 March 1429, of which extracts read as follows:

> King of England, and you, Duke of Bedford, calling yourself Regent of the kingdom of France; you William de la Pole, earl of Suffolk; John lord Talbot; and you Thomas lord Scales, calling yourselves lieutenants of the said Bedford: pay back the King of Heaven [for his royal blood]; deliver the keys of all the good cities you have taken and violated in France to the maid who has been sent here by God, the King of Heaven. ... and you, archers, noble soldiers and others besieging the good city of Orleans, go away, for God's sake, back to your own country. ... King of England, if you do not do so, I am in command of the army, and wherever I encounter your men in France, I shall make them leave, whether they wish to or not; and if they will not obey, I shall have them all killed. ... You, Duke of Bedford, ... if you wish to make peace, answer in the city of Orleans, otherwise remember the great detriment which awaits you.[3]

There was certainly no mistaking the tenor of this message, one copy of which was handed to Talbot by Jeanne's heralds[4] the day after she entered Orleans. Clearly both Bedford and Talbot knew of the maid and her mission but they didn't take her message seriously; why should they? The message enraged Talbot and his commanders who threatened to burn one of her heralds at the stake. Meanwhile, until the fall of St Loup the soldiers knew nothing about her; they probably felt that something had put courage into the French but, in typical English fashion, it didn't worry them unduly.

On 6 May the French crossed the river to the south bank by foot and boats, and assaulted the small fort at St Jean le Blanc about 800 yards to the east of Les Augustins. Seeing this, the garrison of Les Augustins charged the French but were beaten off; they in their turn abandoned their fort and withdrew into the much stronger fort of Les Tourelles and its barbican.[5] The French then attacked and took the fort of Les Tourelles on 7 May. Les Tourelles was a typical medieval guard fort on a bridge. To the south of it there was a drawbridge and to the south of that guarding the drawbridge was a barbican. The French first took the barbican, then rushed the drawbridge and a Herculean fight developed; in the midst of this the French threw a temporary bridge across the two spans of the main bridge, which they had destroyed earlier and then assaulted Les Tourelles from the city side. Les Tourelles fell just before nightfall.[6] The courage shown by the French in the fierce hand-to-hand fighting at the various forts can be attributed to the maid who, although wounded before Les Tourelles, was present at all these little battles encouraging her soldiers to rise above themselves. In short, she raised their morale, not to a pitch above that of the English, whose morale was good, but at least to equal it.

It was now obvious to the English commanders that they would not be able to take the city with the reduced numbers under their command and against a strongly reinforced garrison, so they raised their siege on 8 May 1429. Questions have to be asked of the English conduct of the siege, particularly between 30 April and 8 May. Why was nothing done to prevent the reinforcements from entering the city? Why was Jeanne not attacked when she rode out with 500 soldiers on 4 May? Why was there not a coup de main party ready at fort Paris to meet just such a situation, or to come to the aid of the fort at St Loup if and when it was attacked? This was surely a contingency that could have been foreseen once reinforcements reached the city. Why did the English not attack the boat crossing while it was taking place and before the French attacked St Jean le Blanc? Why was a counter-attack not launched at the French in front of Les Tourelles before they had taken the barbican? The medieval reason given was that Jeanne was a witch and had bedevilled the English. The modern reason given was that the French became too strong, but really any commander who made so many fundamental errors of judgement should have been sacked. In addition, Bedford deserves some of the opprobrium; he never once visited Orleans to see for himself how the lynchpin of his strategy was bearing up.

After lifting the siege the English commanders were faced with the classic dilemma of the defence of a frontier – whether it was better to defend by stationing troops along the frontier or by mobile defences further back. They were faced with two possible courses: to keep the army concentrated and withdraw to the north from where they could threaten any French move towards Paris; or to split up and reinforce their garrisons at Jargeau, Meung and Beaugency. They chose the latter course so that they could maintain their threat to Orleans while waiting for Bedford to send reinforcements. Suffolk marched off to Jargeau, while Talbot and Scales, after reinforcing the garrisons at Meung and Beaugency, marched north to Joinville to join up with Sir John Fastolff's force. Talbot and Fastolf now disputed their next move, the latter advocating a withdrawal to the north, while Talbot was for pressing south to relieve Beaugency, which was now under siege. Talbot won the argument and they marched south. Suffolk, the other joint commander, had meanwhile surrendered Jargeau to Dunois' army of about 8,000 on the 12 June; he was taken prisoner and the garrison massacred. About 2 miles short of Beaugency, Talbot came across the French army drawn up in battle array on a hill about 800 yards to his front. The English halted and deployed in battle formation to await the inevitable French charge. But this did not occur and as the English army was too small to attack the French, Talbot decided to march back to Meung and cross the Loire there before marching back along the south bank to the relief of Beaugency.

When they found the French in possession of the south end of the bridge at Meung, Talbot decided to bombard them with cannon that night, the first time this had been done in war, and to assault them early the next morning. The assault was making good progress when they heard that Beaugency had fallen. They were now in a tactically difficult position. They rightly decided to withdraw and began a march towards Janville. They stopped to rest at Patay, where they were caught by surprise the next morning by the French advance guard before they were ready.

The position chosen was in a dip where the archers and the main body were stationed under Talbot while the rearguard under Fastolff was on the rise behind; it was not a good position even as a temporary delaying position. However the French scouts saw them, or rather heard them as they gave a view-halloo to a stag they had flushed! The French spurred on by Jeanne immediately charged and scattered the archers, who had not yet planted their stakes into the ground, and the men-at-arms were overwhelmed. The Parisian militia did not, on this occasion, seem to have distinguished itself. Fastolff and some sixty of his retinue fought their way out of the mêlée and withdrew to Joinville. Talbot was severely wounded in the back and taken prisoner. Following his rather passive conduct of the siege of Orleans, Talbot's decision to overrule Fastolff and make for Beaugency seems to question his strategic sense, while his choice of the position at Patay questions his ability to choose ground for defence. Fastolff seems to have had the better grasp of the strategic issues and he was a good field commander, but he lacked Talbot's charisma. There is no doubt, however, that for quick offensive action no other commander could match Talbot. Fastolff was undoubtedly the sounder general for defensive warfare, Talbot for the opposite.

Militarily, English France had lost the initiative, and after Orleans and Patay all military action was strictly in defence of Normandy and the conquered territories. Indeed, although it may not have seemed so to the English commanders at the time, due to political, diplomatic and economic factors, April 1429 was to be the apogee of the English effort in France. From this date forward English France, though still dominant in France north of the Loire, was to be mainly on the defensive. Bedford's regency was beset with problems in the spring of 1429, which affected the strategy and field performance, keeping Bedford away from Orleans at a critical time.

After their successes at Orleans and Patay the French went onto the offensive to the east of Paris and into Champagne. Jeanne d'Arc had convinced Charles to take Rheims, where the kings of France had traditionally been crowned. This he did and he was crowned king of France in the cathedral on 17 July 1429. Now the political scene was utterly changed. France had two kings: one, Henry, established by treaty, the grandson of the former king, but not yet crowned; and the other, Charles, the disinherited son of the late king but now duly crowned. From here on loyalty was not just a matter of short-term expediency but of long-term allegiance. God had anointed Charles VII, the former Dauphin, while Henry had not yet been crowned, even as king of England! Unless the English wrested the political initiative and defeated Charles on the battlefield, he would dominate events in France in the future.

It was clearly a matter of the utmost political importance that Henry, still a minor, should be crowned king of France, but first he had to be crowned king of England; the Treaty of Troyes was clear on this point. Henry was duly crowned on 6 November 1429 at Westminster and on 16 December 1431, two and a half years after Charles had been crowned, at Notre Dame in Paris. Although there were now two anointed kings of France, there can be little doubt that Charles had won the battle of the kings.

The political initiative now lay with France, and Philippe of Burgundy began to explore the idea of supporting Charles, consequently becoming the object of tempting offers by both the English and the French to keep him on side, or to suborn him into a change of loyalties. Bedford, his brother-in-law, gave control of Paris to Philippe in 1431 together with a number of *bailliages* south of Paris and northwards to Amiens. The Burgundians would now be responsible for law and order within Paris and for its defence, as well as control over the approaches to Paris from the south-west, the south-east and the north. Bedford gave this responsibility to Philippe in the king's name so that Bedford, as regent, remained Philippe's superior and in accepting the responsibility Philippe once again tacitly accepted Henry's sovereignty. Of more practical moment it released English soldiers from garrison duties in Paris and its environs for more essential duties in the defence of Normandy, Maine and the conquered territories, and they retained the fortress of Pontoise, giving them control of the all-important western and river approaches to the city from Rouen.

Having for the moment mollified Philippe, Bedford turned to the serious business of trying to defeat Charles in battle. This was not an easy task. The French still avoided open confrontation in the field but endeavoured to turn matters in their favour by short campaigns to take certain fortresses along the southern and north-eastern frontiers of Normandy. As part of this offensive the French took Louviers in the spring of 1431, only 15 miles south of Rouen; to wavering Normans this was the writing on the wall. For the English it was a major setback: Louviers was the next important place on the Seine towards Paris and the castle of Gaillon nearby controlled the crossing over the river. If England really wanted Henry to rule France the time had come to go onto the offensive and to be seen to gain the upper hand militarily over the French.

Bedford was given two critical bonuses during this difficult period, one political and one economic. Jeanne d'Arc was captured on 24 May 1430 outside the gates of Compiègne on the River Oise. She had left part of her force in Compiègne and attempted to take the bridge between there and Margny on the opposite side of the river when a stronger Burgundian force from the Anglo-Burgundian army nearby drove her back. She and her companions galloped for the safety of Compiègne but were closely followed by the Burgundians. Jeanne and her immediate followers tried to protect the remainder of her troop who crossed the moat into Compiègne, but before she could cross the captain of the fortress raised the drawbridge to secure the city and Jeanne was soon captured on the wrong side of the city walls.[7] This was perhaps a romantic view of her capture; a more prosaic view and one that seems more likely was that on that fateful day Jeanne led a sortie across the bridge from Compiègne to attack a Burgundian outpost on the other side of the river. Her action was seen by Jean of Luxembourg, the army commander, who quickly called for reinforcements and then attacked Jeanne's force of 500. A hot action followed and in the midst of the mêlée an English troop under Sir John Montgomery charged her group in the rear. She and her immediate companions were overwhelmed and the Burgundians took her prisoner;[8] she was later sold to the English for 10,000 crowns.[9] She was held in various castles until she was incarcerated in the castle at Rouen in December. Bedford, knowing that she was no longer a military threat and realizing that she could remain a political problem, washed his hands of her responsibility and handed her over to the French inquisition. They tried her as a witch and then condemned her to be burnt at the stake as a relapsed heretic. The English carried out the sentence on 30 May 1431. Neither Charles VII nor her old comrade in arms Dunois did anything to help, though it is difficult to see what they could have done apart from trying to ransom her. Jeanne's dreadful death was, perhaps, alleviated for her by the English soldier who gave her a crude wooden cross to clutch as the flames engulfed her. The last comment on this sorry episode should be the words of John Tressart, secretary to Henry VI in France: 'We are lost, we have burnt a saint.'[10]

Jeanne was clearly a charismatic leader who was convinced of the righteousness of her cause, which she expressed in religious terms at a time when France's fortunes had reached their nadir. She gave France hope. Although she was given an army by Charles VII, she was never its commander. She was a brave leader of a small group of soldiers who she led from the front. By force of character and religious zeal she was able to convince the French soldier that he was every bit as good as his English opponent. Undoubtedly the raising of the siege of Orleans was a turning point in the war and she achieved this, but it is doubtful if the relief of Orleans was due solely to her. Others, if they had had the spirit, could have done so.

However it is possible that Charles VII would never have been crowned at Rheims, which was a political victory of huge import, if it had not been for Jeanne d'Arc. Her capture, in nothing more than a skirmish, while at the head of a small troop of French soldiers, clearly showed that she believed she was invincible. It must have been a great shock to her to discover that she was not. Nevertheless she was not a witch – she was a brave political agitator who managed to stir the French to action at a pivotal time and she certainly did not deserve to die at the stake.

Bedford's other bonus was that the government in England sent cash to help finance the garrisons in Normandy as well as frequent reinforcements. The cash was vital. It had become obvious, even to parliament in England that due to the devastation caused by the war in northern France and the activities of the *brigands*, that 'English France' could not possibly pay for the war in France as well as the garrisons. At this time the population of Normandy would have been not more than 600,000, or about a quarter of that of England and Wales together, and the costs of the war in France had to be borne by this relatively small number. The average revenue of the crown in England in 1422 was about £135,023 of which £27,365 was taxation directly due to the war. This levy was to pay for the costs of services and materials procured in England for service in France or on the Channel, such as reinforcements, shipping, guns, powder and shot, bows and arrows. But in France Bedford had to rely on the taxes he could extract from the small population of Normandy, which in 1423–4 amounted to 160,829 Livres Tournois (lt) or £24,124. To this he could add the French treasury receipts, which in 1424 amounted to 146,303 lt or £21,945. This total of £46,069[11] had to cover the costs of the war, his household and the civil administration of Normandy. He could also demand taxes from areas he had overrun, but this was not a reliable source of revenue and would anyway be needed to pay for the garrisons established in the new areas. This total fell far short of the amount that Henry V demanded from the estates of Normandy for the army and the garrisons in Normandy in 1421 of 400,000 lt, plus a levy of a further 100,000 lt, or a total of £75,000.[12] Militarily Henry V was no more active in 1421 than Bedford was a decade later and the same costs would have been met by the exchequer in England for both. It can therefore be seen that Bedford was labouring under a shortfall against Henry's own estimates of some £30,000 per year. Parliament's agreement to pay for the garrisons in Normandy must have been a great relief, but it did mean that the council in England and parliament would henceforth take a closer interest in French affairs.

Bedford's first use of the new troops was to besiege Louviers, and to take Gaillon, Louviers eventually falling in 1432 after a siege of nine months. The fortress of Louviers and the nearby castle of Gaillon were then destroyed. The lines of communication between Rouen and Paris on the ground and up the river had been restored but the English had suffered a blow to their prestige. It received another blow when Bedford was defeated at Lagny by Jean Dunois. The French commanders began to take the war to the English in August 1432 and achieved a small but significant success. That May Bedford had decided to take the fortress of Lagny on the Marne. Jean du Dunois arrived with a relieving army on 9 August and immediately attacked the besieging English. In the afternoon on the 10th, Bedford gave the order to withdraw from the barbican after losing some 300 men in the fierce fighting and he hurriedly raised his siege three days later leaving his artillery behind.

In this period of almost constant war, of siege and skirmish, of the boredom of garrison life and the sudden exhilaration of battle, it might be valuable to examine how the English organized their armies in Normandy and the conquered territories. The English armies were never very large yet they managed to confront the French at every turn of the war with forces that were sufficiently large and well organized to assert their superiority over the French, who invariably had larger numbers. By 1429 the army in Normandy was essentially a garrison force defending what today would be deemed a colony. Gone were the days of expansion and glory, gone the days of profit from war. Consequently it became more and more difficult to persuade the knightly class to leave their manors and their responsibilities at home for a period of dull and unprofitable service manning a garrison in Normandy. This reluctance to serve can be seen in the dwindling ratio between men-at-arms, generally the knights and esquires, and archers in the army of Normandy; a ratio which was reduced for reinforcements from 1:3 to 1:10[13] by the council in England. Following this new political reality the army in Normandy evolved to meet the new conditions. During the conquest stage under Henry V the army, like all armies of the period, consisted largely of the retinues of the king and his nobles, and the companies of individual captains and knights, all serving under indentures for stated periods and paid by the king through his ministers. However, once the army withdrew into garrison for the defence of Normandy the old indenture system was found to be inadequate and new arrangements had to be devised to meet the changes ordained by the need for permanent garrisons.

Whilst Bedford was alive the army was indentured to him, as regent and governor, but after his death the army was administered, paid and equipped under the auspices of the council in Normandy. This was a separate department of state with its own bureaucracy under the titular command of the governor. In this respect the army became a regular army in the modern sense with one salient difference: it was an army made up of privately recruited companies which could, and often did, leave the army at the end of the allotted span of their indentures. Consequently, with the exception of the companies of the principle commanders, the army had a constantly changing composition, although the soldiers from a disbanding company might simply join up again with another captain in a newly formed company. However, when the duke of York arrived on his second tour as governor in 1441 he partially reverted to the old system by recruiting captains to his personal retinue. It is not clear whether these men and their companies were part of what might be called the field army or whether the recruitment of captains to his service included potential garrison commanders. Certainly many officers were appointed as captains of specific fortresses as a reward for service, the posts being well paid. Unfortunately many garrison captains left the command of their garrisons to lieutenants in their absence; a factor that under-mined the discipline of the army as it had been established by Bedford and maintained by the council until York's arrival.

The centralized system of control by the council over the army had the advantage that garrisons could easily be adjusted to meet the changing strategic situation along the frontiers, and within Normandy itself. Garrisons could be enlarged, reduced or even removed altogether; something that was more difficult to do if, as under York, captains and their retinues were appointed as garrison commanders for stated periods. The centralized system also made it easier to form a mobile force for operations in the field by augmenting the personal retinues of the commanders with garrison personnel. However, as with bureaucracies everywhere, the council was slow to react and reluctant to take operational decisions. Consequently the council relied on field commanders such as Scales and Talbot, who were answerable directly to the governor, for advice on and conduct of operations.

Command of the army mirrored the civil administration. Normandy was divided initially into two zones: the south-west including all land south and west of the Seine; and the north-east including all land between the sea, the Seine, the Oise and the Somme. Each zone was under the command of a lieutenant general answerable directly to the governor, who was also commander-in-chief. In 1435 Lord Scales took over responsibility for the south-west from the earl of Arundel, while Talbot, who had been ransomed and exchanged for the French leader Xantrailles in 1434 was made lieutenant general of the north-east zone of Normandy. Talbot had returned to France after his release with 800 reinforcements in the spring of the same year, and was soon in action helping Philippe of Burgundy recover lost territory on the duchy's northern borders. Both Scales and Talbot as lieutenant generals were responsible 'for the conduct of the war' within their zones. In 1436 Normandy was divided into three operational zones, the old south-west zone being divided into two at the Loire, with Lord Fauconberg as the new commander of the central zone.

In May 1436 Talbot was made a marshal of France. As such he had two responsibilities over and above the usual juridical responsibilities that went with the office. First, to undertake such operations as he deemed essential for the recovery of France and the defeat of the French, and second, to carry out the muster and review of the necessary forces gathered for these operations. The post of marshal does not seem to have given him overall command of the army in Normandy at that time since operations in the other two zones continued under the zone commanders without any input from Talbot. However in 1441 York made Talbot his lieutenant general for the conduct of the war and he would then have had operational responsibility for all forces throughout Normandy, in effect carrying out the old function of the marshal as commander in the field whenever no specific commander was appointed. The marshal was subservient to the constable who was always also the governor of the duchy, and as such was what we would call the chairman of the council, of which the marshal was a member. It was this council that was responsible for the strategy of the war and for the initiation of major operations. The council itself had both civil and military members, the former drawn from both the Norman community and from English appointees, and it operated as a form of combined cabinet and chief of staff's committee. The Norman element was reduced to two members after 1442.[14]

Politically the scene was changing. Philippe, after a series of successful minor operations with English help, felt the time had come to attempt a rapprochement with the French. Charles welcomed Philippe's initial overtures and signed preliminaries of peace at Nevers in January 1435. But of course this meant very little without the presence of the other principle player, England. Philippe realized that he needed his English ally's consent to his idea for his peace feelers to have any chance of success; he therefore invited the English to attend a peace conference to be held at Arras in July. Cardinal Beaufort led the English delegation while Bedford, who lay seriously ill at Rouen, took no part in the actual proceedings. The two delegations never met, the daily haggling being delivered from one side to the other by two cardinals, the papal legate Albergati and Hugh de Lusignan, legate of the council of Basle. It soon became clear that the two sides could not, and indeed would never reach an agreement over the main issue. It also became clear that unless the issue was settled by some dynastic arrangement it could only be settled by war and neither side held a military advantage. The English and the French points of view over the legitimacy of the monarchy were mutually antagonistic and could never have been reconciled without some compromise by one side. The conference came to a halt, there was nothing further to discuss and the English delegation having rejected the French offer left Arras on 6 September.[15]

However the French still had one possibility: if they could come to an accommodation with Philippe of Burgundy and if they could neutralize him, they might just have sufficient strength to defeat the English. But they needed to overcome Philippe's scruples about his commitments under the Treaty of Troyes, to which he had sworn his allegiance and to which he had put his seal. For Philippe these commitments had served their purpose and he now wanted to get out of his obligations to Henry under the treaty – having few scruples and no personal ties he instructed a team of lawyers to find a way out of his dilemma. They found a legal quibble. Henry V died before Charles VI and consequently did not inherit the crown of France to pass on to his son. Henry VI therefore could not be king of France and so the Treaty of Troyes in this respect was invalid. With a little financial persuasion the two cardinals at Arras soon absolved Philippe from his oath given at Troyes. Philippe and Charles soon made up their differences. Philippe recognized Charles as his king and forswore his bitterness against his father's murderers, while Charles confirmed Philippe in his lands, some of which he had obtained with English help. They signed an accord on 21 September.

The duke of Bedford, regent in England and regent of France, died on 15 September 1435, during the conference of Arras. His wife, Anne of Burgundy, had died two years earlier thus breaking another link between England and Burgundy. For England the defection of Burgundy from the Treaty of Troyes made a mockery of the concept of the dual monarchy; from hereon the retention and defence of Aquitaine, Normandy and Calais became the main goals of English policy in France. The duke of York, appointed lieutenant in Bedford's place, now became responsible for the implementation of this policy in northern France. However this was not going to be an easy task, not so much for the actions taken by the Valois, but once again for divisions within the council in London, and because of the growing influence of the young king Henry VI who achieved his majority the same year.

Gloucester, supported by York and Huntingdon, and with a general belligerency towards the French by the population at large, continued to maintain that a vigorous war policy supported by adequate funds could defeat the Valois in France. Although England had reacted to the Treaty of Arras by voting subsidies for military expenditure in France, it is clear that the necessary money was not readily available. The attitude of the 'war' party in the council was reflected in the views of the commanders in France. Indeed Sir John Fastolff in a memorandum to the council in France after Arras advocated a tough offensive strategy based on two old-fashioned *chevauchées*, one into Artois and one into Burgundy. Fastolff's plan was never adopted. Beaufort, supported by a rising star ,William de la Pole, earl of Suffolk thought an accommodation with Burgundy should be sought in order to preserve trade with the Flemings. Furthermore, due to the parlous state of England's finances the war with France should be confined to the defence of the two duchies while a truce was sought. The problem of the two kings could then be settled in calmer times. These opposing views were evenly balanced within the council but the taxable classes were becoming less and less keen to provide the funds necessary for Gloucester's policy, and young Henry VI was very much more pacific in his attitude to the war than was his uncle. The net result, as will be seen, was that York and his successors were starved of the support needed to carry out Gloucester's policy, while at the same time were unable to pursue a rapprochement with Burgundy because of the half-hearted implementation of a war policy. Meanwhile the population at home, like their counterparts in Normandy, became thoroughly fed up with the war.

However, for the English in France the war still existed, Normandy and the conquered territories had to be defended and if possible the war had to be taken to the French. In February 1435 the citizens of Paris rose up against the English and at the same time the important fortress of Pontoise to the north of Paris fell. Paris was now virtually cut off from the English by Richemont's besieging army and the English garrison retired to the Bastille; eventually on 13 April the city fell. The English garrison surrendered and was allowed to march out to the catcalls of the Paris mob and retired to Rouen. In early May La Hire took Gisors, but the garrison, shut up in the castle, sent to Rouen for help; Talbot moved with his customary speed and surprised La Hire who fled the scene.

Meanwhile Charles was becoming a more formidable and purposeful opponent than he had been in the time of Jeanne d'Arc. He tightened up the civil and military organization of Valois France so that it became a national administration. In particular he allowed

Richemont, the constable of France, to recruit some of the free companies that had formerly been harassing Burgundy. They were to operate against the English as paid companies in French employ. These companies seized Dieppe on 29 October and then, encouraged by a peasants' revolt in the Pays de Caux, moved on down the coast taking Fécamp, Montvilliers and Harfleur. The thrust of this offensive took the English by surprise and by the end of 1435 Richmont had nearly 3,000 soldiers in the Pays de Caux in addition to a peasant army on the rampage.

Unfortunately at about this time military control within Normandy had become so ineffective that the *brigands* were able to control large areas of the countryside or were able to prevent the normal activities of the duchy from taking place. This general laxity included giving safe conducts to known *brigand* leaders and to ransoming them when captured, rather than executing them after trial as had been done formerly. There can be little doubt that they spied on English troop movements and gave information on garrison strengths to the French, which in the 1440s was invaluable. Their activities were helped by non-existent frontier controls and by a lack of patrolling by garrisons in the countryside for which they were responsible. This in turn resulted from a general insufficiency of armed force within Normandy, which became less whenever offensive English operations were undertaken, since garrisons were invariably milked to provide the field armies. The *brigands* meanwhile unsettled the duchy and made the ultimate re-conquest of Normandy by the French easier. Their activities certainly made it easier for French forces to take Dieppe and Harfleur by surprise, helped by treachery from within.[16]

When the French commander, La Hire, with about 1,000 men, attempted to take Rouen by surprise in 1436 he found the city alert and well guarded, so he withdrew to the east. Talbot then heard from his scouts that La Hire's force was in the village of Ry, about 10 miles to the east of Rouen. He quickly set out from Rouen with another 400 men and surprised La Hire and his force in the village; they panicked and were scattered with many casualties. La Hire himself was wounded but managed to get away. This action relieved the pressure on Rouen. Talbot's quick thinking and offensive spirit reflected his experience in Ireland where small operations carried out quickly, efficiently and ruthlessly were decisive.

The threat to Normandy, following the fall of Paris and the French offensive into the Pays de Caux, now gradually subsided as Richemont failed to take Rouen with a half-hearted move in that direction, and then marched north to co-ordinate operations around Calais with Philippe of Burgundy. The latter, concerned to show both English and French that he was an important player in the war, had decided to besiege Calais with the aid of the Flemings. The siege failed but it aroused a strong response in England and the duke of Gloucester was despatched with a relief force. He arrived in time to greet the victorious garrison on their return and then went on a successful *chevauchée* into the lands of Burgundy in Flanders. This foray encouraged the Flemings to revolt against Philippe and involved him in a local campaign over the next two years.

The duke of York, on first being appointed governor in Normandy in February 1436, had landed at Calais bringing with him some 5,000 reinforcements, a welcome addition to the 1,000 men who had landed earlier with Sir Henry Norbury. York marched south to Normandy taking Dieppe on his way. The crisis seemed over for the time being, indeed with the reinforcements, the capture of Dieppe, the successful operations in the Caux and at Ry, the lifting of the siege of Calais, and Gloucester's *chevauchée*, it could be said that English fortunes were bright. It must have looked so to York who in January 1437 convinced the council in Normandy to support an attempt to recapture Pontoise, a fortress on the west bank of the Oise, which controlled movement out of Paris north along the Oise and west towards Rouen along the Seine. A siege in the middle of winter was going to be difficult if not impossible, however it was thought that the fortress might be taken by surprise. Talbot was put in charge of the operation, which he executed with his usual flair and audacity. He arrived with a small force outside Pontoise on the west bank during the night of 12 February to find the river frozen solid; the unsuspecting garrison were celebrating Mardi Gras. During the night he sent a small party across the ice dressed as peasants, so that they could approach the town across the bridge. Meanwhile a larger assault group camouflaged with white sheets and carrying scaling ladders waited beneath the walls; both parties were in position before light. At dawn the 'peasants' sought admission and were allowed in by the guard, they raised the cry 'Talbot, St George' and overwhelmed the guard at the gate. The assault party, on hearing the cry, scaled the walls and within minutes the town was taken, so totally surprised that hardly a blow was struck.

Talbot followed this up by threatening Paris and then went on a lightning campaign to Beauvais, cleared the Vexin of French-held towns, crossed the Seine, took Chevreuse and then returned to Rouen, all between the end of January and the beginning of April. He was again on the march in July to regain the Pays de Caux, successfully completing the siege of Tancarville before relieving Le Crotoy and doing a successful raid into western Picardy. In 1438 the centre of gravity of the war shifted to Aquitaine. The French advanced in several columns towards Bordeaux but the commanders were to discover that this was a very difficult proposition. They failed to drive the Anglo-Gascon forces into Bordeaux. In the following spring the English government sent an army some 3,000 strong under the earl of Huntingdon who rapidly pushed the French back to their starting point.

In the north, 1439 was another year of consolidation ending with the surprise and rout of Richemont's army of 6,000, mainly mercenaries, near Avranches in a night action by Talbot with an army barely 4,000 strong just before the end of the year. Despite these successes, not once did the English manage to bring a major French army to battle or take and hold any significant city; in short they were unable to alter the political scene by military means. All their operations were defensive designed solely to maintain the integrity of the borders of Aquitaine and Normandy. The problems confronting the English were caused mainly by circumstances at home and were the same as they had been since Arras: faction fighting between Beaufort and his 'peace' party and Gloucester and his 'war' party in the council at home; lack of a national leader after Bedford's death; and a shortage of cash. The problems at home within the council were exacerbated when Henry achieved his majority in 1437. He gathered about him his own councillors of whom the chief was William de la Pole, earl of Suffolk, a man more interested in his own advancement than in the king's welfare. The exchequer in England was finding it more and more difficult to meet its obligations and the country was gradually sinking into debt, something that Gloucester and the 'war party' did not seem to appreciate.

As a result of insufficient revenue from the population of Normandy and the rest of occupied France, parliament at home found itself obliged to subsidize the defence of Normandy from taxation in England, which by 1435 had become a regular feature of English aid to Normandy; not a popular matter. The only alternatives were to agree to a peace, which would involve giving up the claim to the French throne or withdrawal from France altogether; the first was politically difficult and the second unthinkable. The cost of subsidizing Normandy amounted to about half of the total lay and clerical subsidy in any one year in England and was certainly more than the country could afford or wished to disburse.

The army establishment in France was a little over 6,000 men whose total cost was estimated by the council in England in 1441 at about £60,000 annually. These men were distributed among thirty-eight different garrisons and included the personal retinues of the field commanders and the master of the ordinance.[17] Although soldiers from garrisons regularly took part in sieges of French-held castles and towns, most of the operations in the field were carried out by the personal retinues of the commanders aided by troops sent out specifically from England and indentured for the campaigning season. The number of these soldiers each year varied from 800 to 2,700 depending on the operational situation and the size of the subsidy voted by parliament.

During this same difficult period for the English, Charles was busily reorganizing his administration, his finances and his army. He re-established Paris as the centre of government where the constable, Richemont, ensured its security and he asked the Estates of the Realm for the restoration of certain direct royal taxes. These included a wealth tax on the burghers and taxes on the provincial nobility. These revenues, which he collected annually, enabled him to reorganize his army on a permanent basis. He was at last in a more financially secure position than his enemies. Perhaps the most significant development that Charles insinuated into the French psyche was the political thought that war was the king's business and not that of his nobles, and that defence of the realm was exclusively his responsibility. Previously the French king had had to rely on the forces of his feudal nobility to wage war, but from about 1438 onwards he gradually built up royal forces, answerable only to him, for military operations ordered by him.

This reorganization, insisted upon by Richemont after his defeat at Avranches, began by enlisting the *ecorcheurs* into formed companies in the king's pay. As Jacques Chartier was to write:[18] 'The king of France imposed such good order on the conduct of his men-at-arms that it was a fine thing. He caused all those men-at-arms to be equipped with good armour and weapons ... and these men-at-arms were paid each month.' Later, in the early 1440s, they were formalized into specific units with a common organization under the command of an officer appointed by the crown. Initially they were organized into large companies *d'ordonnance* consisting of 1,800 men-at-arms, 3,600 archers and 1,800 infantrymen, a total of 7,200 combatants, all mounted.[19] Charles VII raised two of these very large companies; one was stationed near Normandy and the other near Aquitaine. In due course for administrative reasons they were each divided into ten smaller companies, which were housed in royal garrisons near the frontiers with English France. This provided Charles with a potential army over 15,000 strong, easily concentrated for operations, well trained and equipped and led by his own officers. When compared with the English effort of being able barely to maintain an army of 6,000 men, many of whom would have been in garrisons, it can be seen that the military advantage now clearly lay with France. Nevertheless the English in France could certainly meet and probably defeat a single thrust by a French army of one of these large companies, but probably not one into Normandy at the same time as one equally large into Aquitaine. However if the French organized two or more well-co-ordinated and simultaneous advances into Normandy, something that was well within their capabilities, the English there could be overwhelmed.

This reorganization by the French was not their only development in the military sphere. They had significantly improved the organization of their artillery arm. They began to standardize their guns making the provision of shot a simpler business. They mixed the ingredients of their gunpowder at the factory, so to speak, so that gunpowder was issued in grains ready mixed, and consequently they did not have to do this at the gun-site; this ensured an even burn and therefore consistent range. Having begun the standardization of their guns they were able to produce iron shot of standard calibres. Finally they produced efficient gun carriages. This meant that every company would have 'field' guns with it and that siege trains could be moved more speedily from place to place; it also ensured that the guns, once deployed, could be brought into action rapidly. To quote Jacques Chartier again:

He [Charles VII] had a great number of great bombards, great cannons, veuglaires, serpentines, crapaudins, culverins, and ribaudquins, so that never in the memory of man did a Christian king have such a numerous artillery at one time, nor so well furnished with powder, shot and all things necessary to approach and take towns and castles, nor had more carriages to drag them nor gunners more experienced to handle them, which gunners were paid from day to day.[20] The English failed to follow suit.

In the wider context of history it may seem that these improvements to the French military organization and to their artillery were relatively insignificant, but in the context of the war for Normandy they were critical and changed the course of history.

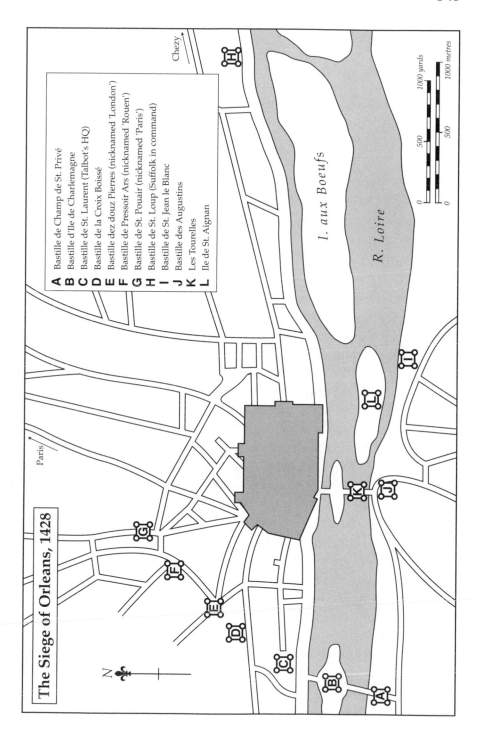

The Siege of Orleans, 1428

A Bastille de Champ de St. Privé
B Bastille d'Ile de Charlemagne
C Bastille de St. Laurent (Talbot's HQ)
D Bastille de la Croix Boissé
E Bastille dez douz Pierres (nicknamed 'London')
F Bastille de Pressoir Ars (nicknamed 'Rouen')
G Bastille de St. Pouair (nicknamed 'Paris')
H Bastille de St. Loup (Suffolk in command)
I Bastille de St. Jean le Blanc
J Bastille des Augustins
K Les Tourelles
L Ile de St. Aignan

Paris

Chezy

I. aux Boeufs

R. Loire

1000 yards
500
0

1000 metres
500
0

Chapter 17

The Loss of Normandy and Aquitaine

'The King's son, lost all his father won'[1]

In 1440 the English army again carried out a successful raid into Picardy and then turned its attention to Harfleur, which it took in October after a siege of four months; Talbot, in recognition of his services, was given the captaincy of the town and fortress. The French meanwhile were forced to attend to a revolt against Charles by the dukes of Alençon and Bourbon, the count of Dunois and his own son, the Dauphin. This was soon dealt with but it took effort away from the main problem, the expulsion of the English from France; the latter seemed not to realize what was going on and certainly failed to take advantage of the situation. The following year, 1441, was to see a gem of a campaign conducted largely by Talbot in which Pontoise became the centre and which showed what the English might have achieved if the forces in Normandy had been properly supported from home. Pontoise, held by the English, was a key fortress on the Oise, commanding that river and to a lesser extent the Seine. It was only 10 miles from St Denis and about a further 3 to the gates of Paris. Charles VII decided to reduce this fortress and take it. He moved his army, some 5,000 strong, to the east bank of the Oise opposite Pontoise early in June; his army had a formidable artillery contingent under his chief of artillery, Jean Bureau.

The French opened proceedings with an artillery bombardment of the English-held barbican protecting the eastern end of the bridge, which though damaging, failed to force the garrison to abandon it. The French of course needed a bridge across the Oise to prosecute their siege successfully and as the only one was in the hands of the English they built a temporary bridge about 2 miles to the south opposite the abbey of St Martin, which they fortified. They then crossed the river in strength and began to dig their encircling trenches around the town, but they had insufficient troops to do this and so most of the north and north-east remained open. The siege proper began with an intense artillery bombardment of the barbican which, together with the three easternmost arches of the bridge at Pontoise, was destroyed. Bureau then concentrated his many guns opposite the south-western perimeter of the town and began to demolish the walls. His artillery made several breaches but by morning the garrison had always made good the damage;[i] this of course could not go on indefinitely and in due course the garrison would run out of materials with which to fill the breaches and then the French could assault. The garrison made many sorties against the French besieging forces but failed to disrupt the artillery sufficiently to stop the barrage.

But relief was on its way. News of the siege had reached Talbot at Rouen and he quickly organized a relief force. He set out on 16 June along the northern bank of the Seine with a convoy of supplies and war stores for the garrison's relief, escorted by about a thousand men. To get to the garrison they had to pass close by the French base at St Martin, but the French, instead of taking this golden opportunity to destroy Talbot and his convoy, tamely shut themselves up in their bastille at St Martin and waited for Talbot to leave! He passed his supplies to the garrison and exchanged some of the personnel for fresh soldiers. He also left lords Scales and Fauconbridge in command. He then marched away, again without interference from the French, to organize another relief convoy, which arrived without interference a few days later. Meanwhile the duke of York, who had been appointed to his second term of office as governor, vice the earl of Warwick who had died in office aged fifty-eight, arrived at Harfleur with some much-needed reinforcements in June. York, with Talbot commanding the vanguard, then set out for the relief of Pontoise early in July with an army estimated to be between two and three thousand men.[2] The French, some 5,000 strong, did not like this development and they withdrew their army, less the garrison at St Martin, to the safety of the east bank of the Oise and awaited events.

Now followed a game of cat and mouse in which the mouse called the tune. York sent a message to Charles by his heralds to the effect

---

i This battering of castle and fortified town walls was possible because of the way they were constructed; they were made by filling the space between stone inner and outer walls with rubble held together with a lime mix. Consequently when the outer wall was breached the rubble generally just spilled out.

that he intended to cross the Oise, thus posing a direct threat to Paris. Charles responded by stretching his army along the complete length of the Oise from Conflans in the south to Creil in the north, guarding every crossing over a frontage of over 30 miles. York meanwhile, on Talbot's advice, marched north away from Pontoise and away from the river, then turned and suddenly descended on Beaumont, about 10 miles north of Pontoise on the river. The French guarding the crossing saw this as the major thrust to cross the river and called in their forces from north and south to oppose any English crossing. However the threat was only a feint. The majority of the English army crossed higher up the river totally unopposed while the French busied themselves with the defence of Beaumont. The French, aware of Talbot's ruthlessness and speed of movement, were immediately thrown into a panic. The first object was to protect the king's person from any threat, but Paris also had to be protected; probably the latter had a higher priority in the minds of most Frenchmen. The French hurriedly crossed back to the west bank of the Oise and destroyed the bridge, putting the river between themselves and the English. Talbot arrived at the abbey the day after Charles had left. Over the next four days the English built a bridge at Neuville a few miles north of the juncture of the two rivers and repaired the bridge at Pontoise.

Charles kept going and crossed the Seine at Poissy, so putting two rivers between himself and the English army. He stayed at the abbey there while he awaited events, much to the derision and opprobrium of the citizens of Paris. It was not long before the English vanguard came up against the French rearguard at the crossing. Although Pontoise had been relieved the problem of destroying the French army and threatening Paris remained. However, Talbot suggested a way out of the impasse, which was approved by York. They would leave a small holding force opposite the French rearguard at Poissy and the rest of the English army would march away unseen. Talbot then moved west to a crossing of the Seine near Mantes, about 13 miles downstream from Poissy, and York moved north to cross the Oise at Neuville, about the same distance from Poissy. Talbot marched away by night and surprised the French at Poissy at dawn next morning after a night march of some 25 miles, indeed Talbot found the bedclothes still warm in the bed where Charles had spent the night at the abbey! The French left in a panic without so much as a token resistance and made for Conflans, where they once more crossed the

Seine and scuttled for the safety of St Denis and Paris. York arrived just too late to corner them at the river crossing, but saw the French marching across his front in some haste, but too far away to stop them.[3]

What effect did this jewel of a campaign have on the general direction of the war? The relative strengths of the armies and the political scene were not affected in any way; it might simply not have happened. However, it did perhaps show that Gloucester and the 'war' party were right. If a successful conclusion was to be a negotiated peace, York and Talbot had shown that it could be a peace negotiated from a position of strength. However, the government in England showed a singular lack of understanding about the situation or were simply not interested anymore.

The French were not slow to react and once they realized that the English had really gone they reopened the siege of Pontoise. The guns, which had been kept in the bastille of St Martin, were wheeled out and took up their old positions outside the walls, while the army once again manned the trenches around the walls after repairing the bridges. The battering began again, however Talbot delivered another relief convoy to the besieged garrison on 16 August and in doing so showed his mettle once more. On hearing of his approach Richemont marched out to meet him near Vigny, about 9 miles west of Pontoise. Talbot's force was no more than an escort for the relief convoy but Richemont dared not attack it. Once night fell Talbot lit campfires, stole away to the north and entered Pontoise at dawn to replenish the garrison before Richemont could interfere. He managed to do this again on 6 September. Bureau's artillery had been battering the walls for several days with accurate and heavy concentrations of fire, making several breaches in the walls all round the town, too many for the defenders to repair. On 19 September Richemont mounted a concerted assault from several different points and after two hours of heavy fighting and the loss of some 500 men the English garrison surrendered. The final concentrated bombardment did in three days what would have taken several months to achieve even as recently as two years previously. From here on sieges would be settled by artillery. Fortifications would change drastically in design and all fortifications would become artillery bastions. Unless England was prepared to spend a great deal more of both her own revenue and that of Normandy and Aquitaine on the defence of English France, she would lose everything. France now had the necessary military organization, a powerful artillery arm and sufficient finance to finally force the English out of France.

In England the 'peace' party in the council had gained the upper hand. Gloucester had virtually retired from active politics after his wife had been found guilty of witchcraft and Henry VI, under the growing influence of Suffolk and with the support of cardinal Beaufort, searched for a way out of the impasse with France. It was clear to the council that if military operations were to be undertaken to maintain the status quo, regular reinforcements of men and equipment had to be sent to Normandy, and to a lesser extent to Aquitaine. Furthermore they had to be on a far larger scale than the reinforcements sent over the past five years; armies of five or six thousand well equipped men had to be able to be fielded in addition to those required for the garrisons. This required money and the government's credit had run out. As a stop-gap it had been decided to send the duke of Orleans, a prisoner in England since Agincourt, to France in 1440 on the understanding that he would explore ways to a peace, much against the wishes and advice of Gloucester. Orleans was released on payment of ransom in November with instructions to examine certain possibilities, one of which was the feasibility of a marriage between Henry VI and a Valois princess. It was not a bad time to explore the possibilities of peace – although Charles had regained Pontoise in September, York and Talbot had shown that England and English armies were still to be feared. Honours were about even.

Charles then opened an offensive along the borders of Aquitaine in 1442, threatening Bordeaux but failing to take the castle at La Réole or Bayonne before his offensive ran out of steam. Meanwhile in Normandy the council found itself increasingly dependent on the council in England for cash and for reinforcements. Consequently policy concerning the defence of Normandy was increasingly made in England in return for the aid so desperately needed. Indeed Talbot, who had returned home to plead for more financial support, came back with 2,500 reinforcements, a great help but not enough. Furthermore Charles's offensive into Aquitaine made the council undecided as to whether the aid sent should go to Aquitaine or Normandy; they were quite certain that they could not do both. In the event their deliberations settled on an expedition to northern France under the command of the duke of Somerset, Beaufort's nephew, in 1443, which was a compromise and met neither requirement.

This expedition did not produce a great military victory nor extend the limits of English possessions in France, indeed it made no difference to the balance of power in France. However, it is of interest in that it shows the costs of raising an army towards the end of the Hundred Years' War, the indifference of the English knightly class towards the continuing war and the increasing importance of artillery. At its inception it seems that neither the king nor Somerset had any clear idea of what they wished the expedition to achieve, although there were valid strategic reasons for offensives from either Normandy or Aquitaine. Action in both theatres was considered urgent but it was finally decided that the expedition should enter Maine and Anjou from Normandy. This was a strategically unimportant area for the defence of Normandy at that time, though it would have been ideal to support an offensive out of Normandy towards the Loire, something that the English could not afford to do either financially or militarily. The expedition left Portsmouth for the Cotentin on the pragmatic ground that the shorter crossing would enable operations to start sooner and there was less chance that the ships would be dispersed by storm. However it is probable that the major factor was that Somerset's brother Edmund, earl of Dorset, happened to be governor of Anjou and Maine.

The size of the army agreed upon was a force of 800 men-at-arms with supporting archers, which, by the usual proportions of the day, would have numbered about 2,400 mounted archers. Artillerymen would also have been recruited, indeed provision was made for twenty cartloads of ribaldquins, and no doubt some guns and bombards would also have been taken. Both Henry and Somerset were concerned that the duke of York, the king's lieutenant in France, should not feel put out by Somerset's command of an independent expedition. A letter was sent from the council to York explaining that the expedition was to cross the Loire 'into ground occupied by the ennemyes and therre use most cruel and mortel warre.'[4] The strategic aim of the expedition seems plausible since there was a general fear that the French would mount an offensive into southern Normandy from their bases in Anjou. Clearly, if successful, the expedition would upset French intentions and remove the southern threat to Normandy. However it has to be seen as a missed opportunity – the 4,500 men of Somerset's army added to the reinforcements sent annually to the army in Normandy, and the usual 1,500 to 2,000 men in various retinues, would have made a formidable field army. Under Talbot's command such a force could well have put France onto the defensive and would have enabled England to negotiate any peace from a position of strength. But it was not to be; Somerset was a relative of Beaufort who had the king's ear and the king was fast losing interest in his kingdom of France.

Preparations for the expedition went ahead in the spring but the recruitment of captains of baronial or knightly status was not going according to plan. Only one banneret and six knights answered the call. This reluctance to join the expedition was symptomatic of a general lack of interest in France and the French wars by the knightly classes at this stage of the Hundred Years' War.

Somerset's army landed at Cherbourg, over a month after the planned date, on 12 August 1443; it included one banneret, Sir Thomas Kyriel, six knights, 592 men-at-arms and 3,949 archers. The proportion of archers to men-at-arms of a little more than 6:1 was rather better than the 10:1 that Talbot achieved in the last batch of reinforcements he had taken to Normandy in 1442. By this period an army that was over strength in archers was in fact a weaker force than one where the proportion was of the order of three to one, for the simple reason that plate armour had become so efficient. Arrows could not penetrate the new armours until the target was less than a hundred yards away and even then penetration was becoming problematic, hence the need for the ribaulds. As he marched south Somerset received some reinforcements from his brother Edmund, earl of Dorset, who joined him, as did the captain Michael Gough with his company.

The details of the operation are open to conjecture since no detailed English records survive and the chroniclers do not all agree, however the accounts given by the Bretons Le Baud and D'Argentré give a more favourable version of the operation than do those of the others. The least flattering accounts simply say that the army marched along the borders of Brittany and Maine, captured the Breton town of La Guerche, laid siege to the town of Pouencé in northern Anjou and then marched back to Normandy in December. If this is all that was achieved by the expedition then Somerset certainly deserved the opprobrium he received on his return to England.

The Breton accounts state that Somerset marched through Maine and Anjou right up to the walls of Angers, laying waste the countryside on his way and in effect carrying out an old-style *chevauchée*.

By these accounts it would seem he carried out his instructions to the letter. He then moved off to the north-west taking Segré and investing Pouancé, while Mathew Gough with a strong party marched to intercept a French relieving force gathering at Chateau Gonthier. Gough defeated the French in a surprise attack, and rejoined Somerset who lifted the siege and went on to La Guerche. When Somerset arrived outside the gates the inhabitants, fearing the consequences of a siege, surrendered and the new duke of Brittany, Francis, bought them off with a danegeld of 20,000 *saluts d'or*. Somerset's action was not well received by the council in England who complained that he had pillaged a Breton town at a time when Brittany was strictly neutral. Indeed he was accused of treachery and ordered to make restitution.

In England it was felt that Somerset had achieved virtually nothing and that he had failed to repay the trust and confidence placed in him, while the cost of the expedition was certainly resented at a time when the king's finances were in difficulties. Judged by the costs of armies of the period, this expedition must have cost the exchequer about £45,000 at a time when it already owed York £20,000 for the pay of the Army in Normandy. Clearly the military situation was getting desperate and yet an expensive and well-equipped expedition was sent to northern France without it being required to assist the hard-pressed army in Normandy. Furthermore, the expedition was independent of the military command structure already in place in northern France.

The inception of Somerset's expedition highlights the arrogance of the Beauforts in the council and the influence of Suffolk on the king; they planned the entire expedition including its objectives without taking advice from York and his commanders in Normandy. York was an opponent of the Beauforts whose protégés were Somerset and Dorset, Somerset's younger brother. The whole incident, including Somerset's elevation to the peerage and his promotion to the rank of duke, reflects the undue influence that the Beauforts and Suffolk had over Henry VI. Nevertheless Cardinal Beaufort, who was now an old man and whose influence was on the wane searched for a way out of the impasse imposed by the Treaty of Troyes. Beaufort and Suffolk, the king's confidant and now the most prominent member of the council, convinced the king that a diplomatic way out of the impasse should be explored. Perhaps an acknowledgement that the king of

England was not also the king of France, in exchange for Normandy and Aquitaine in full sovereignty, was a possible position to aim for in any forthcoming negotiations. England could no longer afford the war and the nobility and knightly classes were no longer interested; besides, problems were mounting up at home and people were beginning to take sides. The king's council nevertheless agreed that the first thing to be achieved was a truce.

Suffolk, with the agreement of the council, opened negotiations with the French, whose ambassadors met him and the English delegation at Tours in April 1444. It seems that Suffolk's brief was to offer to concede Henry's claim to the throne of France in return for certain guarantees concerning Normandy, Maine and Aquitaine, more particularly the sovereignty of Aquitaine and Normandy. Furthermore, to seal such an understanding a marriage was to be arranged between Henry VI and Margaret of Anjou, Charles VII's niece. In due course a truce for two years, eventually extended to four, was agreed in May, but Henry was prepared to give more in order to gain more. It seems that, unbeknown to the council, Henry then gave a personal undertaking to Charles on 22 December 1445 to surrender Le Mans and the county of Maine in return for a truce to last for twenty years.[5] This caught the council in Normandy by surprise and they must now have realized that the king and his council were not really interested in maintaining English power in northern France. Militarily this concession threatened Normandy as it would bring French arms to the southern boundary of the dukedom and made a French invasion of English Normandy both nearer and more likely. The surrender, planned for 30 April 1446, caused outrage in Normandy and at home.

York handed over the lieutenancy of Normandy to Edmund Beaufort, duke of Somerset, in 1444. Somerset failed to make use of the truce negotiated by Suffolk earlier that year to improve the defences of Normandy and there was now no field army in Normandy as York had marched away with his retinue.[6] Le Mans surrendered in March 1448 and the twenty-year truce came fully into force.[7] Outwardly France respected it while she repositioned her well-organized and well-led army towards the frontiers of English Normandy. The writing was on the wall but the English took no particular steps to strengthen their position in Normandy, lethargy and indifference seeming to engulf them. In March 1449 an

Aragonese knight of the Garter, François de Surienne, captured the fortress of Fougères with the connivance of Somerset who clearly profited from the action as most of the plunder estimated at 2 million *ecus d'or* found its way into his pocket.[8] Fougères was a Breton fortress and Brittany was in truce with England, but this stupid and uncalled for action prompted duke Francis of Brittany to ask Charles VII for help. Charles was only too pleased to do so. He claimed that England had broken the truce and his armies crossed the frontier into Normandy.

During the summer and autumn of that year England sent some woefully inadequate reinforcements to Normandy, but Norman towns and fortresses were already falling or changing their allegiance as it became obvious that England neither cared for them nor had the means to defend them.[9] Rouen fell in November and Somerset, after surrendering the castle without a siege although the castle, palace and barbican were prepared and ready to resist,[10] fell back to Caen. In December the French took Harfleur which Henry V thought of as 'the key to the sea of all Normandie.'[11] This siege emphasized the power of the new French artillery – it had taken Henry V thirty-eight days to reduce the fortress to surrender, but Jean Bureau's guns did the business in three days! The French then moved on and took Honfleur, on the other shore of the Seine in January 1450. England was now left with a small part of Normandy only, that which extended along the coast from Caen, through Bayeux to Cherbourg and south to Falaise.

The loss of Rouen followed by that of Harfleur caused a storm of anger in England where no one had realized that the domain in France was so near to catastrophe. Suffolk took the brunt of the opprobrium because the government, which he controlled, had failed to send the necessary reinforcements over the previous year. However an army was raised in haste and put under the command of Sir Thomas Kyriell, a competent and experienced commander. This army, some 2,500 strong, landed at Cherbourg on 15 March with orders to march to Bayeux to make a stand there; Charles with the main French army was slowly advancing towards Caen, about 15 miles to the east. Kyriell was reinforced with a further 1,800 men from the garrisons and retinues of what remained of English Normandy and captured Valognes before marching on towards Bayeux. The French however had two small armies within reach of Bayeux, the closest under the command of the count of Clermont, was about 3,000 strong and was at Carentan, about 20 miles west of Bayeux. The other, under the constable Richemont, was about 2,000 men strong and was at Coutances some 20 miles south-west of Carentan. Kyriell's army was quite large enough to deal with either of these two columns separately, but if they managed to join up Kyriell would be vulnerable.

Kyriell decided to bypass Carentan to the north by a long causeway across the estuary of the River Douve, but lost four hours waiting for the tide. Clermont was now behind him on the road to Bayeux. Kyriell camped for the night about 10 miles to the west of Bayeux by a little stream near the village of Formigny, two hours march from the safety of Bayeux. Clermont stayed the night in Carentan about 8 miles west of Kyriell, but Richemont marched to St Lô where he spent the night, about 15 miles south-west of Kyriell's overnight camp.

Kyriell sent Sir Mathew Gough on ahead with some reinforcements to secure Bayeux and then to return as soon as possible.[12] Kyriell and his army remained at Formigny waiting for Clermont's force. During the night Clermont's scouts brought him definite news that the English were camped at Formigny and Clermont immediately contacted Richemont to suggest that they join forces the next day. Richemont set out promptly along the road from St Lô to Formigny. Kyriell meanwhile prepared his position across the Carentan–Bayeux road in a slight dip with stakes and potholes. Immediately behind the position was a little stream and the road ran over a bridge at this point. He probably had with him no more than 800 men-at-arms and perhaps 2,500 archers, the remainder of his force being made up of bill-men. Kyriell took up the now traditional English defensive position, with men-at-arms possibly two ranks deep stretching about 600 yards from end to end. But now, due to the improved plate armours and the consequent reduction in the lethal range of the archers' fire, the archers were probably in three groups, one at each end and one in the centre in order to cover the whole line with fire. The bill-men would have been behind the men-at-arms; being a small army it was probably too small to have a proper reserve. Judging from the positions he took up Kyriell did not know that Richemont was fast approaching him from the south-west on his left flank.

Clermont's army came in sight at about 3 o'clock in the afternoon, deployed opposite the English out of bowshot range and then waited while they considered their next move. All were conscious of the difficulties ahead of them and the memory of Agincourt and Verneuil still infected the armies of France. However, the more impetuous of the French eventually began to attack, both on foot and on horse, but were beaten back with many casualties and failed to break Kyriell's position. They then wheeled two culverins into position and began a slow battering of the English line, but English archers were so provoked by the gunfire that they ran at the gunners, slew most of them and tried to drag the guns back to their own line. The French were beaten and were beginning to fade away from the battlefield, but instead of vigorously pursuing them Kyriell stood fast. At this critical juncture Richemont's advance guard appeared over the southern horizon – he must have heard the guns for he turned north and hurried to the battle. He came to a ridge about 2,000 yards south of Kyriell's position and from a windmill was able to look at the left flank of the English position from slightly behind. He could see Clermont's routed force fleeing the scene but his own army was strung out on the road behind him. He used the available time until his army reached him to ride over to Clermont and the two agreed to a combined assault. Clermont rallied his own troops and in concert with Richemont's force began an advance against what had been the English left, while Richemont advanced down the ridge. Kyriell meanwhile, on spotting the French approach on his left flank, hastily moved his old right flank forces to the left of his old position to face Richemont to his south. The English army was now facing two enemy forces, one approaching from the west and one from the south, and was outnumbered. As the French pressed their attack the English were slowly beaten back and withdrew towards the bridge. Surrender they would not; some were taken prisoner but most sold their lives dearly. Sir Mathew Gough managed, with a few others, to cut a way out and made for Bayeux, but Sir Thomas Kyriell was taken prisoner.

So ended the last battle on Norman soil, as the last English field army was destroyed in northern France on 15 April 1450. This battle was risky for both the English and the French and the stakes were high. It showed that right to the end English soldiers were still treated with respect by the French, even though the effect of archery was no longer as formidable and lethal as it had been previously. It also showed that the French still remained cautious when faced by the English in a prepared position. The problem for Kyriell was that he had had to move half his small force to face a new direction while under threat of attack, a difficult manoeuvre at the best of times. The battle also highlighted Richemont's generalship – he managed to join up with Clermont at the right time and place, always a difficult prospect and particularly so with the communications available to them in the Middle Ages. How lucky he was that Clermont's army, as a despairing last chance, decided to use their two culverins. Richemont did what Napoleon did three and a half centuries later, he marched to the sound of the guns. If they had not been fired he would have marched on to Bayeux and would have missed the battle being fought at Formigny a mere 4 miles to his north. He was lucky and so was Clermont.

However the writing had been on the wall ever since the surrender of Maine, and the loss of Normandy to the French was inevitable unless England made a real effort. For a moment the news of the defeat at Formigny looked as though it might stir the government to action – an angry and stunned populace demanded it. Fastolff began the process of raising an army of 3,000 men but this took time, a commodity that the French did not intend to waste. They first took Vire after a short battering and siege which lasted six days, Bayeux fell soon after to Clermont and Richemont took Avranches. The outposts quickly fell one after the other thanks to the effectiveness of the French artillery. Caen was next on the list and four columns converged upon it. The French besieging the town and castle were estimated by Burne to be perhaps 20,000 strong.[13] Jean Bureau opened proceedings with a heavy bombardment which continued for three weeks at which point the English garrison under Somerset sued for terms and surrendered on 26 June; the French had had no need to mount an assault. Their artillery had achieved in three weeks what had taken Henry V more than five to accomplish. But the humiliation of the English was not yet over: Falaise, a town and fortress within Talbot's demesne was besieged by Xantrailles and surrendered to him in return for Talbot's release from captivity – he had been surrendered as a hostage after the siege of Rouen. Finally, Cherbourg came under siege from the combined armies of Richemont and Clermont, and Jean Bureau's artillery. The garrison under Thomas Gower put up a stout resistance and caused the French many casualties, but once again it was the artillery that proved decisive. The guns were wheeled onto the sands and waterproofed against the rising tides with tallow and hides[14] so that they could maintain a constant bombardment except at high tide. Cherbourg fell on 11 August 1450 and with it

English rule in northern France came to an end. The loss of Normandy became a major political issue for the rest of Henry VI's reign and was to have an immediate effect on his government.

Many English people lost heavily as a result of the loss of Normandy and Anjou, and the surrender of Maine. At the head of the social ladder people like York, Scales and Talbot lost their lands and the captaincies of various towns and castles, all given by the crown for outstanding service in the past and all providing a useful if not valuable income. However, real hardship faced the people lower down the social scale, who had been encouraged to settle, particularly in Normandy.[15] People who decided to stay in Normandy found themselves in great difficulties, but those who managed to return to England were destitute and they simply added to the thousands of unwanted and out-of-work soldiers. Together they made up a sizeable group of discontented people who were only too willing to make common cause with those, further up the social ladder, who opposed the policies of the king, prominent among whom were dispossessed members of the Anglo-Norman establishment. The only winner in this situation was the duke of Somerset who was granted the sum of 10,000 Lt by the council in London as compensation for the loss of the county of Maine.[16] It was given in order to provide compensation for their loss to the gentlemen and others who lived in the county of Maine; they never received a penny, the whole sum found its way into Somerset's pocket. Somerset returned to England via Calais and notwithstanding his total defeat in Normandy and subsequent disgrace, was elevated by Henry in September 1450 to be constable of England. His predecessor, the duke of York, had been banished to Ireland as the king's lieutenant there, almost certainly to keep him out of the way.

But Henry VI's government then faced other problems as control of the narrow seas passed to the French. With the Norman and Breton coasts now hostile and without a permanent navy Henry was unable to stop damaging French raids on the south coast. All of this affected English trade with the Continent and therefore ultimately with the wealth of the country.[17] Suffolk was later banished for five years by Henry, for whom he had been a loyal servant, and was on his way to exile in Burgundy when sailors in Dover Roads executed him; he was beheaded on the gunwale of a small boat. Suffolk had loyally covered up for Henry whose incompetent government had lost the support of parliament which had the support of the refugees from Normandy, the discharged soldiery and the rebels in Kent, and by a majority of the nobility and the shire knights.

The Kentish rebels of May 1450 were in no sense a rabble of malcontents; neither did they come solely from Kent. They included eighteen esquires, several former sheriffs, and constables of Kent each heading one hundred men. There were also several constables and their contingents from other counties of the south-east[18] led by Jack Cade. They came to London to petition parliament and to protect their king against the traitors about his person having sent a copy of their petition ahead to Westminster. Henry, having had a difficult autumn parliament in 1449, had withdrawn from London but on receiving news of Cade's rebellion hurried back.

The petitioners arrived at Blackheath on 11 and 12 June and immediately built a stockade about their camp as protection against mounted attack. The king gathered an army and marched to Blackheath on 15 June but was dissuaded from further action. Instead Henry sent a herald to discover what the Kentish men wanted. They repeated their previous petition but Henry refused to consider their requests. Two days later the petitioners faded away in the night leaving an empty heath. Henry then sent elements of his army under his own household officers to hunt down the petitioners. One of these patrols under the Staffords was routed in the forests near Sevenoaks. Under the shock of this news Henry ordered his army to step up their pursuit of the rebels only to be faced with mutiny. Realizing that his own force was no longer reliable Henry withdrew to his estates in Lancaster while the rebels reassembled and marched to Southwark. They crossed London Bridge and were opposed by the Tower garrison, fighting broke out but a truce was finally arranged by the archbishop and the bishop of Winchester on promise of pardon in the king's name. The pardons were issued on 1 and 2 July.

The king and his government had survived but they had been rudely shaken.[19] The cause of this unrest can undoubtedly be traced back to the loss of most of Normandy and the realization that Henry's corrupt advisers were largely responsible for the debacle. But the rebellion highlighted the malaise in Henry's own administration. It is hardly surprising that France was lost when government at home was corrupt, ineffectual and grossly negligent in the affairs of 'English France'.

The Treaty of Troyes had been a flawed agreement all along – it might have given Henry V all that he desired but it committed Normandy and England to a continuing conflict, which the former could not afford and the latter was reluctant to finance. The title 'King of France' had always been doubtful and had never been accepted by France south of the Loire. However, once the duke of Burgundy had defected to the cause of the Dauphin and the latter had had himself crowned king of France at Rheims, thanks largely to the efforts of Jeanne d'Arc, England faced an uphill struggle to enforce the conditions of the Treaty of Troyes. Furthermore, after Charles's coronation the title 'King of France' looked even more suspect. At this critical juncture political disagreements in the government at home combined with a fall in the wool price, and unrest at home prevented the necessary military action from being taken. Indeed Henry VI, king of England and France, and the very fount of government, started the rot himself by his voluntary surrender of Le Mans and the county of Maine. But even to the very end England showed that she had the commanders, men-at-arms and archers capable of ensuring the continued occupation of Normandy in sovereignty if that was what was required. However, the politics and the economics of government at home ensured that the king's lieutenant in Normandy never had sufficient military resources to ensure the sovereignty of Normandy nor a government at home with the necessary resolution to support him.

Nevertheless, all was not yet lost; England still held Aquitaine, though a rather smaller Aquitaine than it had been, and she held Calais. If England had had the will she could still have forced France to agree to a lasting peace; but such a peace would once again have had to confront the problem which had started it all, the sovereignty of Aquitaine. The French however were neither able nor ready to move against Aquitaine straight after recovering Normandy; their armies had to be moved about 500 miles to the south. However their intention was clear. But in England, instead of raising an army for service in the duchy, attention was focussed once again on the advisers that Henry had gathered about him. At this time malcontents were using Richard of York's name for their own use as reformers and their demands were being ascribed falsely to him. Richard decided that he had to return from Ireland, where he was the king's lieutenant, in order to clear his name and to take part in the king's council.[20] He went to London via his estates on the borders of Wales to gather his followers and arrived in military array in September. York maintained that his military array was solely for his protection and he felt that as cousin to the king he should be among those who advised him in his council. But others saw him as the only possible alternative to the king of the blood royal. While France was busily positioning herself for the final showdown with England in Aquitaine, England seemed to be drifting towards civil war. Nevertheless one part of the English establishment, parliament, was concerned to do something about the situation. It met at Westminster in November to provide for the defence of the realm, the safekeeping of the seas, the defence of Aquitaine, and to put down and punish rioters, gatherings and insurrections. But parliament's concern about the French and their actions did not affect Henry's government; nothing was done to save Normandy. This was perhaps due to Henry's disinterest, the bad advice given to him by Somerset and the parlous state of England's finances. Tension increased at the end of November when York and his wife's nephew, Norfolk, paraded through the streets of London in strength. But things calmed down when the king, York and most of the nobility rode through the streets of the city together early in December. It was said that 10,000 men-at-arms and archers accompanied them.[21] A second parliament in the New Year petitioned the king to rescind various grants, mainly of land given by him to his advisers and others, and this had a calming effect. York meanwhile returned to Ireland for the remaining seven years of his appointment. In the end, by the spring of 1451 politics in England had calmed down sufficiently for attention to be focussed on Aquitaine.

During this troubled time in England rumours of a forthcoming French invasion of the Isle of Wight became so strong that Henry's government felt obliged to make preparations to meet it if it came about. The French meanwhile garrisoned certain fortresses in Normandy and then sent the remainder of their army to the marches of Aquitaine by both land and sea. By late summer 1450 they had begun their offensive with the capture of the fortresses of Bergerac and Bazas in the autumn. The English, finally realizing that something had to be done, at last took steps to counter the French. Although Lord Rivers was appointed seneschal of Aquitaine on 30 August 1450 and was ordered to raise 4,000 men for its defence, to sail from Plymouth by 21 September the expedition never left.[22]

By summer 1451, Aquitaine had been almost completely overrun by the French, who carried out a swift and brilliant advance into the duchy on several related fronts reminiscent of their campaign into Normandy. After their capture of Bazas and Bergerac they went into winter quarters but the English failed to take advantage of this respite. In the spring the French were on the march once again. One army thrust to the north shore of the Gironde taking Blaye and Bourg and thus, with the aid of eighty to 100 ships from La Rochelle including some from Spain,[23] closed the Gironde to entry by English ships bound for Bordeaux. Another army advanced along the Dordogne taking Libourne and Fronsac, while yet another took Rions on the Garonne. Dax, south of Bordeaux and on the way to Bayonne, was taken by a fourth column. Finally they all converged on Bordeaux, which fell on 30 June 1451 to the count of Dunois. Bayonne fell after siege on 21 August 1451. England had now lost the whole of Aquitaine by conquest after some two and a half centuries, due almost entirely to negligence and disinterest, compounded by a lack of funds. The question of the sovereignty of Aquitaine was now only a matter of historical interest; the French had settled it once and for all. Or had they?

The French, having given generous terms to the Bordelaise and the surrounding country on their surrender and transfer of allegiance, then became overzealous in their bureaucratic control of Bordeaux and the rest of Aquitaine. In particular they imposed a *taille*, or tax, on the inhabitants contrary to the conditions of the treaty of surrender to pay for French garrisons to protect them! A delegation from Aquitaine to Charles objecting to this pointed out that they had sworn allegiance to him and had no need of French troops for their protection. Charles dismissed their petition. After this the Gascons became concerned that their wine trade with England, on which the prosperity of the duchy relied, might be curtailed or taxed, and that the reciprocal grain trade from England would be stopped. Furthermore, heavy handed administration by French officials upset the Bordelaise, used as they had been to an English administration over the past 249 years. Finally it must not be forgotten that the language in Aquitaine was not French, indeed the French were more alien to them than the English.

As a result a secret embassy arrived in London in September 1452 from Aquitaine led by the lord of Lesparre, offering to return to

English allegiance in exchange for certain assurances. The habits of 250 years of English rule die hard and they were not at all happy with the rule imposed on them from Paris. A force of about 4,000 was put under the command of Talbot, the earl of Shrewsbury, by now a man of between sixty and seventy years old, which landed in the Médoc on 17 October 1452. Bordeaux immediately ejected its French garrison and opened its gates to him. Most of the towns and fortresses in the surrounding country did the same, and those that did not were taken by force. By the winter much of Aquitaine had reverted to English rule.

Charles VII, incensed by the English invasion and by the fickleness of the Gascons, made his preparations for a second invasion of Aquitaine over the winter and was ready to strike by the summer of 1453. Meanwhile the English sent two groups of reinforcements to Talbot. These reinforcements brought the English contingent in Talbot's army to between 4,300 and 5,000 men. It is not known if there was an artillery contingent in this force, but by that time it would have been unlikely that a field army did not include artillery. If the past experiences of armies operating out of Aquitaine are any guide there would have been almost as many Gascons in the army as Englishmen, and therefore Talbot's army could have been somewhere between 7,000 and 8,000 strong all told.

Charles meanwhile was ready to put his armies into the field by the summer. He decided to advance on Bordeaux on two separate routes, one along the Dordogne and one from the south through the Landes from St Sever, about 75 miles to the south on the River Adour. Each route had on it a main group followed by a reserve. This is probable bearing in mind the reorganization of the French armies into two large regiments in the 1440s. According to Berry Herald the French heralds put the total strength of the French army at 20,000 men.[24] These were formidable forces to oppose and defeat.

Although Talbot had perhaps as many as 8,000 men in his army, some of these would have been put into garrisons, and a garrison would have been left in Bordeaux itself so it is unlikely that Talbot had more than 6,000 men available as a field force. His strategy therefore had to be one of waiting and watching, followed by a quick strike. His intelligence was good enough for him to know that the French were advancing on two widely separate routes and they obviously hoped that by so doing Talbot would separate his own forces. However Talbot knew that he had to keep his army together as a single force and he hoped that an opportunity would arise for him to defeat one of the French thrusts before the other could come to its aid.

Early in July the northern French thrust put Castillon under siege. This town, on the north bank of the Dordogne, was about 24 miles east of Bordeaux and controlled one of the main bridges across the river. Talbot was reluctant to commit himself at this point believing that the French would be more vulnerable closer to Bordeaux, but unhappily for him his Gascon supporters in Bordeaux demanded action and he was forced to move. He marched out of Bordeaux on 16 July and crossed the Dordogne at Libourne that evening. He had plenty of time as the other French thrust was still some way south in the endless forests of the Landes, and Castillon had not yet fallen. Castillon was only 10 miles away to the east of Libourne. He sent scouts into Castillon to reassure the garrison that help was on its way and to learn from them as much as he could about the French positions and their strength.

On reaching Castillon the French took up most unusual positions for a besieging army. They did not throw up entrenchments around the town, place their artillery within range of the town's walls or dig defensive trenches across the route from Libourne to prevent a relieving army from getting into the town. Instead they made a fortified camp some 2,000 yards to the east of the town between the Dordogne and its small tributary the Lidoire. They made a ditch and palisade on the unprotected side of their camp and placed their guns along its perimeter; the camp had its long axis parallel to the Dordogne. As an outwork they took and fortified the abbey of St Lorent, about 200 yards to the north of the town and about a mile from the French camp. For an attacking army, whose leaders knew it was considerably larger than any Anglo-Gascon army they would have to face, this was a very defensive strategy and one that lacked confidence. Why did they do this? It is suggested[25] that they were afraid of Talbot. The French held him in high esteem – he had a great reputation among them for unorthodoxy and quick movement. By their dispositions the French were clearly more concerned with their own safety than they were with the defeat of their enemy. However, for whatever reason they made an extremely strong defensive position out of their camp and while bottling up the garrison of Castillon they awaited Talbot's arrival.

Talbot's scouts told him about the abbey and the French garrison in it, and also about the French camp, though it is doubtful if they knew its detailed layout or the positioning and number of the guns. Talbot immediately set out with his mounted group, perhaps 500 men-at-arms and 800 archers[26] and arrived at the abbey just before dawn on 17 July. He had marched by the woods on the north side of the Dordogne and had by-passed the town of Castillon. He and his small force rushed the abbey garrison as dawn broke and took them completely by surprise. Many of the garrison were killed but many also escaped and took refuge in the camp. Talbot, having now lost surprise, decided to rest his mounted arm and await his infantry and guns. Everyone then settled down to have a meal at the old garrison's expense, ample food having been left behind in their hurried retreat. At this moment he was told that the French were abandoning their camp and fleeing; apparently watchers on the walls at Castillon could see many horsemen leaving the camp. Talbot, always one for quick decisive action, now threw caution to the winds and instead of veri-fying the observation immediately ordered his men to mount and get ready to attack the camp.

Talbot then committed his little force of 1,300 men to engage about 7,000 in a fortified camp supported by a large number of guns, serpentines and ribaldquins, all alerted and ready. He obviously thought that if the French really were withdrawing a quick attack would pay huge dividends. But the French were not pulling out; what had been seen from Castillon's walls were the French grooms taking the horses off to water, and being a hot dry day they raised a lot of dust. Talbot, who was wearing no armour in deference to his pledge given to the French king on his release as a hostage in 1450, crossed the Lidoire by a bridge close to the Dordogne. He marched his troops to what would seem to have been a specially prepared killing ground between the camp and the river and there deployed them. He must by now have seen that he had led his little force into an impossible situ-ation, nevertheless he ordered his troops to dismount and form a line opposite the southern rim of the camp. He himself remained conspic-uously mounted on a white cob. The order to advance was given and the English marched through a hail of gun and archery fire to the ditch and palisade. English foot soldiers, who had been trailing Talbot's mounted force along the route, were committed to battle as they arrived and with these reinforcements the Anglo-Gascons struggled to defeat the French. The fight lasted about an hour and some of the French were being hard pressed when at this critical moment a mounted squadron of Bretons, who had been hiding in the woods to the north of the camp, rode out and attacked the English right flank. This gave the French the edge and their men-at-arms crossed the ditch to press the English back towards the river. To begin with the English fell back in an orderly withdrawal, but they were gradually overcome; withdrawal became flight and flight rout. It is estimated that about 4,000 Anglo-Gascons eventually took part in the battle, many of whom were killed and the rest either escaped in the woods or were drowned trying to get across the river.

Talbot was found dead on the battlefield together with his son. English Aquitaine, the inheritance of English kings for two and a half centuries, had received a mortal wound. There can be little doubt that Talbot, who was feared and respected by the French, was defeated by his own impetuosity. He was the past master of the quick surprise action with a small mobile force, though he had also shown that he had the patience to conduct a siege successfully. He clearly understood the power and limitation of artillery and therefore probably felt at Castillon that the guns would only have time to fire at him once before he would be among them. What a pity he hadn't the patience to wait for his infantry and his own artillery to come up before engaging the French. He must have realized that the battle, which he was so eager to fight, was politically critical for the continuance of English Aquitaine and yet he treated it as a skirmish; by doing so he gave the duchy to the French.

After the battle it wasn't long before the French were at the gates of Bordeaux. They had taken the fortresses of Cadillac and Blanquefort by the end of September and then advanced for the grand finale, the taking of Bordeaux. Charles decided against an assault on the city but allowed plenty of time for Jean Bureau to bring up his guns. Bureau placed them with skill so that every part of the walls and the city itself could be reached by gunfire. Meanwhile Bordeaux's own small navy of little ships, which had been very active along the Gironde attacking the French besieging forces and keeping the sea open for possible English reinforcements, forced Charles to order a fleet from La Rochelle to clear the Gironde of this menace. It soon became clear to Lord Camoys, the elected leader of Bordeaux's defences, that surrender was inevitable. Negotiations were reopened on 9 October when Lord Camoys and ten of the most senior English and Gascon citizens of Bordeaux went to Montferrand to meet King Charles and a treaty was agreed. The English were allowed to leave freely, the Gascon leaders were banished from France and the city of Bordeaux had to pay an indemnity of 100,000 gold crowns as well as losing certain privileges at the king's pleasure. The city was finally surrendered on 19 October 1453.

This date is usually accepted as being the end of the Hundred Years' War though no peace treaty was drawn up to recognize the fact. England still felt she had a right to territory in France by the normal usages of feudal custom and she still harboured ambitions in France, but *realpolitik* at a time when feudal niceties were on the wane clearly indicated that France had finally pushed England out of the kingdom. True, England still held Calais and was to continue to include the arms of France within those of England until 1801, to show that she still held a lawful claim to the kingdom, but these were minor facets and of little import. The claim to sovereignty over the kingdom of France had been made first by Edward III in 1337 as a result of frustration over his claim to Aquitaine in full sovereignty. But the matter had finally been settled by the one action that was recognized in feudal law, conquest. In France, however, the divisions between the crown and its appenages continued. The quarrel between Charles and Philippe of Burgundy broke out anew and each side looked across the Channel for help in its domestic struggle. But in England all minds were concentrated on the struggle for dominance at court and the slide into the Wars of the Roses.

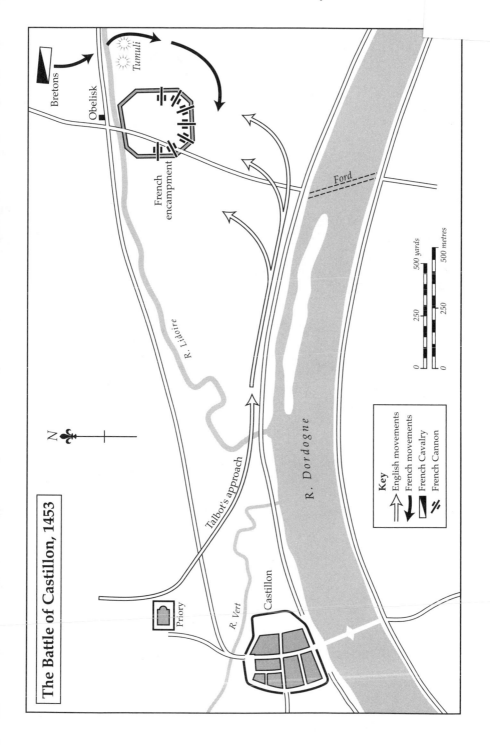

The Battle of Castillon, 1453

Bretons

Tumuli

Obelisk

French encampment

Ford

R. Lidoire

R. Dordogne

Talbot's approach

N

Priory

R. Vert

Castillon

Key
English movements
French movements
French Cavalry
French Cannon

0   250   500 yards
0   250   500 metres

Part 4

THE WARS OF THE ROSES

Chapter 18

Favouritism and Patronage

'let me prophesy,
The blood of English shall manure the ground,
and future ages groan for this foul act.'[1]

The Wars of the Roses have been so called since about the middle of
the nineteenth century, a phrase apparently first coined by Sir Walter
Scott,[2] because they appeared to be dynastic wars between the House
of Lancaster and that of York. These two related branches of the royal
family sometimes used the red rose and the white rose respectively as
heraldic badges. But to use this symbolism, alluded to in his play
Henry VI in the scene in the temple garden, as the defining moment of
the start of the Wars of the Roses is more likely to be a figment of
Shakespeare's fertile imagination and Tudor propaganda than an
historical fact. Indeed, it is a gross oversimplification of the politics of
the time which led to the start of this civil war. It should be understood that these wars were not a period of constant warfare, indeed
the time spent on all the campaigns fought in the wars, which lasted
thirty-four years, amounted to only thirteen weeks and barely
affected the majority of the population. Politically, historians usually
divide the Wars of the Roses into two or three compartments, the
period between 1459 and 1471 being the first wars, and that between
1483 and 1487, the second.

The first period, divided into two by some, is characterized by
political, if not actual, conflict between Henry VI and his supporters,
including his queen, Margaret of Anjou, on the one hand, and
Richard of York and his followers and successors on the other. It
ended with Henry's death in 1471, some ten years after Edward, earl
of March and Richard of York's son, had already been proclaimed
king as Edward IV; Edward died in 1483. Perhaps it is not true to say
that Henry VI was a principle in the early stages of the war. Henry had

always been a weak, easily led person, lacking in resolution, feeble and a near simpleton,[3] he was far more interested in his various foundations than he was in war and sincerely believed that peace with France was the best policy for England. His policy in this respect and his means of achieving it put him in opposition to his uncle, the duke of Gloucester and many other powerful nobles. He also ruled weakly and unfairly at home and gave too much to his court favourites, causing dissent in the council. He had his second bout of madness in 1455 and as a result largely withdrew from the everyday exercise of kingship. Indeed it might be said that the cause of the wars was that there was no legitimate way to remove a king who was unfit to rule.[4] Furthermore there was no such thing as 'His Majesty's Loyal Opposition': whoever had the king's ear controlled him unless the king was strong and fair; unfortunately Henry VI was neither. Nevertheless he remained king in name throughout the period from 1455 to 1461, during which most magnates professed loyalty to him, even though he became a virtual prisoner of the duke of York after 1460. Edward IV was crowned king on 28 June 1461. Henry became king again for a brief period in 1470–1 and was later murdered by agents of Edward IV in 1471 in the Tower of London. Edward IV, the duke of York's son, remained king, except for the brief period of 1470–1 until his death in 1483. Margaret of Anjou, Henry's queen, took a very prominent anti-Yorkist role until the Battle of Towton in 1461; indeed she alone kept his cause alive. After the battle she escaped to France from where she plotted Edward IV's downfall. She returned briefly to England in 1470 but after the Lancastrian defeat and the death of her son at the Battle of Tewksbury she was captured and held until her release and return to France in 1475.

The second historical period covered the time when a Yorkist king, Richard III, and a Tudor aspirant, Henry VII, fought for the throne and later the latter's consolidation of his position. All the wearers of the crown during the Wars of the Roses were supported by a constantly shifting group of magnates and other nobles, either due to a change of loyalties or death.

The crown's supporters came from among the most powerful noble families of the age and it was their ambition that fuelled the wars, rather than enmity between rivals for the throne itself from the houses of Lancaster or York. The fortunes of all the contenders to the throne throughout the wars were settled by battle, generally battle between rival noblemen supporting a particular aspirant or incumbent to the throne. Magnates based support of one side or the other on various causes, which included maladministration by the government, war policy in France, jealousy at court or simply the thirst for power. It is difficult to say why the wars ever actually began and indeed there is much disagreement about this, although there would seem to be three different but interrelated themes, particularly in the first phase. The first was the legitimacy of the two branches of the royal family, the Houses of York and Lancaster, and the use of this schism by their supporters for their own ends. And the second, initially, was simply the jealousy and lust for power of two powerful nobles, a theme which continued with different principles throughout the wars – indeed the wars might more accurately be called the 'Wars of the Magnates.'[5] The third was the failure of Henry VI to provide 'politic rule and governance'; in other words he failed to provide justice in his courts and failed to maintain law and order in his realm without prejudice. This gave nobles the opportunity to pursue their private quarrels without fear of the king's law.

The rupture between the Houses of York and Lancaster had its origin in the deposition of Richard II, of the House of York, by parliament on 29 September 1399. In the absence of a direct heir, parliament then made the formal offer of the crown the next day to Henry Bolingbroke of the house of Lancaster. Henry claimed the throne by right of conquest as well as by right of descent; he was the son of John of Gaunt, duke of Lancaster, Edward III's third son, and his first wife. Henry IV found himself ruling a country in which discord and dispute, caused partly by his accession to the throne, dominated events. However, after a difficult start, he managed to keep the country and his nobles in check during his reign for the next fourteen years. Nevertheless the enmity and the grievances caused by Richard's conduct during his reign and by Henry's usurpation of the throne simmered dangerously near the surface throughout his reign. These problems gradually receded as Henry V, who inherited the throne without challenge, fought and won the Battle of Agincourt and conquered much of northern France, indeed it would seem that they had gone forever. The duke of Bedford, Henry's brother and regent for his infant son, continued Henry's policies in France after his death and maintained peace and some prosperity at home. But when Henry VI came of age and began to pursue his own policies in France and

England, grievances and discord again dominated court life in
England and arrayed one powerful noble against another. When
finally France was lost in 1453 all the old enmities and accusations
surfaced and people took sides. Most nobles were genuinely neutral
concerning the legitimacy of the Lancastrian kings or the fitness of the
Yorkist aspirants to reign, and were content to give their loyalty to
whomsoever wore the crown at the time. However quarrels over land
and royal appointments, often caused by financial difficulties, led to
the shedding of blood and the loss of blood turned to feud; feud found
ready allies in the lust for power around the throne, which depended
on the favour of the king. Change the king and a new group of nobles
would achieve political power with all the favours and grants that
went with it. However, if the king were secure on his throne political
power would remain unchanged and those supporting him would
continue to receive the king's patronage and the benefits that it
brought. These problems might have been overcome had Henry VI
maintained law and order with a firm but fair hand, and been more
even handed in his favours. But this was not to be.

The second cause centred on the rivalry between two royal dukes;
Richard Plantagenet, duke of York, and Edmund Beaufort, duke of
Somerset. The former was an immensely wealthy man and the heir to
the throne until October 1453 when Queen Margaret gave birth to a
boy, Prince Edward. Somerset was a more distant heir to the throne
through his great-grandfather, John of Gaunt, and his third wife. He
was largely dependent on favours from the king for his advancement,
and increasing power and wealth, he had virtually no inherited land
was therefore keen to receive it as a loyal servant of the crown.
Carpenter[6] sees the fact that Somerset had no inherited land as a
positive advantage in that Somerset was always close to the king,
unlike York who had large territorial interests to supervise. York
clearly felt that as the heir to the throne and first cousin to the king he
should, by right, have a place in the council and should be allowed to
offer the king his advice, but of course he was seldom there. However
the king, on Suffolk's advice as lord chamberlain, largely ignored him,
indeed he had been virtually banned from court by his appointment as
king's lieutenant in Ireland in 1447, though he didn't take up the
appointment until 1449.

The quarrel between York and Somerset went back a long way and
almost certainly had its origins in France when Somerset was made

king's lieutenant and commander-in-chief in France, and took over from York in 1444.[7]

York felt that Somerset's appointment smacked of favouritism, particularly since he had himself been appointed initially for a second term as lieutenant only for his appointment to be cancelled in Somerset's favour. Furthermore, Somerset was paid an advance of £25,000[8] to meet his expenses at a time when the government owed York an even larger sum of money for expenses incurred while holding this office. Somerset then failed as lieutenant in France and presided over the loss of Normandy. Even the French remarked on his abysmal conduct in its defence. For York, a considerable landholder in eastern Normandy, owning two counties and three viscomtés, Somerset's withdrawal out of Normandy with little resistance represented a large financial loss. Furthermore the surrender of the cities and fortresses of Rouen and Avranches, where York was captain, without a siege was a stain on his honour.[i]

On Somerset's return to England in August 1450, rather than being required to answer for his conduct before parliament, he was made constable of England and a member of Henry's council. He was soon elevated to the vacant post of the king's chief councillor, previously held by Suffolk, who had been murdered in 1450 on his way to exile. Bordeaux and Aquitaine were then lost to France in June 1451, so compounding Somerset's miserable handling of French affairs. This was too much for York who marched on London with some 4,000 men and camped on Blackheath on 1 March 1452. The king, accompanied by Somerset and many other nobles, including Salisbury and Warwick, marched out to meet York but, after a parley and York had sent away his armed supporters, it became apparent that Somerset was still favoured by the king and York was humiliated.

Unfortunately for York, Somerset's standing at court improved as a result of Talbot's expedition to Bordeaux in October 1452. Talbot and the Gascon nobility soon cleared the French out of Aquitaine, so leaving York somewhat adrift in his dispute with Somerset over French policy. However, when Talbot was killed at Castillon and his

---

i The surrender of a town or fortress without a siege was considered a treasonable offence and unchivalrous, and touched on the honour of the person who was captain, even though he might not have been present at the time.

Anglo-Gascon army routed in August 1453, Henry VI went mad, suffering from what has since been thought to have been catatonic schizophrenia.[9] As a consequence a protectorate was formed in March 1454 and, following precedent, Richard of York was made protector. York himself wanted power, as did his supporters, and Henry's illness presented them with a golden opportunity. They felt, with some degree of truth, that Henry and his council, and particularly Somerset, were solely responsible for England's abysmal performance in France over the previous five years. They were also unhappy with government at home where too many matters were settled by favouritism. They were therefore determined to control events in England which meant removing Somerset and his supporters from office, and replacing them with their own while remaining loyal to their king. Somerset was sent to the Tower pending trial and Salisbury took his place as chancellor.

There now followed a struggle for power, which was set off by events in the north between the old border rivals of the Nevilles and the Percys. Some seven months earlier a bridal party consisting of Sir Thomas Neville and his new bride, Maud Stanhope, were ambushed at Howarth Moor on 24 August 1453 by Lord Egremont, the earl of Northumberland's second son, and a large party of armed Percy retainers. The cause for this ambush lies in a dispute between the two families over land in Yorkshire stemming from the alienation of Northumberland's ancestor by Henry IV for treason fifty years before.[10] However the Nevilles enlisted York's help in their northern quarrel and in exchange offered their support to York in the council; other lords quickly followed suit. Meanwhile the Percys found an ally in Henry Holland, duke of Exeter, who felt slighted that he had not been chosen as protector rather than York. However after the failed ambush Egremont and Exeter rode into the city of York with their armed retainers to establish themselves there but fled when the protector, the duke of York, arrived on the scene; order was soon restored and justice done. Exeter was imprisoned at Pontefract but Egremont remained at large. Later the two northern adversaries came close to blows, each having raised substantial armies, but after a stand-off a few miles apart tempers cooled and both armies drew off. However on 31 October, Egremont and his younger brother Richard, with about 200 men were on their way to York from the Percy manor of Pocklington when they were intercepted by John and Thomas

Neville. The latter had about an equal number of armed men at Stamford Bridge, a Neville manor astride the road to York. The Pocklington men did not like the way things were going and ran away leaving Egremont and his brother prisoners of the Nevilles. York now held Somerset, Exeter and Egremont prisoner. He could be well satisfied with his year as protector, furthermore people could now contrast York's and Salisbury's firm handling of affairs with the weak and partisan government of Henry VI and his chancellor Somerset.

Nevertheless, within the next fifteen months, York and his supporters were thrown into some disarray by two events. First, Queen Margaret gave birth to a son, Edward, on 13 October 1453, so that Richard of York was no longer heir presumptive; and secondly, Henry recovered shortly after Christmas 1454. The king lost no time in reinstalling his favourites at court. Somerset was back in favour and soon set out to unravel York's work. Supported by Northumberland, Exeter and others he forced Salisbury to resign the chancellorship, and assumed it once more himself. Suspecting foul play on Somerset's part, York, Salisbury and Warwick left court and London without taking their leave of the king. The two sides had finally parted.

York and his supporters, including the earls of Salisbury and Warwick, while few in number at court, nevertheless commanded significant military force. These two noblemen were Nevilles, marcher lords from Northumberland and Westmoreland, two areas where troops were always kept on stand-by in case the Scots crossed the border. Warwick also held land in south Wales as well as the lordship of Glamorgan. York himself had the support and the manpower of his lordships in the marcher lands along the border with Wales and in Wales itself, as well as manors in Yorkshire and elsewhere. The three together were a powerful element in the unsettled politics of the day. Opposed to them and ostensibly supporters of Henry VI were primarily Edmund Beaufort, duke of Somerset, the earl of Northumberland, a Percy and the marcher lord of the east march on the border with Scotland and Henry Holland, duke of Exeter. To alienate the two sides further Henry VI gave the lordship of Glamorgan to Somerset in 1453, even though Warwick had held it and administered it well since 1450.[11] Furthermore the Percys were in dispute with the Nevilles over land in Yorkshire. The scene was set for a power struggle around the throne.

York, Salisbury and Warwick, among several other nobles, were then summoned to a great council to be held at Leicester in May 1455 which was largely made up of Somerset's cronies. York read this as a threat and considered a council meeting stacked with Somerset's supporters would lead to his death or at least imprisonment pending trial for treason. York, Salisbury and Warwick failed to answer the summons in the way that Somerset had hoped. While still at Westminster on 18 May Somerset learnt that York, his supporters and their armed retinues were marching rapidly south towards London from near Leeds some 200 miles away. It would seem that York intended to intercept the king on his way to Leicester in order to 'protect' him from his friends for the better governance of the country.

Somerset was caught unawares, having taken no steps to gather an army,[12] and was afraid to remain near London where the population supported York. However he set out for St Albans with the court, the king and as many men-at-arms and archers as he could muster, calling on certain magnates to come with their retinues. But an army gathered in this way took time to muster and time was rapidly running out. The muster was to take place at St Albans and the court made its slow way there.[13] Many in the court could hardly be called allies of Somerset, but were there because of their duties to the king; among these were the earl of Devon and Lord Fauconberg, Salisbury's brother. Also there was the elderly duke of Buckingham who was no friend of Somerset's.

During the march the king was sent several letters by York protesting his loyalty and demanding that a new council chosen by York should advise the king. York's last letter was sent from Ware, barely 20 miles north-east of St Albans and dated the day before so that Somerset and the court realized that York might get to St Albans before them and that York's forces were larger than theirs. They therefore held a council of war at which Somerset suggested that they should forthwith prepare for battle out in the open. Buckingham, however, felt they should make their way to St Albans as planned and enter into negotiations with York while waiting for their reinforcements to arrive. Henry went along with Buckingham's advice and made him constable in place of Somerset. Buckingham was now responsible for the armed forces of the king and he ordered them to march to St Albans.

The king's army arrived at St Albans at about nine o'clock in the morning to find York's army already drawn up on the east side of the town in Key Field. The royal army marched straight into the town from the south. St Albans was a town built mainly along a single street running nearly due north. About one third of the way up this street from the south was a central square where the king, accompanied by Buckingham, raised his banner, so signifying that he was prepared to fight. The central square had a side street leading off to the west. There were three small roads leading into the town from the east – the southernmost, Sopwell lane, where Lord Clifford and his retinue were posted and the middle, or Shropshire lane, where Northumberland and Somerset with their retinues guarded the way into the town. There were no fortifications around the town but there was a ditch partially surrounding it. It began at the road from Watford in the south, circled the town to the east, crossed the northern end of the town and finished where it met the western road out of St Albans. There were wooden gates at each point where the ditch crossed the roads leading into the town. The area between York's camp and the houses on the east side of the main north-south road were filled with scattered trees and gardens. The royal army quickly guarded and barricaded the gates on the three lanes leading into the town from the east. York's army was drawn up in three divisions on slightly rising ground: York's in the north opposite that of Northumberland and Somerset across the Shropshire lane; Warwick's in the middle; and Salisbury's in the south opposite Clifford.

What were these armies like? They were both very small, the king's between two and three thousand strong made up of his personal guard of a few men-at-arms and archers, and the retinues belonging to the principle noblemen accompanying him. Bill-men probably made up the majority of the king's army and there were the fencible men from the towns and villages they passed through on their way. These fencible men were free-born Englishmen between the ages of sixteen and sixty who were liable for military service within the country when called upon by the king or his officers. The king expected reinforcements to come with magnates and knights on their way to the council. Indeed it was said that the duke of Norfolk, a person who was not really committed to either side but who was loyal to the king, was on his way with 6,000 men, as was the earl of Oxford; both arrived conveniently the day after the battle. York too was able to call on considerable military force, but it was not to hand. He had with him about 3,000 men,[14] with probably more men-at-arms and archers than his opponents, but he lacked the royal standard. His best allies were speed of movement and determined action. So far he had shown both.

Fearful that at any time significant reinforcements might arrive to bolster the Lancastrian force and having failed to achieve the surrender of Somerset, York finally decided to attack.

The Yorkists advanced along the Shropshire and Sopwell lanes where they were presumably constricted by hedges on either side or by the depth and width of the ditch. They met determined resistance and as they only attacked on a very narrow front against well-defended stout barricades their greater numbers gave them little advantage. But while they hammered fruitlessly at the barricades the earl of Warwick, with his retinue and the reserve division, crossed the ditch and advanced across the gardens between the two lanes into the centre of St Albans. Their cry of 'A Warwick, a Warwick' and the sight of his banner put the Lancastrians into a panic. Those at the barricades ran off fearful of being attacked from behind with York and Salisbury close on their heels. Within half an hour of Warwick's entry into St Albans the Lancastrians were scattered and it only remained for the Yorkists to overcome the men about the king for their victory to be complete. The king, who had been slightly wounded by an arrow in the neck, was taken to the abbey as a prisoner. Buckingham and the earls of Stafford, Dorset and Wiltshire were also wounded, but Clifford and Northumberland were killed. Somerset, the cause of all the problems, took refuge in the Castle Inn, which was surrounded. He had no intention of giving himself up to face a treason trial so he charged bravely out with several of his retainers and was hacked to death after he had killed four men in his bid for freedom. The battle, while being politically important, was really no more than a skirmish, small judged by the size of later battles in the wars and according to the Paston letters only 120 men were killed.

Fauconberg, Salisbury's brother, Buckingham, Devon, Dorset and Pembroke were rounded up and spared as they were not political allies of Somerset; Wiltshire escaped. York asked the king for forgiveness and was pardoned. Salisbury and Warwick had good reason to be pleased with their work that day: Northumberland and Clifford had been killed; the political map had been redrawn; the king was York's prisoner; and the hated Somerset together with his cronies had been swept away. The next day, 22 May 1455, the victorious

Yorkists rode into London, Warwick leading the way in front of the king, holding the royal sword; York rode on the king's right and Salisbury on his left. No clearer indication could be given to the London crowd that York was now in the driving seat. So first blood had gone to the Yorkists, but the blood that had been spilt at St Albans opened up family feuds and a thirst for revenge; it also left a key player as a bitter enemy. Queen Margaret, mother of the heir to the throne, Prince Edward, was fearful of what might now happen to her son as York, the next closest aspirant to the throne, was made constable of England.

A parliament was called in July, which duly blamed Somerset and two of his minions for the shedding of blood at St Albans; it also pardoned the Yorkist army for its part in the affair. Warwick was made captain of Calais and a new parliament was called to meet in November. During the summer a long-running feud in the south-west between the Courtenays and the Bonvilles broke out afresh. Sir Thomas Courtenay, the earl of Devon's son, and many of his armed retainers murdered Nicholas Radford, Bonville's legal adviser. The earl then occupied the city of Exeter with his armed followers and put Powderham Castle, about 8 miles away to the south, under siege. However, when York was once again made 'Protector and Defensor of this land' by the council in November 1455, which was endorsed by Henry, he moved to stifle this local affray in mid-December. As soon as York was on his way the Courtenays quickly stopped their illegal action and the earl gave himself up; he was brought back to London and committed to the Tower. York had shown that quick decisive action by the central authority could restore and maintain peace in the kingdom, and of course this firm action was contrasted favourably with what had gone before under Somerset's adminis-tration; a contrast which was no doubt intended.

Nevertheless, only two months later York was relieved of his commission as protector by the king in February 1456, no doubt on the advice of Queen Margaret who had left London with her son Prince Edward for the royal duchy of Lancaster, feeling unsafe in London. The king meanwhile remained at Westminster while York continued to supervise many of the functions of government from within the council. However York was not able to supplant Somerset as the driving force of government since too few peers openly supported him, perhaps because he was seen as having achieved his position through force of arms. Nevertheless one person had the king's ear and the will to govern on his behalf, Queen Margaret. When the king joined Margaret in June 1456 at her castle of Kennilworth she ensured that the balance in the political power game changed once again.

Queen Margaret was very assertive and wilful, compromise was not in her nature. Perhaps it should be remembered that Margaret was a French princess more used to government by royal decree and not used to the English form of government by compromise between crown and parliament. She was therefore well aware that her style of government in the king's name might not be appreciated in England and as a consequence she had the defences of the castles of Kennilworth and Leicester improved, the former by the purchase of 26 new Serpentine guns and a culverin.[15] She would of course advise Henry to follow those measures, which supported her primary aim of defending her son's inheritance, and since she didn't trust York, in those which opposed him. The court went with the king, as did Buckingham and supporters of the queen. So once again York was excluded from the king's council as likewise were Salisbury and Warwick. This was mainly of their own choosing because they were afraid that charges would be laid against them for their part in the affray at St Albans. Also they realized that they could be outvoted at the council, which now included the new earl of Northumberland, the son of the earl killed at St Albans, as well as Exeter. Furthermore a partisan parliament could be called either at Kennilworth or Leicester by Queen Margaret and her supporters to charge them with treason. Over the next two years the colour and sympathy of the court changed as Yorkists were removed from their positions in government and replaced by Lancastrians.

The most obvious effect of this slow change, masterminded by the queen, was that her chancellor became keeper of the privy seal in September, and Lancastrians were given the posts of chancellor and treasurer the following month. However the French now temporarily took centre stage, as they landed in Kent and sacked Sandwich in August 1457, an action which for a time made York and Warwick indispensable, the latter being made admiral in place of Exeter. But Warwick's position was being undermined by the treasurer, Thomas Tuddenham, who gradually stopped the funds needed for the maintenance of the fortress of Calais and the wages of its garrison. Warwick found an answer to this problem in typical fashion. He had built up a small fleet of some twelve ships over the previous years and he now made full use of them. In order to provide for the needs of the garrison and his own retinue he turned to piracy in the narrow seas. He attacked a Spanish fleet, capturing six ships, and a little later did the same to the salt convoy from France to the Hanseatic ports in the Baltic, taking much valuable booty; he also opened diplomatic relations with the duke of Burgundy. Warwick now left himself open to charges of piracy and treason. York, meanwhile, moved to his estates at Sandal from where he warily watched the queen build a power base in the royal duchy. Salisbury also left London for his estates in the north. The queen now held the reins of power; the king was feeble and happy to leave the cares of government in his wife's capable and vengeful hands.

Warwick was called back to London in July 1458 to face charges of attacking the Hansa fleet and arrived with 600 of his armed retainers. An enquiry was set up by the council but after a rigorous cross-examination Warwick complained that he was facing a plot to discredit him by the Queen and soon had the London mob on the streets in his support. The riot was quickly suppressed but Margaret had failed to discredit Warwick. Later in October Warwick again went to the court at Westminster but was set on by the royal guard after a brawl between his servants and the guard. He fought free, escaped to his barge in the Thames and sailed for Calais. He claimed the incident had been a deliberate attempt to murder him, which might well have been true, but Margaret laid the incident at his feet and demanded his arrest. She also appointed Somerset, son of the duke killed at St Albans, to the captaincy of Calais. Warwick refused to surrender his post and boldly came back to London to tell the council that as parliament had appointed him only parliament could supplant him. On leaving the council meeting he was attacked by retainers of Somerset and Wiltshire and again fought free, but there was little doubt this time that the queen was responsible for this attempt to murder him.

This brawl led to the next clash of arms. Both Lancastrians and Yorkists saw the way ahead clearly. The Lancastrians ordered 3,000 bows for the royal arsenal[16] and made preparations for war. The queen ordered the sheriffs of every shire to select able-bodied men from the towns and villages for military service and to be ready to answer her call to arms.[17] They also called a meeting of the great council to be held at Coventry in June to which the Yorkists were not invited and which laid indictments against York and his principle supporters. Waverers like Buckingham finally had to choose which side they were on as the queen pressed her advantage. The Yorkists too realized what was afoot and made their plans accordingly. Their leaders called for a meeting at Ludlow and, like the Lancastrians, began to recruit both soldiers and supporters. York was to be joined at Ludlow by Salisbury with his armed followers from the north while Warwick was to cross the channel with his retinue plus part of the Calais garrison and march to the meeting.

The country was alive with noblemen and their retinues, and small armies trying to reach either the banner of the king or that of York. The Lancastrians were trying to prevent the Yorkists from getting together and the Yorkists were trying to avoid them before they had mustered their army. The king was at Nottingham, the queen at Chester and the new duke of Somerset, Sir Henry Beaufort, son of the duke killed at St Albans, was in the West Midlands. York was at Ludlow, close to his estates on the march with Wales, Salisbury was marching to Ludlow from Middleham in north Yorkshire, his own power base, and Warwick was marching from the Channel. Warwick managed to join York at Ludlow having narrowly avoided Somerset's army, which had been ordered to patrol the West Midlands specifically to prevent this from happening. Salisbury, however, was not so lucky. He was intercepted at Blore Heath on 23 September 1459 by part of the royal army under the command of Lord Audley, having avoided Buckingham's army earlier.

The battle at Blore Heath involved two much larger armies than those at St Albans. Lord Audley had about 10,000 men in his army, including a high proportion of men-at-arms and archers, most of whom were untried. Salisbury's army was about half that size, but was composed of experienced semi-professional soldiers from the border country in the north. Salisbury's scouts gave him good warning of the approach of the royal army. He took up a position to the north-east of and overlooking the Wemberton brook, which ran across the Newcastle-under-Lyme to Market Drayton road, about a mile to the west of the aptly named village of Loggerheads. To his right and protecting his right flank he made a wagon laager with his baggage wagons while woods behind him covered his rear. When the royal army arrived they stayed to the south-west of the brook and lined a hedge which ran parallel to the brook. Both sides were defensively prepared. Salisbury tried to negotiate a free passage but when this was denied and while both sides contemplated their next move he took advantage of the delay and strengthened his position by planting stakes along the front of it with a ditch behind.

Audley however took the initiative. About a third of his men-at-arms remained mounted and at about 1.00 p.m. this force advanced across the bridge and over the brook towards the Yorkist army, hoping, no doubt, to break them by a charge. It is not clear what prompted this advance, but it might have been that a withdrawal by part of Salisbury's army into the woods led Audley to think that Salisbury's army was retreating. It may have been, but by the time the mounted men-at-arms had crossed the brook and formed up Salisbury's men had returned to their positions. As with so many battles in the Hundred Years' War, Audley's attack was broken up by archery fire from a protected position and the horsemen withdrew out of arrow range. Lord Audley then led a second charge to break the Yorkist line, but like the first it was repulsed by archery and he lost his life in the attempt. Command now fell on his deputy, John, Lord Dudley. He dismounted most of his men-at-arms and began an attack on foot with about 5,000 men. The fight that followed was long and fierce but gradually Salisbury's men gained the upper hand and the Lancastrians began to flee the battle, leaving some 2,000 dead behind. Salisbury had won the Battle of Blore Heath at a cost to him of about 500 casualties;[18] unfortunately his two young sons were taken prisoner[19] by the Lancastrians in an ambush after Salisbury's army marched from the battlefield.

It seems that the main body of the king's army was only some 10 miles away from Blore Heath and that Henry was well aware of Salisbury's approach, but still failed to concentrate his army for a decisive battle. Perhaps he received conflicting advice, which for an indecisive man would have made inaction the safest thing to do. Salisbury then marched to Ludlow where he joined York and Warwick. Outwardly it would seem that the Yorkists now had the upper hand, but this was not so. There were still two Lancastrian armies in the field, one commanded by Somerset and the other by Buckingham, and while York had received no reinforcements, nobles and their retinues were joining the royal army every day as were contingents from the shires summoned by royal decree. Once again York, who had lost the political battle in the council, now faced a battle against the odds. Nevertheless he sent a letter to the king assuring him of his loyalty and justifying his actions; in response Henry offered a pardon to all except those who had taken part in the Battle of Blore Heath, providing York and his army surrendered.

Receiving no reply to Henry's offer, Queen Margaret ordered the royal armies to march on Ludlow. On coming to Ludford Bridge, just east of Ludlow, on 12 October they found York's army drawn up ready for battle on the far side of the River Teme. However as York, Salisbury and Warwick looked across at the royal army, now some three times larger than their own, they realized that, having rejected the royal pardon, they could expect scant mercy. Their position was made even more difficult when Sir Andrew Trollope accepted the king's pardon and marched the Calais contingent across to the royal army to join the king who was of course his paymaster. This 'treachery' by Trollope was to be repeated by others in the battles to follow and became a major element in the confrontation between the two sides. York and his allies then knew that the game was up. That night York and his second son left for Ireland while Salisbury, Warwick and York's eldest son, Edward, earl of March, left for Calais. The Yorkist army faded away and the Lancastrians plundered Ludlow. Margaret had won; England was now ruled by her French queen.

However, all was not yet settled; the principle Yorkist commanders had got away, they had lost considerable prestige but they were safe. Richard of York was popular in Ireland and well liked, while both the soldiers and citizens of Calais held Warwick in high regard. Margaret now had a problem. She held the reins of power but could not eliminate her rivals because she could not get at them. However she called a parliament in November packed with her supporters, who passed a bill of attainder on the principle Yorkists and she quickly replaced Yorkist sympathizers with her own. She appointed Sir James Butler, earl of Wiltshire to the lieutenancy in Ireland in place of York, and she had already appointed Sir Henry Beaufort, duke of Somerset, to the captaincy of Calais before Ludford Bridge. On paper this was a good start – the two principle appointments within her gift had been given to her two closest supporters but they had yet to take up their appointments before any political advantage could be gained.

Wiltshire did his best to stir up rebellion against York in Ireland but his efforts failed and he was unable to establish himself.

Somerset attempted to land at Calais to take up his appointment but was refused admission. A decision was then taken by the government to assemble an expeditionary force at Sandwich to take Calais by force and ships were arrested to carry an army under Lord Rivers across the Channel. Warwick heard about this force and sent his fleet across to destroy the ships. This they did early in the morning of 15 January, taking Lord Rivers and his family prisoner. Later in March, Warwick left for Ireland with his fleet to confer with York about their future plans and on his return fleets under Sir Baldwin Fulford and the duke of Exeter failed to prevent Warwick from returning safely to Calais in May.[20]

On his return late in May he received news that new preparations had been made at Sandwich to aid Somerset in his siege of Calais; 200 men-at-arms and 200 archers were waiting for suitable weather to cross the Channel as reinforcements for Somerset. In typical fashion Warwick decided to strike first. He sent his own fleet to Sandwich yet again under Fauconberg and Dinham who landed, attacked and defeated the reinforcements and then captured Sandwich. The Yorkists now had a bridgehead in England. On 26 June Warwick joined Fauconberg with a further 1,500 men and an artillery train, and they began a march on London. The populace had been well prepared. The Yorkists had distributed leaflets criticising the government and had much popular support, particularly in London and the south-east, as a result of which people flocked to join Warwick's standard. In London Lord Scales, having offered to defend the city, moved into the Tower with his men and several other Lancastrian lords after his offer had been refused. The London council meanwhile welcomed Warwick and opened the city's gates to him, a judicious move bearing in mind the size of his army, which by now, according to eyewitnesses was more than 20,000[21] strong. On 4 July the city voted a donation of £1,000 to Warwick 'to keep the peace' having provided a baggage train and offered the use of the city's guns. Warwick moved out that day and began his march to the north, leaving Salisbury with sufficient forces to contain Scales in the Tower. He took the Northampton road out of London thinking that the king was still at Coventry and surmising that he would march south towards London. However he had heard that the king might march to Ely instead and so he ordered Lord

Fauconberg to take one half of the army up the London road towards Ely to be certain to intercept the king.

When Warwick reached St Albans he received definite information that the Lancastrian army was on the London road; in fact it had moved out of Coventry shortly after Warwick had landed in Kent. The king and Buckingham, his principle commander, had decided to wait for Warwick at Northampton where they prepared a suitable defensive position to the south of Northampton by the River Nene. On hearing this Warwick sent messengers to Fauconberg to turn west at Ware and join him at Dunstable. The Lancastrian army was in no hurry; they knew that Warwick was marching north and were more concerned that they were ready for him than they were to press on to London. Also they knew that other lords were on their way to join them. Once again the longer they could put off a confrontation the stronger they would get, although they were well aware that York might land from Ireland with considerable force and join up with Warwick in the future.

How did these two armies compare? Taking the leaders first there were already changes to those of five years previously. The Lancastrian leaders now included the duke of Buckingham, the earl of Shrewsbury (son of the earl killed at Castillon in 1453 and Buckingham's son-in-law), Viscount Beaumont (another of Buckingham's sons-in-law), Lord Egremont, Sir Humphrey Stafford, Sir John Talbot, Sir Thomas Percy and Sir Edmund Grey, lord of Ruthin. Although Northumberland was on his way to join them they were not really a representative selection of the peers of England, however they had the king with them. In contrast the Yorkist commanders now contained a wider spectrum of the nobility. They included the duke of Norfolk, the earls of Warwick and of March (York's eldest son), Viscount Bourchier and Lords Abergavenny, Audley (son of the Audley killed at Blore Heath), Fauconberg, Say and Scrope; Lords Clinton and Stanley might also have been there. York was expected from Ireland with his younger son, the earl of Rutland, and Salisbury was besieging the Tower in London. Clearly more peers had joined the Yorkist standard since Ludford Bridge. Also with Warwick's army there was a strong contingent of the cloth: the papal legate and the archbishop of Canterbury travelled with them from London, as well as four other bishops. These clerics were unlikely Yorkist supporters, almost certainly there to arbitrate and to try to prevent bloodshed.

The Yorkist army was the larger of the two, perhaps 20,000, whereas the Lancastrian was unlikely to be more than 15,000 strong, however the latter had the advantage in artillery, which by now and after the Battle of Castillon was a proven and important part of a field army. These were large numbers of men and only a relatively small proportion of them would have been fully armoured men-at-arms and properly equipped mounted archers; there were possibly no more than 1,500 to 2,000 men-at-arms on each side and maybe 6–8,000 archers. There would have been well over 15,000 fencible men in the two armies, men like the Shrewsbury contingent of fifty-one men summoned for service by the king,[22] other town levies and levies from the shires. The basic equipment of these men would have been the jack and a helmet; their helmets were probably visorless salets or a kettle hat. If they had been in battle before on the victorious side they may also have had a shirt of mail pillaged from the dead and possibly gauntlets and a mail hood. Their weapons would have included the bill, a sword or falchion and a dagger. Compared with the fully armoured man-at-arms from the ranks of the knights, nobles and their retainers these men were not particularly well protected. But they had significant advantages: they were much more mobile and because their armour was nothing like as heavy they didn't tire so easily or become dehydrated.

The royal army took up a strong position outside the walls of Northampton to the east of the Buckingham road. They had the River Nene at their backs and a water-filled ditch to their front. They had had ample time to improve these natural defences with stakes driven into the banks of the ditch. The royal army was organized in three divisions, that of Lord Grey on the right, Shrewsbury with Lords Egremont and Beaumont in the centre and Buckingham on the left. The king's tent and his immediate guard were behind Buckingham's division. The artillery was stationed on the right of Grey's division from where they could cover the front of the Lancastrian army with enfilade fire. They were ready and reasonably confident but wary of Warwick's growing reputation.

The Yorkist army approached up the Towcaster road with the vanguard under the earl of March and the duke of Norfolk on 10 July 1460. They halted on some higher ground to the south-west of the Lancastrian position and while the rest of the army came up to them Warwick sent a delegation headed by the bishop of Salisbury with a petition for the king. But Buckingham would not allow them access to the king. Warwick then sent his herald across twice more to try and negotiate a peaceful settlement, but these efforts were also rebuffed and so, receiving no answer, the Yorkist army began its attack in pouring rain at about 2.00 p.m. They advanced in column of divisions, led by Warwick and March, and made for the Lancastrian right wing held by Lord Grey. As they approached the heavy downpour made the going slippery and as soon as they got within bowshot range they were greeted by a fierce volley of arrows. They halted, replied with their own archery fire and then pressed on. Surprisingly the Lancastrian guns did not open fire – they couldn't; the rain had damped the powder and so the guns, so well sited, took no part in the battle. As the Yorkist soldiers came up to the ditch and tried to claw their way up the banks they were given a helping hand by the men of Grey's division[23] who had turned their coats and laid down their arms. It seems that Grey had somehow got a message through to Warwick telling him of his intention and no doubt the Yorkists offered an inducement. Warwick warned his own men not to harm those wearing Lord Grey's badge of the ragged staff. This act of treachery opened the whole Lancastrian line to the Yorkists who now began to roll the line up from the right. The Lancastrians could not adjust their line in time within the confined space of their position and many now did their best to get away. But there was only one way out and that was across the swollen River Nene where several lost their lives trying to get away. As to the remainder, Warwick had ordered his army to spare the common men and the king, but the nobles were given no quarter. The duke of Buckingham, Lords Beaumont and Egremont and the earl of Shrewsbury were all killed defending the king, but Henry was unharmed and once again found himself the prisoner of the Yorkists. Henry was escorted to Delapré Abbey nearby where he spent the next three days before being taken to London. The political balance had changed once again at a cost of the lives of some 300 soldiers and four peers.

Warwick and his prisoner arrived in London on 16 July and Warwick immediately took over the processes of government, appointing his supporters to the important posts of chancellor and treasurer. Lord Scales and others were still being besieged in the Tower but Warwick allowed Lords Scales and Hungerford to go free on 19 July on its surrender. Boatmen later murdered Scales as he was on his way up-river to sanctuary at Westminster. Across the Channel Somerset's abortive siege of Calais had reached stalemate, but as news of the victory at Nottingham arrived across the sea it was clear that Somerset was in a hopeless position, and when Warwick returned to Calais Somerset bought his freedom by surrendering the castle at Guisnes. However, Queen Margaret and Prince Edward were still at large in the north of England, the Lancastrian power base, and the country was split on a north-south basis. Northampton had not been decisive and a catalyst was needed to swing the country one way or the other.

York was destined to be the catalyst. He landed near Chester in early September and then toured his estates in Wales gathering his supporters before going on to London, which he reached on 10 October. He had his sword carried before him in regal fashion as he made his way to Westminster to meet the assembled lords in parliament. By his demeanour he clearly expected to be greeted as the future king, but the lords greeted him in silence and the impasse was only relieved by the archbishop of Canterbury who asked him if he wished to meet the king. Nevertheless it was clear to all that he expected to sit on the throne in due course. He however realized that he could not simply seize the crown, as his support would melt away; he had to proceed legally to achieve his ambition. The means lay to hand. Warwick had sent out writs on 30 July to summon a parliament to meet on 7 October, originally to cancel the acts of attainder against himself and other Yorkists. York thought he could use this parliament to achieve his aim.

On 24 October parliament passed the 'Act of Accord', as it became known, by which it was agreed that York or his heirs should become king on Henry's death. The following day Henry acquiesced and signed away his son's inheritance. This was greeted as a sensible compromise by all in the south; it recognized the status quo but at the same time upheld Henry as the rightful king, notwithstanding the fact that he was virtually York's prisoner. Furthermore parliament ordered that all royal officers should give obedience to York, as the heir to the throne, as they would do to the king. This was particularly useful since it made it lawful for York to raise troops to put down rebels and others.[24] But this compromise was bitterly contested by Queen Margaret who saw her son, Edward, being denied his rightful inheritance by the accord. She was at that time in Wales with Jasper Tudor, earl of Pembroke, raising supporters for her cause. She left him to continue the good work and took ship for Scotland where she hoped to raise more support for which she was quite prepared to pay by ceding Berwick to Scotland in return for military aid. Somerset meanwhile had crossed over from France and joined up with the earl of Devon. They collected their supporters in the south-west, marched rapidly north from Corffe Castle and reached York by mid-November where they were joined by the earl of Northumberland and Lords Clifford and Roos, who had been actively recruiting in the north. The duke of Exeter and the earl of Wiltshire and their contingents also joined this rapidly growing Lancastrian army. All of a sudden the Lancastrian menace to York's ambitions had materialized once again. York was forced to act.

York had to divide his forces, sending his eldest son, the earl of March, to Wales to confront Pembroke, leaving Warwick in London to guard the king, supervise the government and also protect the south-east from French raids. He then marched north with an army of about 6,000 men to meet and beat the Lancastrian uprising, expecting to collect more men on the march. York had his younger son Edmund of Rutland with him, and was accompanied by Salisbury and his son Sir Thomas Neville. They left London on 9 December and arrived at Sandal Castle, York's old home and base near Wakefield on 21 December. The march north had not been uneventful; Andrew Trollope and his men had ambushed part of York's vanguard near Worksop, but failed to stop York. They arrived at Sandal to find that the lieutenant of the castle had been unable to gather sufficient supplies for York's army due to the threat of Lancastrian forces in the neighbourhood, and because of their scarcity in the middle of winter.

Lack of supplies was not an unusual problem for armies in the Middle Ages; they seldom travelled with sufficient food and forage for the whole army and relied on buying or taking provisions on the way. Consequently one of York's first tasks was to find food and forage for his army, which he did by sending out foraging parties. However, due to the presence of Lancastrian forces in the area these had to be quite large bodies of armed men. York also suffered from a lack of reliable information about the Lancastrians in the area, indeed his information seems to have been rudimentary. He obviously knew from his lieutenant at the castle that some Lancastrian forces were in the neighbourhood but he didn't know where they were or in what strength. There were actually seven different contingents within 3 miles of the castle all spread out because of the problem of finding forage and provisions. Nevertheless they were obviously in touch with each other and probably trumpet calls or shouts could be heard from one contingent to another. The area was well hedged so it would not have been easy to see what was going on.

There now followed a minor stalemate: York couldn't march out and engage Somerset because the latter would not concentrate his army, and Somerset could not get at York in the castle because he had no siege artillery. By now York had about 8,000 men in his army while Somerset probably had more than 12,000; both armies had the usual proportions of men-at-arms and archers but had large numbers of bill-men. York spent an uncomfortable and rather bleak Christmas in his castle. On 30 December one of the Yorkist foraging parties to the north of the castle was on its way back when it was attacked by Somerset's own contingent. The foraging party must have been several hundred strong as was Somerset's force and a fierce battle ensued, but now things became untidy and mistakes were made. On York's arrival at Sandal, Lord John Neville had gone to see him to seek permission to raise troops in the area, which York willingly gave him thinking they were to be raised for his cause. But Neville, unbeknown to York and in contrast to most of the Neville family, was a closet Lancastrian and he now marched onto the scene with his new recruits, not to come to the aid of York's foraging party but to destroy it. York himself could see the mêlée from the tower of the castle and marched out with part of the garrison to the aid of his foraging party; he left Salisbury to come on as soon as he could with the remainder of the army from the castle. However as York approached he must have realized that something was amiss; Neville was on the wrong side! Nevertheless there was no turning back now, determined action might yet resolve the situation and so York resolutely led his troops into battle.

Back in the castle Salisbury was preparing to march out with the remainder of York's army to come to his aid about half a mile away to the north. By the time Salisbury reached York others, not yet seen by York and Salisbury, had heard the clash of arms and like vultures they came to the feast. York's army was beginning to press Somerset hard when they were attacked on each flank, by Andrew Trollope and

Exeter on their left and by Lord Roos on their right. A fierce fight now ensued and honours were about even when Lord Clifford marched up from his camp at Sandal Magna and charged York's army in the back. Surrounded, the fight went out of York's army and men fled the scene if they could get away or laid down their arms. Richard Plantagenet, duke of York, was hacked down after being unhorsed and refusing quarter, and some 3,000 men died in the Yorkist cause that day, including York's younger son Edmund, earl of Rutland, who was cut down in the pursuit by Lord Clifford on Wakefield Bridge.[ii] Also killed was Salisbury's son Thomas Neville and many experienced captains. Salisbury was captured by some of Trollope's men and executed the following day.

The battle at Wakefield had moved the political pendulum slightly in favour of the Lancastrians but the fruits of victory were not yet theirs to taste. Could Queen Margaret's supporters march to London, free the king and take over the government? On the face of it, Queen Margaret only had to march south, but this was not as easy as it seems. Edward, earl of March, now the duke of York, was in Gloucester with an army some 11,000 strong made up of his own men and new recruits gathered from Wales. Also, the earl of Warwick was still in London with a sizeable army supported by the citizens of the city and he held the king. Furthermore the Yorkist army at Wakefield had not been decisively defeated; it should be remembered that York had marched north with an army about 8,000 strong but only 3,000 were killed or died as a result of the battle.[25] Other armed Yorkists, perhaps 5,000 strong, were also still at large somewhere in Yorkshire. Margaret had won a battle but she was far from winning the war. However her ally Jasper Tudor, earl of Pembroke, had gathered an army from his own estates in Carmarthen and Pembroke and had joined forces with the earl of Wiltshire who had landed in south-west Wales with an army of mercenaries recruited mainly from Brittany and Ireland. This joint force, 8,000 strong, made its way towards Worcester. Almost certainly Pembroke had received news of the Battle of Wakefield, and had been ordered to meet the main Lancastrian

---

ii Accounts and interpretations of Edmund's death vary, but since he was present on the battle-field he was almost certainly clad in armour and therefore a legitimate casualty of a vigorous pursuit, but an unnecessary casualty since he could have been taken prisoner.

army somewhere near Northampton before Queen Margaret marched on London. But York too had received the news, knew that his father had been killed in battle, that his younger brother had been killed without mercy by Lord Clifford and that Salisbury had been executed the day after the battle. York, formerly the earl of March, was only seventeen years old but he was determined to avenge the deaths of his father and his brother.

York knew that Pembroke had been in south-west Wales gathering an army to join Queen Margaret's main force, indeed he had been sent to Wales specifically to watch and, if possible, destroy Pembroke's army before it could link up with Margaret's main force. He was positioned at Gloucester, from which he could march to intercept any move by Pembroke. When he heard that Pembroke was on the march he moved to Hereford to deny him the bridge. He was now in a pivotal position, both geographically and in intent. He had the choice, he could still march to London to join Warwick before Queen Margaret could reach the city, or he could turn on Pembroke before joining Warwick. When he was told that Pembroke was outflanking the River Wye by moving to the north of Leominster, Edward reacted promptly and marched the 17 miles north to Mortimer's Cross to bar Pembroke's way.

Edward, duke of York, arrived at Mortimer's Cross probably on the afternoon of 1 February and took up positions to the west of the little River Lugg and astride the road to Croft Castle and Ludlow. Edward divided his largely Welsh army of about 11,000 men into three divisions. He put Walter Devereux in command of the vanguard on the right of his line, took command of the main guard in the centre himself and gave the rear guard on the left to Sir William Herbert. Early on 2 February Pembroke's army came into sight and took up positions opposite those of York's army, with Wiltshire and his mercenaries on the left opposite Devereux and Owen Tudor's division on the right opposite Sir William Herbert. Pembroke himself faced Edward of York. Pembroke's army was smaller than York's, perhaps by 2,000 men, but in terms of fighting power was probably about the same since Wiltshire's mercenaries were professional soldiers who would have been equipped to a higher standard than the majority of soldiers opposite them. Both armies would have had perhaps 1,000 fully armed men-at-arms and between 4 and 5,000 archers; the remainder would have been bill-men from the estates of the principles and from the fencible men in the areas under their influence; neither side had field artillery.

Both sides looked at each other and adjusted their lines until about midday when Pembroke's army began a general advance. No doubt showers of arrows accompanied the advance and the defence replied in kind, but neither the advance nor the defence were unduly discomfited by the arrow storm indicating that armour was improving and that the ordinary soldier was beginning to be better protected. As might be expected, Wiltshire's professionals gradually forced Devereux's division back until they broke and ran for safety behind the river. But while their local fight was going on Pembroke's division was locked in a very even battle with York's. Every foot was contested until gradually York and his division gained the upper hand and forced Pembroke to retreat. Meanwhile on York's left Owen Tudor marched his division to the left of Herbert's, hoping to outflank it and attack the Yorkist line from the left or from behind. This was a difficult manoeuvre to accomplish within sight of enemy troops; before he could complete his move and while still in a fairly loose formation Herbert attacked Tudor's division. Tudor's force was checked, scattered and sought safety to the south. The battle was over; Pembroke's division had also been defeated and had run for safety to the west. What happened to the victorious mercenaries? Their leader, Wiltshire, having seen what had happened to the rest of Pembroke's army, took to his heels and escaped,[iii] the mercenaries then simply sat down and took no further part in the battle. Why should they? Their paymaster had fled! The Battle of Mortimer's Cross was a bloody affair; the Lancastrians had nearly 4,000 casualties at a cost of a few hundred of Edward's army. Pembroke fled abroad but his father Owen Tudor was executed the next day.

The Battle of Wakefield took place on the 30 December 1460 and that of Mortimer's Cross on 2 February 1461, thirty-four days later. What had Queen Margaret and her Lancastrian army been doing during that time? It is probable that her victory at Wakefield was an unexpected bonus and that she was not yet ready to march on

---

iii Wiltshire was the great escapist of the Wars of the Roses, having run away at St Albans in 1455 and Mortimer's Cross in 1461. He was to escape again at the battle of Towton in 1461 but was caught later.

London; she was certainly waiting for Pembroke's army and promised Scottish mercenaries. The latter of course had been bought by the promise of the return of Berwick to Scotland and with the sweetener of the promise of the marriage of Prince Edward to one of James III's sisters. The treaty of Lincluden had sealed these arrangements. Others who made up the reinforcements were the shire levies from the north and some French mercenaries. Judging by their behaviour these reinforcements were attracted more by the prospect of loot than anything else; as in the past both the Scots and the northern men were feared and respected in the south as hardy fighting men and rapacious looters.

Queen Margaret eventually began her march south towards London on or about 20 January, presumably expecting to be joined by Pembroke on the march. Her route, straight down the Great North Road, was marked by the towns her army pillaged on the way: Grantham, Stamford, Peterborough, Huntingdon and Royston. Both sides pillaged towns and villages en route during the wars, particularly if they were known to be loyal to the opposing side. In this case all the looted towns sympathized with the Yorkist cause, but the looting by the queen's army, said to be 25,000 strong, was so thorough and on an altogether larger scale than ever before that it had the effect of spreading fear like a wave before it. Indeed as the queen's army approached London panic reined. Fear of this northern rabble turned out to be a good Yorkist recruiting agent as armed volunteers poured into London to serve under Warwick.

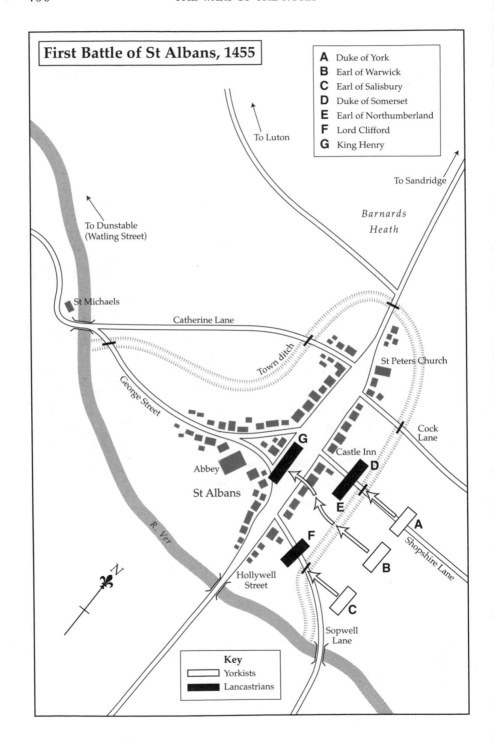

First Battle of St Albans, 1455

A Duke of York
B Earl of Warwick
C Earl of Salisbury
D Duke of Somerset
E Earl of Northumberland
F Lord Clifford
G King Henry

To Luton

To Sandridge

Barnards Heath

To Dunstable
(Watling Street)

St Michaels

Catherine Lane

Town ditch

St Peters Church

George Street

Cock Lane

Castle Inn

G

D

Abbey

E

St Albans

A

Shopshire Lane

R. Ver

F

B

N

Hollywell Street

C

Sopwell Lane

Key

Yorkists

Lancastrians

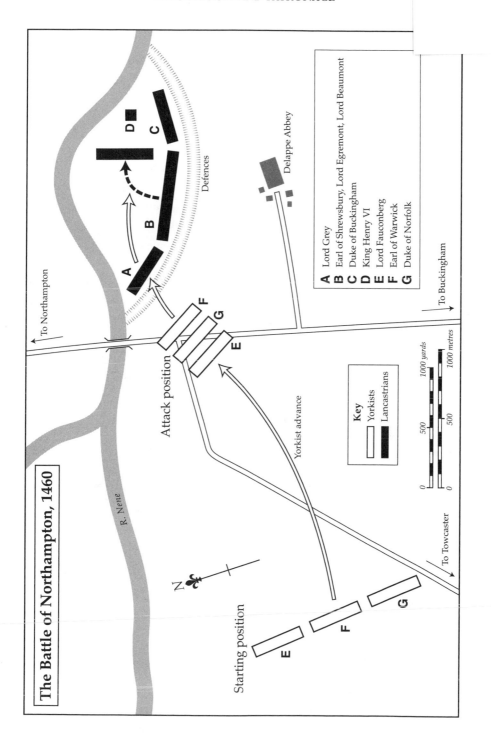

The Battle of Northampton, 1460

To Northampton

R. Nene

Starting position

N

Yorkist advance

Attack position

Defences

To Towcaster

To Buckingham

Delappe Abbey

Key
Yorkists
Lancastrians

0   500   1000 yards
0   500   1000 metres

A Lord Grey
B Earl of Shrewsbury, Lord Egremont, Lord Beaumont
C Duke of Buckingham
D King Henry VI
E Lord Fauconberg
F Earl of Warwick
G Duke of Norfolk

Chapter 19

The Battle of Towton

'Now sways it this way, like a mighty sea
Forc'd by the tide to combat with the wind;
Now sways it that way, like the self-same sea
Forc'd to retire by fury of the wind.'[1]

Warwick now had to decide what to do next. He had sent the duke of
Norfolk off to recruit in East Anglia, and Bonville and Bouchier to the
southern counties to do the same. Rumour had it that Queen
Margaret's army was only a few days' march away to the north, but
Warwick seemed in no hurry. He waited until his recruiters returned
and meanwhile elevated his brother, John Neville, to the peerage as
Lord Montagu, and had himself and two others elected to the Garter.
Only the king of course could enact these promotions, but Henry,
now a puppet king, was Warwick's prisoner and the king would do as
he was told. Margaret's army was making its slow way south, seemingly in no hurry to get to London and possess the king. They must by
now have heard of the destruction of Pembroke's army and were
probably wary of getting too far south with the possibility of York's
army hurrying towards London from the west and coming behind
them. Warwick also must have heard of York's victory so he was
probably waiting for York to join him. The panic in London caused
by the queen's slowly approaching army forced his hand. According
to reports Warwick left London with the king and a large army, but
almost certainly not as large as the 25,000 he was reputed to have
with him.

The direct route for the Queen's army to London would have taken
it through Ware and Waltham but for some reason it veered off to the
west and made towards Dunstable. The Yorkists covered both routes
to London because the duke of Norfolk with the vanguard left
London on the road to Ware and Royston, and joining Warwick at St
Albans later. Probably both armies covered both routes and neither

wished to miss the other; the inclination of both was to take the westerly route because of the possibility that York might join Warwick. The queen's army would have hoped that they might meet and defeat York before he could join up with Warwick, or at least prevent such a juncture, while Warwick would have hoped that York would have joined him before he met the queen's army. Both armies needed to meet and fight the other – a decision had to be arrived at by battle, so neither side was trying to avoid the other.

Warwick arrived at St Albans on 13 February and immediately took up defensive positions in and around the town. He had an outpost of some 200 archers and men-at-arms at Dunstable and a large contingent of archers in St Albans itself, but otherwise his main force was concentrated to the north of the town. From the layout of Warwick's positions it would seem that he expected the queen's army to approach down either the Baldock road or the Luton road. He himself commanded the main force to the north of St Albans on Barnard's Heath, with the rearguard under Lord Montagu, his brother, behind him on the outskirts of the town facing west. His vanguard under the duke of Norfolk was to the north of his own position near Sandridge. His army was well posted for an expected advance by the queen's army either from Baldock or Luton and could easily be switched to meet an actual threat from either direction.

But the queen's army did not come from either Baldock or Luton, it came from Dunstable. The first contact between the two armies came on 16 February when the Lancastrian army overran the outpost at Dunstable killing or capturing everyone there. Warwick received unreliable news of this attack that evening but took no measures to either verify it or to adjust his positions to meet a threat from that direction. Early the next morning elements of the Lancastrian army suddenly appeared in the centre of St Albans where the men stationed there drove them back to their starting point at the bridge over the river with heavy casualties. Word was sent to Lord Montagu who quickly adjusted his position to meet a threat coming out of the town from the south, but the Lancastrians, under their field commander Somerset, also adjusted their battle plan. They sent scouts to find another way into the town and soon reported that the lane to the north of their previous approach was unguarded. The Lancastrians then advanced once again down the Dunstable road and the lane, and again met the force in the town, but this time they were able to attack

them from two sides so that before long they overwhelmed this group
and occupied the town. The army then paused for rest and regrouping
before turning north to confront Montagu's division with overwhelming strength at about noon.

Montagu, realizing the plight he was in, sent a messenger appealing
for urgent help. His division then put up a desperate fight hoping they
would be reinforced before they were overpowered. But the
messenger took time to find Warwick who took time to rally his
division among the hedges and small fields in which they were posted.
Meantime Montagu's bitter fight was gradually coming to its end as
his division was slowly pushed north by sheer weight of numbers. It
was at this point that treachery intervened. The contingent from Kent
in the Yorkist army fighting under their leader, Lovelace, decided to
throw in their lot with the Lancastrians and the fight went out of
Montagu's division as the Kentish men deserted. Warwick had by
now gathered the remainder of his army and was hastily marching
south to the aid of his brother, even riding on ahead with his mounted
men-at-arms and archers leaving his infantry to follow as fast as they
could. But as they approached the scene of the fight they realized from
retreating soldiers that they were too late. Warwick called off his
counter-attack and withdrew northwards.

The king, Henry VI, was abandoned by the Yorkists and was
found later that evening seated under a tree guarded by Lord Bonville
and Sir Thomas Kyriel. They were both assured of their safety by
Henry but were nonetheless executed the next morning by the
Lancastrians on Queen Margaret's orders after she had asked her
seven-year-old son, Prince Edward, what punishment they should
receive. He is reputed to have said, 'Let them have their heads taken
off.'[2] Many other Yorkists were also put to death on the queen's
orders, a factor that probably influenced their own behaviour
towards prisoners from then on. As a result of this second battle of
St Albans the king and queen were re-united and the Yorkist army
had withdrawn. This was hardly a crushing victory for the
Lancastrians, more the end of round one in which the Yorkist army
had received a bloody nose. The total numbers reported killed that
day including casualties from both sides on the battlefield vary from
1,916 to 7,500[3] and were more likely to be nearer the lower figure.
So far as is known both the Yorkist mainguard and rearguard
marched away in good order after nightfall.

A further significant casualty was Warwick's self-esteem and reputation, both suffered from this his first defeat in battle, which stemmed largely from his own mistakes. He had failed to appreciate the significance of the loss of his detachment at Dunstable and as a consequence had failed to realign his army to face the threat. Also he had undoubtedly spaced the divisions of his army too far apart, bearing in mind the closeness of the country surrounding St Albans. In those days it was vital for each constituent part of an army to be in touch with the others, if not actually within sight, especially when battle was imminent. Furthermore, it was almost axiomatic that a commander should be able to see most of the elements of his army immediately prior to battle. Warwick failed to meet these criteria.

After her victory the citizens of London expected Queen Margaret's army to arrive at any moment and went in dread of the thought; they sent a delegation to the Lancastrian army to negotiate the city's surrender while the mayor kept the city under guard. But the queen was as worried as the citizens about the indiscipline of her army and although some rode into London, she withdrew her army to Dunstable. The gates of the City remained firmly shut. This would seem to have been an opportunity lost, but she had never been popular in London and if elements of her army had begun to loot in London she would very soon have loosed a hornet's nest. Meanwhile Warwick made his way towards Gloucester and joined the duke of York and his army at Chipping Norton in the Cotswolds. Although the Yorkists had been beaten at St Albans a large part of the army went with Warwick to join up with York, together making a very formidable army, well able to meet anything the Lancastrians could put into the field. York of course commanded a victorious army, which now grew not only as a result of the merger with Warwick but also because other Yorkist commanders joined it. In contrast Queen Margaret's army began to shrink as northern contingents deserted with their loot. Meanwhile the Lancastrian army was getting short of provisions and tried to arrange for victuals to be sent out to them from London, but the citizens prevented this.

Queen Margaret reluctantly turned north as the duke of York, accompanied by Warwick, rode into London at the head of his army to a rapturous welcome on 26 February. Queen Margaret had lost a golden opportunity. It is possible that as the king was now with them they felt that protocol required them to put plans before Henry for approval before action, but Henry was notoriously unable to make up his mind and quite incapable of giving firm direction. This must have been galling in the extreme for Margaret's commanders and for her, for she had gambled everything for the sake of her husband and her child. However her army was short of provisions, was a long way from the source of its supplies so the queen and her commanders may have felt the need to return to the north to provision and recruit.

It must not be forgotten that Warwick's army at St Albans was reputed to be 25,000 strong and that the queen's was as large, two exceptionally large armies for this time when armies were usually no more than ten to twelve thousand strong. Although these are probably exaggerated numbers and they were not all combatants, many being artisans and administrators, they all needed to be fed; furthermore there would have been at least 10,000 horses with each army and they needed forage. When these numbers are set against the population of the average town of the time of between five to eight thousand people it can be seen that the very problem of feeding such large masses of men and horses was Herculean. The towns themselves were nearly all market towns and therefore attracted the produce of the surrounding countryside. But once an army of this size had marched or encamped in the area there was precious little left for the citizens of the town, let alone for an army nearby for any length of time. Furthermore, the very presence of an army would have disrupted the usual process of the collection and provision of food and fodder to a town. Add to this the problem of loyalties in which a town might be loyal to the opposite faction and it is easy to understand the problems faced by army commanders, none of whom seemed to have an adequate commissariat.

This problem was obviously well understood by the duke of York who, before he marched north out of London on 13 March had collected a large number of wagons loaded with victuals for his army,[4] which were parked outside the city. Wagon trains, like artillery trains, had become an essential element of armies in the later Middle Ages. However, since much reliance was put on the possibility of gaining sustenance en route it is probable that wagon trains were reduced to the minimum size possible, but nevertheless they still constituted a problem. Partly due to the problems of feeding large armies loyal towns were absolutely essential to an army on the march, which tended to move from loyal town to loyal town. Having sent harbingers on ahead to the next town known to be loyal, armies would arrange for provisions to be available for them on arrival; these provisions would be paid for. In contrast, if an army had to go via towns loyal to the other side, as did Queen Margaret's on the march south after the Battle of Wakefield, they would pillage the town and burn any stores of food and forage found that they did not need for themselves. Food on the hoof if not wanted was also killed, to deny them to the other side. Of course the flip side to all this was that an army which burnt and looted its way on the march would be most unpopular and make its leaders unpopular too. Popularity in a civil war was important and this very fact acted as a brake on the behaviour of armies.

Therefore, notwithstanding Edward's foresight, the army would still have needed to gather provisions and particularly fodder on the march, as in the Hundred Years' War in France. Indeed it seems extraordinary that commanders recruited such large armies since at least a third of them were made up from shire and town levies. These people were not mounted or particularly well armoured or armed, indeed they were remarkably like the French peasant levy, though equipped to a slightly higher standard. They were a problem to feed, slow on the march and of a lower combat value than the horsed and armoured men-at-arms and mounted archers of the retinues and contract companies owing allegiance to magnates. There was, however, a very necessary role for which they could have been used. Loyal towns needed to be guarded, but perhaps this was not such an easy task as most towns were not fortified or walled. Combat in the field could then have been left to the nearly professional companies of the magnates. These could move swiftly from place to place, had a high combat value, were well disciplined and were more easily sustained in the field. Furthermore, these were generally the elements of the armies of the day that forced the decisions. The lesson had been learnt before: Edward III, the Black Prince and Henry V had all commanded small, efficient, well-disciplined and well-equipped armies, which had routinely defeated very large French armies. However in the Wars of the Roses both sides tended to field large armies, a result of bastard feudalism and the wish of towns and counties to show their loyalty, which if they were on the winning side might entail a reward in due course. It must be remembered that both sides were similarly equipped and there was no disparity in weaponry as there had been against the French, therefore the possibility of having flanks turned by a larger army was a very real danger. Armies faced each other in lines before combat and so if one side produced a really large army it could always envelop the other side unless it had secure flanks or was equally as large.

Edward, duke of York, had arrived with his army in London on 26 February and had immediately put in hand the necessary measures to pursue Queen Margaret and the Lancastrian army northwards. But first there was a political statement to be made; he was declared King Edward IV on 4 March 1461 at the Palace of Westminster. Now each side in the war had its own king. The Lancastrians had Henry, feeble in the head, unable to make decisions, not a leader of men, easily swayed and the grandson of the usurper Henry IV, while the Yorkists were led by Edward IV, a tall, good-looking, eighteen year old, already a proven leader in battle, a decision maker and a political leader. The contrast could not have been greater: the steel in the Lancastrian cause and army came from Queen Margaret and the duke of Somerset, while that of the Yorkists resided in Edward IV and his ally the earl of Warwick. Yorkist propaganda ensured that Edward was popular everywhere and people flocked to serve under his banner. Edward and his advisers took advantage of the fact that he was now the lawful king of England and used the bureaucratic machinery to call on thirty-three counties for their support. He also issued a proclamation in which he offered pardon to all who submitted within the next ten days with the exception of certain named individuals and those who earned more than 100 marks a year. This was an astute political ploy, which gave the common soldier the opportunity to opt out of the war while isolating the Lancastrian leadership and the knights and gentlemen who supported them.[5]

Notwithstanding these Yorkist measures, on the political front the war still had to be won. Warwick marched out of London to the Midlands on 7 March to recruit, followed by Lord Fauconberg with the vanguard of the Yorkist army on 11 March. Edward followed with the mainguard of the army on 13 March. They were on their way to the Lancastrian heartlands in the north. Meanwhile the Lancastrian army withdrew slowly northwards, looting on the way. They reached the city of York several days later. Edward reached Nottingham on 22 March. Warwick reached Pontefract on 27 March where Edward joined him later. Pontefract Castle was formidable and an excellent base for Edward's army before crossing the River Aire and confronting the Lancastrian army.

On reaching Pontefract Warwick immediately sent scouts north to find the Lancastrian army while waiting for the mainguard to close up to him; he also sent Sir John Radcliffe, Lord Fitzwalter, to seize the bridge across the Aire at Ferrybridge, a logical first step on the road to York. On his arrival, Fitzwalter found the bridge already destroyed by the withdrawing Lancastrians and immediately set his men to work to repair the bridge or at least to make it passable for small bodies of men to cross at a time. Fitzwalter did this soon enough but failed to keep an adequate watch. Early in the morning of 28 March his outpost at the bridge was surprised by Lord Clifford with about 500 of his retainers from the border country in the north. Fitzwalter and most of his men were killed, although some managed to get away and warn Warwick who told Edward who must have arrived at Pontefract late on 27 March. Edward immediately ordered his army to close up to the river where they found Clifford had posted his men in defensive positions on the north bank overlooking the bridge; this was a strong position guarded by marshes on the flanks from which his archers could cover the actual crossing. He was in a position to command the bridge for as long as he had sufficient men to do the job, but once action was joined casualties mounted.

The Yorkists were able to produce overwhelming archery fire to support their efforts to cross and gain the bridge, where a fierce and bloody hand-to-hand fight developed. It had been temporarily repaired by laying a few planks along the old partially destroyed bridge and was only wide enough for one or two men to fight at a time. Clifford's defence made the seizure of the bridge an expensive matter; many men on each side were killed while others slipped and drowned in the freezing waters of the river below. Eventually Clifford was forced to withdraw as Warwick had many more men at hand and Clifford was not reinforced. But he might have been forced to retire by another development; his flank scouts reported that part of the Yorkist vanguard under Fauconberg had crossed the Aire at Castleford, about 3 miles away to the west and was threatening his position from the flank. On hearing this he realized it was time to pull out and join the Lancastrian main army. But he had left it too late. Mounted troops from Fauconberg's force, riding fast, managed to intercept Clifford and his men near Dintingdale, 6 miles to the north before he could reach the main Lancastrian positions. A fierce fight followed in which Lord Clifford was killed by an arrow in the neck. Sir John Neville, the turncoat at the Battle of Wakefield,[6] was also killed, as were most of Clifford's men. King Edward and the main body of the Yorkist army crossed the River Aire that evening and settled for the night just south of the village of Saxton, about a mile from Towton. They spent a cold and miserable night around their campfires and it is doubtful if anyone got a hot meal to cheer them up or a tent to sleep in as the wagon train was probably still miles behind. They would have lain on the ground huddled in their cloaks for warmth waiting for the dawn. In contrast the Lancastrian army would have been well fed and would have spent the night in tents sheltered from the elements. However, before it grew dark that night scouts of the Yorkist vanguard would have seen the Lancastrian army just to the south of the village of Towton and would have reported back to Fauconberg who would have told Warwick and Edward. They knew now that battle in the morning was inevitable.

It grew light at about 6 o'clock that morning on a cold grey day, the wind was gusty and it was snowing. Men on both sides knew there was a stern test ahead. For the commanders, Edward on the Yorkist side and Somerset for the Lancastrian, the forthcoming battle was to be the decider. Who should rule England, Henry VI or Edward IV? Everyone recognized that life could not go on with two kings claiming the throne, besides which too many nobles were irrevocably committed to one side or the other, for them the political see-saw had to stop some time and the time was nigh. Blood feuds had to end and the slate rubbed clean so that the country at large could resume its ordered life. Towton was to be the decisive battle that both sides wanted.

The two armies stirred at dawn, the Lancastrian to pack up their tents, have some breakfast and prepare to meet the Yorkist army. The latter, glad to move after their cold night, formed up in their divisions with Fauconberg in the lead, followed by Warwick and then Edward with the reserve. The vanguard stopped on the high ground south of Towton Vale barely 500 yards from the Lancastrian army. Warwick's division came up behind them and to the right, with Edward's behind and to the left. Across the valley Somerset had drawn up the Lancastrian army with his own division on the right opposite King Edward and Northumberland's division to his left opposite Warwick.

Both armies had a small reserve drawn up behind the centre of their line; both armies also put their archers in front of their men-at-arms and bill-men. The facing lines were about 800 yards long. Some sources say that Somerset had hidden a small force of mounted men-at-arms in Castlehill Wood on the left of the Yorkist position between it and the River Cock, but this is not certain, and seems unlikely. Edward Hall[7] said that the Lancastrian army was 60,000 strong and the Yorkist 48,640. As usual these figures are wildly exaggerated, however if we follow Boardman's logic[8] for the calculation of numbers on the battlefield using the noblemen present as an indication, we can get a fair total. The Lancastrians had 2 dukes, 2 earls, 1 viscount, 8 lords and 24 knights in the field as well as 52 esquires, gentlemen and yeomen. If each duke was able to bring say 2,500 men to the army, the viscount 1,000 and each lord perhaps 400, the knights 100 each and the others an average of 25 each, a total of about 13,000 men is arrived at. If Henry VI's own retinue, less his personal guard is added of say 3,000 men, the total from indentured retinues climbs to 18,000 men. To this should be added the fencible men from the shires and towns who answered Henry's call to arms, a figure of perhaps a further five or six thousand men; the city of York for instance sent 1,000 men to the army at Towton. The total has now reached 24,000, men to which should be added Scottish soldiers sent to Queen Margaret under the terms of the Treaty of Lincluden, and some French mercenaries – say a further 3,000 – and a possible and credible figure of 27,000 for the Lancastrian army emerges.

The Yorkist army was not as large. It had four main contributors – Edward, Warwick, Norfolk and Fauconberg. Edward had about 11,000 men in his army when he defeated Pembroke at Mortimer's Cross, and although he had had some casualties, it is probable that these were made up from his estates in the Welsh border country before he left for London. Warwick joined Edward in the Cotswolds after the Second Battle of St Albans with his own men, possibly 3,000 strong, and elements of the rearguard that day, say a further 2,000 men. Fauconberg had perhaps 400 men of his own. Together these forces make a round total of about 16,500, men to which should be added the men of London and the southern shires to make an army of about 22,000. This army faced one perhaps 5,000 men larger on that cold Palm Sunday morning of 29 March. But the duke of Norfolk had yet to join them. Where was he? The duke was a terminally ill man who was nevertheless gamely marching north with about 5,000 men from his own estates and from East Anglia; he was about a day's march behind Edward's army. No doubt Edward would have left a herald behind at Pontefract to contact Norfolk as he marched north, bringing him up to date and urging him to join the rest of the army as quickly as he could. The composition of both armies would have been in proportion to their total numbers and made up of the same elements. The Lancastrian army would have had about 2,500 men-at-arms, some 12,500 archers and around 12,000 bill-men, while the Yorkist would have had about 2,000 men-at-arms, 11,000 archers and 9,000 bill-men – large numbers of armed men for the forthcoming hand-to-hand fighting.

Both armies probably organized themselves for the forthcoming battle in dead ground, ground that is out of sight of the other side. As the Yorkist and Lancastrian armies simultaneously crested the hill on which they made their position, they both gave a great shout when they saw their opponents. What would they have seen? Commanders, knights, men-at-arms and archers all distributed along the line of soldiers, some commanders on horseback; men and horses armoured, lances carried vertically and banners emblazoned with heraldic devices. Thousands of marching men, some in bright plate armour and the others in jacks and helmets, carrying bills or halberds, with swords and bucklers by their side.

The Lancastrian army would have deployed their bill-men, dismounted men-at-arms and knights in about forty ranks one behind the other with their archers out in front; a significantly larger army than the Yorkists, whose foot soldiers and dismounted men would only have made up about thirty ranks. It was always important in those days to impress the opposition with the strength and composition of one's own army and so each side would have noted the banners of the noblemen and knights present in the army opposite. Also, they would have taken note of the discipline with which they marched to their positions and finally they would have noted the mass of the army opposite. All these factors contributed to or reduced the morale of the armies about to do battle. In this case all in both armies could see that the Lancastrian army was about a quarter larger than the Yorkist, but the Yorkist army had their king with them whereas the Lancastrian king was skulking in York. Consequently the morale factor would have been about even between the larger army and the one with the king in its midst.

Another important factor, as in all battles, was the ground and whether its potential to help or hinder had been made full use of. In this case the Lancastrian army halted on high ground about 1,000 yards south of Towton, covering the road to Ferrybridge on its left and that to Castleford on its right. They had a clear view to their front over a gentle depression, Towton Dale, to the high ground opposite. This high ground was between 600 and 800 yards to the south and level with their own position. The depression became quite pronounced as it fell away to the River Cock on their right, indeed there was a steep drop of over a hundred feet closer to the Yorkist position and the river itself lay between steep banks. To the left of the Yorkist position was Castlehill Wood. Neither side had any great advantage from the ground, but if the Yorkist army was forced to retreat it had to do so over open ground, gently falling away to the south, a boon for any Lancastrian pursuit. However the withdrawal route for the Lancastrians became narrower as they went north, between the river and the village of Towton, so making it easier for them to stabilize their line on a shorter front if they needed to. But if they were pushed north-west to the line of the River Cock, which was in flood, they would be in great difficulty. The other factor which could influence the battle was, of course, the weather.

There was a pause of about two hours after each army gained their starting position and during this time the marshals would adjust their lines and individuals would prepare to fight. Archers would hammer stakes into the ground as a handicap to mounted men-at-arms, string their bows and stick ready arrows into the ground at their feet. Men-at-arms would adjust their armour, unsheathe their swords or take the covers off their poleaxes, bill-men would do the same with their bills and all would send a silent prayer to God. After saying Mass to the various parts of the army priests would go along the lines offering absolution. Captains would ensure that their men knew what they had to do and commanders like Edward, Warwick, Somerset and Northumberland would ride or walk along their ranks giving encouragement and reassurance to all. Both sides were ready. The wind was blowing snow into the Yorkists faces.

Then at about 9 o'clock the wind suddenly changed direction and blew the snow towards the Lancastrians. Fauconberg immediately took advantage of this once the wind had steadied and advanced his archers. They would have been placed out in small groups, checkerboard fashion and possibly eight to ten ranks deep right across the front of the army, so that every archer could bring his bow to bear and volleys of concentrated fire would have been possible. Edward Hall[9] said that Fauconberg ordered his archers to shoot one flight and then to stand still; this they did and the Lancastrians followed suit but shot all or most of their arrows. However, due to the wind those of the Yorkist archers found their mark whereas the Lancastrian arrows fell short, something that they would not necessarily have realized as they were peering into the snow. When the Lancastrian arrow storm died down the Yorkist archers began to shoot again; they probably carried two quivers full of arrows each, forty-eight arrows. Fauconberg ordered them to advance once more and pick up the Lancastrian arrows lying on the ground. They were then able to loose several more volleys at the massed ranks opposite causing many casualties. The combined effect of the wind and snow more than made up for the smaller number of the Yorkist archers. The Yorkist arrow storm must have reduced the Lancastrian numbers significantly and Somerset, seeing this, in an effort to avoid further casualties, was forced to give up his prepared position on the ridge. He ordered his whole line to advance and soon both sides were hotly engaged.

A series of desperate individual fights developed all along the line with men hacking and thrusting at each other. The noise must have been deafening with the sound of weapon on armour, the shouts of those fighting for their lives and the groans of the wounded. As a man went down in the front row another would step forward to take his place. Soon, as at Agincourt, dead and wounded men lay in piles all along the front and men on both sides would pause in their grizzly business to pull the bodies out of the way or have to fight their way around these islands of dead and wounded. Knights and men-at-arms would pause in their own fight, give their place to another in the rank behind while they cooled off and if they were lucky get a drink of water before once more joining the fray. This frenetic fight went on for several hours as Edward's army was forced gradually back by the larger Lancastrian army.

It was at this point that a small mounted force charged out at the left flank of the Yorkist army from Castlehill Wood. It is open to doubt that this force lay hidden throughout the battle until this moment; it is much more likely that Somerset or Andrew Trollope ordered a knight to take a troop of mounted men-at-arms and try to work his way along the Cock, turn up the steep slope into the woods and then to charge out at the flank of the Yorkist line. This would have been quite possible, unlikely to have been spotted in the bad visibility and certainly not heard with the noise of battle. It would only have needed about twenty mounted men to charge out at the left end of the Yorkist line to cause panic and disarray. Such a move coming at a time when the Yorkist line was being hard pressed might have been decisive. But the Yorkist line did not panic; it reeled back but did not give way. Edward committed his reserve and stabilized the situation but the left-hand half of his army was now facing the depression down to the River Cock to the north-west, while the right-hand half was still facing north. Somerset followed up the charge of his cavalry and was pressing Edward hard with his greater numbers when in the nick of time Norfolk with his division of 5,000 fresh men marched onto the battlefield to the right of Warwick. This reinforcement forced Northumberland's division to fall back. The opposing lines now faced each other diagonally in a north-east to south-west direction so that the River Cock was behind the right wing of the Lancastrian army. Many in Northumberland's division found themselves in the Dale between the two areas of high ground when Norfolk's division marched down the hill towards them.

Norfolk's fresh troops made all the difference. Edward must have wondered how much longer his weary army could hold on – after four or five hours of close fighting they were at their last gasp. But Norfolk's arrival raised morale. It was at this point in the battle that Lancastrian soldiers began to make good their escape. While many of Northumberland's division made good their escape to Towton and beyond, Somerset's division had to retreat over the River Cock. The triumphant Yorkists forced the Lancastrian soldiers down the slippery slope and into the river. Many were drowned trying to get across the river but many more were cut down in the meadow and on the banks by Yorkist men-at-arms, now mounted. Fighting even continued into the river, where so many bodies pilled up that others were able to cross by this human bridge. For the Lancastrians, what began as a fairly orderly retreat ended in a complete and bloody rout. The river ran red and the meadow has ever since been called the Bloody Meadow.

A further obstacle for the routed Lancastrians escaping the Yorkist pursuit was to the north where the road to York crossed the formidable River Wharfe at Tadcaster. Apparently Somerset ordered the destruction of the bridge across the river in order to gain time to get Henry and his family out of York and on their way to Scotland. In this he was successful but his action caused the deaths of many of his soldiers caught the wrong side of the bridge; indeed more died here than at the much smaller River Cock. It must be emphasized that pursuit after battle was a very definite and important phase of war, and always has been. In this case a vigorous pursuit was very important, particularly in the case of escaping knights and nobility who could otherwise lead the ranks in yet another battle at some future date. Also, it must not be forgotten that the capture of a nobleman or a famous knight would bring some reward.

The duke of Somerset, the duke of Exeter and Lord Roos escaped the carnage to join Henry, Queen Margaret and the Prince of Wales in York whence they made good their escape to sanctuary in Scotland. But others were not so lucky; the duke of Buckingham, the earl of Northumberland, Lord Dacre, Lord Welles, Lord Willoughby, Lord Manly and Sir Andrew Trollope were killed on the battlefield, or died from their wounds shortly after. The heralds said at the time that altogether 28,000 men died in battle or in the pursuit that day. The following day a further forty-two knights and esquires were executed for treason. The earl of Devon, a sick or wounded man, was taken in York and beheaded; the earl of Wiltshire was finally captured in Cumberland and was taken to Newcastle where he was executed. This was the bloodiest battle ever fought on English soil.

Towton was a finely balanced struggle, which was decided by the duke of Norfolk's fresh division joining the fray. Somerset and Northumberland, helped by the advice of the professional soldier Sir Andrew Trollope, made no mistakes, indeed their mounted flank attack might well have ended the struggle there and then. They had the larger army at all times, even when Norfolk joined the battle, but they failed to prevail. Possibly the presence of King Edward and the royal banner made all the difference. The earl of Warwick was also an experienced and battle-hardened commander. The two together clearly inspired their forces to great effect and at no time more effectively than when the army was gradually being forced back after the flank attack by Somerset's cavalry. Lord Fauconberg also took a prominent part in the battle and his direction of the Yorkist archers in the early stages of the battle made a great contribution to the final result – not only due to the casualties they inflicted but also because they forced a change on the Lancastrian battle plan right at the very start of the battle.

The Lancastrian rout at Towton was not as complete as Edward would have wished. He had destroyed the majority of the nobles who had supported King Henry, but had failed to capture and eliminate the dukes of Somerset and Exeter. Queen Margaret, with Henry and her son Edward, reached Scotland in safety with about 1,000 armed followers. There her first act was to cede Berwick to Scotland under the terms of the Treaty of Lincluden. She and Henry were housed by Scotland's Queen mother, Mary of Guelders, James II's widow, at the palace of Linlithgow. So the heart of the Lancastrian cause was safely out of reach within the kingdom of Scotland, and this heart, notwithstanding that it had been severely wounded at Towton, was beating still. Margaret must have realized that Henry's days as king of England, except purely as a legitimate figurehead, were over. Her hopes for the future resided in her son, Edward, Prince of Wales, then seven years old. She still had a fairly strong hand, had the backing of the Scots and was a French princess who could call on support from her mother country. Somerset had survived and the three great Percy strongholds in the East March of Alnwick, Bamburgh and Dunstanburgh were still held by Lancastrian garrisons, each of them accessible by sea.

Except for people in the north-east of England and those who had personal reasons for supporting the Lancastrian cause, however, most of the population and the remaining nobility must have turned to Edward with relief. So far he seemed to live up to their expectations of kingship. He certainly met the military criteria but whether he was going to uphold the law for the benefit of his subjects without favour remained to be seen. However, he certainly fitted the part and most people wished him well.

Edward remained in the north until May, having witnessed the execution of the earl of Wiltshire in Newcastle on the 1st of the month. He had travelled north from York after the battle, staying in Durham and Newcastle. His progress in the north through country loyal to the Percys, the Cliffords and the Dacres had to be done with care and diplomacy. His first act was to make Laurence Booth, the bishop of Durham and a Lancastrian, his confessor. This was a shrewd move, providing the bishop remained loyal to his new supplicant for his was a powerful office in the north in both the spiritual and the secular worlds. He then set out for London to arrange the important political event of his coronation on 28 June. The sooner he was anointed and crowned the sooner would his authority be absolute. Henry VI, the anointed king of England had absconded and lived outside his kingdom thereby giving up his authority. Edward left Warwick, Fauconburg and Montagu in the north to pacify the area after the rout of Towton. A joint Scottish-Lancastrian force crossed the border to besiege Carlisle, which Queen Margaret had also promised the Scots in return for their help. The invading force in the West March soon withdrew over the border after Lord Montagu relieved Carlisle and Bishop Booth remained loyal when put to the test. In June a Lancastrian raiding force under Lords Roos, Dacre and Gray rode through the East March down to Brancepeth Castle south of Durham where they raised Henry's standard but they found little enthusiasm in the area. Indeed Bishop Booth called out the local levies and scattered this embryo Lancastrian revolt before it had time to grow.

For a turbulent age, Edward was remarkably lenient with those Lancastrians who had survived the many battles of the previous two years: he had only fourteen noblemen attainted and ninety-six non-nobles. Many of these had already been killed in the battles or died shortly after. However, it was important that Edward attracted some of the die-hard Lancastrians away from their allegiance to Henry, particularly in the north of England and along the Scottish border. It was equally important that he rewarded those who had shown their loyalty to him and his father. He was largely able to do this by giving attainted land and estates to his supporters and by a redistribution of posts in the government. Edward's punishments and rewards helped to establish his reign, if not among all the Lancastrian nobility and gentry then at least among the people. Warwick, for instance, received various royal offices as well as numerous estates, which formerly belonged to the Percys in Yorkshire and the Cliffords in Westmoreland. Of equal importance was that Warwick was given the wardenship of the East March, normally a Percy office, so in effect becoming warden of the whole march with Scotland.

Lord Fauconberg was made earl of Kent while Lord Bourchier was made earl of Essex, and his son was ennobled as Lord Cromwell. The old royal title of duke of Clarence was conferred on Edward's younger brother George, then eleven years old, with the aim of consolidating a Yorkist dynasty. The greatest losers were the Percys, the Cliffords and lords Dacre and Roos. However in some cases Edward showed mercy and trust to his former enemies. He did not confiscate the duke of Buckingham's estates but left them held by his widow for his grandson, and likewise he left the earl of Shrewsbury's estates in trust for his son, who was only twelve years old.

Having had her invasion of the Channel Islands stopped Queen Margaret now turned her attention to the possibilities offered by the fortresses on the north-east coast. Any initiative from this quarter, however, needed both French and Scottish assistance and this took time to arrange. In Wales she still had influential friends, in particular Sir Jasper Tudor, earl of Pembroke and Sir Henry Holland, duke of Exeter. These nobles controlled the garrisons of four formidable castles, Carreg Cennen, Denbigh, Harlech and Pembroke, and together they constituted a threat which Edward could not ignore. So he decided to go on a judicial progress through Kent, Sussex, Hampshire, Wiltshire and Gloucestershire, which would leave him well placed to move on into Wales and subdue the Lancastrian fortresses. However, after progressing up the Welsh marches and into the Midlands he returned to London for his first parliament. He then mobilized his artillery and commissioned Lords Herbert and Ferrers, formerly Sir William Herbert and Sir Walter Devereux, his commanders of the rearguard and vanguard respectively at the Battle of Mortimer's Cross, to raise volunteers from Wales and the marches for a campaign into the north of Wales. They set out in the early autumn. Pembroke Castle was captured on 30 September and in October Pembroke and Exeter were defeated in the field by Herbert near Caernarvon. The two castles of Denbigh and Carreg Cennen fell in January and May 1462, the latter being demolished soon after.[10] However Harlech still stood out for Henry, although for the time being the Lancastrian cause in Wales was in tatters.

Queen Margaret was as yet unable to make full use of the Lancastrian castles in the north because neither French nor Scottish support, though promised, was yet ready. Edward therefore hoped to subdue them before any such help could materialize and his commanders in the north eagerly set about the task. In September 1461 the old Percy stronghold of Alnwick Castle surrendered, shortly followed by the castle of Dunstanburgh. Here Sir Ralph Percy surrendered and submitted to Edward who took a calculated risk in a gesture of forgiveness by allowing Sir Percy to remain in command at the castle.

When he heard that Queen Margaret had gone to France in April 1462 to plead for help with her cousin Louis XI, it became vital for Edward to create and maintain good diplomatic relations with both Scotland and France. If he could do this he would deny Henry the secure base and the military resources that he would need to regain the throne.

Margaret did her best to solicit help from Louis and, as in Scotland, pawned an important English possession, Calais, in return for military help in a secret agreement signed at Chinon on 24 June 1462. The fact that Calais, for the moment, had a loyal Yorkist garrison did not seem to worry Louis since once he had provided the help he had promised, Calais legitimately became his; all he had to do was take it. But Calais remained tantalizingly out of his reach; it lay surrounded by Burgundian territory and the Duke of Burgundy refused to let a French army cross his frontier. Perhaps it was because the wool staple was still at Calais that he denied Louis access, for an unhindered flow of wool to Flanders was an important factor in his diplomacy. Wool was vital for the wealth and well-being of the citizens of Flanders and thus for the duke himself; it was essential therefore that he maintained good relations with the English king no matter who he may be.

In the north-east Lord Dacre abandoned the castle of Naworth and Tailboys surrendered the castle of Alnwick at the end of July while Sir Richard Tunstall took Bamburgh. Meanwhile, following a raid by Warwick into Scotland in June, Mary of Guelders came to Carlisle to agree a temporary truce along the border to last until 24 August, which no doubt Edward and Warwick hoped might become more permanent. Notwithstanding these Yorkist successes in the north the populace of Northumberland remained obstinately loyal to the Lancastrian cause. Clearly if Margaret and Henry could establish a foothold in the north-east once more their chances of raising the country against Edward would improve significantly. Unfortunately all the castles in the north-east were now, nominally, held by Edward's captains but one of them, Sir Ralph Percy, might be lured back to his old allegiance. Margaret sailed from France to Scotland with forty-three ships and 800 French soldiers in October 1462,[11] collected King Henry and about 1,200 of her supporters and some Scottish troops and then set out for Bamburgh where they landed on 25 October. The new Lancastrian campaign had begun with a motley force of Frenchmen, Scots, followers of the northern nobility, the duke of Somerset and her own and Henry's retinues.

Bamburgh soon surrendered. At Dunstanburgh Sir Ralph Percy turned his coat again and declared for Henry, taking the castle with him, while Alnwick surrendered after a short siege being short of supplies. All three of these great fortresses were back in Lancastrian hands within a surprisingly short time. Henry raised his standard and expected the gentry to come flocking to it with their followers, but he had a miserable return. Edward reacted promptly and forcibly. Within five days of the landing he had despatched Warwick to the north again together with a commission to raise the northern levies and snuffed Margaret's offensive in the bud. Realizing that overwhelming force was being arrayed against her she set sail for Scotland once again on 13 November to collect reinforcements but a storm at sea scattered her ships and four were wrecked on the Northumbrian coast, including her own. She, Henry and de Brézé managed to get to Berwick in an open boat but most of her small expeditionary force perished; some lost their lives to local levies on Holy Island but most drowned, a few were taken prisoner.[12] The duke of Somerset, Lords Pembroke and Roos and Sir Ralph Percy were left behind in Bamburgh Castle while Lords Hungerford and Whittingham were in Alnwick and Sir Richard Tunstall in Dunstanburgh.

Meanwhile Edward had gathered a large army, which included thirty-nine peers and their retinues.[13] The army got as far as Durham on its march north where Edward fell ill with measles, leaving Warwick to conduct the campaign. Warwick made his headquarters at Warkworth Castle and put all three Lancastrian-held castles under siege. Bamburgh and Dunstanburgh surrendered on 26 and 27 December respectively and so the focus of attention shifted to Alnwick and the border. Margaret was expected to cross the border and make a foray for the relief of her castles with her Scottish allies. Edward's intelligence was accurate, George Douglas, earl of Angus and warden of the Scottish east march, gathered a strong mobile army and crossed the border probably on 2 or 3 January arriving in Alnwick on 5 January. Warwick raised his siege once he knew that a Scottish army was on its way, but kept his army nearby. The French garrison was half starved and probably would not hold out for much longer, but the besiegers were hardly better off, not because of a lack of food but because of the weather. The Scottish relief force meanwhile reached the castle and 300 French soldiers of the garrison made a sortie, joined the relief force and rode away, watched by Warwick's men. The few English soldiers left behind surrendered on terms shortly after. This little episode was seen as a triumph by some in Scotland but in reality both sides missed a chance. Warwick had it in his grasp to inflict a serious setback to Henry and his cause but failed to take advantage of the opportunity offered. As to the Scots having found no besiegers at the castle, they suspected a trap and rode away as soon as the French had joined them.

Once again, in his efforts to placate the Lancastrians in the north, Edward dealt leniently with the commanders taken at the castles. Somerset was allowed to buy himself a pardon and had all his lands and titles restored to him; he was then employed on the Yorkist side at the siege of Alnwick. Sir Ralph Percy was given another chance and the captaincy of both Bamburgh and Dunstanburgh castles, notwithstanding the fact that he had betrayed his allegiance to Edward once already. Sir Ralph Grey was given the captaincy of Alnwick Castle.

One may wonder why Edward failed to use his artillery, which he had mobilized and sent north to Newcastle by ship for the campaign. Apart from the fact that his great guns were offloaded from ships on arrival nothing more was heard of them even though the guns could have been decisive, battering each castle into submission very quickly. The answer possibly lies in the difficulties they would have faced in moving them from the dockside in Newcastle to the three castles under siege in winter along bad roads and tracks. Siege guns were heavy and bulky items; they needed an extensive train supporting each gun with stone or iron shot and gunpowder. Siege guns at that time were still usually carried on wagons and offloaded onto a firing cradle on site, so a crane would have been needed at each site. With three castles to subdue, a minimum of four guns would have been needed, providing the guns were taken from one siege to another. The artillery train would have taken many days to reach the castles and be placed in their firing positions; perhaps Bamburgh and Dunstanburgh had already surrendered before the guns could arrive. These were good reasons for not using the artillery but the most likely reason is the strategic position of the castles on a traditional Scottish invasion route. If they had been battered by a bombardment they would have been of little use against either a Scottish or a Lancastrian invasion across the border unless they were repaired, and that would have been costly and time consuming. It is therefore probable that Edward mobilized his artillery as a threat and a propaganda measure, well knowing that news of this would reach Henry and his commanders.

After the surrender of Alnwick Castle Edward and his army returned to the south leaving Warwick and his brother Lord Montagu to guard the border and stamp out any signs of Lancastrian revolt. However, in March 1463 Sir Ralph Percy once again changed his coat and put the castles of Bamburgh and Dunstanburgh back into Henry's allegiance. Sir Ralph Grey soon followed his example and did the same in May with Alnwick Castle. In July, Henry, Margaret, Mary of Guelders with her son James III of Scotland, and de Brézé suddenly crossed the border and laid siege to the castle at Norham. Presumably this was done with a view to enlarging the Lancastrian enclave inland, but in reality this siege was more in Scotland's interests than that of the Lancastrians although it would have opened up another route into Northumberland. However, Warwick clearly had word that this might happen as he wrote to Bishop Booth on 11 July saying that the king's enemies had crossed the border in force and requested that a force of Clergy and all men of military age within the Church lands be defensibly arrayed and assembled at Durham on 15 July 1463. He and Montagu then marched north with the local levies and put the invaders to flight some eighteen days after they had begun their siege. Henry, Margaret and their supporters then fled to Bamburgh hotly pursued by Warwick's men. They arrived safely, Margaret and her son set sail for France via Flanders, while Mary of Guelders, James III and Henry returned to Scotland.

On the diplomatic front Edward made significant progress. He signed a truce with France and Burgundy at Hesdin in October, the main condition of which, from Edward's perspective, was that Louis XI should give no more help to Henry and Margaret, which effectively prevented them from using France as a base. In December Edward achieved a truce with Scotland to last for a year and there was a real possibility that Henry might be extradited to England, as of course he was a refugee in Scotland. Indeed Edward claimed that since he was not a subject of James III he was a rebel and a traitor.[14] This was unlikely to happen while Mary of Guelders remained regent for James III, but unfortunately for Henry she died in December that winter as did another powerful Scottish supporter of his cause, the earl of Angus. Henry's protector in Scotland, the chancellor, Bishop Kennedy, took him to St Andrews for greater safety in January but eventually sent him to Bamburgh at the end of February. So now

Bamburgh Castle became the centre of the Lancastrian cause in 1464. Messages of support were received from all over the country giving the impression that Henry only had to make a positive move for the country to rise up in his support. Perhaps this was wishful thinking. Henry had never made a positive move in his own cause and was unlikely to do so now; he needed either military aid from France and Scotland or a powerful English nobleman to emerge and rally to his support. Both France and Scotland had been effectively sidelined by Edward's diplomacy and Queen Margaret, the main Lancastrian motivator and decision maker, was living with her son in poverty in a house provided by her father, René of Anjou, in the duchy of Bar in France.

Providentially a powerful English nobleman did emerge. The duke of Somerset, who had been pardoned and befriended by Edward after the siege and fall of Bamburgh Castle in December 1462, and who had been sent to Wales by Edward for his own safety, now turned his coat and declared for Henry. Early in 1464 he travelled to Newcastle, where some 200 of his retainers had been incorporated into the garrison after he was sent to Wales. His aim was to overcome the Yorkist garrison and turn Newcastle into another Lancastrian stronghold. But his intentions were discovered before he arrived and his retainers were disarmed and detained.[15] Somerset then moved on north to Bamburgh. His arrival there put heart and effort into the Lancastrian cause; during March and April they managed to take over the castle at Norham as well as the castle at Skipton in Craven in Yorkshire, the seat of the Clifford family. However Edward, who had been on a progress in the south putting down rebellious outbreaks, heard of Somerset's betrayal and returned to London to organize military operations to stamp out the Lancastrian hold in Northumberland before it could spread any further.

Meanwhile, in his efforts to conclude a longer lasting truce or treaty with the Scots to supersede the current one-year truce, Edward had invited a Scottish delegation for talks to be held in Newcastle on 6 March. However, due to increased Lancastrian activity in the north-east the meeting was postponed to the end of April and was to be held in York for security reasons. Warwick was entrusted with the negotiations on Edward's behalf and sent his brother Sir John Neville, Lord Montagu, to escort the Scottish delegation from the border to York. Once he reached Newcastle volunteers flocked to Montagu's banner and by the time he left that city he had with him a small army of between 5,000 and 6,000 men, including men-at-arms and archers. As Montagu marched north to meet the Scottish delegation, Somerset with the Lancastrian army of some 5,000 men marched out of Alnwick to intercept him on the road south of Norham. The armies met at Hedgeley Moor on 25 April. Somerset had with him most of the Lancastrian hierarchy including Lords Roos and Hungerford, and Sir Ralph Percy. The resulting clash of arms was not in any way decisive although Sir Ralph Percy was killed. Montagu carried on to the border and then successfully escorted the Scottish delegation to York.

On 27 March Edward had made a public announcement that he was going to march north with an army finally to eliminate the Lancastrian enclave in Northumberland. He sent out writs of array to the sheriffs of over thirty counties calling on their fencible men to muster at Leicester, where he would join them. He also, once again, mobilized some of his artillery or 'great ordinance' including the guns 'Dijon', 'London', 'Newcastle', 'Richard Bombartel' and 'Edward'.[16] But Edward had other matters on his mind beside his wish to defeat the Lancastrians – he was in love and his route north took him conveniently close to the manor of his loved one, Elizabeth Wydeville. He halted on his march north at Stony Stratford and then before dawn on 1 May he rode to Grafton, the seat of Earl Rivers, with a few of his household, pretending to go hunting. There he married Elizabeth in secret, they consummated the marriage after the ceremony and he remained there with her for the next four days before riding to join his army at Leicester on 10 May. Elizabeth was the widow of Sir John Grey of Groby who had been killed at St Albans fighting for the Lancastrians and was four years older than Edward. She was the daughter of Richard Wydeville, Earl Rivers, a staunch Lancastrian, and Jacquetta of Luxembourg, Dowager Duchess of Bedford, and she had two young sons. She was, by all accounts, a beautiful woman with long gold hair, but she was also ambitious and ruthless, and as a commoner considered totally unfit to be queen of England. Furthermore, she had five brothers and five sisters all of whom would expect to profit from her marriage. Nevertheless Edward was besotted by her and queen she became.

While Edward had been dallying with his new and secret bride, Montagu had marched back towards Newcastle when he heard that

Somerset had arrived at Hexham with the Lancastrian army on
14 May. Hexham was only 21 miles away to the west and so without
further ado he set off and reached Hexham on 15 May. Of the two
armies Montagu's was by far the larger, perhaps 6,000 men, while
Somerset's was reported to be as few as 600, an unlikely figure as he
had had about 5,000 with him at Hedgeley Moor. Nevertheless the
issue was never in doubt. Montagu had arrived on high ground overlooking the meadow and the stream, and while his own men took up
positions along the ridge Somerset's were hurriedly getting into some
semblance of order. The Yorkists charged down the hill and soon
overwhelmed Somerset's smaller army. Sir Henry Beaufort, duke of
Somerset, was taken prisoner and executed the following day. Lords
Roos and Hungerford were captured in woods nearby and taken to
Newcastle where they were executed two days later. Montagu soon
learnt from prisoners that King Henry was lodged at Bywell Castle
and immediately despatched a troop to capture him, but Henry had
already learnt of the disaster at Hexham and had fled, leaving behind
his coronetted helmet and his sword. In reward for his victory
Montagu was made earl of Northumberland and warden of the East
March.

Hexham had dealt the Lancastrian cause in the north a fatal blow
but the four northern castles of Alnwick, Dunstanburgh, Norham and
Bamburgh still remained in Lancastrian hands. Warwick, who had
arrived in the north shortly after Hexham immediately took charge of
the lightning siege campaign that followed. On 23 June Warwick and
Montagu appeared before the castle of Alnwick with the army and
demanded its surrender. The garrison agreed to do so providing their
lives were spared. The next day the castles of Dunstanburgh and
Norham surrendered. Then on 25 June Warwick arrived before
Bamburgh and demanded its surrender, offering pardons to all but the
two commanders, Sir Ralph Grey and Sir Humphrey Neville. Grey
answered defiantly and so the siege went ahead. Warwick had the
royal arsenal with him and placed the guns to cause a breach in the
walls. Before long the walls were breached, the besiegers swept
through and took the castle. The garrison, including Humphrey
Neville, were spared. Grey was not so fortunate; he had been
concussed by falling masonary and was led away in a daze to face trial
and execution later in the south. The Battle of Hexham and the taking
of the northern castles, which followed, totally eliminated the

Lancastrian enclave in the north of England, furthermore the safe haven in Scotland had been denied to them by Edward's diplomacy. The leading Lancastrian nobles and knights had been swept away. Henry remained in hiding, moving from safe house to safe house for about a year until he was betrayed and captured in a wood near Clitheroe in Lancashire in July 1465, and was escorted to the Tower of London where he lived in reasonable comfort. Meanwhile Queen Margaret lived in straightened circumstances in France with her son Edward, Prince of Wales. Harlech Castle still survived as a bastion of Lancastrian power in north Wales but it seemed now that at last Edward was probably secure on his throne.

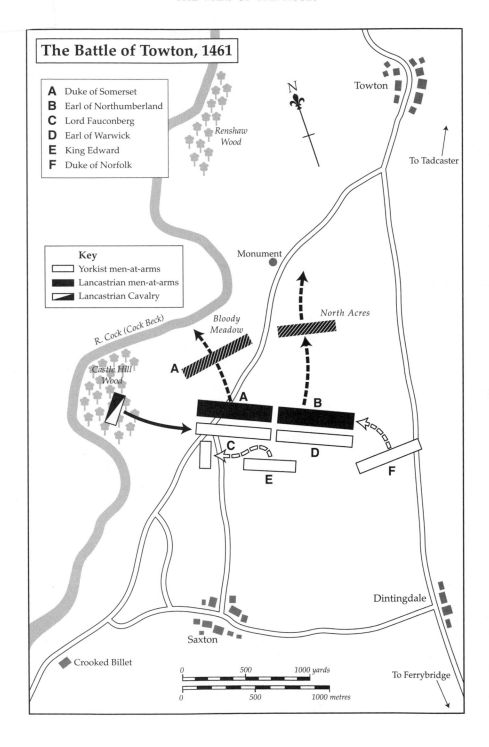

The Battle of Towton, 1461

A Duke of Somerset
B Earl of Northumberland
C Lord Fauconberg
D Earl of Warwick
E King Edward
F Duke of Norfolk

Key
☐ Yorkist men-at-arms
■ Lancastrian men-at-arms
◨ Lancastrian Cavalry

N

Towton

To Tadcaster

Renshaw Wood

Monument

North Acres

Bloody Meadow

R. Cock (Cock Beck)

Castle Hill Wood

A

A

B

C

D

E

F

Dintingdale

Saxton

◆ Crooked Billet

To Ferrybridge

0   500   1000 yards

0   500   1000 metres

Chapter 20

Edward Flees and Returns

'Did Henry die of "pure displeasure, and melancholy"'[1]
or
'was he "Stykked with a Dagger"'?[2]

As a result of his diplomacy, Edward managed to maintain peace in the countryside at large and peace with his neighbours. He showed even-handedness in the dispensation of his law to all: the nobles, the gentry and commoners. Above all, he showed a remarkable lack of vindictiveness towards his former enemies, a very unusual trait for the times. These achievements instilled confidence in his government and that confidence greatly improved his ability to obtain credit to bridge the time gap between revenues agreed from taxation and expected from customs, and their realization; and also between these and his actual expenditure.

In the main crown revenues were expended on the crown's household, its government, its law and on the permanent military establishments on the Marches with Scotland and in the garrison of Calais. The latter was usually met from the customs on wool but these had declined over the past five years from an average of £30,000 per year to about £25,000.[3] The shortfall could only be met by either increased taxation or credit. Edward had twice received grants of taxation for military purposes and was reluctant to go cap in hand to parliament yet again for the maintenance of his permanent garrisons. He therefore had to rely on credit and indeed did so through the Act of Retainer in 1466, which allowed the garrison in Calais to be paid by the wool staplers and for them to recover their money through the profit on the wool customs charged at Calais.[4] As a result of this, a cutback in his household expenses and improvements in the management of crown lands Edward was largely able to eliminate the crown's debts and face the future with confidence.

Once solvency had been achieved, Edward's thoughts turned to France and he claimed the throne of France as the rightful king, as had all English kings since Edward III. A new expedition to France would be popular with all elements of society and finance for such a venture could certainly be obtained. To this end treaties were concluded with all France's neighbours in 1468 but most importantly with Burgundy and Brittany. His intention and his diplomatic achievements pleased everyone but Warwick who was by now a disgruntled and dissatisfied magnate. In too many ways Edward, his cousin, was beginning to show that he could make up his own mind and did not always need the benefit of Warwick's experience and advice. In particular this manifested itself in Edward's policy towards France, which was by then openly hostile. Warwick favoured rapprochement and alliance with France – indeed he had hoped to arrange a marriage between Edward and Louis XI's sister to cement friendship between the two countries – was in marked contrast to Edward's own French policy in which he favoured an alliance with Burgundy.

The possibilty of a relationship with the French king came to nothing as a result of Edward's secret marriage to Elizabeth Wydeville, which led to growing antagonism between Edward and Warwick. Edward's gradual enrichment of the Wydevilles and their growing influence at court certainly offended him. Warwick the 'Kingmaker' was an over-powerful magnate who believed the king should follow his advice and virtually do his bidding, but Edward insisted on pursuing his own agenda. Through Edward's good offices every one of the queen's sisters was married off to an earl, whereas Warwick met opposition from Edward himself to his plans to marry his two daughters to Edward's younger brothers, George of Clarence and Richard of Gloucester. Although Edward remained friendly towards Warwick, it became clear to their contemporaries that the king was on a collision course with his most powerful subject.

Meanwhile, in July 1468 Louis XI paid for an expedition under Jasper Tudor in Wales to raise the Lancastrian banner there and to link up with Harlech Castle, still in Lancastrian hands. But this raid was snuffed out by the Herberts and was followed by the surrender of the castle in August. In September and October of the same year Louis patched up his quarrels with Brittany and Burgundy. Charles of Burgundy agreed not to help the English, notwithstanding that he had married Edward's sister Margaret in March. Louis, having secured his flanks with the two dukedoms, began to stir the English pot, seeing in Warwick a means of neutralizing Edward's declared ambitions in France. Edward had recently received a generous grant of taxation from parliament for an expedition to France, but this came to nothing largely due to Louis' rapprochement with Brittany and Burgundy. Nevertheless Edward felt he had to justify the grant and so on the pretence that Margaret of Anjou was about to invade England he sent his fleet to sea. They returned after suffering autumn gales in the Channel in November and having achieved absolutely nothing. It was not long before people realized that the whole exercise had been a sham and that £18,000[5] had been granted unnecessarily and had probably gone into Edward's pocket. This little episode did not endear Edward to the taxpayers, something that Warwick was quick to exploit.

George, duke of Clarence, the king's brother, had come of age in 1466 and although he was given estates and honour by Edward he was not given any governmental responsibility and this irked him. Warwick, who assiduously cultivated Clarence's friendship, began to influence him against his brother, exploiting his grievances. Edward called a great council meeting in Coventry to heal the wounds but Warwick and Clarence, though receiving gifts and favours, remained unsatisfied. Warwick wished to govern the country and control its foreign policy. In particular he favoured a rapprochement with France, perhaps because Louis XI had promised him lavish gifts. It was probably at about this time that Warwick's thoughts became treasonable.

In the spring of 1469 Edward's attention was drawn once more to the north of England where two uprisings took place. The first, under the leadership of Robin of Holderness, was an apparently local affair demanding the restoration of the Percys to their old earldom of Northumberland. The new earl, John Neville, Warwick's brother, soon put this down. But towards the end of May another rising occurred, led by a man known as Robin of Redesdale, probably Sir William Conyers.[i]

i It is not clear whether Robin of Redesdale was Sir William Conyers or his brother Sir John. As Sir William had married Warwick's niece the second Redesdale rising is most likely to have been led by him. Perhaps the first rising was actually led by his brother John. Either way Warwick's brother failed to catch the leader of the first rising, probably by intent, when he put the rising down.

This uprising had started a little later than the first and probably earlier than it was meant to. Warwick's brother easily put it down but it started up again under the same alias but with new impetus in June 1469. This time it looked like a Neville conspiracy, since its backers all seemed to be Warwick supporters in Yorkshire about his manor of Middleham. However, it had some popular backing too.

In its infancy the second Redesdale rising did not seem to amount to much and Edward, having decided to deal with it himself, sent letters to the earls of Devon and Pembroke requiring them to raise troops in the West Country and in Wales, and to meet him in the Midlands. He also sent orders to the Tower to mobilize his artillery and to various cities demanding contingents of archers and others. Meanwhile he travelled north, spending a week with the queen at Fotheringhay Castle. However on 10 July, when he had reached Newark, he suddenly turned and marched south to Nottingham to await promised troops and the forces raised by Devon and Pembroke that were on their way to Northampton. Presumably he had been given reliable reports of the size of the forces marching south under Conyers and realized they were a formidable threat. Edward would have tied this to the rumours of plotting by Warwick, Clarence and the archbishop of York, Warwick's younger brother George. Also, he must have known that they had met on board Warwick's ship the *Trinity* at Sandwich in mid June.

Shortly after this the betrothal of Warwick's daughter Isabel to Clarence was announced in defiance of Edward's wishes, after dispensation from the Pope had been received.[ii] The three plotters remained in London after the announcement and prepared the ground for their subsequent actions by distributing leaflets in Kent and London. These roughly echoed those of Robin of Redesdale's saying that the king had gathered advisers about him who were only interested in their own advancement and that he ignored the advice of his blood relations, Warwick and Clarence, to the detriment of the country. Further, the leaflets compared Edward's behaviour to that of Edward II, Richard II and Henry VI. Warwick was a good propagandist and had used this ploy before to prepare the ground before him. However, early in July the three plotters went to Calais, where Warwick was captain, and

ii Clarence and Isabel were second cousins.

where the archbishop married Clarence and Isabel on 11 July. Two days later Warwick and Clarence landed in Kent and made their way to Canterbury where they awaited reinforcements.

All the pieces in the forthcoming struggle were now on the board. Edward was immobile at Nottingham, awaiting Pembroke and Devon and their forces from Wales as well as the various contingents of fencible men called up from cities and shires. Robin of Redesdale, Sir William Conyers, was marching south with a sizeable army, the prior of Crossland gave the impossible figure of 60,000 men,[6] which if divided by ten might be about right; in any case it was apparently about three times the size of the army with the king. Warwick and Clarence were in Canterbury gathering their own army before marching on London. Conyers, discovering that Edward was at Nottingham, by-passed the city in an effort to reach Warwick before Pembroke and Devon met up with Edward. The latter on their march from Wales became separated; Pembroke's force had a majority of men-at-arms while Devon had most of the archers; each commander might have had perhaps 2,000 men in their divisions. It was reported that the two commanders quarrelled over billeting in Banbury and as a consequence they separated. However, even if that was the case, it is much more likely that they became separated because of the different rates of march between a largely mounted force and one that was marching on its feet. Furthermore, they probably did not expect to run into rebel forces and so had not been grouped for action; so far as they knew they thought they were on a peaceful though hurried march to join up with Edward and the main army. Indeed they had probably not yet heard of Conyers' rapid march south and did not realize the difficult position that faced Edward or the proximity of Conyers' army.

Warwick meanwhile, having set out his manifesto, invited all who agreed with him to join him at Canterbury. Large numbers flocked to his standard and he left Coventry for London on 18 July with a sizeable army; he was well received there, indeed the city gave him a loan of £1,000. This money was almost certainly a form of bribe to ensure the good behaviour of Warwick's troops and the safety of the citizens of London, and did not necessarily reflect the political views of the city and its leaders. However Warwick was anxious to get on and join Sir William Conyers and his army before Edward could concentrate his forces. He therefore left London with his army on the road to Nottingham after a short stay, having sent a strong mounted contingent on ahead to join Sir William Conyers as soon as possible.

To the north the armies of Pembroke and Conyers became aware that the other was close by; they camped for the night either side of the River Cherwell overlooking a crossing, which Pembroke took the precaution of guarding. Early the next morning, 26 July 1469, Conyers' army attacked Pembroke's and a fierce fight took place for possession of the crossing. Pembroke's force, while giving a good account of itself, suffered from a lack of archers and was gradually forced back. It managed to disengage and reform a short distance away where it was joined by Devon and his force, but just as Pembroke's troops were increased to near parity with those of Conyers, so Warwick's advance force joined Conyers. Early in the afternoon Conyers, now reinforced by Warwick's mounted troops, renewed the struggle. Pembroke's and Devon's army, seeing troops wearing Warwick's badges and thinking that his whole army had joined the struggle, took to their heels and ran. Pembroke and his brother were taken prisoner but Devon managed to get away.[7]

The Battle at Edgecote Moor, though a relatively minor affair, had significant political repercussions. Firstly it made Warwick undoubtedly the most powerful man in the land, secondly, it put Edward in his power, and thirdly, he was able to get rid of many of his political opponents. He had the two Herbert brothers, Pembroke and Sir Richard Herbert executed without trial and for no apparent reason the day after the battle, thus ridding himself of rivals in Wales. The Herberts were in no way involved in treason, indeed they were on their way to aid their lawful sovereign whom Warwick still professed to serve. Edward meanwhile, unaware of the fate of Pembroke's army at Edgecote Moor, made his way south towards Northampton to rendezvous with Pembroke and Devon. He heard of their defeat and presumably of Warwick's part in it on 29 July when he was near Northampton, and as the news spread so his army deserted him. He was found by Warwick's brother George, the archbishop, near Olney, south of Northampton, with only a few of his friends and retainers making his way to London and was escorted as a prisoner to Coventry. Warwick received him there and then sent him first to Warwick Castle and then later to Middleham. On 12 August Earl Rivers and Sir John Wydeville, the queen's father and brother, were both taken as prisoners and executed on Warwick's orders purely out of antagonism and because they were the senior members of the Wydeville faction at court. The unfortunate earl of Devon was caught and killed by a mob in Somerset.

Warwick had made a clean sweep of his rivals in court and he held the king as his prisoner but he was to find, as the duke of York had discovered when he held Henry VI, that his problems now began. He claimed he was Edward's loyal servant and had only removed his advisers, but he expected Edward to do his bidding. Edward was very much his own man and had no intention of doing as Warwick wished, furthermore Warwick was to find that the majority of the lords and barons did not support him. Once the king was no longer clearly on the throne to provide law and order, violence broke out again. In East Anglia the duke of Norfolk laid siege to Caister Castle, in Gloucestershire the Berkeley and Talbot families engaged in a private war over the Berkeley inheritance. There were further outbreaks of violence in Lancashire and Yorkshire where the duke of Gloucester and Lord Stanley came to blows over the ownership of land, and riots broke out in London. In the north Sir Humphrey Neville of Brancepeth and his brother Charles raised King Henry's standard in revolt. Warwick, responsible now for the maintenance of law and order, called for volunteers to put the rebellion down, however when they failed to come he realized that he needed the king's authority. Consequently Edward was released in September and made public appearances in York and Pontefract after which the volunteers were raised and Warwick was despatched to the north to quell the rebellion. The revolt was soon crushed and Sir Humphrey Neville taken prisoner, tried and executed for treason in front of Edward. Edward next summoned his brother, the duke of Gloucester, the earls of Arundel, Essex, Northumberland and Suffolk and also, William, Lord Hastings and other members of his council from London to attend him in York. He then moved south escorted by his loyal council to enter London in state in the middle of October.

By the standards set previously in the Wars of the Roses it was to be expected that Edward would enact bloody revenge on Warwick and all who had supported him, but this was not Edward's way, as he had shown after Towton. Instead he continued to show friendship to Warwick and others but nevertheless made certain adjustments of the gifts within his power, of which two were particularly important. He first transferred the Pembroke lands in Wales, which had been assumed by Warwick after Pembroke's execution by him following the Battle at Edgecote Moor, to Richard of Gloucester, and secondly he released Sir Henry Percy from the Tower where he had been held since 1464. Percy was the traditional heir to the earldom of Northumberland, an area where it was important for Edward to have friends and allies. As the earldom of Northumberland had been given to Sir John Neville, Lord Montagu, Warwick's brother, as a reward for his victory at Hexham he was compensated with the lands of the erstwhile earl of Devon. It was now possible to restore Sir Henry Percy to the traditional Percy title and lands in the north. To cement the friendship and loyalty between the new Marquis Montagu and the king, his son George was married to Edward's eldest daughter, Elizabeth, and made the duke of Bedford. Consequently, notwith-standing the outcome of the battle at Edgecote Moor and Edward's subsequent imprisonment by Warwick, he would seem to have emerged in a stronger position than before. However Warwick too had done well in the power stakes – his daughter had married the king's heir and his nephew had married the king's daughter, but of prime importance to him he had thinned the ranks of Wydevilles around the king. Nevertheless, Edward now knew where he stood with Warwick who could no longer be trusted. Of equal concern would be the loyalty of both the new earl of Northumberland and Warwick's brother Sir John Neville, Marquis Montagu.

Despite regaining his freedom and freedom of action by returning to London Edward knew that the country was ill at ease. The smell of treason had to be cleared away before Edward could feel secure on his throne. A catalyst was needed and it appeared in the shape of an outbreak of lawlessness between two families in Lincolnshire. In March 1470 Richard, Lord Welles, with his son Sir Robert Welles and his sons-in-law, Sir Thomas de la Lande and Sir Thomas Dymmock, drove Sir Thomas Burgh of Gainsborough and his family from their manor house, burnt it down and carried off their possessions.

They miscalculated badly. Burgh was Edward's Master of the Horse and Edward decided to come to his servant's aid. He summoned Lord Welles and Sir Richard Dymmock to him in London to answer for their actions and at the same time announced that he was going to go to Lincolnshire to restore order. Welles and Dymmock duly appeared before the king, were questioned and pardoned, but detained at his pleasure. Edward then sent out writs to summon an army to meet him at Grantham on 12 March. Sir Robert Welles turned to his second cousin, the earl of Warwick, for help. Warwick was only too glad to take this opportunity to confront Edward and hopefully push him off the throne. Sir Robert Welles was told to raise volunteers in Lincolnshire but to wait until Warwick had left London before taking any action. Clarence meanwhile asked to see Edward and by doing so delayed Edward's departure from London; they met at Baynard's Castle on 6 March, where Clarence explained that he could not accompany the king as he was going westwards to see his wife, an excuse that Edward accepted. Edward then marched off towards Grantham and, once he had gone, Clarence left the capital, not to see his wife but to join Warwick who had left London earlier.

In Lincolnshire, meanwhile, Sir Robert Welles had spread various rumours that Edward was coming to conduct a bloody assize and not merely to calm the unrest earlier in the month. Sir Robert made a call to arms and many volunteers flocked to his banner. Edward meanwhile, was marching north in the company of the dukes of Norfolk and Suffolk, the earls of Wiltshire and Worcester and Lords Hastings and Howard and their retinues. When Edward reached Waltham Abbey on 7 March he heard of Sir Robert Welles's call to arms but continued on his way north, arriving at Royston the day after and Huntingdon on 9 March. By now he knew that the Lincolnshire men had been joined by many more from Yorkshire, indeed it was reported that Sir Robert Welles had 100,000 men-at-arms in his army.[8] Clearly this is another exaggeration but it certainly meant that Sir Robert had a very large following. Edward, on hearing of the size of Sir Robert's army, had ordered Lord Welles and Sir Thomas Dymmock to be brought to him and after questioning them discovered their complicity in the uprising. He ordered Lord Welles to write to his son warning him that unless he laid down his arms and submitted, he and Sir Thomas Dymmock would lose their lives.

Sir Robert meanwhile marched off towards Leicester to join Warwick and Clarence. However, when he received Edward's letter he turned back towards Stamford hoping to save his father's life. Edward reached Stamford on 12 March where he heard that Warwick and Clarence had reached Leicester. He soon discovered from his scouts that Sir Robert Welles's army was drawn up in battle array near Empingham about 5 miles away to the west. Edward now showed admirable resolution and immediately marched to face Sir Robert. He drew up his own army in battle order, called for Lord Welles and Sir Thomas Dymmock to be brought before him and had them executed for treason in front of both armies. At this Sir Robert's army advanced shouting 'a Warwick, a Warwick' and 'a Clarence, a Clarence' clearly indicating their allegiance and the complicity of both Warwick and Clarence in the armed revolt. Edward retaliated by ordering his artillery to fire a barrage and immediately followed it up by charging the forces opposite, who, after some initial resistance, soon fled the scene. The battle, such as it was, became known as the Battle of Loosecoat Field from the large number of livery jackets abandoned on the field by the fleeing Lincolnshire men. These jackets bore the liveries of Warwick and Clarence and clearly endorsed their complicity in the whole plot.

Loosecoat Field was a temporary watershed. After the battle Warwick and Clarence did their best to raise volunteers in the north and the south-west without much luck. People were reluctant to put their heads on the block to support Warwick and to put Clarence on the throne in place of Edward. On 2 April Edward publicly condemned both Warwick and Clarence as 'rebels and traitors'.[9] They fled first to Lancashire, where they hoped to gain help from Lord Stanley who clearly felt the risks to be too great to aid them, and then to Exeter to take ship for Calais, where Warwick was still captain. On his way Warwick sailed into Southampton hoping to seize his old flagship the *Trinity* and any other ships docked there, and ready for sea, but he was thwarted by Sir Anthony Wydeville, the new Lord Rivers.[iii] After his failed raid Warwick sailed on for Calais. When they arrived off Calais the commander there in Warwick's absence, Lord Wenlock, refused them entry saying it would be unsafe and so they sailed down the Channel to seek sanctuary in France. On their way Warwick's little fleet fell in with a fleet of Flemish merchant ships and, unable to resist the temptation, attacked them, taking several prizes and much booty as well as killing or drowning many of their crews. On hearing this Charles of Burgundy mobilized a fleet to attack Warwick but before they could do so Lord Howard, who had been

---

iii It is not clear whether Warwick sailed from Exeter with a small fleet of ships or was sailing alone and then managed to take some small ships either on the way or at Southampton, but he certainly arrived off Calais with a small fleet.

ordered to sea by Edward to confront Warwick, found and attacked Warwick's fleet. After a sharp fight several of Warwick's prizes were seized but Warwick managed to reach Honfleur in safety with much of his pirated loot intact. Warwick now sought the protection of Louis of France, who gave it grudgingly, but was blockaded in Honfleur by the combined fleets of the Burgundians and Lord Howard. In June Howard withdrew his fleet from the blockade in order to meet threats to the English east coast from the Hanseatic fleet, while the Burgundians sailed back to their Flemish ports to refit. Warwick took this opportunity to sail down the coast to Barfleur and La Hogue, further away from the possibility of a raid by either the English or the Burgundian fleets.

Warwick had for some time been a protégé of Louis XI of France and his arrival in France was fortuitous for French plans. Louis knew of Edward's wish to go to war against France and of course Edward's sister was now duchess of Burgundy and Burgundy was at the time a threat to France. Louis had also given sanctuary to Margaret of Anjou, Henry VI's queen, since she had fled from England with her son Edward in July 1463. Now, seven years later, Louis held most of the cards he needed for Henry to be put on the throne of England once more and have an acquiescent, if not friendly, England across the Channel. He knew that with Henry as king England would not interfere with his plans to overcome Burgundy, indeed he might even be able to arrange an Anglo-French alliance against Burgundy. Louis was a crafty schemer and was not to be diverted from his aim. But to achieve his aims against Burgundy he had to do two things. He had to arrange reconciliation between Queen Margaret and her bitterest foe Warwick who together might then be able to push Edward off the throne. Warwick of course would need Louis' help to do this and in particular he would need men, money and ships.

Louis' first contributory aim was soon realized: Warwick went down on bended knee to Queen Margaret to plead for her forgiveness, indeed it is reported that she kept him there for a quarter of an hour before pardoning him! This must have been a humiliating experience for this arrogant and over-mighty nobleman. Nevertheless, the two, Margaret and Warwick, needed each other. Margaret to ensure that her son Edward, Prince of Wales, became king in due course and Warwick to become the undisputed first counsellor to the crown and the most powerful man in the realm. The betrothal of

Anne Neville, Warwick's daughter, to Prince Edward on 25 July sealed this alliance just three days after their parent's reconciliation. However, Anne was to be left in Margaret's care, as a hostage for Warwick's loyalty after he had invaded England and overcome Edward IV; furthermore, Prince Edward was to remain with his mother. Edmund, duke of Somerset, heir to his elder brother Henry, executed after the Battle of Hexham in 1464, and Sir John Courtenay, heir to the earldom of Devon, two of Margaret's closest supporters, were to go with Warwick. Warwick was now in the position of the punter who has backed both horses for a win in a two-horse race, his elder daughter was married to the heir to the Yorkist throne, Clarence, and his younger daughter was betrothed to the heir to the Lancastrian throne, Prince Edward. Surely now he couldn't lose – all he had to do was to cross the Channel. Louis had agreed to provide the money, the ships and some of the men, but there was a problem: the Anglo-Burgundian fleet was back on station; not only did it prevent Warwick from setting sail but it also raided down the coast of Normandy. The Burgundians considered Warwick a pirate and were determined to capture him so they were content to join Edward's fleet to prevent Warwick from crossing the Channel.

Warwick's presence in France ensured Burgundian sympathy for Edward and made an Anglo-Burgundian alliance against France more likely. Duke Charles of Burgundy was of course Edward IV's brother-in-law so that there was family pressure for his support for Edward. However Charles had no particular preference for either claimant to the English throne – he was only interested in the continuing flow of wool from England to his Flemish cloth towns and the possibility of English help in his ongoing quarrel with France. The resolution of Louis' aims, however, rested on a regime change in England and this depended on a successful campaign in England by Warwick. Nevertheless the reconciliation between Margaret and Warwick left Clarence in an invidious position. While Edward remained on the throne and without a direct heir Clarence filled that station, but if his father-in-law Warwick was successful in the venture and Henry VI was restored to the throne, he would become sidelined. This was clearly recognized and so he was designated 'residual heir' in case the Lancastrian line should fail.[10] However Clarence, who had been declared a traitor by Edward for his support for Warwick's recent rebellion, was clearly an unreliable ally. He had already behaved treacherously towards his brother, might he not do the same towards his father-in-law in order to obtain a pardon and maintain his position as heir to the throne? The alliance between Louis, Warwick, Margaret and Clarence had many fault lines!

Warwick's invasion fleet was kept in port by the blockading fleets of England and Burgundy throughout the summer, and then early in September a fierce storm blew up in the Channel and the blockading fleets were scattered. By 9 September the storm had blown itself out and they quickly put to sea. Warwick and his men landed near Exeter four days later.

Warwick's allies struck first. Late in July, before Warwick left France, his brother-in-law Lord Fitzhugh of Ravensworth began a rebellion in the West Riding of Yorkshire, quickly followed by another in Cumberland. Both these uprisings involved gentlemen and yeomen connected with the Neville family, indeed most were directly connected to Warwick as the lord of Middleham.[11] As soon as he heard of the rebellion in the north Edward moved to crush it and very soon it evaporated. He was still in Yorkshire when Warwick landed near Exeter but quickly marched south to confront him. He got as far as Doncaster where he halted and waited for the forces, which he had authorized John Neville, Marquis Montagu, to raise on his behalf and had assembled at Pontefract. Montagu, however, was marching now not to join Edward but to join his brother Warwick.

Warwick, meanwhile, had begun his march north and in due course was to be joined by Lord Stanley and the earl of Shrewsbury and their contingents. His army was estimated to be some 30,000 strong according to the Coventry City records,[12] certainly an exaggeration, but clearly it was large. Edward with perhaps no more than 3,000 men was now sandwiched between the armies of Warwick and Montagu. Edward halted at Doncaster where his army was dispersed in billets in the villages round about and while Edward was at dinner with his commanders he received the devastating news that Montagu had turned coat and was not far away. Indeed he was so close that Edward himself was endangered. He was in an impossible situation, trapped between the armies of the two brothers with less than half the number of men opposed to him.

Edward took the one course open to him, he abandoned his army and fled the scene together with his closest advisers and supporters. They rode south-east to the Wash obtained boats and crossed the

Wash by night to King's Lynn on the opposite shore where they arrived late on 30 Serptember. Here, two days later, they boarded three ships and sailed across the sea to Holland, where Edward was given shelter by the governor of Holland, Louis of Gruthuyse in Alkmaar. Edward was not exactly a welcome guest in Burgundy, but duke Charles gave him reluctant sanctuary.

In England, once it was confirmed that Edward had fled, rioting broke out in London and Kent, and Warwick hurried south to London to restore order and to restore Henry VI to the throne. Edward's queen fled from the Tower and sought sanctuary at Westminster where on 2 November 1470 she gave birth to Edward's first son, another Edward. Margaret meanwhile remained in France with the prince of Wales, while Warwick assumed an uneasy position of authority with his puppet king Henry in tow. Events on the Continent now dictated those in England. Both Louis of France and Charles of Burgundy wanted English support for their own purposes, war against the other. Louis knew he had the support of Warwick and that Henry had always been in favour of rapprochement with France, he also had Queen Margaret and her son at his court. An Anglo-French alliance against Burgundy should have been achievable fairly soon, but Warwick would not move without Margaret's authority, she wouldn't give it until she was safely in England and she didn't yet trust Warwick to uphold their bargain. Furthermore the wool revenue once again dictated events; an Anglo-French alliance and war against Burgundy might cut off this lucrative source of funds for the English royal purse, as Burgundy was the main buyer of wool for the Flemish cloth trade. England under either king was therefore more likely to side with Burgundy; certainly this was so with the merchants who provided much of the finance for war and amongst the barons who provided most of the trained manpower. So although Louis was straining at the leash to go to war against Burgundy, the leash in the shape of Lancastrian England was neither ready to go to war nor certain that war with France against Burgundy was the right policy.

In Burgundy Charles still refused to see Edward or to give him any useful help, but he was well aware of Louis' intent and the possibility of English help in any eventual war against him if Edward was back on the throne. On 3 December Louis' patience broke and he published what was to all intents and purposes a declaration of war against Charles of Burgundy; his troops were soon on the march. The French quickly took St Quentin and were threatening Amiens when Charles responded by seeing Edward and backing his bid to invade England to take back his crown. Louis' precipitate action against Charles had Warwick's backing and his promise that he would lead an English army against Burgundy as Louis' ally;[13] to all intents and purposes England was now at war with Burgundy as an ally of France. All the pieces were now in place for the dramatic events that were to follow. Warwick was all powerful in England, Edward had received Charles's backing but was still in Holland, Margaret was still in France, and apart from providing support to the rival English camps Louis and Charles were now too involved in their own affairs to interfere in England's. The race was now on between Margaret and Edward; whoever crossed over first with sufficient support, was likely to control future events. Would Margaret overcome her mistrust of Warwick before Edward could gather the necessary support and finance? Edward at least was well aware that he had to move fast if he was to have any chance at all.

Edward won the race. He secured a loan from his brother-in-law and paid for 300 Flemish hand gunners, 900 English soldiers[14] and thirty-six ships[15] to carry his small force across to the east coast of England. He embarked at Flushing on 2 March 1471 but was held up by contrary winds.[16] He finally sailed on 11 March and dropped anchor off Cromer on 12 March. Scouts were immediately sent ashore to discover if the duke of Norfolk would be willing and able to help and to get up-to-date news of the situation in the country at large. They returned with the news that East Anglia was awash with Lancastrian supporters and that Norfolk was in prison. Edward decided to sail on up the coast to Yorkshire and seek support there. It was at about this time that Warwick learnt that Edward had arrived and he began the process of mobilizing his own forces. Unfortunately a storm blew up and Edward's fleet was scattered. The next morning, 14 March, Edward found his ship alone in the Humber estuary off the coast by the village of Kilnsea on the Ravenspur. He landed with Lord Hastings and about 500 men, went to the village for the night and sent out riders to find out what had happened to the rest of his fleet. Later that day he was reunited with his brother Richard, duke of Gloucester, with about 300 men, who had landed near the village of Welwick about 4 miles away, and Earl Rivers with another 200 who had come ashore at Paull about 12 miles further up the estuary.

On 15 March Edward was reunited with the rest of his small force, all of whom had come ashore safely. They then began their march inland making for Hull, but their way was barred by a force of six or seven thousand militiamen, under the command of Sir John Westerdale, the priest of Keyingham, which lay en route, and a gentleman called Martyn du Mer. The force opposing Edward was too large to defeat in battle but he managed to convince Sir John and his officers that he had simply come to claim his inheritance as duke of York, as had Henry Bolingbroke seventy-two years before. He was allowed to go on his way to Hull where the garrison was hostile and the gates closed against him, so he marched on to York some 40 miles further inland. When he was about 3 miles from the city the city recorder, Thomas Conyers, rode out to advise him that he would not be allowed to enter York and that if he did he might be trapped. Edward felt that if he turned back now his cause would be lost irretrievably, so decided to put a bold face on it and demand entry. He continued towards York and on halting outside the gates was told that since he came only to reclaim his inheritance as duke of York he would be allowed to enter the city, but only with sixteen men; the rest of his force would have to remain outside the walls. He entered York on 18 March with an ostrich feather in his cap, the badge of the Prince of Wales, and shouting 'King Harry, King and Prince Edward!'[17] By evening, after he had charmed the city councillors, his whole force was allowed in to spend the night in the city providing they left in the morning. The next day Edward turned south and went via Tadcaster, a town loyal to the earl of Northumberland, and Wakefield to Sandal.

So Edward had gained entry to his kingdom, but only just. He had been lucky with the militias after he landed and had had an unenthusiastic though not hostile reception at York. The fact that the earl of Northumberland had not raised the north against him meant that others would be reluctant to come forward to do so. However, Edward could not rely on Northumberland's neutrality so he turned south towards the Midlands where his own and Lord Hastings's influence was greatest. He made for Sandal Castle, his family seat, and arrived there on 20 March. Montagu, Warwick's brother, was only 7 miles away at Pontefract but did not interfere; his very presence forced Edward to move on.

Edward received a sizeable reinforcement when he reached Nottingham. Six hundred well-armed men rode in to join him under the two knights, Sir William Parr and Sir James Harrington; Edward's army was now probably a little over 2,000 strong, but its strength lay in the fact that it was a well-equipped, nearly professional force. Learning that the duke of Exeter and the earl of Oxford were at Newark with about 4,000 men from East Anglia, Edward marched to confront them. Exeter and Oxford deserted their army during the night and made good their escape; their army simply melted away.

Having scared Exeter and Oxford away, Edward then turned due west and marched the 40 odd miles to Leicester, the agreed rendezvous for expected reinforcements. Three thousand well-equipped soldiers arrived here led by men largely from Lord Hastings' estates. These were most welcome; Edward now had a viable well-organized army at his command. But the opposition had not been idle since Edward landed. Warwick arrived at Coventry on 27 March with an army of six or seven thousand, perhaps a thousand more men than Edward had in his, and settled down in the walled city while he waited for Clarence, Montagu, Oxford and Exeter to join up with him. On 29 March Edward's army arrived before Coventry and Edward challenged Warwick to come out and fight, but Warwick, expecting to be reinforced within the next few days, declined the invitation. Edward then drew off to the town of Warwick, about 10 miles south of Coventry.

This was an interesting strategic move – although from here he could not prevent reinforcements arriving for the earl of Warwick from the north and east he could intercept those coming from Wales and the west country, and most importantly he was now between the earl and London. On 3 April forces loyal to Edward met and dispersed Exeter's reinforcements near Leicester but failed to prevent all of them from reaching Coventry. At about this time both Montagu and Oxford managed to join Warwick whose army was now considerably larger than Edward's, however Warwick failed to take the initiative as he was waiting for Clarence who had 4,000 men with him. Warwick was clearly afraid of his erstwhile protégé and, perhaps unwisely, trusted in Clarence.

However Clarence must have realized that he would be left in an invidious position should Warwick win and Margaret return. He had also been in touch with Edward through the good offices of their sister the duchess of Burgundy. Clarence was hedging his bets. Both sides therefore waited for him with some anxiety, but Edward was between Clarence and Warwick, and overlooked Clarence's approach route. On 3 April he heard that Clarence was nearing Warwick on the Banbury road and marched to intercept him. The two armies faced each other, but Edward's was by far the larger, possibly by now 7,000 strong. At this point Clarence, who always wanted to be on the winning side, had to make up his mind either to fight for his brother or his father-in-law. He decided on the former and after an emotional pardon and greeting the two armies marched together into the town of Warwick. Clarence's army added to Edward's made the joint force of between ten and eleven thousand men almost as large as Warwick's, and Edward once again challenged Warwick to come out to settle matters by pitched battle; Warwick declined a second time. It was at this point, on 5 April that Edward decided to march to London.

Time was of the essence. All the main antagonists in England must by now have heard that Margaret and the prince of Wales had embarked for England on 24 March and were expected at any time, news that might have convinced Edward that he needed to be in London to control events. Somerset and Courtenay, earl of Devon, on hearing the news that Margaret was on her way left Henry in the care of Warwick's brother, George, archbishop of York, and hurried off to be able to greet Margaret when she landed. In London panic reigned among Henry's supporters as news came that Edward was on his way south. Archbishop York and other Lancastrians paraded Henry through the streets in the vain hope of cementing loyalty to their cause, but it did not impress the citizens or the common council of the city who decided not to oppose Edward when he reached London. George Neville, the archbishop, realizing that he had no means of preventing Edward's entry, sent a letter to Edward at St Albans on 10 April offering his submission, and that night Yorkists seized the Tower.

The next day Edward rode triumphantly into London ahead of his army. He went to St Paul's to offer thanks and then went to the archbishop's palace to find Henry. It is reported that the two kings shook hands and embraced, and that Henry said, 'My cousin of York, you are very welcome. I know that in your hands my life will not be in danger.'[18] Edward had Henry escorted back to the Tower for safety together with the archbishop. Edward next went to Westminster to be reunited with his queen and to see his baby son, whom he had never seen. However there was no time to dally – Warwick was fast approaching London. He had set out in pursuit of Edward on 6 or 7 April so would be approaching London on the 11th or 12th. Edward had to assemble his army and march north fast. On Good Friday and the following day, Edward's army made hectic preparations for the battle that had to come. Edward had to defeat Warwick before he could join up with Margaret, while Warwick was under some pressure to defeat Edward and present himself as the victor to Margaret; each man needed to eliminate the other.

Edward left London at about 4 o'clock in the afternoon on Saturday 12 April, reinforced by men and artillery from London, and began his march north up the road towards St Albans with about 10,000 men; he took Henry with him, a useful card in case of difficulties. About 10 miles up the road at Barnet his patrols met Warwick's and drove them out of the town; this would have been at about 5 o'clock, half an hour before dusk. Edward's men pursued Warwick's and a little way north of the town saw Warwick's army drawn up across the road ready for battle. This army was considerably larger than Edward's but nothing like as large as the reported 30,000. Battle was inevitable the next day and Edward, not willing to be caught forming up in the morning by the larger army opposite him, closed up and deployed his army in battle order during the night. Warwick was well aware that the Yorkist army was only a shot away to his front but didn't realize how close it actually was. He ordered his artillery to carry out a bombardment throughout the night but due to the closeness of their opponents' positions most of the shot went clean over their heads and very few casualties resulted. Edward had forbidden his own artillery from replying and had ordered complete silence from his army so that he might gain an element of surprise the next morning.

A very foggy dawn broke on 13 April, with both sides able to hear but not see the other. Warwick had deployed his army with his vanguard under Lord Oxford on his right and his rearguard under Exeter on his left; in the centre Montagu commanded the mainguard; Warwick himself commanded the reserve which he drew up behind the centre. Edward, with Clarence close by, commanded his centre, with Gloucester and the vanguard on his right flank and Hastings on his left. Warwick's army was deployed along a slight ridge either side of the Barnet–St Albans road and probably stretched for about 500 yards either side; his right flank and part of his centre was protected by a thick hedge. Usually in the Middle Ages one army deployed exactly opposite the other, so that the right-flank division was opposite the left flank division of the army opposite and so on. However, in this case, due to a night deployment by Edward's army, Warwick's right flank overlapped Edward's left and Edward's right flank did the same at the other end of the opposing lines. This was to have a crucial effect on the forthcoming battle; furthermore, due to the fog neither side was aware of this asymmetrical deployment.

At between 4 and 5 o'clock in the morning Edward opened proceedings with a volley of arrows and the fire of his guns before charging into the ranks of Warwick's army, who replied in kind. Very soon Hastings's division found itself outflanked by Oxford's who overlapped them due to their original starting positions; before long they were forced back and then broke and fled towards Barnet, closely pursued by Oxford's men. Luckily, the fog prevented the main and vanguards of Edward's army from seeing the defeat and pursuit of their own rearguard on the left, so they fought on. Meanwhile on Edward's right flank the same thing was beginning to happen. Gloucester's division overlapped Exeter's and was beginning to force it back when Warwick reinforced it with the reserve and steadied it. In the centre Edward, leading by example, was hotly engaged and the battle was very even, although Edward's initial charge had forced Montagu's division back a little way. It was not long before some of Hastings's division reached London and spread the rumour that Edward had lost the day, but while they were galloping south fortune took a twist.

Oxford managed to rally about 800 of his division and marched back to the battle. Confusion now reigned as Oxford's men came back to the battle to their old positions, but out of the fog towards the right flank of Montagu's division and from the direction in which they might have expected Edward's men if he had decided on a flank attack by a reserve. Montagu's men, seeing them, and taking them to be Edward's, shot at them as they came out of the fog at which Oxford's men shouted 'treason, treason' and fled the battle. Montagu's men, perhaps losing concentration and distracted by Oxford's, were pressed harder by Edward's mainguard and then suddenly they broke. The shambles on the Lancastrian right flank was said to have arisen from the similarity of Oxford's heraldic badge worn by his troops to those of Edward's; the former wore a star with streamers while the latter wore a sun with rays,[19] easily confused especially in the fog. Following the mix-up, Edward's army soon put Warwick's to flight and by 10 o'clock he was the clear victor. Both the earl of Warwick and his brother marquis Montagu had been killed and Exeter severely wounded. The latter survived and was taken to sanctuary at Westminster; the earl of Oxford escaped the battlefield and got safely away to Scotland. Edward's army lost the Lords Cromwell, Say and Mountjoy and 'many other good knyghts, and squiers, gode yemen, and many othar meniall servaunts of the Kyngs'. In all, the casualties that day from both sides were said to be as many as 4,500 men.

Edward returned to London where he had Warwick's and Montagu's bodies displayed naked on the steps of St Paul's for three days to prevent rumours being spread that they were still alive. Edward was greeted with joy, gave thanks at St Paul's for his victory and King Henry was once again lodged in the Tower. But Edward could not linger in London; he now had firm intelligence of Queen Margaret. She had landed with her son the prince of Wales at Weymouth on Easter Day, 13 April, in the evening, the day before Edward won the Battle of Barnet. She immediately rode to Exeter where Edmund, duke of Somerset, and his brother John, the earl of Devon and many others greeted her. On Easter Monday she heard the news of Edward's victory at Barnet and of Warwick's and Montagu's deaths. This must have been a staggering blow to her and her cause, but particularly to Prince Edward's future prospects; nevertheless she was determined to continue. She knew that Jasper Tudor, earl of Pembroke, was already in Wales raising an army in her cause, so she resolved to march north-eastwards towards Bristol and Gloucester.

No doubt Margaret hoped to meet up with Pembroke at one of the crossings of the river Severn before marching on London to do battle with Edward. A glance at the map will show that there are several routes along this way that Margaret's army could take in order to march to London. There is the route from Exeter through Dorchester and Blandford, then the more direct route that goes through Yeovil, Shaftesbury and Salisbury; there is another from Bath, yet another from Bristol and then one more from Gloucester. Margaret was marching around the rim of the wheel and had many available spokes on which to advance to London. Edward, on the other hand, was at the hub. He knew that the threat from the north no longer existed and although there were rumours of a threat from Thomas Neville, Lord

Fauconberg's bastard son, in Kent, it had not yet materialized and any such threat was unlikely to be co-ordinated with Margaret's approach from the west. Edward had the advantage of working along interior lines and providing he had the western routes and those from Kent watched he would have plenty of time to march his army to intercept either threat.

Edward did indeed send out scouts to watch the various approaches and Margaret did her best to deceive him by sending small parties along each of the spokes in turn in order to distract Edward and lure him from the hub along the wrong spoke. But Edward, having shown that he was capable of swift and determined movement, now showed that he could be patient as well. He waited at Windsor to see if Margaret made a definite move along one route or another before he made his own move; this also gave him time to gather fresh forces after the Battle of Barnet. He made use of the Tower armoury to replace lost and damaged weapons and, most importantly, to reinforce his artillery for he now had both Warwick's guns and those of the Tower arsenal. Meanwhile Margaret marched up towards Wells. Edward probably realized that she was not confident enough to challenge him without either Pembroke's rein-forcements from Wales or Thomas Neville's from Kent. He left Windsor on 24 April and went slowly westwards without really committing himself to either the route to Gloucester or the routes from Salisbury or further south. But clearly the information he received had begun to indicate that Margaret was definitely moving towards a juncture with Pembroke, because instead of marching due west to Reading he went north-west to Abingdon, where he arrived on 27 April and rested there all of the next day waiting for news. Realizing that the Severn crossings at Gloucester, Tewkesbury or Worcester would be crucial to Margaret, he marched along the road to Gloucester with his army hoping to confront Margaret before she could join up with Pembroke. He made a forced march of 30 miles to Cirencester on 29 April. Having heard that Margaret was at Bath he left Cirencester that evening and took up positions in fields about 3 miles away on the Bath road, but his scouts reported no sign of the enemy.

Next morning Edward decided to march towards Bath and reached Malmesbury, but again there was no sign of Margaret's army. She, or rather Somerset her commander, had managed to lure Edward southwards towards Bath, but in fact her army had marched to Bristol where it had spent the night, was refreshed and had now been reinforced by Lancastrian supporters. The next day, 2 May, they marched out towards Chipping Sodbury but instead of continuing towards Edward they swung left and made for Gloucester and the first crossing point of the Severn. Edward marched towards Sodbury Hill, about a mile out of the town, but as he approached his scouts reported no sign of the enemy. Margaret had given Edward the slip once again but at the same time had made her own intentions crystal clear. But Edward was still between her and London and was, if anything, slightly closer to Gloucester than she was.

About 3.00 a.m. that night Edward was told that Margaret's army was marching through the night to Gloucester via Berkeley. Realizing that he had been tricked and that Gloucester was Margaret's immediate destination, he sent messengers to Sir Richard Beauchamp, governor of the city and constable of the castle, warning him of Queen Margaret's approach. Edward commanded him to close the gates against her and to be ready to defend both city and castle; he also said he would be marching to their relief should Margaret's army decide to besiege or bombard them. Edward's messengers must have left at about 4 in the morning on 3rd May for their 25-mile ride, arriving in time for Beauchamp to alert the city's and castle's defences and close the gates before Margaret's army arrived there at about 10 o'clock the same morning. Richard Beauchamp, son and heir to Lord Beauchamp, had been appointed by Edward and was his staunch supporter. When Margaret arrived before the gates and demanded entry, she was refused. Realizing that this game of bluff could not go on for ever, Margaret marched to Tewkesbury, arriving about 4.00 p.m. the same afternoon.

The Lancastrian army made for the ford across the Severn, but the foot soldiers lagged behind. They were exhausted having marched the 36 miles during the night and that day 'in a fowle contrey, all in lanes and stonny wayes, betwyxt woodes, without any good refresshynge'. Edward was some 6 or 7 miles behind and to the east of Margaret's army but was almost as exhausted. However, they made faster progress as they marched north along the open country of the Cotswolds with their scouts out ahead and on their flanks, and in three battles or divisions. The Lancastrian army decided to make their stand at Tewkesbury. On 3 May they took up a strong position with the town and the abbey at their backs and in front of them 'fowle lanes, and deep dykes, and many hedges, with hylls and valleys, a ryght evil place to approche, as cowlde well have been devised'. At about the same time as Margaret and her army reached Tewkesbury, Edward reached Cheltenham, some 5 miles away. Having received definite intelligence that the Lancastrian army was waiting for him at Tewkesbury, he marched on for another 3 miles and halted for the night.

Margaret's army was drawn up in three divisions: Sir Edmund Beaufort, the Duke of Somerset on the right, Lord John Wenlock with Prince Edward in the centre and Sir John Courtenay, the earl of Devon on the left. Queen Margaret, after reviewing and encouraging her army, left it before the battle and went to a religious house in Tewkesbury not far behind. In all the Lancastrian army had some six or seven thousand men-at-arms, footmen and archers as well as some artillery. They were placed in a strong position with their flanks protected by the Coln brook on their right and the Swillgate brook on their left; because of the dykes and hedges 'it was right hard to approche them nere, and come to hands.' There was a small hillock to their right front. Edward approached in three divisions: his vanguard under his brother Richard, duke of Gloucester, the mainguard he kept under his own command and he put the rearguard under the command of Lord Hastings. Edward kept his brother Clarence where he could keep an eye on him. Edward's army consisted of between five or six thousand men, smaller than that of his enemy, but he had more men-at-arms and archers, and many more guns. It should be remembered that there was still a significant difference between the personal protection of a man-at-arms in his full plate armour and that of the bill-men whose protection was still much as it had been thirty years before. Consequently the side with the most men-at-arms and guns had a definite advantage; this advantage lay with the king but it was largely cancelled out by the superior numbers of the Lancastrians and the excellent position they had taken up.

As Edward's army approached Margaret's he noticed a wooded park on his left flank beyond the hillock and, remembering his experience at Towton, sent 200 mounted men-at-arms to it to ensure that no Lancastrian force was hiding there. He also told them that if they found no one there they should, at their own discretion, join the main battle if and when an opportunity occurred for them to intervene on the flank or rear of the enemy. As the rest of his army closed up to the Lancastrians, Gloucester wheeled to the left and Hastings to the right; the guns were placed all along the front. Gloucester was therefore opposite Somerset, Edward opposite the prince of Wales and Hastings opposite Devon. The battle began with a cannonade from Edward's guns, replied to in kind from those of the Lancastrians, and followed by several flights of arrows from the Yorkist archers. Edward then advanced to attack. Somerset's division suffered badly from the opening firefight and so, leaving some of his men in their old positions, he marched round to his right under cover to attack Gloucester's division on its left flank. Once Gloucester saw them he quickly adjusted his front and met them squarely. He was pushed back initially but when men from Edward's division reinforced him he gradually forced Somerset back up the hillock. As soon as Somerset's men could be seen from the park as they reached the top of the hillock, the 200 men-at-arms charged them in the back. Somerset's division disintegrated and men fled the scene towards Tewkesbury, but many were caught and slaughtered in what is known to this day as the Bloody Meadow. After that it was not long before the rest of the Lancastrian army began to be forced back, hard pressed as they were now by the whole of Edward's army, then resistance suddenly collapsed and every man escaped as well as he could, pursued by the victorious Yorkists.

Shortly after the battle Edward went to the abbey church to give thanks for his victory and there saw many Lancastrian fugitives from the battle seeking sanction. The abbey had never been authorized as a sanctuary and so all were soon dragged out to stand trial for treason. Among those taken in the abbey was Edmund Beaufort, duke of Somerset, who was to be tried by a court martial the next day. He and others were judged by the constable, the duke of Gloucester, and the marshal, the duke of Norfolk, found guilty of treason and were executed forthwith. The verdict was not surprising; Somerset, like his brother and his father, had consistently backed the Lancastrian cause. He was the great-grandson of John of Gaunt, duke of Lancaster, and a potential claimant to the throne. Somerset is a good example of the blood feuds that arose between noble and knightly families as a result of this war. His father had been killed at the First Battle of St Albans while his brother, who had been pardoned by Edward after the siege of Bamburgh in 1462, then reneged and fought against Edward at

Hexham, only to be defeated and executed. Others were also executed for treason, but many were pardoned and allowed to go. Lancastrian battle casualties included Edward, prince of Wales, Lord Wenlock and Sir John Courtenay, the earl of Devon, and Somerset's younger brother John Beaufort. The number of casualties is not known other than the fact that those of the Yorkist army were light. Politically this battle sealed the fate of the Lancastrian cause; with the prince of Wales dead, Henry a prisoner in the Tower and the main Lancastrian commander dead, the Yorkists had finally prevailed. Queen Margaret had not yet been found but she was once again a fugitive. The Lancastrian cause had been struck down but the corpse still twitched.

After the battle Edward moved north to Worcester where he arrived on 7 May. It was here that he received the welcome news of Margaret's capture; she had been found in a poor religious house not far from Tewkesbury the day after the battle. He also heard rumours of rebellion in the north and in Kent. He decided to deal with the problem in the north first and sent out summons for a muster at Coventry where he arrived on 11 May. While at Coventry Margaret was brought before him and then sent to the Tower. Edward also sent messengers throughout the country to spread the news of his victory, the deaths of Somerset and Prince Edward, and the capture of Queen Margaret. The news obviously had some effect, particularly in the north where the potential rebellion just petered out, but another reason soon became clear: the earl of Northumberland, who in the absence of Warwick and the Neville clan was now all powerful in the north remained loyal to Edward. Indeed he came south to meet the king on 14 May at Coventry, not dressed for war with hundreds of his armed followers but in friendship and accompanied only by a few of his companions; no surer sign of peace in the north could have been given. Edward's gamble in 1469 of releasing Sir Henry Percy from imprisonment in the Tower and his restoration to the earldom of Northumberland had paid off handsomely.

However, he also had news of events in Kent. Thomas Neville, Fauconberg's bastard son, had been sent to sea by the earl of Warwick before the Battle of Barnet to practise piracy in the Channel. In this he was very successful and volunteers flocked to join him, he attacked and robbed several Portugese ships causing problems between Portugal, an old ally, and England. He then went to Calais where more men joined him and finally landed in Kent late in April where he began to stir people up against the king, and indeed forced them by threats and violence to join his rebellion.[20] On 12 May Neville sailed up the Thames to London with many ships and men, supported by many more overland from Kent; altogether he had assembled between sixteen and seventeen thousand men with which he hoped to threaten and harass the city of London. Neville said he had come to fetch King Henry from the Tower and demanded entry to the city for himself and his army, but the mayor and aldermen barred his way. Neville, learning of the battle at Tewkesbury, had struck too late to help the Lancastrian cause.

Edward, on hearing the news from London, was forced to act. He heard about Neville's arrival at London on 14 May and immediately sent 1,500 well-armed men in haste to reinforce the city's militia and protect the Queen and his son. He then moved out of Coventry for London with his army the next day.

The rebels attempted to cross the Thames by way of London Bridge but were frustrated by the mayor and citizens so set part of it on fire. They then tried their hand at a landing from the ships but were again defeated. They offloaded some guns from their ships and set up batteries on the south bank of the river but were outgunned and forced to move out of range by the city's own, more numerous, guns. Neville's men next tried to force their way into the city at Cripplegate and Aldgate but were beaten back by the citizens' militia.[21] The rebels drew off and made camp at Blackheath where they remained for three days, finally dispersing on 18 May. Realizing that he had lost the initiative and the possibility of seizing London and releasing King Henry and Queen Margaret, Neville withdrew. He, with the troops from Calais, rode to Sandwich while his sailors embarked on his ships and sailed down the Thames to Sandwich where they landed;[22] Edward meanwhile marched into Kent with his army to disperse the remnants of the rebellion and was on his way to Sandwich when Neville surrendered and sought the king's pardon. He handed over his ships to the duke of Gloucester as a measure of his goodwill on 26 May and duly received Edward's pardon.

King Henry died on 23 May in the Tower. It was said that he died of 'pure displeasure, and melancholy' but it is more likely that he was murdered. Indeed it was surmised that 'he was stykked with a dagger by the handes of the duke of Gloucester,'[23] probably on Edward's orders; Gloucester was at that time constable of the Tower.

Nevertheless it is just possible that the author of the 'Arrival' had reported Henry's death accurately – after all, what had he to live for? He was in prison, his wife was in prison, his son had been killed at the Battle of Tewkesbury, his principle supporters had been killed in battle or executed shortly after, and his cause, the continuation of the Lancastrian dynasty on the throne of England, was totally crushed. The Yorkists had finally won the wars between the two royal houses – the Wars of the Roses.

Edward was now undeniably king of England and he had secured the throne by his political and military courage. Edward, when it was needed, showed that he could be patient as well as decisive. He was a good tactical commander and strategist, and he led by example. He never once in the 435 days between his return on 14 March 1471 and the death of Henry showed the indecisiveness that was one of Henry's hallmarks; he was a determined man who never lost sight of his ultimate aim, the throne of England. But perhaps Henry had the last laugh; within ten years of Henry VI's death he had become a popular saint to whom many miracles were attributed. He remained so until he was largely forgotten some fifty years later when the process of canonization became lost within the papal bureaucracy.

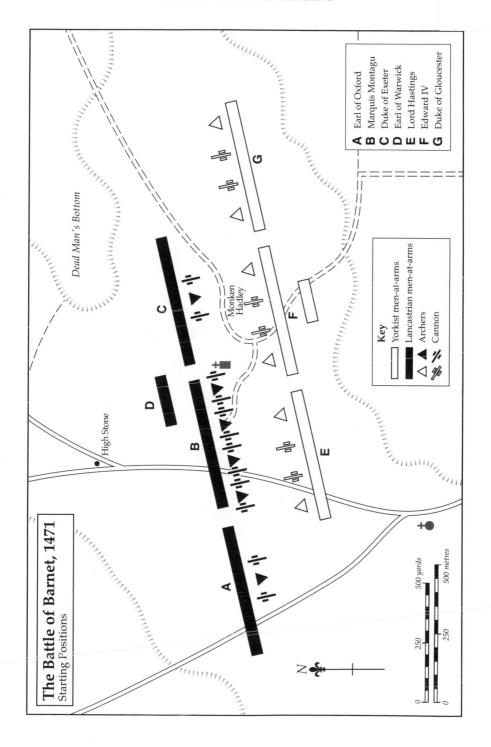

The Battle of Barnet, 1471
Starting Positions

Dead Man's Bottom

High Stone

Monken Hadley

A

B

C

D

E

F

G

N

Key

Yorkist men-at-arms

Lancastrian men-at-arms

Archers

Cannon

A Earl of Oxford
B Marquis Montagu
C Duke of Exeter
D Earl of Warwick
E Lord Hastings
F Edward IV
G Duke of Gloucester

500 yards

250

0

500 metres

250

0

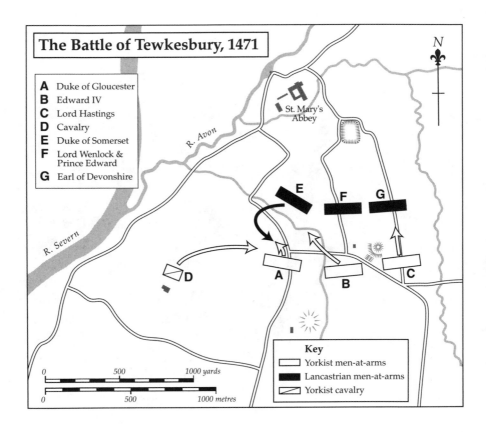

The Battle of Tewkesbury, 1471

A Duke of Gloucester
B Edward IV
C Lord Hastings
D Cavalry
E Duke of Somerset
F Lord Wenlock &
   Prince Edward
G Earl of Devonshire

St. Mary's
Abbey

R. Avon

R. Severn

N

Key
Yorkist men-at-arms
Lancastrian men-at-arms
Yorkist cavalry

0   500   1000 yards
0   500   1000 metres

Chapter 21

The Battle of Bosworth Field

'A horse! A horse! My kingdom for a horse!'[1]

Edward IV was now secure on his throne. No nobleman was in a position to threaten him from within the country and no candidate for the throne remained outside of his immediate family, although Henry Tudor, who was holed up in Wales with his uncle and had no support among the nobility, was a remote possibility. The wars, while mainly affecting the persons and fortunes of the nobility and the knights of the shires, had also touched the gentleman in his manor, the yeoman on his farm and the men of the shires and boroughs liable for the shrieval and city call to arms. Furthermore, there had been a great deal of lawless behaviour between the followers of competing magnates. Additionally and not necessarily due to the wars there existed an endemic lawlessness throughout the country at this time, as indeed there had been throughout the century.[2] What was needed now was the enforcement of the king's law without fear or favour and this is what Edward set out to provide. It was also important for Edward to reduce his need for taxation through parliament and so to this end he accelerated his reforms of the management of the royal estates.

Nevertheless two problems remained and they were centred round two powerful men: the duke of Clarence, Edward's younger brother and the earl of Oxford, Warwick's brother-in-law. Oxford had escaped the carnage of Barnet and had reached France safely, via Scotland, where Louis XI of France gave him sanctuary and aid. Louis was always on the lookout for a tool with which to destabilize the kingdom across the Channel and he clearly thought that Oxford could be the tool he needed. Clarence having been pardoned by Edward on 3 April 1471, when their armies met near Coventry, had nevertheless been kept on a short lead by Edward who did not yet trust him. Indeed Edward failed to give Clarence any office of state or position of authority after the battles of Barnet and Tewkesbury. Clarence saw his lack of authority in the affairs of the kingdom as a slur on his loyalty and ability. He was an unstable and inept man who yet yearned to be recognized as the most powerful man in the kingdom after Edward. His ambiguous position rankled and his resentment grew.

Meanwhile events across the Channel once again influenced politics in England. Louis, after giving help to Queen Margaret and the Lancastrians, continued to stir the pot in England, firstly by trying to entice the Scots to cross the border, secondly by giving aid to the earl of Oxford, and thirdly by supporting Jasper Tudor in Wales. Jasper sailed for France but unfortunately his ship was driven by bad weather to seek shelter in a Breton port. Duke Francis, Edward's ally, wisely kept Jasper and his nephew Henry Tudor as his prisoners. Louis' aggressive policy towards England convinced Edward, by the summer of 1472, to consider going to war against France as an ally of Burgundy and he did his best to prepare English opinion for this eventuality. Indeed it was said that 'The principle object of the King was to encourage the nobles and people to engage in war against France.'[3] It was even reported that one of Edward's supporters in parliament argued that external wars were a safeguard against problems at home,[4] a dictum that is no less true today.

After the Tudors sailed for France, John de Vere, earl of Oxford, became the principal thorn in Edward's side. Oxford with Louis' help began to raid the Calais marches without much success. He next tried his luck across the Channel, landing at St Osyth in Essex on 28 May 1473 with several followers, no doubt hoping to raise volunteers before marching inland; the de Vere family estates were not far away. However he was forced to put to sea again by the rapid response of the earl of Essex. His next foray against Edward took him to St Michael's Mount in Cornwall where he and Viscount Beaumont landed on 30 September with 397 armed men. Edward sent John Fortescue to prosecute a siege. Guns were sent down under the master of the ordinance and ships were put on station to enforce a proper blockade, at the same time lenient terms were offered to de Vere's garrison. Before long men began to desert and by the time de Vere and Beaumont themselves surrendered early in February 1474 only eight or nine men remained with them. Oxford was imprisoned in Hammes Castle within the March of Calais and was not to be heard of again for a further ten years. So ended the last flicker of the Lancastrian flame. But Clarence's name became linked with Oxford's treasonable activities in the rumours of the day.[5]

Once Oxford's abortive invasion attempt had been dealt with, Edward's attention once more focused on France. He managed to convince parliament that war with France was the best way of preventing continuing interference by France in English affairs. He also had to convince the nobility, the knights and gentlemen that war was the right and proper thing to do. These men would be the backbone of any force raised to cross the Channel and they were not too keen on the prospect. Money could only come by way of parliament and opinion there relied on the support of the very people who would provide him with his fighting men and who would, by and large, be those who would be taxed to provide the money. Although he failed to rouse the country, Edward did, eventually, raise the money for an expedition.

In November 1472 the lords agreed a special tax of their income from land and other sources of one tenth[i] and the commons agreed a similar tax from non-aristocratic income to pay the wages of 13,000 archers for one year, a sum estimated at £118,625.[6] However this money was to be reimbursed to taxpayers if the army had not been mustered by 27 September 1474, a proviso presumably made as a result of the grant made to Edward in 1468 for war with France, which did not happen, and which he kept. Parliament laid down complicated rules for the collection and retention of this tax, requiring Edward's officers to show that indentures had been drawn up before funds could be released. In April 1473 the lords confirmed their grant and allowed it to be paid into the exchequer; this realized the paltry sum of £2,461 3s 4d, a very unlikely one tenth portion of all aristocratic income from land in one year.

By the time parliament met in July 1474 it was revealed that the sum of £31,410 13s 1½d had been collected from the original levy on incomes, but as yet nothing had been handed to the king's exchequer. However it was expected that a further £62,094 0s 4d would be forthcoming from the tenths and fifteenths agreed in 1473. This made a

---

i This was unusual, normally a tax of a tenth or a fifteenth was on the value of 'moveables', or property excluding land.

shortfall of £22,659 3s 2½d against the original estimate for the service of 13,000 archers for one year. The king, realizing that the money collected would not pay even for the number of archers enlisted, asked parliament to make up the balance, a further £5,147 3s 7½d,[7] presumably because the figure of 13,000 archers was unobtainable and he had to settle for less. Indeed the actual final figure for the archers for the French expedition totalled 10,173 according to the tellers' rolls.[8]

By January 1475 no money had been passed from parliament to the exchequer, apart from the Lords' contribution. Parliament was already four months behind its own deadline for the muster of the army. The bureaucracy didn't seem to understand that the muster wouldn't take place because contracts of service would not be signed without some money up front; this applied all through the ranks of the army from the nobleman to the archer. Contracts were for one year's service from the date of signing and the first quarter's wages were usually paid within a month of the signing; if this was an unlikely event then individuals would not sign. However parliament suddenly woke up and realized that without money the muster was an unlikely event. They released what money had been collected and additionally on 15 March granted a one and one-third fifteenths and tenths to raise the outstanding amount needed, estimated at a further £51,147 7s 7½d. This was more than was needed to pay the archers alone so presumably the extra, a sum of just over £33,635 8s, was available to pay for men-at-arms, artillery and gunners, or for the various extras such as carpenters, miners, surgeons and others. Nevertheless the king still had insufficient finance with which to pay his army and for its administration. He therefore bullied and pleaded with his richer subjects to donate money for his expedition in what became known as 'The First Benevolence.'[9] This took the form, in London, of putting all people with an income of £10 annually or more, or who had personal property valued at more than £100, in front of Edward's commissioners.[10] They would then be bullied into contributing to the king's war fund; no doubt similar scenes took place all over the country. In due course Edward got the money he needed.

In the end, 10,173 archers were mustered as well as 1,278 men-at-arms and 192 contingent leaders. A further 387 artisans of one sort or another were also recruited.[11] The whole including elements of the households of the king and the nobles probably amounted to about 13,000 men, all of whom had to be transported across the Channel together with as many as 15,000 horses, plus guns, wagons and various military stores. It had been difficult to recruit the necessary number of men-at-arms, still the backbone around which armies grouped for battle. The proportion of archers to men-at-arms was nearly 8:1 compared with the ideal of 3:1. One of the noblemen who joined this expedition was Henry Percy, earl of Northumberland, who at that time had recently been reappointed to the wardenship of the East March.[12] He was able to leave following a treaty with Scotland that was signed on 30 July 1474. His inclusion in the expedition also shows that the north of England must have been reasonably happy with Edward's rule.

The expedition mustered in June 1475 at Dover and set sail for Calais early in July, escorted by warships with 3,000 archers on board. There might have been twenty or more ships fitted out as warships, no doubt carrying early ships' cannon, but with the fire-power of the archers they would have been formidable adversaries should any French ship have decided to interfere with the crossing. Henry V transported his invasion force to Normandy in 1415 from Southampton in 1,500 ships, but nothing like this number were required this time for the much shorter crossing from Dover to Calais. Since the army was being transported to a safe and friendly port it was carried out over a period of several days and the arrested ships might have made several crossings, consequently it is unlikely that more than 500 ships were involved. Also, by this date, fifty years later, ships were already bigger, could take more cargo in their holds and with more deck space could carry more men and horses.

This was a very well organized and equipped expedition and was larger than anything that Henry V took to France, but it lacked experienced leaders. Commynes commentated[13] that this was an army without experience, certainly in warfare on the Continent; but then, to a lesser extent, that of France was also inexperienced. Nevertheless it was enough to frighten Louis. After a sojourn of about a month in Calais Edward finally got his army on the march and advanced into Artois. The French army was not far away at Amiens and at this point Louis sent ambassadors to Edward to explore peace terms. Edward agreed to meet Louis to discuss their differences.

The meeting took place on a bridge across the Somme at Picquigny near Amiens, at which Louis agreed to buy Edward off with a payment of 75,000 gold crowns to meet his expenses, together with an annual pension of a further 50,000 crowns. The treaty of Picquigny, signed on 29 August 1475, also provided for the withdrawal of Edward's army and a ten-year truce, furthermore the two kings agreed that the Dauphin, Charles, should marry Elizabeth, one of Edward's daughters. According to Commynes, after the treaty was signed Louis invited the English army to Amiens as his guests; many took up his invitation and drank themselves insensible. So ended Edward's war with France. Presumably the down payment and the annual pension went into Edward's coffers because nothing was ever repaid to the taxpayers, though he did remit three quarters of the amount allotted by parliament but not yet collected.[14] From a financial point of view the problems of paying for war across the Channel put the king very firmly in the hands of parliament and this made it essential that the king and his advisers advocated a cast-iron case for the need for war. In this case the king had to cajole and persuade in order to raise the money because enthusiasm for the war did not exist, as a result of which propaganda became a necessary tool of government.

Edward, in treating with Louis, had been politically pragmatic. He wasn't fit enough to lead an army in the field, he was fat and dissolute, and was no longer the powerful young man who had fought so valiantly in the hand-to-hand fighting at Towton fourteen years before. Furthermore his army, although both well equipped and provided, was not the disciplined and experienced army that Henry V had commanded. Also the military power of Burgundy was deployed elsewhere and France was no longer the divided country that had opposed Henry. Finally the country at home was unenthusiastic about war with France – perhaps they could see an unending war ahead without much profit. As to Burgundy, Duke Charles was more than a little annoyed at the treaty concluded by his brother-in-law with his enemy Louis. Charles felt he had been let down, and did not acknowledge that his own failure to keep his promise of military assistance to Edward was a prime reason for Edward's accommodation with Louis. It meant that from now on Burgundy would have to deal with France by itself and Charles recognized that without the threat of English intervention he was not powerful enough to take on France single-handed. Louis, a clever politician, had really been the winner; as he boasted to Commynes: 'I kicked the English out of France much more easily than did my father – he had to do it by force of arms but I used venison pies and good wine!'[15] Perhaps Edward was a winner too – he had refilled his coffers and appeared to have earned a useful income. But the income was not as assured as it seemed. According to Polydore Vergil, Louis:

> began almost openly to deny payment of the money which he had promised; and so by wrangling and shifting, had already defrauded the king of England of one years trybute, which the king determined to revenge by dint of the sword.[16]

On his return to England Edward heard of the loss of his former brother-in-law, the duke of Exeter. Exeter had fought against Edward at the Battle of Barnet where he was wounded, but escaped to sanctuary at Westminster Abbey. Later Edward had him taken to the Tower. It seems that Exeter had either volunteered to go on the French expedition or was forced to. He fell overboard and was conveniently drowned on the journey home. According to the Milanese envoy to the Burgundian court of Duke Charles, Edward had given specific orders to the sailors to throw his brother-in-law overboard.[17]

The Yorkist dynasty was now firmly established: Edward had two brothers and two sons. The royal estates, under his astute management, were providing a proper income for the royal household and Edward was at last solvent, the first English king to be so for many generations. Law and order were being imposed fairly throughout the land. Abroad, Edward had truces with both France and Scotland, and his sister, Margaret, was married to Charles of Burgundy. Matters should have been set fair for a period of peaceful prosperity. However the Yorkist dynasty was not as stable as it might seem.

Clarence's name was frequently linked by rumour with various treasonable activities, added to which he failed to maintain law and order within his own lands, and violently breached the law twice in April 1477. On one occasion he abducted one of his wife's former attendants and had her taken across four counties to his home base of Warwick to be tried by magistrates under threat for poisoning his wife. She was found guilty and hanged, all in the space of three hours. Clarence's wife Annabel had actually died six weeks after giving birth to her third child.[18] Shortly after this Clarence burst into the royal council chamber in Westminster declaring the innocence of two men who had been tried and found guilty of witchcraft against Edward, one of whom was a member of Clarence's own household. This was too much for Edward who ordered Clarence to come before him at Westminster where he publicly denounced him; three weeks later, in June, Clarence was arrested. He was finally attainted and died while under arrest in 1478, drowned in a butt of Malmsey wine,[19] almost certainly on the orders of his brother Edward.

It will be remembered that the Treaty of Picquigny not only stipulated that a pension should be paid to Edward but also that Edward's daughter Elizabeth was to be betrothed to the Dauphin. Not only did Louis fail to pay his debts but he also failed to keep his promise regarding Elizabeth. In 1482 Mary of Burgundy was killed in a riding accident and her young sister became the heir to the duchy of Burgundy. Senior politicians in Burgundy, despairing of Maximillian's support against France, decided to placate France and turned to Louis instead. He reacted quickly and the Treaty of Arras was soon signed and sealed with the betrothal of the infant heiress to the Dauphin. Edward thus lost this diplomatic battle as well as his pension and the hope of family alliance between England and France. From England's point of view this was an unfortunate event that would ultimately give France both Flanders and Artois, and upset the wool trade. France would also be able to close up to the Calais pale and extend her control over the coast all the way from Boulogne to Dunkerque.

At about this time attention shifted to Scotland where James III, through ambassadors had betrothed his son, James, to Edward's younger daughter Cecily, presumably in an effort to consolidate the truce between the two countries. But after Louis broke his promise to Edward concerning Elizabeth and had concluded the treaty of Arras, James, with Louis' encouragement, broke his truce with Edward and allowed cross-border raids to start again. Edward's response was to send a naval raid up the Firth of Forth in 1481 but, encouraged by James's brother, Alexander, duke of Albany, who was in exile at Edward's court, he ordered his brother, Richard, duke of Gloucester, to lead an expedition across the border into Scotland in 1482. Apart from humbling the Scots the aim of the expedition was to put Albany on the throne, and by agreement with him take Berwick and a slice of Scottish land back into the realm of England. Richard marched north burning and pillaging as he went. Edinburgh was then taken and

James captured, but Richard, seeing that not a man had come to join the duke of Albany,[20] opened negotiations with his prisoner and after arranging a truce marched south to the border. Lord Stanley meanwhile had managed to take Berwick after a short siege and so the town reverted once more to the crown of England. As Christine Carpenter says: 'the return of Berwick was militarily and psychologically significant' and for the first time for many years the north of England felt secure from the Scots.[21]

The house of York reigned supreme when on 9 April 1483 Edward died after a short illness. He was only forty-one years old and apparently died from a cold, or perhaps pneumonia, after fishing. He recovered sufficiently in the middle of his illness to make a new will and to arrange for the care and succession of his son Edward. He left what was to all intents and purposes a secure and financially independent monarchy, with a nobility and a landed class who may not have liked him but nevertheless respected and accepted him. Edward V was a boy of twelve when his father died and was in the care of Anthony Wydeville, Earl Rivers, his maternal uncle and guardian at Ludlow; Edward's brother Richard, duke of York, and his sisters were with the queen at the Tower. Richard, duke of Gloucester, who had been nominated as protector by Edward before he died, was at Middleham in Yorkshire. Sir Thomas Grey, marquis of Dorset, and the queen's eldest son by her first marriage to Sir John Grey, who had died in 1461, held the Tower of London. Lord Hastings, the captain of Calais, was also in London. In addition to these another player was at hand, Henry Stafford, duke of Buckingham. Buckingham was married unhappily to the queen's sister and was another remote claimant to the throne, being the senior candidate from Thomas of Woodstock's line, Edward III's youngest son. He was another very wealthy man having received half the Bohun inheritance, but he was also an ambitious man. He had been prevented by Edward IV from taking up certain official appointments, mainly in Wales and on the March, and was resentful of the Wydevilles and their influence at court, considering them upstarts. The scene was set for the dramatic events of the next few weeks.

Edward IV had appointed a minority council to rule in his son's name and, following precedent, named Richard of Gloucester as protector and chairman of this council. The council soon had its first meeting at which it was decided that Edward V's coronation should

be held on 4 May and that he should be brought to London for it
beforehand. Gloucester was still at Middleham and so was not
present at this meeting but once Hastings informed him of the coronation date, he hurried south with several hundred armed men.
Buckingham got in touch with Gloucester, and they agreed to meet at
Northampton. It was here that Richard hatched his plot to usurp the
crown.[22] He was a ruthless man and one of his characteristics during
the following eight weeks was his total unpredictability – he caught
everyone unawares.

It should be realized that the Queen's family, the Wydevilles, were a
greedy and grasping lot who had taken full advantage of Elizabeth
Wydeville's position as queen to advance themselves socially and to
increase their political power; they were actively disliked by many of
the established nobility. Gloucester and Buckingham were afraid that
the Wydevilles would influence the boy king against them and others
if he remained under the guardianship of Earl Rivers. It seemed to
them that the king had to be taken from the protection of the
Wydevilles to prevent him and the minority council from being dominated and controlled by them. Hastings on the other hand had always
been a loyal supporter of Edward IV and a close friend, and while he
disliked the Wydevilles his loyalty was now given wholeheartedly to
the boy king Edward V.

Hastings made the first move; he realized that if Earl Rivers arrived
in London with the king and a large escort while Dorset held the
Tower the Wydevilles would dominate the council. Consequently he
managed to persuade Rivers to come with a relatively small escort for
the king, less than 2,000 armed men. Rivers did as he was bid and left
Ludlow with the boy king to take him to London for his coronation.
When they reached Stony Stratford, Rivers heard that Richard was 14
miles away near Northampton. Rivers and his nephew, Sir Richard
Grey, left the king in the charge of their retinue and rode the few miles
north to greet Richard. They all had a convivial evening together but
the next morning, 30 April, quite unexpectedly Rivers and his nephew
were arrested. Richard then dismissed Rivers' escort and escorted
Edward V to London with his own men; they arrived on 4 May.

However, news of Rivers' fate reached the queen that same night,
30 April. Fearing for her life and that of her children she quickly took
her son, Richard, Duke of York and her other children to sanctuary at
Westminster. She was joined there later by her eldest son, Dorset,

from the Tower. Once in London Richard of Gloucester assumed his responsibilities as protector and, as chairman of the minority council, he set a new date of 22 June for Edward's coronation. On 13 June at a council meeting held in the Tower, Richard suddenly accused Hastings of treason and without more ado had him seized and executed without trial, not even allowing him time to confess his sins. This was murder and gave the first hint to others that Richard had his eye on the throne; furthermore he could not legally have accused Hastings of treason since that crime could only be enacted against the sovereign, and Richard was merely the protector.

Edward V on arriving in London had been lodged at the Tower, a perfectly proper place for him to be as the Tower was a royal palace as well as an arsenal and a prison. However, this took him away from his mother and out of the reach of the Wydevilles. If Richard had indeed already embarked on his plan to usurp the crown, Edward's brother Richard, duke of York, also stood in the way and he was in sanctuary with his mother. Richard of Gloucester was only fourth in line to the throne, the third being Clarence's infant son. Clearly Richard had to extract his nephew from the queen's protection in sanctuary at Westminster if he wished to usurp the crown.

Richard made the plausible excuse that the duke of York should be with his brother before the coronation in his plea with the queen to release him from sanctuary at Westminster on 16 June, but he backed it up with armed force by surrounding the abbey with his men. Knowing that she could not prevent Gloucester from taking her son by force she reluctantly gave Richard of York into Gloucester's doubtful care; Dorset managed to escape. The following day Richard of Gloucester cancelled the parliament that was due to meet after the coronation. It was then put about that Edward V and the duke of York were bastards on the grounds that Edward IV had been pre-contracted in marriage before his marriage to Elizabeth Wydeville[23] and were therefore not legitimate candidates for the throne. However, as there were no witnesses to the contract as required by law, this development was received with some scepticism and in any event this was a matter for an ecclesiastical court to decide, which Richard failed to convene. Ignoring Clarence's son's prior claim to the throne Richard of Gloucester then had his claim to the throne first announced in London on 22 June. Three days later Earl Rivers, his nephew Sir Richard Grey, Sir Thomas Vaughan, the king's chamberlain, and Sir Richard Haute were executed at Pontefract Castle on Richard's orders without trial or lawful charge. Nothing more was heard or seen of Edward V or the duke of York.[24] The only other obstacle to his claim lay in the person of Clarence's son, the earl of Warwick, aged eight. Richard claimed that as his father Clarence had been declared a traitor and was attainted by Edward IV, his son had no legitimate claim on the crown, and anyway he was already in Richard's care. The way was now clear for Richard's coup. On 26 June Buckingham led a delegation of some of the nobility to Richard to beg him to take the throne, which he was pleased to do, but there was one thing left to be done to make his case cast iron.

Richard might have reached this point by his own efforts and machinations but there can be little doubt that he was encouraged and supported by Buckingham, who had most to gain by the downfall of both the Wydevilles and Lord Hastings. Richard had to show that he had a legitimate claim to the throne to make his case watertight. To this end he arranged to have a noted preacher, Dr Ralph Shaw, declare at St Paul's that the late king, Edward IV, was also a bastard. He claimed that the duke of York, who had been killed at the Battle of Wakefield, had not fathered his brother Edward IV and that their mother had committed adultery. His evidence rested entirely on his similarity to his father, both of whom were dark and small. Edward IV in contrast was tall and fair, as were his sons, bastards all! Ralph Shaw may not have believed what he preached but he was under threat, and Richard was present at the time with many of his armed men. Richard then commanded the judges and magistrates of the city, together with the mayor and aldermen, to assemble in the Old Hall where Buckingham, accompanied by other nobles, convinced them, under threat, of the truth of Richard's claims. Richard had written to Lord Neville earlier in June asking him to ride to London with his affinity. By 21 June it was reported by Simon Stallworth in a letter that 20,000 of the lord protector's and Buckingham's men were in London.[25] This number is unlikely but certainly a large number of Richard's armed supporters were in London at that time; indeed by the time of Richard's coronation the earl of Northumberland and his armed following were also in London. The next day Richard, dressed regally and accompanied by Buckingham and others with a considerable armed escort, rode through the city to Westminster where he claimed the throne. He was crowned King Richard III on 6 July 1483.

So Richard's usurpation was complete and he now faced the usual problems of kingship in the Middle Ages, maintaining even-handed relations with his nobles and providing law and order throughout the land. He set about this with determination and not a little success, but a throne achieved by force and treachery, and bought by gifts of land and position, is not one established on firm ground. Before long murmuring against Richard was to be heard in various quarters and, more worryingly, the name of Henry Tudor was heard as a possible replacement. Among those rewarded by Richard, apart from Buckingham, was Lord Howard, who became the duke of Norfolk, and the Stanley brothers, Thomas Lord Stanley and Sir William. However, Lord Stanley was married to Margaret Beaufort, Henry Tudor's mother, and this itself would always make him an unreliable supporter. Margaret Beaufort meanwhile had been in touch with Queen Elizabeth, still in sanctuary at Westminster. They had agreed that a marriage between Margaret's son, Henry Tudor, and Edward's eldest daughter, Elizabeth of York would be a politically astute move after Henry had taken the crown, and they resolved to pursue the idea secretly.[26]

At about this time Richard made his nine-year-old son, Edward, the prince of Wales, but unfortunately he died three months later, a tragedy that was seen as divine justice, but more importantly it left Richard without an heir. However, the first crack in Richard's support came from Buckingham. He had been well rewarded after Richard's coup, receiving much of Lord Hastings's land holdings and many of his official positions, particularly those in Wales and along the March, but it seems his greed was insatiable – he wanted more and Richard had no more to give. It is of course conceivable that Buckingham realized that the princes had been murdered by Richard since they had never been seen in public even though Richard might have benefited from showing them.[27] In these circumstances Richard would only have had to deal with possible support for the princes who had been declared bastards and were therefore not eligible to wear the crown. Buckingham might have encouraged Richard to take the crown to provide firm kingship rather than the minority rule, which would otherwise have been the case. After Edward V's declared illegitimacy the way was clear for Richard to seize the crown anyway without murdering the princes, an act which Buckingham may never have contemplated. It is quite possible that Buckingham thought that he might be able to take the throne himself or that he would be better off if he supported Henry Tudor's claims, but whatever his reasons, and they are not known, he decided to lead a rebellion against Richard in October 1483. As Christine Carpenter points out,[28] this was in no sense a rebellion of a particular geographic area, but rather was it one supported by Edward IV's former household and it took root in the south of the country. It had two political effects: it made Richard realize that he could no longer rely on the old bureaucratic hierarchy set up by his brother; and it made Henry Tudor a recognizable alternative as king, since it appears that the aim of the rebellion was to replace Richard by Henry. Buckingham failed to gain support from Wales or the Marches and significantly failed to gain the support of the Stanleys, notwithstanding the fact that Lord Stanley was related to Henry Tudor by marriage. Lord Stanley, Richard's steward of the household, was well rewarded for his loyalty, being granted his wife's forfeited estates.

Buckingham's rebellion was due to start sometime in the middle of October with simultaneous uprisings in Kent, Wiltshire, Berkshire and Devon. Meanwhile Buckingham himself was to lead a force from his castle at Brecon and march down the Marches gathering men from Wales as he went to meet up with those mustered at Exeter, Salisbury and Newbury. The Kentish men were to muster at Maidstone and threaten London. To muster such a disparate army at any time would have been difficult, but in the fifteenth century well nigh impossible to do with any precision. Be that as it may, Richard heard rumours of the uprising and had them confirmed from captured messages from Brecon to the other leaders and to Brittany, where Henry Tudor lay waiting for the off, backed by Duke Francis. Richard meanwhile had not been idle, he had confirmation of the revolt on 10 October when at Lincoln and he immediately sent out commissions of array to summon an army to muster at Leicester on 25 October. He also had it proclaimed that there would be a free pardon for all yeomen and commoners who gave up their arms and dispersed; large numbers took advantage of his offer. But Richard also put a price on the heads of the leaders: for Buckingham the princely sum of £1,000, for Dorset 1,000 marks, the same for the bishops of Salisbury and Exeter, and 500 marks for captured knights.

As a consequence Buckingham's movements were closely watched and Richard was well aware of his march down the Wye valley in appalling weather. Meanwhile recruits failed to come in, rather were they deserting Buckingham's force. By the time he reached Weobley, about 9 miles north-west of Hereford, he realized the game was up. He slunk away from his camp in disguise taking refuge in the house of one of his followers, Ralph Bannister, at Wen, about 10 miles north of Shrewsbury, but was handed over to the sheriff. Richard III moved to Coventry where he was joined by the Stanley and Percy contingents and by about 24 October he must have received news of Buckingham's capture. He marched south to Salisbury, entering it unopposed at the end of the month and there on 2 November he had Buckingham executed for treason. He then turned west for Exeter, where once again rebel forces had evaporated. He was back in London by 25 November having thoroughly extinguished Buckingham's rebellion. The Kentish force failed to materialize.

Buckingham had clearly been premature in his uprising, other important magnates were not yet ready to take the plunge, if indeed they had made up their minds, particularly the Stanleys and the Percys from the North Midlands and the North. These were the families who had profited most from Richard's usurpation. Henry Tudor crossed the Channel with a force reputed to be 5,000 strong in fifteen ships all paid for by a loan from Duke Francis in support of the rebellion. But when he discovered what had happened to Buckingham and his rebellion, having arrived off Plymouth, he wisely put to sea again for France. Henry Tudor's time had not yet come.

During 1484 events in England were largely dictated by events in France and Brittany. Duke Francis still held the whip hand, Henry Tudor was his prisoner in the loosest sense and a valuable prisoner too. Francis had to decide whether it was more advantageous for him to accede to Richard's plea to give Henry up or to support him. Richard did his best to pressurize Francis to give up his prisoner. Meanwhile Louis XI died on 30 August 1483 and pressure by France on Brittany eased while the boy king Charles VIII assumed royal powers through a regency council. At the same time several of Edward IV's old supporters crossed the Channel and gave their allegiance to Henry; these included Sir Edward Wydeville, the earl of Dorset and Bishop Courtenay.

This encouraged Henry, no doubt under the influence of his mother Margaret Beaufort, to declare in the cathedral at Rennes on Christmas Day 1483 that he would marry Elizabeth of York once he was king; it also made Henry a rather more important card in Duke

Francis' hand. However, relations between Richard and Francis were patched up and Henry saw in this rapprochement a threat to his continuing sanctuary at the Breton court; he also got wind of a conspiracy to arrest him and hand him over to Richard. He realized the danger he was in and made good his escape to France.

From now on nothing seemed to go Richard's way. The first blow was the escape of John de Vere, earl of Oxford, from Hammes Castle in the Calais pale where he had been held a prisoner since his abortive rebellion at St Michael's Mount ten years previously. John de Vere made his way to Montargis and joined Henry there at the French court. Next, the captain of Hammes Castle, James Blount, defected together with John Fortescue, who held an important office in Calais itself. Blount's wife then held the castle at Hammes in Henry's name. These defections to Henry put the loyalty of the Calais garrison under suspicion and Richard appointed the reliable Sir James Tyrell as deputy in command for John his bastard son.

In March 1485 Anne Neville, Richard's wife, died leaving him open to damaging rumours that he had poisoned her and that he intended to marry his niece Elizabeth of York. These rumours were particularly harmful because Richard had inherited the Neville lands in the north through his marriage to Anne. Richard was getting uneasy and fearful so moved to Nottingham to be nearer his own power base and to be in the centre of the country so as to be able, more easily, to face any threat, from whichever direction it might come. He abandoned London as he clearly felt unsafe there.

Henry meanwhile, hearing of Richard's military preparations and the rumours of Richard's intentions towards Elizabeth of York, realized that if either or both were true he would have to make his bid for the crown soon or abandon it altogether. The longer Henry waited the stronger Richard would get. Henry now had both Yorkists and Lancastrians in his following and crucially he at last got financial support from the French government. He moved to Rouen in the spring of 1485 and began the business of hiring ships and fitting them out for war. Richard countered by sending his fleet to sea to patrol the Channel and appointed Viscount Lovell to take charge of the defence of the south coast. While these moves and counter-moves were taking place Henry sent out his spies to discover the lie of the land at home. He discovered that the Stanleys would definitely support him and that the earl of Northumberland would be an unenthusiastic supporter of

Richard and at best neutral. He discovered that south Wales, where Sir William Stanley, Lord Stanley's brother, held office was a possible entry-point for his bid for the crown, also of course it was the home ground of his uncle the earl of Pembroke. He received assurances of support from others among whom importantly was Sir Rhys ap Thomas. It is probable that the latter's promise of support finally convinced Henry to land in south Wales.

Henry set sail from Honfleur at the mouth of the Seine on 1 August 1485 in a fleet commanded by the French admiral Guillaume de Casenove and sailed down Channel for Wales. His fleet was not spotted or intercepted by the English fleet; again it must be stressed that it was almost impossible in those days for ships of a fleet to remain on station. The fleet arrived at Milford Haven, where Henry landed, on 8 August. Henry's invasion army was small; it included his own followers and some Norman troops supplied by France, in all, according to Polydore Vergil, some 2,000 men. This was a pitifully small number with which to grab a kingdom, particularly one on the alert and armed; Henry desperately needed volunteers to join his banner. In his first three days on Welsh soil very few came to join him and then he heard that Sir Rhys ap Thomas and Sir John Savage were actually getting ready to bar his path, contrary to indications he had received previously. However Pembroke sent a troop of armed men to join him, which was comforting. Nevertheless morale in his small band was very low.

Henry countered by sending messages to Sir Rhys ap Thomas to promise him the lieutenancy of Wales once he was king if he would support him now. The bribe worked and morale steadied. Henry let it be known that he was on his way to Shrewsbury and Sir Thomas joined him en route 'with a great band of soldiers'. At Shrewsbury money and messages of support came in but of more immediate importance so did some reinforcements for his small army, when Sir Gilbert Talbot rode in with 500 men at Newport, about 16 miles east of Shrewsbury. Sir William Stanley also rode in but only accompanied by a small troop and they left soon after. The Stanleys had a problem. A few days before Henry Tudor's landing Lord Stanley had asked permission to leave the court and Richard had granted this on condition that Lord Stanley left his son, Lord Strange, behind as a hostage. Once Richard heard of Henry's landing, four or five days later he summoned Lord Stanley back to court, the latter failed to answer the summons pleading sickness, but clearly if the Stanley's moved too soon Lord Strange would pay with his life. No doubt Sir William Stanley's brief meeting with Henry was to explain their difficulty and that therefore any help they could give would have to be at the last moment. It seems he pledged their support but were reluctant to be seen to join forces; he did however promise a further meeting after he had seen his brother.

As soon as he heard of Henry's landing Richard sent out summons for the array of fencible men and called for a muster of his army at Leicester. He hoped that sizeable contingents would arrive under commissions of array in addition to the retinues of the earl of Northumberland, the duke of Norfolk and possibly that of Lord Stanley. Richard also sent letters of array to many prominent families ordering them to join him at Nottingham 'upon pain of forfeiture unto us of all that ye may forfeit and lose', as he said in a letter to the Vernon family. As a result of his commissions and his threats Richard hoped for an army of perhaps 20,000 men if everyone remained loyal and arrived in time. But some contingents had a long way to go to get to the muster. Northumberland had perhaps 140 miles to go after gathering his forces from a wide area, Norfolk had at least 80 miles to go while contingents from London and the south would have had to travel much the same distance; it would take several days for this army to muster.

If it is assumed that orders were sent out as soon as Richard heard of Henry's landing then they would have been sent out on or about 12 or 13 August. Those farthest away, such as the earl of Northumberland, would not have received these orders until 15 or 16 August after hard riding by the messengers. It is unlikely therefore that the earl's forces could have reached the muster before 20 or 21 August. Norfolk had mustered his own forces on 16 August at Bury St Edmunds and would therefore have arrived at Leicester on 19 August. Richard's household knights came up from London under Sir Robert Brackenbury, the constable of the Tower, and would have arrived at about the same time. Consequently Richard's army would have assembled at Leicester on or by 21 August, and the longer he waited there the larger his army would become, providing his summons was answered.

One prominent person who did not answer the call from his lord and master was Sir John Paston who disregarded an entreaty from the duke of Norfolk, and no doubt there were others. Lord Stanley, however, had no inhibitions. He intended to be on the winning side, whichever it was. He gathered his men and marched not to Leicester but to Atherstone, about 16 miles to the south-west. Lord Stanley was being very careful; he could easily claim he was en route to join Richard, but he could just as easily join Henry. Henry rode off to rejoin his army at Lichfield on Friday 19 August and Sir William Stanley rode to join his own troops at Stone. The next day Sir William made a forced march of about 38 miles to join up with his brother, Lord Stanley, at Ratcliffe Culey a mile north of Atherstone. Henry also marched that day in the same direction and made camp at Whitemoors, between Shenton and Stoke Golding, about 4 miles east of Atherstone. Henry had a little over 5,000 men with him including by now many deserters from Richard's army and cause; the Stanleys had between them about 6,000. By itself Henry's army was much too small to face Richard's 12,000 men or more, and would simply be swept away, but in combination with the Stanleys he had a fighting chance of winning the day when battle commenced. The 21st was spent with another meeting between Henry, Sir William and Lord Stanley, but once again although pledging support they refused to join forces at that time. After this meeting the Stanleys marched their combined force in the night to the high ground south of the hamlet of Near Coton. From his position Lord Stanley might have seen Richard's camp on the high ground near Sutton Cheney, about a mile away to the south, and Henry's camp on the Whitemoors about 2 miles away to the south-west. Lord Stanley had positioned himself very cleverly: he was in a position to come to the aid of either side, at the same time he could not yet be deemed a traitor by either Richard or Henry, yet his intervention, if it came, would be decisive. That evening Sir John Savage, one of the Stanley faction, marched in to Henry's camp with his following. Battle the next day was now inevitable.

It should be stressed that, other than Polydore Vergil's account written perhaps twenty years later but based on eyewitness statements, the Battle of Bosworth is very poorly documented. Slim archaeological evidence exists but no one knows exactly where the various forces took up their battle stations. Furthermore the marsh referred to by Polydore Vergil no longer exists. Its position can be surmised from two streams, unfortunately one runs from east to west north of the probable battlefield and the other in the same direction but to the south of the battlefield. Therefore the marsh could have been either to the north of Ambion Hill or to the south of it, but was probably at the junction of the two streams. As a further complicating point the exact camp locations of the three forces are not known. Three possibilities exist and each has its adherents. Everyone seems to agree that King Richard camped for the night of 21 August at or near Sutton Cheney and that Henry Tudor camped at Whitemoors about 2½ miles away to the west. A spur of high ground runs west from Sutton Cheney, which then slopes down towards the junction of the two streams; the ground rises again on the west side of the streams to Whitemoors, a few hundred yards away. All of this can be seen today.

The problem arises with the Stanley contingent. Some have it to the south of Ambion Hill, the high ground running west from Sutton Cheney, some split it into two with Lord Stanley to the north and Sir William to the south, and some have it to the north of Ambion Hill. It is militarily unlikely that a force of 6,000 men would have been split into two, making neither a decisive force and making each vulnerable to attack. Furthermore, such a split would have put one of the two behind the marsh, so this possibility is discounted. As to whether the Stanleys camped to the north or the south of Ambion Hill, this would have depended on the position of the marsh, however it is thought that they marched to a position to the north of Ambion Hill after their meeting with Henry on 21 August. If they had marched to the south they would have had to cross Henry's own line of march, an unlikely event in the dark. Furthermore the Stanleys would certainly not have positioned themselves so that Richard's army lay across their lines of communication to their home area in the North-West Midlands. Therefore it is probable that the Stanleys camped to the north of Ambion Hill and, because they would not have wanted to cross the marsh to deploy, the marsh must have been to the south-west of Ambion Hill.

Both sides broke camp early on 23 August and everyone knew that a battle was imminent. It is unlikely that any of the commanders had viewed the probable battlefield the day before and so they relied on their scouts to brief them as to the topography and the position of the enemy. Richard's scouts clearly briefed him well because Richard's army moved quickly to establish themselves on the high dominating ground of Ambion Hill before Henry's army, or indeed that of the Stanleys could get there. Henry's army had a slightly longer distance to go and had to cross a stream and then march up the hill. They also had to avoid the marsh by marching round it to the north-west, as it was said 'with the sun on their backs', but the marsh protected their flank as they wheeled right into line to face Richard's army. By the time Henry's advance guard under John de Vere, earl of Oxford, could see their way to the top of Ambion Hill Richard's advance guard under the duke of Norfolk was already in possession of the hill and spread out in line along the top of it. Once again it can be seen that good scouts and local intelligence were crucial to armies of the day. They ensured that armies not only met for battle but also avoided each other when they were not ready. They were also essential in deciding the layout of an army and its exact position. Richard's scouts served him well, but the Stanleys clearly had very good local intelligence and probably good scouts too; Henry was not so fortunate in either sense. Richard commanded the main guard of his army drawn up behind Norfolk with the earl of Northumberland and his forces behind him and facing north to protect Richard's main guard from attack in the flank by the Stanleys should they decide to take Henry's side. Henry's army was so small that it didn't really have a mainguard and a rearguard; Henry himself commanded a small mounted force that took up position behind Oxford. Sir Gilbert Talbot was on Oxford's right flank with his small band and Sir John Savage with his contingent on the left. Henry placed Oxford, an experienced soldier, in command of his army, but Richard, an experienced soldier himself, retained command and had both Norfolk and Northumberland, both capable commanders, to support him. The Stanleys, led by the troops of Sir William, marched south to the high ground astride the Shenton to Market Bosworth road and about half a mile north of Ambion Hill.

The three forces were now on their start lines and each could see the other. Henry must have been daunted by the task confronting him: he commanded the smaller army, and faced one on dominating ground. He had now to either abandon his quest altogether or attack the superior army on the high ground above him. If he gave up now he knew he would be hunted down relentlessly; there was really only one course open to him – he had to hazard everything in an attack on Richard's army up the hill. But first before giving the order to advance he sent a herald over to the Stanleys requesting that Sir William join him and take station on the left of his line. He received a pretty brusque reply to the effect that he should put his own troops in order first and that they would then join him at an appropriate time; Henry, realizing that he would not get any firmer promise of support, gave the orders to prepare to advance. Lord Stanley's mind was not yet made up; his son Lord Strange was still held by Richard. Indeed Lord Strange had earlier tried to escape but on recapture confessed to the treason of his uncle but not to any on the part of his father. Sir William was then declared a traitor and must somehow have known about it before the battle because he showed none of his brother's diffidence about declaring his hand. He advanced his own 3,000 mounted men and many of his brother's troops to a pivotal position to the right of Richard's position and to the left of Henry's, but between the two and probably no more than 200 yards away. Richard probably thought the Stanleys in their original position were going to support him, but couldn't be sure, however when he saw Sir William's men move to their ambivalent position his mind was made up and he gave the order for Lord Strange's execution. Luckily for Lord Strange the order was not carried out either due to the haste and confusion of battle or to disloyalty.

The royal army opened proceedings by firing at Oxford's line with both artillery and archers. Oxford, realizing that he could be defeated at a distance concentrated his division for an advance up the hill; the sooner they closed for the hand-to-hand struggle under the covering fire of his own archers and cannon the better. Both sides had artillery;[ii] Sir Robert Brackenbury would have brought Richard's guns from the Tower and Henry's guns were either French or Burgundian. However it was Richard's army that forced the issue; Norfolk ordered his line to advance and they rushed down the hill at the smaller army below. It soon closed with Oxford's line and a fierce hand-to-hand struggle ensued. But although Oxford commanded the smaller army his orders to shorten his front produced a more concentrated force to overcome. Norfolk's men would have lost cohesion in their rush downhill and meeting a very concentrated block of men tended to flow down the sides of Oxford's division leaving themselves open to attack from Oxford's two wings under Sir John Savage and Gilbert Talbot. Furthermore their own artillery and archers could not fire on

---

ii The guns of both sides were probably culverins firing a ball weighing about four pounds; they were mounted on a wheeled carriage and could be elevated and depressed.

Oxford's division once Norfolk's men began their charge; in contrast Henry's artillery and archers could continue to fire until the two armies closed, no doubt causing many casualties. Norfolk's men pulled back after the initial struggle and the two sides faced each other once again.

Henry, seeing the predicament his small army was in, galloped over towards Sir William Stanley's force, accompanied by about fifty knights, to plead with him to enter the battle on his behalf straight away. Richard saw this move from his position on the hill and recognized the banners of his enemy. He clearly decided that he could settle matters there and then by eliminating Henry with one swift charge. He was taking a risk but if he could eliminate his rival his crown would be secure. Richard, with several hundred mounted knights charged down the hill into Henry's little band, which they scattered. Richard killed Henry's standard bearer but failed to close with Henry. Once the initial charge was over the action degenerated into a series of individual fights as the mounted men milled about and Richard sought out Henry. Richard and his knights would soon have accounted for all of Henry's knights as well as Henry himself but at this point Sir William Stanley overcame his hesitation and charged Richard's mounted force in the flank. King Richard was unhorsed and died fighting on his feet; his own men were either killed or galloped away. The battle lasted about two hours and perhaps a thousand men lost their lives in the battle. The Plantagenets, whether Lancastrian or Yorkist were swept away for ever.

Northumberland, having taken no part in the battle, marched his division away to the north. Lord Stanley, reunited with his son, rode down to where Henry was and greeted him. Norfolk had been killed in the fighting with Oxford's division and his son the earl of Surrey, together with most of his division, broke off the bloody fight with Oxford's division and did their best to escape to the south. Richard's army was defeated and scattered and Henry Tudor was the victor. Richard was stripped of his armour, thrown naked over the back of a horse and taken to Newark where he was displayed for two days before Franciscan friars were allowed to take his corpse for burial. The crown circlet from Richard's helmet was found and it is said that Lord Stanley placed it on Henry's head to loud cheers from his knights and soldiers. The Tudor dynasty had begun with the crowning at Bosworth Field of King Henry VII.

Henry had been lucky in the battle and as so often before in the Wars of the Roses the outcome was settled by treachery: principally that of the Stanleys and the earl of Northumberland, but also that of Sir Rhys ap Thomas, Sir John Savage and Sir Gilbert Talbot. Clearly Richard was not trusted and once he had spent all that his brother Edward had accumulated in his treasury, and distributed the land he had seized from those he had attainted, there was nothing left with which to bribe potential supporters. Since he could no longer buy loyalty, when the opportunity came for change those who might have benefited from loyal support failed to give it. Richard was a good field commander as he had proved on his campaign in Scotland in 1482; he was also a brave man. He was clearly under pressure; perhaps he sensed disloyalty about him and took a fleeting opportunity to settle matters once and for all. He was undoubtedly over-hasty in leading the last cavalry charge of the Middle Ages – if he had shown a little more patience he would surely have won the day. He had the larger army with the most artillery and he held the dominant ground; waverers like Lord Stanley and the earl of Northumberland would probably have supported him if it looked as though he was going to win. Norfolk's division being the larger and fighting downhill would almost certainly have overcome Oxford's. Sir William Stanley's charge was a spur of the moment decision, he saw an opportunity and he took it; he could just as easily have supported his king and had he done so would no doubt have had the charge of traitor withdrawn. The lesson of the Battle of Bosworth Field is that loyalty on the battle-field is priceless.

As to Richard III, he had been a loyal and active supporter of his brother Edward IV while he was alive, and had apparently been a good uncle to his nephews. Nevertheless, when minority rule guided by the Wydevilles and Lord Hastings seemed to be the probable political future for the country, together with his own eclipse, the prospect became too much for such an ambitious man to tolerate. Once the idea of seizing the crown had taken root in his mind, possibly implanted by Buckingham, each step was taken logically and ruthlessly. He became king after executing five potential opponents, all without trial, and the murder of his two nephews. No amount of courage and capability on the battlefield can compensate for such a record. Richard III received his just deserts on the field at Bosworth.

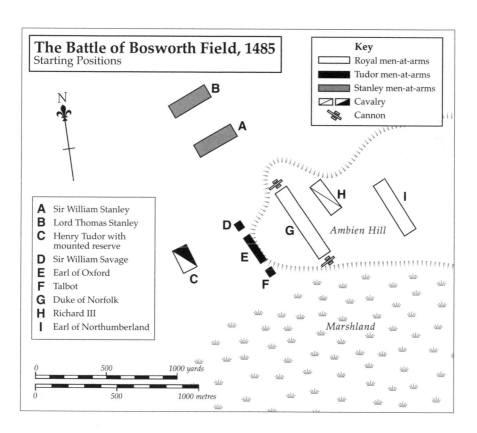

The Battle of Bosworth Field, 1485
Starting Positions

Key
Royal men-at-arms
Tudor men-at-arms
Stanley men-at-arms
Cavalry
Cannon

N

B
A
H
I
D
G
Ambien Hill
E
C
F

A Sir William Stanley
B Lord Thomas Stanley
C Henry Tudor with
   mounted reserve
D Sir William Savage
E Earl of Oxford
F Talbot
G Duke of Norfolk
H Richard III
I Earl of Northumberland

Marshland

0   500   1000 yards

0   500   1000 metres

Postscript

Although the Battle of Bosworth Field had been decisive in that it had swept away the Plantagenets for ever and inaugurated the Tudor dynasty. Henry Tudor was not as firmly on the throne as he might have wished. Inevitably there were murmurings against his rule and, although most could be ignored and overcome by good government, one particular problem could not just be brushed aside. It focused about the person of the earl of Warwick, Clarence's son, who was nine years old at the time of the Battle at Bosworth. Although his name was used, Warwick took no part in the insurrection that began early in 1487. On his accession Henry has taken the young Warwick under his protection and had at first put him under the care and tutelage of his mother, Margaret Beaufort, countess of Richmond. Later he was to be kept at the Tower of London where he was kept a prisoner until Henry VII had him executed in November 1499[1] because of his involvement with Perkin Warbeck in a plot to escape from the Tower.

During a revolt led by Lord Lovell and John Stafford in 1486, which was quickly extinguished, the old battle cry of 'A Warwick, a Warwick' was heard once again. This gave the priest Richard Simons the idea of grooming Lambert Simnel, a young lad much the same age as Warwick, to impersonate the earl. In due course he took him to Ireland where he presented him as the earl. Very soon he had convinced Sir Thomas Fitzgerald, brother of George Fitzgerald, earl of Kildare and former deputy lieutenant in Ireland, that the young 'earl', Lambert Simnel, was who he said he was. Early in the New Year Henry heard of this development and to convince doubters paraded the real earl in London. However, to the sceptical, this youth could just as easily have been an impostor as the one in Ireland and not everyone was convinced that Henry's 'Warwick' was the real one. The earl of Lincoln was not convinced. One 'Warwick' was held by Henry VII who naturally would not relinquish the crown in his favour, the other was free in Ireland ready to claim his inheritance. Why not back him and bring back a Yorkist king?

Lincoln went to Flanders and was joined there by Lovell where a plot was hatched with money and resources funded by Margaret of Burgundy, Edward IV's sister. Henry, on hearing of the growing menace to his crown, expected an invasion from Flanders in April, probably in East Anglia, reasoning that any invasion backed by Margaret would come from Flanders and would land there. But Lincoln and Lovell sailed to Dublin, having been contacted by the Fitzgeralds, to join forces with them and other backers of Lambert Simnel. They landed at Dublin on 5 May and took the pretender under their wing. On 24 May 1487 Lambert Simnel was crowned King Edward VI in Dublin. Henry meanwhile soon realized his first guess was wrong and moved to Kenilworth in late April to be in the centre of the country. From here he ordered the muster of an army at Nottingham and to await a large contingent promised by the Stanleys. Lincoln and Lovell meanwhile set out from Dublin and landed at Furness in Lancashire on 4 June. They quickly moved inland and crossed the Pennines. They had with them perhaps 2,000 German and Swiss mercenaries under the command of Martin Schwartz, paid for by Margaret, and a few thousand Irish soldiers under the command of Thomas Fitzgerald, as well as their own retinues. They expected to be joined by Lord Scrope of Bolton and Lord Scrope of Masham in Yorkshire with many Yorkshiremen; they marched rapidly south and were at Newark on 15 June. Northumberland meanwhile arrived at York with many of his followers, not to support the uprising, but to suppress it and to secure York against it. The Stanley contingent under Lord Strange arrived at the muster on 14 June, larger it was said than the whole rebel army and 'all fair embattled'. Although initially Henry appeared undecided about what to do, once his scouts brought him the definite information that the rebel force was near Newark he marched his army to Radcliffe, 14 miles away, and camped for the night. Early next morning his scouts made contact with the rebel army drawn up for battle on the east of the River Trent by East Stoke. There were said to have been between five and eight thousand of them, mainly Irish and the German mercenaries but relatively few Englishmen.

Very little is known about the ensuing battle and what is comes from Vergil's account.[2] We know that there were some 4,000 rebel casualties, mainly Irishmen who were ill-equipped to fight against Henry's army. The vanguard of the king's army, commanded by Lord

Oxford, seems to have won the battle on its own. Lincoln led the rebel army in a determined attack as soon as Oxford had deployed. Gillingham speculates that Lincoln did this because it was his only hope, the king's army being several times the size of his own, and its best chance was to attack before the royal army was ready.[3] Indeed the battle began at about nine o'clock in the morning and was over before the mainguard of Henry's army arrived at the battlefield. Lovell fled the scene but Lincoln, Schwartz, Fitzgerald and Broughton were all killed. The Scropes were soon scattered by Northumberland and never joined the main rebel force; they were imprisoned in the south and eventually released. Lambert Simnel was captured and ended his days working in the royal kitchens. The last attempt to change the king by force in the Middle Ages was over, though there would be many Yorkist intrigues to come.

The earl of Northumberland had maintained peace in the north, which was perhaps an indication that the north of England was reasonably happy with the state of affairs in England under Henry VII. After the battle Henry went on progress via York and Durham to Newcastle before turning south with a settled and peaceful country behind him. England seemed content under the firm rule of the Tudors and in the main the nobility and the gentry accepted Henry's rule, whether they had formerly favoured the Lancastrian or Yorkist claimants to the throne.

There can be little doubt that in the Middle Ages warfare had changed England but also that England had changed warfare. Plantagenet aggression in pursuit of their perceived feudal rights moulded Scotland and France into two distinct countries. The English style of warfare changed tactics and organization on the ground throughout Western Europe. The need for armed force for periods longer than forty days, and to be available for service abroad, changed the composition of armies from feudal service to contract service and eventually, in France, to regular paid service in the king's employ. The need for contract service and guaranteed financial backing increased the powers of parliament over that of the crown; it also began a crude system of national debt to cover the time lapse between parliamentary agreement to provide finance and the actual receipt of the funds agreed. The solution to this problem enhanced the power of the merchants of the city of London. The growing complexity of warfare forced improvements in government decision making and the administrative system to support it. The wars against France highlighted the need for king's ships to be always available and they in due course evolved into the Royal Navy. The fact that these existed and were needed to protect our coasts and our trade, plus the fact that the Tudor dynasty was not so concerned about its feudal rights on continental Europe, turned English eyes away from the Continent and outward across the seas.

Appendix

Short Biographies of Prominent Names

Throughout the Middle Ages certain names keep reappearing and it is easy to become confused when a particular name is repeated over many years. These names belong to royal princes, prominent noblemen and knights whose heirs continued the name and title. When a nobleman died without a male heir the title could become extinct unless a daughter passed it on to her husband. If the title became extinct the king could resurrect the title to reward faithful service. In this case the title, while being the same, would descend down through a different family. Titles belonging to noblemen who were attainted for treason usually reverted to the crown and the king might then give the title to another person who would pass it on down his own family. The names listed below occurred and reoccurred throughout the period covered in this book. Also included are some others who became prominent in their time but who were untitled.

Arundel, earl of, KG. Deputy commander of the rearguard of Edward III's army on the Crécy campaign. This division was placed to the left of the prince of Wales's division at the Battle of Crécy in 1346.

Arundel, earl of, Sir Richard Fitz-Allen. Saw service in France in 1369 and again in 1380. He took Cherbourg in 1383. Commanded the naval force that intercepted a Franco-Flemish wine convoy off Margate in 1387, took fifty prizes and 19,000 tuns of wine. He relieved Brest from siege the same year. He was a member of both Edward III's and Richard II's councils. He was a member of the continental council during Richard II's reign. He was one of the five appellant lords who fought and defeated Lord Oxford at Radcot Bridge in December 1387. He commanded the abortive expedition to Brittany in 1388. He was found guilty of treason in 1397 and executed.

Arundel, earl of, Sir Thomas Fitz-Allen. Commanded an English expeditionary force sent to aid the duke of Burgundy to raise the siege of Paris in 1411. He was involved in a quarrel over land with Talbot in 1413, which resulted in the latter being imprisoned in the Tower. He died of fever (dysentery?) at the siege of Harfleur in 1415.

Arundel, earl of (brother of Sir Thomas?). He campaigned success-fully in Maine and Anjou in 1434. He was lieutenant general for the south-west zone of Normandy answerable to the governor. He was fatally wounded on operations at the mouth of the Somme and captured in 1435.

Audley, Sir James. One of the knights detailed to advise and guard the Black Prince at Crécy in 1346. Stayed with the prince through all his later campaigns. Fought at Poitiers being one of the mounted men-at-arms in the prince's counter-attack; accepted king Jean's surrender on the prince's behalf. He was with the prince at Najero in 1366. He was killed in 1369 at the siege of La Roche sur Yon.

Audley, Lord. Commanded the Lancastrian army at Blore Heath where he lost his life in 1459.

Balliol, Sir Edward, son of Sir John Balliol (see below). Landed in Fife with a small army of Scots and English in August 1332 and defeated a Scottish army at Dupplin Moor near Perth on 12 August. He had been helped and supported by Edward III and had given his fealty to Edward before the start of his campaign. He was crowned King of Scotland at Scone on 24 September 1332. Three months later he was defeated at Annan and fled across the border. In May 1333 Edward III and Balliol besieged Berwick, which they took after the defeat of the Scottish army at Halidon Hill. Following the battle Balliol ceded the town and castle of Berwick to Edward. In June 1335 he granted the southern counties of Scotland to Edward III and shortly after he did homage to Edward III for his kingdom of Scotland, however he was again driven out of Scotland in 1342. He gave up his kingdom to Edward III in January 1356 and never again entered Scotland.

Balliol, Sir John. Elected King of Scots on the advice of and with the backing of Edward I on 30 November 1292 and did homage to Edward I for his kingdom a month later. However his council concluded an alliance with France in October 1295 promising aid between the two countries should either be attacked by England. Following Edward's campaign into Scotland in 1296, the storming of Berwick and the defeat of the Scottish army at Dunbar, Balliol surrendered his kingdom and his crown to Edward, he was then sent to England and retired to his estate at Bailleul in France in 1299. He died in 1313.

Beaufort, Henry, cardinal and bishop of Winchester, second son of John of Gaunt, duke of Lancaster. He was chancellor of England in 1403–4 and again under Henry V in 1413–17. As a member of the council during Henry IV's minority prevented his nephew, the duke of Gloucester, from exercising power in England after Henry V's death and while Bedford the regent was in France. He was again chancellor in 1424–6. He was a close adviser to Henry VI after he achieved his majority and was leader of the peace faction in the council realizing that the continuing war against France could not be sustained financially. He was an extremely wealthy man and loaned large sums to the crown. He died in 1447.

Beaumont, Sir Henry. As the earl of Buchan, one of the disinherited. Served in Edward Balliol's army at Dupplin Moor and later acted as one of Edward III's advisers at Hallidon Hill.

Bedford, John, Duke of, earl of Kendal and Richmond, Henry IV's third son. He was created duke in 1414. He was warden of the East March with Scotland 1403–14. He was guardian of England during Henry V's absence in France on his Agincourt campaign and during his conquest of Normandy. He commanded a fleet of ships that defeated the French blockading fleet at Honfleur in 1416. After Henry's death he became regent of France on behalf of the infant king Henry VI and held the appointment until his death. He married Anne of Burgundy, Duke Philippe's sister in 1423. While he was regent his army won the Battle of Cravant and he personally commanded the army at the Battle of Verneuil in 1424. The siege of Orleans, which took place against his better judgement, marked the apogee of his attempt to fulfil the conditions of the Treaty of Arras. He became responsible for the trial, by the French Inquisition, of Joan of Arc after she was captured. She was convicted as a heretic and burnt at the stake. He was also protector of England in 1425–6 and chief councillor in 1433–4. He died without issue in 1435.

Bedford, duke of, Sir George Neville. Son of Sir John Neville, Marquis Montagu. Elevated to the dukedom as a mark of friendship by Edward IV in 1469 and married Edward's eldest daughter Elizabeth.

Bolingbroke, Sir Henry, earl of Derby, duke of Hereford. Eldest son of John of Gaunt, duke of Lancaster. He was one of the lords appellant and fought at Radcot Bridge. After accusing and being accused by the duke of Norfolk of treason they were ordered by Richard II to fight a judicial duel that Richard then stopped before it began and banished both contestants. While Bolingbroke was abroad his estates were confiscated by Richard II, but he returned to claim his estates in 1399 while Richard was away in Ireland. Richard was then deposed and Bolingbroke was crowned King Henry IV the same year.

Buckingham, earl of, Sir Thomas of Woodstock, later duke of Gloucester, Edward III's youngest son. He commanded the fleet that put a garrison into Brest in the winter of 1377. He commanded a *chevauchée* out of Calais in 1380–1. He was a member of the continental council during Richard II's reign. He was one of the five appellant lords who fought and defeated lord Oxford at Radcot Bridge in December 1387. He was found guilty of treason in 1397, was imprisoned at Calais and later murdered, probably on the orders of his nephew Richard II.

Buckingham, 1st duke of, Sir Humphrey Stafford. Made KG in 1429. He served in France and was lieutenant general in Normandy, governor of Paris and constable of France in the 1430's. He was made captain of Calais in 1442–51. He was made constable of England just before the First Battle of St Albans in May 1455 and commanded the Lancastrian forces at the battle where he was wounded. He was present at the confrontation between Lancastrian and Yorkist forces before Ludford Bridge in October 1459. He was killed at the Battle of Northampton on 10 July 1460.

Buckingham, 2nd duke of, Sir Henry Stafford. Son of the above, married to Queen Elizabeth's sister, Catherine Wyderville. He was a remote claimant to the throne being the senior descendant of Thomas of Woodstock, Edward III's youngest son. He took a prominent part in Richard III's seizure of the throne and the imprisonment of Edward V in the Tower of London. He was well rewarded for his support by Richard III being made chief justice and chamberlain of Wales, and steward of the marcher lordships, also the Bohun inheritance, taken from the family on his father's attainder after the Battle of Northampton was restored to him. He rose in rebellion against Richard III in 1483, was defeated, captured and executed.

Calveley, Sir Hugh. Served with his 'free company' under the French commander du Guesclin in Spain in 1365 but left and joined the Black Prince's army with his company for the Najero campaign in 1366; he commanded the rearguard of the army at the battle. He joined Lancaster for his *Grande Chevauchée* in 1373.

Chandos, Sir John, KG. One of four knights detailed to advise and guard the prince of Wales at the Battle of Crécy in 1346. He was the prince's chief adviser at the Battle of Poitiers in 1356. As king's lieutenant in France supervised the handing over of territories from the French after the treaty of Brétigny; also took the homage of the principle nobles and towns of Aquitaine to Edward. He, together with John of Gaunt, commanded the vanguard of the Black Prince's army on his Najero campaign in 1366. He was killed in a minor skirmish near Poitiers in 1369.

Clarence, duke of, Thomas earl of Aumale. Henry IV's second son. Commanded an expeditionary force of 4,000 to aid the Armagnacs in the French civil war in 1412. Landed at Calais but arrived too late to affect the issue and went on his way to Bordeaux, burning and looting until bought off by payment of 210,000 gold crowns. Present at the siege of Harfleur in 1415, evacuated sick, probably dysentery. He commanded the vanguard of Henry V's army in 1417 and was present at the siege and sack of Caen. He was present at the siege of Rouen and was later killed at the Battle of Baugé on 22 March 1421.

Clarence, George, duke of, 2nd son of Richard, duke of York. Edward IV's younger brother, became the earl of Warwick by his marriage to Sir Richard Neville's daughter after the 'Kingmaker's' death at the Battle of Barnet. Rebelled against Edward IV in 1469 and again in 1470 and against Henry VI in 1471. He was involved in treason in

1473 and again in 1477. He was drowned in a butt of Malmsey wine in the Tower of London on the orders of his brother Edward IV in 1478.

Clifford, Sir Robert. Fought at Bannockburn in command of one of the English mounted divisions.

Clifford, lord of Skipton. Present at the First Battle of St Albans in the Lancastrian army on 21 May 1455 and killed in the battle.

Clifford, Lord, Sir John, son of the above. Present at the Battle of Wakefield on 30 December 1460, he murdered the youngest son of the duke of York at Wakefield Bridge in the pursuit after the battle. Defended the bridge across the Aire at Ferrybridge and was killed while on his withdrawal to join the main Lancastrian forces at Towton in March 1461.

Courtenay, Sir John, earl of Devon. Commanded the rearguard of Queen Margaret's army at the Battle of Tewkesbury in 1471, killed in the battle.

Crabbe, Sir John. He was a Flemish pirate and adventurer. He was taken into Scottish service and used to update and restore the defences of Berwick and its castle. He supervised its defence in the siege of 1319. He was captured by Sir Walter Manny in 1332 and ransomed by Edward III, he was then used at the siege of Berwick by Edward in 1334 where he supervised the bombardment.

Dagworth, Sir Thomas. Deputy lieutenant in Brittany in 1346. Rebuffed Charles de Blois at Finisterre in June 1346 and later defeated him and took him prisoner at La Roche-Derrien in Brittany. He was ambushed and killed in Brittany in 1351.

De la Pole, Sir. Brother of Sir William (?) de la Pole, later duke of Suffolk. Ordered to maintain the siege of Mont St Michel, but disregarded his orders and raided to Angers in 1423, surprised and defeated by Aumale and taken prisoner.

Derby, earl of, Sir Henry of Grosmont. See Lancaster.

Devereux, Sir Walter. Commanded the vanguard of the duke of York's army at Mortimer's Cross in February 1461, made Lord Ferrers after the battle.

Douglas, Sir James. Fought at Bannockburn in Walter the Steward's division of the Scottish army. Fought in the Weardale campaign of 1327. Was killed in Spain while fighting the Moors in 1330.

Douglas, Sir Archibald. The guardian and regent of Scotland during the minority of king David II. Raided into England in 1333, commanded the Scottish army at Halidon Hill where he was killed.

Douglas, Sir William. He commanded the Scottish army that took Berwick in November 1355 but withdrew when confronted by Edward III. He commanded the first Scottish contingent of a hundred men-at-arms to serve in France for the French king in 1356. He was present at the Battle of Poitiers and was one of king Jean's war council at the battle. He was severely wounded but survived.

Douglas, earl of, Sir James. Commanded part of the Scottish army in 1388 and was killed at Otterburn by forces under command of Henry Hotspur.

Douglas, earl of, Sir Alexander. Created duke of Touraine by Charles VII of France in 1424. He landed in France in April 1424 with Scottish reinforcements, perhaps 3,000 strong for the Scottish army serving as allies of France. He was killed at the Battle of Verneuil while commanding the Scottish division in August 1424.

Erpingham, Sir Thomas, KG. He commanded the English archers at the Battle of Agincourt in 1415.

Exeter, duke of, Sir Thomas Beaufort, earl of Dorset. He commanded reinforcements for Henry V's army in Normandy in 1418 and remained as a divisional commander in Normandy. He was present at the siege of Rouen and accepted its surrender on Henry V's behalf on 19 January 1419. He cleared northern Normandy of French forces and captured Dieppe in 1419.

Exeter, duke of, earl of Huntingdon, Sir John Holland. Half brother of King Richard II. He was a famous tourneyer, tourneying in Spain in 1386–7. He went on pilgrimage to Palestine in 1394. He murdered Sir Ralph Stafford in 1385, went into sanctuary to escape retribution. Married Elizabeth of Lancaster in 1386 after seducing her and gained the patronage of the lands of John of Gaunt. He was made a Knight of the Garter in 1381. He was created earl of Huntingdon in 1387 and made duke of Exeter in 1397. He was made great chamberlain of England, admiral of the west and captain of Brest in 1389. He became warden of the West March with Scotland and captain of Calais in 1398. He accompanied Richard II on his expedition to Ireland in 1399 but remained there when Richard returned to England and captivity. He supported the rebellion against Henry IV in 1400 and was caught while attempting to flee the country and executed.

Exeter, duke of, Sir Henry Holland. Involved in the ambush at Howarth Moor in August 1453 and was later imprisoned for this breech of the peace. Fought in the Lancastrian army at Towton but managed to escape to Scotland in 1461. Went to join the earl of Pembroke in Wales in the autumn of 1461 and was joint commander of a small army defeated at Caernavon by Lord Herbert in October. Commanded the rearguard of Warwick's army at Barnet in 1471 where he was severely wounded, he was taken to sanctuary at Westminster, later imprisoned in the Tower of London, and released to accompany Edward IV's expedition to France in 1475. Was lost at sea during the Channel crossing on the expedition's return.

Fastolff, Sir John, KG. He became deputy constable of Bordeaux in 1412. He was present at the siege of Harfleur in 1415 and at Agincourt the same year. Took part in the campaign to conquer Normandy. Was knighted during the campaign and made constable of Fécamp and captain of the Bastille in Paris. He was made a councillor of France and governor of Anjou and Maine in 1423. He led Bedford's offensive into Maine and Anjou in 1424 with Lord Scales. He fought at the Battle of Verneuil in 1424 where he captured the duke of Alençon. He commanded a relief convoy bringing sustenance to the army besieging Orleans in 1429 from Paris when it was attacked near Joinville by Clermont's army, which he defeated at the 'Battle of the Herrings'. He was present with Talbot at the Battle of

Patay but managed to escape capture. He was present at the congress of Arras in 1435 and retired from active service five years later. He built Caister Castle in East Anglia from his profits of war, built up a small mercantile fleet that plied the east coast and built a town house near the court in London. He died in 1459.

Fauconberg, William Neville, Lord, earl of Kent. The earl of Salisbury's brother. He was made joint commander of the garrison of Pontoise by Talbot in 1441 but surrendered three months later after a fierce artillery barrage by the French. He was present at the First Battle of St Albans in 1455 as a member of the court. He commanded Warwick's fleet that sailed out of Calais and captured Sandwich for the Yorkists in May 1460. Fought with Warwick at the Battle of Northampton in 1460. He commanded the vanguard of the Yorkist army at the Battle of Towton in 1461; he was made earl of Kent after the battle.

Gloucester, earl of. Sir Gilbert Clare. Fought and died at the Battle of Bannockburn without issue.

Gloucester, duke of, Sir Thomas of Woodstock. Youngest son of Edward III. See Buckingham.

Gloucester, duke of. See Humphrey, duke of Gloucester.

Hastings, William Lord. He was made a peer by Edward IV in 1461. He married Sir Richard Neville, earl of Warwick's sister. He was a long-time friend and loyal supporter of Edward IV. He accompanied king Edward with his retinue at the Battle of Loosecoat Field in March 1470. He was with king Edward in March 1471 when he landed at the Ravenspur in his bid to regain the crown. He reinforced Edward's little army at Leicester with 3,000 of his own retainers in March 1471. He commanded the left flank division in Edward's army at the battle of Barnet in April 1471 and the rearguard at the Battle of Tewkesbury. He was made captain of Calais in 1471. He was appointed a member of the minority council to rule in Edward V's name under the protector, Richard of York, by Edward IV before he died. He informed Richard, duke of Gloucester, and Buckingham of Edward's death. Seized on Richard III's orders at a council meeting at the Tower of London and immediately executed without trial for treason in 1483.

Herbert, Sir William. See Pembroke.

Holland, Sir Thomas, KG. Ordered to protect the prince of Wales at the Battle of Crécy.

Humphrey, Duke of Gloucester, Henry IV's fourth son. He was wounded at Agincourt. He captured Cherbourg on 29 September 1418 and was present at the siege of Rouen. After the death of Henry V he became protector in England while Bedford the regent was in France but was denied the exercise of power. He married Jacqueline, countess of Hainault, and then in October 1324 landed with an army of 5,000 to recover her inheritance, having done this he went on *chevauchée* through Flanders to Brussels and then retreated and embarked for England as Burgundy collected his forces to oppose him. He did irreparable damage to the Anglo-Burgundian alliance and to Bedford's position in France.

Knolles, Sir Robert. Joined Lancaster's Normandy campaign with 800 men from Brittany in 1356 and secured Lancaster's base at Montebourg. He served on Edward III's Rheims campaign in 1359 with his 'free company' of 3,000 men from Brittany. He, together with three others, was appointed to command the *chevauchée* in 1370 that landed at Calais and then burnt and pillaged its way to Paris where the garrison refused, under Charles V's orders, to come out and fight.

Kyriel, Sir Thomas. The only banneret in Somerset's army that landed at Cherbourg in 1443, and then campaigned into Maine without much effect. Commanded the small army sent to oppose the French and retrieve the situation in Normandy in March 1450, was defeated at Formigny the following month. Fought with the Yorkists under the earl of Warwick at the Second Battle of St Albans in 1461, was left behind by the defeated Yorkists to guard Henry VI who assured him he would come to no harm. However he was executed the next day on orders of Queen Margaret on 17 February 1461.

Lancaster, duke of, earl of Derby, Sir Henry of Grosmont. Son of Henry, earl of Lancaster. He was created earl of Derby in 1337, earl of Lancaster in 1345 and duke of Lancaster in 1351. He was a founder member of the order of the Garter. He was one of Edward III's most trusted lieutenants and an outstanding soldier. He first saw active service in Scotland. He accompanied Edward III on the Cambrai campaign in 1339. He commanded in Aquitaine, 1344–6 and was present at the siege of Calais, 1346–7. He returned to Aquitaine, 1349–50. He commanded a warship in the battle off Winchelsea in 1350. He went on crusade to Prussia, 1351. He campaigned in Normandy in 1356 and besieged Rennes in 1357, was bought off by a payment of 100,000 crowns. He was a divisional commander on the Rheims campaign, 1359–60. He was one of the English delegates at Brétigny who drafted the treaty in 1360. He was king's lieutenant in Brittany in 1356–8. He died in 1361.

Lancaster, duke of, Sir John of Gaunt. Edward III's third son and 2nd duke; he was given the title in 1362 on the death of Henry of Grosmont. He accompanied Edward III on his Rheims campaign in October 1359. Accompanied the Black Prince on his Spanish campaign and was present at the Battle of Najero in April 1367. Went on *chevauchée* from Calais in 1369. Accompanied the Black Prince at the siege and sack of Limoges in 1370. Commanded the *Grande Chevauchée* of 1373. He negotiated the truce of Bruges with the French in 1375. He married Constanza, daughter of King Pedro of Castille in 1385 and consequently had a legitimate claim to the Castilian throne. He was the king's lieutenant in Aquitaine in 1388 and made duke of Aquitaine by Richard II in 1390.

Manny or Mauny, Sir Walter. As lord of Mauny in France he accompanied Philippa of Hainault for her wedding to Edward III in 1327. He was knighted in 1331, made a baron in 1347 and a knight of the Garter in 1359. He campaigned with Edward Balliol in Scotland in 1332. He campaigned in Brittany in 1342, Gascony in 1345 and was present at the siege of Calais in 1347. He served on Edward III's Rheims campaign in 1359–60. He was with Lancaster (John of Gaunt) on his *chevauchée* in 1369. He died in 1372.

March, earl of, Sir Roger Mortimer. Fought at Bannockburn. Defeated Edward Bruce in Ireland in 1318. Became Queen Isabella's lover after the overthrow of Edward II. Generally held responsible for Edward II's murder. Made earl of March in 1328. Died 1330.

March, earl of, Sir Edmund Mortimer, great-grandson of Edward III's second son, Lionel duke of Clarence. Captured by Owen Glendower in Wales in 1402 and married his daughter. He became the subject of a dynastic plot led by Henry Percy, earl of Northumberland, to replace Henry IV in 1403. He was granted full title to the family lands by Henry V. He again became the subject of a dynastic plot to replace Henry V in 1415 but alerted the king to the danger. He died in 1425.

March, earl of, Sir Edward. The duke of York's eldest son, inherited his father's title on the latter's death at the Battle of Wakefield in 1460 and later became king Edward IV.

Montfort, Jean de, duke of Brittany and earl of Richmond. He was confirmed in the earldom, which his family had held for several generations, by Edward III after supporting his campaigns in Brittany. He was taken prisoner by Charles de Blois at the Battle of Nantes in 1341 but ransomed later.

Mowbray, Sir Philip. Captain of Stirling Castle in 1313–14. Surrendered the castle after the Battle of Bannockburn in 1314.

Norfolk, duke of, earl of Nottingham, Sir Thomas Mowbray, KG. He held the joint command with Arundel of the naval interception of a Franco-Flemish wine convoy off Margate in 1387. He was one of the five appellant lords who fought and defeated Lord Oxford at Radcot Bridge in December 1387. He became warden of the East March with Scotland in 1390 and captain of Berwick; was made captain of Calais in 1390. He arrested the duke of Gloucester on Richard II's order and imprisoned and later murdered the duke at Calais; as earl marshal oversaw the execution of his father-in-law, the earl of Arundel. He was elevated to the dukedom of Norfolk in 1397 and was banished for life by Richard II in 1398 after he and Hereford accused each other of treason. Died in Venice aged thirty-three in 1399.

Norfolk, duke of, Sir John Howard. Present at the Battle of Northampton in July 1460. Led his division to the battle of Towton in 1461 arriving at a critical time so ensuring Edward IV's victory. He was a terminally ill man and died the same year.

Norfolk, duke of, Sir John Howard. Served in his uncle's division at the Battle of Towton in 1461. He inherited the title on his uncle's death. He was one of Edward's commanders at the Battle of Loosecoat Field in March 1470. He was imprisoned by Warwick after Edward fled to Flanders in 1470 but was released on Edward's re-assumption of the throne in 1471. Gave his support to Richard III and was killed at the Battle of Bosworth Field in 1485.

Northampton, earl of, William Bohun. Earldom created by Edward III in 1337. Made constable of England in 1338. With Edward III on Cambrai campaign 1339. Commanded an army in Brittany in 1342 and again in 1345, made king's lieutenant in Brittany. He was present at the siege of Caen 1346. Commanded the division on the left at Crécy. Present at the siege of Calais 1346–7.

Northumberland, Henry Percy, 1st earl. Accompanied Edward III on his Picardy expedition in 1355. Marshal of England 1376–7 and constable in 1399. Enobled in 1377. Was warden of the East and West Marches towards Scotland, lost the latter position in 1396. Supported Henry Bolingbroke (later King Henry IV) when he landed on the Yorkshire coast in 1398. Met Richard II on his return from Ireland in 1398 and escorted him as a prisoner to Chester. Defeated the Scots at Homildon Hill in 1402. Supported his son's (Hotspur's) rebellion in Cheshire in 1403 but on his defeat and death submitted to Henry IV; was stripped of his wardenship of the East March. Was in rebellion in 1405 and driven into exile in Scotland. Returned and rebelled again in 1408 but was defeated and killed at Bramham Moor.

Northumberland, 2nd earl. Killed at the First Battle of St Albans on 21 May 1455.

Northumberland, 3rd earl, Sir Henry Percy. Son of the earl killed at St Albans. Made member of the council in 1456. Staunch Lancastrian, killed at the Battle of Towton on 29 March 1461.

Northumberland, 4th earl, Sir Henry Percy. Son of the earl killed at Towton. Was imprisoned in the tower in 1461 following the Battle of Towton. He was released in 1469, restored to the earldom of Northumberland by Edward IV in 1470 and was instrumental in maintaining peace in the north of England on Edward's return from Flanders in 1471. Was in London in July 1483 with his armed affinity to support Richard of Gloucester at his coronation. He commanded the rearguard division, mainly his own supporters from the north of England, in Richard's army at the Battle of Bosworth; took no part in the battle and marched his division away. He later submitted to Henry VII and retained his lands and title.

Oxford, earl of, Sir John de Vere. Responsible for the defence of London and the Essex coast in 1339; commanded a fleet of ships in 1340. Fought at Crécy in the prince of Wales's division in 1346. Accompanied the Black Prince on his *chevauchée* into Languedoc in 1355. Shared command of the vanguard with the earl of Warwick at Poitiers in 1356.

Oxford, earl of, Sir Robert de Vere. Member of Richard II's alternative council in 1387. Defeated by the Lords appellant at Radcot Bridge. Tried for treason and found guilty by parliament in 1387, fled the country.

Oxford, earl of, John de Vere. He accompanied the earl of Warwick to Calais for the marriage of his daughter to the duke of Clarence in 1469. He commanded the right wing of Warwick's army at the Battle of Barnet in 1471 but escaped to France via Scotland after the battle. He occupied St Michael's Mount in rebellion against Edward IV for three months in 1473, surrendered and was taken prisoner and imprisoned in Hammes Castle in the Calais Pale. He escaped from Hammes in 1483 and gave his loyalty to Henry Tudor, earl of Richmond in France. He accompanied Henry Tudor in his bid for the throne in 1485 and commanded the mainguard of Henry's army at the Battle of Bosworth Field. He commanded the vanguard of Henry VII's army at the Battle of Stoke in 1487.

Pembroke, earl of, Sir Aymer de Valence. Fought at Bannockburn, led the Welsh contingent of 3,000 men back to Carlisle after the defeat. He died in 1324.

Pembroke, earl of, Sir John Hastings. Married Edward III's fifth daughter Margaret. Joined the Black Prince in Gascony in 1369.

Appointed king's lieutenant in Aquitaine in 1373 and on his way to take up his appointment his convoy was attacked and destroyed at La Rochelle by Castilian galleys in June 1373; he was taken prisoner and later ransomed.

Pembroke, earl of, duke of Bedford, Sir Jasper Tudor. Second son of Sir Owen Tudor and Katherine of France (Henry V's dowager queen) and half brother to Henry VI. He was present, as a member of the court, at the First Battle of St Albans in 1455. His father Sir Owen Tudor was executed after the Battle of Mortimer's Cross in 1461 but Pembroke managed to escape after his army was defeated. Became prominent in Queen Margaret's court and travelled on her behalf to France and to Scotland to solicit help for her cause. He backed the abortive French invasion of Wales in 1468. After the defeat of the Lancastrian cause at Tewkesbury he accompanied his nephew Henry Tudor (later Henry VII) to exile in Brittany and on his return from exile to fight the Battle of Bosworth and claim the crown. Sir Jasper Tudor was then elevated to the dukedom of Bedford by his nephew. He died childless in 1495.

Pembroke, earl of, Sir William Herbert. Fought at Mortimer's Cross in 1461 where he commanded the rearguard on the left flank of the Yorkist line, created Lord Herbert after the battle. He was created earl of Pembroke in 1468. Defeated by Sir William Conyers army at Edgecote Moor on 26 July 1469 when marching to join Edward IV at Northampton. Was executed without trial the following day by order of the earl of Warwick.

Percy, Sir Henry. Younger son of the earl of Northumberland killed at St Albans, and brother of the 3rd earl killed at Towton. He was captain of the castle at Dunstanburgh and surrendered to Edward IV in September 1461, was pardoned and allowed to remain in command of the castle. He declared for Henry in October 1462 when Queen Margaret invaded Northumberland from Scotland. After the failure of this offensive he again surrendered the castle, was pardoned once more and given the captaincy of both Dunstanburgh and Bamburgh castles. He turned his coat once again in March 1463 and put both castles into Henry's allegiance. He was killed at the Battle of Hedgeley Moor on 25 April 1464.

Rempston, Sir Thomas. He crossed into Brittany from Normandy in 1426 and took the small town of St James de Beauvron where he was besieged by Arthur de Richemont, the constable of France, with an army many times the size of his garrison; however he put them to flight by use of a stratagem. He was later joined by the earl of Suffolk and they jointly marched on Rennes forcing Duke Jean of Brittany into a three months' truce as the forerunner of a treaty by which Duke Jean accepted that Henry VI was the lawful king of France.

Rivers, the earl, Sir Richard Wydeville. Knighted in 1426. Married the duke of Bedford's widow, Jacquetta of Luxembourg in 1436. Saw service in France. Created Lord Rivers in 1448, made constable of England the same year. Appointed seneschal of Aquitaine in August 1450 and was to take an army to Aquitaine later that year but it never sailed. Father of Edward IV's queen, Elizabeth Wydeville. He was executed on the earl of Warwick's orders after Edward IV became Warwick's prisoner on 12 August 1469.

Rivers, the earl, Sir Anthony Wydeville, son of Sir Richard, brother of the queen. Frustrated Warwick's attempt to seize his old ship the *Trinity* after the Battle of Loosecoat Field on his way to Calais in March 1470. Fought at the battles of Towton and Barnet where he was wounded. Accompanied Edward IV on his return to England from Flanders in 1471. He was for a short time constable of England and captain of Calais. Became the boy king Edward V's guardian on the death of Edward IV. Executed on Richard of Gloucester's orders in June 1483.

Salisbury, 2nd earl of, Sir William de Montagu. Accompanied the Black Prince on his *chevauchée* into Languedoc in 1355. Shared command of the rearguard with Suffolk at Poitiers in 1356.

Salisbury, 6th earl of, Sir Thomas Montagu. He was made a knight of the Garter in 1414 and was a member of Henry VI's minority council. He was present at the siege of Harfleur in 1415 and fought at the Battle of Agincourt. King's lieutenant in south-west Normandy in 1420. He commanded the main body of the duke of Clarence's army at Baugé but arrived too late to prevent Clarence's death in 1421. He defeated the Franco-Scottish army at Cravant in July 1423 and commanded a division of Bedford's army at the Battle of Verneuil. He captured both

Le Mans and Mayenne in 1425. Took the fortress of Meulan on the Seine in March 1424. Occupied Paris in July 1428. Commanded the army at the siege of Orleans in October 1428. Was fatally wounded by a cannot shot on 24 October and died on 3 November 1428.

Salisbury, earl of, Sir Richard Neville. Accompanied Henry VI to meet the duke of York at Blackheath in March 1452. Made Chancellor of England in 1454. Relieved of the appointment in January 1455 after Henry VI's recovery. Fought in the Yorkist army at the First Battle of St Albans on 21 May 1455. Intercepted with his army at Blore Heath in 1459 by Lord Audley and his army, defeated them and joined up with Warwick and other Yorkists at Ludlow and from there left for Calais. On Warwick's return in 1460 besieged the Tower of London and maintained peace in London during the Battle of Northampton in 1460. Fought with the duke of York at the Battle of Wakefield, was taken prisoner and executed the following day, 31 December 1460.

Scales, Lord. Took joint command of Bedford's offensive into Maine and Anjou with Sir John Fastolff in 1424. Joined Talbot at the siege of Orleans in 1429. After the siege was raised joined Fastolff and Talbot in an operation to relieve Beaugency, which failed. He was at Patay shortly after where the English army was overwhelmed by a larger French army. He was made lieutenant general of south-west Normandy on the death of Arundel in 1435. He became garrison commander, together with Lord Fauconbridge, of Pontoise in 1441. But three months later was forced to surrender the fortress after a fierce artillery bombardment. He took over the Tower of London with his retinue in May 1460 to hold it for the Lancastrians. He surrendered the Tower after the Battle of Northampton and was allowed to go free, but was murdered by boatmen on his way to sanctuary in Westminster in July 1460.

Somerset, earl of, elevated to rank of duke, Sir John Beaufort. Son of John of Gaunt's legitimized eldest bastard son. Commanded the abortive expedition to northern France in 1443. Ridiculed and banned from court as a result of the expedition. Died in 1444.

Somerset, duke of, Sir Edmund Beaufort, earl of Dorset, brother of Sir John. Inherited the title after the death of his elder brother. He was captured at Baugé in 1421 and later ransomed. He was made lieu-tenant in Maine in 1427 and king's lieutenant in Normandy in 1444. He surrendered Rouen without a siege in November 1449 and Caen after a three week artillery battering in June 1450. He presided over and was blamed for the expulsion of the English from Normandy in 1450. Became constable of England in September 1450. Staunch Lancastrian, he was present and killed at the First Battle of St Albans on 21 Mary 1455.

Somerset, duke of, Sir Henry Beaufort, son of Sir Edmund. Appointed captain of Calais in 1458. Commanded Lancastrian forces at the Second Battle of St Albans on 14 February 1461. Commanded the Lancastrian army at the Battle of Towton in March 1461, escaped to Scotland. Landed with Queen Margaret's small army in Northumberland in October 1462. Remained in command of Bamburgh Castle after Margaret's return to Scotland for reinforce-ments. Surrendered the castle on terms on 26 December 1462 and was pardoned, was then employed at the siege of Alnwick Castle by the Yorkists. He was sent for his own safety to Wales bur turned his coat and went to York to fight once more for the Lancastrian cause. He went on to Bamburgh Castle to command the Lancastrian army of about 5,000 men based on the castle and that of Alnwick. Commanded the Lancastrian army at the Battle of Hedgely Moor on 25 April but withdrew. Commanded the Lancastrian army at the Battle of Hexham on 15 May 1464, taken prisoner and executed on 16 May.

Somerset, Sir Edmund Beaufort, younger brother of Sir Henry Beaufort. Greeted Queen Margaret at Exmouth after her landing from France in April 1471. Acted as her chief adviser and commanded her army on its march north to Tewkesbury. Fought at the Battle of Tewkesbury, was defeated and taken prisoner. Tried for treason the following day, found guilty and executed on 5 May 1471.

Stafford, Sir Ralph, made earl of Stafford by Edward III in 1351. Accompanied duke of Lancaster on his *Grande Chevauchée* in 1373.

Stafford, Sir Henry, duke of Buckingham. Edward IV's brother-in-law was married to Queen Elizabeth's sister. Led a parliamentary dele-gation to Richard of Gloucester in 1483, after Edward IV's death to persuade him to take the throne. Rose in rebellion in 1483, was captured and executed for treason on 2 November 1483.

Suffolk, earl of, Sir Robert Ufford. Accompanied the Black Prince on his *chevauchée* into Languedoc in October 1355. Shared command of the rearguard with Salisbury at Poitiers in 1356. Made marshal of England in 1359. Accompanied duke of Lancaster on his *Grande Chevauchée* in 1373.

Suffolk, earl of, Sir Michael de la Pole. Son of Sir William a successful merchant and creditor of Edward III. Created earl by Richard II in 1385. Chancellor of England 1381–6. Impeached by parliament in 1386. Member of Richard II's alternative council in 1387. Tried for treason by parliament in 1387, found guilty and fled the country.

Suffolk, earl of, Sir Michael de la Pole. Attended the Council of Constance as personal representative of Henry IV in 1409. Fought and died at Agincourt, 1415.

Suffolk, earl of, later duke of, Sir William de la Pole. He was the son of Sir Michael who died at Agincourt. Knight of the Garter in 1421. Present at the Battle of Cravant in 1423. Recaptured the town of Ivry in June 1424. Commanded the vanguard of Bedford's army before the Battle of Verneuil. Relieved the garrison of St James de Beauvron in March 1426 and occupied Dol de Bretagne. Commanded the army at the siege of Orleans after the death of Salisbury in 1428, failed to prosecute the siege properly and lost overall command of the army. Taken prisoner at Jargeau in June 1429 but later ransomed. He led Henry VI's delegation to France to negotiate his marriage to Margaret of Anjou in 1444 and a truce. As a member of Henry VI's council agreed to surrender the county of Maine as the price for extending the truce of Tours in 1447. He was involved in the arrest and death of Humphrey duke of Gloucester in 1447. He was impeached by parliament for defeat in France and banished from England, beheaded by sailors on his way to exile in Burgundy in 1450.

Talbot, Sir John, 1st earl of Shrewsbury, count of Clermont. He was imprisoned in the Tower of London in 1413 after a quarrel with the earl of Arundel that epitomized his quarrelsome nature as shown again in his feud with Lord Ormond in Ireland; indeed he was so bellicose and combative that it was decided that he would be better employed in France. However he showed much initiative in his campaign against Owen Glendower in Wales in 1404 and again in Ireland in 1414–19 where he was lieutenant. He was taken to France by the duke of Bedford to be one of his commanders in 1419. He took Pontorson by siege in 1427 and was made governor of Maine and Anjou the same year and took Le Mans shortly after. He was given joint command of the army at the siege of Orleans in 1429 with Lord Scales. He raised the siege when the French garrison and reinforcements became significantly larger than his besieging army. He tried to relieve Beaugency in 1429 but failed, his small army was overwhelmed by a larger French army at Patay; he was wounded in the back and taken prisoner. He was ransomed in 1434 and returned to duty as lieutenant general of the north-east of Normandy in 1435. He was made a marshal of France in 1436. He took Pontoise in 1437 after surprising the garrison. In 1439 he routed Richemont's army in a night attack just before Christmas. He was made York's (governor of Normandy) lieutenant general responsible for the conduct of the war in 1441. In 1441 he carried out operations about Pontoise to relieve pressure by the French on the fortress town; he completely out-manoeuvred the French army forcing them to raise their siege and retreat to Paris. He was given as a hostage to the French after the surrender of Rouen by Somerset in 1449 and was exchanged for the surrender of Falaise in 1450. At the request of the Gascons of Aquitaine Henry VI's government agreed to send an army to Bordeaux in 1453 and Talbot was put in command. The French invaded Aquitaine stopping at Castillon where Talbot attacked them in July 1453; he was defeated and killed at the ensuing battle.

Talbot, Sir John, earl of Shrewsbury, 2nd son of the first earl. He arrived too late with his retinue to aid Henry at St Albans in May 1455. He commanded the centre division of the Lancastrian army at the Battle of Northampton on 10 July 1460 where he was killed.

Talbot, Sir John, earl of Shrewsbury, 3rd earl. Cousin of the above, he was with the Lancastrian army at the Second Battle of St Albans in 1461, he was killed at Towton in 1461.

Talbot, Sir John, earl of Shrewsbury, 4th earl. Son of the above, he was twelve years old when his father died. He joined Warwick for the latter's rebellion against Edward IV in 1470, but was with Clarence when Edward IV returned in 1471 and joined Edward. He fought in Edward's army at both the battles of Barnet and Tewkesbury in 1471.

Talbot, Sir Gilbert. Cousin of the above. Joined Henry Tudor before the Battle of Bosworth Field. Fought with Henry VII in the earl of Oxford's division at the Battle of Stoke in 1487.

Trollope, Sir Andrew. Commanded a contingent of the Calais garrison that came over with the earl of Warwick in 1459 to join the Yorkist army at Ludlow. Accepted the king's pardon and changed sides joining the king's army before Ludford Bridge. Fought on the Lancastrian side at the battles of 2nd St Albans and Towton in 1461; was killed at Towton.

Tudor, Sir Edmund, earl of Richmond. He was enobled by his half brother Henry VI in 1452, he died in 1456.

Warwick, earl of, Sir Thomas Beauchamp. Accompanied Edward III on the Cambrai campaign in 1339. Commanded a fleet of ships in 1340. Fought in Brittany in 1342. Fought at the siege of Caen in 1346. Fought in the prince of Wales's division at Crécy in 1346. Present at the siege of Calais, 1346–7. Accompanied the prince of wales on his *chevauchée* through Languedoc in 1355. Shared command of the vanguard with the earl of Oxford at Poitiers in 1356. King's lieutenant in France 1360–1. One of the English delegates at Brétigny who drafted the treaty in 1360. Accompanied the duke of Lancaster on his *Grande Chevauchée* of 1373. One of the five appellant lords who fought and defeated Lord Oxford at Radcot Bridge in December 1387. Found guilty of treason in 1397 and banished to the Isle of Man.

Warwick, earl of, count of Aumale, Sir Richard Beauchamp, KG, son of Sir Thomas. Member of Henry V's embassy to Burgundy in 1413 to seek a treaty. Commanded a division of Henry V's army during the conquest of Normandy. Isolated Rouen from the north before the siege and captured Cadence and Quilleboeuf on the Seine west of Rouen. Was captain of Calais from 1423. Commanded the siege of Pontorson in May 1427.

Commanded the abortive siege of Montargis in July 1427. Governor and king's lieutenant in Normandy from 1437 until his death in 1439.

Warwick, earl of, Sir Richard Neville, the 'Kingmaker'. Accompanied Henry VI to meet the duke of York at Blackheath in March 1452. Supported the duke of York in his confrontation with Somerset after 1454. Fought in the Yorkist army at the First Battle of St Albans on 21 May 1455. Captain of Calais 1456–61. Commanded the Yorkist army at the Second Battle of St Albans on 17 February 1461. Commanded the mainguard of the Yorkist army at the Battle of Towton on 29 March 1461. Commanded Yorkist forces that carried out the successful sieges of the Lancastrian castles in Northumberland in 1463 and again in 1465. Married his daughter to the Duke of Clarence, Edward IV's younger brother against the king's wishes in Calais on 12 July 1469. Landed in Kent in support of 'Robert of Redesdale's' uprising on 13 July 1469 and marched north with an army ostensibly to support the king but in fact to support the uprising. Supported Sir William Conyers' (Robert of Redesdale's) army in its confrontation and defeat of Pembroke's and Devon's army at Edgecote Moor in July 1469. Took Edward IV prisoner the same month, but was obliged to release him in September. Complicit in Sir Robert Welles's revolt and the Battle of Loosecote Field in March 1470. Forced out of England shortly after when he was declared a rebel and a traitor and attacked a Flemish convoy in the Channel with his own small fleet. Took refuge in Honfleur after his fleet was attacked by Lord Howard and scattered, was given sanctuary by Louis of France who arranged a reconciliation between Warwick and Queen Margaret who was also in sanctuary in France. Sailed to England and landed at Exmouth with an army to put Henry VI back on the throne on 13 September 1470. Marched to Coventry and from there with help from his brother, Marquis Montagu, forced Edward IV to flee. Restored Henry VI to the throne in October but failed to prevent Edward IV from returning to England in 1471. Killed at the Battle of Barnet on 14 April 1471.

Warwick, earl of, son of duke of Clarence. Put under the tutelage of Margaret Beaufort, Henry VII's mother, by Henry VII after Bosworth. Removed to the Tower of London shortly before the rebellion of Lambert Simnel. Implicated in Perkin Warbeck's attempt to escape from the Tower. Executed on orders of Henry VII in November 1499.

Willoughby, Lord. Commanded a division of Salisbury's army at Cravant in 1421.

Wiltshire, earl of, Sir James Butler. Present at the First Battle of St Albans on the Lancastrian side, but escaped capture after the battle. Was present at Ludford Bridge. Was appointed lieutenant in Ireland by Queen Margaret on Henry VI's behalf in 1459 but was prevented from taking up the appointment. Joined the earl of Pembroke's army with a force of French mercenaries in 1461 and was defeated at the Battle of Mortimer's Cross but escaped during the battle. He fought at Towton under Somerset but escaped the carnage; he was captured later in Cumberland and taken to Newcastle where he was executed for treason on 1 May 1461.

York, duke of, Sir Edward Plantagenet. Saw service with Henry when prince of Wales in Wales. Became a close supporter of Henry V after the latter removed the stigma recorded in parliament against his father. Commanded the vanguard of Henry V's army before Harfleur and at Agincourt. Died at Agincourt 1415.

York, duke of, Sir Richard Plantagenet. Son of the earl of Cambridge who was executed after the Southampton plot. Inherited the title after his uncle's death at Agincourt. Made a knight of the Garter in 1433 and became king's lieutenant in France in 1436 after the duke of Bedford's death. Recaptured Dieppe in 1436. Became governor of Normandy in 1439. Commanded the Pontoise campaign of 1441 with Sir John Talbot. Handed over the appointment of king's lieutenant in France to the duke of Somerset in 1444. Made king's lieutenance in Ireland in 1447. Returned to England in 1452 gathered 4,000 armed supporters and camped on Blackheath to await the king, later arrested and held for three months. Was protector of the realm from March 1454 to February 1456. Commanded the Yorkist army at the First Battle of St Albans on 21 May 1455. He was killed at the Battle of Wakefield, 30 December 1460.

York, duke of, Sir Edward Plantagenet, earl of March, son of Sir Richard. He was crowned King Edward IV on 4 March 1461.

Notes

Chapter 1 The Nation

1 Contamine, P., 'The French Nobility and the War' from Fowler, *The Hundred Years War*, p. 138.
2 See Zeigler, *The Black Death*. See Ch 2 for a general view of the plague in Western Europe. See also Lander, *Conflict and Stability in 15th Century England*, pp. 21 and 22.
3 *Ibid.* The figures quoted are taken from J.C. Russell, *British Medieval Population*, p. 287.
4 For a good idea of how the higher nobility travelled see Stratton, *Some Aspects of Medieval Travel*, pp. 77–97.
5 See *The Canterbury Tales*, particularly the General Prologue and within that the descriptions of the knight, his son the esquire and the yeoman. The new translation by David Wright published by the Oxford University Press in 1985 is probably the most readable and easily understood.

Chapter 2 Preparing for War

1 See Glossary.
2 See Glossary.
3 Baldwin, *The King's Council in England during The Middle Ages*, pp. 74–5.
4 *Ibid.*, pp. 163–7.
5 *Ibid.*, p. 178.
6 Powicke, *Military Obligation in Medieval England*, p. 183.
7 *Ibid.*, p. 247.
8 Schuyler, *The Financing of the Hundred Years' War*, pp. 10–11.
9 Hibbert, *Agincourt*, pp. 27–8.
10 Figures taken from receipt rolls and quoted in Newhall, *The war finances of Henry V and The Duke of Bedford*, pp. 172–98.
11 *Ibid.*
12 *Ibid.*, p. 197.
13 Pollard, *John Talbot and The War in France*, pp. 32–4.
14 Hewitt, 'The organisation of War under Edward III', p. 3.
15 Powicke, *op. cit.*, pp. 119–20.
16 Alban, 'English Coastal Defence'.
17 Hewitt, *op. cit.*, p. 33.
18 Hewitt, *The Horse in Medieval England*, pp. 42–3.
19 Hewitt, *The Organisation of War under Edward III*, pp. 41–2.
20 Powicke, *op. cit.*, pp. 88–9.

21 *Ibid.*, p. 79.
22 Pollard, *op. cit.*, p. 69.
23 Gillingham, *The Wars of the Roses.*
24 Hewitt, H.J., *op. cit.*, pp. 34–6.
25 Hibbert, C., *op. cit.*, p. 34.
26 Nicolas, *History of The Battle of Agincourt*, pp. 165–6.
27 Pollard, *op. cit.*, pp. 103–4.
28 Pollard, *op. cit.*, pp. 109–10.
29 Gillingham, *op. cit.*, p. 97.
30 *The Boke of Noblesse*, J.G. Nichols (ed.), p. 76. Quoted in Keene, *England in the late Middle Ages*, pp. 21–2, note 24.
31 Barker, *The Tournament in England*, pp. 139–40.
32 Barber and Barker, *Tournaments, Jousts, Chivalry and Pageants*, p. 41. See also Sumption, *The Hundred Years War*, Vol. 11, pp. 33–4.
33 Seward, *The Hundred Years War*, p. 78.
34 Dillon and St John Hope, *Pageant of the Birth, Life and Death of Richard Beauchamp*, p. 28.
35 Bradbury, *The Medieval Archer*, p. 165 and note 6.
36 Boardman, *The Battle of Towton*, p. 49. See also Gillingham, *op. cit.*, p. 47.
37 Wylie and Waugh, *The Reign of Henry V*, Vol. 2, pp. 33–4.
38 Croft, *Scotland from the Earliest Times to 1603*, pp. 231–2.

Chapter 3 The Army at War

1 Pisan, *The Book of Fayttes of Arms and of Chivalrye*, p. 225.
2 Bouet, Honoré, *The Tree of Battles*, p. 189.
3 Avesbury, *De Gestis Mirabililus Regis Edwardi Teritii*. Letter from Edward III to his son and the council on his 1339 Campaign in the Cambresis.
4 *Ibid.*
5 Le Baker, *Chronicon.*
6 Froissart.
7 *Ibid.*
8 *Ibid.*
9 *Ibid.*
10 Walsingham, *Historia Anglicana*, p. 284.
11 Hay, 'The Division of the Spoils of War', Vol. 4, 1954.
12 *Ibid.*
13 Lewis, 'The Last Medieval Summons', Vol. 73.
14 Newhall, *The English Conquest of Normandy*, p. 223.
15 Taken from Twiss (ed.), *The Blacke Booke of the Admiral*, Vol. I and set out in Appx IV of Hibbert's *Agincourt.*
16 Newhall, *op. cit.*, p. 229.
17 Newhall, *op. cit.*, p. 228.
18 Newhall, *op. cit.*, p. 230.
19 Quoted in Rowe, 'Discipline in the Norman Gamsous' and taken from the 'Collection des Quittances' Q.60.1048 (March 1429) at the Bibliothèque Nationale, Paris.

20 Barnie, *War in Medieval Society*, p. 37.
21 Pisan, *op. cit.*, p. 223.
22 McFarlane, K. B., 'A Business Partnership in War and Administration', pp. 290–310.
23 Newhall, 'The War Finances of Henry V'.
24 Postan, 'The Costs of the Hundred Years' War'.
25 Figures concerning Sir John Fastolff's war profits are taken from McFarlane, 'The Investment of Sir John Fastolff's Profits of War'.
26 Gask, 'The Medical Staff of King Edward the Third'.
27 From the list of Henry V's household stall set out in full in Harris, *The History of Battle of Agincourt*.
28 MacKinney, *Medical Illustrations in Medieval Manuscripts*, p. 39.
29 *Ibid.*, p. 66.
30 *Ibid.*, p. 74.

Chapter 4 The War at Sea, the Ships and their Crews

1 Quoted in Rodger, *The Safeguard of the Sea*, p. 117. Said in the House of Commons and reported in PR, IV, 79.
2 Burly, 'The Victualling of Calais' pp. 49–67.
3 Landström, *The Ship*, p. 71.
4 Hewitt, 'The Organisation of War under Edward III' from Fowler (ed.), *The Hundred Years War*.
5 Hewitt, *The Horse in Medieval England*.
6 Richmond, 'English Naval Power'. Details taken from pages 1–15.
7 Richmond, *ibid.*, pp. 1–15.
8 PRO Exchequer accounts, 1480: E.404/77/1/38; and 1484: E.404/78/3/43.
9 Rodger, *op. cit.*, p. 107.
10 Moore, 'Accounts and Inventories', pp. 20–6 and pp. 167–73.
11 Hewitt, *op. cit.* and also see Newhall, *The English Conquest of Normandy*, p. 31, note 154.
12 Wylie and Waugh, *The Reign of Henry V*, Vol. 2, p. 323.
13 Campbell, 'England, Scotland and the Hundred Years War', pp. 83–4.
14 Richmond, *op. cit.* Figures takes from the table at pp. 12–15.
15 Richmond, 'The Keeping of the Seas during the Hundred Years War', pp. 283–98.
16 Hewitt, *op. cit.*, p. 77.
17 Hewitt, *op. cit.*, p. 80.
18 Roger, *op. cit.*, p. 123.
19 Wylie and Waugh, *op. cit.*, Vol. 2, p. 376.
20 Wylie and Waugh, *op. cit.*, Vol. 2, p. 388, and 'Blacke Book of the Admiraly', Vol. 2, p. 211 and Vol. 3, p. 437.
21 Wylie and Waugh, *op. cit.*, Vol. 2, p. 388 and 'Blacke Book of the Admiralty', Vol. 3, p. 437.
22 Roger, *op. cit.*, p. 132.
23 Stanford-Reid, 'Sea Power in the Anglo-Scottish War', pp. 7–23.

24 Roger, *op. cit.*, p. 144.
25 Ford, 'Piracy or Policy', pp. 63–77 for figures of ships seized.
26 Hay, 'The Division of the Spoils of War'.
27 Keen, *The Laws of War*, p. 140.

Chapter 5 The Bannockburn and Weardale Campaigns
 1 Froissart, *Froissart in Britain*, p. 5.
 2 Barron, *The Scottish War of Independence*.
 3 Maxwell, *The Chronicle of Lanercost*, p. 195.
 4 Scott, *Robert the Bruce*, p. 87.
 5 Knighton, *Chronicum*, p. 452.
 6 Scott, *op. cit.*
 7 Gray, *Scalacronica*, p. 143.
 8 Maxwell, *op. cit.*, p. 207.
 9 Gray, *op. cit.*, p. 142.
10 *Ibid.*, p. 144.
11 Maxwell, *op. cit.*, p. 225.
12 Main sources for the battle were the near contemporary chronicles *The Brus*, *The Chronicle of Lanercost* and the *Scalacronica*. Also Barron, *op. cit.*, Scott, *op. cit.*, and Mackenzie, *The Battle of Bannockburn*.
13 Froissart's Chronicles, from *Froissart in Britain*, *op. cit.*, pp. 16–17.
14 Froissart, *Chronicles of England, France and Spain*.
15 Rogers, *The Wars of Edward III*, p. 12, in a translation of the chronicle written by Jean Le Bel, a Hainaulter who served in this campaign in the contingent from Hainault. The chronicle was written in 1352.
16 The story of the Weardale campaign has been taken from Froissart's chronicles, but Froissart based his account on the chronicle of Jean Le Bel; that which is relevant to the Weardale campaign is translated in *op. cit.*, pp. 4–19.
17 Rogers, *op. cit.*, p. 20.

Chapter 6 The Battle of Halidon Hill
 1 Attributed to Pope Martin V, 1417–1431.
 2 Nicholson, 'The Siege of Berwick', pp. 19–42.
 3 Nicholson, *Ibid*.
 4 Maxwell, *The Chronicle of Lanercost*, p. 190.
 5 Nicholson, *op. cit.*
 6 Brie (ed.), *Brut*, p. 281.
 7 Lucas, 'John Crabbe', pp. 334–50.
 8 Morris, 'The Archers at Crécy', p. 431.
 9 Harleian MS.
10 Brie, *op. cit.*, p. 286.
11 According to the Meaux chronicler in *Chronica Monasterii de Melsa*, p. 370; however, the same chronicler gives the strength of the Scottish army as 90,000 so perhaps his testimony is not entirely reliable, never-

theless it confirms the account given by the chronicler Wyntoun, ii, 401–2 from Historians of Scotland Series.

12 Nicholson, *op. cit.*, p. 42. Also Croft, *Scotland from the Earliest Times*, p. 178.
13 Gray, *Scalacronica*.

Chapter 7 The Battle of Neville's Cross and the Capture of a King

1   Said by Edward III's chamberlain at Berwick on the difficulty of collecting taxes in southern Scotland.
2   Rogers, *The Wars of Edward III*, Source 31, translation of an original letter, pp. 48–50.
3   Nicholson, *Edward III and the Scots*.
4   Lewis, 'The Last Medieval Summons', pp. 2–26.
5   Sumption, *The Hundred Years War*, pp. 552–3.
6   Lewis, *op. cit.*, pp. 2–26.
7   Sumption, *op. cit.*, pp. 552–3.
8   Schuyler, *The Financing of the Hundred Years War*, p. XVII.
9   *Ibid.*
10 *Ibid.*
11 Campbell, 'England, Scotland and the Hundred Years War', p. 199.
12 A Scottish mark was worth 160 English pennies, therefore this ransom of 100,000 marks amounted to £66,666 sterling, an increase over the original ransom demand of £26,666.
13 Campbell, *op. cit.*
14 *Ibid.*
15 *Ibid.*
16 Prestwich, *The Three Edwards* p. 82.
17 Ramsay, *A History of the Revenues of the Kings of England*, Table 1, p. 292. Heavy expenditure continued until 1340 but after 1337 the majority of war expenditure was as a result of the war with France.

Chapter 8 The Crécy Campaign

1   Froissart, *Chronicles*.
2   Cuttino, 'Historical Revision' pp. 468–9.
3   See Le Patourel, 'Edward III and the Kingdom of France', pp. 173–89, for a reasoned case that the attainment of the throne of France was in fact the main cause for Edward's war with France.
4   Villani, *Cronica* and quoted in Rogers, *The Wars of Edward III*, p. 84.
5   Villani, *op. cit.*, p. 84.
6   Aungier, French Chronicle of London.
7   *Ibid.*
8   Sumption, *The Hundred Years War*, Vol. 1, pp. 399–400.
9   Perroy, *The Hundred Years War*, pp. 114–15. The size of this army is uncertain; Perroy says 12,000, but Sherborne in 'Indentured Retinues and English Expeditions to France', p. 735 and note 4, estimates 5,000,

a more likely figure. The difference in the figures might well have been made up by Bretons as the 5,000 refers to the English contingent; nevertheless the higher figure is almost certainly too high.

10 Sumption, *op. cit.*, p. 496.
11 Barber, *Life and Campaigns of the Black Prince*, p. 14. Letter of Bartholomew Burghersh to the archbishop of Canterbury.
12 The exact numbers are not known. However Sir James Ramsay in his 'The Strength of English Armies', p. 224 gives a figure, taken from Walter Wettwang's accounts (he was keeper of the wardrobe accounts), of those embarked in England for the expedition and therefore probably the most reliable. His figures include 1,200 lances, 1,743 light horse (probably hobilars), 3,680 archers and 3,500 Welsh embarked for the campaign. A 'lance', according to Contamine, *War in the Middle Ages*, included a knight and his esquire, equipped similarly to himself, plus a servant and a groom. If a 'lance' meant this then there would have been 2,400 well-equipped men-at-arms in addition to the light horse, making a total army strength of 11,323 soldiers.
13 Le Bel, *Chronique*.
14 Baker, *Chronicon*.
15 Froissart, *op. cit.*
16 See also Morris, 'The Archers at Crécy', pp. 427–36.
17 Rothero, *The Armies of Crécy and Poitiers*, p. 32.
18 Froissart, *op. cit.*
19 Froissart, *op. cit.*
20 Viollet-le-Duc, *An Essay on the Military Architecture of the Middle Ages* pp. 153 & 154.
21 Perroy, *op. cit.*, p. 119.
22 Le Bel, *op. cit.*, Vol. 2, pp. 102–10. Gives a good account of the battle on which this account is largely based. Le Bel wrote it shortly after from accounts given to him by Jean de Hainault and others who were present at the battle.

Chapter 9 The Siege of Calais

1 King Edward's words to King Philippe's messenger at the siege of Calais as reported by Froissart.
2 Sumption, *The Hundred Years War*, p. 578.
3 Zeigler in *The Black Death*, p. 135 estimates the population of London at, between sixty and seventy thousand in 1348, while Perroy, in *The Hundred Years' War*, p. 49, estimated the population of London in 1328 at about 40,000.
4 Sumption, *op. cit.*
5 Le Bel, *Chronique*.
6 Froissart, *op. cit.*
7 The quotes in this paragraph are all taken from Froissart, *op. cit.*
8 Hewitt, *The Organisation of War under Edward III*, p. 59.

9 See Tout, 'Some Neglected Fights', pp. 726–80.

10 Perroy, *op. cit.*, p. 45.

11 Hewitt, *The Black Prince's Expedition*, pp. 20–21. However le Bel says that the prince crossed to Bordeaux with 1,200 men-at-arms and 4,000 archers; quoted in Rogers, *The Wars of Edward III*, p. 150.

12 Barber, *The Life and Campaigns of the Black Prince*, p. 93.

13 Rogers, *The Wars of Edward III*, pp. 154–5. Rogers quotes a letter from Sir John Wingfield to the bishop of Winchester, dated 24 December 1355, in which he states that the area about Carcassonne and Limoux produced revenue for the wages of 1,000 men-at-arms in addition to 100,000 *écus* towards the cost of the war. In addition Narbonne gave war subsidies to the amount of 400,000 *écus*. The whole area through which the prince and his army rode was very prosperous. This letter is reproduced in full by Barber, *op. cit.*, pp. 50–2.

Chapter 10 The Battle of Poitiers and a King Ransomed

1 Froissart, *Chronicles*, book one, 1968, pp. 129–30. Reported as being said by Cardinal de Périgord to King Jean II, before truce negotiations began the day before the Battle of Poitiers.

2 Burne, *The Crécy War*, p. 262. See also *Robert of Avesbury's chronicle*, pp. 462–5.

3 Barber, *Life and Campaigns of the Black Prince*, p. 57.

4 Hewitt, *The Black Prince's Expedition*, pp. 108–12.

5 Barber, *op. cit.*, p. 72. Geoffrey le Baker was a contemporary of the Black Prince and wrote his account of the battle sometime between 1358 and 1360 as a result of speaking to eyewitnesses. It is the most detailed and the most contemporary account available.

6 See the *Anonimalle Chronicle*, p. 36. This chronicle was written some twenty years after the event and supports Hewitt's view.

7 Froissart, *op. cit.*, p. 127.

8 Hewitt, *op. cit.*, p. 114.

9 Burne, 'The Battle of Poitiers' pp. 21–52.

10 Perroy, *The Hundred Years War*.

11 Viollet-le-Duc, *An Essay*, p. 155.

12 Of the twenty-six original members of the Order of the Garter, Edward III and the Black Prince were the only royals who were members; then came Henry, 1st duke of Lancaster, the earls of Warwick, Stafford and Salisbury and the lords Mortimer and Mohun, followed by fourteen English knights and two Gascons. Taken from *The Black Book of the Order of the Garter* published in 1724. The quotes that follow are also taken from *The Black Book*.

Chapter 11 The Rheims Campaign and the Prince in Spain

1 The duke of Lancaster's advice to Edward III during the negotiations for the Treaty of Brétigny and an ever-present risk to both French and

English monarchs throughout the Hundred Years' War. Froissart's *Chronicles* quoted by Rogers in *The Wars of Edward III*, p. 182.

2   Burne, *The Crécy War*, pp. 327–8.
3   *Ibid.*, pp. 351–2, and Delachenal, *Charles V*.
4   Prince, 'The Strength of English Armies', p. 368.
5   *The Anonimalle Chronicle*, pp. 44–5.
6   See Froissart, *op. cit.* Froissart's account of the negotiations for the treaty of Brétigny are reproduced by Rogers, *op. cit.*, pp. 181–3.
7   Details of the territories to be ceded included the Agenais, including Agen; Belleville; Gaure: the Limousin, including Limoges; Périgord, including Périgueux; Poitou, including Poitiers; Thouars; Quercy, including Cahors.
8   Barber, *Edward*, p. 180.
9   *Ibid.*, pp. 189–90.
10   See Prince, *A Letter of the Black Prince*, pp. 414–18.
11   Barber, *op. cit.*, p. 217.
12   Froissart, *Chronicles*, translated by Geoffrey Brereton, p. 178.
13   Barber, *op. cit.*, pp. 225–6.
14   Keen, *The Laws of War*, p. 122.
15   Froissart wrote of the siege of Limoges in his first book covering the period between 1322 and 1378, but his main sources of information for this book were Jean le Bel and Chandos Herald. Le Bel, however, finished writing his chronicle in 1361, nine years before the 'massacre'. It is therefore probable that Froissart's only source for his version of events would have been Chandos Herald.
16   Rogers, *op. cit.*, pp. 194–5.
17   Sherborne, 'Indentured Retinues', pp. 727–30.
18   Sherborne, *The Cost of English Warfare*, p. 138 and note 1.
19   Prestwich, *The Three Edwards*, p. 203.

Chapter 12 The Tyrant and the Usurper

1   Attributed to the duke of Gloucester on hearing of French proposals for a permanent peace after the truce of Leulinghen in 1389. See note 12 below.
2   Gillespie, 'King of Battles?' from *The Age of Richard II*, p. 140.
3   Sherborne, 'The Cost of English Warfare', p. 146.
4   Sherborne, 'Indentured Retinues', p. 731.
5   For details of the costs of the expedition, the numbers in the army and the matter of scutage see Lewis, 'The Last Medieval Summons', pp. 1–26; and Palmer, 'The Last Summons', pp. 771–5.
6   Keen, 'England in the Late Middle Ages', p. 276.
7   Myres, 'The Campaign of Radcot Bridge', pp. 20–33.
8   *Ibid.*, pp. 138–9.
9   Palmer, 'The Anglo-French Peace Negotiations', pp. 81–94.
10   Keen, *op. cit.*, p. 289 and note 27.

11 McHardy, A.K. Haxey's Case, 1397. From 'The Age of Richard II, ed. by James L. Gillespie, p. 104. See also Rotuli Parliamentorum, Vol. 111, p. 339.
12 Ibid., p. 408.
13 McHardy, op. cit., p. 104.
14 Shakespeare, Richard II Act 11 Scene 1, lines 210–11.
15 Keen, op. cit., p. 314.
16 Curry, 'The Hundred Years War', p. 93.

Chapter 13 The Agincourt Campaign
1 Revelations, ch VI, verse 2.
2 Allmand, Lancastrian Normandy, p. 8.
3 Wylie and Waugh, The Reign of Henry V, Vol. 2, p. 1.
4 Pugh, 'The Southampton Plot of 1415'.
5 Allmand, Henry V, p. 79 and note 55.
6 Wylie, op. cit., p. 3.
7 Ibid., p. 7.
8 Nicolas, History of the Battle of Agincourt, p. 192.
9 Ibid., p. 192, note 'c', Monstrelet's description of the siege.
10 Ibid., p. 193.
11 Taylor and Roskell (tr and eds), Gesta Henrici Quinti, p. 39.
12 Monstrelet, Chroniques d'Enguerrand de Monstrelet.
13 Ibid., p. 217.
14 Seward, The Hundred Years War, p. 161.
15 Nicolas, op. cit.
16 Ibid., p. 98.
17 Wylie, op. cit., p. 157.
18 Ibid., p. 175.
19 Allmand, op. cit., pp. 94–5.
20 Nicolas, op. cit., p. 129.
21 Wylie, op. cit., p. 225.
22 Nicolas, op. cit., p. 134.
23 As written by the Frenchman, Jean de Fevre, who fought on the English side, forty years after the battle. See Wylie, op. cit., p. 196 and note 3.
24 Ibid., p. 199.
25 Wylie, op. cit., p. 250.

Chapter 14 The Conquest of Normandy
1 Dante, the Florentine poet and philosopher, quoted in Speed (ed.), Those who Fought, p. 42.
2 Allmand, Lancastrian Normandy, p. 5.
3 Wylie and Waugh, The Reign of Henry V; Vol. 2, p. 361 and Rodger, The Safeguard of the Sea, pp. 143–4.
4 Keen, England in the Later Middle Ages, pp. 364–5 and note 11.
5 Rodger, op. cit., p. 144.
6 Newhall, The English Conquest of Normandy, p. 59 and note 119.

7Seward, *Henry V as Warlord*, p. 105.
8*Ibid.*, pp. 66–7.
9*Ibid.*, p. 76 and note 213.
10*Ibid.*, p. 80.
11Newhall, *op. cit.*, p. 269 and note 1.
12*Ibid.*, p. 272
13*Ibid.*, p. 278, note 51.
14Burne, *The Agincourt War*, p. 154.

Chapter 15 The Rise of Bedford and Talbot

1Hobbes, 'Leviathan (1651)', pt 1, ch 13. See *Oxford Dictionary of Quotations*, 4th edn, p. 340.
2Newhall, *The English Conquest of Normandy*, p. 294 and note 153.
3*Ibid.*, p. 293 and note 171.
4*Ibid.*, pp. 213–15.
5Burne, *The Agincourt War*, p. 185.
6*Ibid.*, pp. 184–93. See also Burne, 'The Battle of Cravant', pp. 172–8.
7Waurin, *Recueil des Croniques et Anchiennes Histoires*. Waurin fought in the English army at Agincourt and was present at Cravant.
8Burne, *op. cit.*, p. 197.
9This date is disputed, some say the surrender was on 15 August. But see Simpson, 'The Campaign of Verneuil', pp. 93–100.
10Newhall, *op. cit.*, p. 316 and note 276.
11Burne, *op. cit.*, p. 213.
12Wolffe, *Henry VI*, pp. 40–1.
13Seward, *The Hundred Years War*, p. 203.
14Burne, *op. cit.*, pp. 219–20.
15Allmand, *Lancastrian Normandy*, pp. 31–2, and Seward, *op. cit.*, pp. 207–8.
16Information on the artillery at Orleans taken from Viollet-le-Duc, *Encyclopédie Médiévale*, pp. 461–2.
17Jollois, *Histoire du Siege d'Orleans*, pp. 42–6.
18See Pollard, *John Talbot and the War in France*, for detailed account of military action under Talbot, also see Talbot, *The English Achilles*.
19Lot, *L'Art Militaire des Armées au Moyen Age*, p. 37.
20For a fuller account of these groups see Allmand, *op. cit.*, pp. 229–34 and Rowe, 'John Duke of Bedford'.
21Seward, *op. cit.*, p. 212.
22*Ibid.*, p. 212.

Chapter 16 The Two Kings of France

1Sackville-West, *St Joan of Arc*, pp. 304–6.
2*Ibid.*, pp. 145–50.
3*Ibid.*, pp. 304–6.
4*Ibid.*, p. 117.
5*Ibid.*, pp. 152–4.
6*Ibid.*, pp. 157–60.

7   *Ibid.*, pp. 213–16.
8   Burne, *The Agincourt War*, p. 264.
9   Keen, *England in the Late Middle Ages*, p. 388.
10 Sackville-West, *op. cit.*, p. 284.
11 Figures taken from Newhall, 'The War Finances of Henry V', pp. 196–7.
12 *Ibid.*, p. 189.
13 Pollard, *John Talbot and the War in France*, p. 34, see also Keen, *op. cit.*, p. 406.
14 See Pollard, *op. cit.*, pp. 36–40 for army organization after 1429.
15 Keen, *op. cit.*, pp. 389–90.
16 Allmand, *op. cit.*, pp. 237–8.
17 Pollard, *op. cit.*, pp. 32–4.
18 Chartier, Jacques, 'Chronique Française du Roi de France Charles VII', quoted by Speed in *Those who Fought*, p. 197.
19 Contamine, *War in the Middle Ages*, p. 169.
20 Chartier, *op. cit.*, p. 202.

Chapter 17 The Loss of Normandy and Aquitaine

1   Wolffe, *Henry VI*, p. 210. This was part of a jingle going the rounds in London at the time.
2   Burne, *The Agincourt War*, p. 295.
3   *Ibid.*, pp. 293–392 and see Talbot, *The English Achilles*, pp. 120–5.
4   PPC, V, 260.
5   Stevenson, *Letters and Papers*, pp. 638–42. See also Allmand, *Lancastrian Normandy*, p. 46.
6   Wolffe, *op. cit.*, p. 210.
7   Stevenson, *op. cit.*, pp. 696–718. Gives several orders from Henry VI to Mathew Gough and Foukes Eton, esquires, concerning the handing over of the town and castle of Le Mans to the French.
8   Jones, 'Somerset, York and the Wars of the Roses', p. 301, note 2.
9   Stevenson, *op. cit.*, see pp. 619–34 for a list dated 1450 of 'The Cities, Towns, Castles and Fortresses in France and Normandy taken from the English by the French during the Administration of the Duke of Somerset'.
10 Jones, *op. cit.*, p. 305.
11 See Allmand, *op. cit.*, p. 3.
12 Burne, *op. cit.*, p. 316.
13 *Ibid.*, p. 324.
14 *Ibid.*, p. 325.
15 Wolffe, *op. cit.*, p. 211.
16 Stevenson, *op. cit.*, pp. 718–22. The point is made in a list of questions to be asked by the council of the duke of Somerset respecting his misconduct in Normandy.
17 Wolffe, *op. cit.*, pp. 219–20.
18 *Ibid.*, pp. 231–8.
19 *Ibid.*, p. 240.

20 *Ibid.*, p. 244.
21 *Ibid.*, p. 249.
22 Labarge, *Gascony, England's First Colony*, p. 218.
23 Stevenson, *op. cit.*, pp. 479–80.
24 Wolffe, *op. cit.*, p. 265.
25 Burne, *op. cit.*, p. 334.
26 *Ibid.*, p. 336.

Chapter 18 Favouritism and Patronage

  1 Shakespeare, *Richard II*, Act IV, Sc 1, lines 136–8. The bishop of Carlisle berates Henry Bolingbroke for saying that he would ascend the throne after Richard II had been taken prisoner at Chester in 1399.
  2 Lander, *Crown and Nobility*, p. 57.
  3 Storey, *The End of the House of Lancaster*, pp. 33–42.
  4 Carpenter, *The Wars of the Roses*, p. 137.
  5 Storey, *op. cit.*, for a general view of the political manoeuvrings and conflicts of the magnates, which led to the Wars of the Roses.
  6 Carpenter, *op. cit.*, p. 119.
  7 Jones, 'Somerset, York and the Wars of the Roses', pp. 285–307. For a detailed background to the quarrel between York and Somerset.
  8 Storey, *op. cit.*, p. 72.
  9 Pollard, *The Wars of the Roses*, p. 22. See also Gillingham, *The Wars of the Roses*, pp. 73–4 and Wolffe, *Henry VI*, pp. 270–1 and notes 13 and 14.
 10 Gillingham, *Ibid.*, pp. 76–8, and Wolffe, *ibid.*, p. 274.
 11 Weir, *Lancaster and York, the Wars of the Roses*, pp. 178–9.
 12 Armstrong, 'Politics and the Battle of St Albans', p. 13.
 13 Armstrong, *ibid.*, p. 17.
 14 Armstrong, *ibid.*, p. 28.
 15 Wolffe, *op. cit.*, p. 302.
 16 Gillingham, *op. cit.*, p. 102.
 17 Weir, *op. cit.*, p. 218.
 18 Haigh, *The Military Campaigns of the Wars of the Roses*, based on account at pp. 17–19.
 19 Gillingham, *op. cit.*, p. 104.
 20 Gillingham, *op. cit.*, pp. 109–10.
 21 Gillingham, *op. cit.*, p. 111. Clearly a gross exaggeration and as Gillingham says a figure traditionally used to mean 'a great many'.
 22 Goodman, *The Wars of the Roses*, p. 36.
 23 Gillingham, *op. cit.*, p. 114.
 24 Wolffe, *op. cit.*, p. 325.
 25 Haigh, *op. cit.*, p. 37.

Chapter 19 The Battle of Towton

  1 Shakespeare, *Henry VI*, part 3, scene V, lines 5–8. King Henry describing the Battle of Towton.

2 Weir, *Lancaster and York*, p. 270.
3 Goodman, *The Wars of the Roses*, p. 47 and note 47.
4 Goodman, *Ibid.*, p. 156.
5 Haigh, *The Military Campaigns of the Wars of the Roses*, p. 56.
6 Boardman, *The Battle of Towton*. This account of the action at Ferrybridge is based on that at pp. 66–77.
7 Hall, *Chronicle*.
8 Boardman, *op. cit.*, p. 104.
9 Boardman, *op. cit.*, p. 115 and note 10.
10 Goodman, *op. cit.*, p. 58.
11 Wolffe, *Henry VI*, p. 334.
12 Gillingham, *op. cit.*, p. 144.
13 Goodman, *op. cit.*, p. 60.
14 Wolffe, *op. cit.*, p. 335.
15 Haigh, *op. cit.*, p. 78.
16 Haigh, *op. cit.*, p. 83.

Chapter 20 Edward Flees and Returns

1 Warkworth, *A Chronicle of the First Thirteen years of the Reign of King Edward the Fourth*.
2 Fabyan, *New Chronicles of England and France*, p. 662.
3 Carpenter, *The Wars of the Roses*, p. 166.
4 *Ibid*.
5 Gillingham, *The Wars of the Roses*, p. 160.
6 *Ibid.*, p. 161.
7 Haigh, *The Military Campaigns of the Wars of the Roses*, pp. 100–2.
8 *Ibid.*, p. 107.
9 Seward, *The Wars of the Roses*, p. 152.
10 Wolffe, *Henry VI*, p. 341. See also Lander, *Crown and Nobility*, pp. 252 and 257.
11 Pollard, *Lord Fitzhughe's Rising in 1470*, p. 171.
12 Gillingham, *op. cit.*, p. 183.
13 Myers, *The Outbreak of War*, p. 114/5.
14 Warkworth, *op. cit.*, p. 13.
15 Haigh, *op. cit.*, p. 115.
16 Bruce, *Historie of the Arrivall of Edward IV*. Most of the details concerning Edward IV's return to England and subsequent restoration come from this MS written at the time by a person in his entourage. Details found from other sources are noted as such.
17 Warkworth, *op. cit.*, p. 14.
18 Gillingham, *op. cit.*, p. 195.
19 Warkworth, *op. cit.*, p. 16.
20 Warkworth, *op. cit.*, p. 19.
21 Richmond, 'Fauconberg's Kentish Rising', pp. 673–92. Richmond gives a full account of this rising well supported by notes.

22 Richmond, *op. cit.*
23 Fabyan, *op. cit.*, p. 662.

Chapter 21 The Battle of Bosworth Field

1 Shakespeare, *King Richard III*, Act 5, Scene 4, line 7. Said by King Richard on being unhorsed at the battle of Bosworth Field.
2 Lander, *Conflict and Stability*, pp. 101–3. Lander, *Crown and Nobility*, pp. 11–12.
3 *Ibid.*, p. 226, quoting from the Second Continuation of the *Croyland Chronicle* in Fulman, p. 557.
4 Gillingham, *The Wars of the Roses*, p. 216.
5 Lander, *op. cit.*, p. 246.
6 Lander, *op. cit.*, p. 230.
7 Figures taken from Lander, *op. cit.*, pp. 231–2.
8 See Lander, *op. cit.*, pp. 236–7 and appendix E, p. 321.
9 Vergil, *English History*, p. 161.
10 Lander, *op. cit.*, p. 234 and note 57 for more information on the 'Second Benevolence'.
11 *Ibid.* Appendix E, p. 321.
12 Storey, 'The Wardens of the Marches', p. 615.
13 Commynes, *Memoires.*
14 Carpenter, *The Wars of the Roses*, pp. 197–8.
15 Quoted by Desmond Seward in *The Wars of the Roses*, p. 224.
16 Vergil, *op. cit.*, p. 169.
17 Seward, *op. cit.*, p. 224. See also Fabyan, *New Chronicles of England and France*, p. 663.
18 Lander, *op. cit.*, p. 247 and notes.
19 Vergil, *op. cit.*, p. 167.
20 *Ibid.*, p. 170.
21 Carpenter, *op. cit.*, p. 199.
22 Vergil, *op. cit.*, p. 174.
23 Carpenter, *op. cit.*, p. 209. See also Weir, *The Princes in the Tower.*
24 For a clear and reasoned case that the princes were murdered by Richard III see Weir, *op. cit.*, first published by the Bodley Head Ltd, 1992.
25 Gillingham, *op. cit.*, p. 221.
26 Vergil, *op. cit.*, p. 196.
27 Weir, *op. cit.*, pp. 179–80.
28 Carpenter, *op. cit.*, pp. 212–13.

Postscript

1 Weir, *The Princes in the Tower*, p. 239.
2 Vergil, *Historia Anglicana*, pp. 24–7.
3 Gillingham, *The Wars of the Roses*, p. 252.

Glossary

Aketon or **haketon**. A padded jacket with long sleeves, worn by foot soldiers as a simple form of armour, also worn by knights and men-at-arms under the hauberk to prevent the mail from rubbing.

Appenage. A dependent territory given to the son of a king or prince.

Bailliages. Bailleywicks, towns or cities under the jurisdiction of a baillie appointed by the crown.

Balinger. A shallow-draft ship with both oars and sails, often used as a warship. They were usually between 50 and 85 feet overall and could displace as much as 35 tons. They were long and narrow with much less draft than a cog but more than a galley. One built for Henry IV in about 1410 had 24 oars a side in addition to a square sail.

Bannerole. A small banner, perhaps no longer than nine inches by three inches on the fly, fastened to a small spike on the top of a commander's helmet displaying his badge for recognition purposes in battle.

Barbacane or **barbican**. A fortified outwork, generally made of a ditch and palisade, and sometimes of stone. It was built to protect a town gate or castle entrance or bridge. In due course they became quite complicated stone outworks with towers.

Barded horse. A barded horse was a horse which carried steel or leather armours covered with cloth trappings falling nearly to the ground.

Barehide. An undressed hide or one with its hair removed.

Barge. A shallow-draft ship with both sails and oars of the same type as a balinger but generally larger and often used as a warship.

Bascinet. A conical helmet that left the face uncovered, though visors were often attached to them. They were worn either over a camail or the latter was attached to it by lacing.

Bastide. A small town or a village in the south-west of France, enclosing a market place, a church and sometimes a chateau. In those bastides where no chateau existed the church was generally a fortified church. It was generally walled or the outside houses were continuous and their outside walls, which had no windows, served as the walls of the bastide. A gateway and tower or a barbican usually protected the entrance. Many bastides had a deep ditch or even a moat surrounding the walls.

Bill. A bill was originally a staff weapon adapted from an agricultural hedging tool with a sharp point to the end. They were later refined into the halberd.

Bistoury. A fine-bladed surgeon's knife used for making incisions.

Blazon. A coat of arms, displayed on shields, jupons and tabards, and the trappings of horses.

Bombard. A heavy siege cannon usually fired from a solid wooden platform laid on the ground; some had a bore of 17 or 18 inches in diameter. A good example of a bombard is 'Mons Meg' at Edinburgh Castle.

Brigandine. A tunic of cloth or leather with many small steel plates riveted to it.

Brigands. Groups of people who operated against the English in Normandy from the early 1420s onwards. According to the modern French view they were patriots and partisans, but the English simply considered them outlaws. Those who had taken the oath of fealty generally ended their career on the block, while those who had not graced the gallows as common criminals. Their numbers increased when the French were doing well and reduced when they were not.

Brow. A portable bridge carried on board ship and used to cross from ship to shore; a gangway.

Camail. A mail hood worn over the head under a bascinet or other helm and falling onto the shoulders.

Carrack. A type of ship that gradually replaced the cog in northern waters. It originated in the Mediterranean and was a carvel built ship with a lateen sail. By th time of its introduction into northern waters it carried both a lateen sail and a square sail on two masts and by the middle of the fifteenth century a third mast had been added. It became the main type of ship for warships and had high castles both fore and aft. By the end of the Wars of the Roses they had become large ships with an unloaded displacement of 500 tons. They began to carry guns on board by about 1410.

Cat. A covered wooden tower on wheels. Carpenters built them on the spot the same height as the curtain walls or towers of the castle or town being besieged. Inside the cat were platforms with stairs between them to the top story where a draw bridge was placed so that it could be lowered onto the walls. The cat was covered with wet skins as protection against fire. When all was ready the cat would be wheeled into position against the walls and an assault party would climb up to the top platform, the drawbridge would be lowered and the assault party would cross over to the walls under covering fire from archers and crossbowmen.

Cheveteyn de la Guerre. Literally 'Chief of the War', we would call such an appointment 'Commander-in-Chief'. The word 'cheveteyn' gradually became 'chieftain'.

Coat armour. An expression that refers to the tabards worn over plate armour in the fifteenth century to distinguish the wearer from those not entitled to armourial bearings. Only noblemen, knights and esquires would be entitled to wear a heraldic tabard; they were worn to distinguish these men in battle to their followers and showed that they could probably stand a ransom and were worth taking prisoner; this saved many lives.

Cog. The usual merchant ship in northern waters until the late fifteenth century. It was clinker built and had a single mast with a square sail; those used as warships had high castles fore and aft as well as one at the top of the mast. They were beamy, deep-keel ships and were very seaworthy but were unable to steer close to the wind. At the beginning of the Hundred Years' War they varied from about 10 tons burthen to about 200 tons, however by 1415 cogs of 500 tons burthen were not uncommon.

Cortes. The Castilian parliament.

Courser. A horse like a modern hunter and often used in war.

Cuir-boulli. Literally boiled leather. When armour was made of this it was shaped to fit while still wet. It was a light and effective form of protection for the knees and elbows and was often used as horse armour.

Cuissarts. Protection for the thighs made of strips of steel riveted through leather, padded and covered on the outside with cloth, generally silk or velvet and brightly coloured. The work was known as pourpointerie and was often also used to protect the forearms. The cuissarts were more comfortable to wear when riding than plate armour and were worn from the middle of the fourteenth century to the early fifteenth century.

Culverin. A field gun, mounted on a carriage that fired an iron ball of about 20 lb weight.

Danegeld. A tax imposed by and paid to an invading army to buy them off to prevent the burning and looting of property.

Destrier. A warhorse. These were specially bred animals, larger than a hack, able to carry the weight of a man in armour and trained for war.

Ecorcheurs. So called because they sometimes flayed the skin off their prisoners during torture, were in fact the fifteenth-century equivalent of the brigands of earlier times but who operated in those areas of France controlled by the Valois; brigands still operated in Normandy. The ecorcheurs were unemployed soldiers, of whom there were many, who banded together under a captain and made their living by pillage, extortion and ransom. A band might include ex-soldiers from Burgundy, England, France and Scotland all co-operating in a single enterprise.

Escheator. An officer of the crown responsible for ensuring the return of the lands of a fief to the crown on the death of the tenant who died without having a successor qualified to inherit under the original grant. There was usually an escheator for each county and they were represented in the king's council by the escheator-general.

Estates. Regional assemblies in France with limited executive powers but no tax-raising powers. However they were essential to approve taxes imposed by the crown or new laws. That of Paris provided the political forum for the Îsle de France.

Falchion. A single-edged curved sword.

Fascine. A large bundle of sticks bound together. They were used to fill ditches outside a castle or town wall at a siege. Usually between six and ten feet long and three or four feet in diameter.

Fencible men. Freeborn Englishmen between the ages of sixteen and sixty. Providing they were fit they were liable for military service within the country for a maximum of forty days. They were called out by the king, or on his behalf, and mustered by the local sheriff. They were paid by the king once they crossed their county boundary. Serfs could not be fencible men.

Free Companies. A recognized company of unemployed soldiers under a knight or sometimes under an elected leader made up of redundant soldiers of many nationalities operating in France. They were often based in a castle that they had seized and ruled a particular area from which they extracted taxes. Some free companies roamed the countryside robbing and pillaging.

Galley. These boats were the traditional warship in the Mediterranean, where they were carvel built and carried a lateen sail. However they were also built in northern waters where they were based on the Viking longships, were clinker built and had a square sail. The two types had merged by about the beginning of the fifteenth century. They were used as warships by the French and English and by France's ally Castille. They were narrow, shallow-draft ships but nothing like as seaworthy as the cogs and carracks and could not carry cargo. A large galley could have sixty oars a side and a keel length of 180 feet. The oars were up to 23 feet long and were propelled by five oarsmen. Galleys had a top speed under oars of about 9 knots and under sail downwind of about 12 knots. They all had a ramming beak at the bows and often a small cannon on the deck in the bows.

Gambeson. A tight-fitting quilted garment stuffed with wool and worn underneath chain mail to prevent chafing. No longer worn after about 1335 due to improvements in armour, particularly the increasing use of plate armour.

Hanse. Short for the Hanseatic League, a trading alliance set up in 1358 by some north German states.

Harness. An expression used, not only for a horse's harness but also for the weapons and armour of the person who rode it.

Hastiludes. The tournaments.

Hauberk. A shirt of mail reaching to mid-thigh.

Hobilar. Originally the name for a Scottish mounted infantryman, adopted by the English after the Weardale campaign. The *Chronicle of Lanercost* referring to the Scottish army says it included 'the conformity of the villages who are called hobilars'. A Scottish hobilar rode to war but fought on his feet; he rode a pony or hack and carried a spear and a sword as well as his provisions and a cloak. English hobilars were often used as scouts and flank guards.

Jack. A jack was a small coat falling to the thigh and made up of several thicknesses of leather or felt and studded with steel rivets or plates. It was the usual protection worn by archers and bill-men.

Jaques. Rebellious peasants, collectively known as the jaquerie. These peasants rebelled against authority in northern France after Poitiers and caused hardship and misery in the areas that they overran. They were finally defeated and scattered by troops of Charles of Navarre in 1358.

Jupon. A sleeveless tight-fitting jacket worn over plate armour; it was decorated with the wearer's coat of arms or a national insignia, such as the Cross of St George.

Lance. A long spear used by mounted men-at-arms and knights. First weapon used in the tournaments by jousting knights. A crenelled lance was one that had its sharp point removed and replaced by a small wooden coronet, which would break off on striking the armour of an opponent in the lists.

Lance. A collective noun used to designate a knight and his immediate following of an esquire, a groom and a servant. The esquire had to be armed and mounted like his master the knight.

Letters of Marque. Letters issued by the sovereign to license a person to arm a ship and to use it to capture enemy shipping.

Liege homage. The acceptance of the king as one's sovereign lord. In practice it meant that one accepted the king's law and was obliged to support the king with one's armed manpower at war whenever called upon to do so. This homage had to be given by those owning land direct from the king. It was also usually expected from those lower down the social scale who might own or rent land direct from a magnate in which case the homage would be given to the magnate.

March. The march was the frontier between two countries, as between England and Scotland.

Mouton d'Or or **florin.** A coin valued at 4 shillings Sterling.

Oyer and **Terminer.** Literally to hear and determine. It was a progress of judges and sergeants appointed by the king to investigate and punish treasons, felonies, disturbances and insurrections. The king sometimes led these commissions.

Palfrey. A well-bred riding horse, but not as strong as a destrier or a courser.

Pâtis. A local and illegal tax imposed by English garrisons and the free companies on the area surrounding their garrison for approximately a day's ride. Garrison commanders and their men looked upon this as one of their perks, and for the free companies it was often their only form of pay. Until the time of Henry V officials kept a blind eye on the practice. This was an unofficial impost on the surrounding population and garrison commanders kept the proceeds. It was a protection racket and its collection relieved the boredom of garrison life.

Pavise. A large shield, about the height of a man, made of planks of wood covered with boiled leather. It was mainly used by crossbowmen and was carried into action by a paviseur who held it upright on the ground to give some protection to the crossbowman, particularly when he bent to span his crossbow. At sieges the paviseur would be dispensed with and the pavise was propped upright with a wooden leg. They were also hung on the rails of ships to give protection against arrows.

Peel. A defensive stone tower, usually entered by ladder at the first floor. They were common both sides of the Anglo-Scottish border and in some parts of the Highlands.

Pontes. French word for a brow or gangway.

Pourpointerie. Thickly quilted material generally used as backing for metal defences riveted to it.

Purveyance. The buying of supplies or commodities at a fixed price by purveyors for the crown, the price being fixed by the crown.

Quitclaim. A feudal charter by which an overlord renounced any claim he might have on his liegeman, including that of liege homage itself, or by which any one lord renounced claims held against another.

Rachâts. An illegal tax imposed by garrison commanders and free company leaders on the surrounding countryside. This was a common practice throughout France and eventually made illegal by both the English and French authorities.

Ribald or **Ribaldquin.** A type of cannon made from several small-bore barrels held together with steel bands like a fascine and mounted on a carriage. The barrels could be fired individually or all at the same time. It was a weapon mainly used by castle garrisons to cover a breach in the walls and produced a very effective spread of shot against a breaching party. However when used on a carriage in the field it produced an effect like the grapeshot of a much later era or perhaps of a machine gun. Properly placed it significantly enhanced the fire of archers against massed men-at-arms, either mounted or on foot, and was beginning to be adopted by armies in the field. It was used by the French at the Battle of Castillon.

Routier. A soldier belonging to a free company.

Schiltron. A compact mass of spearmen often as deep as it was wide. It was a Scottish attack formation, very vulnerable to massed archery fire but relatively immune to a cavalry charge; it had great penetrating power against a line of men-at-arms.

Scutage. A tax on a knight's fee in lieu of personal service.

Sergeant. Originally one of the twenty-four men, usually knights who were required to be in attendance on the king's person and who were used to arrest traitors and other offenders.

Serpentine. An early form of musket fired from the shoulder. It had a wooden stock or sometimes a wooden shaft that could be stuck into the ground. The serpentine fired a small iron or lead ball about half an inch in diameter. It was ideal for castle defence and was used by the French at the Battle of Castillon; it was first seen about 1440. It was so called because of its trigger mechanism, which resembled a serpent.

Signet. The signet was a small personal seal used by the sovereign to authenticate his orders and requirements and to authorize private and some official documents.

Staple. The staple was a designated selling point for various commodities on the Continent. On 5 April 1347 Edward III established the wool staple at Calais, which also became the staple for tin, lead and feathers, other English exports. Continental merchants buying any of these commodities had to go to Calais to purchase them. This particularly affected the Flemish cloth makers and later when the duke of Burgundy inherited Flanders Burgundian foreign policy.

Sumpter. A pack-horse.

Tally. A short wooden stick issued by the exchequer, or on its behalf, that represented a debt owed by the exchequer. Tallies were issued in identical pairs and were marked with notches to represent the sum owed and also had the exact amount written on them. One tally was issued to the officer responsible for payment and its copy to the creditor who had to present it to the paying officer for payment to be made. Sometimes a single tally was made and this was split down the middle, one half being kept by each party; when payment was claimed the two halves would be compared and if they matched payment was made.

Trappings. Long cloth horse coverings draped over the horse that fell almost to the ground. They were originally intended to deflect arrows or lance thrusts in battle and were usually embroidered or printed with the armorial insignia of the rider; in due course they were used in tournaments only.

Trébuchet. A large siege engine made of wood with a throwing arm up to 50 feet long pivoted close to one end between two upright posts. The throwing arm was powered by a large counterweight hung from the short end of the arm; a sling was fastened at the long end of the throwing arm into which a stone of between two and three hundred pounds was placed. Such a stone could be thrown in a high trajectory for about 300 yards. To throw the stone a winch hauled the long arm down to near ground level and when the throwing arm was released the weight at the short end pulled that end towards the ground and pivoted the long end and the sling in a wide arc overhead, releasing the stone.

Trephine. A surgeon's small hand drill.

Tun. A large barrel or cask used to transport wine and used as a measure of volume; it gradually applied to other containers including chests of the same volume. A tun equalled two butts or pipes, four hogsheads or eight barrels. A beer barrel contained 36 gallons. A full tun weighed approximately one ton.

Vintaine. Twenty soldiers raised by shrieval summons; usually foot soldiers, either archers or bill-men, but could also be men-at-arms, hobilars or mounted archers.

Vintenar. A junior officer in charge of a Vintaine.

Wappinshaw or **Wapenshaw.** An inspection of arms by sheriffs required to be held regularly by law in Scotland of all those liable to be called for military service, i.e. those having more than £10 per year income.

Wardrobe. The office of the wardrobe was originally the crown office that was responsible for paying for military service; this function was gradually taken over by the exchequer in the mid fourteenth century but the wardrobe remained responsible for paying the army in the field until the end of the century.

Bibliography

Abbreviations

AHR	American Historical Review
BIHR	Bulletin of Inst of Hist Research
BJRL	Bulletin of the John Ryland's Library
CM	Camden Miscellany, Royal Historical Society
CPR	Calendar of Patent Rolls
CUP	Cambridge University Press
EcHR	Economic History Review
EETS	Early English Text Society
EHR	English Historical Review
HA	History Association
HJ	Historical Journal
HT	History To-day
JAHR	Journal of Society of Army Hist Res
JMedH	Journal of Medieval History
JmilHis	Journal of Military History
LUP	Liverpool University Press
MM	Mariners Mirror
MS	Medieval Studies
MUP	Manchester University Press
NMS	Nottingham Medieval Studies
OUP	Oxford University Press
P&P	Past and Present
POPC	Proceedings and Ordinances of the Privy Council
PR	Pipe Rolls
PRO	Public Record Office
SAHR	Society of Army Historical Research
SHR	Scottish History Review
Spec	Speculum
STS	Scottish Text Society
TBC	Transactions of the Buchan Club
TRHS	Trans of the Royal Historical Society
Vi	Viator
YUP	Yale University Press

Printed Record Sources
'The Blacke Booke of the Admiralty', trans by Travers Twiss, 1871.
CPR 1436–41.
POPC, Vol. 5.
PRO, Exchequer accounts, 1480, E404/56/3/29.
PRO, Exchequer accounts, 1480, E404/77/1/38.
PRO, Exchequer accounts, 1480, E404/78/3/43.

Primary Sources
Anonimalle Chronicle, 1333–81, ed by V.H. Galbraith, MUP, 1927.

Aungier, G.J., *French Chronicle of London*, trans by Camden series XXVIII, 1844.

Baker, Geoffrey le, *Chronicon*, ed E.M. Thompson, H Rolls series, Oxford, 1889.

Barbour, J., *The Brus*, ed and trans by G. Eyre Todd, 1907.

Benet, John, *Chronicle for the Years 1400–1462*, ed by G.L. and M.A. Harriss in Camden Miscellany, XXIV, RHS, 1972.

Bonet, Honoré, *The Tree of Battles*, ed and trans by G.W. Coopland, Liverpool, 1949.

The Black Book of the Order of the Garter, published 1724.

Brie, F.W.D., *Brut*, ed by EETS, 1906.

Bruce, J., *Historie of the Arrival of Edward IV, AD 1471*, Camden Society, 1838.

Chandos Herald, *Life of the Black Prince by the Herald of Sir John Chandos*, ed by M.K. Pope and E.C. Lodge, Oxford 1910, reprint 1974.

Charny, Geoffroi de, *The Book of Chivalry*, EETS.

Chaucer, Geoffrey, *The Canterbury Tales*, trans by David Wright, OUP, 1985.

Chronica Monasterii de Melsa, Rolls series, Vol. ii.

Croyland Chronicle, continuation, 1459–1486, ed by N. Pronay and J. Cox, 1986.

Devon, Frederick, Issue Rolls of Thomas de Bremtingham (44 Ed III), London 1835.

Evans, J., *The Unconquered Knight*, a chronicle of Don Pedro Nino, trans 1929.

Fabyan, R., *New Chronicles of England and France*, ed by H. Ellis, London 1811.

Froissart, J., *Chronicles*, translated from the French by Lord Berners and published in six volumes 1901–3.

Froissart, J., *Chronicles*, selected, translated and edited by Geof Brereton, Penguin, 1968.

Froissart, J., *Chronicles of England, France and Spain*, condensed version of Thomas Johnes of Haford's version (1803–10), adapted by Dunster, H.P., J.M. Dent & Co., 1853.

Froissart, J., *Froissart in Britain*, ed Henry Newbolt, London, 1900.

Froissart, J., *Historian*, ed by Palmer, J.J.N., Woodbridge, Ottawa, 1981.

Gairdner, J. (ed.), *Three Fifteenth Century Chronicles*, Camden Society, 1880.

Gairdner, J. (ed.), *The Paston Letters 1422–1509*, 3 vols, Edinburgh, 1910.

Giles, J.A. (ed.), *Chronicles of the White Rose of York, matters relative to the reign of Edward IV*, 1845.

Gray, Sir Thomas, *Scalacronica*, ed by J. Stevenson, Edinburgh, 1836.

Hall, Edward, *Chronicle*, ed by Henry Ellis, 1809.

Harleian MS, 4690, f82, Brit Mus.

Harriss, G.L. and M.A. (eds), *John Benet's Chronicle for the Years 1460–1462*, Camden Miscellany, RHS Vol. XXIV, 1972.

Knighton, Henrici, *Chronicum*, Monachi Leycesternsis, ed by J.R. Lumby, Rolls series, 1889–93.

Le Bel, Jean, *Chronique*, ed by J. Viard and E. Déprez, 2 vols (1904–5).

Le Bel, Froissart, de Monstrelet, *Chronicles of the Hundred Years' War*, ed by P.E. Thompson, Folio Society, London, 1966.

Maxwell, Sir H., *The Chronicle of Lanercost, 1272–1346.*

Monstrelet, Enguerand de, *Chroniques d'Enguerand de Monstrelet*, ed by L. Douet d'Arcq, Paris, 1857–62.

Munroe, C. (ed.), *Letters of Margaret of Anjou*, Camden Society, 1863.

Nicolas, Sir H. (ed.), *Proceedings and Ordinances of the Privy Council of England*, Vol. V, London 1837.

Nichols, J.G. (ed.), *The Boke of Noblesse*, Roxburghe Club, 1860.

Paston Letters, ed by J. Gairdner, London, 1904.

Pisan, Christine de, 'The Book of Fayttes of Armes and of Chivalrye', trans by William Caxton, ed by A.T.P. Byles, EETS, 1937.

Pronay, N. and Cox, J. (ed.), *Croyland Chronicle Continuation, 1459–1496*, 1986.

Robert of Avesbury's Chronicle, ed by E.M. Thompson, Rolls series, London, 1889.

Rous, John, *Life of Richard Beauchamp, Earl of Warwick*, Cottonian MS; Julius, E. IV.

Rowe, B.J.H., 'A contemporary account of the Hundred Years' War', EHR Vol. 41, 1926.

Stevenson, J. (ed.), *Letters and Papers Illustrative of the Wars of the English in France*, Rolls series, 2 vols, 1861–4.

Stevenson, J. (ed.), *Narratives of the Expulsion of the English from Normandy, 1449–1450*, Rolls series, London, 1863.

Stevenson, J. (ed.) *The Scalacromica of Sir Thomas Grey*, Edinburgh, 1836.

Taylor, F. and Roskell, J.S. (trans and eds), *Gesta Henrici Quinti, The Deeds of Henry V*, Oxford, 1975.

Vergil, Polydore, *Three Books of Polydore's English History, comprising the Reigns of Henry VI, Edward IV and Richard III*, from an early translation, ed Sir Henry Ellis, Camden Society, 1844.

Vergil, Polydore, *Anglica Historia*, AD 1485–1537, ed by J.O. Halliwell, Camden Series 1950.

Walsingham, Thomas, *Historia Anglicana*, ed by H.T. Riley, Calendar of Close Rolls series, 1863–4.

Warkworth, John, *A Chronicle of the First Thirteen Years of the Reign of King Edward the Fourth*, ed by J.O. Halliwell, Camden Society, 1839.

Warwick Pageant, The, Chronicles of Richard de Beaumont, earl of Warwick.

Waurin, Jean de, *Recueil des Croniques et Anchiennes Histoire de la Grande Bretagne*, ed by W. and E. Hardy, Rolls series, 1864–1891.

Secondary Sources

Alban, J.R., 'English Coastal defence; some XIV Century Modifications within the System', from *Patronage, the Crown and Provinces in Later Medieval England*, ed by R.A. Griffiths.

Allmand, C.T. (ed.), *Society at War, The Experience of England and France during the Hundred Years' War*, Edinburgh, 1973.

Allmand, C.T., 'War and Profit in the Late Middle Ages', HT, 15 (1965).

Allmand, C.T., *War, Literature and Politics in the Late Middle Ages*, ed by Copeland, LUP, 1976.

Allmand, C.T., 'The War and the Non-Combatant', from *The Hundred Years' War*, ed by K.A. Fowler, London, 1971.

Allmand, C.T., *The Hundred Years' War*, CUP, 1988.

Allmand, C.T., 'The Aftermath of War in XVth Century France', History, Vol. 61, 1976.

Allmand, C.T., *Henry V*, YUP, London, 1992.

Allmand, C.T., *Lancastrian Normandy, 1415–1450; The History of a Medieval Occupation*, OUP, 1997.

Allmand, C.T., 'The Anglo-French Negotiations of 1439', BIHR, Vol. 40, 1967.

Anderson, W., *Castles of the Middle Ages*, London, 1970.

Anderson, W., *Castles of Europe*, Ferndale Editions, London, 1980.

Armitage-Smith, S., *John of Gaunt*, 1904.

Armstrong, C.A.J., 'Politics and the Battle of St Albans', BIHR, Vol. 33, 1960.

Armstrong, C.A.J., 'Some Examples of the Distribution of News in England at the Time of the Wars of the Roses', from *Studies in Mediaeval History*, ed by F.M. Powicke, Oxford, 1948.

Ashdown, C.H., *Armour and Weapons in the Middle Ages*, London, 1925.

Ashdown, C.H., *European Arms and Armour*, Barnes and Noble Books, 1995.

Ayton, Andrew, 'English Armies in the Fourteenth Century', from *Arms, Armies and Fortifications in the Hundred Years' War*, ed by Anne Curry and Michael Hughes, Boydell Press, 1994.

Bagley, J.J., *Margaret of Anjou*, Batsford, 1948.

Baldwin, J.F., *The King's Council in England during the Middle Ages*, Clarendon Press, Oxford, 1913.

Barber, R., *The Knight and Chivalry*, London, 1970.

Barber, R., *Life and Campaigns of the Black Prince*, Boydell Press, 1986.

Barber, R., *Edward, Prince of Wales and Aquitaine: A Biography of the Black Prince*, Allen Lane, Penguin Books Ltd, 1978.

Barber, R. and Barker, J., *Tournaments, Jousts, Chivalry and Pageants in the Middle Ages*, Boydell Press, 1989.

Barbour, John, *The Bruce*, ed by W.W. Skeat, STS, Vol. II, Edinburgh, 1894. Also ed by W.M. Mackenzie in 1909.

Barker, J.R.V., *The Tournament in England, 1100–1400*, Boydell Press, 1986.

Barnie, J., *War in Medieval Society; Social Values and the Hundred Years' War, 1337–99*, London, 1971.

Barron, E.M., *The Scottish War of Independence*, Inverness, 1914.

Barron, C., 'The Tyranny of Richard II', BIHR, Vol. 41 (1968).

Barrow, G.W.S., *Robert Bruce*, London, 1965.

Barrow, G.W.S., 'The Aftermath of War: England and Scotland in the late XIIIth and early XIV Centuries', TRHS, 5th Ser, Vol. 28 (1978).

Bartlett, C. and Embleton, G., *English Longbowman, 1330–1515*, Warrior series, Vol. 11, Osprey Press.

Bayley, C.C., 'The Campaign of 1375 and the Good Parliament', EHR, Vol. 55 (1940).

Bean, J.M.H., 'Plague, Population and Economic Decline in England in the Later Middle Ages', EcHR, 2nd Ser, XV (1963).

Bean, J.M.W., *Henry IV and the Percys*, History, Vol. 44 (1959).

Bennet, M., *The Battle of Bosworth*, Gloucester, 1987.

Bennet, M., *Agincourt, Triumph against the Odds*, London, 1991.

Blair, C., *European Armour, 1066 to 1700*, London, 1958.

Blakeway, M., *An Archer in the Army of Edward III*, 1962.

Blyth, J.D., 'The Battle of Tewkesbury', Transactions of the Bristol and Gloucestershire Archaeological Society, LXX, 1961.

Boardman, A.W., *The Medieval Soldier in the Wars of the Roses*, Sutton Publishing Ltd, 1998.

Boardman, A.W., *The Battle of Towton*, Sutton Publishing Ltd, 1994.

Bornstein, D., 'Military Manuals in Fifteenth Century England', MS, Vol. 37 (1975).

Bradbury, J., *The Medieval Archer*, Boydell Press, 1985.

Bridbury, A.R., 'The Black Death', EcHR, 2nd Ser, XXVI (1973).

Bridbury, A.R., 'The Hundred Years' War, Costs and Profits' from *Trade, Government and Economy in Pre-industrial England*, ed by D.G. Coleman and A.H. John, 1976.

Brindley, H.H., 'Medieval Ships', MM, Vols II and III.

Brooks, F.W., *English Naval Forces, 1199–1272*, London, 1962.

Broome, D.M., 'The Battle of Poitiers', EHR, 53 (1928).

Brown, A.L., 'The English Campaign in Scotland, 1400', from *British Government and Administration*, studies presented to S.B. Chrimes, ed by H. Hearder and H.R. Loyn, Cardiff, 1974.

Brown, H., *History of Scotland*, Cambridge, 1911.

Bryant, A., *The Story of England*, Vol. 2, London, 1963.

Burly, S.J., 'The Victualling of Calais 1347–65', BIHR, Vol. 31 (1958).

Burne, Alfred H., *The Crécy War: A Military History of the Hundred Years' War from 1337 to the Peace of Brétigny, 1360*, Greenhill Press, London, 1977.

Burne, Alfred H., *The Agincourt War: A Military History of the latter part of the Hundred Years' War from 1369–1453*, Greenwood Press, London, 1976.

Burne, Alfred H., 'The Battle of Formigny (15 April 1450)', Army Qtly, July 1953.

Burne, Alfred H., 'The Battle of Cravant (30 July 1423)', Army Qtly, July 1955.

Burne, Alfred H., 'The Battle of Poitiers', EHR, 63 (1938).

Burne, Alfred H., 'Cannons at Crécy', Royal Artillery Journal, Vol. 77, No. 4.

Burne, Alfred H., 'John of Gaunt's Grande Chevauchée', HT, Vol. 9, Feb 1959.

Burne, Alfred H., 'When Artillery Made History; Artillery at Castillon, 1453', Royal Artillery Journal, Vol. 75, No. 4.

Burnie, J., *War in Medieval Society, 1377–99*.

Campbell, J., 'England, Scotland and the Hundred Years' War', from *Europe in the Late Middle Ages*, ed by B. Smalley, J. Hale and J.R.L. Highfield, London, 1965.

Carpenter, Christine, *The Wars of the Roses, Politics and the Constitution in England, c. 1437–1509*, CUP, 1997.

Carpenter, Christine, 'The Beauchamp Affinity, a Study of Bastard Feudalism at Work', EHR, Vol. 95 (1980).

Carruthers, A.R., 'The Site of the Battle of Bannockburn', extr from *Scottish War of Independence*, by E.M. Barron, Appx. Also from the same book, 'The Declaration of Arbroath'.

Chew, H.M., 'The Ecclesiastical Tenants-in-chief and Writs of Military Summons', EHR 41 (1926).

Cipolla, C., 'Currency Depreciation in Medieval Europe', EcHR, 2nd Ser, XV (1963).

Clephan, C.M., 'The Ordinance of the Fourteenth and Fifteenth Centuries', *The Archaeological Journal*, 68 (1911).

Coleman, C.H.D., 'The Execution of Hastings: A Neglected Source', BIHR (1980).

Commynes, P., *Memoires*, ed by J. Calmette and G. Durville, Paris, 1924–5.

Contamine, P., *War in the Middle Ages*, trans by Michael Jones, Basil Blackwell Publishers Ltd, Oxford, 1984.

Contamine, P., 'The French Nobility and the War', from *The Hundred Years' War*, ed by K. Fowler, Macmillan, 1971.

Croft, Dickinson, W., *Scotland from the Earliest Times to 1603*, 3rd edition, Oxford, 1977.

Curry, A.E., *The Hundred Years' War; British History in Perspective*, Macmillan Press Ltd, 1993.

Curry, A.E. and Hughes, M., *Arms, Armies and Fortifications in the Hundred Years' War*, Boydell Press, 1994.

Curry, A.E., 'The First English Standing Army? Military organization in Lancastrian Normandy, 1420–1450', from *Patronage, Pedigree and Power in Later Medieval England*, ed by C. Ross, Gloucester and Ottawa, 1979.

Cuttino, G.P., 'Historical Revision, the Causes of the Hundred Years' War', Speculum, XXXI, 1950.

Davis, R.H.C., *The Medieval Warhorse*, 1989.

Dawson, Ian, *The Wars of the Roses*, History in Depth, Macmillan Educational series, Nelson, 1994.

Devon, Frederick, Issue Rolls of Thomas de Bremtingham (44 ed III), London, 1835.

Dillon, Viscount and W.H. St John Hope, *Pageant of the Birth, Life and Death of Richard Beauchamp, Earl of Warwick, KG, 1389–1439*, 1914.

Draper, G.I.A.D., 'The Law of Ransom during the Hundred Years' War', extract from Revue de Droit Penal Militaire, 1968.

Duffy, C., *Siege Warfare: The Fortress in the Early Modern World, 1494–1660*, London, 1979.

Duncan, A.A.M., 'The War of the Scots, 1306–23', TRHS, 6th Ser, Vol. 2, 1991.

Duncan, A.A.M., 'The Community of the Realm and Robert Bruce', SHR, Vol. 45, 1991.

Dunham, W.H., *Lord Hastings' Indentured Retainers, 1461–83* (1955).

Edge, David and Paddock, J.M., *Arms and Armour of the Medieval Knight*, Bison Books Ltd, 1988.

Foulkes, C.J., *Armour and Weapons*, Oxford, 1909.

Ford, C.J., 'Piracy or Policy; the Crisis in the Channel, 1400–03', TRHS, 5th Ser, Vol. 29, 1979.

Foster, J., *Some Feudal Coats of Arms*, first published by James Parker & Co., 1901, republished by Crécy Books, 1984.

Fowler, K.A. (ed.), *The Hundred Years' War*, Macmillan, London, 1971.

Fowler, K.A., *The Age of Plantagenet and Valois*, 1967.

Fowler, K.A., *The King's Lieutenant, Henry of Grosmont, First Duke of Lancaster*, 1969.

Fryde, E.B., 'Parliament and the French War, 1336–40', from *Essays in Medieval History*, presented to Bertie Wilkinson, Toronto, 1969.

Fryde, E.B., 'The English Farmers of the Customs', TRHS, 5th Ser, Vol. IX (1959).

Fryde, E.B., 'Edward III's Wool Monopoly, a XIVth Century Royal Trading Venture', HA, XXXVII (1952).

Gairdner, J., 'The Battle of Bosworth', Archaeologica, Vol. 55 (1897).

Galbraith, V.H., 'The Battle of Poitiers', EHR, 54 (1939).

Gask, G.E., 'The Medical Staff of King Edward III, from *Sidelights on the History of Medicine*, ed by Cope, Z., London, 1957.

Gaupp, F., 'The Condottiere John Hawkwood', History 23 (1938–9).

Gies, Francis, *The Knight in History*, Hale, London, 1984.

Giles, J.A. (ed.), *Chronicles of the White Rose of York*, 1845.

Gillespie, James L., *The Age of Richard II*, Sutton Publishing Ltd, 1997.

Gillespie, James L., 'Richard II and his Knights, a Study in Chivalry and Patronage', JMedH 13 (1987).

Gillingham, J., *The Wars of the Roses, Peace and Conflict in Fifteenth Century England*, Phoenix Press, London, 1981.

Gillingham, J. and Holt, J.C. (eds), *War and Government in the Middle Ages*, CUP, 1984.

Goodman, A., *The Wars of the Roses, Military Activity and English Society 1452–97*, Routledge and Kegan Paul, London, 1981.

Goodman, A., *John of Gaunt; the Exercise of Princely Power in Fourteenth Century Europe*, Harlow, 1992.

Goodman, A., 'The Military Sub-contracts of Sir Hugh Hastings, 1380', EHR, 95, 1980.

Grant, A., *Independence and Nationhood, Scotland 1306–1469*, London, 1984.

Gray, H.L., 'Incomes from Land in England in 1436', EHR, Vol. 49, 1934.

Green, H., 'A/Q at Agincourt' (extract from The Army Quarterly).

Griffiths, R.A., 'The Duke of York's Intentions in 1450 and the Origins of the Wars of the Roses', J Med H, Vol. 1 (1975).

Griffiths, R.A. (ed.), *Patronage, the Crown and the Provinces in Later Medieval England*.

Griffiths, R.A., *The Reign of Henry VI*, London, 1981.

Griffiths, R.A., 'Local Rivalries and National Politics: the Percies, the Nevilles and the Duke of Exeter, 1452–55', Spec, Vol. XLIII, No. 4, Oct 1968.

Guth, D.J., 'Richard III, Henry VII and the City of London, Politics and the Dun Cow', from *Kings and Nobles in the Later Middle Ages*, ed by R.A. Griffiths and J. Sherborne.

Haigh, Phillip, A., *The Military Campaigns of the Wars of the Roses*, Sutton Publishing Ltd, 1995.

Hale, J.R., 'The Early Development of the Bastion, 1440–1534', from *Europe in the Late Middle Ages*, ed by B. Smalley, J. Hale and J.R.L. Highfield, London, 1965.

Hallam, Elizabeth (ed.), *Chronicles of the Age of Chivalry*, Weidenfeld & Nicolson Ltd, London, 1987.

Hallam, Elizabeth (ed.), *The Wars of the Roses*, Weidenfeld & Nicolson Ltd, London, 1988.

Hammond, P.W., *The Battles of Barnet and Tewksbury*, Sutton Publishing Ltd, 1990.

Hardy, R., *Longbow: A Social and Military History*, Patrick Stephens, Cambridge, 1976.

Harriss, G.L., *King, Parliament and Public Finance in Medieval England to 1369*, Oxford, 1975.

Harriss, G.L., 'War and the Emergence of Parliament, 1297–1360', JMedH, Vol. 2, 1976.

Harriss, G.L., 'Cardinal Beaufort – Patriot or Userer', TRHS, 5th Ser, Vol. XX (1970).

Harriss, G.L., 'The Struggle for Calais, an Aspect of the Rivalry between Lancaster and York', HER, Vol. LXXV, No. CCXCIV, Jan 1960.

Harriss, G.L., 'Preference at the Medieval Exchequer', BIHR, Vol. 30, 1957.

Harvey, J.H., *The Black Prince and his Age*, London, 1976.

Harvey, S., 'The Knight and the Knight's Fee in England', P&P, 49, 1970.

Hatcher, J., *Plague, Population and the English Economy 1348–1530*, Cambridge, 1977.

Haward, W.I., 'Economic Aspects of the Wars of the Roses in E. Anglia', EHR, Vol. 41 (1926).

Hay, D., 'The Division of the Spoils of War in Fourteenth Century England', TRHS, 5th Ser, Vol. 4, 1954.

Heath, E.G., *Archery, a Military History*, London, 1980.

Heath, Ian, *Armies of the Middle Ages*, Vol. 1, The Wargames Research Group, 1993.

Henneman, J.B., 'The Military Class and the French Monarchy in the Late Middle Ages', AHR, 83 (1978).

Hewitt, H.J., *The Black Prince's Expedition of 1355–57*, Manchester, 1958.

Hewitt, H.J., *The Organisation of War under Edward III*, MUP, 1966.

Hewitt, H.J., 'The Organization of War under Edward III', from *The Hundred Years' War*, ed by K.A. Fowler, London, 1971.

Hewitt, H.J., *The Horse in Medieval England*, London, 1983.

Hibbert, C., *Agincourt*, B.T. Batsford Ltd, 1978.

Hicks, M.A., *Richard III and his Rivals: Magnates and their Motives in the Wars of the Roses*, Hambledon, 1993.

Hicks, M.A., *Who's Who in Late Medieval England*, Shepheard-Walwyn, London, 1991.

Hicks, M.A., 'Descent, Partition and Extinction: the Warwick Inheritance', BIHR 52, 1979.

Hicks, M.A., *Bastard Feudalism*, Longman, London & New York, 1995.

Hill, D.R., 'Trebuchets', Viator, Vol. 4 (1973).

Hill, M.C., *The King's Messengers, 1199–1377*, London, 1961.

Hime, H.W.L., *The Origin of Artillery*, London, 1915.

Hogg, O.F.G., *The Royal Arsenal*, Oxford, 1963.

Hooker, J.R., 'Notes on the Organization and Supply of the Tudor Military under Henry VII', Hungtington Library Qtly, Vol. 23, 1959–60.

Hopkins, R., *Knights*, Collins and Brown, London.

Hunt, R.W., Pontin, W.A. and Southern, R.W. (eds), *Studies in Medieval History*, presented to F.M. Powicke, Oxford, 1984.

Hunt, Tony, *The Medieval Surgery*, Boydell Press, 1992.

Hurley, V., *Arrow against Steel; the History of the Bow*, New York, 1975.

Jack, R.I., 'The Battle of Northampton, 10th July 1460', P&P, Vol. 2.

Jacob, E.F., *Henry V and the Invasion of France*, London, 1947.

Jarman, R.H., *Crispin's Day, The Glory of Agincourt*, London, 1979.

Johnson, Charles, 'The System of Account in the Wardrobe of Edward I', TRHS, 4th Ser, Vol. VI.

Johnson, J.H., 'The System of Account in the Wardrobe of Edward II', TRHS, 4th Ser, Vol. XII.

Jollois, J.B.M., *Histoire du Siège d'Orléans*, Vol. 1, 1883.

Jones, M.K., 'Edward III's Captains in Brittany; England in the Fourteenth Century'. Proceedings of the 1985 Harlaxton Symposium, ed by Ormorod, W.M. Woodbridge, 1986.

Jones, M.K. and Vale, M., *England and Her Neighbours, 1066–1453*, London, 1989.

Jones, M.K., 'Somerset, York and the Wars of the Roses', EHR 411 (1989).

Jones, Michael, 'John Beaufort, duke of Somerset and the French Expedition of 1443', from *Patronage, the Crown and the Provinces in Later Medieval England*, ed by Ralph, A. Griffiths.

Keegan, J., *The Face of Battle*, Jonathan Cape Ltd, London, 1976.

Keen, Maurice, *Chivalry*, YUP, New Haven and London, 1984.

Keen, M.H., *The Laws of War in the Late Middle Ages*, Methuen & Co Ltd, London, 1965.

Keen, M.H., *England in the Late Middle Ages*, Methuen & Co Ltd, London, 1973.

Keen, M.H., 'Brotherhood in Arms', HA, Vol. XLVII (1962).

Keen, M.H., 'The End of the Hundred Years' War, Lancastrian France and Lancastrian England', from *England and her Neighbours, 1066–1455*, essays in honour of Pierre Chaplais, Hambledon Press, London, 1989.

Keen, M.H. and Daniel, M.J., 'English Diplomacy and the Sack of Fougères in 1449', HA, Vol. LIX (1974).

Keeney, B.C., 'Military Service and the Development of Nationalism in England, 1272–1327', Spec, Vol. 22, 1947.

Kenyon, J.R., 'Artillery and the Defences of Southampton, Circa 1360–1680', Fort, 3 (1977).

Kepler, J.H., 'The Effects of the Battle of Sluys upon the Administration of English Naval Impressment, 1340–43', Spec, 48 (1973).

Kirby, J.L., 'The Financing of Calais under Henry V', BIHR, Vol. XXIII (1950).

Koch, H.W., *Medieval Warfare*, Bison Books, London, 1978.

Labarge, M.W., *Gascony, England's First Colony, 1204–1453*, Hamish Hamilton, 1980.

Lander, J.R., *The Wars of the Roses*, London, 1965.

Lander, J.R., *Crown and Nobility 1450–1509*, Edward Arnold, London, 1976.

Lander, J.R., *Conflict and Stability in Fifteenth Century England*, Hutchison University Library, London, 1959.

Lander, J.R., 'Attainder and Forfeiture, 1453–1509', HJ, Vol. IV (1961).

Lander, J.R., 'Henry VI and the Duke of York's Second Protectorate', BJRL, Vol. XLIII (1960).

Landström, Björn, *The Ship*, Allen & Unwin, 1961.

Le Patourel, J., 'Edward III and the Kingdom of France', HA, 43 (1958).

Le Patourel, J., 'The King and the Princes in Fourteenth Century France', from *Europe in the Late Middle Ages*, ed by B. Smalley, J. Hale and J.R.L. Highfield.

Le Patourel, J., 'The Treaty of Brétigny 1360', TRHS, 5th Ser, Vol. 10 (1960).

Lewis, N.B., 'The Organization of Indentured Retinues in Fourteenth Century England', TRHS, 4th Ser, Vol. 27 (1945).

Lewis, N.B., 'The Recruitment and Organization of a Contract Army, May to November 1337', BIHR, Vol. 37 (1964).

Lewis, N.B., 'The Last Medieval Summons of the English Feudal Levy, 13th June 1385', EHR, Vol. 73 (1958).

Lewis, N.B., *Indentures of Retinue with John of Gaunt, Duke of Lancaster, Enrolled in Chancery, 1367–1399*, pp. 77–85.

Lewis, N.B., 'The Summons of the English Feudal Levy, 5th April 1327', from *Essays in Medieval History*, presented to Bertie Wilkinson, ed by T.A. Sandquist and M.R. Powicke, Toronto, 1969.

Lewis, N.B., 'Article VII of the Impeachment of Michael de la Pole', EHR, Vol. 42 (1927).

Lewis, P.S., 'France in the Fifteenth Century: Society and Sovereignty', from *Europe in the Late Middle Ages*, ed by B. Smalley, J. Hale and J.R.L. Highfield, London, 1965.

Lodge, E.C., 'Edward I and His Tenants-in-Chief, TRHS, 4th Ser, Vol. VII.

Lot, Ferdinand, *L'Art Militairedes Armées au Moyen Age*.

Lucas, H.S., 'John Crabbe, Flemish Pirate, Merchant and Adventurer', Spec, Vol. 20, 1945.

Lyle, Helen, 'The Rebellion of Jack Cade', HA (1950).

MacDermott, M., Translation of *Military Architecture of the Middle Ages*, by Viollet-le-Duc, Greenwood Press, 1977.

MacDonald, R.J., 'Medieval Artillery in an Expedition Overseas', JAHR, 1921.

Mace, Frances A., 'Devonshire Ports in the 14th and 15th Centuries', TRHS, 4th Ser, Vol. VIII.

McFarlane, K.B., 'A Business Partnership in War and Administration, 1421–45', EHR, Vol. 78 (1963).

McFarlane, K.B., 'War, the Economy and Social Change', P&P, No. 22 (1962).

McFarlane, K.B., 'Parliament and Bastard Feudalism', TRHS, 4th Ser, Vol. XXVI (1944).

McFarlane, K.B., 'England and the Hundred Years War', P&P, No. 22 (1962).

McFarlane, K.B., 'The Investment of Sir John Fastolff's Profits of War', TRHS, 5th Ser, Vol. 7 (1957).

McFarlane, K.B., 'Bastard Feudalism', BIHR 20 (1945).

McFarlane, K.B., *The Nobility of Later Medieval England*, Oxford, 1971.

McFarlane, K.B., 'The Wars of the Roses', Proceedings of the British Academy, Vol. 50, 1964.

McGuffie, T.H., 'The Long Bow as a Decisive Weapon', HT, 5 (1955), pp. 737–41.

MacKenzie, W.M., *The Battle of Bannockburn: a study in Medieval Warfare*, Glasgow, 1913.

MacKenzie, R.M., *The Kingdom of Scotland*, Chambers, 1940.

MacKinney, L., *Medical Illustrations in Medieval Manuscripts*, The Wellcome Historical Medical Library, 1965.

McKisack, May, *The Fourteenth Century, 1307–1399*, OUP, 1959.

Maddicott, John, 'The Origins of the Hundred Years' War', HT, May 1986.

Mallett, M.E., *The Florentine Galleys in the Fifteenth Century*, Oxford, 1967.

Miller, E., *War in the North. The Anglo-Scottish Wars of the Middle Ages*, Hull, 1960.

Moore, Allen, 'Accounts and Inventories of John Starlyng, Clerk of the King's Ships to Henry IV', MM, Vol. 7.

Morgan, D.A.L., 'The King's Affinity in the Polity of Yorkist England', TRHS, 5th Ser, Vol. 23 (1973).

Morris, C., 'The Plague in Britain', HJ, Vol. XIV (1971).

Morris, J.E., *Bannockburn*, Cam, 1914.

Morris, J.E., 'Mounted Infantry in Medieval Warfare', TRHS, 3rd Ser, Vol. 8 (1914).

Morris, J.E., 'The Archers at Crécy', EHR, 12 (1897).

Morton Nance, R., 'A Trader and a Man of War, Late XIV Century', MM, Vol. 2.

Myers, A.R., 'The Outbreak of War between England and Burgundy in February 1471', BIHR, XXIII (1960).

Myres, J.N.L., 'The Campaign of Radcot Bridge in December 1387', EHR, Vol. 42 (1927).

Neillands, R., *The Hundred Years' War*, Routledge, London, 1990.

Newark, P., *Medieval Warfare*, London, 1979.

Newhall, R.A., *The English Conquest of Normandy, 1416–1424, a study in XV Century Warfare*, YUP, New Haven and London, 1924.

Newhall, R.A., *Muster and Review, a Problem of English Military Administration; 1420–1440*, Cambridge, Mass, 1940.

Newhall, R.A., 'The War Finances of Henry V and the Duke of Bedford', EHR, 36 (1921).

Nicholson, R., 'The Siege of Berwick, 1333', SHR, 40 (1961).

Nicholson, R.J., *Edward III and the Scots. The Formative Years of a Military Career, 1327–1335*, Oxford, 1965, also Edinburgh, 1971.

Nicholson, R.J., *Scotland: The Later Middle Ages*, Edinburgh, 1974.

Nicolas, Sir N. Harris, *History of the Battle of Agincourt and of the Expedition of Henry V into France in 1415*. Includes 'Henry V's Orders for War' in Appx VIII, London, 2nd edn, 1832 (repr 1970).

Norman and Pottinger, *English Weapons and Warfare, 449–1660*, Dorset Press, 1985.

Oakeshott, R.E., *A Knight and his Armour*, London, 1961.

Oakeshott, R.E., *A Knight and his Weapons*, London, 1964.

Oakeshott, R.E., *A Knight and his Horse*, London, 1964.

Oakeshott, R.E., *A Knight and his Castle*, London, 1965.

Oakeshott, R.E., *The Sword in the Age of Chivalry*, London, 1964.

O'Connell, A.L., *Of Arms and Men*, Oxford, 1989.

Oman, C.W.C., *The Art of War in the Middle Ages, AD 1378–1485*, London, 1924, repr Ithaca 1960, 2 vols, 2nd vol covers period 1278–1485.

O'Neil, B.H., *Castles and Canon; a Study of Early Artillery Fortifications in England*, Oxford, 1960.

Ormrod, W.M., *Political Life in Medieval England, 1300–1450*, British History in Perspective, Macmillan Press, London, 1995.

Palmer, J.J.N., 'The Last Summons of the Feudal Army in England', EHR 83 (1968).

Palmer, J.J.N., 'Charles VI and Richard II: The Hundred Years War from 1380–1399'.

Palmer, J.J.N., 'The Anglo-French Peace Negotiations 1390–1386', TRHS, 5th Ser, Vol. 16 (1966).

Palmer, J.J.N., 'The War Aims of the Protagonists and the Negotiations for Peace', chapter in *The Hundred Years' War*, ed by K.A. Fowler, London, 1971.

Palmer, J.J.N., 'The Impeachment of Michael de la Pole in 1386', BIHR, Vol. 42 (1969).

Patrick, J.M., *Artillery and Warfare during the XIII and XIV Centuries*, 1961.

Payne-Galway, Sir Ralph, *The Crossbow*, 1904.

Perroy, E., *The Hundred Years War*, trans by W.B. Wells, London, 1951, and Capricorn Books, New York, 1965.

Perroy, E., 'The Anglo-French Negotiations at Bruges, 1374–77', CM, Vol. 19 (1952).

Perroy, E., 'Franco-English Relations, 1350–1400', History 21, 1936–7.

Phillpotts, C., 'The French Plan of Battle during the Agincourt Campaign', EHR, January 1984.

Pistono, S.P., 'Henry IV and Charles VI, Confirmation of the 28 Year Truce', J Med H, Vol. 3.

Plucknett, A.F.T., 'The Place of the Council in England in the XVth Century', TRHS, 4th Ser, Vol. 1.

Pollard, A.E., *John Talbot and the War in France, 1427–53*, London, 1983.

Pollard, A.J., *The Wars of the Roses*, Macmillan Press Ltd, London, 1988.

Pollard, A.J., 'Lord Fitzhughe's Rising in 1470', BIHR, Vol. 52 (1979).

Pollard, A.J., 'The Tyranny of Richard III', J Med H, Vol. 3 (1977).

Postan, M., 'The Costs of the Hundred Years' War', P&P, No. 27, April 1964.

Postan, M.M., 'The Fifteenth Century', EcHR, Vol. IX (1939).

Powicke, M.R., *Military Obligation in Medieval England*, Oxford, 1962.

Powicke, M.R., 'The English Aristocracy and the War', from *The Hundred Years War*, ed by K. Fowler, Macmillan, London, 1971.

Powicke, M., 'Lancastrian Captains', from *Essays in Medieval History*, presented to Bertie Wilkinson, ed by T.A. Sandquist and M. Powicke, Toronto, 1969.

Prebble, J., *The Lion in the North*, Secker and Warburg, London, 1971.

Prestwich, M., *The Three Edwards, War and State in England 1272–1377*, Methuen and Co Ltd, 1981.

Prestwich, M., *Armies and Warfare in the Middle Ages, The English Experience*, YUP, Newhaven and London, 1996.

Prestwich, M., 'English Armies in the Early Stages of the Hundred Years War; A Scheme in 1341', BIHR, Vol. 56 (1983).

Prestwich, M., 'Victualling Estimates for English Armies in Scotland During the Early XIV Century', EHR, Vol. 82 (1967).

Prestwich, M., 'Cavalry Service in Early Fourteenth Century England', from *War and Government in the Middle Ages*, essays in honour of J.O. Preswick, ed by J. Gillingham and J.C. Holt, Ottawa, 1984.

Prince, A.E., 'The Strength of English Armies in the Reign of Edward III', EHR, 46 (1931).

Prince, A.E., 'The Payment of Army Wages in the Reign of Ed III', Spec, Vol. XIX (1944).

Prince, A.E., 'A Letter of the Black Prince Describing the Battle of Najera in 1367', EHR, Vol. 41 (1926).

Prince, A.E., 'The Indenture System under Edward III', from *Historical Essays in Honour of James Tout*, ed by J.G. Edwards, Manchester, 1933.

Prince, A.E., 'The Importance of the Campaign of 1327', EHR, Vol. 1 (1935).

Prynne, M.W., 'Henry V's Grace Dieu', MM, Vol. LIV (1968).

Pryor, J.H., 'The Transportation of Horses by Sea during the Era of the Crusades', MM, 68 (1982).

Pugh, T.B., 'The English Baronage and the Income Tax of 1436', BIHR, Vol. 26 (1953).

Pugh, T.B., 'The Southampton Plot of 1415', from *Kings and Nobles of the later Middle Ages*, ed by R.A. Griffiths and J. Sherborne.

Ramsay, Sir James M., *A History of the Revenues of the Kings of England, 1066–1399*, Oxford, Clarendon, 1925.

Ramsay, Sir James M., 'The Strength of English Armies in the Middle Ages', EHR, Vol. 29 (1914).

Ramsay, Sir James M., *Lancaster and York*, Oxford, 1892, 2 vols.

Redstone, V.B., 'Mercenaries of Henry of Lancaster, 1327–1330', TRHS, 3rd Ser, Vol. VII.

Reid, R.R., 'The Office of the Warden of the Marches, its Origin and Early History', EHR, Vol. XXXII (1917).

Richardson, H.G., 'Illustrations of English History in the Medieval Registers of the Parliament of Paris', TRHS, 4th Ser, Vol. X.

Richardson, H.G. and Sykes, G.O., 'The Governance of Medieval England' (1963).

Richmond, C.F., 'The Keeping of the Seas during the Hundred Years' War, 1422–1440', HA 49 (1964).

Richmond, C.F., 'English Naval Power in the XVth Century', HA, Vol. 52 (1967).

Richmond, C.F., 'The War at Sea', from *The Hundred Years' War*, ed by K. Fowler, London, 1971.

Richmond, C.F., 'The Battle of Bosworth', HT, Vol. 25 (August 1985).

Richmond, C.F., 'Fauconberg's Kentish Rising of May 1471', EHR, Vol. 85 (1970).

Richmond, C.F., 'The Nobility and the Wars of the Roses, 1459–61', NMS, Vol. 21 (1977).

Robinson, Gregory, 'The Medieval Artist, His Value as a Witness in Nautical Affairs', MM, Vol. II (1912).

Robinson, W.C., 'Money, Population and Economic Change in Late Medieval Europe', EcHR, 2nd Ser, Vol. XII (1959).

Rodger, N.A.M., *The Safeguard of the Sea*, HarperCollins, London, 1997.

Rogers, Clifford J., 'Edward III and the Dialectics of Strategy, 1327–60', TRHS, 6th Ser, Vol. 4 (1994).

Rogers, Clifford J., *The Wars of Edward III*, Boydell Press, 1999.

Rogers, C.J., 'The Military Revolutions of the Hundred Years' War', J Mil Hist, 57 (1993).

Roskell, J.S., *The Commons in the Parliament of 1422*, Manchester, 1953.

Ross, Charles, *The Wars of the Roses*, Thames and Hudson, London, 1976.

Ross, Charles, *Edward IV*, London, 1974.

Ross, Charles (ed.), *Patronage, Pedigree and Power in Late Medieval England*, Gloucester, 1979.

Ross, C.D., 'Forfeiture for Treason in the Reign of Richard II', EHR, Vol. 71 (1956).

Rothero, C., *The Armies of Crécy and Poitiers*, Men-at-arms series, Vol. III.

Rowe, B.J.H., 'Discipline in the Norman Garrisons under Bedford 1422–35', EHR, Vol. 46 (1931).

Rowe, B.J.H., 'A Contemporary Account of the Hundred Years War', EHR, Vol. 41 (1926).

Rowe, B.J.H., 'John, Duke of Bedford and the Norman Brigands', EHR, Vol. 47 (1932).

Rowe, B.J.H., 'The Grand Conseil under the Duke of Bedford', from *Essays in Medieval History*, ed by H.E. Salter, Oxford.

Runyan, T.J., 'Merchantman to Man-of-War in Medieval England, from *New Aspects of Naval History*, ed by Symonds, C.L., Annapolis, 1981.

Russell, F.H., *The Just War in the Middle Ages*, Cambridge, 1975.

Russell, J.C., *British Medieval Population*, Albuquerque, 1948.

Russell, P.E., *The English Intervention in Spain and Portugal in the Time of Edward III and Richard II*, Oxford, 1955.

Sackville-West, Vita, *St Joan of Arc*, Folio edn, 1995.

Sanders, I.J., *Feudal Military Service in England*, Oxford, 1956.

Saul, Nigel, 'Henry V and the Dual Monarchy', HT, May 1986.

Scammell, Jean, 'Robert the Bruce and the North of England', EHR, Vol. 63 (1958).

Schuyler, B.T., 'The Financing of the Hundred Years' War, 1337–68'.

Scott, Ronald McNair, *Robert the Bruce, King of Scots*, Edinburgh, 1982.

Sellman, R.R., *Medieval English Warfare*, Methuen & Co Ltd, London, 1960.

Sellman, R.R., *Castles and Fortresses*, Methuen & Co Ltd, London, 1954.

Seward, D., *The Hundred Years War*, Constable and Co, London, 1978.

Seward, D., *Henry V as Warlord*, Sidgewick and Jackson Ltd, 1987; also by Penguin Books, 2001.

Seward, D., *The Wars of the Roses*, Constable, London, 1995.

Shakespeare, William, *Richard II*, also *Richard III*.

Sherborne, J.W., 'John of Gaunt, Edward III's retinue and the French Campaign of 1369', from *Kings and Nobles in the Late Middle Ages*, a tribute to Charles Ross, ed by Griffiths, R.A. and Sherborne, J., Glos, 1986.

Sherborne, J.W., 'The Battle of La Rochelle and the War at Sea, 1372–5', BIHR, Vol. 42 (1969).

Sherborne, J.W., 'Indentured Retinues and English Expeditions to France, 1369–80', EHR, Vol. 79 (1964).

Sherborne, J.W., 'The Cost of English Warfare with France in the Late XIV Century', BIHR, Vol. 1 (1977).

Sherborne, J.W., 'The English Navy; Shipping and Manpower, 1369–89', P&P, Vol. 37 (1967).

Simpson, M.A., 'The Verneuil Campaign', EHR, Vol. 49, 1934.

Smail, R.C, *Art of War, in Medieval England*, ed by A.L. Poole, Oxford and New York, 1958.

Speed, Peter (ed.), *Those who Fought: An Anthology of Medieval Sources*, Italica Press, New York, 1996.

Stanford-Reid, W., 'Sea Power in the Anglo-Scottish War, 1296–1328', MM, Vol. 46 (1960).

Stanford-Reid, W., 'Trade, Traders & Scottish Independence', Spec, Vol. 29 (1954).

Steel, A., 'The Financial Background of the Wars of the Roses', HA, Vol. 40, 1955.

Storey, R.L., *The End of the House of Lancaster*, Barrie and Rockcliffe, London, 1966.

Storey, R.L., 'The Wardens of the Marches of England towards Scotland, 1377–1489', EHR, Vol. 72 (1957).

Stratton, Grace, 'Some Aspects of Medieval Travel', TRHS, 4th Ser, Vol. VII.

Sumption, J., *The Hundred Years War*, Vol. I, 'Trial by Battle', Faber & Faber, London, 1990.

Sumption, J., *The Hundred Years War*, Vol. II, 'Trial by Fire', Faber & Faber, London, 1999.

Talbot, Hugh, *The English Achilles, the Life and Campaigns of John Talbot 1st Earl of Shrewsbury*, Chatto and Windus Ltd, London, 1981.

Templeman, G., 'Edward III and the Beginnings of the Hundred Years War', TRHS, 5th Ser, Vol. 11 (1952).

Terry, S.B., 'The Financing of the Hundred Years War, 1337–1360', 1914.

Thompson, A.H., 'The Art of War to 1400', J Med H, Vol. VI.

Tinniswood, J.T., 'English Galleys, 1272–1377', MM, Vol. XXXV, 1949.

Tipping, C., 'Cargo Handling of the Medieval Cog', MM, 80 (1994).

Tout, T.F., 'Chapters in the Administrative History of Medieval England', HA, Vol. IV.

Tout, T.F., 'Firearms in England in the XIV century', EHR, Vol. XXVI (1911).

Tout, T.F., 'Some Neglected Fights between Crécy and Poitiers', EHR, Vol. 20 (1905).

Tuck, A., *Crown and Nobility (1272–1461)*, Fontana Press, London, 1985.

Tuck, J.A., 'Why Men Fought in the Middle Ages', HT, 33 (April 83).

Turnbull, S., *The Book of the Medieval Knight*, Arms and Armour Press, London, 1985.

Turner, H.L., *Town Defences in England and Wales*, London, 1971.

Unger, Richard W., *The Ship in the Medieval Economy, 600–1600*, Montreal, 1980.

Vale, M.G.A., 'New Techniques and Old Ideals: The Impact of Artillery on War and Chivalry at the End of the Hundred Years War' from *War, Literature and Politics in the Late Middle Ages*, ed by C.T. Allmand, Liverpool, 1976.

Vale, M.G.A., *War and Chivalry: Warfare and Aristocratic Culture in England, France and Burgundy at the End of the Middle Ages*, London, 1981.

Vale, M.G.A., 'Sir John Fastolff's report of 1435; a New Interpretation Reconsidered', MS, Vol. 17 (1973).

Vale, M.G.A., 'The Last Years of English Gascony, 1451–53', TRHS, 5th Ser, Vol. XIX (1969).

Vale, M.G.A., *English Gascony, 1399–1453*, Oxford, 1970.

Vale, M.G.A., *Charles VII*, London, 1974.

Verbruggen, J.F., *The Art of Warfare in Western Europe during the Middle Ages (from the Eighth Century to 1340)*, Eng trans, Amsterdam and New York, 1976.

Viard, J., 'Le Siège de Calais', Vol. 39 (1929).

Viollet-le-Duc, *Annals of a Fortress*, Sampson Low, 1975.

Viollet-le-Duc, *Encyclopédie Médiévale*, Normandie Roto Impression SA, Lonrai, 1995.

Viollet-le-Duc, *An Essay on the Military Architecture of the Middle Ages*, trans by M. Macdermott. Originally pub by J.H. and J. Parker, Oxford and London, 1960, and reprinted by Greenwood Press, Connecticut, 1977.

Wailly, Henri de, *Crécy, 1346. Anatomy of a Battle*, Blandford Press, 1987.

Waites, B., 'The Fighting Galley', HT, Vol. 18 (1968).

Warner, P., *The Medieval Castle. Life in a Fortress in Peace and War'*, London, 1971.

Warner, P., *Sieges of the Middle Ages*, London, 1968.

Warren, John, *The Wars of the Roses and the Yorkist Kings*, Hodder & Stoughton, 1995.

Webster, B., 'David II and the Governance of Fourteenth Century Scotland', TRHS, Vol. ?

Weir, Allison, *Lancaster and York, The Wars of the Roses*, Jonathan Cape, 1995.

Weir, Allison, *The Princes in the Tower*, Pimlico, 1993.

White, Lyn, jnr, *Medieval Technology and Social Change*, Oxford, 1962.

Wilkinson, F., *Arms and Armour*, A&C Black Ltd, London, 1963.

Willard, J.F., 'Taxes upon Moveables of the Reign of Edward II', EHR, Vol. 29 (1914).

Williams, M.R., 'Methods of Manufacture of Swords in Medieval Europe Illustrated by the Metallography of some Examples', Gladius, Vol. 13 (1977).

Wise, T., *Medieval Warfare*, New York, 1976.

Wise, T., *Wars of the Roses*, Men-at-Arms series, Osprey, London, 1983.

Wollfe, Bertram, *Henry VI*, Eyre & Methuen, London, 1981.

Wright, N.A.R., 'Pillagers and Brigands in the Hundred Years War', JMedH, Vol. 9 (1983).

Wylie, J.H. and Waugh, W.T., *The Reign of Henry V*, 3 vols, CUP, 1919.

Wylie, J.H., 'Notes on the Agincourt Roll', RHS, 3rd S34, Vol. 5, 1911.

Zeigler, P., *The Black Death*, Collins, 1969.

Index